Effective Use of Microsoft Enterprise Library

Microsoft .NET Development Series

John Montgomery, *Series Advisor*
Don Box, *Series Advisor*
Martin Heller, *Series Editor*

The **Microsoft .NET Development Series** is supported and developed by the leaders and experts of Microsoft development technologies including Microsoft architects and DevelopMentor instructors. The books in this series provide a core resource of information and understanding every developer needs in order to write effective applications and managed code. Learn from the leaders how to maximize your use of the .NET Framework and its programming languages.

Titles in the Series

Brad Abrams, *.NET Framework Standard Library Annotated Reference Volume 1: Base Class Library and Extended Numerics Library*, 0-321-15489-4

Brad Abrams and Tamara Abrams, *.NET Framework Standard Library Annotated Reference, Volume 2: Networking Library, Reflection Library, and XML Library*, 0-321-19445-4

Keith Ballinger, *.NET Web Services: Architecture and Implementation*, 0-321-11359-4

Bob Beauchemin, Niels Berglund, Dan Sullivan, *A First Look at SQL Server 2005 for Developers*, 0-321-18059-3

Don Box with Chris Sells, *Essential .NET, Volume 1: The Common Language Runtime*, 0-201-73411-7

Keith Brown, *The .NET Developer's Guide to Windows Security*, 0-321-22835-9

Eric Carter and Eric Lippert, *Visual Studio Tools for Office: Using C# with Excel, Word, Outlook, and InfoPath*, 0-321-33488-4

Eric Carter and Eric Lippert, *Visual Studio Tools for Office: Using Visual Basic 2005 with Excel, Word, Outlook, and InfoPath*, 0-321-41175-7

Mahesh Chand, *Graphics Programming with GDI+*, 0-321-16077-0

Krzysztof Cwalina and Brad Abrams, *Framework Design Guidelines: Conventions, Idioms, and Patterns for Reusable .NET Libraries*, 0-321-24675-6

Anders Hejlsberg, Scott Wiltamuth, Peter Golde, *The C# Programming Language*, 0-321-15491-6

Alex Homer, Dave Sussman, Mark Fussell, *ADO.NET and System.Xml v. 2.0—The Beta Version*, 0-321-24712-4

Alex Homer, Dave Sussman, Rob Howard, *ASP.NET v. 2.0—The Beta Version*, 0-321-25727-8

James S. Miller and Susann Ragsdale, *The Common Language Infrastructure Annotated Standard*, 0-321-15493-2

Christian Nagel, *Enterprise Services with the .NET Framework: Developing Distributed Business Solutions with .NET Enterprise Services*, 0-321-24673-X

Brian Noyes, *Data Binding with Windows Forms 2.0: Programming Smart Client Data Applications with .NET*, 0-321-26892-X

Fritz Onion, *Essential ASP.NET with Examples in C#*, 0-201-76040-1

Fritz Onion, *Essential ASP.NET with Examples in Visual Basic .NET*, 0-201-76039-8

Ted Pattison and Dr. Joe Hummel, *Building Applications and Components with Visual Basic .NET*, 0-201-73495-8

Dr. Neil Roodyn, *eXtreme .NET: Introducing eXtreme Programming Techniques to .NET Developers*, 0-321-30363-6

Chris Sells, *Windows Forms Programming in C#*, 0-321-11620-8

Chris Sells and Justin Gehtland, *Windows Forms Programming in Visual Basic .NET*, 0-321-12519-3

Paul Vick, *The Visual Basic .NET Programming Language*, 0-321-16951-4

Damien Watkins, Mark Hammond, Brad Abrams, *Programming in the .NET Environment*, 0-201-77018-0

Shawn Wildermuth, *Pragmatic ADO.NET: Data Access for the Internet World*, 0-201-74568-2

Paul Yao and David Durant, *.NET Compact Framework Programming with C#*, 0-321-17403-8

Paul Yao and David Durant, *.NET Compact Framework Programming with Visual Basic .NET*, 0-321-17404-6

For more information go to www.awprofessional.com/msdotnetseries/

Effective Use of Microsoft Enterprise Library

Building Blocks for Creating Enterprise Applications and Services

Len Fenster

Addison-Wesley

Upper Saddle River, NJ • Boston • Indianapolis • San Francisco
New York • Toronto • Montreal • London • Munich • Paris • Madrid
Capetown • Sydney • Tokyo • Singapore • Mexico City

The publisher offers excellent discounts on this book when ordered in quantity for bulk purchases or special sales, which may include electronic versions and/or custom covers and content particular to your business, training goals, marketing focus, and branding interests. For more information, please contact:

U.S. Corporate and Government Sales
(800) 382-3419
corpsales@pearsontechgroup.com

For sales outside the United States, please contact:

International Sales
international@pearsoned.com

This Book Is Safari Enabled

The Safari® Enabled icon on the cover of your favorite technology book means the book is available through Safari Bookshelf. When you buy this book, you get free access to the online edition for 45 days.

Safari Bookshelf is an electronic reference library that lets you easily search thousands of technical books, find code samples, download chapters, and access technical information whenever and wherever you need it.

To gain 45-day Safari Enabled access to this book:

- Go to http://www.awprofessional.com/safarienabled
- Complete the brief registration form
- Enter the coupon code I9ML-V92N-DISD-RCML-69AY

If you have difficulty registering on Safari Bookshelf or accessing the online edition, please e-mail customer-service@safaribooksonline.com.

Visit us on the Web: www.awprofessional.com

Library of Congress Cataloging-in-Publication Data

Fenster, Len.
Effective use of Microsoft Enterprise Library : building blocks for creating enterprise applications and services / Len Fenster.
p. cm.
Includes bibliographical references and index.
ISBN 0-321-33421-3 (pbk. : alk. paper)
1. Microsoft .NET. 2. Enterprise application integration (Computer systems) I. Title.

QA76.76.M52F46 2006
005.2'768—dc22

2006009616

ISBN 0-321-33421-3
Text printed in the United States on recycled paper at RR Donnelly in Crawfordsville, Indiana.
First printing, June 2006

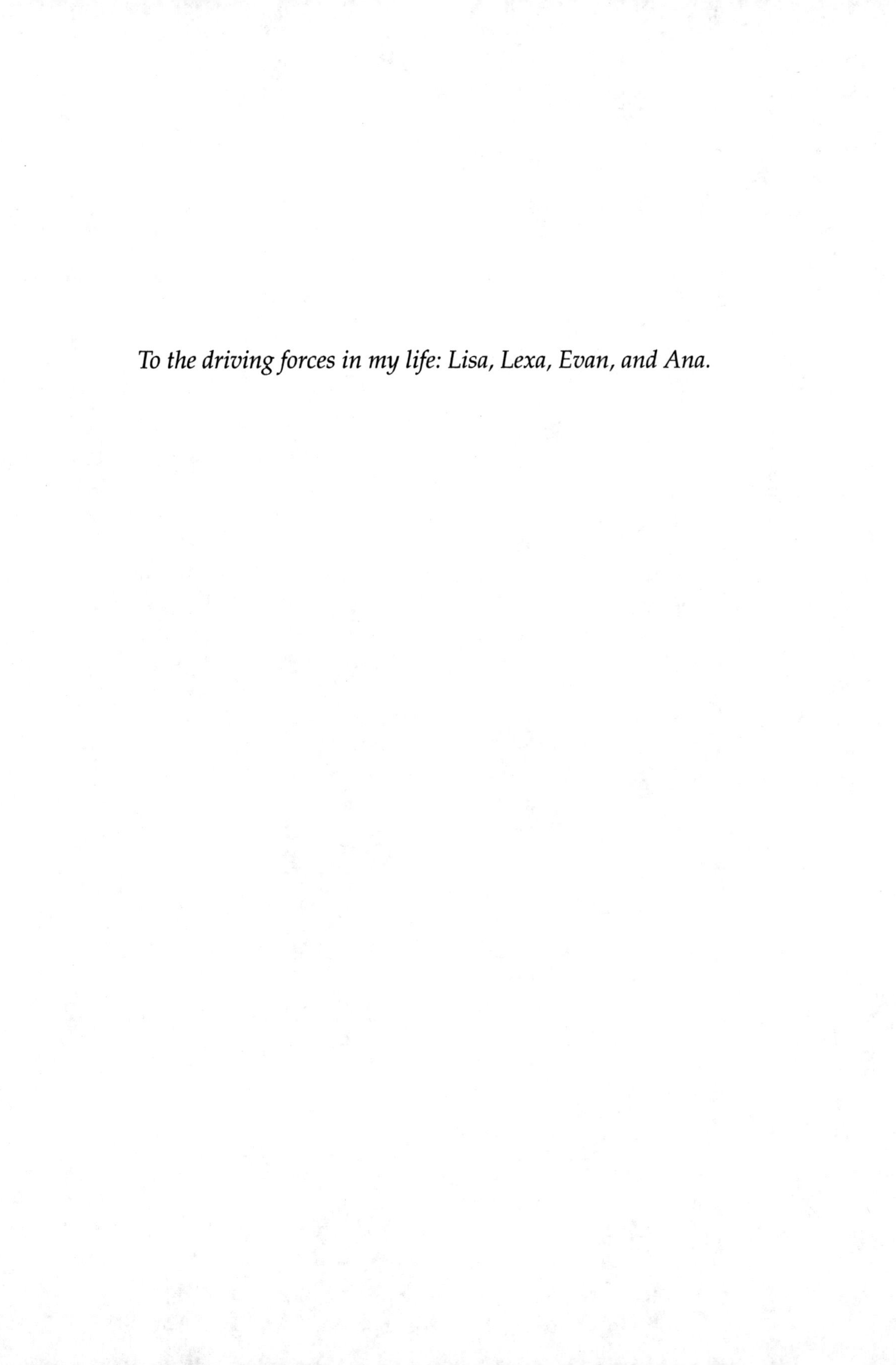

To the driving forces in my life: Lisa, Lexa, Evan, and Ana.

Contents at a Glance

Contents

Figures

Tables

Foreword

BEING A DEVELOPER isn't easy. Generally this is a good thing, or the job would get boring very quickly. Each project brings new requirements and new technical challenges, and the backdrop of products and platform versions is constantly evolving.

Amid all the excitement, though, there's still a considerable amount of déjà vu in development: the feeling that you've written the exact same code many times before. This happens because real-world needs often require developers to write generic code at a higher level of abstraction than provided by base platform capabilities—often for application infrastructure or cross-cutting features that feature in enterprise line-of-business applications.

Not only is it boring writing more or less the same code again and again, but it's also inefficient and can lead to consistency and quality problems. To address this, for a number of years the Microsoft patterns & practices team has been producing reusable, extensible, and configurable source code components called *application blocks*. We started off with a very simple data access helper class that we called the Data Access Application Block, but we quickly moved to many other areas, including exception management, logging, authorization, caching, and offline smart client support. These blocks demonstrate proven practices and are designed to meet the most common enterprise application requirements out-of-the-box, but they are also customizable and extensible to meet each organization's or project's unique requirements.

While the original generation of application blocks was generally very well received by the .NET developer community, most would agree that Enterprise Library marked the beginning of a new era for code-based guidance from the patterns & practices team. Enterprise Library includes functionality similar to that previously released as standalone blocks, but internally it was completely overhauled to feature much-improved consistency across blocks; extensibility to easily support new requirements; ease of use through simpler APIs, documentation, and samples; and integration between blocks that are often used together in applications.

In addition to the changes within the deliverable itself, the other big improvement that arrived with Enterprise Library was the formation of a community—thousands of developers, testers, and architects—sharing problems, solutions, experiences, and extensions with each other and with the patterns & practices team, communicating using our GotDotNet community site, blogs, Webcasts, and events. This community has dramatically increased the value of Enterprise Library by delivering insights and feedback on experiences far beyond what the patterns & practices team could possibly come up with on our own.

Even though Lenny Fenster is a Microsoft employee, it was through this public community that the patterns & practices team really got to know him. Lenny's role involves working with customers every day, on real projects, and this gave him both the opportunity to use Enterprise Library on these projects, as well as the insight into new customer challenges that weren't addressed by Enterprise Library but seemed to be asking for a similar solution. Armed with this insight, Lenny created the Data Mapping Application Block as an extension to Enterprise Library and shared it with the community—and now, with readers of this book as well!

When the time came to update Enterprise Library for the upcoming release of .NET Framework 2.0, the patterns & practices team was lucky enough to be able to "borrow" Lenny from his customer work so he could work as a core member of the Enterprise Library development team. Not only did this allow the patterns & practices team to benefit from his recent customer experiences, but it also gave Lenny first-hand experience with what it takes to build a patterns & practices deliverable. While this book focuses on the .NET Framework 1.1 release of Enterprise Library, most of the concepts are still relevant for the new .NET Framework 2.0 release. Lenny's expertise and experience on the development team have put him in a unique position to teach developers how to use Enterprise Library most effectively.

So thanks to Lenny—and to all of you as well—for your support of Microsoft patterns & practices and your willingness to give back to the community!

—*Tom Hollander, product manager*
Microsoft patterns & practices
http://msdn.microsoft.com/practices
http://blogs.msdn.com/tomholl

Preface

DEVELOPING APPLICATIONS that fit the needs of many enterprises is of keen interest to CIOs, CTOs, architects, and developers because it typically requires many resources in terms of time and money to develop the core foundational services needed to support these applications. Microsoft has provided guidance for developing these services and code for supporting them. *Effective Use of Microsoft Enterprise Library* fills the void on how to "put all the blocks together." With this void filled, architects and developers will be equipped to create solid Service-Oriented Architectures (SOAs) based on the Microsoft recommended best practices in an easy and repeatable manner.

How, you ask? Read on.

Today many companies are faced not only with the challenge of how to create a robust application that leverages as many of the features and functions of Microsoft .NET as they can, but they are also faced with the challenge of architecting these applications so that they can reap the benefits that Service-Oriented Architectures are promising to deliver both now and in the future. Imagine helping your child to create a model of the Sphinx from a box of several hundred random Lego blocks and you might get a good sense of an architect's emotions when first faced with the prospect of designing an enterprise-level application for a particular CxO.

Microsoft provides help, though, by delivering guidance on how to architect enterprise-level applications so that they can leverage the features and functions of .NET. It provides this help in the form of Prescriptive

Architecture Guidance (PAG) documents. PAG documents detail the different layers, components, and services that architects should consider when designing their applications. Think of the PAGs as the picture of the Sphinx on the Lego blocks box. Microsoft also provides the Lego blocks—in the form of the application blocks for .NET. An **application block** is code that implements one of the components or services in one of the layers that make up an application.

So, what's the problem?

The problem is that there is no instruction manual or documented process for using the Lego blocks to create the application blocks. With which block should you start? Should all the blocks be used? Are there blocks missing from the box? How should they best be assembled together?

This book will serve as the instruction manual for how to take the blocks that Microsoft provides to create the picture on the box. This book will help you reshape some of the blocks as needed and see how new blocks can be created. It also looks at the tools Microsoft provides to help you fit the blocks together and where the new initiatives from Microsoft around Service-Oriented Architecture fit with the current application blocks for .NET.

A Brief History of Application Blocks

The benefits associated with reusing software assets have been touted for many years. Today developers spend a significant amount of time and energy searching for software libraries or code that provides functionality they need in an effort to avoid "reinventing the wheel." It is commonplace for developers to first search the Internet for code samples or reusable software libraries with the thought that "this must have been done before." Sometimes solutions can be located; other times they cannot. However, even when software libraries that solve common application problems can be located, using them is not without its challenges. The design and quality of an asset, as well as the future direction of that asset, must be assessed. Any dependencies upon which the asset relies must also be evaluated to determine whether using it will cause a company to move away from its own strategic vision.

The Microsoft application blocks were intended to help by providing a library of core assets needed for most enterprise applications. This began with the introduction of the original Data Access Application Block in April 2002. The block was popular because it was simple to understand (it had a very simple interface and no dependencies) and it covered the majority of common operations most projects required for accessing a Microsoft SQL Server database.

Over the next few years, more application blocks were introduced; however, those that followed the Data Access Application Block were met with varying degrees of acceptance. Overall, each application block was considered successful, but as more and more application blocks were created, issues began to arise about using them. These issues revolved around the following matters.

- **Consistency.** The application blocks were created by different teams at Microsoft over several years with no overall guidelines for consistency. The result was that application blocks varied widely in their approach and packaging. Users of the application blocks found it difficult to understand how each new block fit together. Additionally, because the blocks were inconsistent in their approach, many users found it difficult to get them to work together in the same project.
- **Configuration.** Most of the application blocks relied on complex configuration with little or no tooling support or validation that could help configure the application correctly. Configuring an application block entailed manually creating and modifying XML files and testing the results at runtime. This was one of the most common problems that users of the original blocks faced when trying to use them.
- **Complexity.** Many of the application blocks that followed the Data Access Application Block were difficult to understand. Yet to become productive with an application block, a developer needed to quickly ramp up by understanding how to configure, develop, and extend the block. There was a lack of samples and tutorials that could help a developer get up to speed very quickly on an application block. Additionally, the documentation that was provided with the appli-

cation blocks did not convey enough information for most developers to understand how to use the blocks.

- **Dependencies.** Companies sometimes wanted to use a block but found that they didn't want to accept the dependencies of that application block. Many times an application block had a hard dependency on other application blocks. For example, many blocks relied on the Exception Management Application Block. However, if an enterprise had no desire to use the Exception Management Application Block, it had to choose between removing the dependency manually or not using the application block at all. Also, the original Logging Application Block had a dependency on the Enterprise Instrumentation Framework (EIF). Users who didn't want to use the EIF could not use the logging block.

Enterprise Library is the evolution of the application blocks. It is not a product from Microsoft insomuch that you don't purchase a license for it. Additionally, all the source code for Enterprise Library is released to the public. These facts alone make it much different from any product that Microsoft releases. Enterprise Library's seven application blocks—Configuration, Data Access, Caching, Exception Handling, Logging and Instrumentation, Security, and Cryptography—are *truly* a library that can solve common challenges encountered in enterprise applications. It is not a part of the .NET Framework, but rather it is intended to fill what may be perceived as "gaps" in the Framework until such time that the .NET Framework absorbs those features.

The vision for Enterprise Library was to take the lessons that were learned with the original application blocks to not only create a set of the most fundamental application blocks needed for most enterprise applications, but to create an entire ecosystem in which Microsoft customers, partners, community members, and the patterns & practices team can deliver reusable assets that can be combined into code libraries based on the needs of an enterprise. The core philosophy behind Enterprise Library is defined by four principles that guide the development of all of the application blocks in the library.

- **Consistency.** Every application block should apply consistent design patterns and implementation approaches. This should make it easy for someone who understands one block to understand and use another block and thus become productive quickly.
- **Extensibility.** Application blocks must include defined extensibility points that let developers customize the behavior of the blocks by plugging in their own code. The goal is to anticipate the need for extensions and minimize the need to modify the core elements through custom code. By designing an application block for extensibility, the application block is able to adapt to different environments and has a greater chance of "fitting" into an enterprise than it might otherwise have had were it not designed this way.
- **Ease of Use.** For developers to embrace an application block, it must be easy to use. Therefore, the Enterprise Library team provided
  - *The Enterprise Library Configuration Tool.* As configuring the application blocks proved to be one of the most difficult aspects of usability, a graphical configuration tool was created to improve on this experience. The Configuration Tool makes it much easier to create, modify, remove, and validate configuration information for all of the application blocks that ship with Enterprise Library. This eliminates the need to have to manually modify XML files to get an application block to function correctly.
  - *A simpler installation procedure.* Setting up a development environment to use any of the application blocks has been made simpler.
  - *Clear documentation and samples.* The documentation for every application block includes key scenarios for how that application block might be used and includes walkthroughs for how to perform the most common tasks.
- **Integration.** Application blocks should be designed to work well together and tested to ensure that they do. However, it should also be possible to use one application block independently of another one. Throughout Enterprise Library, the integration of application blocks has been designed with the goal of loose coupling. This allows the application block on which another block depends to be

completely replaced with another asset without causing any issues to the calling block.

Lastly, it is important to point out that Enterprise Library is intended to serve as architectural guidance embodied in the code. Although it ships with the full source code, thus allowing any user the ability to modify it, care should be given before the block is modified, because each application block is intended to enforce best practices for solving specific challenges common to an enterprise-level application. In fact, in many of the chapters in this book I compare the design for an application block to the guidance that has been published by the Microsoft patterns & practices team. For many of the application blocks, the implementation of the application block is a direct result of following the guidance that lays out the blueprint for that particular block.

For example, the design for the Data Access Application Block focuses on how to use database providers in the data layer of an application. The guidance for this can be found in the *Application Architecture for .NET: Designing Applications and Services* publication.[1] Also, the Caching Application Block is an implementation of the guidance prescribed in the *Caching Architecture Guide for .NET Framework Applications*.[2] The Data Mapping Application Block that I created and provide more detail about in Chapter 9 and Appendix A is intended to be an implementation of the guidance for creating and using data access logic components in a distributed application, which is also promoted in the Architecture for .NET: Designing Applications and Services publication.

About This Book

Current .NET developers and architects will be interested in this book because it centers on how to use the Enterprise Library application blocks and recommended best practices from Microsoft to produce enterprise applications. I assume that the reader has experience with either Visual Basic.NET or C#. I have included code samples in both languages at every

1. Found at http://msdn.microsoft.com/library/default.asp?url=/library/en-us/dnbda/html/distapp.asp.
2. Found at http://msdn.microsoft.com/library/default.asp?url=/library/en-us/dnbda/html/CachingArch.asp.

point that I thought it was important to show how to take advantage of a block or to show how the block works.

I believe that most readers will fall into two groups: those who want to know how the Enterprise Library application blocks have been designed and how to take advantage of that design to extend Enterprise Library so that it better fits their needs, and those who just want more information about how to configure and develop an application to use Enterprise Library without any desire to extend any of the application blocks or to create their own.

I have tried to address the needs of both groups in this book. Each chapter addresses either a different application block in Enterprise Library or a specific aspect of Enterprise Library that is important to call out (e.g., the configuration design-time features or how to build a custom application block). For each application block, I begin with a detailed explanation of how the block is designed, the available extension points in that application block, and at least one custom, real-world example of how to create your own extension to that application block. I conclude each chapter with a walkthrough of how to configure the application block and write code to reap the benefits that the block provides.

If you don't care about the design or extensibility features of a block, you can skip right to the chapter's final section. If you already know the basics about how to configure and develop an application to use a block but want to know more about how to extend the block to suit your needs, read the first section. If you want to know as much as possible about a block, read the chapter from start to finish.

This book is organized into the following nine chapters and three appendixes.

Chapter 1: Configuration Application Block Runtime

This chapter is important for several reasons. It shows how the Configuration Application Block has been designed so that an enterprise application can use it to easily read and write configuration data while remaining completely decoupled from the actual storage type and location where that configuration data is contained. More significantly, however, this chapter is valuable because all the other application blocks that exist in Enterprise Library have a dependency on the Configuration Application Block. The

Configuration Application Block is the only application block that is a dependency of the other blocks. Because all of the application blocks are driven by configuration, it is critical to understand the role that this block plays in providing functionality for the other blocks. Many of the real-world extensions to Enterprise Library in this book rely on at least a basic understanding of the configuration runtime.

Chapter 2: Configuration Application Block Design-Time

This chapter is also important for all the reasons that the first chapter is important. One of the major design goals for Enterprise Library was to make it easy to configure the application blocks. The design-time features of the Configuration Application Block provide the features that are used to accomplish this goal. When designing extensions to any of the application blocks or creating a completely new application block, it is important to understand how the design-time features of the Configuration Application Block work so that any new extensions can also be made easy to use and configure.

Chapter 3: The Data Access Application Block

The Data Access Application Block provides a set of classes and interfaces that encapsulate many of the best practices that Microsoft recommends for designing a data layer. Specifically, Enterprise Library's Data Access Application Block provides a solution that satisfies the requirements for using database providers to produce cleaner and more manageable code. A new design goal with this version of the Data Access Application Block was to increase the probability that code using this block can be ported between different types of databases.

Chapter 4: The Caching Application Block

The Enterprise Library's Caching Application Block is an implementation of the Solution Blueprint for caching that is promoted in the *Caching Architecture Guide for .NET Framework Applications*. As a result, it exposes a simple and consistent programming interface that allows the code for an application to be written so that it is indifferent as to the type of caching store that is used. This allows the code for an application to remain unchanged even if the location where the cached data is stored changes.

Chapter 5: The Exception Handling Application Block

Enterprise Library's Exception Handling Application Block is a policy-driven system that lets an administrator determine *how* specific exceptions are handled in an application and a developer concentrate on *why* and *where* exceptions should be handled. The block is an implementation of the best practices promoted by the Microsoft patterns & practices team. This application block provides a very simple programming interface so that developers for the application don't need to be concerned about how an exception gets handled. This allows the code for an application to remain unchanged even if a change is made to the way an exception is handled or exception handlers are added or removed for a particular scenario.

Chapter 6: The Logging and Instrumentation Application Block

The Logging and Instrumentation Application Block provides a standard and consistent way to log and instrument messages independent of whether the message is destined for an event log, file, database, MSMQ, or WMI event. This application block is designed to make it easy for developers to incorporate logging and tracing functionality into an application without needing to know anything about how, where, or even if a message gets logged. In this chapter I show how the Logging and Instrumentation Application Block can be extended to provide capabilities to log information to other data sources if the features that are provided out-of-the-box do not fit your needs.

Chapter 7: The Security Application Block

The primary design goal for the Security Application Block was to make it easy for an enterprise to add authentication, authorization, role membership, security cache, and profile membership features to their applications. The Security Application Block ships with a relational security database, security database administration console, and security providers for that database that make it easy for an application to add security features without having to rely on some other external user store, for example, Microsoft Active Directory. At the same time, it is understood that many enterprises already have a system in place that stores information about its users, credentials, and roles in the enterprise. The Security Application Block has been designed so that it can easily be extended to meet the needs of these enterprises. In this chapter I show you how to do just that.

Chapter 8: The Cryptography Application Block

The Cryptography Application Block makes it easier for developers to add functionality to their applications for encrypting data, decrypting data, and creating and comparing hashes. The Cryptography Application Block uses many of the assets that exist in the .NET Cryptography API, while also eliminating some of the complexities that are associated with using it.

Chapter 9: Building an Application Block

All the chapters up until this point show how to extend the features of an application block so that it can fit the particular needs of an enterprise. The extensibility of Enterprise Library, however, does not end with the ability to just extend each application block. The Enterprise Library team expects—in fact, it promotes—the creation of new application blocks that solve the particular needs of enterprises. The application blocks that ship with Enterprise Library solve many of the challenging issues that are faced by most enterprise applications; however, there is no belief that they will solve all of them. If none of the application blocks that ship with Enterprise Library can solve your reoccurring challenge, then it is perfectly reasonable to create a new application block that can solve this need and can serve as a peer to the application blocks that ship with Enterprise Library. In this chapter I walk you through the steps that are needed to create a new application block that will solve your problems.

Appendix A: The Data Mapping Application Block

In Chapter 9 I describe the steps to create a new application block. This new block, the Data Mapping Application Block, is intended to make it easier for developers to create data access logic components that subscribe to the best practices as promoted by the Microsoft patterns & practices team. In this appendix I provide details with respect to the design of that application block and how to configure and develop an application to use it.

Appendix B: Building a .NET Managed Data Provider

In Chapter 3 I describe the database providers that ship with Enterprise Library and show how to extend the Data Access Application Block by creating a new database provider. A prerequisite for a database provider is the existence of a .NET managed data provider that exposes an implementation for the interfaces that need to be returned by that database provider. In this appendix I show how to create a .NET managed data provider for the rare cases where you need one that does not already exist.

Appendix C: Enterprise Library for the .NET Framework 2.0

This book explains the design of Enterprise Library for the .NET Framework 1.1 and how to extend, develop, and configure Enterprise Library's application blocks. In January 2006, Enterprise Library for the .NET Framework 2.0 was released. In this appendix I highlight the important differences between Enterprise Library for the .NET Framework 1.1 and Enterprise Library for the .NET Framework 2.0.

Acknowledgments

I WOULD FIRST LIKE to thank the technical reviewers for this book—Bill Ryan, Brian Davis, Klaus H. Probst, and Les Smith—for taking the time to review the manuscript and for all of your valuable feedback. Your suggestions were enormously helpful in making certain that the book was on target and that the tone was appropriate for the targeted audience.

Special thanks go to Scott Densmore and Tom Hollander. Your tough, but fair, reviews were critical to reshaping the book into what it is today. You were instrumental in pointing out important areas that needed to be discussed and never seemed shy about telling me areas that should be cut or areas that didn't seem "quite right." The book would be but a shell of its current form were it not for your insight.

My editors, Joan Murray, Jessica D'Amico, Jim Markham, and Rebecca Greenberg, guided me through the writing of this book. Your advice has been invaluable. There has been much that I have learned about writing a book through this experience. Whenever things looked bleak, you never seemed to lose faith in me and were always encouraging. Thank you for that.

Amber, you were the only one that was by my side every night, even until three in the morning. You're a good dog.

Lexa, Evan, and Ana, I tried not to let the writing of this book take away from our time together; however, I know that there were times that it was difficult. I thank you for constantly understanding when Daddy had to be writing and I apologize for the "grouchy mornings" when I was up writing all night. Your love helped keep the candle burning at both ends.

Lisa, thank you for your love and patience. I could not have done this without you behind me all the way. I apologize for the nights, weekends, holidays, and vacations that were missed so that this book could be written. I appreciate your constant encouragement and your patience when there was always just "a little more left to be written." I look forward to making up for the time that was missed during the year it took to write this book. I love you.

About the Author

Len Fenster is the lead architect for .NET Development for Microsoft Consulting Service's U.S. East Region. During his last eight years at Microsoft, he has focused on helping many enterprises create robust applications based on Microsoft technology. Most recently, Len has been working with the Microsoft patterns and practices team on the next version of Enterprise Library. Even before his career with Microsoft, Len led a global team of developers and architects that built distributed applications based on Microsoft technologies. Since the advent of .NET, Len has served as an enterprise architect for Microsoft Consulting Services and has leveraged his considerable experience to help many enterprises incorporate .NET into their own technology strategies. Len speaks on a regular basis to companies and at architecture forums about architecting solutions based on .NET and service oriented architecture.

1 The Configuration Application Block Runtime

WHY START THIS book with a discussion of the Configuration Application Block? After all, there certainly must be more interesting topics than reading and writing configuration data for an application. True as that may be, the Configuration Application Block is the most important block in Enterprise Library. All other blocks depend on the Configuration Application Block to provide the functionality that drives their specific behavior. The application blocks that ship with Enterprise Library are no different than most applications and assemblies in this respect: they require some form of configuration information to operate properly. Understanding the design of the Configuration Application Block will help you grasp the concepts of the other application blocks. In short, the Configuration Application Block is the "glue" that combines the other application blocks into one "library."

This chapter describes how the Configuration Application Block has been designed to allow a loose coupling to exist between an enterprise application or application block and the data stores that contain its configuration data. It details how the Configuration Application Block manages the configuration data internally and includes detailed information on how specific features in the Configuration Application Block work. It discusses how configuration data must be structured for it to be read and written by the Configuration Application Block, and how StorageProviders and Transformers are used to achieve the design goal of decoupling an application from the form and storage location of its configuration data.

This chapter also describes how to create new StorageProviders and Transformers to extend the capabilities of the Configuration Application Block and looks at the classes that are used to manage configuration data and the role of each. The chapter concludes by showing how to take advantage of these classes to read and write configuration data for an application.

What Is the Configuration Application Block?

The previous version of Enterprise Library's Configuration Application Block was called the Configuration Management Application Block. In Enterprise Library, the word *Management* has been dropped from all application blocks that had it as part of their name. There are a few reasons for this. First, configuration management is a larger discipline than this block really addresses. Second, all the application blocks provide management of some kind, so including *Management* as part of the name seemed superfluous.

Like the Configuration Management Application Block, Enterprise Library's Configuration Application Block is designed to ease the burden of storing and retrieving configuration information from an underlying data store and ensure the security and integrity of the configuration data. At the heart of the Configuration Application Block is the ability to decouple read and write operations for configuration data from the specifics of its underlying data store. It accomplishes this through **StorageProviders**, objects that transfer data between an application and a particular configuration data store (e.g., an XML file, the Windows Registry, or a database).

The Configuration Application Block also provides a simple application programming interface for performing the most common configuration tasks, like reading and writing configuration data. Retrieving configuration data, for example, only requires a single line of code. Additional methods and classes also exist to handle atypical configuration scenarios. While StorageProviders existed in the previous versions on the Configuration Application Block, some enhancements have been made to Enterprise Library's version that distinguishes it from its predecessor.

- **Transformers.** Transformers are new with Enterprise Library's version of the Configuration Application Block. Transformers are objects that are responsible for transforming the data returned from a configuration store into a form that an application can use. Enterprise Library's Configuration Application Block ships with the `XmlSerializerTransformer`, a generic Transformer that takes configuration information and serializes/deserializes it via the `XmlSerializer` object.
- **Design-time capability.** Configuring the previous application blocks consisted of manually editing XML files. I am certain that many developers have spent endless hours debugging applications only to find that the issue was due to an error in the configuration information. In this version, the Microsoft patterns & practices team—the creators of Enterprise Library—has introduced the **Enterprise Library Configuration Tool**, a graphical, design-time configuration tool that is intended to be used for entering and editing an application's configuration information. This tool eliminates the burden of having to manually edit the configuration information and thus reduces the probability of configuration errors. The Configuration Tool will be examined in detail in the next chapter.

Lastly, if the needs of a particular enterprise application cannot be completely provided by the features that ship right out of the box, you can extend the Configuration Application Block by creating custom Storage-Providers and Transformers. Both of these constructs are covered in detail later in this chapter.

Design of the Configuration Application Block Runtime

There are two parts to the Configuration Application Block: the runtime and the design-time (the design and features of the design-time are covered in the next chapter). The runtime component focuses on simplifying the reading and writing of configuration data, which allows applications to be loosely coupled with their configuration data stores, and providing a model that allows a developer to extend the capabilities of the block for situations where the Configuration Application Block doesn't perfectly fit an enterprise's needs (e.g., the need to store configuration data in a relational database other than Microsoft SQL Server).

Reading and Writing Configuration Data

The first step to being able to read and write configuration data in an application is to determine the in-memory representation of that data. Without that, nothing else matters. This representation might be as simple as a string or as complex as an object graph.

For the Configuration Application Block to read and write this data, it must be able to represent the data in a serial format. The Configuration Application Block requires that an object representing configuration information supports XML serialization. This way, the data in an object that is described as public classes, fields, properties, primitive types, arrays, and embedded XML in the form of `XmlElement` or `XmlAttribute` objects will get serialized. When the Configuration Application Block saves the state for such an object, it uses the `XmlSerializer` to save the public properties and fields as XML. When it recreates the object, it deserializes it from this XML.

An example might help illustrate this point. Imagine that you have a simple Windows application that can contain numerous tabs; each tab has different background colors, labels, and data in it. The number of tabs in the application, label for the tags, background color, and information on the tab are all configurable. To represent this information, a `TabConfig` class can be defined that contains an array of `ApplicationTab` objects. An `ApplicationTab` object contains information like the name of the tab, the background color, and a string to display on the tab. Listing 1.1 shows what the `ApplicationTab` class might look like so that it supports XML serialization.

LISTING 1.1: ApplicationTab Class Sample

```
[C#]
/// <summary>
/// Represents the information for a tab.
/// </summary>
public class ApplicationTab
{
      private Color tabColor;
      private string label;
      private string message;
```

```
    /// <summary>
    /// Default constructor
    /// </summary>
    public ApplicationTab() {}

    /// <summary>
    /// Don't save this attribute.
    /// Provided to facilitate getting/setting
    /// background color of tab through code.
    /// </summary>
     [XmlIgnore]
    public Color TabColor
    {
         get
         {
              return this.tabColor;
         }
         set
         {
              if (! value.IsEmpty)
                   this.tabColor = value;
         }
    }

    /// <summary>
    /// Used to serialize the color for the tab.
    /// Will be serialized with tag of TabColor.
    /// </summary>
     [XmlElement("TabColor")]
    public string BackColor
    {
         get
         {
              ColorConverter colorConverter = new ColorConverter();
              return colorConverter.ConvertToString(TabColor);
         }
         set
         {
              if (value != null)
              {
                   ColorConverter colorConverter =
                        new ColorConverter();
                        TabColor =
                        (Color)colorConverter.ConvertFromString(value);
              }
         }
    }
...
}
```

```
[Visual Basic]
Public Class ApplicationTab
     Private myTabColor As Color
     Private myLabel As String
     Private message As String

     ' Default constructor
     Public Sub New()
     End Sub

     ' Don't save this attribute.
     ' Provided to facilitate getting/setting
     ' background color of tab through code.
     <XmlIgnore> _
     Public Property TabColor() As Color
          Get
               Return Me.myTabColor
          End Get
          Set
               If (Not Value.IsEmpty) Then
                    Me.myTabColor = Value
               End If
          End Set
     End Property

     ' Used to serialize the color for the tab.
     ' Will be serialized with tag of TabColor.
     <XmlElement("TabColor")> _
     Public Property BackColor() As String
          Get
               Dim colorConverter As ColorConverter = _
                    New ColorConverter()
               Return colorConverter.ConvertToString(TabColor)
          End Get
          Set
               If Not Value Is Nothing Then
                    Dim colorConverter As ColorConverter = _
                         New ColorConverter()
                    TabColor = CType(colorConverter.ConvertFromString _
                         (Value), _ Color)
               End If
          End Set
     End Property

...
End Class
```

All public fields and properties will be serialized except for those that are explicitly marked with the `XmlIgnore` attribute. In Listing 1.1, the `TabColor` property will not be serialized because it is attributed with `XmlIgnore`, but the `BackColor` property will be serialized as a `TabColor` element because it is attributed as `XmlElement("TabColor")`.

Other public properties, like `Label` and `Message`, which are not shown in Listing 1.1, will just be serialized with the name of that property because they are not attributed in any way. The `TabConfig class` contains a public property that allows the entire array of `ApplicationTab` objects to be serialized and deserialized. The complete source code for this chapter is on the book's Web site. When this application uses the Configuration Application Block to save its configuration data, it might look Listing 1.2.

LISTING 1.2: Sample Configuration for the ApplicationTab Class

```
<?xml version="1.0" encoding="utf-8"?>
<TabConfig>
  <xmlSerializerSection type="Defining_Config_Info.TabConfig, Defining
      Config Info, Version=1.0.2119.14112, Culture=neutral,
      PublicKeyToken=null">
    <TabConfig xmlns:xsd="http://www.w3.org/2001/XMLSchema"
           xmlns:xsi="http://www.w3.org/2001/XMLSchema-instance">
      <Tabs>
        <ApplicationTab>
          <TabColor>Green</TabColor>
          <Label>Tab1</Label>
          <Message>This is Tab1</Message>
        </ApplicationTab>
        <ApplicationTab>
          <TabColor />
          <Label>Tab Numero Duo</Label>
          <Message>This is Tab2</Message>
        </ApplicationTab>
        <ApplicationTab>
          <TabColor />
          <Label>Tab3</Label>
          <Message>This is the third tab</Message>
        </ApplicationTab>
      </Tabs>
    </TabConfig>
  </xmlSerializerSection>
</TabConfig>
```

Decoupling Physical Storage Location

Although I have described how the configuration data needs to be represented in order to be serialized and deserialized by the Configuration Application Block, I have not mentioned anything about *where* it gets stored. That is because a developer does not need to know anything about location for the configuration data. By using the Configuration Application Block, determining *where* configuration data gets stored is more of an operational issue than it is a development decision.

The Configuration Application Block uses a different set of configuration data, known as **configuration metadata** or **metaconfiguration**, which tells it where to store the application configuration data. The metaconfiguration is always stored in the application domain configuration file (i.e., app.config or web.config), so the Configuration Application Block always has one place to go to read it. The application configuration data, like that shown in Listing 1.2, can be placed in a separate data store, separated from the metaconfiguration.

While this feature may seem trivial at first, it is actually quite powerful. The application can be completely ignorant about the physical location of its configuration data. It does not need to know whether the configuration data is stored in a file, the Windows Registry, a relational database, or some other type of data store. Thus, you don't need to write code to store configuration data in one of those particular data stores. At a later date, if the personnel responsible for the operations and maintenance of the application decide to change the location for where the configuration data should be stored, they merely have to modify the metaconfiguration for the application; no code needs to change.

StorageProviders and Transformers are the keys to insulating applications from the physical storage location and providing an extensible model that allows for custom storage locations (see Figure 1.1).

- A StorageProvider allows an application to have its metaconfiguration stored in a data store other than the one that houses the application data.

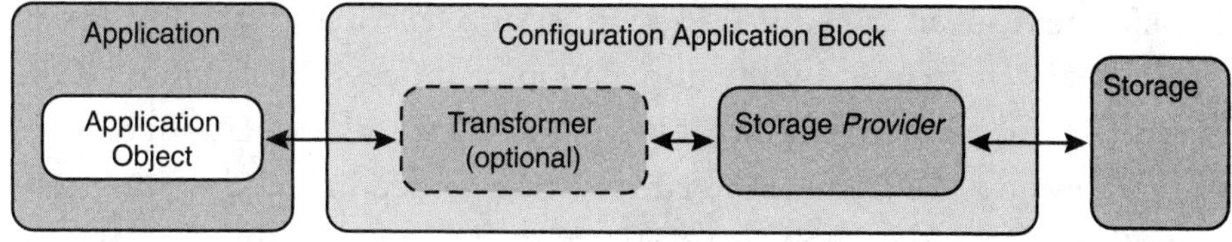

FIGURE 1.1: Reading and Writing Configuration Objects

- The `IStorageProviderReader` interface defines the interface that is used to read configuration information from a storage location.
- The `IStorageProviderWriter` interface defines the interface that is used to write configuration information.
- The `ITransformer` interface transforms configuration setting objects between the application and the StorageProvider.

Enterprise Library ships with four StorageProviders: the XmlFileStorageProvider, the AppConfigFileStorageProvider, the RegistryStorageProvider, and the SqlStorageProvider. As the names imply, these are used for reading and writing configuration data from and to XML files (other than the application domain configuration file), the application configuration file, the Windows Registry, and Microsoft SQL Server respectively.

StorageProviders have just two responsibilities: reading configuration data from a particular data source and writing data to a particular data source. The XmlFileStorageProvider, for example, points to a file that contains particular configuration settings and accepts and returns objects of type `XmlNode`. The design behind the other StorageProviders is the same except that RegistryStorageProvider has code that reads and writes to Registry keys, and SqlStorageProvider uses database connections, commands, and stored procedures for reading and writing to Microsoft SQL Server.

I mentioned earlier that configuration data must be serialized and deserialized. This job, however, is not the responsibility of a StorageProvider. Once the data is read or written, the StorageProvider's job is complete. Serializing and deserializing the configuration data is the job of a Transformer. Enterprise Library ships with an `XmlSerializerTransformer`. This

Transformer uses an `XmlSerializer` to serialize and deserialize the data to a form that can be used by the application or process. By default, all the Enterprise Library application blocks leverage the `XmlFileStorageProvider` and `XmlSerializerTransformer` for reading and writing configuration data from and to XML files. Figure 1.2 shows how an `XmlSerializerTransformer` and an `XmlFileStorageProvider` can be combined to serialize and deserialize configuration data to and from an XML format and to read and write that configuration data to an XML file.

When you save configuration data using the `XmlSerializerTransformer`, the `XmlSerializer` is used to serialize the configuration data to an `XmlNode` object. If you also use the `XmlFileStorageProvider`, then the XML is written to the predefined file. When the configuration data is read, the reverse process happens: the `XmlFileStorageProvider` reads the data from the XML file and returns an `XmlNode` object. Then the `XmlSerializerTransformer` deserializes the data and returns it to the application block, which then returns it to the application. If the RegistryStorageProvider is used instead of the `XmlFileStorageProvider`, the data is read and written using the Registry. Using a specific Transformer does not necessitate using a particular StorageProvider; the two are distinct from one another and can be assembled in any combination.

Providers in Enterprise Library

The ability to decouple the configuration data from a specific data store or format is not a result of a specific implementation for a StorageProvider or Transformer. It is a result of the **Provider Model Design Pattern** that exists

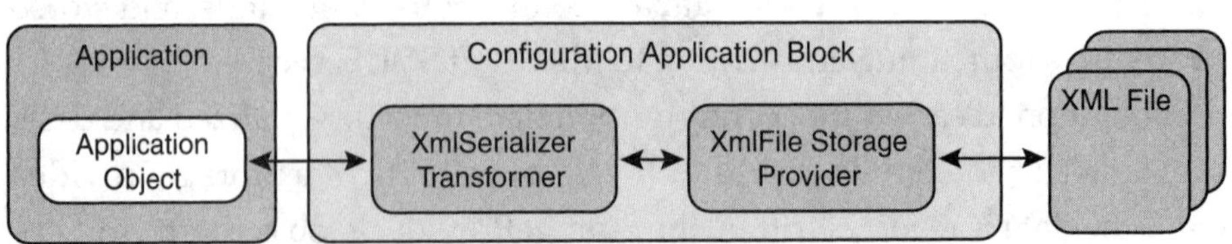

FIGURE 1.2: Reading and Writing to XML Files

in the Configuration Application Block. This pattern allows an easy-to-understand interface to be used while also providing complete control over the internals of what occurs when an implementation of that interface is called. A **provider** is a contract between an interface and an application or process that consumes that interface. The provider is the implementation of the interface separated from the interface itself.[1]

There are some common characteristics for providers. A concrete, provider implementation should derive from an abstract base class or interface that is used to define a contract for a particular feature. The `XmlFileStorageProvider`, for example, derives from the `StorageProvider` base class. This base class in turn typically derives from a common provider base class. In Enterprise Library, all providers either directly or indirectly implement the `IConfigurationProvider` interface. This provider base class is used to mark implementers as a provider and forces the implementation of a required method and property common to all providers.

For example, when configuration data is read, the Configuration Application Block uses its metaconfiguration data to determine which implementation of the `IStorageProviderReader` interface it should instantiate; when configuration data is written, the Configuration Application Block uses its metaconfiguration data to determine which implementation of the `IStorageProviderWriter` to instantiate. Since applications typically read data from the same data store to which they write data, the Configuration Application Block only allows one StorageProvider for both operations. The Configuration Application Block is not written to know anything about a specific implementation for a StorageProvider, though; it is written to use the `StorageProvider` interface. Through its metaconfiguration, it determines which instance of the provider to use at runtime.

A closer look at the design for StorageProviders and Transformers can help you understand how this pattern is used in the Configuration Application Block and throughout all the Enterprise Library application blocks.

---

1. Summarized from Rob Howard's *Provider Design Pattern, Part 1 and 2* at http://msdn.microsoft.com/library/default.asp?url=/library/en-us/dnaspnet/html/asp04212004.asp

The `IConfigurationProvider` Interface and the `ConfigurationProvider` Class

Enterprise Library follows the Provider Model Design Pattern by requiring that all providers implement the `IConfigurationProvider` interface in order for the Configuration Application Block to properly create them. The `IConfigurationProvider` interface is very straightforward—it consists of a property called `ConfigurationName` and a method named `Initialize`. The Configuration Application Block also includes an abstract base class named `ConfigurationProvider` that implements the `ConfigurationName` property of the `IConfigurationProvider` interface. This is included to make it easier to create providers. Thus, providers do not need to explicitly implement the `IConfigurationProvider` interface, but can instead derive from the `ConfigurationProvider` base class and implement the `Initialize` method. This method initializes the provider to the correct state and context used by the factory creating it.

The `Initialize` method accepts an object representing the current `ConfigurationView` and uses it to obtain the provider's runtime configuration data. The `ConfigurationView` base class signifies a wrapper around a specific type of configuration information. For example, a Storage-Provider expects the `ConfigurationView` to be of type `RunTimeConfigurationView` because it holds the metaconfiguration data which has, among other things, configuration information specific to a configuration data store (e.g., information about the name of the file for an XmlFileStorage-Provider). In the Data Access Application Block, a database provider expects a `DatabaseConfigurationView` because a `DatabaseConfigurationView` contains configuration data specific to that type of database provider (e.g., connection information for connecting to Microsoft SQL Server).

The `ConfigurationView` is very important because it isolates a provider from having to know anything about how to retrieve the data that is needed. This lets an application that uses these providers respond to changes in the underlying configuration data store. If an `XmlFileStorageProvider` is used because configuration data is held in an XML file, and that XML file is modified outside of the application, the configuration runtime is made aware of this fact and the new configuration data can be retrieved and used. This is extremely effective, as it also allows configuration data to be cached by the Configuration Application Block without concern for that data becoming stale.

It is also important to recognize that the configuration runtime is caching the configuration data and therefore there is no need (and it is not recommended) to cache references to this data yourself. How, exactly, the Configuration Application Block is able to recognize and respond to a change that has occurred in a particular configuration data store is an implementation detail in a specific StorageProvider.

The `IStorageProviderReader` and `IConfigurationChangeWatcherFactory` Interfaces and the StorageProvider Class

To read configuration data from a particular data store, a StorageProvider must implement the `IStorageProviderReader` interface. As such, any implementation of an `IStorageProviderReader` must implement the `Initialize` method so that the Configuration Application Block can initialize the StorageProvider to its correct state and context.

In addition to inheriting from the `IConfigurationProvider` interface, the `IStorageProviderReader` interface also inherits from the `IConfigurationChangeWatcherFactory` interface. This allows the configuration runtime to recognize and react to changes that occur in the StorageProvider's data source. `IConfigurationCacheWatcherFactory` defines a single method: `CreateConfigurationChangeWatcher`.

Since the `IStorageProviderReader` interface implements the `IConfigurationChangeWatcherFactory` interface, any class that implements `IStorageProviderReader` must also have a `CreateConfigurationChangeWatcher` method. This method must return an `IConfigurationChangeWatcher`, which provides a StorageProviderReader with the ability to watch for changes in a particular configuration data store. Unfortunately, even if this functionality is not needed, it is still required that a `StorageProviderReader` return an `IConfigurationChangeWatcher`.

In this scenario, a ChangeWatcher that does nothing must be created and returned. Scott Densmore, the lead software development engineer for Enterprise Library, has written an example of a `ChangeWatcher` that does nothing and that can be used in these situations. For more

TABLE 1.1: Implementation Requirements to Support the IStorageProviderReader Interface

Method/Properties	Description
`SectionName`	Gets or sets the configuration section name for which the storage is configured.
`CreateConfigurationChangeWatcher`	Creates an object that is responsible for watching for changes in the underlying storage mechanism for configuration persistence. When a change occurs, this object must raise its `ConfigurationChange` event.
`Read`	Reads the configuration from storage.

information on this `ChangeWatcher`, see Scott's blog at http://blogs.msdn.com/scottdensmore. Creating an `IConfigurationWatcher` that actually does do something is the most difficult task in creating a `StorageProviderReader`. This is true for several reasons, which are discussed later in this chapter.

Similar to the `ConfigurationProvider`, the Configuration Application Block supplies an abstract `StorageProvider`[2] base class to make creating `StorageProviderReaders` easy. To create a `StorageProviderReader`, you only need to derive from the `StorageProvider` class and implement the `Initialize`, `CreateConfigurationChangeWatcher`, and `Read` methods. Table 1.1 lists the methods and properties that a derived StorageProvider class needs to implement to support the `IStorageProviderReader` interface.

The `IStorageProviderWriter` Interface

The `IStorageProviderWriter` interface represents a StorageProvider writer for configuration data. Only the Write method needs to be imple-

2. Long before it was released, the `StorageProvider` used to implement both the `IStorageProviderWriter` and `IStorageProviderReader` interfaces. It was changed shortly before release to only implement the `IStorageProviderReader` interface to support StorageProviders that only need read-only data. The 'Reader' suffix, however, was never added on to the name for this class.

mented to support the `IStorageProviderWriter`. The Configuration Application Block calls the `IStorageProviderWriter`'s `Write` method to save configuration data to storage.

Enterprise Library StorageProviders

Enterprise Library ships with four StorageProviders: XmlFileStorageProvider, AppConfigFileStorageProvider, RegistryStorageProvider, and SqlStorageProvider. All of these StorageProviders inherit from the `StorageProvider` base class and implement the `IStorageProviderWriter`, as illustrated in Figure 1.3. Each StorageProvider has been created to read and write configuration data from a different data store.

- The XmlFileStorageProvider reads and writes configuration data from and to the XML files.
- The AppConfigFileStorageProvider represents a StorageProvider to read and write data to an application domain configuration file (i.e., app.config or web.config). This allows the metaconfiguration and configuration data to exist in one file, since the metaconfiguration data will always reside in the application domain configuration file.
- The RegistryStorageProvider reads and writes configuration data from and to the Windows Registry. The RegistryStorageProvider existed in the previous Configuration Block and was introduced to Enterprise Library shortly after its initial release. As such, the design goals and implementation details are the same as they were in the previous version of the Configuration Block. For security reasons, only the Current_User, Local_Machine, and Users registry hives are supported
- The SqlStorageProvider reads and writes configuration data from and to a Microsoft SQL Server database table (the `Configuration_Parameters` table). A trigger exists on this table that updates information to be used for detecting changes to the configuration data that occur outside of a particular application. Like the RegistryStorageProvider, the SqlStorageProvider existed in the previous Configuration Block and was introduced to Enterprise Library shortly after its initial release.

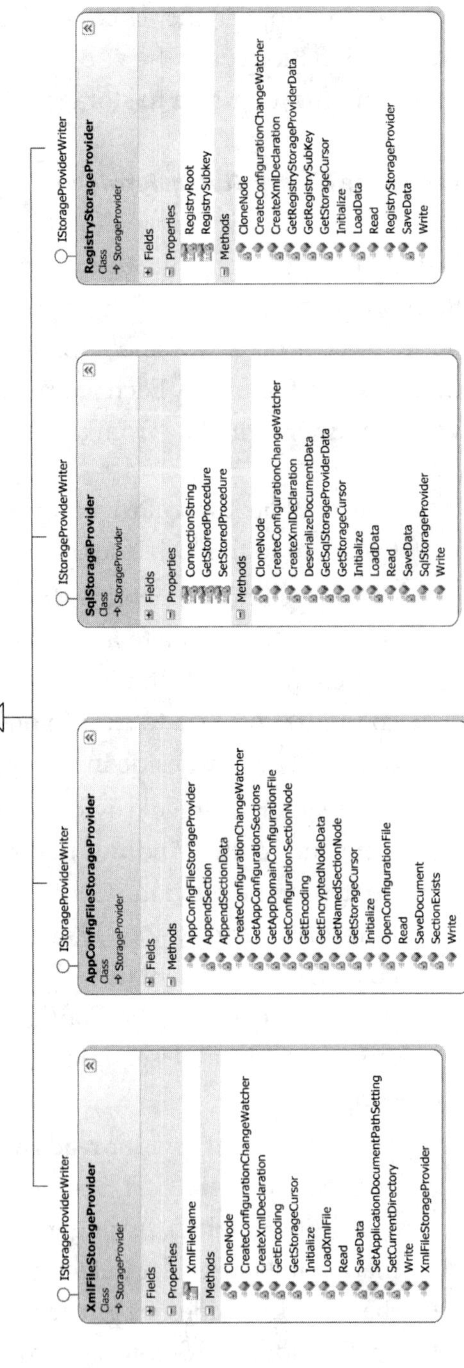

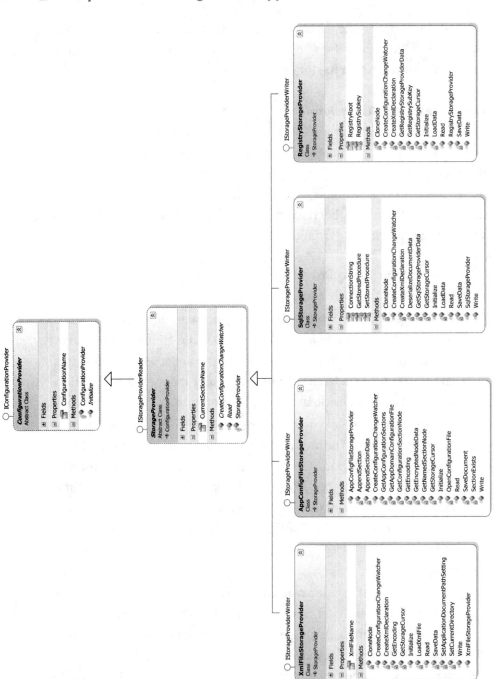

FIGURE 1.3: StorageProviders in Enterprise Library

A Custom StorageProvider: DatabaseStorageProvider

When Enterprise Library was initially released, it only shipped with the XmlFileStorageProvider. If you wanted to store configuration data somewhere besides XML files, there were few choices but to create your own custom StorageProvider. Soon after the initial release, the Enterprise Library Team released a patch that included several extensions. Three of these are the AppConfigFileStorageProvider, RegistryStorageProvider, and the SqlStorageProvider.

Still, these additional providers don't negate the possible need for a custom StorageProvider. What if an enterprise has standardized on a relational database technology other than Microsoft SQL Server yet prefers to have configuration data stored in a database? Are they left with having to choose between using Enterprise Library and their standard relational database?

The answer is no. Recall that subscribing to the Provider Model Design Pattern only exposes an application to the interface for a provider; an application is not bound to a particular implementation of a provider. If a different provider is needed to meet a particular circumstance, it can be developed and used without any code modifications to an application.

This section walks you through the details for creating a custom StorageProvider. This provider uses the Data Access Application Block for abstracting away the details involved with connecting to different types of relational database engines. (The Data Access Application Block is covered in Chapter 3, so you may not understand all of its features. At this point, it is only necessary to understand one of the primary concepts behind the Data Access Application Block: subscribing to the Provider Model Design Pattern allows an application or service to abstract away the details with connecting to a particular data store.) I leverage this feature to enhance the `SqlStorageProvider`. Since this new StorageProvider will no longer be specific to Microsoft SQL Server, I've named it `DatabaseStorageProvider`.

There are five steps to create this custom StorageProvider and one step to configure it.

1. Set up the database (specific to this StorageProvider).
2. Create a class that acts as the data transfer object for the provider. The sole purpose for this class is to represent the data needed for a particular provider.

3. Create the ConfigurationChangedEventArgs and ConfigurationChangingEventArgs classes that are specific to this StorageProvider.
4. Create a ConfigurationChangeWatcher class that is specific to the StorageProvider.
5. Create the StorageProvider.
6. Configure the new StorageProvider for an application.

Figure 1.4 depicts steps 2–5.

Step 1: Set Up the Database

This step is not needed for every custom StorageProvider, but it is necessary for this one. A modified SQL script from the one that is used for Enterprise Library's SQLStorageProvider can be used to create the database for this StorageProvider. This script makes it easy to extend a database with a table for storing an application's configuration data, stored procedures for retrieving and storing this data, and a trigger that will update a `DateTime` field to signify that the configuration data has been modified. To use a database other than Microsoft SQL Server, you will need to modify this script.

Step 2: Create the Data Transfer Object

The first task is to create a data transfer object to represent the information needed for reading and writing configuration data from and to the database. To represent this information, I have encapsulated three strings: one for holding the name of the database instance, one for holding the name of the stored procedure that will retrieve the configuration data, and one for holding the name of the stored procedure that will set the configuration data.

The `DatabaseStorageProviderData` class is derived from the abstract `StorageProviderData` class, as shown in Figure 1.4. In this model, it is the StorageProviderData classes that actually maintain the information about their respective StorageProvider. The `DatabaseStorageProviderData` class is a serializable class that contains properties for getting and setting the three strings mentioned in the previous paragraph. Listing 1.3 shows the code for the `DatabaseStorageProviderData`.

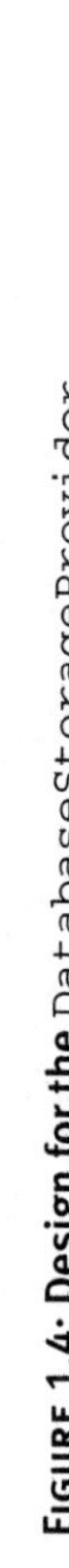

FIGURE 1.4: Design for the `DatabaseStorageProvider`

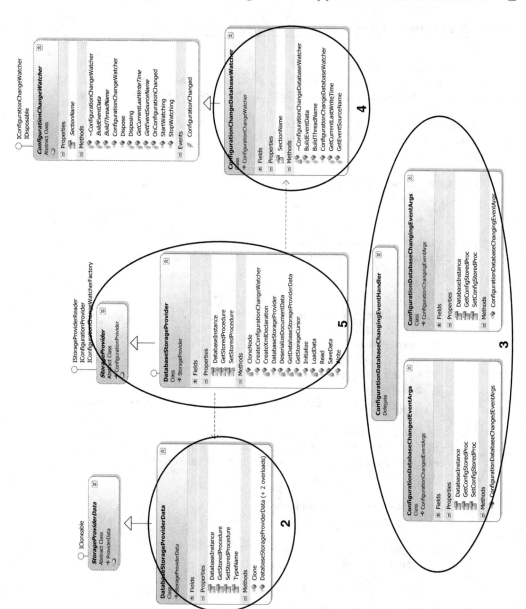

Listing 1.3: DatabaseStorageProviderData Class

```
[C#]
[XmlRoot("storageProvider",
    Namespace=ConfigurationSettings.ConfigurationNamespace)]
public class DatabaseStorageProviderData : StorageProviderData
{
      private string databaseInstance;
      private string getStoredProcedure;
      private string setStoredProcedure;

      public DatabaseStorageProviderData() : this(string.Empty)
      {
      }

      public DatabaseStorageProviderData(string name) :
          this(name, string.Empty, string.Empty, string.Empty)
      {
      }

      public DatabaseStorageProviderData(
               string name,
               string dbInstanceString,
               string getStoredProcedure,
               string setStoredProcedure) :
               base(name,
                  typeof(DatabaseStorageProvider).AssemblyQualifiedName)
      {
           this.databaseInstance = dbInstanceString;
           this.getStoredProcedure = getStoredProcedure;
           this.setStoredProcedure = setStoredProcedure
      }

      [XmlAttribute("databaseInstance")]
      public string DatabaseInstance
      {
          get { return databaseInstance; }
          set { databaseInstance = value;}
      }

      [XmlAttribute("getStoredProcedure")]
      public string GetStoredProcedure
      {
          get { return this.getStoredProcedure; }
          set { this.getStoredProcedure = value; }
      }

      [XmlAttribute("setStoredProcedure")]
      public string SetStoredProcedure
      {
```

```
        get { return this.setStoredProcedure; }
        set { this.setStoredProcedure = value; }
    }

    [XmlIgnore]
    public override string TypeName
    {
        get
        {
            return
            typeof(DatabaseStorageProvider).AssemblyQualifiedName;
        }
        set
        {
        }
    }
}

[Visual Basic]
<XmlRoot("storageProvider", _
        Namespace:=ConfigurationSettings.ConfigurationNamespace)> _
Public Class DatabaseStorageProviderData : Inherits StorageProviderData
    Dim databaseInstance As String
    Dim getStoredProcedure As String
    Dim setStoredProcedure As String

    Public Sub New()
        Me.New(String.Empty)
    End Sub

    Public Sub New(ByVal name As String)
        Me.New(name, String.Empty, String.Empty, String.Empty)
    End Sub

    Public DatabaseStorageProviderData(_
            String name, _
            String dbInstanceString, _
            String getStoredProcedure, _
            String setStoredProcedure)
        MyBase.New(name, _
            GetType(DatabaseStorageProvider).AssemblyQualifiedName)
            Me.databaseInstance     = dbInstanceString
            Me.getStoredProcedure     = getStoredProcedure
            Me.setStoredProcedure     = setStoredProcedure
    End Sub

    <XmlAttribute("databaseInstance")> _
    Public Property DatabaseInstance() As String
        Get
            Return databaseInstance
```

```
            End Get
            Set
                databaseInstance = Value
            End Set
        End Property

        <XmlAttribute("getStoredProcedure")> _
        Public Property GetStoredProcedure() As String
            Get
                Return Me.getStoredProcedure
            End Get
            Set
                Me.getStoredProcedure = Value
            End Set
        End Property

        <XmlAttribute("setStoredProcedure")> _
        Public Property SetStoredProcedure() As String
            Get
                Return Me.setStoredProcedure
            End Get
            Set
                Me.setStoredProcedure = Value
            End Set
        End Property

        <XmlIgnore> _
        Public Overrides Property TypeName() As String
            Get
                Return _
                GetType(DatabaseStorageProvider).AssemblyQualifiedName
            End Get
            Set
            End Set
        End Property
    End Class
```

Step 3: Create the Classes That Are Specific to This StorageProvider

This is the least straightforward part of creating a StorageProvider. The first task that needs to be completed for enabling a StorageProvider to detect changes in the underlying data store is to create `ConfigurationChanged-EventArgs` and `ConfigurationChangingEventArgs` for it. These classes are used as the arguments that get passed to the Configuration Application Block when a change occurs. They need to contain data for the `Configura-`

tionChanged event to make it easy for event handlers to understand where a change may have occurred.

The classes are specific to the data described in the data transfer object for that StorageProvider. So, instead of passing in a filename like that used for XmlFileStorageProvider, the ConfigurationChangedEventArgs and ConfigurationChangingEventArgs for the DatabaseStorageProvider need the name of the DatabaseInstance and two stored procedures. It would be ideal to derive these from abstract base classes and simply supply the new values needed. However, in Enterprise Library, the ConfigurationChangedEventArgs is not an abstract base class.

Figure 1.5 shows the design for the ConfigurationChangedEventArgs in Enterprise Library. Because it assumes a file-based configuration is used, the base class, ConfigurationChangedEventArgs, contains member variables and properties relevant to a configuration file. This variable and property are vestigial for the SqlStorageProvider's and RegistryStorageProvider's ConfigurationChangedEventArgs. When these StorageProviders were created (which occurred after the initial release of Enterprise Library), their ConfigurationChangedEventArgs were derived from the base ConfigurationChangedEventArgs class and simply ignored the variable and property pertaining to the file. There's not really any harm done in doing this; passing in an empty string for the file name to the constructor will not cause any issues if the data store is not actually a file.

This may seem like blasphemy to object-oriented "purists," and some architects are not comfortable with vestigial properties and ignoring variables. For the benefit of these architects, I have included a modified Configuration Application Block on the book's Web site. The modifications include the ConfigurationChangedEventArgs class, an abstract base class, and a new ConfigurationFileChangedEventArgs class that derives from it (and is a sibling to ConfigurationSqlChangedEventArgs and ConfigurationRegistryChangedEventArgs). This code is intended solely for those who *must* have a pure approach; other than that there is very little benefit to using it. In fact, I believe it to be a best practice to not modify the code supplied with Enterprise Library, but rather to wrap and extend it as needed. This makes it much easier to maintain and migrate your work as the Enterprise Library team releases patches and updates. Therefore, for the

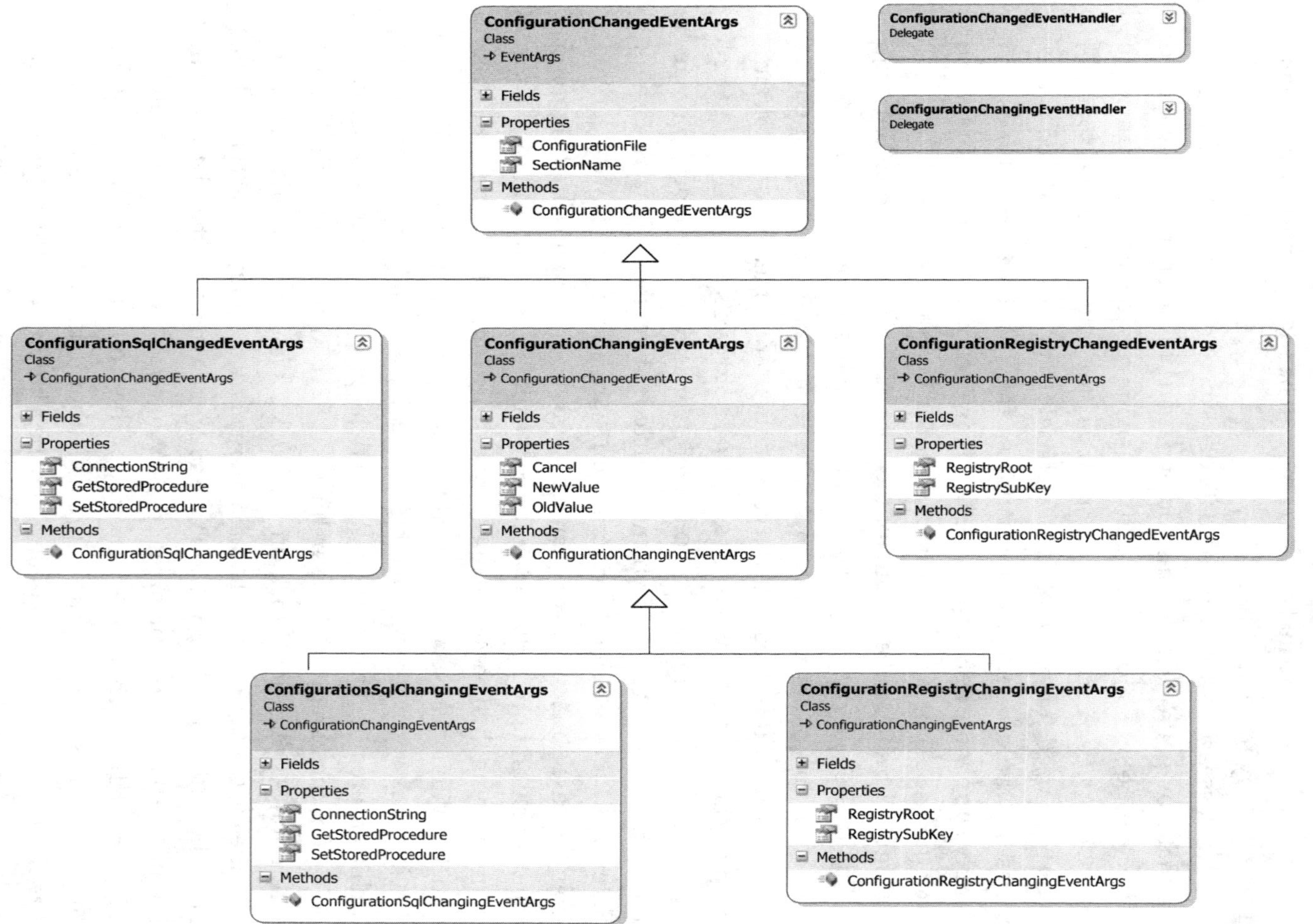

FIGURE 1.5: Enterprise Library's `ConfigurationChangedEventArgs` Design

remainder of this example I have taken the "nonpurist" approach with respect to the `ConfigurationChangedEventArgs`.

Once it is understood that the file parameter will be ignored, the actual code for the `EventArgs` classes can easily be created. Listing 1.4 shows the code for the `ConfigurationDatabaseChangedEventArgs` class. The `ConfigurationDatabaseChangingEventArgs` is the exact same code except that it derives from `ConfigurationChangingEventArgs` instead of `ConfigurationChangedEventArgs`.

LISTING 1.4: ConfigurationDatabaseChangedEventArgs Class

```
[C#]
[Serializable]
public class ConfigurationDatabaseChangedEventArgs :
ConfigurationChangedEventArgs
{
     private readonly string dbInstance;
     private readonly string getConfig;
     private readonly string setConfig;

     public ConfigurationDatabaseChangedEventArgs(
          string dbInstance,
          string getConfig,
          string setConfig,
          string sectionName) : base(String.Empty,sectionName)
      {
          this.dbInstance = dbInstance;
          this.getConfig =  getConfig;
          this.setConfig =  setConfig;
     }

     public string DatabaseInstance
     {
          get { return this.dbInstance; }
     }

     public string GetConfigStoredProc
     {
          get { return this.getConfig; }
     }

     public string SetConfigStoredProc
     {
          get { return this.setConfig; }
     }
}
```

```
[Visual Basic]
<Serializable> _
Public Class ConfigurationDatabaseChangedEventArgs : _
                    Inherits ConfigurationChangedEventArgs
     Private ReadOnly dbInstance As String
     Private ReadOnly getConfig As String
     Private ReadOnly setConfig As String

     Public Sub New(_
               ByVal dbInstance As String, _
               ByVal getConfig As String, _
               ByVal setConfig As String, _
               ByVal sectionName As String)
                         MyBase.New(String.Empty,sectionName)
          Me.dbInstance = dbInstance
          Me.getConfig = getConfig
          Me.setConfig = setConfig
     End Sub

     Public ReadOnly Property DatabaseInstance() As String
          Get
               Return Me.dbInstance
          End Get
     End Property

     Public ReadOnly Property GetConfigStoredProc() As String
          Get
               Return Me.getConfig
          End Get
     End Property

     Public ReadOnly Property SetConfigStoredProc() As String
          Get
               Return Me.setConfig
          End Get
     End Property
End Class
```

Step 4: Create the `ConfigurationChangeDatabaseWatcher`

Now the `ConfigurationChangeDatabaseWatcher` can be created. This is the class that will raise the `ConfigurationChanged` event when the configuration data for a `DatabaseStorageProvider` has been modified. I know that Microsoft SQL Server 2005 and the .NET 2.0 Framework make it much easier to have a database call back into application code upon a change in the database; however, for now, I'll use what is available in the .NET 1.1 Framework to poll the configuration table and compare the *lastmoddate* value with the last one kept by the `DatabaseStorageProvider`. Incidentally, when the SQL script for this StorageProvider was run, an update trigger was created on the database table, so that modifications made to the table outside of an application that uses the `DatabaseStorageProvider` will still be detected.

Fortunately, Enterprise Library has taken the difficulty out of creating a `ConfigurationChangeWatcher`. An abstract base class, aptly named `ConfigurationChangeWatcher`, does all the "heavy lifting" that is needed. The `ConfigurationChangeWatcher` class spawns a background thread that will poll the derived class' `GetCurrentLastWriteTime` method to determine if a change has occurred. It compares this `DateTime` with a `DateTime` variable that it keeps to represent the last known update. If the value for the `GetCurrentLastWriteTime` is greater than the value for the local variable, the local variable is set to the `GetCurrentLastWriteTime` value and the `ConfigurationChanged` event is raised.

The `ConfigurationChanged` event expects the `ConfigurationChangedEventArgs` specific to that data store; for the `DatabaseStorageProvider`, this is the `ConfigurationDatabaseChangedEventArgs` created as the first task for this step. The base class retrieves this via the abstract BuildEventData method. Other than a few other helper methods that are used for diagnostic purposes, this is all that needs to be done to create a derived `ConfigurationChangeWatcher`.

Thus, the major activity that needs to be completed to create a new `ConfigurationChangeWatcher` is implementing the `GetCurrentLastWriteTime` method that is specific to the configuration data store. The value that is returned from this method begins the change notification process. The `ConfigurationChangeDatabaseWatcher's GetCurrentLastWriteTime` method is shown in Listing 1.5. The full source code for this class is on the book's Web site.

Listing 1.5: ConfigurationChangeDatabaseWatcher's GetCurrentLastWriteTime

```
[C#]
protected override DateTime GetCurrentLastWriteTime()
{
     DateTime currentLastWriteTime = DateTime.MinValue;
     Database db;
     try
     {
          db = DatabaseFactory.CreateDatabase(this.dbInstance);
```

```
        }
        // When the Config Console is used to modify this information,
        // the database factory has to be used to dynamically build the
        // dbInstance
        catch (ConfigurationException)
        {
            ConfigurationContext ctx =
                runtimeConfigurationView.ConfigurationContext;
            try
            {
                DatabaseProviderFactory factory =
                            new DatabaseProviderFactory(ctx);
                db = factory.CreateDatabase(dbInstance);
            }
            catch (Exception e)
            {
                throw new
                    ConfigurationException(
                    SR.ExceptionConfigurationDbInvalidSection(
                        SectionName),e);
            }
        }
        catch (Exception e)
        {
            throw new
                ConfigurationException(
                SR.ExceptionConfigurationDbInvalidSection(
                    SectionName),e);
        }

        IDataReader dataReader =
                db.ExecuteReader(this.getConfig, this.SectionName);
        if( dataReader.Read() )
            currentLastWriteTime = dataReader.IsDBNull( 1 ) ?
            DateTime.MinValue : dataReader.GetDateTime( 1 );
        dataReader.Close();
        return currentLastWriteTime;
    }

    [Visual Basic]
    Protected Overrides Function GetCurrentLastWriteTime() As DateTime
        Dim currentLastWriteTime As DateTime = DateTime.MinValue
        Dim db As Database
        Try
            db = DatabaseFactory.CreateDatabase(Me.dbInstance)

        ' When the Config Console is used to modify this information,
        ' the database factory has to be used to dynamically build the
        ' dbInstance
```

```
        Catch e1 As ConfigurationException
            Dim ctx As ConfigurationContext = _
                runtimeConfigurationView.ConfigurationContext
            Try
                Dim factory As DatabaseProviderFactory = _
                    New DatabaseProviderFactory(ctx)
                db = factory.CreateDatabase(dbInstance)
            Catch e As Exception
                Throw New _
                    ConfigurationException( _
                        SR.ExceptionConfigurationDbInvalidSection( _
                        SectionName),e)
            End Try
        Catch e As Exception
            Throw New _
                ConfigurationException( _
                SR.ExceptionConfigurationDbInvalidSection( _
                SectionName),e)
        End Try

        Dim dataReader As IDataReader = _
            db.ExecuteReader(Me.getConfig, Me.SectionName)
        If dataReader.Read() Then
            currentLastWriteTime = IIf(dataReader.IsDBNull(1), _
            DateTime.MinValue, dataReader.GetDateTime(1))
        End If
        dataReader.Close()
        Return currentLastWriteTime
    End Function
```

The `GetCurrentLastWriteTime` method shown in Listing 1.5 is specific to the needs for the `DatabaseStorageProvider`. It creates a `Database` object via the Data Access Application Block and uses this object to get a `DataReader` that contains the last modified time, *lastmoddate,* for a configuration section. (The Data Access Application Block is covered in much more detail in Chapter 3.) Notice that there is no code that is specific to Microsoft SQL server in Listing 1.5. The information for connecting to the database and retrieving and providing data to it are maintained by the Data Access Application Block.

If the *lastmoddate* is greater than the last date and time that the base `ConfigurationChangeWatcher` class has recorded, then that class determines that a change has occurred and the `ConfigurationChanged` event is raised.

Otherwise, the thread sleeps for a predefined period before it calls the Data Access Application Block again.

Step 5: Create the DatabaseStorageProvider

The `DatabaseStorageProvider` is very similar to the `SqlStorageProvider`. Upon saving configuration data, the data is serialized and then saved in a database. When being retrieved, the data is fetched from the database and the configuration data is deserialized. The main differences are in the private `LoadData` and `SaveData` methods. Instead of specifically calling Microsoft SQL Server to retrieve and update information in a database, the Data Access Application Block is used.

Thus, the code for retrieving and updating the configuration data in the database is very similar to the code that exists for the `GetCurrentLastWriteTime` method in the `ConfigurationChangeDatabaseWatcher`. However, instead of just retrieving and updating the *lastmoddate,* the data for the configuration section is retrieved. Listing 1.6 shows the LoadData method. The full source code is on the book's Web site.

LISTING 1.6: DatabaseStorageProvider's LoadData Method

```
[C#]
private XmlDocument LoadData()
{
     string xmlData;

     Database db;
     try
     {
          db = DatabaseFactory.CreateDatabase(DatabaseInstance);
     }
     // When the Config Console is used to modify this information,
     // the database factory has to be used dynamically to build the
     // dbInstance
     catch (ConfigurationException configEx)
     {
          ConfigurationContext ctx =
               runtimeConfigurationView.ConfigurationContext;
          try
          {
               DatabaseProviderFactory factory =
                    new DatabaseProviderFactory(ctx);
               db = factory.CreateDatabase(DatabaseInstance);
```

```
        }
        catch (Exception e)
        {
            throw new
                ConfigurationException(
                    SR.ExceptionConfigurationDbInvalidSection
                    (CurrentSectionName), e);
        }
    }
    catch (Exception e)
    {
        throw new
            ConfigurationException(
                SR.ExceptionConfigurationDbInvalidSection
                (CurrentSectionName), e);
    }

    lock(this)
{
        try
        {
            IDataReader dataReader =
                db.ExecuteReader(
                    GetStoredProcedure,
                    CurrentSectionName);
            if( !dataReader.Read() )
                return null;
            else
                xmlData = dataReader.IsDBNull(0) ?
                              null : dataReader.GetString(0);
            dataReader.Close();
        }
        catch (Exception e)
        {
            throw new
                    ConfigurationException(
                        SR.ExceptionConfigurationDbInvalidSection
                        (CurrentSectionName), e);
        }
    } //End lock

    if (xmlData == null || xmlData.Trim().Equals(String.Empty))
    {
        throw new
              ConfigurationException(
                  SR.ExceptionConfigurationDbInvalidSection
                 (CurrentSectionName));
    }
    return DeserializeDocumentData(xmlData);
```

```
}

[Visual Basic]
Private Function LoadData() As XmlDocument
    Dim xmlData As String
    Dim db As Database

    Try
        db = DatabaseFactory.CreateDatabase(DatabaseInstance)
        ' When the Config Console is used to modify this information,
        ' the database factory has to be used dynamically to build the
        ' dbInstance
    Catch configEx As ConfigurationException
        Dim ctx As ConfigurationContext = _
            runtimeConfigurationView.ConfigurationContext
        Try
            Dim factory As DatabaseProviderFactory = _
                New DatabaseProviderFactory(ctx)
            db = factory.CreateDatabase(DatabaseInstance)
        Catch e As Exception
            Throw New _
                ConfigurationException _
                    (SR.ExceptionConfigurationDbInvalidSection _
                    (CurrentSectionName), e)
        End Try
    Catch e As Exception
        Throw New ConfigurationException _
                (SR.ExceptionConfigurationDbInvalidSection _
                (CurrentSectionName), e)
    End Try

    SyncLock Me
        Try
            Dim dataReader As IDataReader = _
                    db.ExecuteReader( _
                    GetStoredProcedure, _
                    CurrentSectionName)
            If (Not dataReader.Read()) Then
                Return Nothing
            Else
                xmlData = IIf(dataReader.IsDBNull(0), _
                        Nothing, _
                        dataReader.GetString(0))
            End If
            dataReader.Close()
        Catch e As Exception
            Throw New ConfigurationException _
                (SR.ExceptionConfigurationDbInvalidSection _
                (CurrentSectionName), e)
```

```
        End Try
    End SyncLock

    If xmlData Is Nothing OrElse xmlData.Trim().Equals(String.Empty) _
    Then
        Throw New ConfigurationException _
                (SR.ExceptionConfigurationDbInvalidSection _
                (CurrentSectionName))
    End If
    Return DeserializeDocumentData(xmlData)
End Function
```

Step 6 (Post-Creation): Changing the Metaconfiguration

Configuring an application to use the DatabaseStorageProvider is a matter of configuring the values in the metaconfiguration for a specific configuration section. I have not yet detailed how you can use the Enterprise Library Configuration Tool to make this a very simple process, so for now you still need to configure this "by hand." The code in bold in Listing 1.7 shows how I have modified the metaconfiguration for the sample application that was described at the beginning of this chapter to use the `DatabaseStorageProviderData` instead of the `XmlFileStorageProviderData`.

LISTING 1.7: Application Domain Configuration File Modified to Use the DatabaseStorageProvider

```
<?xml version="1.0" encoding="utf-8"?>
<configuration>
  <configSections>
    <section name="enterpriselibrary.configurationSettings"
          type="System.Configuration.IgnoreSectionHandler, System,
          Version=1.0.5000.0, Culture=neutral,
          PublicKeyToken=b77a5c561934e089" />
  </configSections>
  <enterpriselibrary.configurationSettings
          xmlns:xsd="http://www.w3.org/2001/XMLSchema"
          xmlns:xsi="http://www.w3.org/2001/XMLSchema-instance"
          applicationName="Tabbed App"
          xmlns="http://www.microsoft.com/practices/enterpriselibrary/
                  08-31-2004/configuration">
  <configurationSections>
    <configurationSection
          xsi:type="ReadOnlyConfigurationSectionData"
          name="dataConfiguration" encrypt="false">
          <storageProvider xsi:type="XmlFileStorageProviderData"
               name="XML File Storage Provider"
```

```
                path="dataConfiguration.config" />
                <dataTransformer
                     xsi:type="XmlSerializerTransformerData"
                     name="Xml Serializer Transformer">
                     <includeTypes />
                </dataTransformer>
    </configurationSection>
    <configurationSection name="TabConfig" encrypt="false">
       <storageProvider xsi:type="DatabaseStorageProviderData"
          name="Database Storage Provider"
          databaseInstance="EntLibExtensions"
          getStoredProcedure="EntLib_GetConfig"
          setStoredProcedure="EntLib_SetConfig" />
       <dataTransformer xsi:type="XmlSerializerTransformerData"
          name="Xml Serializer Transformer">
            <includeTypes />
       </dataTransformer>
    </configurationSection>
  </configurationSections>
  <keyAlgorithmStorageProvider xsi:nil="true" />
  <includeTypes>
     <includeType name="DatabaseStorageProviderData"
          type="EnterpriseLibrary.Extensions.Configuration.
          DatabaseStorageProviderData, EnterpriseLibrary.Extensions,
          Version=1.0.0.0, Culture=neutral, PublicKeyToken=null" />
  </includeTypes>
</enterpriselibrary.configurationSettings>
</configuration>
```

Note that the `includeType` element also needs to be added to the metaconfiguration. Because the `DatabaseStorageProvider` is not compiled as part of the Configuration Application Block, the Configuration Application Block cannot automatically recognize how to create an instance of this provider. The Configuration Application Block needs to be told which assembly to use to create this provider. The `includeType` element provides the Configuration Application Block with this information.

After this configuration section has been modified to store its information in a database instead of an XML file, the results can be viewed in the centralized database. Figure 1.6 shows an example of these results.

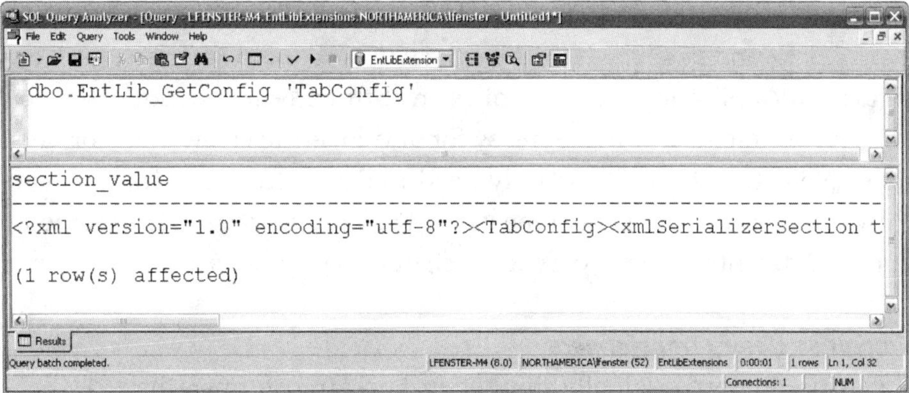

FIGURE 1.6: Result of Using the DatabaseStorageProvider

The `ITransformer` Interface and the `TransformerProvider` Class

The Enterprise Library version of the Configuration Application Block not only allows an application to be agnostic as to the data store in which its configuration data is held, but it also allows an application to be indifferent as to the structure of the data in the data store. **Transformers**, new in this version of the Configuration Application Block, translate between the format of the in-memory representation of the data and the format that is used by a StorageProvider. Earlier in this chapter, I demonstrated serializing an object that contains configuration data into an XML representation. The `XmlSerializerTransformer` that is included with Enterprise Library was used to *transform* the object into XML.

Applications are not required to configure a Transformer. If there is no Transformer, configuration settings objects are returned to the application in the same form as provided by the StorageProvider. If an `XmlSerializerTransformer` isn't used to deserialize XML, a consuming application has to deal with XML representation of the configuration object instead of the actual object. For this reason, it is often useful for an application to be configured to use a Transformer. This allows both the application and the StorageProvider to deal only with the representation of the data that each cares about (e.g., XML for the XMLFileStorageProvider) and not have to understand anything about creating classes from that representation.

The `ITransformer` interface has three methods: `CurrentSectionName`, `Serialize`, and `Deserialize`. Like the `StorageProvider` class, the Configuration Application Block supplies an abstract `TransformerProvider` class that is intended to make it easy for developers to create Transformers. To create a Transformer, you only need to derive from the Transformer-Provider class and implement the `Deserialize` and `Serialize` methods. Table 1.2 describes the purpose for each of these methods.

Enterprise Library Transformers

Enterprise Library originally shipped just one Transformer: the `XmlSerializerTransformer`. Figure 1.7 illustrates how this Transformer derives from the abstract `TransformerProvider` base class and implements the `ITransformer` interface. This design allows other Transformers to be created and used in place of the `XmlSerializerTransformer`. After the initial release of Enterprise Library, the `MvpSerializerTransformer` was shipped with the Enterprise Library Extensions project as an alternate to using the `XmlSerializerTransformer` under special circumstances.

`XmlSerializerTransformer`. The Enterprise Library `XmlSerializerTransformer` can feed an `XmlNode` returned from a StorageProvider to the .NET `XmlSerializer` class so that it can be transformed into an object graph that represents configuration data. The `XmlSerializerTransformer` provides a generic way to serialize and deserialize configuration data without being bound to a specific object type.

The `Serialize` method wraps the results obtained from serializing the configuration data object with an element named *xmlSerializationSection*

TABLE 1.2: Methods Needed by a Derived Transformer to Support the ITransformer Interface

Method	Description
Deserialize	Deserializes the configuration data coming from storage.
Serialize	Serializes the configuration data coming from the calling assembly and maps it into something that the StorageProvider can understand.

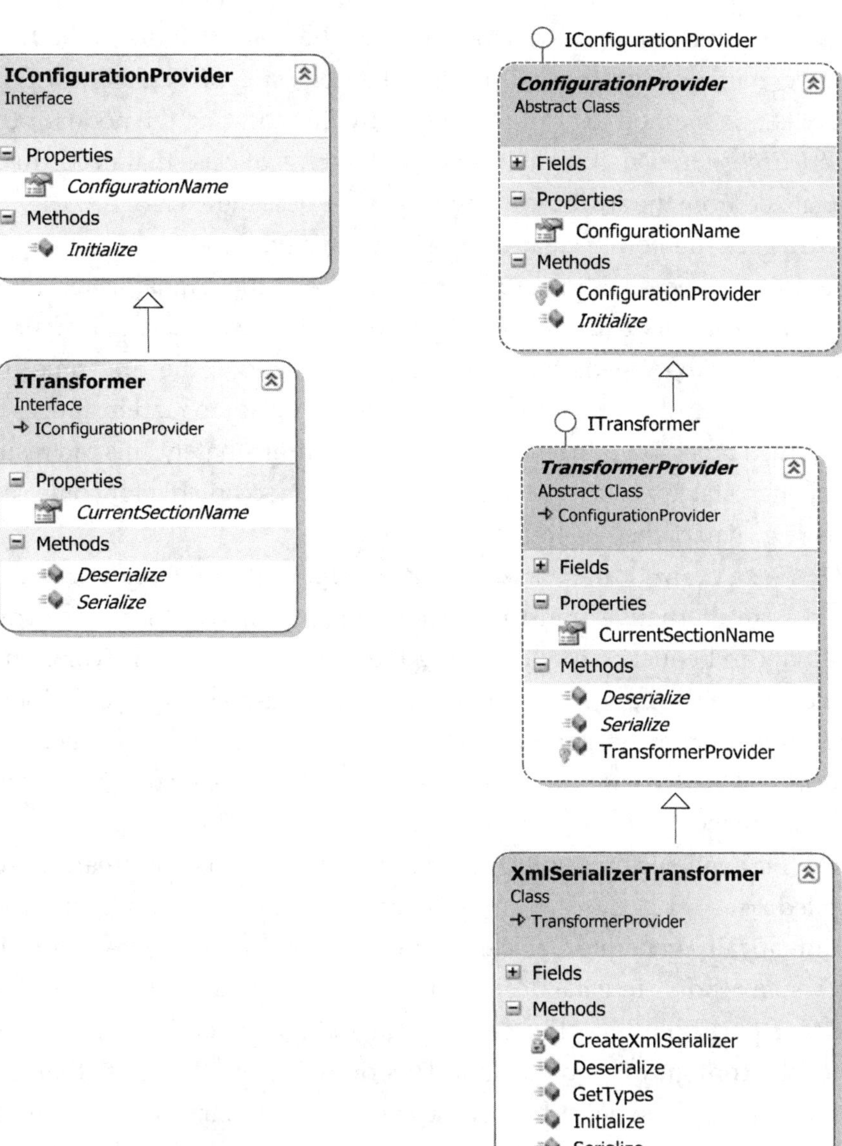

FIGURE 1.7: Enterprise Library Design for Transformers

and an attribute named *type*. The value for the *type* attribute is the fully qualified name of the configuration data's object type. This allows the `Deserialize` method to work in reverse by first locating the node for the *xmlSerializationSection*. It then determines the type of class that needs to be deserialized from the attribute named *type*, and uses the `XmlSerializer's` `Deserialize` method to create a class from this type.

Because a generic `XmlSerializer` is used, the Transformer must inspect a specific node (the serializationNode) in the XML to determine the type of object that needs to be created. Furthermore, the first time the `XmlSerializer` object is used it must generate a class to read instances of the received type, compile it, and then load it. Unfortunately, this can result in very high startup costs and may prove to be unacceptable for some scenarios (e.g., smart client solutions).

`MvpSerializerTransformer`. The `MvpSerializerTransformer` is offered as an alternative Transformer that can be used to reduce the startup costs that can be incurred when using the `XmlSerializer`. It works just like the `XmlSerializerTransformer` except that it uses precompiled serializers rather than the generic `XmlSerializer`, so there is no need to inspect the XML to determine the type of class that needs to be serialized and deserialized.

A tool is available on Daniel Cazzulino's blog that lets you create a precompiled `XmlSerializer` for any serializable class.[3] The custom serializer is automatically generated at design-time and the tool integrates nicely with Visual Studio. To get a design-time version of a custom `XmlSerializer` for a particular type, the `Mvp.Xml.XGen` tool must be associated and run for the configuration data class. This produces another class that can be used to perform serialization of the configuration data class. Figure 1.8 illustrates setting the Custom Tool property for the `TabConfig` class shown earlier in this chapter to Mvp.Xml.XGen to create the `TabConfigSerializer` class.

Once this class has been created, compiled, and deployed, it can be used by the `MvpSerializerTransformer` to serialize and deserialize a specific

3. See http://weblogs.asp.net/cazzu/archive/2004/10/21/XGenToolRelease.aspx.

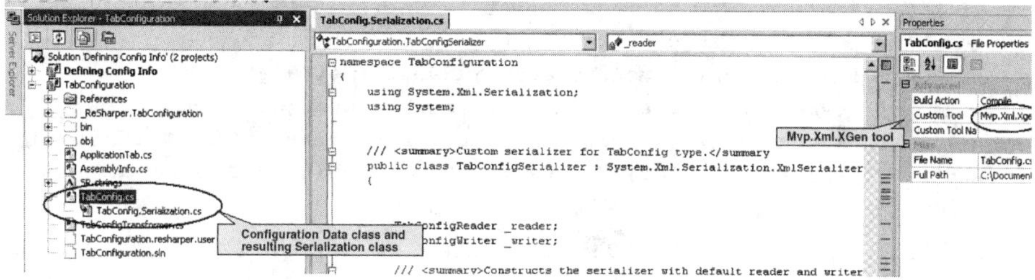

FIGURE 1.8: Using Mvp.Xml.XGen to Create a Serializer

configuration data class; in the example used throughout this chapter, that is the `TabConfig` class. To use the `MvpSerializerTransformer` instead of the `XmlSerializerTransformer`, the configured Transformer must be replaced in the metaconfiguration and an include type must be added so the Configuration Application Block knows to load the proper assembly and type. Listing 1.8 highlights the changes that must be made to the metaconfiguration for the sample application to use the `MvpSerializerTransformer` instead of the `XmlSerializerTransformer`. The lines in bold highlight the changes that need to occur (some formatting has been done to enhance readability).

LISTING 1.8: Metaconfiguration Changes to use the MvpSerializerTransformer

```
...
<configurationSection name="TabConfig" encrypt="false">
     <storageProvider xsi:type="DatabaseStorageProviderData"
          name="Database Storage Provider"
          databaseInstance="EntLibExtensions"
          getStoredProcedure="EntLib_GetConfig"
          setStoredProcedure="EntLib_SetConfig" />
     <dataTransformer xsi:type="MvpSerializerTransformerData"
          name="Mvp Serializer Transformer"
          serializationType="TabConfiguration.TabConfigSerializer,
          TabConfiguration, Version=1.0.2131.41118, Culture=neutral,
          PublicKeyToken=null" />
</configurationSection>
...
<includeTypes>
     <includeType name="DatabaseStorageProviderData"
          type="EnterpriseLibrary.Extensions.Configuration.
```

```
            DatabaseStorageProviderData, EnterpriseLibrary.Extensions,
            Version=1.0.0.0, Culture=neutral, PublicKeyToken=null" />
        <includeType name="MvpSerializerTransformerData"
            type="EnterpriseLibrary.Extensions.Configuration.
            MvpSerializerTransformerData, EnterpriseLibrary.Extensions,
            Version=1.0.0.0, Culture=neutral, PublicKeyToken=null" />
    </includeTypes>
    ...
```

Creating a Custom Transformer

Most enterprises will probably never need a custom Transformer. However, for the rare case where the `XmlSerializerTransformer` or `MvpSerializerTransformer` is not good enough, I will take you through the steps to create one.

Creating a custom Transformer is not as arduous an exercise as creating a custom StorageProvider. There is no need to watch for configuration changes; a custom Transformer can be created by just deriving a new provider class from the abstract `TransformerProvider` base class and overriding the `Serialize` and `Deserialize` methods.

Listing 1.9 shows a Transformer that doesn't use the `XmlSerializer`. This Transformer, the `BinaryTransformer`, serializes a configuration data class to its binary representation and deserializes it back again. This is not a bad option if you know that the schema for the configuration data is stable and the configuration data does not need to be modified in the data store which houses it. There are, however, a few items that should be recognized when using this Transformer.

- The configuration data class must be `Serializable` in the remoting sense of the word. That is, the `SerializableAttribute` attribute should be applied to indicate that instances of the type can be serialized.[4]
- The StorageProvider that is configured to save and load the data for this Transformer must know how to deal with binary data. The

4. See http://msdn.microsoft.com/library/default.asp?url=/library/enus/cpref/html/frlrfstserializableattributeclasstopic.asp for more information

`DatabaseStorageProvider` shown earlier in this chapter has special methods for saving and retrieving binary data.

- The configuration data will not be as easy to modify as it would be with the two Transformers provided by Enterprise Library. Because the configuration data will be stored as binary and not XML, the configuration data will have to be deserialized into an object graph and modified through an application instead of natively through an editor like Notepad or Visual Studio.
- If the schema for the configuration data changes, it will be more difficult to modify the existing configuration data to match this schema.

LISTING 1.9: Custom BinaryTransformer

```
[C#]
public class BinaryTransformer : TransformerProvider
{
    public override object Serialize(object value)
    {
        ArgumentValidation.CheckForNullReference(value, "value");

        byte[] buffer = null;

        using (MemoryStream ms = new MemoryStream())
        {
            BinaryFormatter formatter = new BinaryFormatter();
            formatter.Serialize(ms, value);
            buffer = new byte[ms.Length];
            ms.Position = 0;
            ms.Read(buffer, 0, (int)ms.Length);
            ms.Flush();
        }

        return buffer;
    }

    public override object Deserialize(object section)
    {
        object returnConfigObject = null;
        BinaryFormatter formatter = new BinaryFormatter();

        using (MemoryStream ms = new MemoryStream((byte[])section))
        {
            returnConfigObject = formatter.Deserialize(ms);
        }

        return returnConfigObject;
```

```
        }

        public override void Initialize
                (ConfigurationView configurationView)
        {
        }
    }

    [Visual Basic]
    Public Class BinaryTransformer : Inherits TransformerProvider

        Public Overrides Function Serialize _
                (ByVal value As Object) As Object

            ArgumentValidation.CheckForNullReference(value, "value")

            Dim buffer As Byte() = Nothing

            Dim ms As MemoryStream = New MemoryStream()
            Try
                Dim formatter As BinaryFormatter = _
                        New BinaryFormatter()
                formatter.Serialize(ms, value)
                buffer = New Byte(ms.Length - 1) {}
                ms.Position = 0
                ms.Read(buffer, 0, CInt(ms.Length))
                ms.Flush()
            Finally
                If TypeOf ms Is IDisposable Then
                    Dim disp As IDisposable = ms
                    disp.Dispose()
                End If
            End Try

            Return buffer
        End Function

        Public Overrides Function Deserialize
                (ByVal section As Object) As Object

            Dim returnConfigObject As Object = Nothing
            Dim formatter As BinaryFormatter = New BinaryFormatter()

            Dim ms As MemoryStream = _
                    New MemoryStream(CType(section, Byte()))
            Try
                returnConfigObject = formatter.Deserialize(ms)
            Finally
                If TypeOf ms Is IDisposable Then
                    Dim disp As IDisposable = ms
```

```
                disp.Dispose()
            End If
        End Try

        Return returnConfigObject
    End Function

    Public Overrides Sub Initialize _
            (ByVal configurationView As ConfigurationView)
    End Sub
End Class
```

The `BinaryTransformer` can be configured in an application as a custom Transformer. Special hooks exist in Enterprise Library to call out to custom-built Transformers without needing to know intricate details about the data that a Transformer might need. In the case of the `BinaryTransformer`, it is especially useful because no additional information needs to be configured. The `MvpSerializerTransformer`, on the other hand, needed to know the type and assembly name for the class that was created with the `Mvp.Xml.Gen` tool. The `BinaryTransformer` does not need any additional information. If it did, though, a property named `Attributes` exists that can be used to pass configuration data to a custom Transformer. `Attributes` is a `Dictionary` object. A custom Transformer can get the values for the configuration data it needs by accessing a particular item in the `Attributes Dictionary` by name.

However, since none of that needs to be set for the `BinaryTransformer`, configuring an application to use this Transformer just involves modifying the metaconfiguration to replace the current Transformer with this one. In Listing 1.10, I have replaced the configuration for the `MvpSerializerTransformer` with the `BinaryTransformer`.

LISTING 1.10: Metaconfiguration Changes to Use the BinaryTransformer

```
...
<configurationSection name="TabConfig" encrypt="false">
    <storageProvider xsi:type="DatabaseStorageProviderData"
        name="Database Storage Provider"
        databaseInstance="EntLibExtensions"
        getStoredProcedure="EntLib_GetConfig"
        setStoredProcedure="EntLib_SetConfig" />
    <dataTransformer xsi:type=" CustomTransformerData"
        name="Binary Transformer Provider"
        serializationType=
```

```
            "EnterpriseLibrary.Extensions.BinaryTranformer,
                EnterpriseLibrary.Extensions" />
</configurationSection>
...
```

Managing Configuration Information

An application is able to take advantage of StorageProviders and Transformers to decouple itself from configuration data because the Configuration Application Block manages the work to make this happen. The Configuration Application Block also caches the configuration data for an application while still allowing the application to respond to changes that may occur in the underlying configuration data. This section focuses on the classes that exist in this block that provide these capabilities. Figure 1.9 illustrates how the classes in the Configuration Application Block work together to accomplish this.

Configuration Sections

Configuration settings for a block are grouped together and referred to as a **configuration section**. The Configuration Application Block accesses the data in a configuration section through an application's metaconfiguration. As illustrated in the previous section, the metaconfiguration includes information about the configuration storage location for a configuration section and the type of Transformer and StorageProvider that is needed to read from and write to this storage location.

Listing 1.11 shows two configuration sections as part of the metaconfiguration for an application. The first configuration section holds information for the Data Access Application Block and is named *dataConfiguration*. The metaconfiguration shows that the Configuration Application Block will use an `XmlFileStorageProvider` for storing the configuration data in a file named dataConfiguration.config. Furthermore, it will use an `XmlSerializerTransformer` for transforming the data from this StorageProvider into the object that is needed by the application. The configuration data for the Data Access Application Block contains information that is needed to connect to the relational databases that this application will use. That configuration data is kept in the dataConfiguration.config file. This is indicated by the value for the `XmlFileStorageProvider` in the metaconfiguration.

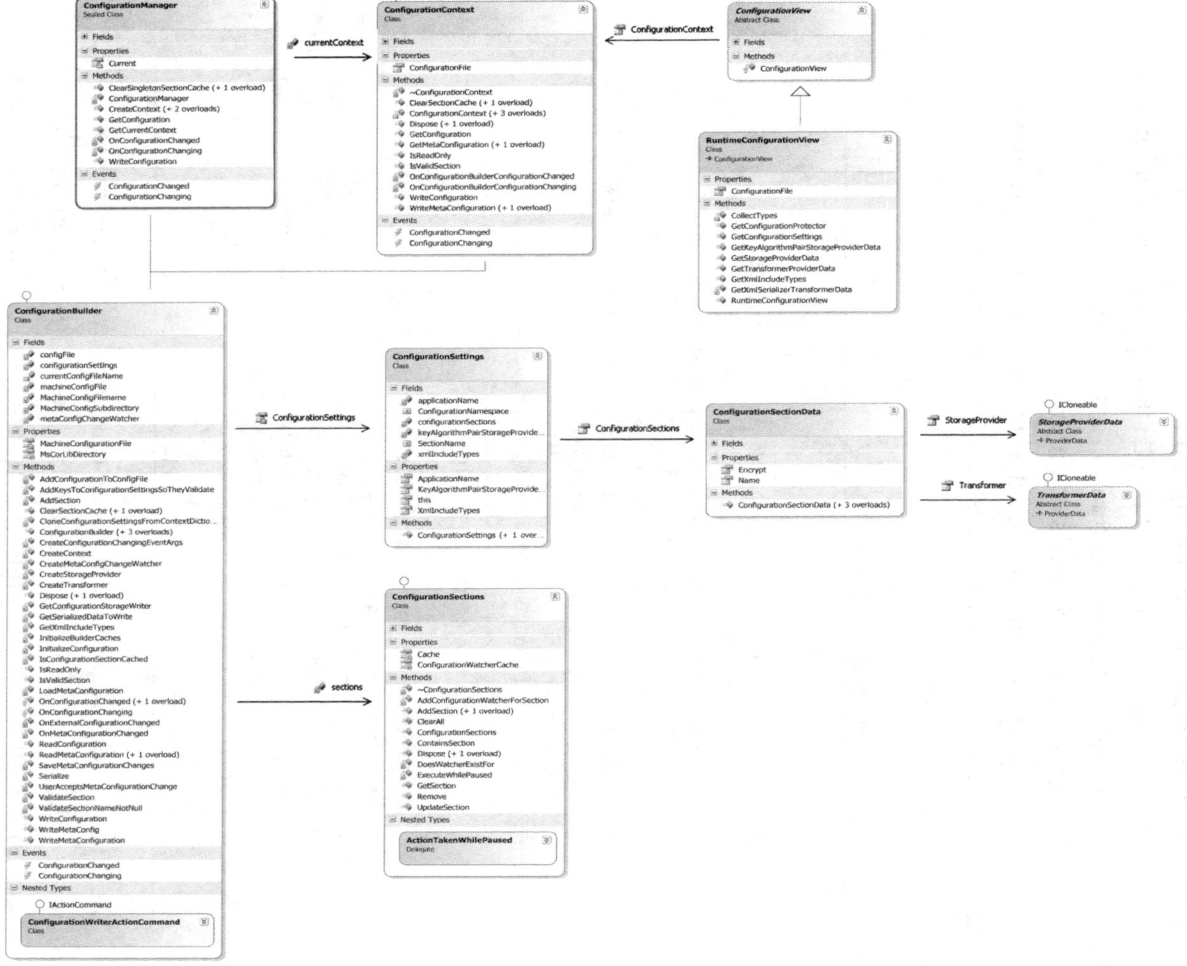

FIGURE 1.9: Design of Enterprise Library's Configuration Application Block

The second configuration section contains metaconfiguration for housing the special configuration information that this application needs. In this example, that is the `TabConfig` configuration data highlighted earlier in this chapter. This configuration section is configured to use a `DatabaseStorageProvider` to keep the configuration data in a relational database and an `XmlSerializerTransformer` to transform the data into the object graph needed by the application.

LISTING 1.11: Sample Configuration Sections

```
...
<configurationSections>
    <configurationSection xsi:type="ReadOnlyConfigurationSectionData"
          name="dataConfiguration" encrypt="false">
      <storageProvider xsi:type="XmlFileStorageProviderData"
          name="XML File Storage Provider"
          path="dataConfiguration.config" />
      <dataTransformer xsi:type="XmlSerializerTransformerData"
          name="Xml Serializer Transformer" />
    </configurationSection>
    <configurationSection name="TabConfig" encrypt="false">
      <storageProvider xsi:type="DatabaseStorageProviderData"
          name="Database Storage Provider"
          databaseInstance="EntLibExtensions"
          getStoredProcedure="EntLib_GetConfig"
          setStoredProcedure="EntLib_SetConfig" />
      <dataTransformer xsi:type="CustomTransformerData"
          name="Binary Transformer Provider"
          type="EnterpriseLibrary.Extensions.BinaryTranformer,
               EnterpriseLibrary.Extensions" />
    </configurationSection>
  </configurationSections>
...
```

The internal `ConfigurationSections` class keeps a cache of the configuration sections and `ConfigurationChangeWatchers` used to detect changes in the underlying configuration data stores. This means that caching the configuration settings in application code does not provide any performance benefits. If an application still chooses to cache configuration settings, then it is that application's responsibility to ensure that any changes to the configuration data are synchronized so that no portion of the application uses stale data. For this reason, the Microsoft patterns & practices team recommends that an application just let the Configuration Application Block handle the cache of configuration settings.

The `ConfigurationSettings` Class

Every application block includes a class that allows the configuration data for that block to be retrieved. This class can usually be recognized by the application block's suffix: *Settings*. Aside from the fact that the configuration data for the Configuration Application Block is the metaconfiguration, the Configuration Application Block is no different. The metaconfiguration for an application can be retrieved via the `ConfigurationSettings` class.

Information about the configuration sections can be accessed to retrieve data about the StorageProvider and Transformer configured for a section. Additionally, information about the `XmlIncludeTypes` needed by the Configuration Application Block, the name of the application, and an encryption key that can be used to encrypt the configuration data in the configuration sections can also be obtained. Table 1.3 lists the properties of the `ConfigurationSettings` class.

Table 1.3: ConfigurationSettings Properties

Property	Description
`ConfigurationSections`	Returns a collection of the configuration sections that have been configured for an application.
`ApplicationName`	Returns the name of the application as it appears in the metaconfiguration.
`this[string] / Me(string)`	Indexer for retrieving or setting a specific configuration section. For example, `ConfigurationSettings["dataConfiguration"]` would retrieve the configuration section for the Data Access Application Block shown in Listing 1-11.
`KeyAlgorithmPairStorage-ProviderData`	Retrieves the `KeyAlgorithmPair's` StorageProvider information that can be used to encrypt the data in a configuration section.
`XmlIncludeTypes`	Retrieves the collection of all include types that the Configuration Application Block needs.

Often times, the data that is contained in a configuration section must be protected. For example, the configuration section for the Data Access Application Block contains configuration data used to create connection strings to backend databases. This kind of sensitive information must be protected from those who should not see it. The Configuration Application Block allows the data in a configuration section to be protected by a combination of an encryption key and symmetric algorithm. This information is represented in the Configuration Application Block as a `KeyAlgorithmPair`.

When encryption for a configuration section has been enabled, the StorageProvider that is responsible for reading and writing the configuration data for that section uses an instance of the `ConfigurationProtector` class that is part of the Configuration Application Block. The `ConfigurationProtector` class gets the `KeyAlgorithmPair` information from ConfigurationSettings and makes functions available to the StorageProviders for easy encrypting and decrypting of the configuration data.

By default, the keys are saved in plaintext files. Any user or application with access to the plaintext file can read the key and use it to decrypt the configuration sections. Therefore, additional protection for this file should be implemented. An excellent option is to protect the file with the Data Protection API (DPAPI). The Enterprise Library Configuration Tool provides a wizard that can be used to create a key/algorithm pair. This wizard also enables DPAPI protection for the master key file. DPAPI is part of the operating system and can protect files in situations where other security measures, such as access control lists (ACLs), cannot. (Chapter 2 shows how to accomplish this by using the wizard provided by the Enterprise Library Configuration Tool.) For more information about DPAPI, see Chapter 8 in this book and the book *Writing Secure Code,* Second Edition, by Michael Howard and David C. LeBlanc.

`XmlIncludeTypes` allow the Configuration Application Block to be extended with object types that are not compiled in one of the base application blocks that ship with Enterprise Library. Some of the previous examples showed how Enterprise Library's Configuration Application Block can be extended by creating new StorageProviders and Transformers. But how does the Configuration Application Block know which type and assembly to use to create an instance of this class? The answer is that it uses `XmlIncludeTypes`.

The XmlIncludeTypes that are defined in the metaconfiguration, and thus maintained by the ConfigurationSettings, indicate which new types of objects the Configuration Application Block needs to instantiate at runtime.

The ConfigurationBuilder Object

The ConfigurationBuilder object is an internal class to the Configuration Application Block and represents the engine that manages the Storage-Providers and Transformers that read and write the configuration data. When a ConfigurationBuilder object is created, it reads the metaconfiguration data from the application domain file (i.e., app.config or web.config) and stores this information in its private ConfigurationSettings member variable.

The ConfigurationBuilder contains the methods and events needed to read, write, and detect when changes are made to configuration files. In addition to a ConfigurationSettings member variable, the ConfigurationBuilder also maintains a ConfigurationSections variable. As mentioned earlier, the ConfigurationSections class keeps a cache of the configuration sections. Subsequent attempts to read configuration data use the cached data and do not reread information from the configuration storage. The Configuration Application Block can clear this cache for any and all configuration sections via the ClearSectionCache method if the StorageProvider detects that configuration data has changed in storage. If the cache is cleared, the next request for configuration information will access the configuration settings from the defined storage location.

The ConfigurationContext Object

The ConfigurationBuilder is intended to serve as a private, internal engine that manages the reading, writing, and caching of configuration information. Applications must use the ConfigurationManager and ConfigurationContext objects for reading, writing, and caching configuration and metaconfiguration data. The ConfigurationContext is not the way most applications will access configuration data; the ConfigurationManager (which is covered next) is intended to be the more common means.

The ConfigurationContext is intended to be used under special circumstances where an application or process needs more control of the configuration data than what the `ConfigurationManager` provides. The `ConfigurationContext` simply wraps around a `ConfigurationBuilder` object to read and write configuration and metaconfiguration data. It is actually the `ConfigurationBuilder` object that uses a StorageProvider and Transformer to do the heavy lifting of reading, writing, and transforming configuration data.

Whereas the `ConfigurationManager's GetConfiguration` and `WriteConfiguration` methods only support reading and writing configuration and metaconfiguration data using the application domain configuration file, the `ConfigurationManager's CreateContext` method can be used to create a `ConfigurationContext` object from a file other than an application domain configuration file. For example, an assembly that requires its own configuration independent of the host application might need to use this to retrieve metaconfiguration from a file other than the application domain configuration file. The file has to follow the same schema as the application domain configuration file, but other than that there are no constraints.

The `ConfigurationContext` object represents a read-only set of configuration data indexed by configuration section name. As such, it can be used to pass read-only configuration information throughout an application. The Configuration Application Block uses the `ConfigurationContext` by passing it throughout various methods so that all blocks in an application can consume their respective configuration information. This allows the configuration block to read in all of the configuration information once and pass that information around to all of the objects that need to get populated. Listing 1.12 shows how to get the object held in the `ConfigurationContext` for the *TabConfig* section.

LISTING 1.12: Using the ConfigurationContext to Obtain Configuration Settings for a Section

```
[C#]
ConfigurationContext context = ConfigurationManager.GetCurrentContext();
string file = context.ConfigurationFile;
object data = context.GetConfiguration("TabConfig");

[Visual Basic]
Dim context As ConfigurationContext = ConfigurationManager.GetCurrentContext()
Dim file As String = context.ConfigurationFile
Dim data As Object = context.GetConfiguration("TabConfig")
```

In the previous examples, the `ConfigurationFile` property and the `GetConfiguration` method were used to obtain the desired objects. The `ConfigurationContext` class contains many more properties and methods that can be used to read, write, and validate configuration data. Table 1.4 lists the `ConfigurationContext's` public methods and properties.

It might also be necessary to leverage a `ConfigurationContext` if an application or process needs to dynamically access configuration data without direct access to the underlying configuration data store. Such a need exists in the `DatabaseStorageProvider` example described earlier in this chapter. Under normal runtime conditions, the `DatabaseStorageProvider` works without any problems. However, a complexity occurs when this StorageProvider is configured with an application like the Enterprise Library Configuration Tool. I'll dive deeper into this tool and the Configuration Design-Time tool in the next chapter. For now, you just need to

TABLE 1.4: ConfigurationContext Methods and Properties

Method/Property	Description
`ConfigurationFile`	Gets the configuration file used by the current context.
`ClearSectionCache`	Removes all sections from the internal cache.
`GetConfiguration`	Returns configuration settings for a configuration section.
`GetMetaConfiguration`	This overloaded method gets the metaconfiguration for the configuration manager.
`IsReadOnly`	Gets a value indicating whether a section in configuration is read-only.
`IsValidSection`	Determines if a section name is valid in the current configuration file.
`WriteConfiguration`	Writes the configuration for a section to storage.
`WriteMetaConfiguration`	This overloaded method writes the metaconfiguration for the configuration manager to the configuration file.

understand that because this StorageProvider relies on the configuration information of another application block (i.e., the Data Access Application Block), situations can occur when it cannot get this configuration information through the normal means.

When this occurs, a `ConfigurationException` is thrown and the `DatabaseStorageProvider` reacts by trying to access the Data Access Application Block's configuration information via the `ConfigurationContext`. This is a perfectly acceptable way to create a `Database` object and everything else flows through perfectly fine.

The `ConfigurationManager` Object

The other exposed interface for reading and writing configuration data is the `ConfigurationManager` object. The `ConfigurationManager` is simply a façade over the current `ConfigurationContext` class and is provided to make it easy to read and write configuration data. It provides static methods to read and write configuration settings for a specified configuration section. The static methods of the `ConfigurationManager` class simply use the current `ConfigurationContext` object to do its work. Table 1.5 lists the methods that can be used to read and write configuration data.

Developing with the Configuration Application Block

A primary design goal for the Configuration Application Block is to make it simple to save and retrieve configuration data. This design goal is achieved via the `ConfigurationManager` object that was just discussed. Many applications will only need to leverage two static methods exposed by this object: `GetConfiguration` and `WriteConfiguration`.

`GetConfiguration` is used for reading configuration data in a configuration section, and `WriteConfiguration` is used for saving data for a configuration section back to the configuration data store. Additional methods exist for handling change events to the underlying configuration data store and clearing the configuration cache to enforce that configuration data is reread from this store.

Occasionally, an application or assembly may need more functionality than the `ConfigurationManager` provides. For example, an assembly may

TABLE 1.5: **ConfigurationManager** Public Methods and Events

Method/Event	Description
ClearSingletonSectionCache	This overloaded method removes a section from the internal cache.
CreateContext	Gets a new instance of the ConfigurationContext class with the specified ConfigurationDictionary.
GetConfiguration	Returns configuration settings for a user-defined configuration section.
GetCurrentContext	Gets the ConfigurationContext for the current ConfigurationManager.
WriteConfiguration	Writes the configuration for a section to storage.
ConfigurationChanged (Event)	Occurs after the configuration is changed.
ConfigurationChanging (Event)	Occurs before the configuration is changed.

need to be created that cannot access the configuration data for a configuration section through the `ConfigurationManager`, like the `DatabaseStorageProvider` example shown earlier. The `ConfigurationContext` exists to handle these more advanced configuration needs.

The following sections detail how you can use the `ConfigurationManager` and `ConfigurationContext` objects to address all of these points.

Reading Configuration Data

One of the most common needs for many applications is to read configuration data. Often a developer needs to write code that accesses a specific data store (e.g., a file or database) and reads configuration data from well-defined sections in this store. If the location or type of data store changes, the code in the application may need to be rewritten.

The `ConfigurationManager's` static `GetConfiguration` method addresses these issues. Because the knowledge about how and where to get configuration data is handled by the Configuration Application Block, you do not need to write code that is specific to any one physical store. Instead, you can use the GetConfiguration method to retrieve the configuration data for a particular configuration section. The Configuration Application Block does the rest.

Listing 1.13 demonstrates how to call the GetConfiguration method to retrieve configuration data for the TabConfig object that was shown earlier in this chapter.

LISTING 1.13: Reading Configuration Data with the ConfigurationManager

```
[C#]
object configInfo = ConfigurationManager.GetConfiguration("TabConfig");
if (configInfo is TabConfig)
     appConfig = configInfo as TabConfig;

[Visual Basic]
Dim configInfo As Object = _
     ConfigurationManager.GetConfiguration("TabConfig")
If TypeOf configInfo Is TabConfig Then
     appConfig = IIf(TypeOf configInfo Is TabConfig, _
          CType(configInfo, TabConfig), CType(Nothing, TabConfig))
End If
```

Note that the return value from the GetConfiguration method must be cast to the appropriate runtime type. Also note that no code is written that is specific to accessing data from a file, database, or registry. You don't need to know where the configuration data is being stored. Not only does this ease the development effort, but it also allows the application to be more flexible to any changes that may occur to the underlying configuration store.

Writing Configuration Data

The ConfigurationManager provides a complementary method to GetConfiguration with the WriteConfiguration method. WriteConfiguration is used to write configuration data back into the physical configuration data store.

The sample application described at the beginning of this chapter lets users change different characteristics of the tabs (e.g., background color and tab label) that exist in the application. When the application is closed, this configuration data is automatically written back to the physical data store by way of the `ConfigurationManager's WriteConfiguration` method. Listing 1.14 shows the code for this. The `configTabs` variable is an instance of the object that represents the configuration data. To write the configuration data back to the configuration data store, the `WriteConfiguration` method is called with the name of the configuration section and the object that represents the configuration data for that section.

LISTING 1.14: Saving Configuration Data with the ConfigurationManager

```
[C#]
private void frmConfigInfo_Closing(
                    object sender,
                    System.ComponentModel.CancelEventArgs e)
{
     ConfigurationManager.WriteConfiguration("TabConfig",configTabs);
}

[Visual Basic]
Private Sub frmConfigInfo_Closing( _
                    ByVal sender As Object, _
                    ByVal e As System.ComponentModel.CancelEventArgs)

     ConfigurationManager.WriteConfiguration("TabConfig",configTabs)

End Sub
```

Detecting Change Notification

When a StorageProvider detects that configuration data has changed in the physical data store, it fires a `ConfigurationChanged` event. The `ConfigurationBuilder` receives this event and clears that section from its cache so that it is reread the next time it is requested.

Sometimes it may be valuable for other parts of an application to also be aware when a change has been made to the configuration data in the physical configuration data store. For example, the sample application used throughout this chapter displays a dialog to end users notifying them that a change to the underlying configuration data store has changed and asks if it should immediately account for this change. To accomplish this, an application can handle the `OnConfigurationChanged` event notification. Listing 1.15 shows how this is accomplished in the sample application.

LISTING 1.15: Detecting Configuration Changes

```
[C#]
ConfigurationManager.ConfigurationChanged += new
          ConfigurationChangedEventHandler(OnConfigurationChanged);
...
private void OnConfigurationChanged(object sender,
                    ConfigurationChangedEventArgs e)
{
    if (e.SectionName.Equals(tabConfigSectionName) && !(this.isClosing))
    {
          DialogResult dialogResult =
               MessageBox.Show(
                    SR.ConfigurationChangedMessage,
                    SR.ConfigurationChangedCaption,
                    MessageBoxButtons.YesNo);
          if (dialogResult == DialogResult.Yes)
          {
               configurationChanged = true;
          }
     }
}

[Visual Basic]
Private ConfigurationManager.ConfigurationChanged += New _
          ConfigurationChangedEventHandler(OnConfigurationChanged)
...
Private Sub OnConfigurationChanged(ByVal sender As Object, _
               ByVal e As ConfigurationChangedEventArgs)

     If e.SectionName.Equals(tabConfigSectionName) AndAlso _
          Not(Me.isClosing) Then

          Dim dialogResult As DialogResult = _
               MessageBox.Show(_
                    SR.ConfigurationChangedMessage, _
                    SR.ConfigurationChangedCaption, _
                    MessageBoxButtons.YesNo)
          If dialogResult = DialogResult.Yes Then
               configurationChanged = True
          End If
     End If
End Sub
```

Clearing Cached Configuration Data

The configuration data for each configuration section that gets loaded by the Configuration Application Block is cached. The Configuration Application Block will use the configuration data from its cache first and will only go out to the physical data store if the configuration does not exist in cache. When a change occurs in the underlying data store, the cache is cleared.

There may be instances where it is desirable to specifically clear the cache so the Configuration Application Block will read the configuration data from the physical data store. You can use the `ConfigurationManager's` `ClearSingletonSectionCache` method to do this. If the `ClearSingletonSectionCache` method is called with no parameters, all configuration sections will be cleared from the cache; if it is called with a section name, only that section's data will be cleared from the cache. Listing 1.16 shows how to clear the configuration data for the TabConfig configuration section from the cache.

LISTING 1.16: Clearing the Cache of Configuration Data

```
[C#]
ConfigurationManager.ClearSingletonSectionCache(tabConfigSectionName);

[Visual Basic]
ConfigurationManager.ClearSingletonSectionCache(tabConfigSectionName)
```

Accessing Configuration Data Through ConfigurationContext

Under special circumstances, the `ConfigurationManager` might not provide all the capabilities that are needed to accomplish a task. You can use the `ConfigurationContext` when you need more control over configuration data. For example, sometimes it is not desirable to obtain the metaconfiguration data for an application or assembly from an application domain configuration file. The `ConfigurationContext` supports using a file other than the application domain configuration file for reading and writing metaconfiguration.

Listing 1.17 illustrates how to create a `ConfigurationContext` from a file other than the application domain configuration file. The one caveat is that the file has to follow the same schema as the application domain configuration file.

LISTING 1.17: Accessing Data Using the ConfigurationContext

```
[C#]
ConfigurationContext context =
     ConfigurationManager.CreateContext("differentfile.config");

[Visual Basic]
Dim context As ConfigurationContext =
     ConfigurationManager.CreateContext("differentfile.config")
```

Another special circumstance is when the configuration data needs to be retrieved and/or created in an application or process without the benefit of a backing store, as in the `DatabaseStorageProvider` example described earlier in this chapter. When the `DatabaseStorageProvider` is being configured with the Enterprise Library Configuration Tool (I'll show how this is possible in the next chapter), it is not actually running in an application. Yet it still needs to dynamically build the `DatabaseInstance`.

Because all application blocks have a provider factory class that accepts a `ConfigurationContext` in its constructor, this factory can be fed the `ConfigurationContext` to retrieve specific configuration information for that block. The `DatabaseStorageProvider` uses the `DatabaseProviderFactory` and a `ConfigurationContext` to obtain the configuration data from the Data Access Application Block. Listing 1.18 shows where this occurs in the code for the `DatabaseStorageProvider`.

LISTING 1.18: The DatabaseStorageProvider's Use of the ConfigurationContext

```
[C#]
Database db;
try
{
    db = DatabaseFactory.CreateDatabase(DatabaseInstance);
}
// When the Config Console is used to modify this information,
// the database factory has to be used dynamically to build the
// dbInstance
catch (ConfigurationException configEx)
{
    ConfigurationContext ctx =
     runtimeConfigurationView.ConfigurationContext;
```

```
        try
        {
             DatabaseProviderFactory factory =
              new DatabaseProviderFactory(ctx);
         db = factory.CreateDatabase(DatabaseInstance);
        }
...

[Visual Basic]
Dim db As Database
Try
     db = DatabaseFactory.CreateDatabase(DatabaseInstance)
' When the Config Console is used to modify this information,
' the database factory has to be used dynamically to build the
' dbInstance
Catch configEx As ConfigurationException
     Dim ctx As ConfigurationContext = _
          runtimeConfigurationView.ConfigurationContext
     Try
          Dim factory As DatabaseProviderFactory = _
               New DatabaseProviderFactory(ctx)
          db = factory.CreateDatabase(DatabaseInstance)
     End Try
End Try
...
```

By using the `ConfigurationManager` for most applications and the `ConfigurationContext` for atypical scenarios, the Configuration Application Block can help you accomplish most of the configuration scenarios that exist for enterprise applications and services.

Summary

This chapter covered the design concepts that make up the Configuration Application Block. A primary design goal for the Configuration Application Block is to allow an application to be decoupled from the form and location of the configuration data that it uses. A major part of this chapter focused on how StorageProviders and Transformers can be used to accomplish this goal. It also detailed how new StorageProviders and Transformers can be created to extend Enterprise Library's Configuration Application Block should the need arise.

Another design goal was to make developing against the Configuration Application Block very straightforward. That is the reason why a façade exists with static methods for getting and writing configuration data. And if the StorageProviders and Transformers that ship with the Configuration Application Block are sufficient for the needs of an application, then a developer may never even need to know that they exist. The configuration of StorageProviders and Transformers is more of an administrative detail than it is a development detail.

The overarching point that you should now understand is that you don't need to be involved with storing and retrieving configuration information for an application and where or how the configuration data gets saved and retrieved. Instead, this lets you concentrate on developing a solution to the business needs at hand. Furthermore, the code for the application is isolated from changes if configuration data is moved from one store to another. Rather than modifying any code, only metaconfiguration data needs to be changed.

2

The Configuration Application Block Design-Time

A COMMON COMPLAINT ABOUT the application blocks before Enterprise Library was that configuration was often a challenging, tedious, and error-prone activity. The Enterprise Library team worked hard to design and develop design-time features and tools to address this issue. These features are intended to not only make the exercise of configuring an application straightforward and simple, but to also provide extensibility points to let you add your own design-time features if you need to.

This chapter first highlights how to use the Enterprise Library Configuration Tool to take advantage of the features provided by the Configuration Application Block's runtime. Specifically, it describes how to use the tool to create and modify configuration sections, configure StorageProviders and Transformers, and enable encryption of the configuration data in configuration sections. It continues with an in-depth examination of the Configuration Application Block's design-time features and design. It concludes with an example of how to extend Enterprise Library's design-time features by adding design-time support for the `DatabaseStorageProvider` that was created in Chapter 1.

Configuration and the Enterprise Library Configuration Tool

Chapter 1 explained how the Configuration Application Block's runtime stores the metaconfiguration data for a section in the application domain configuration file (i.e., app.config or web.config), how it provides capabilities to encrypt configuration settings using a key and symmetric algorithm, and how Enterprise Library's features can be configured for an application by using an XML editor to modify the XML for those features. This section introduces the Enterprise Library Configuration Tool, a Windows application that provides developers and administrators with the ability to easily configure application blocks, StorageProviders, Transformers, encryption information, and more.

Essentially, the Enterprise Library Configuration Tool is a part of the Configuration Application Block that you can use to configure any application or block that uses the Configuration Application Block's design-time features without the need for an XML editor. The Enterprise Library Configuration Tool uses the Configuration Application Block to not only read and write the configuration information contained for an application, but to also load the design-time objects for each application block.

The design-time objects for an application block are populated with information obtained from their corresponding configuration runtime objects. For example, the configuration nodes for the Data Access Application Block shown in Figure 2.1 (e.g., connection string nodes and database type nodes) retrieve their configuration information from the runtime components of the Data Access Application Block. The Configuration Application Block populates these runtime objects by getting the configuration settings from the StorageProvider that is configured for that block. The design-time components then use that information to display the settings in the Enterprise Library Configuration Tool.

As you modify the configuration settings at design time, the application block design-time objects update their corresponding runtime objects to reflect the changes. When you save an application through the Enterprise Library Configuration Tool, the design-time objects perform validation on the data and report any failures. If the configuration is valid, then the Configuration Application Block writes the metaconfiguration to the application domain configuration file, and the configured StorageProviders write to their respective data stores.

Each application block provides support for its design-time configuration by leveraging the design-time classes that are part of the Configuration Application Block. This is accomplished by implementing the interfaces, deriving from the classes, and overriding the methods that are exposed by the Configuration Application Block. This entails creating classes to represent configuration nodes, configuration menu items, and a configuration design manager. As I cover each of the other application blocks in later chapters, I demonstrate how to use this tool to easily configure that block's features as well.

To begin using the Enterprise Library Configuration Tool, click *Start > All Programs > Microsoft patterns & practices > Enterprise Library June 2005,* and then click *Enterprise Library Configuration.* Figure 2.1 illustrates some of the primary features of the Enterprise Library Configuration Tool.

Creating a Configuration Section

You can use the Enterprise Library Configuration Tool to create, modify, and remove configuration sections for an application. You can choose to either create a new application configuration file or to open an existing one. A nice thing about this tool is that it works with existing application domain configuration files. If you already have developed a Web application and decide to use some of the features of Enterprise Library at a later date, you can point the Enterprise Library Configuration Tool at the web.config file for the Web application. This simply appends the metaconfiguration that it needs, but it doesn't modify any of the other configuration data that is contained in it.

1. To create a new application, click the New button (the first one) on the toolbar; to open an existing application, click the Open button (the second button) on the toolbar. Alternatively, you can use the menu items or context-sensitive menu.

   This creates an Application node as the root of an application configuration's hierarchy.

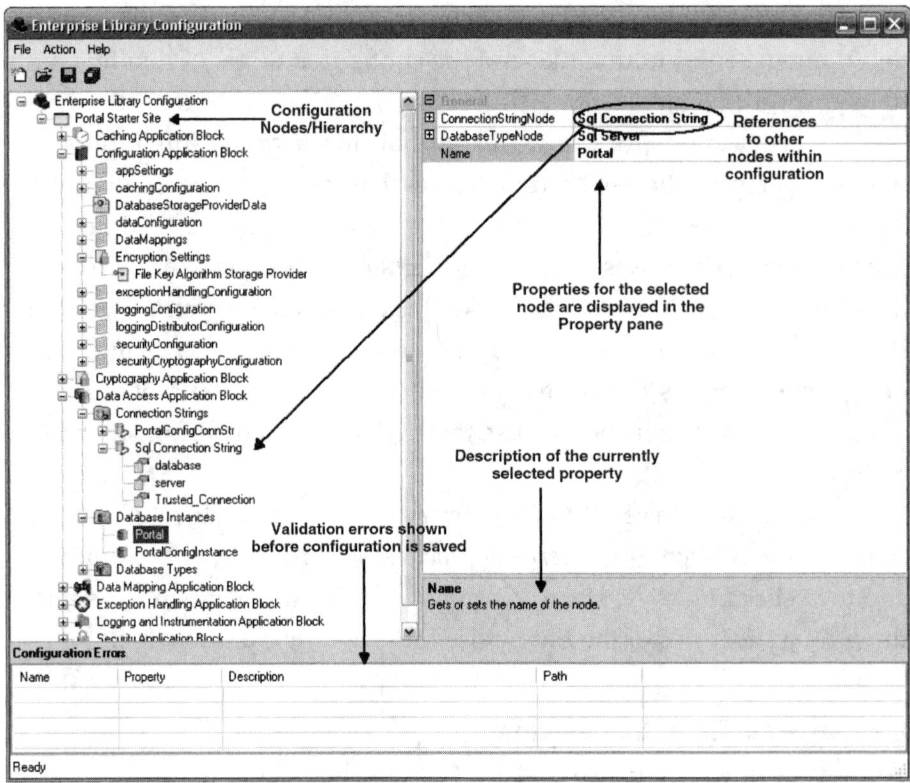

FIGURE 2.1: Enterprise Library Configuration Tool

2. You can rename this node to make it more meaningful for the application by right-clicking and selecting *Rename* or by changing the value for the Name property that appears in the Property pane on the right when the application node is selected.
3. If you are creating a new application configuration file, the `ConfigurationFile` property will need to be populated with the filename and location for this configuration file.
4. After you have opened or created an application, you can add the Configuration Application Block. To add this, right-click the *Application* node and select *New > Configuration Application Block.* Because all of the other application blocks in Enterprise Library rely on the Configuration Application Block for retrieving and saving their con-

FIGURE 2.2: Adding a Configuration Section

figuration information, adding any other application block will automatically add the Configuration Application Block too.

5. You can create a new configuration section by right-clicking the *Configuration Application Block* node and selecting *New > Configuration Section.* You can change this name the same way that you renamed the Application node in step 2.

Figure 2.2 shows a new application configuration file named *Tabbed Application.* It has a Configuration Application Block and a new configuration section named Tab *Config Info.*

After you have created a configuration section, you can configure it to use a StorageProvider and Transformer. The following sections describe how to do configure these.

Configuring StorageProviders

To configure StorageProviders and Transformers, you just add or change the application's metaconfiguration. These modifications can be automated by using the Enterprise Library Configuration Tool. A configuration section must have one StorageProvider to read and write configuration data and may optionally have one Transformer to change the form of the data. To add a StorageProvider, right-click on the *Configuration Section* node and select *New.* This displays a list containing all the available StorageProviders and Transfomers. The StorageProviders that are available with Enterprise Library are XmlFileStorageProvider, AppConfigFileStorageProvider, RegistryStorageProvider, and SqlStorageProvider. You can also configure a custom StorageProvider using the Enterprise Library Configuration Tool. The following sections describe these StorageProviders.

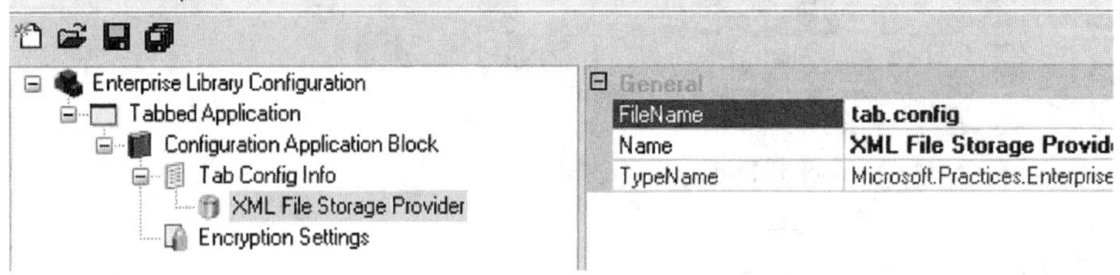

FIGURE 2.3: Configuring the XMLFileStorageProvider

The XmlFileStorageProvider

The XmlFileStorageProvider is probably the most popular StorageProvider because it was the only one that shipped with the initial release of Enterprise Library and is the default StorageProvider when another application block is added to the configuration for an application. Configuring an XmlFileStorageProvider amounts to configuring the location and name for the external XML file it uses. Relative paths—paths relative to the location of the application domain configuration file—are supported. If a path isn't specified, the file will be created in the same folder as the application domain configuration file. Any path entered must be valid and must exist at the time the application block attempts to read or write configuration data. In other words, the Configuration Application Block will not create directories for paths that don't exist. To set this property, change the value of the `FileName` property in the Property Panes dialog.

Figure 2.3 illustrates an added XmlFileStorageProvider with a renamed `FileName` property. The data for this configuration section is in a file named *tab.config*.

Listing 2.1 shows the app.config file for this application.

LISTING 2.1: App.config file After Adding an XMLFileStorageProvider

```
<configuration>
  <configSections>
    <section name="enterpriselibrary.configurationSettings"
        type="System.Configuration.IgnoreSectionHandler,
        System, Version=1.0.5000.0, Culture=neutral,
        PublicKeyToken=b77a5c561934e089" />
  </configSections>
```

```
  <enterpriselibrary.configurationSettings
      xmlns:xsd="http://www.w3.org/2001/XMLSchema"
      xmlns:xsi="http://www.w3.org/2001/XMLSchema-instance"
      applicationName="Tabbed Application"
      xmlns="http://www.microsoft.com/practices/enterpriselibrary/
            08-31-2004/configuration">
  <configurationSections>
    <configurationSection name="Tab Config Info" encrypt="false">
      <storageProvider xsi:type="XmlFileStorageProviderData"
            name="XML File Storage Provider" path="tab.config" />
      <dataTransformer xsi:nil="true" />
    </configurationSection>
  </configurationSections>
  <keyAlgorithmStorageProvider xsi:nil="true" />
  <includeTypes />
</enterpriselibrary.configurationSettings>
</configuration>
```

Because the XmlFileStorageProvider is configured to store its configuration data in a file named tab.config, a tab.config file now exists in the same directory. This file, currently empty because no configuration data has been saved to it yet, will be populated once configuration data for an application has been saved. For example, Listing 2.2 might be a fair representation of the contents in the tab.config file if this configuration represents the Listing 1.1 in Chapter 1 for saving an application's tab configuration.

LISTING 2.2: Tab.config File After Saving Configuration Data

```
<?xml version="1.0" encoding="utf-8"?>
<TabConfig>
  <xmlSerializerSection type="Defining_Config_Info.TabConfig, Defining
        Config Info, Version=1.0.2119.14112, Culture=neutral,
        PublicKeyToken=null">
    <TabConfig xmlns:xsd="http://www.w3.org/2001/XMLSchema"
            xmlns:xsi="http://www.w3.org/2001/XMLSchema-instance">
          <Tabs>
            <ApplicationTab>
              <TabColor>255, 128, 64</TabColor>
              <Label>Uno</Label>
              <Message>This is Tab1</Message>
            </ApplicationTab>
            <ApplicationTab>
              <TabColor>255, 0, 128</TabColor>
              <Label>Tab Numero Duo</Label>
              <Message>This is Tab2</Message>
            </ApplicationTab>
            <ApplicationTab>
```

```
                <TabColor>255, 255, 128</TabColor>
                <Label>Tab Number Three</Label>
                <Message>Tab numero tria</Message>
              </ApplicationTab>
            </Tabs>
      </TabConfig>
    </xmlSerializerSection>
  </TabConfig>
```

The AppConfigFileStorageProvider

With the XmlFileStorageProvider, the configuration data for each configuration section gets saved in its own XML file. Some architects prefer to have all the configuration data, including metaconfiguration, for an application reside in the application domain configuration file instead. The AppConfigFileStorageProvider is designed to fit this requirement. This StorageProvider allows the configuration data for a configuration section to be saved and retrieved from the application domain configuration file. To use this StorageProvider, right-click on the *Configuration Section* node and select *New > Application Configuration Storage Provider.*

Because a configuration section can only have one StorageProvider configured for it, if a StorageProvider has already been configured for this configuration section, you will first need to remove it by selecting the StorageProvider node, right-clicking it, and selecting *Remove.* There is nothing to prevent you from erroneously adding more than one StorageProvider to a configuration section if editing the XML with an editor. The Enterprise Library Configuration Tool, however, understands this to be invalid and will prevent more than one StorageProvider from being added to a single configuration section. This is one example of how the Configuration Tool increases productivity by helping to prevent configuration errors from occurring.

Once you have added the AppConfigFileStorageProvider for a configuration section, you don't need to do any other configuration for it. It uses the name of the file that was set for the Application node to determine where to save the configuration data for this section. Optionally, you can rename the StorageProvider the same way as the other configuration nodes thus far. This is generally true for all configuration nodes in the Enterprise Library Configuration Tool.

There is no need for separate configuration files like the tab.config file that was shown earlier; all the metaconfiguration and configuration data is saved in the application domain configuration file. Listing 2.3 represents what the configuration data might look like in the application configuration file.

LISTING 2.3: Application Configuration File When Using the AppConfigFileStorageProvider

```
<configuration>
  <configSections>
    <section name="enterpriselibrary.configurationSettings"
        type="System.Configuration.IgnoreSectionHandler,
        System, Version=1.0.5000.0, Culture=neutral,
        PublicKeyToken=b77a5c561934e089" />
  </configSections>
  <enterpriselibrary.configurationSettings
        xmlns:xsd="http://www.w3.org/2001/XMLSchema"
        xmlns:xsi="http://www.w3.org/2001/XMLSchema-instance"
        applicationName="Tabbed Application"
        xmlns="http://www.microsoft.com/practices/enterpriselibrary/
            08-31-2004/configuration">
  <configurationSections>
    <configurationSection name="Tab Config Info" encrypt="false">
      <storageProvider xsi:type="AppConfigFileStorageProviderData"
            name="ApplicationConfigurationFileStorageProvider" />
      <dataTransformer xsi:type="XmlSerializerTransformerData"
            name="Xml Serializer Transformer">
    </configurationSection>
  </configurationSections>
  <keyAlgorithmStorageProvider xsi:nil="true" />
  <includeTypes />
</enterpriselibrary.configurationSettings>
</configuration>
<TabConfig>
  <xmlSerializerSection type="Defining_Config_Info.TabConfig, Defining
        Config Info, Version=1.0.2119.14112, Culture=neutral,
        PublicKeyToken=null">
    <TabConfig xmlns:xsd="http://www.w3.org/2001/XMLSchema"
        xmlns:xsi="http://www.w3.org/2001/XMLSchema-instance">
          <Tabs>
            <ApplicationTab>
              <TabColor>255, 128, 64</TabColor>
              <Label>Uno</Label>
              <Message>This is Tab1</Message>
          </ApplicationTab>
            <ApplicationTab>
                  <TabColor>255, 0, 128</TabColor>
              <Label>Tab Numero Duo</Label>
```

```
                <Message>This is Tab2</Message>
            </ApplicationTab>
            <ApplicationTab>
                <TabColor>255, 255, 128</TabColor>
                <Label>Tab Number Three</Label>
                <Message>Tab numero tria</Message>
            </ApplicationTab>
        </Tabs>
        </TabConfig>
    </xmlSerializerSection>
</TabConfig>
```

Incidentally, an `XmlSerializerTransformer` was added to the configuration for this section for the application to run properly. Adding Transformers to an application are covered a little later in this chapter.

The RegistryStorageProvider

Another approach to eliminate the need for separate configuration files for each configuration section is to save and retrieve the configuration data from the Windows Registry instead of files. To create a RegistryStorageProvider, right-click on the *Configuration Section* node and select *New> Registry Storage Provider.* Configuring the RegistryStorageProvider involves setting the `RegistryRoot` property and `RegistrySubKey` property. The combination of these properties gives the StorageProvider enough information to locate the proper key.

The `RegistryRoot` property represents the root key of the registry tree where this StorageProvider will read and write the configuration data for this configuration section. A drop-down list exists for the `RegistryRoot` property to ensure that the value for this property is one of the ones shown in Table 2.1.

The `RegistrySubkey` property represents the subkey in the configured registry root where this StorageProvider will read and write the configuration data for this configuration section. You can enter a subkey path by separating the subkeys with the backslash character (for example, Software\Company\Application). If any key in the subkey path does not exist, it will be created when the Configuration Application Block writes the settings. The RegistryStorageProvider will create a subkey underneath the location that is specified for this property with the name of the configuration section.

TABLE 2.1: Possible `RegistryRoot` Values for the RegistryStorageProvider

Option	Registry Key
CurrentUser	HKEY_CURRENT_USER
LocalMachine	HKEY_LOCAL_MACHINE
Users	HKEY_USERS

Figure 2.4 illustrates the sample application described in Chapter 1 configured with a RegistryStorageProvider. The `RegistryRoot` property is set to *LocalMachine* and the `RegistrySubkey` property is set to *Software\ SomeCompany\TabbedApplication.*

When the configuration data for this application is saved, the Registry keys will be created if they do not already exist. The configuration data for the TabConfig configuration section will be saved and retrieved from the *Software\SomeCompany\TabbedApplication\TabConfig* key underneath the HKEY_LOCAL_MACHINE registry root. Figure 2.5 depicts how the configuration data will be stored in the Windows Registry.

The SqlStorageProvider

The SqlStorageProvider allows configuration data to be read from and written to a Microsoft SQL Server database table. To create a SqlStorageProvider, right-click on the *Configuration Section* node and select *New > Sql Storage Provider.* Table 2.2 describes the properties that must be configured

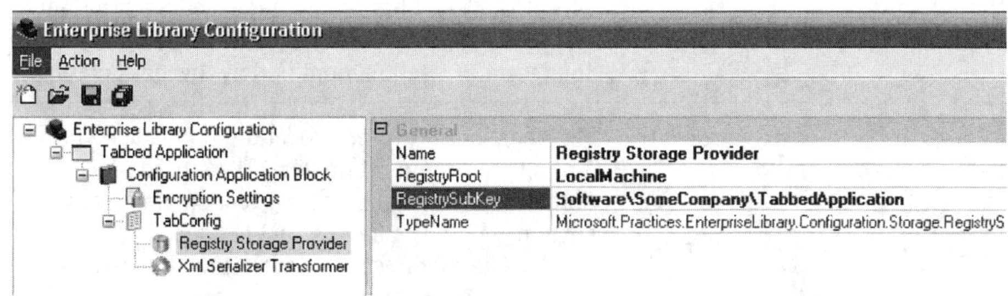

FIGURE 2.4: Configuring the RegistryStorageProvider

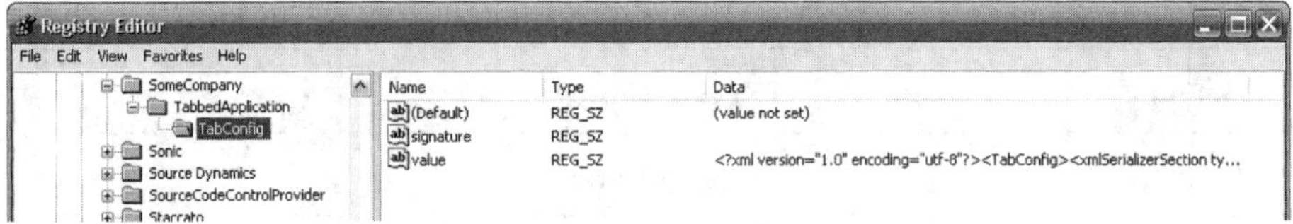

FIGURE 2.5: Results from Using the RegistryStorageProvider

for this StorageProvider, `ConnectionString`, `GetConfigStoredProcedure`, and `SetConfigStoredProcedure`. The combination of these properties provides the SqlStorageProvider with enough information to save and retrieve the configuration data for a given configuration section.

Enterprise Library ships with a SQL Script called SqlStorage.sql that you can use to create the database table, stored procedures, and a trigger that allows the SqlStorageProvider to operate properly. This script is located in the src\Configuration\Scripts directory where Enterprise Library is installed. Figure 2.6 illustrates what the configuration properties might

TABLE 2.2: Required Properties for the SqlStorageProvider

Configuration Property	Description
`ConnectionString`	The connection string used for connecting to the database. The connection string must conform to a valid SQL Server connection string
`GetConfigStoredProcedure`	The name of the stored procedure that is used to retrieve configuration data. The stored procedure accepts an NVarChar parameter called SectionName and returns the configuration data contained in the configuration section identified by this parameter.
`SetConfigStoredProcedure`	The name of the stored procedure that is used for storing the configuration data. The stored procedure accepts two parameters: section_name and section_value. The first parameter, section_name, is an NVarChar parameter that contains the name of the configuration section. The second parameter, section_value, is an NText parameter that contains the configuration data.

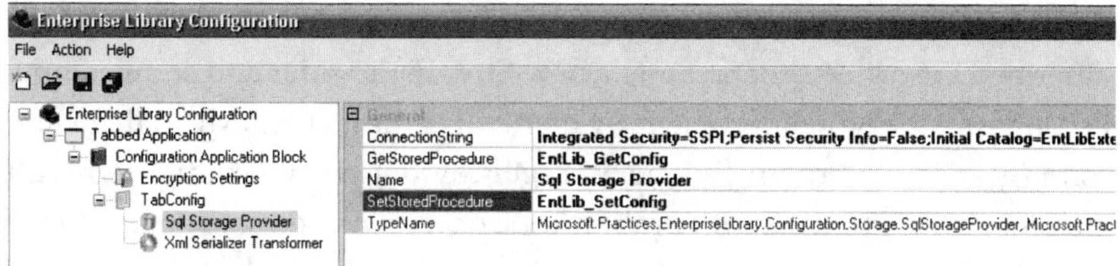

FIGURE 2.6: Configuring the SqlStorageProvider

look like for the SqlStorageProvider in the Enterprise Library Configuration Tool.

When the configuration data for this application is saved, the configuration data will reside in the Configuration_Parameter table (by default) in the database indicated by the connection string. A trigger exists on this table that allows the SqlStorageProvider to recognize when configuration data has changed for a particular section, even if it is changed from outside an application using the Configuration Application Block. Figure 2.7 illustrates executing a SQL query with the Microsoft SQL Server Query Analyzer to view the configuration data for a configuration section.

Custom StorageProviders

The Configuration Application Block also allows custom StorageProviders to be configured with the Enterprise Library Configuration Tool. The sec-

```
select * from Configuration_Parameter
```

	section_name	section_value	lastmoddate
1	TabConfig	<?xml version="1.0" encoding="utf-...	2005-05-04 11:49:14.420

FIGURE 2.7: Using the SqlStorageProvider

tion "A Custom StorageProvider: DatabaseStorageProvider" in Chapter 1 described the process for creating a new StorageProvider and showed how to configure the StorageProvider by manually editing the XML in the metaconfiguration. Alternatively, the StorageProvider can be configured with the Enterprise Library Configuration Tool; however, to do so, you must take one additional step when creating the StorageProvider.

A custom StorageProvider's `Attributes` property plays a vital role in providing the ability to read the metaconfiguration that is set for it. The `Attributes` property is a `NameValueCollection` of configuration items. When a custom StorageProvider is configured, the metaconfiguration properties that the provider needs must be configured in this `Attributes` property. For example, the custom DatabaseStorageProvider shown in Chapter 1 needs the same kind of information as the SqlStorageProvider: connection information for connecting to the database, the name of a stored procedure for retrieving configuration data, and the name of a stored procedure for saving configuration data. The Enterprise Library Configuration Tool provides an editor that makes this process a bit easier.

In Figure 2.8, a custom StorageProvider has been added by right-clicking on the Configuration Section node and selecting *New > Custom Storage Provider.* I have configured this custom StorageProvider to use the DatabaseStorageProvider by using the Type Selector dialog that is provided by the Configuration Tool. This utility enforces that the type selected implements the `IStorageProvider` interface. When the DatabaseStorageProvider was selected, the tool entered the fully qualified type name of the DatabaseStorageProvider as the value for the `TypeName` property. The `TypeName` property is important because it determines the actual StorageProvider that will be created. I then configured the parameters needed by the DatabaseStorageProvider by adding items in the NameValueItem Collection Editor, which displays when the ellipses button is clicked for the `Attributes` property.

But how does the DatabaseStorageProvider know how to use the items in the `Attributes` property? The answer is that the DatabaseStorageProvider needs to look for the values contained in the Attributes collection when it is initialized.

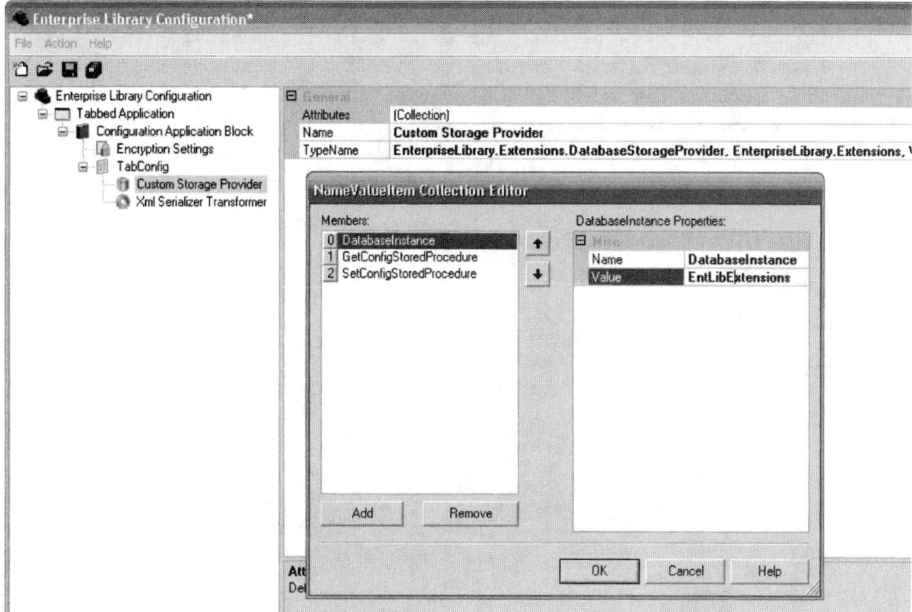

FIGURE 2.8: Configuring a Custom StorageProvider

First of all, you don't need to create a data transfer object (e.g., `DatabaseStorageProviderData`) when creating this type of custom StorageProvider. Instead, the StorageProvider uses the `CustomStorageProviderData` class that is provided by the Configuration Application Block. In the `Initialize` method for the StorageProvider, the `CustomStorageProviderData`'s `Attribute` collection should be queried for the necessary items, and these values can be stored in member variables for the StorageProvider. Listing 2.4 shows how the `Initialize` method would need to be created for the `DatabaseStorageProvider` to query the `Attributes` property for the data it needs.

LISTING 2.4: `Initialize` Method for the Custom DatabaseStorageProvider

```
[C#]
public override void Initialize(ConfigurationView configurationView)
{
    ArgumentValidation.CheckForNullReference
```

```
        (configurationView, "configurationView");
    CustomStorageProviderData custData = GetStorageProviderData();
    this.databaseInstance = custData.Attributes["DatabaseInstance"];
    this.getStoredProc=
        custData.Attributes["GetConfigStoredProcedure"];
    this.setStoredProc=
        custData.Attributes["SetConfigStoredProcedure"];

    GetStorageCursor(configurationView);
}

[Visual Basic]
Public Overrides Sub Initialize _
        (ByVal configurationView As ConfigurationView)

    ArgumentValidation.CheckForNullReference _
         (configurationView, "configurationView")
    Dim custData As CustomStorageProviderData = _
        GetStorageProviderData()

    Me.databaseInstance = custData.Attributes("DatabaseInstance")
    Me.getStoredProc = custData.Attributes("GetConfigStoredProcedure")
    Me.setStoredProc = custData.Attributes("SetConfigStoredProcedure")

    GetStorageCursor(configurationView)
End Sub
```

Custom StorageProviders are nice because they make it easy for you to create new StorageProviders and "snap them into" the Configuration Tool with little effort. When a StorageProvider is created, it leverages the design-time properties that have been established for all custom StorageProviders. Namely, these are the `TypeName` and `Attributes` properties.

Sometimes, however, it is desirable to create a StorageProvider that works more like the StorageProviders that ship with Enterprise Library. This allows many benefits, such as validation of the metaconfiguration data in the tool. To accomplish this, the features and functions of the configuration design-time tool need to be leveraged (this is described later in this chapter).

Configuring Transformers

A configuration section can have up to one Transformer to change the configuration data provided by the StorageProvider into the format needed by the application and then transform it back again from the application to the

StorageProvider. As mentioned in Chapter 1, Enterprise Library shipped with a single Transformer, the `XmlSerializerTransformer`, and the `MvpSerializerTransformer` was released later. This section shows how to configure both of these Transformers and how to configure a custom Transformer, like the `BinaryTransformer` shown in Chapter 1.

The `XmlSerializerTransformer`

The `XmlSerializerTransformer` allows configuration data to be serialized to and deserialized from XML. It serializes objects to an `XmlNode` and deserializes them from an `XmlNode` into the appropriate type. Each of the StorageProviders that ship with Enterprise Library was designed to work with the `XmlSerializerTransformer`. They each accept and return an object of type `XmlNode` in order to store and retrieve the serialized object to and from the configuration data store.

To use an `XmlSerializerTransformer` for a configuration section, right-click on the *Configuration Section* node and select *New > Xml Serializer Transformer.* Because a configuration section can only have one Transformer configured, if a Transformer already exists for this configuration section you will first need to remove it by selecting the Transformer node, right-clicking on it, and selecting *Remove.*

`XmlIncludeTypes` can be added so that a Transformer can properly create object types that it does not explicitly know about. Any custom providers that don't ship with Enterprise Library fall into this category. The Transformer must know the assembly and type name for such an object so that it can create them. Figure 2.9 shows a configuration section that has

FIGURE 2.9: Adding an `XmlSerializerTransformer` to a Configuration Section

been configured to use an XmlFileStorageProvider and an `XmlSerializerTransformer` that contains one `XmlIncludeType`.

The `MvpSerializerTransformer`

The `MvpSerializerTransformer`, introduced in Chapter 1, works very much like the `XmlSerializerTransformer` except that it uses a predefined and compiled class that derives from an `XmlSerializer` in an effort to negate the startup cost associated with the `XmlSerializer`. To use an `MvpSerializerTransformer` for a configuration section, right-click on the *Configuration Section* node and select *New > Mvp Serializer Transformer,* then select the specific type you will use to serialize the configuration data into an object. This is the class that was created with the `Mvp.Xml.XGen` tool. The fully qualified typename for this class needs to be specified as the `SerializerType` for this property.

The Enterprise Library Configuration Tool makes this task much easier by using a Type Selector dialog to automatically fill in the fully qualified name for the selected class which derives from `XmlSerializer`. The `SerializerType` is important because it determines which object the `MvpSerializerTransformer` will instantiate to serialize and deserialize the configuration data.

Figure 2.10 illustrates how to add an `MvpSerializerTransformer` to a configuration section and how to use the Type Selector utility to select an appropriate object type for it.

Custom Transformers

The Configuration Application Block allows custom Transformers to be configured with the Enterprise Library Configuration Tool in the same way that StorageProviders can be configured. The concept is exactly the same.

Figure 2.11 illustrates adding a custom Transformer to a configuration section by right-clicking on the *Configuration Section* node and selecting *New > Custom Transformer.* After the Transformer has been added, you need to select the specific type of Transformer by using the Type Selector utility. In this case, the Type Selector only shows classes that implement the `ITransformer` interface. This allows the `BinaryTransformer` that was created in Chapter 1 to be selected.

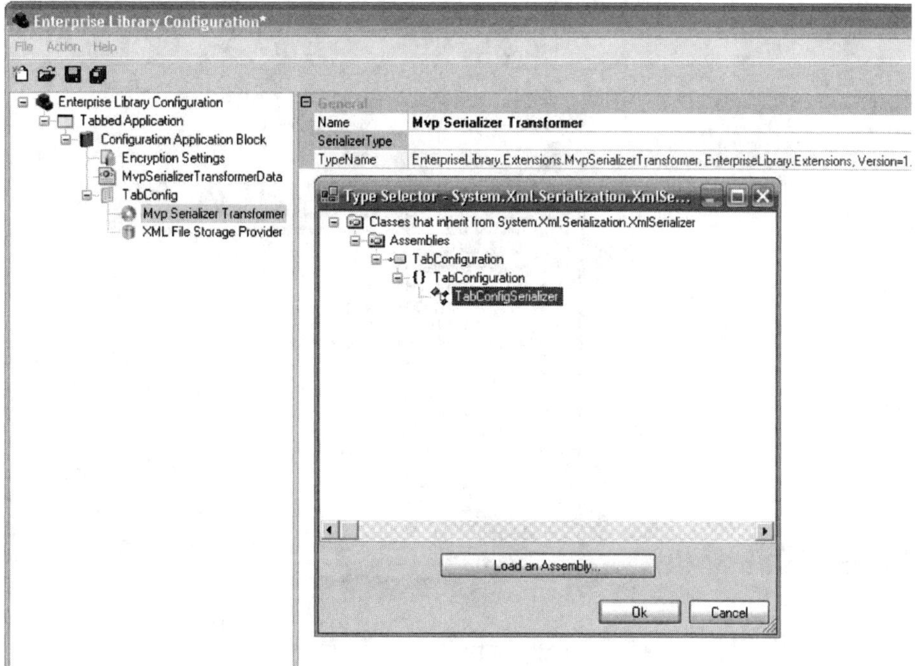

FIGURE 2.10: Configuring a Section to Use the `MvpSerializerTransformer`

You don't need to add items to the `Attributes` property because the `BinaryTransformer` does not need additional information to operate properly. Therefore, there is no need to encapsulate a `CustomTransformerData` in the `BinaryTransformer` provider or query for the `Attributes` in its `Initialize` method. If a custom Transformer did need to obtain additional configuration data, it would need to implement a strategy similar to that for the custom StorageProvider mentioned earlier—except that it would use the `CustomTransformerData` class instead of the `CustomStorageProviderData` class.

Encrypting Configuration Data

As described in Chapter 1, the Configuration Application Block's runtime features support encrypting configuration sections for an application using

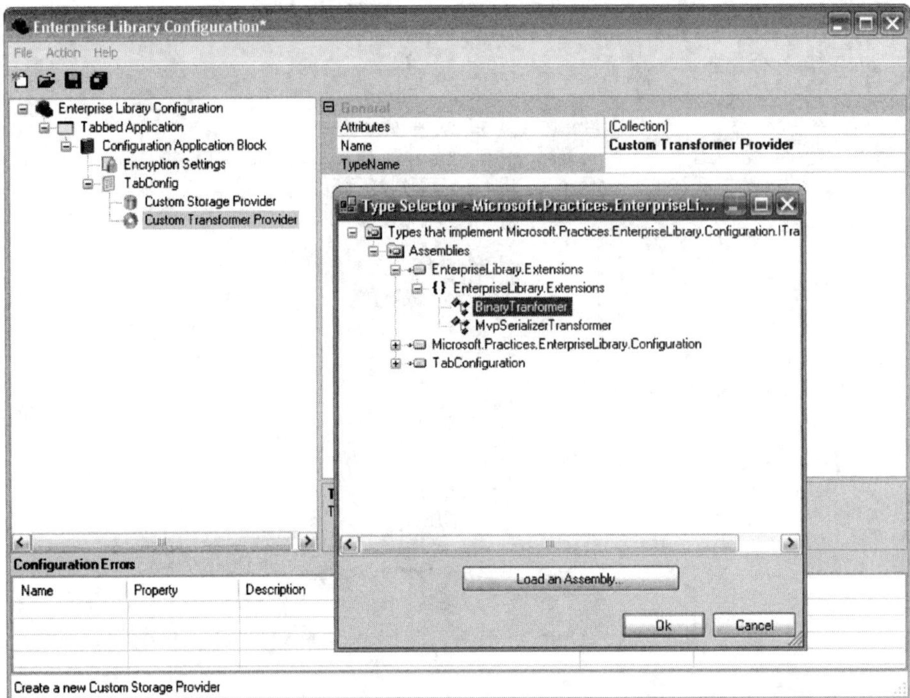

FIGURE 2.11: Adding a Custom Transformer to a Configuration Section

a single key/symmetric algorithm pair. By default, the key is saved in a plaintext file and the file should really be further protected with technologies like the Data Protection API (DPAPI). The Enterprise Library Configuration Tool provides a wizard you can use to both create the key/algorithm pair and enable DPAPI protection for the master key file.

Follow these steps to create the `KeyAlgorithmPair`.

1. Right-click the *Encryption Settings* subnode and then choose *New > File Key Algorithm Storage Provider.*
2. Do one of the following:
   - To create a new key, click *Create a new key algorithm pair.*
   - If you have already created a key, you can load it. Continue with step 5.

3. Select which symmetric algorithm to use to encrypt the configuration sections. Figure 2.12 illustrates selecting the Rijndael algorithm.
4. Either generate a new key or enter/modify a key that has been generated.
5. Select the file that will store the key. This is the file that should be protected
6. To protect the file with DPAPI, select the *Enable DPAPI protection* option.

   DPAPI operates in either User or Machine mode. In User mode, the ability to decrypt the file is restricted to the account of the user who was logged in when the file was encrypted. Machine mode restricts

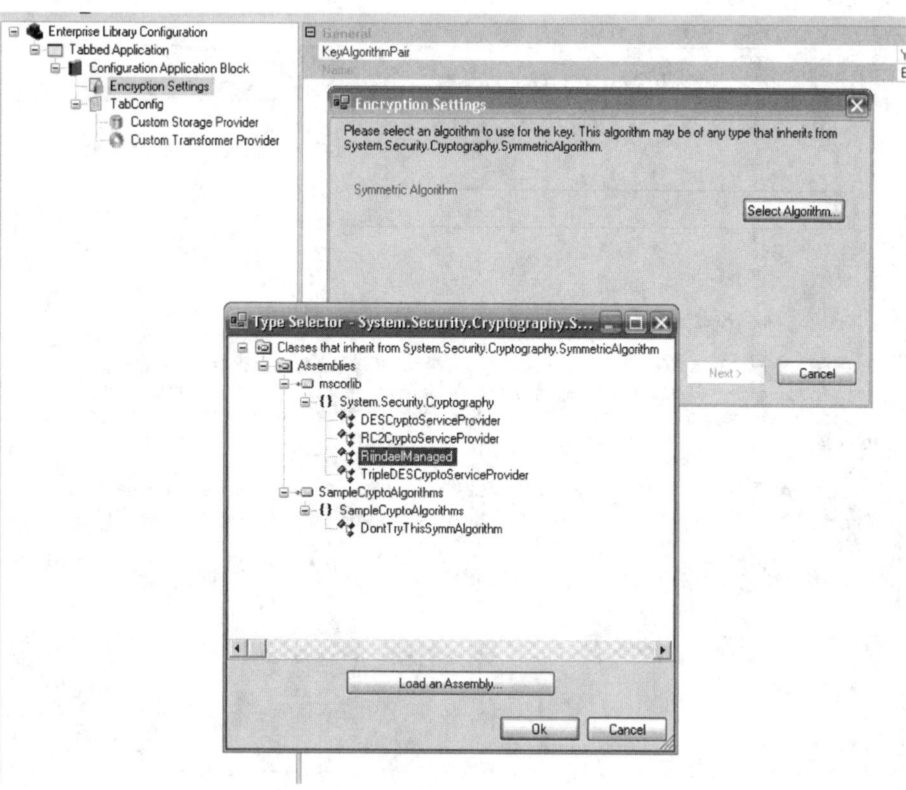

FIGURE 2.12: Selecting a Symmetric Algorithm

the ability to decrypt the file to the computer used when the file was encrypted. This means that any user with an account on that computer can decrypt the file. If you select Machine mode, you can use additional security features (e.g., ACLs) to lock the file down even further.

Figure 2.13 illustrates using the File Key Algorithm Storage wizard to enable DPAPI protection in User mode.

After the key has been created, a node for a File Key Algorithm StorageProvider will be added underneath the Encryption Settings node. The only settings you can change for this node are to switch it from one DPAPI mode (User/Machine/None) to another. If you want to make other

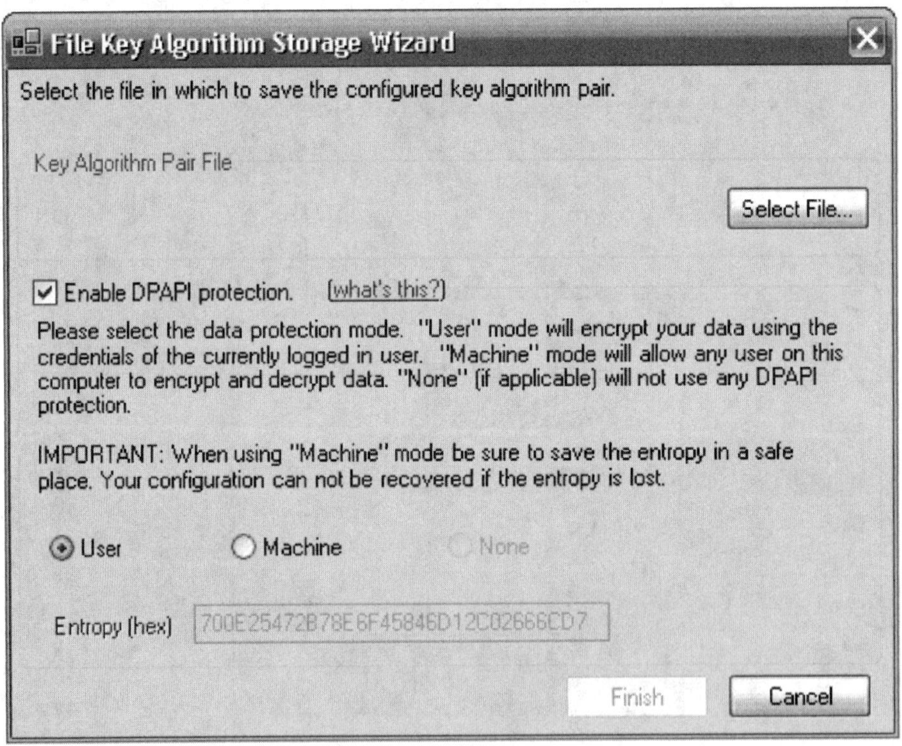

FIGURE 2.13: Using the File Key Algorithm Storage Wizard

FIGURE 2.14: The Configuration Hierarchy of the File Key Algorithm StorageProvider

changes, like selecting a new symmetric algorithm or generating a new key, you will need to create a new `KeyAlgorithmPair`. Figure 2.14 illustrates the configuration hierarchy after the `KeyAlgorithmPair` has been created.

You can use this `KeyAlgorithmPair` to encrypt the configuration data in any configuration section for an application. After creating the `KeyAlgorithmPair`, you can enable encryption for a configuration section by simply changing that section's `Encrypt` property from `False` to `True`. Figure 2.15 illustrates turning encryption on for the TabConfig configuration section.

Now when the configuration data in this section is viewed, it will look something like Figure 2.16.

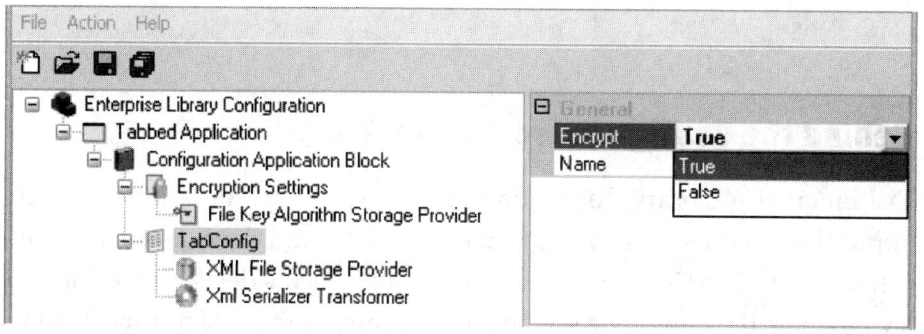

FIGURE 2.15: Enabling Encryption for a Configuration Section

```
00000000  E3 1A FB 4C 77 61 06 1B  2C 62 D1 9F C3 EE 26 D8  ...Lwa...b....&.
00000010  03 6F 80 23 36 D7 34 5F  8E 8F D9 0E 53 73 B0 B3  .o.#6.4_....Ss..
00000020  1D A1 9E 56 E9 28 3F 94  7F 8F 58 63 E4 CA 0F A2  ...V.(?...Xc....
00000030  5A F1 8C 5C BD 72 FE C0  0C 45 1B 2D 9F 12 13 64  Z..\.r...E.-...d
00000040  4D 30 51 82 ED 42 C9 4D  5D 52 4D 79 54 D6 BF 3A  M0Q..B.M]RMyT..:
00000050  81 1F 64 DC CE 95 B8 DD  F1 06 20 12 33 37 27 B5  ..d.........37'.
00000060  43 16 DB E5 EF 6E EF 04  2E 11 A0 34 D3 BD 4D 30  C....n.....4..M0
00000070  0C 1D 15 D7 1D 25 43 AF  3C D1 44 6C 95 A1 C9 08  .....%C.<.Dl....
00000080  7C 91 52 FB 7F 02 93 E9  A2 B2 BE DB BC 1C EA B8  |.R.............
00000090  99 0C F8 4F 4A CF 9B AF  22 6F 4A E3 FF 8A 82 8C  ...OJ..."oJ.....
000000a0  4A C5 C4 23 C8 EB 5B D7  4E 0B 0F 67 10 DA 40 B6  J..#..[.N..g..@.
000000b0  BE 91 50 55 01 22 56 46  C8 2A DE E7 1B 17 00 1C  ..PU."VF.*......
000000c0  52 0A 1D 1D C0 C9 EC CF  F1 DF 2D 23 63 0C 7F 8F  R.........-#c...
000000d0  3E DD 8C 2F BD C2 EF 6E  67 C0 52 7A 2F C4 2F 03  >../...ng.Rz/./.
000000e0  73 B6 7F 9A 38 9B DD B8  62 DF D0 A0 51 A1 71 7E  s...8...b...Q.q~
000000f0  B9 98 FB DD 26 2E 77 A8  42 D1 52 45 BB B7 74 F2  ....&.w.B.RE..t.
00000100  F4 B3 EF AC 44 AC 45 6F  56 76 ED 95 D4 04 9E 70  ....D.EoVv.....p
00000110  1D 86 D9 81 91 C2 48 E4  7C B3 F3 53 CD BA B3 8A  ......H.|..S....
00000120  CC 26 33 13 3A 5E 9E 0E  8D 20 1E 4E 08 E7 AF 50  .&3.:^.....N...P
00000130  61 B3 3F 99 B7 5C 3A 66  A8 21 92 E5 1A 10 22 ED  a.?..\:f.!....".
00000140  A4 41 50 D5 31 A5 BA 9C  7D 10 56 C3 72 CD 48 A7  .AP.1...}.V.r.H.
00000150  28 D7 8E 4E E6 AB E2 70  63 A9 30 A6 18 96 A7 BF  (..N...pc.0.....
00000160  8A FF DD 3A 2E 0D BE 08  86 0D 72 19 84 90 F5 5D  ...:......r....]
00000170  E4 D9 2E FD 52 5E 6D A2  D1 AA C7 53 9F E2 31 27  ....R^m....S..1'
00000180  70 60 A4 0C F6 91 53 24  D4 C7 AE 51 C5 50 BF 0C  p`....S$...Q.P..
00000190  5E E3 EB 08 3D 26 E7 16  6C 91 FE 86 A1 31 9A D5  ^...=&..l....1..
000001a0  D6 85 1D 23 30 19 89 99  97 76 91 0F 40 DD AE BF  ...#0....v..@...
000001b0  EB A1 24 F6 60 4A F5 6E  39 C9 58 E6 1F 8B ED A1  ..$.`J.n9.X.....
000001c0  D3 0A CF F8 5A AE E2 85  C1 BD CB 21 F8 BF 41 06  ....Z......!..A.
000001d0  0B E6 0A 9A 76 1C B8 35  CF FB 32 AF 28 C1 2C A4  ....v..5..2.(.,.
000001e0  8B 6B 43 12 03 7D C5 3C  F8 C6 2A 79 59 CD 36 8C  .kC..}.<..*yY.6.
000001f0  35 2A 94 24 09 1D 32 A0  B1 DE D8 5D 96 1F 9A BE  5*.$..2....]....
00000200  6E BE 5A B3 01 D9 19 1F  82 A5 58 33 A2 63 A5 D8  n.Z.......X3.c..
00000210  84 4D 4D 15 3B D4 85 A9  3B A8 28 EB 87 5C 1A 0A  .MM.;...;.(..\..
00000220  08 99 5C 72 3B F7 0D 4B  7B 91 5C 5C 8C 6C D6 11  ..\r;..K{.\\.l..
00000230  82 1D DF DD 69 72 50 FD  84 00 6A 3D 09 C5 64 28  ....irP...j=..d(
00000240  7F F4 2E D6 06 B9 A5 2E  44 1C F1 08 9D 1D 5F 65  ........D....._e
00000250  F7 17 B6 E0 2F 5A 8A D0  BE 42 97 46 F5 9C B0 B9  ..../Z...B.F....
00000260  20 FF 16 79 DD A7 28 0A  17 47 49 F1 90 1A E1 A5   ..y..(..GI.....
00000270  4B 15 44 20 28 AF 9B F4  61 EA 27 A9 54 EE F3 8E  K.D (...a.'.T...
00000280  0A 13 71 94 E3 1F 01 F2  90 94 2D 6E D8 10 D9 49  ..q.......-n...I
00000290  DF 63 C3 6F 78 3B 04 5F  B0 34 04 2C DC E6 14 CD  .c.ox;._.4.,....
000002a0  BE 7A 48 A3 7D B7 74 C6  79 02 6A 25 CD A7 CD C3  .zH.}.t.y.j%....
000002b0
```

FIGURE 2.16: Encrypted Configuration Section Data

Behind the Configuration Design-Time

The Enterprise Library Configuration Tool is really just a Windows Form application that uses the design-time features in the Configuration Application Block. The Configuration Application Block's design-time features are based on the same concepts and architecture as the design-time features for .NET Windows Forms and ASP.NET applications: the classes in the `System.ComponentModel` namespace. Exposing the Configuration Application Block's design-time features has many benefits. It provides a single, consistent model that all application blocks can use to display, validate, and update the configuration data for their runtime components. It also gives you design-time configuration capabilities for adding your own Storage-Providers, Transformers, application blocks, and extensions to application blocks.

Figure 2.17 depicts several concepts. First, it illustrates how the Enterprise Library Configuration Tool uses the design-time features in the Configuration Application Block to achieve its needs. It also emphasizes that the Configuration Application Block's design-time objects rely on its runtime objects for saving and retrieving configuration information. Lastly, it shows how client applications that are built to use Enterprise Library will either directly or indirectly use the Configuration Application Block's runtime features for storing and retrieving either their own custom configuration information or the configuration information needed for the Enterprise Library application blocks to function properly.

The following sections describe the concepts behind the Configuration Application Block's design-time and how it uses the classes contained in the `System.ComponentModel` namespace. They include a discussion of how you can use the design-time features in the Configuration Application Block to provide new design-time features in the Enterprise Library

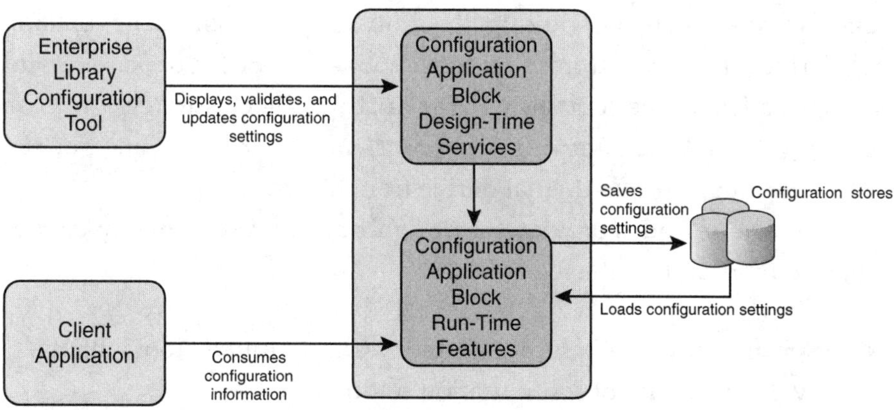

FIGURE 2.17: High-Level Design of the Configuration Application Block's Design-Time

Configuration Tool and walks you through an example of creating such an extension.

Using the `System.ComponentModel` Namespace

Enterprise Library's Configuration design-time is based heavily on the .NET `System.ComponentModel` namespace. This namespace includes base classes and interfaces for implementing attributes and type converters, binding to data sources, licensing components, and more. The namespace provides Enterprise Library with a valuable service-based model that is not only used to implement its runtime and design-time behavior for components and controls, but it also allows Enterprise Library's design-time experience to be extended. Some of the interfaces used by the Enterprise Library Configuration design-time are `IComponent`, `IContainer`, `ISite`, `IServiceProvider`, and `IServiceContainer`.

The `IComponent` Interface

The `IComponent` interface defines the functionality that must exist for all components. The `System.ComponentModel.Component` class is the default implementation of this interface and is the base class for all components in the common language runtime that marshal by reference. Components are especially important because they can access services from a container that owns the component. In Enterprise Library, the abstract `ConfigurationNode` class—and therefore any class that derives from `ConfigurationNode`—is a component. Figure 2–18 illustrates how the `ConfigurationNode` class derives indirectly from `System.ComponentModel.Component` and shows just a few of the concrete `ConfigurationNode` classes (e.g., `XmlIncludeTypeNode`, `StorageProviderNode`, `TransformerNode`, and `ApplicationConfigurationNode`) that derive from this base class.

Configuration nodes provide the design-time representation of configuration settings and do the following.

- Determine how the Enterprise Library Configuration Tool will display the hierarchy of configuration settings
- Control which properties are exposed in the graphical interface

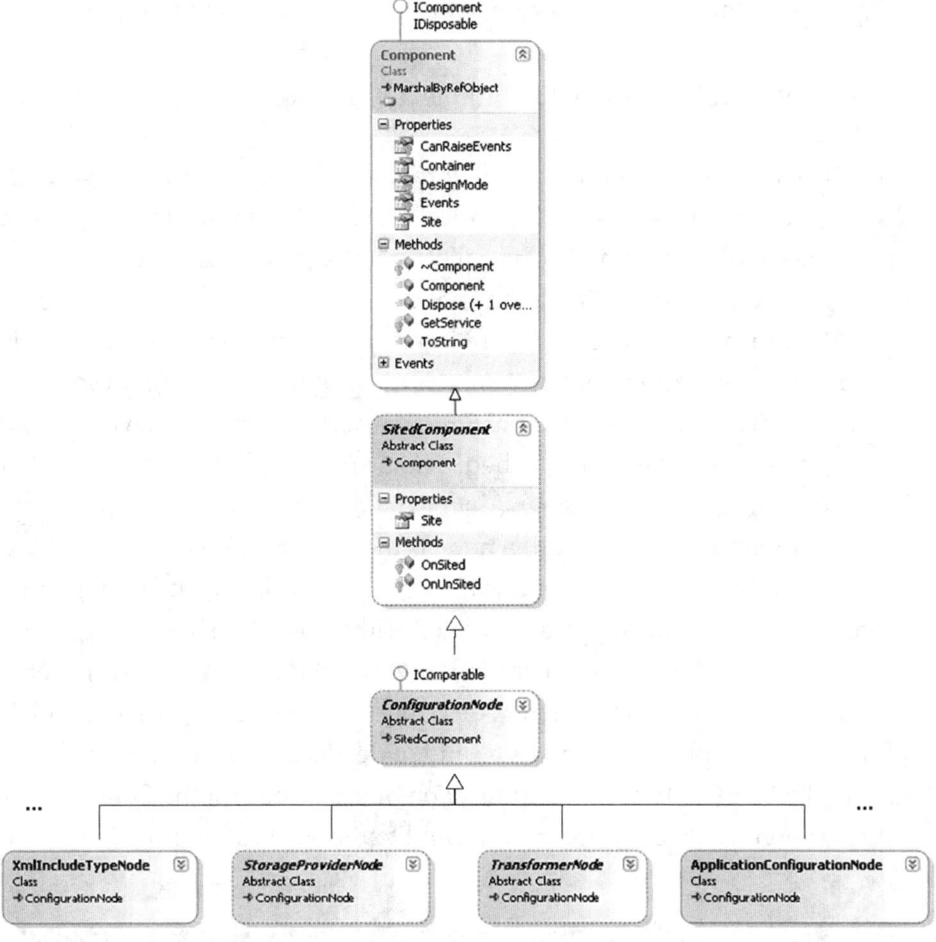

FIGURE 2.18: `ConfigurationNode` **Derives From** `Component`

- Enable the validation for the values a user assigns to a configuration node
- Contain references to the runtime data classes

The left pane of the Enterprise Library Configuration Tool displays the configuration nodes in a configuration tree (see Figure 2.19). When a user selects a configuration node, the collection of settings associated with that configuration node display in the Property pane.

When an application's configuration is created or opened, the Enterprise Library Configuration Tool first creates an application configuration node and adds it to the `SolutionConfigurationNode`, the top-level node to which all other nodes are attached. The `SolutionConfigurationNode` is always named *Enterprise Library Configuration.*

The application configuration node is the parent for all application block nodes that are added to that application's configuration. Child nodes underneath the application node are associated with application blocks. Figure 2.19 shows an application that is configured to use the Data Access Application Block; therefore, the application node is the node labeled *Application1* and the Data Access Application Block is a child node. Because all application blocks depend on the Configuration Application Block, a node for the Configuration Application Block also appears as a child to the application node.

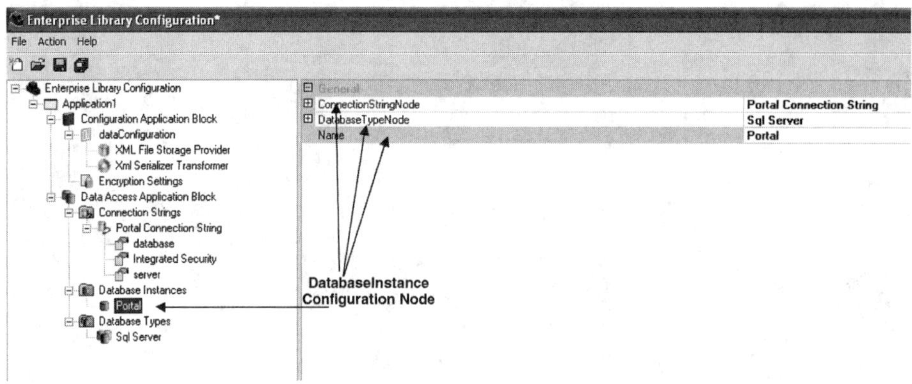

FIGURE 2.19: Configuration Nodes and the Property Pane

Configuration nodes have properties that allow them to be maintained in parent-child relationships with other nodes. Each node can have at most one parent node, but it can have multiple child nodes. The parent-child relationship of nodes allows configuration settings to be organized in a logical hierarchy at design time. The Enterprise Library Configuration Tool uses this hierarchical relationship to construct the configuration tree.

All configuration nodes derive from the abstract `ConfigurationNode` base class. A `ConfigurationNode`'s public properties are exposed and editable at design time as properties displayed within the node's Property pane. In Figure 2.19, the *DatabaseInstance* node is referencing a `DatabaseType` node and a `ConnectionString` node. Clicking the plus sign next to the node's settings will let you edit the settings for the node. The `Name` property is also exposed and editable for this node. Every configuration node includes the public property `Name`, which represents the name of the node that is displayed in the tree view.

The `IContainer` Interface

The `System.ComponentModel.IContainer` interface defines the functionality that must exist for a **container,** an object that encapsulates and tracks zero or more components. The `IContainer` interface defines the properties and methods that must exist to wrap around a collection of components. The `Components` property returns a `ComponentsCollection`; the `Add` and `Remove` methods allow components to be added to and removed from the collection.

The `Container` class is the default implementation of the `IContainer` interface. In addition to the `Components` property and the `Add` and `Remove` methods, the `Container` class also provides a `CreateSite` method for creating a `Site` (explained next) for a given component in the container, and a `GetService` method for retrieving a service object for a specified type. By using a container in an application, application-wide services can be retrieved throughout the entire application. In Enterprise Library, the `ConfigurationDesignHost` class implements the `IContainer` interface and is the container for all the classes that derive from `ConfigurationNode`. Figure 2.20 shows the `ConfigurationDesignHost`'s properties and methods.

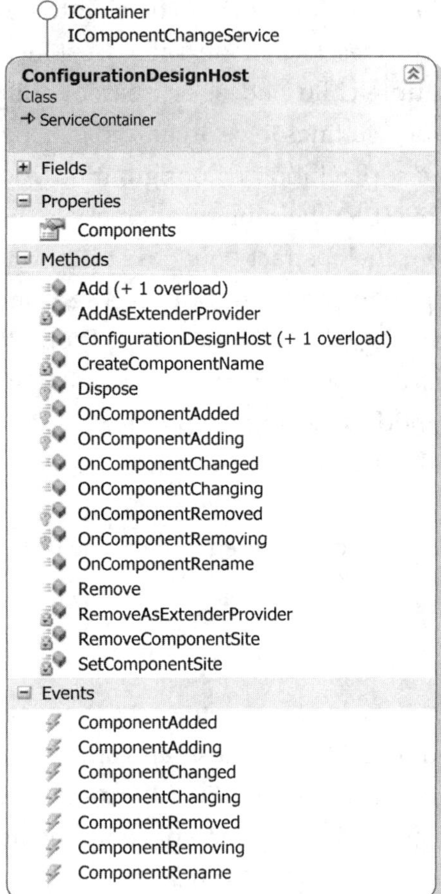

Figure 2.20: Properties and Methods of `ConfigurationDesignHost`

The `ISite` Interface

A **site** "glues" a component to the container it lives in and enables communication between the two. The `ISite` interface defines the properties needed to enable service retrieval by a component. In Enterprise Library, the `ConfigurationNodeSite` class implements the `ISite` interface. It binds configuration nodes with the `ConfigurationDesignHost`. Figure 2.21 shows the properties and methods for the `ConfigurationNodeSite`. Two notable properties are the `Component` and `Container` properties; these are used to bind the two together.

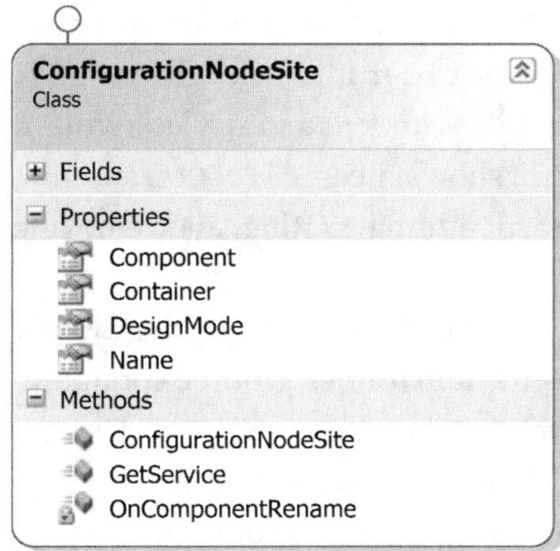

FIGURE 2.21: Properties and Methods of `ConfigurationNodeSite`

The `IServiceProvider` and `IServiceContainer` Interfaces

The `IServiceProvider` and `IServiceContainer` interfaces derive from the `System` namespace. A **service object** is an object that provides custom support to other objects. Services are powerful because they allow for a loose coupling between the interface that defines a service and the classes that implement it. Components can request a service and retrieve an instance that they can use, but they never need to know anything about the implementation of the service.

The `IServiceProvider` interface defines a mechanism for retrieving a service object. A **service container** is, by definition, a service provider. In addition to providing services, it also provides a mechanism for adding and removing services. To obtain a service at design time, the `GetService` method of a component sited in design mode can be called.

Designers and other objects can add or remove services at design time as well. When a service is added, it can be added with instructions to promote it. When a service is promoted, it is added to all parent service containers until the top of the service container tree is reached. This allows a designer to provide a global service that other objects in the process can use.

Enterprise Library's abstract `ServiceContainer` class implements both the `IServiceContainer` and `IServiceProvider` interfaces. The `ConfigurationDesignHost` derives from the `ServiceContainer` class; thus, it is also a `ServiceContainer`. Figure 2.22 shows the `ServiceContainer`'s methods. Notice the methods that exist for adding, getting, and removing services.

The `ConfigurationDesignHost` is created when the Enterprise Library Configuration Tool starts, and it acts as the hub for design-time configuration-related objects and services. As previously mentioned, this class is a container for configuration nodes and design-time services.

As configuration nodes are added to an application's configuration, the `ConfigurationDesignHost` object creates an object of type `Configura-`

FIGURE 2.22: Properties and Methods of `ServiceContainer`

`tionNodeSite` for the nodes. At this point, the component is known to be **sited** and is fully functional. Since the `ConfigurationNodeSite` object implements the `ISite` interface, it lets the configuration node access the services hosted by the `ConfigurationDesignHost` object.

Table 2.3 lists the services initialized by the `ConfigurationDesignHost` object when it is created.

Because a configuration node can access the container via the `Site` property that has been set for it, the node can perform actions requiring services by calling `Site.GetService(Type)`. `IServiceProvider.GetService(Type)` allows dynamic retrieval of services from the container. Thus, new configuration nodes can be created and dynamically added to the `ConfigurationDesignHost` that can access and use the services provided by the Enterprise Library's Configuration design-time.

Configuration Hierarchies

Configuration hierarchies maintain a logical structure and grouping for configuration settings. Configuration nodes can have a parent node, child nodes, and sibling nodes. Every configuration hierarchy has a single root node.

Hierarchies must conform to the `IUIHierarchy` interface. The `IUIHierarchy` interface can prove useful because it has methods to search for nodes either by node type or by name. This becomes especially important when a configuration node needs to reference another configuration node in an application. For example, Figure 2.19 shows a `DatabaseInstance` node for the Data Access Application Block referencing a `ConnectionString` node and a `DatabaseType` node. The `IUIHierarchy` interface provides this configuration node with the capability to return a list of the types of these nodes (i.e., `ConnectionString` node and `DatabaseType` node) that have already been configured for the application.

Configuration Menu Items and Commands

Configuration menu items and commands provide the user interface for launching configuration-related actions at design time. For example, as

Table 2.3: Services Initialized and Added by the `ConfigurationDesignHost`

Service	Description
`NodeNameCreationService`	Generates a unique name for a node. All child nodes under a parent node must have a unique name. The Configuration Application Block uses this service to create a new name when a node is created with the same name as a sibling node.
`UIHierarchyService`	Provides a container and management services for objects that implement the `IUIHierarchy` interface. The command to create an application configuration node creates an `IUIHierarchy` object for the application and adds this hierarchy to the collection maintained by the `UIHierarchyService` class.
`ConfigurationErrorService`	Collects configuration and validation errors. The application block design managers use this service to report errors that occur when an application block configuration is opened or saved. The command to validate configuration nodes also uses this service to report validation errors.
`NodeCreationService`	Creates configuration nodes. It allows design managers to map runtime configuration data types to configuration node types. Configuration nodes also use this service to create child nodes based on runtime configuration object types.
`XmlIncludeTypeService`	Adds `XmlIncludeTypes` to the metaconfiguration data. It is typically used when providing extension points to existing applications.
`LinkNodeService`	Links one configuration node to another. A configuration node can have a property that specifies another configuration node as the value for that property. Configuration nodes use this service to create a link between the two nodes.
`MenuContainerService`	Adds menu items to a menu. Configuration nodes use this service to create menu items to be added to the context menu for that node.

depicted in Figure 2.23, a command on the Data Access Application Block `ConnectionStrings` configuration node lets users create new connection strings as child nodes.

Actions are exposed as configuration menu items. Configuration menu items are classes that derive from the `ConfigurationMenuItem` class. Com-

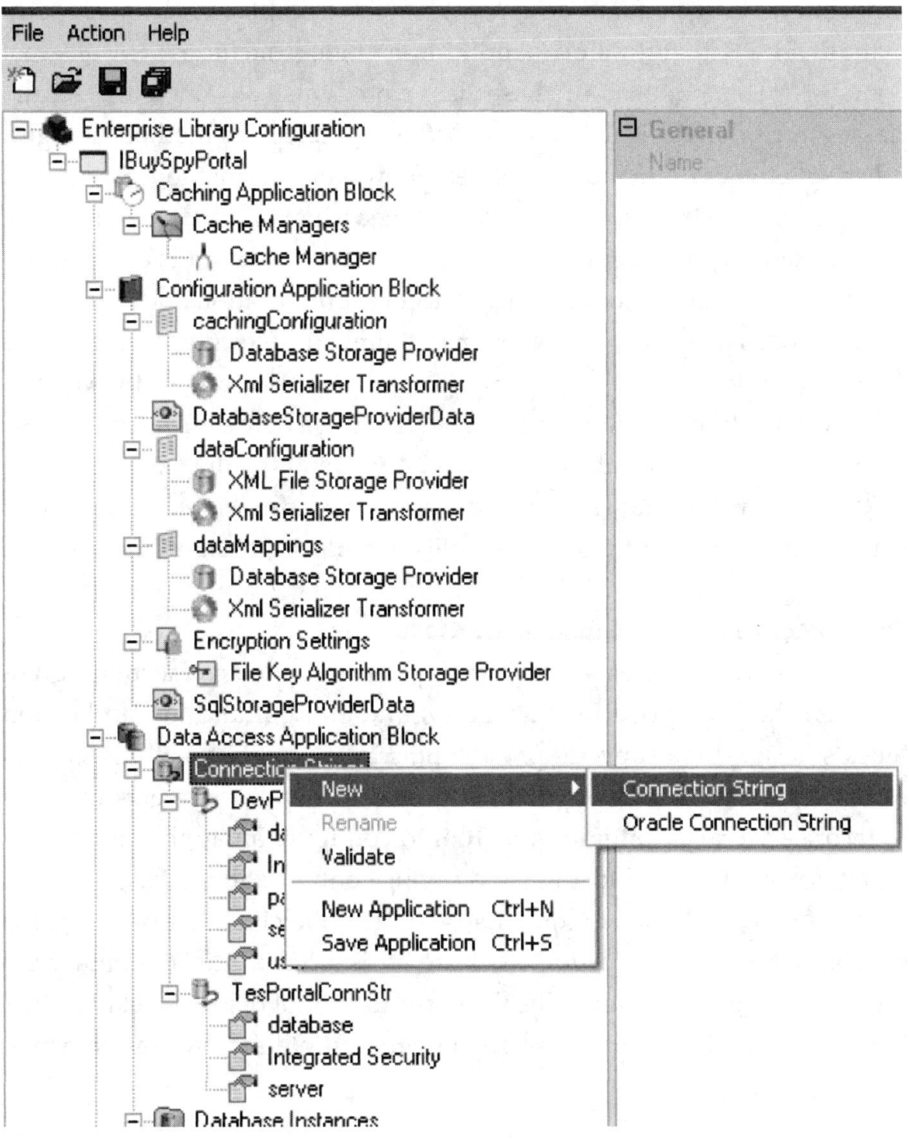

FIGURE 2.23: Configuration Menu Items and Commands

mon menu items that exist for many configuration nodes are New, Rename, Remove, Validate, New Application, and Save Application. You can add custom menu items to a configuration node by overriding the `OnAddMenuItems` method.

A configuration node command determines the action performed when a user selects a menu item. The Enterprise Library Configuration design-time follows the command design pattern[1] in its implementation for commands. The Configuration Application Block includes an abstract `ConfigurationNodeCommand` base class from which all concrete `Command` classes must derive. The base class defines an `Execute` method that gets called when the command is executed. However, this method passes control to a derived class' implementation of the virtual `ExecuteCore` method.

For example, the `AddChildNodeCommand` command adds a configuration node as a child of the currently selected configuration node. The logic for the actions that take place when this command is executed resides in the `AddChildNodeCommand`'s `ExecuteCore` method. You can add new commands to the design-time experience by deriving a new class from the `ConfigurationNodeCommand` class and implementing the `ExecuteCore` method. Figure 2.24 shows a small sampling of the concrete commands that exist as part of the Configuration Application Block's design-time features.

The `ConfigurationDesignManager` Class

The `ConfigurationDesignManager` provides the connection point between the Enterprise Library Configuration Tool and an application block's design-time support. The `ConfigurationDesignManager` creates menu items and commands that are invoked as a user interacts with the Enterprise Library Configuration Tool to configure an application block, and it is responsible for loading and saving configuration data.

The `ConfigurationDesignManager` is also the class that provides the capability for new application blocks to be "snapped into" the Enterprise Library Configuration Tool. The Configuration Tool discovers classes that implement the `IConfigurationDesignManager` interface by examining the

---

1. *Design Patterns: Elements of Reusable Object-Oriented Software*, by Erich Gamma, Richard Helm, Ralph Johnson, and John Vlissides. Addison-Wesley, 1995.

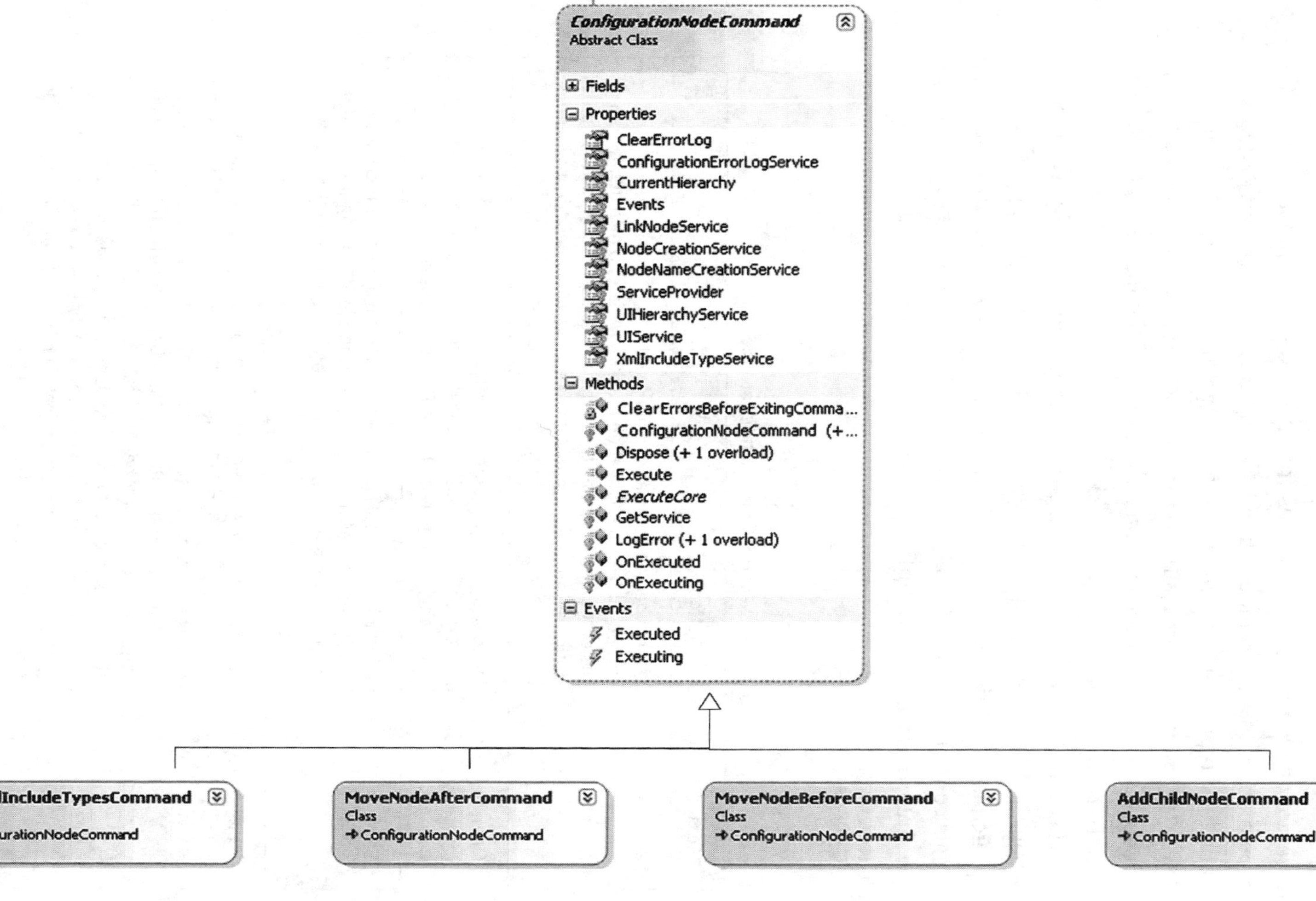

Figure 2.24: `ConfigurationNodeCommand` **Hierarchy**

assembly attributes for assemblies that it knows about, instantiating the type defined in the `ConfigurationDesignManagerAttribute`, and validating the type as an implementation of `IConfigurationDesignManager`. The `IConfigurationDesignManager` interface defines four methods: `Register`, `Open`, `Save`, and `BuildContext`. Table 2–4 details the significance of each of these methods.

The `ConfigurationDesignManager` determines the actions that occur when the Enterprise Library Configuration Tool is used to open or save an application's configuration information. For example, when an application that is configured to use the Data Access Application Block is opened with the Enterprise Library Configuration Tool, the following actions take place.

Table 2.4: `IConfigurationDesignManager` **Interface Methods**

Method	Description
Register	Called when an application configuration node is selected. This method allows an application block to register a new menu item. This menu item contains the command to add the application block configuration to the current application and relates the menu item to its corresponding configuration node.
Open	Called when an application's configuration file is opened. This method loads the configuration data for all application blocks by calling each configured StorageProvider's `Read` method.
Save	Called when an application's configuration information is saved. This method saves all of an application block's configuration information to storage by calling each configured StorageProvider's `Write` method.
BuildContext	Creates an in-memory representation of the application block's configuration settings. This method does not require that these settings exist in configuration storage. The `BuildContext` method can construct configuration settings based on the state of the configuration settings of other application blocks. This allows an application block to be configured dynamically. (To see an example of using the `ConfigurationContext` to dynamically access the configuration settings for an application block, refer to the description of the DatabaseStorageProvider in Chapter 1.)

1. The `ConfigurationDesignManager`'s `Open` method is called for both the Configuration Application Block and the Data Access Application Block.
2. The Configuration Application Block reads the configuration metadata about all configuration sections from the application domain configuration file (i.e., app.config or web.config).
3. The configuration information for the Data Access Application Block is read from the configured StorageProviders and the `BuildContext` method is used to maintain it in the Configuration Application Block's current `ConfigurationContext` object.
4. The Data Access Application Block's runtime components are instantiated with the information contained in the current `ConfigurationContext`.
5. The `ConfigurationDesignManager`'s `Register` method is called for each application block. This allows the Enterprise Library Configuration Tool to populate the configuration nodes, menus items, and commands. The settings that are displayed for each configuration node are obtained from the node's corresponding runtime object. For example, the `DatabaseTypeNode` configuration node encapsulates the Data Access Application Block's `DatabaseTypeData` object.
6. Users can add, delete, or modify the configuration settings.
7. As information is modified for the properties of a configuration node, the application block design-time objects update their runtime objects to reflect the changes.
8. When the configuration information is saved in the Enterprise Library Configuration Tool, each `ConfigurationDesignManager`'s `Save` method is called. This lets each design-time object perform validation on the data that exists in the runtime objects and report any failures through the tool.
9. After validation succeeds, each application block writes the new configuration data to its respective data stores: the Configuration Application Block writes the settings to the application domain configuration file, and the Data Access Application Block uses its config-

ured StorageProvider and Transformer to save its new configuration settings to the appropriate data store.

Example: Design-Time Configuration

Chapter 1 showed how the metaconfiguration data for the DatabaseStorageProvider can be manually entered and modified in the application domain configuration file. While it is entirely possible to take this route for all of the configuration data for an application, you should avoid it when at all possible. Entering and editing configuration data with an XML editor requires detailed knowledge of the particular configuration's schema, and there is no way to automatically validate the settings until runtime. A better route to go is using a tool like the Enterprise Library Configuration Tool to modify, validate, and save configuration information.

This chapter has shown how to use the Enterprise Library Configuration Tool to configure the runtime features in the Configuration Application Block. It has also detailed the architecture behind the design-time features in the Configuration Application Block and promoted how such features allow for great extensibility in the entire design-time experience. This example proves that point. This section walks through the tasks that are involved in adding design support and extending the Enterprise Library Configuration Tool by adding design-time features for the DatabaseStorageProvider.

As previously mentioned, a configuration node encapsulates a group of logically related runtime configuration settings for display and modification at design time. When you select a configuration node, the Enterprise Library Configuration Tool displays the properties associated with that configuration node in the Property pane. The configuration node's properties are the most granular level at which configuration settings can be altered.

The first task for extending the design-time experience of the Enterprise Library Configuration Tool is to create a project that will contain the classes that represents the new `ConfigurationNode` and `ConfigurationDesignManager`. Some thought must be given to determine which configuration node settings should be exposed. You expose the settings of a configuration node by creating the configuration node with public properties to reflect the values stored in its associated runtime configuration object. The `DatabaseStorageProviderNode` contains the following public properties: `Name`, `DatabaseInstance`, `GetConfigStoredProcedure`, `SetConfigStoredProcedure`, `TypeName`, and `DatabaseStorageProviderData`.

- **`Name`**. Because the public Name property is defined in the base `ConfigurationNode` class, it does not need to be redefined. This property represents the name of the node that is displayed in the configuration hierarchy. Because it is a public property, it is also displayed in the Property pane of the Enterprise Library Configuration Tool.
- **`DatabaseInstance`**. This example requires that the `DatabaseInstance` property contain data by attributing it as `[Required]`. This property is especially interesting because I am referencing a `ConfigurationNode` in the Data Access Application Block through the `LinkNodeService` (described earlier in the discussion of the services that the `ConfigurationDesignHost` initializes).

  To indicate which type of node I am referencing, I have attributed this property with the `[ReferenceType(typeof(InstanceNode))]` attribute. I have also specified the `[Editor]` and `[BaseType]` attributes. The `Editor` attribute allows a special editor to be used in the Property pane for this property. In this case, the `ReferenceEditor` is being used to make it easier to ensure that users add references to other `InstanceNode`s that already exist in the application's configuration. The `ILinkNodeService` provides the ability to create the reference to another `ConfigurationNode`.
- **`GetConfigStoredProcedure`**. This example uses the `GetConfigStoredProcedure` property to set and get the name of the stored procedure that will retrieve configuration information. I am requiring that this property contain data by attributing it as `[Required]`. If no value is set for this property, the configuration settings will fail validation and an error will display in the Enterprise Library Configuration Tool's Configuration Errors window.
- **`SetConfigStoredProcedure`**. This example uses the `SetConfigStoredProcedure` property to set and get the name of the stored

procedure that will save configuration information. I am requiring that this property contain data by attributing it as `[Required]`.

- **TypeName**. I am exposing the `TypeName` property with the `[ReadOnly]` attribute so users will be able to see the fully qualified type name for this `ConfigurationNode` but will not be able to edit its value.
- **DatabaseStorageProviderData**. The `DatabaseStorageProviderData` class contains a property for accessing the runtime `DatabaseStorageProviderData` object. However, since I don't want end users to be able to view this property, I am preventing it from being displayed in the Enterprise Library Configuration Tool by attributing it with `[Browsable(false)]`. All of the other properties just discussed set the properties of their corresponding runtime counterparts; that is, the `DatabaseStorageProviderData` class that was created in the last chapter.

Listing 2.5 includes the code for creating the `DatabaseInstance` property for the `DatabaseStorageProviderNode` class. The full source code is on the book's Web site.

LISTING 2.5: `DatabaseStorageProviderNode` Class

```
[C#]
[ServiceDependency(typeof(ILinkNodeService))]
[ServiceDependency(typeof(IXmlIncludeTypeService))]
[ServiceDependency(typeof(INodeCreationService))]
public class DatabaseStorageProviderNode : StorageProviderNode
{
    private InstanceNode instanceNode;
    private ConfigurationNodeChangedEventHandler
              onInstanceNodeRemoved;
    private ConfigurationNodeChangedEventHandler
              onInstanceNodeRenamed;
    private DatabaseStorageProviderData databaseStorageProviderData;

...

     [Required]
     [Editor(typeof(ReferenceEditor), typeof(UITypeEditor))]
     [ReferenceType(typeof(InstanceNode))]
     [SRCategory(SR.Keys.CategoryGeneral)]
```

```
    public InstanceNode DatabaseInstance
    {
        get { return instanceNode; }
        set
        {
            ILinkNodeService service =
                GetService(typeof(ILinkNodeService))
                as ILinkNodeService;
            instanceNode = service.CreateReference
                 (instanceNode, value, onInstanceNodeRemoved,
                    onInstanceNodeRenamed) as InstanceNode;
            this.databaseStorageProviderData.DatabaseInstance =
                String.Empty;
            if (instanceNode != null)
            {
                this.databaseStorageProviderData.DatabaseInstance =
                    instanceNode.Name;
            }
        }
    }

 ...
}

[Visual Basic]
<ServiceDependency(GetType(ILinkNodeService)), _
ServiceDependency(GetType(IXmlIncludeTypeService)), _
ServiceDependency(GetType(INodeCreationService))> _
Public Class DatabaseStorageProviderNode : Inherits StorageProviderNode

    Private instanceNode As InstanceNode
    Private onInstanceNodeRemoved As _
            ConfigurationNodeChangedEventHandler
    Private onInstanceNodeRenamed As _
            ConfigurationNodeChangedEventHandler
    Private databaseStorageProviderData As _
            DatabaseStorageProviderData

...

    <Required, Editor(GetType(ReferenceEditor), _
        GetType(UITypeEditor)), ReferenceType(GetType(InstanceNode)), _
        SRCategory(SR.Keys.CategoryGeneral)> _
    Public Property DatabaseInstance() As InstanceNode
        Get
            Return instanceNode
        End Get
        Set
            Dim service As ILinkNodeService = _
```

```
                    GetService(GetType(ILinkNodeService))
                Dim ILinkNodeService As as instanceNode = _
                    IIf(TypeOf service.CreateReference _
                    (instanceNode, Value, onInstanceNodeRemoved, _
                    onInstanceNodeRenamed) Is InstanceNode, _
                    CType(service.CreateReference (instanceNode, _
                    Value, onInstanceNodeRemoved, _
                    onInstanceNodeRenamed), InstanceNode), _
                    CType(Nothing, InstanceNode))
                Me.databaseStorageProviderData.DatabaseInstance = _
                    String.Empty
                If Not instanceNode Is Nothing Then
                    databaseStorageProviderData.DatabaseInstance _
                    = instanceNode.Name
                End If
            End Set
        End Property
...
End Class
```

Since I am creating a new assembly, a new class that implements the IConfigurationDesignManager interface is needed to properly register, open, and save the configuration information for the DatabaseStorage-ProviderNode. If I were adding a ConfigurationNode to an assembly that already exists, I would modify the ConfigurationDesignManager that already exists instead of creating a new one. The ConfigurationDesign-Manager is primarily needed to register the new ConfigurationNode and associate menu items and commands with it.

An XmlIncludeType also needs to be added so the Configuration Application Block knows how to create the DatabaseStorageProvider-Data type. Because the Configuration Application Block uses the service model provided by the System.ComponentModel namespace, I can simply request the XmlIncludeTypeService to accomplish this. In fact, because requesting the services outlined in Table 2.3 is such a common activity, the Configuration Application Block provides a ServiceHelper utility class to make requesting these services easier. In the code for the Configura-tionDesignManager's Register method, shown in Listing 2.6, I use the ServiceHelper class to request both the NodeCreationService and the

XmlIncludeTypeService. The full source code for this assembly is on the book's Web site.

LISTING 2.6: Register Method for the ExtensionsConfigurationDesign-Manager

```
[C#]
INodeCreationService service =
            ServiceHelper.GetNodeCreationService(serviceProvider);
nodetype = typeof(DatabaseStorageProviderNode);
service.AddNodeCreationEntry(
            NodeCreationEntry.CreateNodeCreationEntryNoMultiples(
            new AddChildNodeCommand(serviceProvider, nodetype),
            nodetype, typeof(DatabaseStorageProviderData),
            SR.DbStorageProviderNodeMenuName));
IXmlIncludeTypeService includeTypeService =
            ServiceHelper.GetXmlIncludeTypeService(serviceProvider);
includeTypeService.AddXmlIncludeType(
            ConfigurationSettings.SectionName,
            typeof(DatabaseStorageProviderData));

[Visual Basic]
Dim service As INodeCreationService = _
            ServiceHelper.GetNodeCreationService(serviceProvider)
Dim nodetype = GetType(DatabaseStorageProviderNode)
service.AddNodeCreationEntry( _
            NodeCreationEntry.CreateNodeCreationEntryNoMultiples( _
            New AddChildNodeCommand(serviceProvider, nodetype), _
            nodetype, GetType(DatabaseStorageProviderData), _
            SR.DbStorageProviderNodeMenuName))
Dim includeTypeService As IXmlIncludeTypeService = _
            ServiceHelper.GetXmlIncludeTypeService(serviceProvider)
includeTypeService.AddXmlIncludeType( _
            ConfigurationSettings.SectionName, _
            GetType(DatabaseStorageProviderData))
```

Finally, a new assembly attribute needs to be added to the Assembly-Info.cs (or vb) file, because the Enterprise Library Configuration Tool will look for a value for this attribute to determine whether it should load an included ConfigurationDesignManager. Listing 2.7 shows adding the ConfigurationDesignManagerAttribute to the AssemblyInfo file for a ConfigurationDesignManager named ExtensionsConfigurationDe-signManager.

LISTING 2.7: Assembly Attribute Needed to Recognize `ExtensionsConfigurationDesignManager`

```
[C#]
[assembly :
    ConfigurationDesignManager(
    typeof(ExtensionsConfigurationDesignManager))
]

[Visual Basic]
<assembly : _
    ConfigurationDesignManager( _
    GetType(ExtensionsConfigurationDesignManager))
>
```

Once this assembly has been compiled and deployed so the Enterprise Library Configuration Tool can access it (e.g., copy this assembly to the same directory as the tool), a DatabaseStorageProvider can be added and used as easily as any of the StorageProviders that ship with Enterprise Library's Configuration Application Block. Figure 2.25 shows how I have modified a configuration section by removing the XmlFileStorageProvider and adding a new DatabaseStorageProvider.

Thus, the design-time experience provided by the Configuration Application Block and the Enterprise Library Configuration Tool has been extended without modifying any of the code that ships with Enterprise Library. A separate assembly was created that was able to be used to

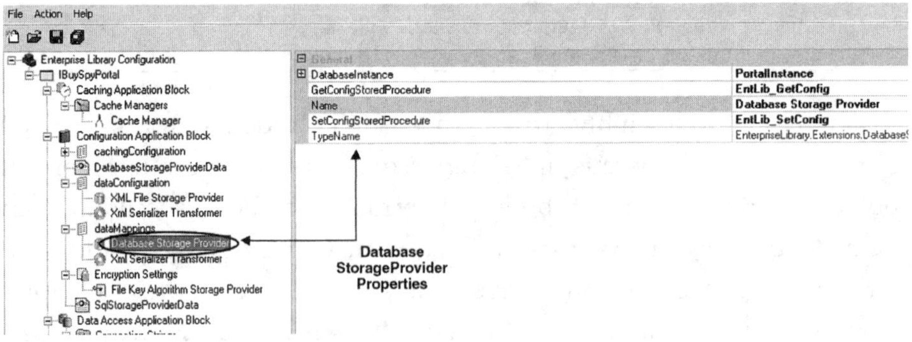

FIGURE 2.25: `DatabaseStorageProvider` **Configuration Node**

dynamically add new capabilities to the Enterprise Library Configuration Tool. The experience for using this new functionality is no different than using any of the application blocks that ship with Enterprise Library. In fact, as you will see in later chapters, each application block uses the same process that I have just outlined to add its own unique features to the Configuration Tool.

Summary

This chapter began with a description of how to use the Enterprise Library Configuration Tool to easily create or modify the runtime features provided by the Configuration Application Block. It showed how the Enterprise Library Configuration Tool can be used to add, remove, and modify the metaconfiguration for an application. It discussed how the Configuration Application Block's design-time features not only provide the basis from which the Enterprise Library Configuration Tool is formed, but how they are designed to allow enterprises to extend the tool as the need exists. It described how the Configuration Application Block's use of the classes in the `System.ComponentModel` namespace helps provide this service-based model. The chapter concluded with an example showing how the tool can be extended by taking advantage of the design-time features provided by the Configuration Application Block.

There are two major principles you should now recognize. The first is that the design-time features for the Configuration Application Block are based on the `System.ComponentModel` namespace; these are the same design-time features that are used for Windows Form-based and ASP.NET applications. These foundation classes allow Enterprise Library to provide a rich service-based, design-time experience.

The second, and somewhat related, point is that the Configuration Application Block has been designed for extensibility so that enterprises can add new features as needed. Furthermore, the model and process that an enterprise uses to extend the features of Enterprise Library are the very same model and process that each application block uses to supply its own unique features.

3

The Data Access Application Block

MOST ENTERPRISE-LEVEL applications store information in some type of relational database. As a result, these applications often need to execute database commands such as Transact-SQL statements or stored procedures. The commands are used to perform database updates, retrieve data values, retrieve multiple rows of data, and even retrieve XML data. The need for this type of functionality is at the core of almost every enterprise-level application.

However, developers often find themselves duplicating code to open and close database connections, assign parameters to database commands, and perform similar database operations throughout the various applications that they build. The Data Access Application Block is designed to address these inefficiencies by providing methods that encapsulate the logic needed to perform the most common database operations with a minimal requirement for custom code. Furthermore, its design provides a consistent interface for performing these database operations regardless of the ultimate data source that is being used.

This chapter begins by explaining the differences between Enterprise Library's Data Access Application Block and the versions of the Data Access Application Block that have preceded it. (One of the major differences is the introduction of database providers.) It discusses the design of database providers and why they are at the core of this version of the Data

Access Application Block. It describes how to create a new database provider, complete with design-time capabilities, that extends the ability of the Data Access Application Block to use data sources other than Microsoft SQL Server, Oracle, or DB2.

The chapter then highlights how to configure database providers for an application and how to take advantage of a database provider's methods and properties to access and update data from a database. The chapter concludes by showing how to design the data tier for a distributed application so that it not only takes advantage of the features that Enterprise Library's Data Access Application Block provides, but so it also adheres to the guidance prescribed by the Microsoft patterns & practices team.

What Is the Data Access Application Block?

The **Data Access Application Block** provides a set of classes and interfaces that encapsulate many of the best practices that Microsoft recommends for designing a data layer.[1] Specifically, Enterprise Library's Data Access Application Block provides a solution that satisfies the requirements for using data access helper components to produce cleaner and more manageable code. The Data Access Application Block also uses an abstract base class that defines a common interface for these components. This lets you write code that uses the Data Access Application Block to be very portable; that is, the code can generally remain unchanged when switching between different databases (e.g., from a Microsoft SQL Server database to an Oracle or DB2 database). By making the most of the Data Access Application Block, an enterprise can do the following.

- Maintain consistent data access practices, both in an application and across the enterprise.
- Reduce difficulties in changing the physical database target.
- Relieve developers from having to learn different programming models for different types of databases.

1. See Application Architecture for .NET: Designing Applications and Services at http://msdn.microsoft.com/library/default.asp?url=/library/en-us/dnbda/html/distapp.asp.

- Reduce the amount of code that needs to be rewritten when porting applications to different types of databases.
- Provide a single point of interception for data access monitoring and testing.
- Allow developers to abstract the data access code from the code related to business logic. This has the benefit of reducing and simplifying the code that usually exists in data access logic components.

Earlier versions of the Microsoft Data Access Application Block provided an implementation for data access helper components. These versions, however, focused solely on providing support for Microsoft SQL Server. The data access helper component for the previous versions was named `SqlHelper`. Separate implementations of the entire application block were then made available for Oracle and OLE DB. The data access helper components in those implementations were named `OracleHelper` and `OleDbHelper` respectively. Although these components were very similar, there was no single application block that focused on providing a uniform and consistent interface across different database vendors.

All of the features that existed in the previous versions of the Data Access Application Block still exist in the Enterprise Library version. The primary difference, however, is that the data access helper components in the Enterprise Library version have not been designed just for Microsoft SQL Server and then ported to support other database vendors. Instead, a generic abstract base class, named `Database`, has been designed that serves as the uniform interface for all types of databases. This class, coupled with a `DatabaseFactory` class that uses configuration data to create concrete implementations of the `Database` class, provides new benefits.

- Code can be written against the base class' interface so it is agnostic as to the underlying data source. For example, code can be written to consume data from and provide data to an Oracle database so that it is no different than the code needed to work with a SQL Server database.

  If an application must be ported from one data source to another, very little, if any code needs to be changed. Not only does this enhance database portability, but it also provides for "developer portability" as it gives developers a consistent interface that is independent of the type of database that may be needed.

It is also important to note that just because an application is "database portable," this doesn't eliminate the need to retest that application after it has been ported to another database. Occasionally, differences may exist in the way one database vendor supports certain functionality (e.g., retrieving an "identity" value) that may ultimately cause unforeseen differences in an application. While the Data Access Application Block strives to support database portability, it cannot guarantee it.

- The ultimate data source that is used by an application is determined at runtime from configuration information. Not only does this allow an application to switch from one data source to another without needing to restart, but it also allows new data sources to be created and "snapped in" on the fly.

  If you need support for a database provider other than those supplied by Enterprise Library (i.e., Microsoft SQL Server, Oracle, and DB2), you can create that database provider (or if available, download one from a site like www.gotdotnet.com) and plug it into the configuration data for any application.

Design of the Data Access Application Block

The design of the Data Access Application Block focuses on providing a simple but consistent interface for performing the most common database operations needed by applications today. The combination of the `DatabaseFactory` class, a database provider class, and a database command wrapper class allows an application to perform database operations against relational databases while remaining decoupled from the databases that it is using. Furthermore, the design provides an extensible model that allows new database providers to be used by the application block if the ones provided with Enterprise Library don't meet the needs of an application.

This section defines these classes and describes how the `DatabaseFactory`, database providers, and database command wrappers work together to achieve the design goals set forth with this version of the Data Access Application Block. It also demonstrates how to extend the application block by creating and configuring a new database provider.

Database Providers

Centralizing generic data access functionality is a best practice. The patterns & practices publication entitled *Architecture for .NET: Designing Applications and Services*[2] refers to centralized components as Data Access Helper Components. In Enterprise Library these components are called **database providers** because they follow the Provider design pattern (see Chapter 1 for more information about this design pattern), and each concrete implementation is developed specifically for the type of database that it is intended to access.

Using database providers to centralize data access operations produces code that is cleaner and more manageable than repeating the same generic data access routines throughout an application. Database providers are core to the Data Access Application Block. They meet the criteria of a Data Access Helper Component outlined in the *Architecture for .NET* publication because they:

- Abstract the data access API programming model from the data-related business logic, thus reducing and simplifying the code that typically resides in an application's data layer
- Hide connection management semantics
- Isolate data source location and authentication (through connection string management)
- Encapsulate transaction enlistment
- Centralize data access logic for easier maintenance, minimizing the need for data-source-specific coding skills throughout the development team and making it easier to troubleshoot data access issues
- Isolate data access API versioning dependencies from data access logic components

---

2. See http://msdn.microsoft.com/library/default.asp?url=/library/en-us/dnbda/html/distapp.asp.

The design goals of the Data Access Application Block consider performance, developer productivity, externalized configuration management, and database transparency. The Data Access Application Block aims to perform at 5 percent of ADO.NET efficiency, reducing the number of objects and classes, and ensuring that the block works identically independent of the database used.

Enterprise Library ships with three concrete database providers: `SqlDatabase`, `OracleDatabase`, and `DB2Database`. Figure 3.1 shows the relationship between the three classes that ship with Enterprise Library and the abstract base class named `Database`. You can find more database providers at the Enterprise Library's gotdotnet workspace[3] for data sources like OleDb and MySql.

The `Database` Class

If you were familiar with previous versions of the Data Access Application Block, you will notice that many of the methods that belonged to the `SqlHelper` class have now been moved to a new abstract base class named `Database`. This is good because, prior to this version, a lot of code had to be replicated as new classes were developed to deal with data sources other than Microsoft SQL Server. Therefore, it made sense to refactor the redundant code into a base class and allow derived classes to override this functionality and add new functionality as needed.

Many of the `Database` class methods listed in Table 3.1 are virtual functions, so derived classes can override them should they have the need. Also, instead of returning an object specific to one data source (e.g., `SqlDataReader`, `SqlCommand`) like they did in the previous versions, these methods return objects that represent a generic data interface (e.g., `IDataReader`, `IDbCommand`).

This level of abstraction is important because it lets you remain agnostic as to the underlying database with which you are working. (This chapter later explains how you can create an instance of a class that is derived from the `Database` class and execute a database command without speci-

3. See gotdotnet.com/codegallery/codegallery.aspx?id=295a464a-6072-4e25-94e2-91be63527327.

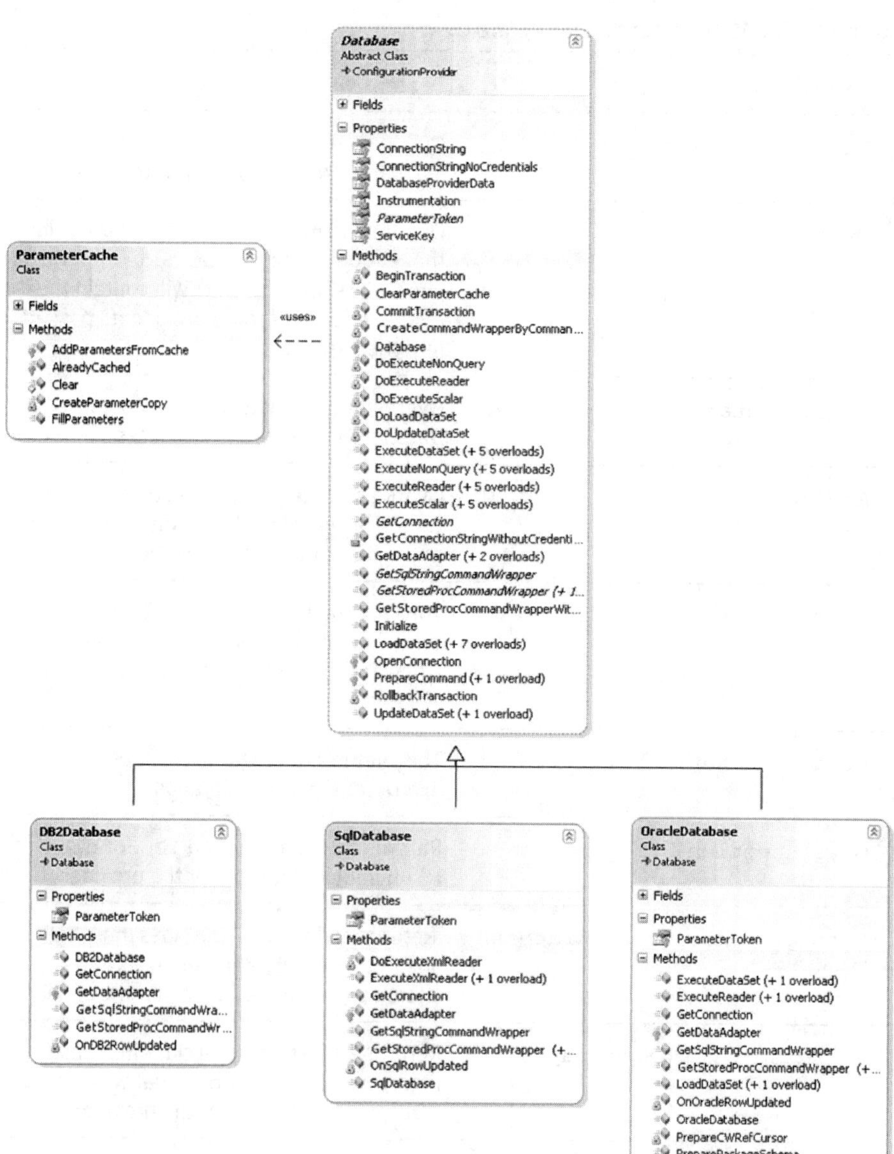

FIGURE 3.1: Enterprise Library Database Providers

fying whether the data source is Microsoft SQL Server, Oracle, or DB2.) Listing 3.1 shows code written in such a way that it is agnostic as to the underlying data source. In this example, the `DatabaseFactory` class is used to

TABLE 3.1: The Methods for the `Database` Class

Method	Description
`ExecuteNonQuery`	Overloaded methods used to execute commands that do not return any rows or values.
`ExecuteReader`	Overloaded methods used to return a class that supports the `IDataReader` interface. The `DataReader` object will contain the results returned for the arguments passed into the method.
`ExecuteDataset`	Overloaded methods for returning a DataSet for the arguments passed into it.
`ExecuteScalar`	Overloaded methods that return a single value. The value is always the first column of the first row returned by the command.
`LoadDataSet`	This method is similar to `ExecuteDataset`, except that instead of returning a new DataSet object, it adds data to an existing DataSet.
`UpdateDataset`	This method propagates changes recorded in a DataSet back to database.
`GetConnection`	Returns an instance of an `IDbConnection` implementation for the provider.
`GetStoredProcCommandWrapper`	Returns an instance of a class implementing `DbCommandWrapper` that wraps a stored procedure command for the provider.
`GetSqlStringCommandWrapper`	Returns an instance of a class implementing `DbCommandWrapper` that wraps a SQL query command for the provider.
`GetDataAdapter`	Exposes a class that returns the `IDataAdapter` interface.
`ParameterToken`	Returns the parameter token used to delimit parameters for a specific type of database.
`ClearParameterCache`	New to this version of the Data Access Application Block. This method clears the parameter cache. Since there is only one parameter cache that is shared by all instances of this class, this clears all parameters cached for all databases.

create an instance of a class that is derived from the `Database` class. The code accesses a database with the alias of `PortalDatabase`; however, there is no code that specifies the actual type of data source that is used. A generic `DataReader` is then used to populate a grid in the user interface.

LISTING 3.1: Using the `Database` Class to Remain Agnostic to the Data Source

```
[C#]
Database db = DatabaseFactory.CreateDatabase("PortalDatabase");
int divId = 1;
using (IDataReader dataReader = db.ExecuteReader("GetCustomers",divId)
{
  customerGrid.DataSource = dataReader;
  customerGrid.DataBind();
}

[Visual Basic]
Dim db As Database = DatabaseFactory.CreateDatabase("PortalDatabase")
Dim divId as Integer = 1
Dim dataReader As IDataReader = db.ExecuteReader("GetCustomers",divId)

customerGrid.DataSource = dataReader
customerGrid.DataBind()

dataReader.Close()
```

The `SqlDatabase` Class

Technically, in Listing 3.1 an instance of the `Database` class is not created. It is not possible to create an instance of the `Database` class because it is an abstract class and cannot be instantiated. Rather, you must create a derived class that overrides the abstract methods. The `SqlDatabase` class is the concrete database provider that ships with Enterprise Library for centralizing data access to a Microsoft SQL Server database.

Any class that derives from the `Database` class must override the `Database` class' abstract methods and properties; otherwise, it must also be marked as abstract and cannot be instantiated. The abstract methods and properties (not including overloads) of the `Database` class are `GetConnection`, `GetStoredProcCommandWrapper`, `GetSqlStringCommandWrapper`, `GetDataAdapter`, and `ParameterToken`.

When implemented in the `SqlDatabase` class, these methods return values that are specific to working with a Microsoft SQL Server database. For example, the `GetConnection` method will return a `SqlConnection`.

The `SqlDatabase` class uses the features provided by the Microsoft SQL Server .NET Managed Provider to return values specific to working with Microsoft SQL Server. Table 3.2 lists the methods and properties provided by the `SqlDatabase` class.

One of the methods listed in Table 3.2 is not defined by the base `Database` class. This method, `ExecuteXmlReader`, is used solely with a Microsoft SQL Server database. It is defined in the derived `SqlDatabase` class and not in the base `Database` class because it uses functionality that is not provided by every type of database. The `SqlDatabase` provider takes advantage of the `SqlCommand` object (through the `SqlCommandWrapper`, described later in this chapter), which provides an `ExecuteXmlReader` method. The `ExecuteXmlReader` method allows forward-only, stream-based access to XML data. Retrieving data as XML is beneficial if you need to process XML, minimize the performance overhead of creating a DataSet, and don't require a disconnected cache of data.

A drawback to using `ExecuteXmlReader` is that it reduces the ability to remain completely agnostic as to the underlying database, because an instance of the `SqlDatabase` class must be explicitly created (or cast to). Contrary to Listing 3.1 where a generic database provider was used, Listing

TABLE 3.2: `SqlDatabase`'s Methods and Properties

Method	SqlDatabase-Specific Instance
`GetConnection`	Returns a `SqlConnection`.
`GetStoredProcCommandWrapper`	Returns a `SqlCommandWrapper`.
`GetSqlStringCommandWrapper`	Returns a `SqlCommandWrapper`.
`GetDataAdapter`	Exposes the underlying `SqlDataAdapter` that is used for accessing data in a Microsoft SQL Server database.
`ParameterToken`	Gets the parameter token used to delimit parameters for a SQL Server database, which is the @ character.
`ExecuteXmlReader`	Returns an `XMLReader` (created from `SqlCommand.ExecuteReader`).

3.2 illustrates explicitly using a `SqlDatabase` provider so the `ExecuteXmlReader` method can be called.

LISTING 3.2: Calling `SqlDatabase`'s `ExecuteXmlReader` Method

```
[C#]
SqlDatabase db =
     DatabaseFactory.CreateDatabase("PortalDatabase") as SqlDatabase;

int divId = 1;
DbCommandWrapper dbCommandWrapper =
db.GetStoredProcCommandWrapper("GetCustomers",divId)

StringBuilder readerData = new StringBuilder();
XmlTextReader reader = null;

// XmlTextReader does not support IDisposable so it can't be
// used with a using keyword
try
{
     reader = (XmlTextReader)
     db.ExecuteXmlReader(dbCommandWrapper.Command);

     reader.MoveToContent();
     for (      string value = reader.ReadOuterXml();
                value != null && value.Length != 0;
                value = reader.ReadOuterXml())
     {
          readerData.Append(value);
      }
}
finally
{
      if (reader != null)
      {
           reader.Close();
     }
     dbCommandWrapper.Command.Connection.Close();
}


[Visual Basic]
Dim db As SqlDatabase = _
     IIf(TypeOf DatabaseFactory.CreateDatabase("PortalDatabase") _
     Is SqlDatabase, CType(DatabaseFactory.CreateDatabase _
      ("PortalDatabase"), SqlDatabase), CType(Nothing, SqlDatabase))

Dim divId As Integer = 1
```

```
Dim dbCommandWrapper As DbCommandWrapper = _
     db.GetStoredProcCommandWrapper("GetCustomers",divId)

Dim readerData As StringBuilder = New StringBuilder()
Dim reader As XmlTextReader = Nothing

Try
     reader = (XmlTextReader)
     db.ExecuteXmlReader(dbCommandWrapper.Command)

     reader.MoveToContent()
     Dim value As String = reader.ReadOuterXml()

     Do While Not value Is Nothing AndAlso _
               value.Length  0
          readerData.Append(value)
          value = reader.ReadOuterXml()
     Loop
Finally
     If Not reader Is Nothing Then
          reader.Close()
     End If
     dbCommandWrapper.Command.Connection.Close()
End Try
```

The `OracleDatabase` Class

Microsoft SQL Server is not the only Relational Database Management System (RDBMS) available to enterprises. Oracle is another popular choice for many. Ensuring that support for Oracle databases exists in a common data layer is a demand that must be met for any viable design. Enterprise Library's version of the Data Access Application Block goes a step further than its predecessors by providing the `OracleDatabase` class, a database provider for Oracle.

Just like `SqlDatabase`, `OracleDatabase` needs to override the abstract functions defined in the `Database` class. Instead of relying on the Microsoft SQL Server .NET Managed Provider, the `OracleDatabase` database provider relies on the Microsoft .NET Managed Provider for Oracle. It uses this managed provider's implementation to return values specific to working with an Oracle database. Table 3.3 lists the methods exposed by the `OracleDatabase` database provider.

It is worth noting that although they do not return values that are specific to using an Oracle database, the `ExecuteDataSet`, `LoadDataSet`, and

ExecuteReader methods have been overridden in the OracleDatabase class. The OracleDatabase's private PrepareCWRefCursor method gives a clue as to why. All three of the overridden methods first call PrepareCWRefCursor, which adds a ref cursor as an additional output parameter to the stored procedure if a ref cursor hasn't already been added.

Oracle is unique in its use of ref cursors. A **ref cursor** is a pointer into a result set returned by a PL/SQL query. Unlike a normal cursor, a ref cursor is a reference to a cursor that can be set to point to different result sets at execution time. A ref cursor output parameter must be used to pass a result set from an Oracle stored procedure back to a calling application. By encapsulating this logic in the OracleDatabase class, a calling application can still call a stored procedure in a way that lets it remain agnostic as to the underlying database. That is, the intricacies involving ref cursors are hidden from any caller of the ExecuteDataSet, LoadDataSet, and ExecuteReader methods, which allows for support of the database transparency design goal.

TABLE 3.3: OracleDatabase's Methods and Properties

Method	OracleDatabase-Specific Instance
GetConnection	Returns an OracleConnection.
GetStoredProcCommandWrapper	Returns an OracleCommandWrapper.
GetSqlStringCommandWrapper	Returns an OracleCommandWrapper.
GetDataAdapter	Exposes the underlying OracleDataAdapter that is used for accessing data in an Oracle database.
ParameterToken	Gets the parameter token used to delimit parameters for the Oracle Database, which is the ":" (colon) character.
ExecuteDataSet	Returns a DataSet for the arguments passed into it.
LoadDataSet	Fills a DataSet for the arguments passed into it.
ExecuteReader	Returns a DataReader for the arguments passed into it.

Another distinguishing attribute of the `OracleDatabase` database provider is its use of an internal `OracleDataReaderWrapper` class. This class implements the `IDataReader` interface and is used to wrap the `OracleDataReader` object that is returned from the `ExecuteReader` method. DataReaders provide strongly typed accessor methods that return column values as .NET Framework types. Examples of strongly typed accessors are `GetInt32`, `GetString`, and so on.

Most methods of the `OracleDataReaderWrapper` class merely pass through to the `OracleDataReader` class; however, a few exceptions are the `GetBoolean`, `GetByte`, and `GetGuid` methods. Oracle databases do not support a native data type for Guid or Bit. The `OracleDataReaderWrapper` class provides type conversion for these methods. The overrides for `GetBoolean` and `GetByte` use the `System.Convert.ToBoolean()` and `System.Convert.ToByte()` methods respectively for type conversions.

The `GetGuid` method has also been overridden to properly cast the data returned from the `GetGuid` method of the `OracleDataReader` into a proper Guid. By performing the data type conversions before results are returned from the `OracleDatabase` database provider, type conversions are not needed by a calling application, and the code to access the results from a database can remain agnostic as to the actual database that is being used.

One caveat: While the `ExecuteReader` methods will use the `OracleDataReaderWrapper` to perform type conversions, the `LoadDataSet` method will not. When a DataSet is filled by the Oracle `DataAdapter`, the native `OracleDataReader` is used, so the `OracleDataReaderWrapper` is of no use. If a Guid is needed by a calling application, you will need to write custom code to convert the returned `byte[]` value into a Guid.

The `DB2Database` Class

Another popular RDBMS used in many enterprises is the IBM DB2 database. While the Data Access Application Block ships with a database provider for DB2, it is not included in the default EnterpriseLibrary.sln solution file. This is because the DB2 code relies on the DB2 .NET Managed Provider from IBM (IBM.Data.DB2) and many developers may not have this provider installed. So as not to burden developers who do not have it installed to either install the provider or suffer through compiler errors, the

Enterprise Library team decided not to include it in the default solution. Instead, a DB2 database provider is provided as a separate project, `Data.DB2.csproj`, and is included in an alternate solution file, Data.sln.

The DB2 database provider isn't much different from the other database providers mentioned so far. Just like the SQL and Oracle database providers, the DB2 database provider must override the abstract methods defined in the base `Database` class. The overridden methods return values that are specific to working with a DB2 database (see Table 3.4).

Database Command Wrappers

Database commands and parameters are handled differently across database systems. One way to handle the differences among types of databases is to include a multitude of overloaded methods in the `Database` class that perform operations like deriving and getting parameter values. This is what the versions of the Data Access Application Block preceding Enterprise Library did. In this version, however, Enterprise Library has introduced the concept of a database command wrapper.

A **database command wrapper** is a class that handles commands and parameters in a specific way depending on the type of database that it is intended to support. An abstract `DbCommandWrapper` base class provides

Table 3.4: `DB2Database`**'s Methods and Properties**

Method	`DB2Database`-specific Instance
`GetConnection`	Returns a `DB2Connection`.
`GetStoredProcCommandWrapper`	Returns a `DB2CommandWrapper`.
`GetSqlStringCommandWrapper`	Returns a `DB2CommandWrapper`.
`GetDataAdapter`	Exposes the underlying `DB2DataAdapter` that is used for accessing data in a DB2 database.
`ParameterToken`	Gets the parameter token used to delimit parameters for the DB2 database, which is the @ character.

an interface that is implemented by database-specific command wrappers. There is a one-to-one mapping between a database provider and a database-specific command wrapper. For example, the SQL database provider uses a SQL database command wrapper, and the Oracle database provider uses an Oracle database-specific command wrapper. Figure 3.2 depicts the database command wrappers that are included with Enterprise Library.

Two of the abstract methods listed earlier in the section "Database Providers" are `GetStoredProcCommandWrapper` and `GetSqlStringCommandWrapper`. Both of these methods must return an object that derives from the abstract `DbCommandWrapper` base class. The `GetStoredProcCommandWrapper` returns a new database command wrapper. It requires a parameter for the name of the stored procedure and accepts optional parameters that represent the values for a stored procedure's parameters. The `GetSqlStringCommandWrapper` also returns a new database command wrapper but requires a string that represents a SQL statement. These command wrappers can then be used to set additional properties that might be required to update or retrieve data from an underlying database (such as parameter information required by a stored procedure). Table 3.5 lists the `DbCommandWrapper`'s methods and properties.

Handling Parameters and the `ParameterCache`

In Listing 3.2, a `DbCommandWrapper` was returned from the Data Access Application Block by calling the `GetStoredProcCommandWrapper` method. The stored procedure, `GetCustomers`, was used to retrieve data from the backend data source. This particular stored procedure expects a single parameter that represents a company's division ID for which a set of customers should be retrieved. A significant point to recognize from this listing is that no attributes were set for this stored procedure parameter; only the value for the parameter was supplied. In this example, the `Database` class used the `DeriveParameter` methods in ADO.NET to dynamically discover attribute information about a stored procedure's parameters. This is known as **dynamic parameter discovery.**

One downside to dynamic parameter discovery is that it requires a separate roundtrip to the backend database to collect the information about the parameters' attributes. To minimize the impact of this additional roundtrip,

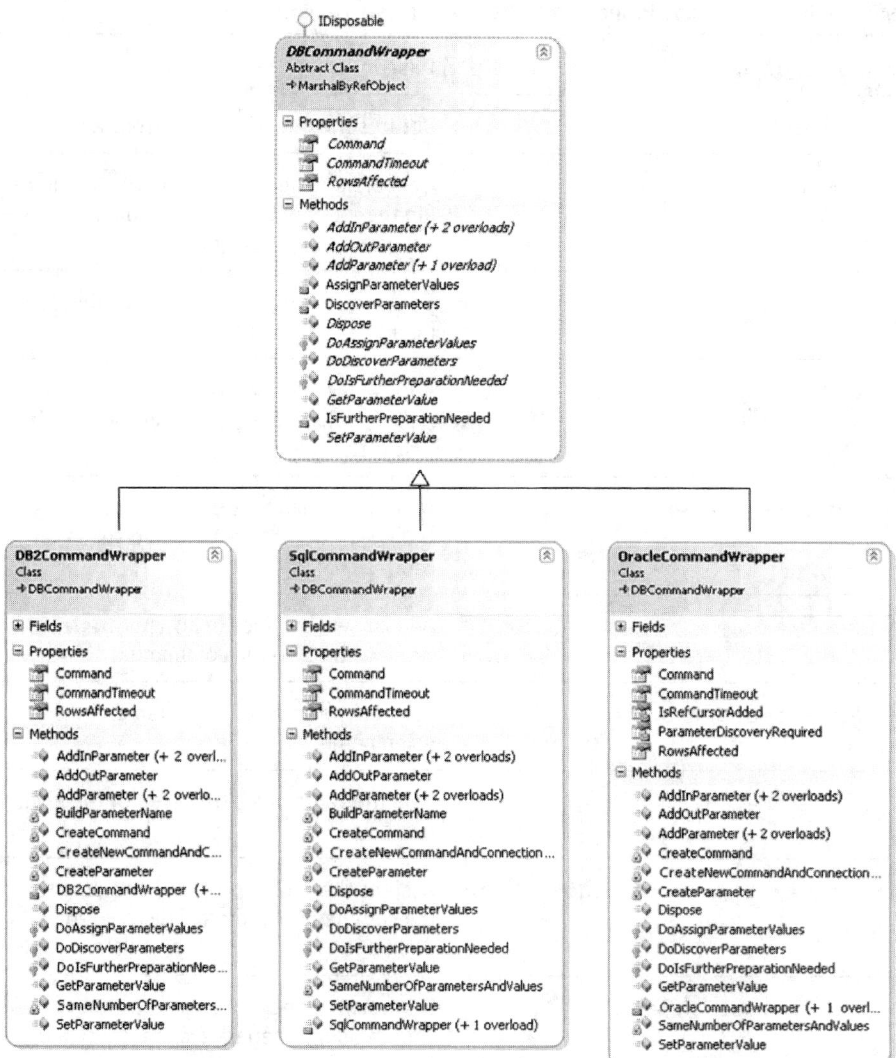

FIGURE 3.2: Enterprise Library Database Command Wrappers

the Data Access Application Block caches the information about the parameters that it discovers. The `ParameterCache` class provides the cache that stores the parameter information for each procedure call. Therefore, subsequent calls to the same stored procedure will not require a roundtrip.

TABLE 3.5: Methods and Properties of the `DbCommandWrapper` Class

Property/Method	Description
`Command`	Returns the underlying `IDBCommand`.
`CommandTimeout`	Gets or sets the wait time before terminating the attempt to execute a command and generating an error.
`RowsAffected`	Gets or sets the rows affected by this command.
`AddInParameter`	Adds a new instance of an `IDataParameter` object to the command set as `Input`.
`AddOutParameter`	Adds a new instance of an `IDataParameter` object to the command set as `Output`.
`AddParameter`	Adds a new instance of an `IDataParameter` object to the command.
`GetParameterValue`	Returns the value of the parameter for the given name.
`SetParameterValue`	Sets the value of a parameter for the given name.
`DoAssignParameterValues`	Assigns the values provided by a user to the command parameters discovered in positional order.
`DoDiscoverParameters`	Discovers the parameters for a stored procedure using a separate connection and command.
`DoIsFurtherPreparationNeeded`	Determines if a stored procedure is using parameter discovery.

An alternative to dynamic parameter discovery is to avoid the roundtrip altogether. You can use the `DbCommandWrapper` that is returned from the `GetStoredProcCommandWrapper` method to set the attributes for the stored procedure's parameters. Methods like `AddInParameter` or `AddParameter` (listed in Table 3.5) can be used to explicitly specify all of the attributes of any particular parameter. Calls can be made to these methods to explicitly specify information like the data type, direction, or size of a parameter.

Explicitly setting the attributes of a stored procedure's parameters is known as **explicit parameter handling.** The benefit to this approach is that it avoids any roundtrips to the database to dynamically discover information about a stored procedure's parameters. The downside is that it more tightly couples the code that makes that database calls to the stored procedures themselves. Thus, if you modify the parameters of a stored procedure, it is highly likely that you will need to modify the code to reflect these changes. Listing 3.3 illustrates how the code in Listing 3.2 can be rewritten to use the `DbCommandWrapper` for explicitly handling parameters.

LISTING 3.3: Explicit Parameter Handling Example

```
[C#]
SqlDatabase db =
     DatabaseFactory.CreateDatabase("PortalDatabase") as SqlDatabase;

int divId = 1;
DbCommandWrapper dbCommandWrapper =
     db.GetStoredProcCommandWrapper("GetCustomers")
dbCommandWrapper.AddInParameter("DivisionID", DbType.Int32, divID);

StringBuilder readerData = new StringBuilder();
XmlTextReader reader = null;

// XmlTextReader does not support IDisposable so it can't be
// used in a using keyword
try
{
     reader = (XmlTextReader)
     db.ExecuteXmlReader(dbCommandWrapper);

      //No change to the rest of the example
...


[Visual Basic]
Dim db As SqlDatabase = _
     IIf(TypeOf DatabaseFactory.CreateDatabase("PortalDatabase") _
     Is SqlDatabase, CType(DatabaseFactory.CreateDatabase _
     ("PortalDatabase"), SqlDatabase), CType(Nothing, SqlDatabase))

Dim divId As Integer = 1
Dim dbCommandWrapper As DbCommandWrapper = _
     db.GetStoredProcCommandWrapper("GetCustomers")
```

```
dbCommandWrapper.AddInParameter("DivisionID", DbType.Int32, divID)

Dim readerData As StringBuilder = New StringBuilder()
Dim reader As XmlTextReader = Nothing

Try
     reader = (XmlTextReader)
     db.ExecuteXmlReader(dbCommandWrapper)

     'No change to the rest of the example
...
```

Because there is a one-to-one relationship between a concrete database provider and a concrete database command wrapper, a database command wrapper is typically accessed via the specific database provider that uses it. Listing 3.3 demonstrates how to obtain a `DbCommandWrapper` from the `SqlDatabase` database provider. In this case, the `DbCommandWrapper` that was returned was a `SqlDbCommandWrapper` because of the one-to-one relationship between a `SqlDatabase` and a `SqlDbCommandWrapper`. Naturally, Enterprise Library ships with database command wrappers for Oracle and DB2 as well. I am not going to discuss the specifics of each of these in any detail because they all work similarly. All three database command wrappers override the abstract methods listed in Table 3.5 with functionality that is specific to their respective type of database.

The `DatabaseFactory` and `DatabaseProviderFactory` Classes

One of the primary factors that differentiate Enterprise Library's Data Access Application Block from its predecessors is the use of the factory pattern for creating database providers. Guidance from the patterns & practices team states that if you want to take on the goal of providing for "no touch" data source transparency, a good design pattern is to implement data access helpers (aka database providers) with a common interface so that a factory pattern can be leveraged.[4]

Not only have database providers with a common interface for Microsoft SQL Server, Oracle, and DB2 been provided in Enterprise Library's version of the Data Access Application Block, but a database

4. Summarized from Application Architecture for .NET: Designing Applications and Services at http://msdn.microsoft.com/library/default.asp?url=/library/en-us/dnbda/html/distapp.asp.

provider factory has also been introduced to help make the goal of database transparency more of a reality. It is still important to recognize that the patterns & practices team does not *guarantee* that database transparency can be achieved simply by taking advantage of the enhanced design. As shown in Listing 3.2, which used specific XML features provided by Microsoft SQL Server, there may still be situations when complete database transparency cannot be achieved.

In addition, the patterns & practices team believes that developer portability is a more common scenario than database portability (aka transparency). That is, they believe it is more common that a single developer will work with various different data sources over many different projects (e.g., working with Microsoft SQL Server on one project and Oracle on the next) than it is for a single application to require transparency among different data sources (e.g., having to work with both Microsoft SQL Server and Oracle in a single application). Whichever case may exist, however, the Data Access Application Block provides you with a consistent interface for performing database operations independent of the actual database that is being used.

When an application needs to perform some type of database operation, it usually does so by calling one of the methods listed in Table 3.1. As long as no methods are used that are specific to a single type of database provider (e.g., `ExecuteXMLReader` for the `SqlDatabase` database provider), then changing an application from relying on one data source to another is a matter of modifying the configuration data for the application. To allow for this, a factory class named `DatabaseProviderFactory` uses the features provided by the Configuration Application Block that retrieve configuration information. The `DatabaseProviderFactory` then determines which instance of a specific database provider should be created (via reflection).

By looking at Listings 3.2 and 3.3, you can infer that the application has been configured so that *PortalDatabase* signifies a Microsoft SQL Server database. This is known because a successful cast to a `SqlDatabase` database provider is possible from the value that is returned from the `CreateDatabase` method. If the application weren't configured for PortalDatabase to signify a Microsoft SQL Server database, then this cast would fail. Figure 3.3 illustrates the relationship between the `DatabaseFactory`, the `DatabaseProviderFactory`, and the `Database` class.

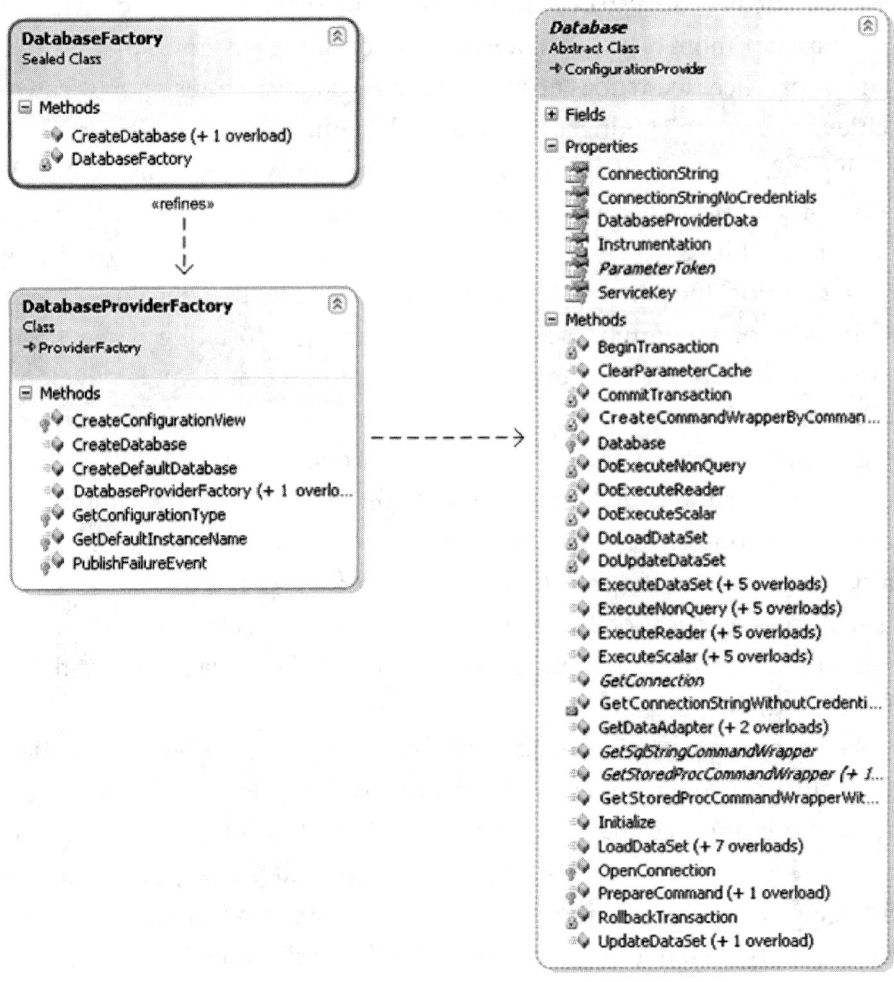

FIGURE 3.3: `DatabaseFactory` **and** `DatabaseProviderFactory`

The `DatabaseProviderFactory` exposes two public methods: `CreateDatabase` and `CreateDefaultDatabase`. `CreateDatabase` accepts a string argument that specifies which instance of a database should be created. In all the listings shown so far, the string PortalDatabase was provided to the `CreateDatabase` method so that the `DatabaseProvider-`

Factory would create the database that had been configured as the PortalDatabase database instance.

A **database instance** is a logical representation of a database, and it contains information about the type of database (e.g., Microsoft SQL Server, Oracle, or DB2) and the physical location of the database as represented by the database connection string. Because a database instance encapsulates this information and this information is read in using features provided by the Configuration Application Block, the code for an application can be written so that it is completely indifferent as to the physical location of a database. Furthermore, the physical location of a database can be changed (e.g., from a development to a test environment) and the application will be made aware of it quickly and without recompilation.

The `CreateDefaultDatabase` method does not accept any arguments. The `CreateDefaultDatabase` method creates a database provider that has been configured in the application as the default database; that is, the database provider that should be returned if no database instance is specified.

Another class, `DatabaseFactory`, refines the `DatabaseProviderFactory` class with static methods that simply pass through to an instance of the `DatabaseProviderFactory` class. This provides a very simple interface for developers, as it allows a database provider to be created without directly having to instantiate a factory class, and it contains a single method: `CreateDatabase`.

`CreateDatabase` contains two overloads: One overload accepts no arguments and wraps around the `DatabaseProviderFactory`'s `CreateDefaultDatabase` method, and the other overload accepts a string and wraps around the `DatabaseProviderFactory`'s `CreateDatabase (string)` method. Both the `DatabaseProviderFactory` and the `DatabaseFactory` classes can be used to obtain a database provider. In all the listings provided so far, the `DatabaseFactory` class—and not the `DatabaseProviderFactory` class—was used.

Creating a Custom Database Provider

While Enterprise Library ships with database providers for three of the most common databases used by enterprise applications today, it is conceivable that many enterprises may need to develop applications that use a database other than one of these three. And while the Data Access Application Block may not supply a database provider for every database that exists, you can still reap the benefits of its design and features. To do so, however, you must create a custom database provider.

A few new database providers have cropped up since the release of Enterprise Library. You can find database providers for MySql and OleDb on the GotDotNet.com community site for Enterprise Library. The sole prerequisite for creating a database provider that can work with the Data Access Application Block is that a .NET managed data provider exists for it. This prerequisite is important because managed providers consist of a set of objects that are used to communicate between a data source and a DataSet. Therefore, if a managed data provider for a specific data store already exists, it is not too difficult to create the classes needed by the Data Access Application Block to work with that data store. However, even if a .NET managed data provider does not yet exist for a particular data source, all hope is not lost; it is possible to create one.

It is with this in mind that I have intentionally picked an example for which a .NET managed provider does not exist. This section creates a database provider that will store and retrieve data in an XML file. My primary reason for picking this database provider is to show that it is feasible to create a database provider for just about any data source that might exist.

A data store does not necessarily need to be a relational database. For example, it is not uncommon for data to be stored in XML files, especially to cache data. A common scenario is a Web site that stores nontransactional semi-static data in XML files. In fact, the well-known IBuySpy portal site uses an XML file (i.e., portalcfg.xml) for just this purpose. It stores data relevant to the site's "look and feel" in an XML file.

Having a database provider that can be used specifically for storing and retrieving data in an XML file allows for greater flexibility. Without such a provider, if the data that drives the look and feel of the IBuySpy portal needed to be moved to a data source other than an XML file, code would need to be written to access the new data source. However, if a database provider for XML files were used to store and retrieve the data, only configuration data would need to be changed to point the application at the alternate data source; no code should need to change in the application.

Since creating a .NET managed provider is really outside the scope of how a database provider uses such a component, I have not included the steps for creating the .NET managed data provider as part of this chapter. Rather, I have included step-by-step instructions for how to create the .NET managed data provider for XML files in Appendix B of this book. The rest of this section will concentrate on how to use this .NET managed data provider to create a database provider that can be used by the Data Access Application Block. This consists of creating two classes: a database command wrapper and a database provider.

Creating a Database Command Wrapper

The first step to creating a custom database provider is to create a database command wrapper class for the data store in question. A database command wrapper must derive from the abstract `DbCommandWrapper` base class and must override the abstract methods defined in this base class. Table 3.5 lists the methods and properties that must be overridden for a concrete database command wrapper.

The concrete database command wrapper in Listing 3.4 that supports the database provider for XML files is named `XmlFileCommandWrapper`. To implement support for parameter handling, the `AddParameter` and `AddInParameter` methods must be overridden to instantiate a class that implements the `IDataParameter` interface and that corresponds to the underlying data source. In this case that class is the `XmlFileParameter`. Also, the `GetParameterValue` and `SetParameterValue` methods must return and set values for this type of object.

Since the need to create an `XmlFileParameter` exists for many of the methods that must be overridden, I have added a `CreateParameter` method much like the ones that exist for the database command wrappers that ship with the Data Access Application Block. This method is used to create a new `XmlFileParameter` object. Listing 3.4 shows two of the functions in the `XmlFileCommandWrapper` that are used to create objects exposed from the .NET managed data provider that this class wraps around. This listing shows how to create a new `XmlFileParameter`, which exposes the `IDataParameter` interface, and how to create a new `XMLFileCommand`, which implements the `IDbCommand` interface.

LISTING 3.4: Database Command Wrapper Methods that Create New Parameters and Commands

```
[C#]
private XmlFileParameter CreateParameter(
     string name, DbType type, int size, ParameterDirection direction,
     bool nullable, byte precision, byte scale, string sourceColumn,
     DataRowVersion sourceVersion, object value)
{
     XmlFileParameter param =
               (XmlFileParameter)this.command.CreateParameter();
      param.ParameterName = BuildParameterName(name);

      param.DbType = type;
      param.Direction = direction;
      param.SourceColumn = sourceColumn;
      param.SourceVersion = sourceVersion;
      param.Value = (value == null)? DBNull.Value : value;

      return param;
}

private XmlFileCommand CreateCommand(
          string commandText, CommandType commandType)
{
     XmlFileCommand newCommand = new XmlFileCommand();
     newCommand.CommandText = commandText;
     newCommand.CommandType = commandType;

      return newCommand;
}

[Visual Basic]
Private Function CreateParameter(ByVal name As String, _
                   ByVal type As DbType, ByVal size As Integer, _
                   ByVal direction As ParameterDirection, _
                   ByVal nullable As Boolean, ByVal precision As Byte, _
                   ByVal scale As Byte, ByVal sourceColumn As String, _
                   ByVal sourceVersion As DataRowVersion, _
                   ByVal value As Object) As XmlFileParameter

     Dim param As XmlFileParameter = CType( _
                    Me.command.CreateParameter(), XmlFileParameter)
     param.ParameterName = BuildParameterName(name)

     param.DbType = type
     param.Direction = direction
     param.SourceColumn = sourceColumn
     param.SourceVersion = sourceVersion
```

```
    param.Value = IIf((value Is Nothing), DBNull.Value, value)

    Return param
End Function

Private Function CreateCommand(ByVal commandText As String, _
                ByVal commandType As CommandType) As XmlFileCommand

    Dim newCommand As XmlFileCommand = New XmlFileCommand()
    newCommand.CommandText = commandText
    newCommand.CommandType = commandType

    Return newCommand
End Function
```

Creating the Database Provider

After creating the database command wrapper, the next step is to create the class that represents the database provider itself. A database provider must derive from the abstract `Database` base class, and several methods and properties must be overridden. Table 3.1 lists the methods and properties that a concrete `Database` class must override.

Methods like `GetDataAdapter` must return objects that allow the Data Access Application Block to correctly utilize the .NET managed provider for that specific data store. The `GetStoredProcCommandWrapper` and `GetSqlStringCommandWrapper` methods must return the specific command wrapper class that was written for this database provider; in this case, that is the `XmlFileCommandWrapper`. You can add other public methods, like `ExecuteXmlReader` for the `SqlDatabase` database provider, to the database provider as you like. For example, the `XmlFileDatabase` database provider shown in Listing 3.5 also includes a method that returns an XmlReader. The full source code for the XML file database provider and .NET managed data provider for XML files are on this book's Web site.

LISTING 3.5: `ExecuteXmlReader` Method for the XML File Database Provider

```
[C#]
public XmlReader ExecuteXmlReader(XmlFileCommandWrapper command)
{
    // OpenConnection calls the GetConnection method
    // which returns a new XmlFileConnection class for this
    // database provider
```

```
        IDbConnection connection = OpenConnection();
        PrepareCommand(command, connection);

        XmlFileCommand xmlFileCommand = command.Command as XmlFileCommand;
        try
        {
            return DoExecuteXmlReader(xmlFileCommand);
        }
        catch
        {
            connection.Close();
            throw;
        }
    }

    public XmlReader ExecuteXmlReader(
            XmlFileCommandWrapper command, IDbTransaction transaction)
    {
        PrepareCommand(command, transaction);

        XmlFileCommand xmlFileCommand = command.Command as XmlFileCommand;
        return DoExecuteXmlReader(xmlFileCommand);
    }

    private XmlReader DoExecuteXmlReader(XmlFileCommand xmlFileCommand)
    {
        try
        {
            DateTime startTime = DateTime.Now;

            //XmlFileCommand exposes a method that will return the data
            //in the file in an XmlReader
            XmlReader reader = xmlFileCommand.ExecuteXmlReader();
            return reader;
        }
        catch
        {
            throw;
        }
    }

    [Visual Basic]
    Public Function ExecuteXmlReader(
        ByVal command As XmlFileCommandWrapper) As XmlReader

        ' OpenConnection calls the GetConnection method
        ' which returns a new XmlFileConnection class for this
        ' database provider
        Dim connection As IDbConnection = OpenConnection()
        PrepareCommand(command, connection)
```

```
    Dim xmlFileCommand As XmlFileCommand = _
                IIf(TypeOf command.Command Is XmlFileCommand, _
                CType(command.Command, XmlFileCommand), _
                CType(Nothing, XmlFileCommand))
    Try
        Return DoExecuteXmlReader(xmlFileCommand)
    Catch
        connection.Close()
        Throw
    End Try
End Function

Public Function ExecuteXmlReader( _
        ByVal command As XmlFileCommandWrapper, _
        ByVal transaction As IDbTransaction) As XmlReader

    PrepareCommand(command, transaction)

    Dim xmlFileCommand As XmlFileCommand = _
        IIf(TypeOf command.Command Is XmlFileCommand, _
        CType(command.Command, XmlFileCommand), _
        CType(Nothing, XmlFileCommand))
    Return DoExecuteXmlReader(xmlFileCommand)
End Function

Private Function DoExecuteXmlReader( _
    ByVal xmlFileCommand As XmlFileCommand) As XmlReader
    Try
        Dim startTime As DateTime = DateTime.Now

        'XmlFileCommand exposes a method that will return the data
        'in the file in an XmlReader
        Dim reader As XmlReader = xmlFileCommand.ExecuteXmlReader()
        Return reader
    Catch
        Throw
    End Try
End Function
```

Once the database command wrapper and database provider classes have been created, the new database provider is almost ready to be used in an application. From a development perspective, the code that needs to be written to use the new database provider is no different than the code that needs to be written to access and update data for any other database provider. The only exception to this rule is if calls need to be made to methods that are specific to this database provider (e.g., `ExecuteXmlReader`).

The primary task you need to complete specifically for this new database provider is to add configuration data for it to the configuration information for the Data Access Application Block. The next section shows how to configure an application to use the Data Access Application Block and how to develop an application that adheres to the guidance prescribed by the Microsoft patterns & practices team while taking advantage of the benefits provided by the Data Access Application Block.

Using the Data Access Application Block's API

One of the reasons that the Data Access Application Block has been among the most popular application blocks produced by the Microsoft patterns & practices team is that it is very easy to use. It was very important that this remained the case for the Enterprise Library version of the Data Access Application Block as well. The `DatabaseFactory`, database providers, and database command wrappers that were discussed in the previous section all play a role in achieving the design goal for a simple and consistent development API.

Developing an application to use Enterprise Library's Data Access Application Block involves two types of activities: configuring the application with the appropriate database providers and writing code to call the API exposed by the Data Access Application Block to retrieve and update data from a database. This section provides detailed information on both of these tasks. First it details how to configure a database provider so that you can use it in an application, and then it specifies which database provider methods you should use to retrieve and update information and why. The section concludes with an overview of data access logic components and why they are recommended as the typical primary controller for managing database providers in a distributed application.

Configuring a Database Provider

Once the database command wrapper and database provider classes exist, a database provider can be returned by the Data Access Application Block by adding its configuration information to the rest of the configuration information for the Data Access Application Block. By default, the configuration information for the Data Access Application Block is kept separate from the rest of the configuration information for an application. The default setting in the metaconfiguration data (the configuration data that describes information about an application's configuration) is for the configuration data to be stored in an XML file named *dataConfiguration.config.* You can change this location to be a different file, the application domain configuration file (app.config or web.config), the Windows Registry, or a relational database. For details about modifying the metaconfiguration data for an application, see Chapter 1.

The first step in using the Data Access Application Block in an application is to add the block to the overall configuration for the application. Although this can be accomplished manually, the easiest and least error-prone way to do this is to use the Enterprise Library Configuration Tool (see Chapter 2). To add the Data Access Application Block using the Configuration Tool, open the application domain configuration file for the application in the tool, right-click on the application node, and select *New > Data Access Application Block.*

Figure 3.4 shows the resulting configuration hierarchy. A new configuration section is added to the nodes underneath the settings for the Configuration Application Block, and a configuration hierarchy has been created to hold the settings for the Data Access Application Block.

Configuring a database provider so that it can be used by the Data Access Application Block involves adding several elements to the configuration for the block. The elements are database type, connection string, and database instance.

Adding a Database Type

The database type specifies information about a database provider so that it can be created by the Data Access Application Block. You must add an XML element to the configuration data that specifies a logical name and fully qualified assembly name for a database provider. To add a database type to the Data Access Application Block, right-click the *Database Types* configuration node and select *New > Database Type.*

The Property pane for the new configuration node will contain properties for the logical name of this database type and the `TypeName` for this

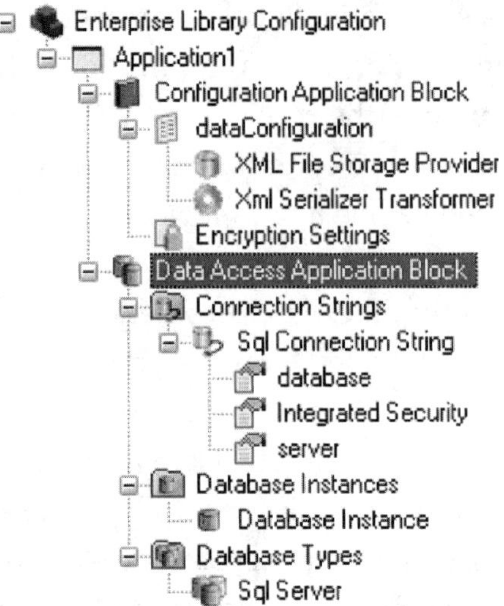

FIGURE 3.4: Hierarchy after Adding the Data Access Application Block to an Application

database type. The `TypeName` is the fully qualified assembly name for a database provider. Click on the ellipses in this property to display the Type-Selector dialog. This only shows the classes that the Configuration Tool is aware are subclasses of the abstract base `Database` class.

Figure 3.5 illustrates adding a database type that represents the custom `XmlFileDatabase` database provider to the configuration for the Data Access Application Block.

There is no limit to the number of database types that you can add to the configuration for an application. Because Enterprise Library automatically added a database type for the `SqlDatabase` database provider when the block was added to the application's overall configuration, adding the `XmlFileDatabase` database type resulted in two database types for this application. Listing 3.6 illustrates the section of the configuration data that has been modified due to the additional database type (the listing has been formatted for legibility purposes).

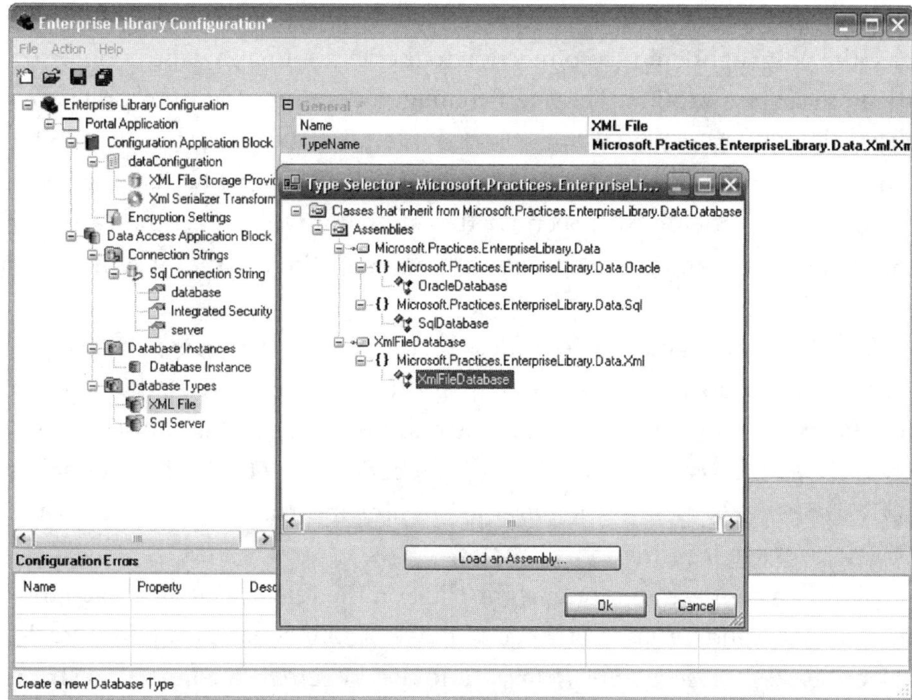

FIGURE 3.5 : Adding the `XmlFileDatabase` Database Type to the Data Access Application Block

LISTING 3.6: Resulting Configuration from Adding a New Database Type

```
<databaseTypes>
     <databaseType
          name="Sql Server"
          type="Microsoft.Practices.EnterpriseLibrary.Data.Sql.
               SqlDatabase, Microsoft.Practices.EnterpriseLibrary.Data,
               Version=1.0.0.0, Culture=neutral, PublicKeyToken=null"/>
     <databaseType
          name="XML File"
          type="XmlFileDatabase, XmlFileDatabase, Version=1.0.0.0,
Culture=neutral, PublicKeyToken=null" />
```

Adding a Connection String

The connection string specifies the physical location of a database. A database provider uses the information contained in the connection string to open the particular data source. For a database provider to successfully get past the point of opening a connection to the data source, a valid connection string must be supplied. The .NET managed data provider interprets how to handle the connection string it is provided. For example, since the .NET managed provider for XML files does not actually work with a relational database, the provider has been written so that it will expect the value for the database parameter to contain the name of the file that it will use to store and retrieve data.

The .NET managed provider for SQL, on the other hand, expects parameters that contain values for the name of the database server, the name of the database, whether a trusted connection is to be used and optionally a user ID and password (if trusted connection is set to false). Oracle's provider expects these same parameters plus information that represents Oracle package information.

To add a connection string, right-click on the *Connection Strings* configuration node and, unless you need to create a connection string for Oracle, select *New > Connection String*. If you do need to create a connection string for Oracle, select *New > Oracle Connection String*. This will add a special configuration node for dealing with Oracle package information.

Adding a connection string automatically adds configuration nodes for the database, server, and Trusted Connection parameters. If you don't need these parameters, you can remove them by right-clicking on the node and selecting *Remove*. For the `XmlFileDatabase`, the only parameter that is needed is the database parameter; therefore, I have removed all the other configuration nodes. Figure 3.6 shows the resulting connection string after these nodes have been removed and the name of the XML file has been set for the database parameter.

Adding a Database Instance

A **database instance** is the logical representation of a database. It couples the database type with the connection string. This is needed because a particular database provider can be used to access more than one database (e.g., accessing multiple SQL Server databases only requires that the `SqlDatabase` provider is added to the configuration as a database type once).

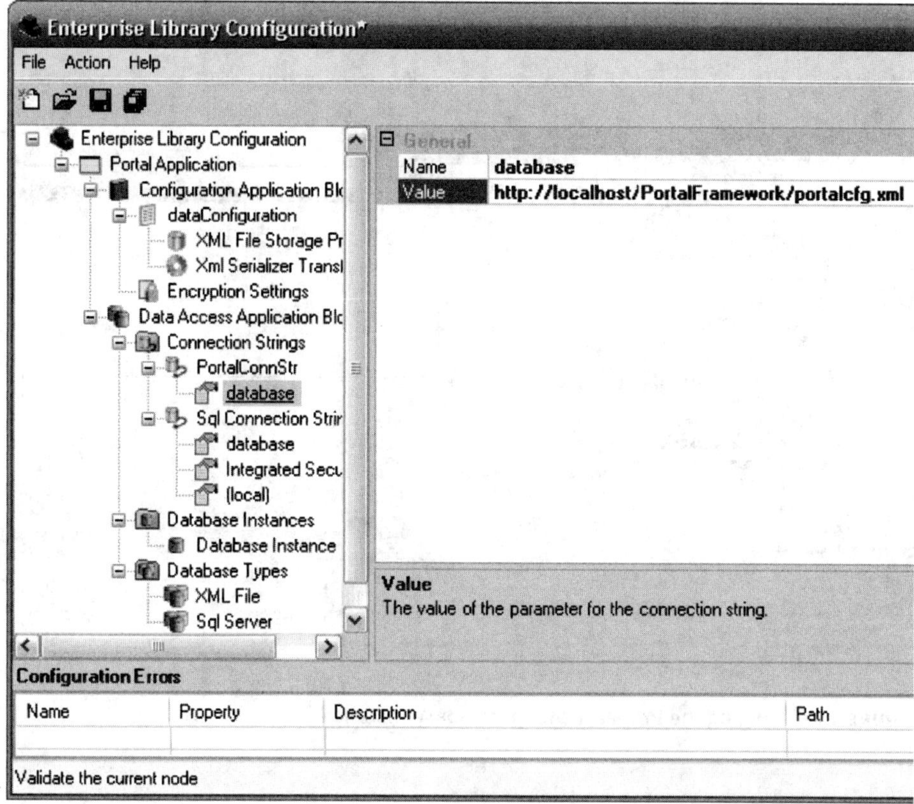

FIGURE 3.6: Setting the Connection String for the `XmlFileDatabase`

To add a database instance, right-click on the Database Instances configuration node and select *New > Database Instance.* The resulting properties for this node will be prepopulated with values based on the connection strings and database types that have already been added to the configuration for this block. To change these settings, choose a new value from the drop-down box for a particular property. For example, Figure 3.7 illustrates changing the instance for the new database instance named *PortalConfiguration* from using the SQL Server database type to using the XML file database type. This change has the effect of creating and returning an `XmlFileDatabase` database provider instead of a `SqlDatabase` database

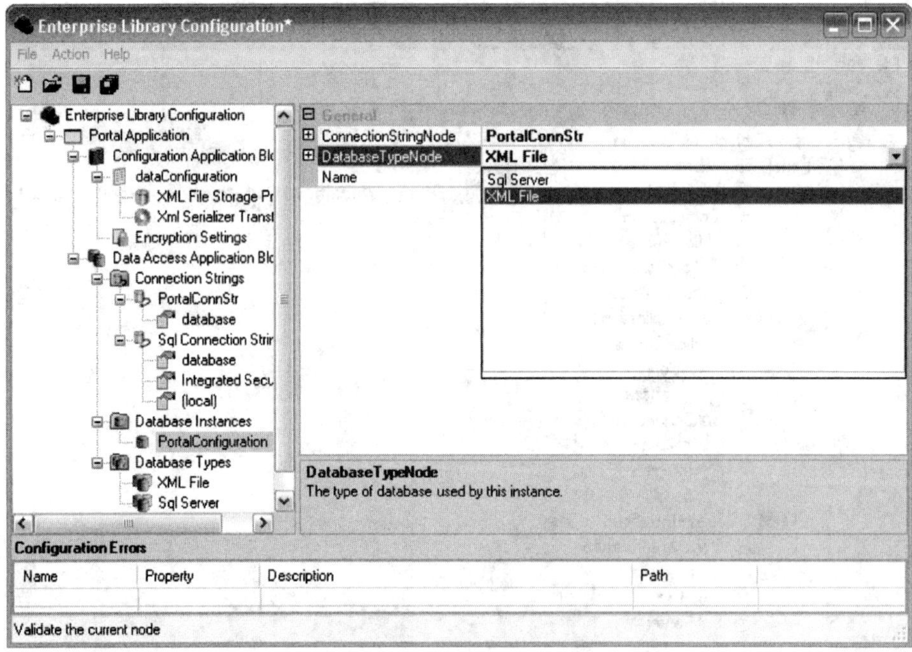

FIGURE 3.7: Changing the Properties for a Database Instance

provider whenever the `CreateDatabase` method is called for the Portal-Configuration database instance.

Listing 3.7 depicts the configuration information that results from making these changes for a new database provider to be supported by the Data Access Application Block. Hopefully, it is evident from this listing that it is far easier and less error-prone to use the Enterprise Library Configuration Tool to make these changes than it would be to manually create or modify this data. The listing has been formatted for legibility purposes.

LISTING 3.7: Resulting Configuration Data for the Data Access Application Block

```
<?xml version="1.0" encoding="utf-8"?>
<dataConfiguration>
  <xmlSerializerSection
     type="Microsoft.Practices.EnterpriseLibrary.Data.Configuration.
          DatabaseSettings,Microsoft.Practices.EnterpriseLibrary.Data,
          Version=1.1.0.0, Culture=neutral, PublicKeyToken=null">
     <enterpriseLibrary.databaseSettings
```

```
        xmlns:xsd="http://www.w3.org/2001/XMLSchema"
        xmlns:xsi="http://www.w3.org/2001/XMLSchema-instance"
        defaultInstance="Portal"
        xmlns="http://www.microsoft.com/practices/enterpriselibrary/
              08-31-2004/data">
    <databaseTypes>
     <databaseType name="Sql Server"
          type="Microsoft.Practices.EnterpriseLibrary.Data.Sql.
               SqlDatabase, Microsoft.Practices.EnterpriseLibrary.
               Data, Version=1.0.0.0, Culture=neutral,
               PublicKeyToken=null" />
     <databaseType name="XML File"
          type="Microsoft.Practices.EnterpriseLibrary.Data.Xml.
               XmlFileDatabase, XmlFileDatabase, Version=1.0.0.0,
               Culture=neutral, PublicKeyToken=null" />
        </databaseTypes>
        <instances>
        <instance name="Portal"
            type="Sql Server" connectionString="Sql Connection String"/>
        <instance name="PortalConfigInstance"
            type="XML File" connectionString="PortalConfigConnStr" />
   <instances>
   <connectionStrings>
       <connectionString name="PortalConfigConnStr">
          <parameters>
            <parameter name="database"
               value="http://localhost/AcePortalStarterSite/
                    PortalFramework/portalcfg.xml" isSensitive="false" />
                 </connectionString>
        <connectionString name="Sql Connection String">
          <parameters>
            <parameter name="database"
                    value="Portal"
                    isSensitive="false" />
            <parameter name="server"
                    value="(local)"
                    isSensitive="false"/>
            <parameter name="Trusted_Connection"
                    value="True"
                    isSensitive="false" />
                   </parameters>
                 </connectionString>
     </connectionStrings>
    <enterpriseLibrary.databaseSettings>
     </xmlSerializerSection>
</dataConfiguration>
```

Once the configuration information for a database instance has been successfully saved, that database instance can then be referenced in code for performing data access and updates against a particular data store. Technically, the name of the database instance can be used even before the configuration information is saved for an application; however, the application will result in runtime errors because it will not be able to find the configuration information for the referenced database instance.

Developing with the Data Access Application Block

For almost all situations, using the `DatabaseFactory` and a known database instance will be the starting point for performing any data access or update procedure. Once the database providers have been configured for an application, they can be used to access and update data in the data source for which they have been configured. Many methods exist that allow database providers to retrieve data from a backend database or add, delete, or modify the data in the database. The following sections detail how to use the Data Access Application Block to retrieve data from a database and update the data in it.

Retrieving Data

Database providers expose many public methods that can be used for accessing data from a backend data source. The method that should be used for a particular situation depends on many details. One of those details is simply the amount or type of data that needs to be accessed. For example, you can use the `ExecuteScalar` method for retrieving a single value, and the `ExecuteNonQuery` method for retrieving multiple values via the output parameters from a stored procedure. Listing 3.8 illustrates how these two methods differ by accessing a stored procedure to get the unique identifier for a customer with the `ExecuteScalar` method, and then using this identifier to obtain more details about that customer with the `ExecuteNonQuery` method.

LISTING 3.8: Using the `ExecuteScalar` and `ExecuteNonQuery` Methods for Retrieving Data

```
[C#]
Database db = DatabaseFactory.CreateDatabase("PortalDatabase");

string customerName = "John Doe";
string sqlCommand = "GetCustomerId";
```

```
DbCommandWrapper dbCommandWrapper =
     db.GetStoredProcCommandWrapper(sqlCommand, customerName);

int custID = (int)db.ExecuteScalar(dbCommandWrapper);

string sqlCommand = "GetCustomerDetails";
DbCommandWrapper dbCommandWrapper =
     db.GetStoredProcCommandWrapper(sqlCommand);

dbCommandWrapper.AddInParameter("CustID",DbType.Int32, custID);
dbCommandWrapper.AddOutParameter("AccountID", DbType.Int32, 4); dbCom-
mandWrapper.AddOutParameter("LocationID", DbType.Int32, 4);
db.ExecuteNonQuery(dbCommandWrapper);

string results = string.Format(CultureInfo.CurrentCulture,
               "Customer Name: {0}, Account ID: {1}, Location: {2}",
               customerName,
               dbCommandWrapper.GetParameterValue("AccountID"),
               dbCommandWrapper.GetParameterValue("LocationID"));


[Visual Basic]
Dim db As Database = DatabaseFactory.CreateDatabase("PortalDatabase")

Dim customerName As String = "John Doe"
Dim sqlCommand As String = "GetCustomerId"
Dim dbCommandWrapper As DbCommandWrapper = _
     db.GetStoredProcCommandWrapper(sqlCommand, customerName)

Dim custID as Integer = 1 = CInt(db.ExecuteScalar(dbCommandWrapper))

Dim sqlCommand As String = "GetCustomerDetails"
Dim dbCommandWrapper As DbCommandWrapper = _
     db.GetStoredProcCommandWrapper(sqlCommand)

dbCommandWrapper.AddInParameter("CustID",DbType.Int32, custID)
dbCommandWrapper.AddOutParameter("AccountID", DbType.Int32, 4);
dbCommandWrapper.AddOutParameter("LocationID", DbType.Int32, 4)
db.ExecuteNonQuery(dbCommandWrapper)

Dim results As String = String.Format(CultureInfo.CurrentCulture, _
                  "Customer Name:{0}, Account ID: {1}, Location: {2}", _
                  customerName, _
                  dbCommandWrapper.GetParameterValue("AccountID"), _
                  dbCommandWrapper.GetParameterValue("LocationID"))
```

In addition to the ExecuteScalar and ExecuteNonQuery methods for accessing particular data values, there are also several other methods you can use to retrieve multiple rows of data. These methods can be categorized by the approaches that are used for retrieving the data: connected access and disconnected access.

Connected Access. No discussion about accessing data would be complete without mentioning DataReaders. **DataReaders** provide noncached read-only, forward-only access to data. Requests are returned as a query executes, and the data is stored in the network buffer until it is requested using the `Read` method. DataReaders are often used to increase an application's performance, because data can be retrieved as soon as it is available and typically only one row of data is stored in memory at any one time to reduce system overhead.

It is important to note, however, that until a DataReader is closed, its connection is exclusively locked. This prevents any other commands from being executed on that same connection. When the DataReader is of no more use, it must be closed for the database connection to be released. The Data Access Application Block handles connection management whenever possible by using the `CommandBehavior.CloseConnection` method to automatically close connections when the DataReader is closed.

A test conducted to determine the best data access method for performance and scalability showed that DataReaders were ideal for retrieving a single record from a database.[5] As more records were retrieved from a database, the performance of the DataReader continually improved over methods like using a DataSet. It was determined that the overhead associated with creation of a DataSet object was responsible for worse performance and an increase in memory overhead.

However, while the tests confirmed that a DataReader is a better choice than a DataSet for applications that require optimized read-only and forward-only data access, the tests also showed that because the DataReader holds a database connection while an application reads data, it limits scalability if the connection is held long enough for contention to occur. Other mechanisms like DataSets or custom data transfer objects (DTOs) only need to hold a connection while they are being populated; once they are filled, the connection may be closed and returned to the pool. This is important

5. From http://msdn.microsoft.com/library/?url=/library/en-us/dnbda/html/BOAGag.asp?frame=true.

because when a delay was introduced to these tests, contention for the database caused the DataSet to outperform the DataReader.

The tests concluded that DataReaders are an excellent solution if there is a need to retrieve multiple rows from a database, use them once, and then discard them. The most important detail to remember when using a DataReader is that the data should be used immediately and the DataReader should be closed as soon as possible. Listing 3.1 illustrated using a DataReader to retrieve multiple rows of customer data from a database and displaying the data in a tabulated form. Note how the DataReader was used immediately to populate the DataGrid and then closed. The DataReader did not explicitly cache the data, manipulate it by using a DataSet or custom object, or pass it to other components. In other words, the listing illustrates how to display the results as quickly as possible for a single use.

Disconnected Access. When data needs to be passed through multiple tiers of an application, interacted with dynamically, cached locally, or extensive processing needs to be performed on it, a more disconnected and stateful approach to working with data is typically needed. There are many different approaches that can be used to work with data in a disconnected fashion; each has its own benefits and liabilities. Three of the most popular ways of working with disconnected data in a .NET environment are generic DataSets, typed DataSets, and custom business entity components or data transfer objects. The following gives an overview of the benefits and liabilities of each of these approaches and how they are supported by Enterprise Library's Data Access Application Block.

A **DataSet** is a disconnected, in-memory representation of relational data. Because it holds no persistent connection to outside resources, it is ideal for packaging, exchanging, caching, persisting, and loading data. A DataSet object contains zero or more DataTable objects, which represent a table in a relational database. A DataTable contains zero or more DataColumns and DataRows, each respectively representing the columns and rows in a relational database table. Additionally, a DataSet may have Relation objects to associate tables together.

The following are the advantages of using a generic DataSet for accessing data in a disconnected manner.

- **Flexibility.** DataSets are designed to handle sets and complex relationships, so you don't need to write custom code to implement this functionality.
- **Serialization.** DataSets natively support serialization when passing across tiers.
- **Data binding.** DataSets can be bound to user-interface controls in ASP.NET and Windows Forms applications.
- **Sorting and filtering.** DataSets natively support sorting and filtering of the data.
- **XML support.** DataSets can be read or written in XML format. This is useful in remote and disconnected applications that can receive the XML format and recreate a DataSet locally.
- **Optimistic concurrency.** DataSets provide built-in functionality to handle optimistic concurrency and support for complex data structures. DataSets are designed to encourage the use of optimistic concurrency for long-running activities like working with the data in a disconnected mode.
- **Extensibility.** Because they are generic, if a database schema is modified, it is possible to expose these modifications with little or no additional code.

The following are some of the disadvantages of using generic DataSets for disconnected access to data.

- **Generalization.** There is no strong typing for the tables or fields of a generic DataSet. Accessing data with a generic DataSet is accomplished by using the collections that are exposed. For example, to access a table, a developer must write code to index into the DataTable collection; to access a particular column, code must be written that indexes into the DataColumn collection. The major disadvantage to this approach is the lack of compile-time checking for the indexer values of the collections. If an invalid table name or column name is specified, the error is trapped at runtime, not design-time. Listing 3.9 shows how to use a generic DataSet to access the customer ID column for the first row in the customer table.

- **High instantiation and marshalling costs.** DataSets result in the creation of several subobjects (DataTables, DataRows, and DataColumns). Therefore, DataSets can take longer to instantiate and marshal than XML strings or custom components. The relative performance of DataSets improves as the amount of data increases, because the overhead of creating the internal structure of the DataSet is less significant than the time it takes to populate the DataSet with data.
- **Private fields.** There is no option for hiding information.
- **Interoperability.** The `DataSet` class is part of ADO.NET and is, therefore, not the best choice in cases requiring interoperability with clients that are not running the .NET Framework.

LISTING 3.9: Accessing Data Using a Generic DataSet

```
[C#]
string customerId =
      (string)dsCustomers.Tables["Customer"].Rows[0]["CustomerId"];

[Visual Basic]
Dim customerId As String =
     CStr(dsCustomers.Tables("Customer").Rows(0)("CustomerId"))
```

The Data Access Application Block makes it easy to return a generic DataSet object from a backend database. Once a database provider has been instantiated, returning a DataSet is as simple as calling the `ExecuteDataSet` method with the name of a stored procedure and parameter array. This is illustrated in Listing 3.10. This method will use dynamic parameter discovery to automatically determine the parameters for the stored procedure. Alternatively, a database command wrapper could have been used to explicitly handle the parameters for the database commands and pass them to the `ExecuteDataSet` method.

LISTING 3.10: Calling `ExecuteDataSet` to Return a DataSet

```
[C#]
int divId = 1;
Database db = DatabaseFactory.CreateDatabase("PortalDatabase");

// Connection is closed by ExecuteDataSet.
DataSet customerDataSet = db.ExecuteDataSet("GetCustomers", divId);
```

```
string customerName =
      (string)customerDataSet.Tables["Customer"].Rows[0]["CustName"];

[Visual Basic]
Dim divId As Integer = 1
Dim db As Database = DatabaseFactory.CreateDatabase("PortalDatabase")

' Connection is closed by ExecuteDataSet.
Dim customerDataSet As DataSet = _
     db.ExecuteDataSet("GetCustomers", divId)
Dim customerName As String = _
     CStr(customerDataSet.Tables("Customer").Rows(0)("CustName"))
```

Typed DataSets. A **typed DataSet** is a DataSet that is associated with an XML schema and contains strongly typed methods, properties, and type definitions based on that schema. Typed DataSets exhibit approximately the same instantiation and marshalling performance as generic DataSets. However, because of the strong-typing, using a typed DataSet instead of a generic DataSet to access data allows for a few additional benefits.

- **Code readability.** Instead of relying on a generic Collection object to access data, typed methods and properties allow a more implicitly meaningful way to access tables and columns. Listing 3.9, which showed how to access the tables and columns for a generic DataSet that represents customer information, could be rewritten to use a typed DataSet instead. This is illustrated in Listing 3.11. The typed DataSet, *dsCustomers,* has a DataTable named *Customers,* and one of the columns in this DataTable is named *CustomerId.* Casting to the appropriate data types is not necessary because a typed DataSet's columns return the appropriate data type instead of returning an object as they do in a generic DataSet.
- **Compile type checking.** Because of the strong-typing, compile type checking and IntelliSense are also available. This makes typed DataSets easier to use than generic DataSets and naturally results in increased developer productivity. Invalid table names and column names are detected at compile-time rather than at runtime.

Listing 3.11: Accessing Data Using a Typed DataSet

```
[C#]
string customerId = dsCustomers.Customers[0].CustomerId;

[Visual Basic]
Dim customerId As String = dsCustomers.Customers(0).CustomerId
```

The following are some of the disadvantages of accessing data as a typed DataSet (in addition to those listed for a generic DataSet).

- **Deployment.** The assembly containing the typed DataSet class must be deployed to all tiers that use the business entity. If the structure of the typed DataSet changes, the assembly containing the typed DataSet class must be redeployed to all applications referencing it.
- **Extensibility issues.** Extra effort needs to be given to allow a typed DataSet to be extended. For example, if the database schema on which a typed DataSet is based becomes modified, the typed DataSet class will need to be regenerated to support the new schema. The regeneration process, however, will not preserve any custom code that was implemented directly in a typed DataSet class. A common best practice for dealing with this is to derive a custom class from the typed DataSet class and add any custom code to the derived class. This will prevent the custom code from being overwritten during the regeneration of a typed DataSet. This is, however, not always straightforward because of the issues presented in the next item.
- **Inheritance.** Creating a well-architected object-oriented hierarchy is difficult when using typed DataSets, because the subobjects created by a DataSet are declared private and a typed DataSet must inherit from a DataSet. This precludes the use of any other base classes.

Even with these disadvantages, the gains in developer productivity from using typed DataSets often makes it a much more attractive way to represent disconnected data than other means. Additionally, the Data Access Application Block makes populating typed DataSets with data extremely easy. The `LoadDataSet` method accepts a DataSet object and a list of names for the DataTables of that DataSet. It populates the DataTables for the supplied DataSet with data from the backend database. This works a bit differently than the `ExecuteDataSet` method, because the `ExecuteDataSet` method returns a new DataSet with generic tables named *Table, Table1, Table2,* and so on. `LoadDataSet` allows a typed DataSet to be passed to and populated by the Data Access Application Block.

Listing 3.12 shows how to populate a new `CustomersDS` DataSet by calling the `LoadDataSet` method. The example then uses the typed properties of the DataSet to retrieve the name of the first customer in the `Customers` DataTable. In this example, only the `Customers` DataTable is populated, even if there are other DataTables in the DataSet, because only the name of the `Customers` DataTable is passed to the `LoadDataSet` method.

LISTING 3.12: Calling `LoadDataSet` to Populate a Typed DataSet

```
[C#]
Database db = DatabaseFactory.CreateDatabase("PortalDatabase");

//Create a new CustomersDS typed DataSet
CustomersDS customerDataSet = new CustomersDS();

// Load the Customer DataTable in the typed DataSet
string[] tableNames = new string[1];
tableNames[0] = "Customers";
int divId = 1;
db.LoadDataSet("GetCustomers", customerDataSet, tableNames, divId);

//Get the first Customer name
string customerName;
if (customersDS.Customers.Count > 0)
{
     customerName = customersDS.Customers[0].CustomerName;
}
else
{
     customerName = String.Empty;
}

[Visual Basic]
Dim db As Database = DatabaseFactory.CreateDatabase("PortalDatabase")

'Create a new CustomersDS typed DataSet
Dim customerDataSet As CustomersDS = New CustomersDS()

' Load the Customer DataTable in the typed DataSet
```

```
Dim tableNames As String() = New String(0) {}
Dim tableNames(0) = "Customers"
Dim divId As Integer = 1
db.LoadDataSet("GetCustomers", customerDataSet, tableNames, divId)

'Get the first Customer name
Dim customerName As String
If customersDS.Customers.Count > 0 Then
    customerName = customersDS.Customers(0).CustomerName
Else
    customerName = String.Empty
End If
```

Custom Business Entity Components. Custom business entity components and data transfer objects are another way that disconnected data can be represented and passed through the multiple tiers of a distributed application. These are custom classes that are designed to represent the data in a backend database; however, these classes do not derive from the `DataSet` class. They can be built entirely from scratch or with a tool, like the XML Schema Designer (xsd.exe) that ships with Visual Studio, to create the class from an XML schema. Many tools also exist today that can automate the creation of these custom classes given the data model for a database. Custom business entities typically contain the following.

- Private member variables to cache the data locally. These fields hold a snapshot of the data in the database at the time the data was retrieved.
- Public properties to access the state of the entity and to access subcollections and hierarchies of data inside the entity.
- Methods and properties to perform localized processing by using the data in the entity component.
- Events to signal changes to the internal state of the entity component.

The following are some advantages of using a custom entity to represent disconnected data.

- **Code readability.** Similar to typed DataSets, strongly typed methods and properties can be used to access data. Listing 3.11 has been rewritten in Listing 3.13 to call the `CustomerId` property of a custom business entity instead of using the properties and methods that are automatically generated with a typed DataSet.

- **Encapsulation.** Custom entities can contain methods to encapsulate simple business rules. These methods typically operate on the disconnected data that is cached in the entity component rather than accessing the live data in the database. For example, in Listing 3.14 the `SetStatus` method changes the status for a customer given the desired customer status and only if the customer meets certain criteria as determined by a set of business rules. This change is not made permanent, however, until another component updates the customer data in the database through the `UpdateCustomer` method. The component that is responsible for the actual database update is discussed later in this chapter in the section Data Access Logic Components.
- **Private fields.** Similar to the encapsulation of business logic, member variables that do not need to be exposed to a consumer of the component can be hidden.
- **Abstraction.** Business entity components can be easily abstracted from a database schema. This allows a consumer of the component to be more decoupled from the actual backend database.
- **Modeling of complex systems.** It is often easier to model complex domain problems and interactions between business entities with custom classes because they do not suffer any disadvantages due to inheritance.
- **Interoperability.** Because custom entity components do not rely on DataSets, they can be designed for interoperability with clients that are not running the .NET Framework.

LISTING 3.13: Accessing Data Using a Custom Business Entity

```
[C#]
Customers customers = new Customers();
string customerId = customers[0].CustomerId;

[Visual Basic]
Dim customers as Customers = new Customers()
Dim customerId As String = customers(0).CustomerId
```

LISTING 3.14: Updating Data with a Custom Business Entity

```
[C#]
// Change the status for the customer
customer.SetStatus(CustomerStatus.Preferred)

//Update the customer via the Customer Data Access Logic Component
CustomerDALC.UpdateCustomer(customer);

[Visual Basic]
' Change the status for the customer
customer.SetStatus(CustomerStatus.Preferred)

'Update the customer via the Customer Data Access Logic Component
CustomerDALC.UpdateCustomer(customer)
```

The main disadvantage associated with using custom entity components as compared to generic and typed DataSets is a possible decrease in developer productivity. This is due to the fact that code must be written to handle many of the features that DataSets provide automatically. Specifically, the following are some of these features.

- **Collections.** A custom entity represents a single business entity, not a collection of business entities. Code needs to be written for one entity to hold multiple business entities of another type.
- **Serialization.** Code often needs to be written to control a custom entity's serialization.
- **Relationships and hierarchies.** Representing relationships and hierarchies of data in and between business entity components needs to be designed and developed.
- **Searching and sorting.** Support for searching and sorting custom entities must be defined and developed. For example, the `IComparable` interface can be implemented to allow entity components to be held in a `SortedList` or `Hashtable` collection.
- **Deployment.** Like typed DataSets, assemblies containing the custom entities must be deployed to all clients that use them.
- **Extensibility issues.** Like typed DataSets, if a database schema is modified, the custom entity that represents the data in that schema may also need to be modified and redeployed.

Custom components or data transfer objects are not uncommon. In fact, they are used to represent data in every Enterprise Library application block. The most common form of data that must be represented in any application block is configuration data. Every application block in Enterprise Library uses a data transfer object to represent configuration data for a particular runtime object. The data transfer objects can be recognized with the name of the runtime object for which it holds the data suffixed with the word *Data.* For example, the data transfer object that holds the configuration data for database providers is named `DatabaseProviderData`. One of the private member variables that this class encapsulates holds information about the connection string for a database provider. That class is named `ConnectionStringData`.

Typically, the most efficient means of populating the private member variables for a data transfer object is to use a DataReader. There is usually no need to incur the performance overhead of using a DataSet in addition to populating the separate member variables contained by a data transfer object.

Updating Data

Just as the Data Access Application Block provides different methods for retrieving data, so too does it provide multiple methods for updating data. Determining when to use a particular method is fairly straightforward. If DataSets are not being used to represent the data that needs to be updated, then the `ExecuteNonQuery` method is the right choice. If, however, generic or typed DataSets are being used, then the `UpdateDataSet` method can take advantage of a DataSet's capabilities for keeping track of the changes that have occurred in the DataSet and updating the database accordingly.

`ExecuteNonQuery`. The previous section, Retrieving Data, stated that the `ExecuteNonQuery` method can be used for retrieving multiple values via the output parameters from a stored procedure. It does not, however, need to be used solely for the purpose of retrieving data. It can also be used to update data without the need for a DataSet or custom entity component. This makes the `ExecuteNonQuery` very useful in situations where there is no need to work with data in a disconnected or distributed manner; instead, a simple database command to update data needs to be executed against the database.

The ExecuteNonQuery will execute the database command that is provided to it and return the number of records that have been affected. Listing 3.15 shows how to use the ExecuteNonQuery method by providing it with the name of a stored procedure that will add a customer record to the database. Dynamic parameter discovery is used for this example; however, explicit parameter handling could just as easily have been used.

LISTING 3.15: Using ExecuteNonQuery to Update Data

```
[C#]
Database db = DatabaseFactory.CreateDatabase("PortalDatabase");
int divId = 1;
string companyName = "CompanyXYZ";
string customerName = "John Doe";
int affectedRecords = db.ExecuteNonQuery("AddCustomer",
                                divId, companyName, customerName);
[Visual Basic]
Dim db As Database = DatabaseFactory.CreateDatabase("PortalDatabase")
Dim divId As Integer = 1
Dim companyName As String = "CompanyXYZ"
Dim customerName As String = "John Doe"
Dim affectedRecords As Integer = db.ExecuteNonQuery("AddCustomer", _
                                divId, companyName, customerName)
```

UpdateDataSet. DataSets are an excellent way to keep track of changes that have occurred in an application, and they are very useful when submitting changes back to a database. This is especially true when an application must work with the data in a disconnected mode, because DataSets were designed with functionality to handle optimistic concurrency. There are four main approaches to managing optimistic concurrency with DataSets.

1. Include only the primary key columns
2. Include all columns in the WHERE clause
3. Include unique key columns and the timestamp columns
4. Include unique key columns and the modified columns

Typically, when optimistic concurrency violations occur, an exception such as DBConcurrencyException is thrown. If this occurs and the update is not in a transaction, the database state will be such that the rows that passed the optimistic concurrency validation will be committed, while the rows that failed the concurrency validation won't be updated. If generic or typed DataSets are used to represent a disconnected view of data, the Data Access Application Block's `UpdateDataSet` method provides the best option for updating the backend database with the changes that have occurred in the DataSet. This method propagates all of the insertions, deletions, and changes for a particular DataTable in a DataSet back to the underlying database.

To accomplish this, the `UpdateDataSet` method relies on the DataAdapter that is exposed for a particular .NET managed data provider. The tables in the section "Design of the Data Access Application Block" listed every concrete database provider that must provide an implementation for the `GetDataAdapter` method. This method must return that .NET managed data provider's implementation of the `IDataAdapter` interface.

For example, the `SqlDatabase` database provider returns the `SqlDataAdapter` that is included with ADO.NET. When the `UpdateDataSet` method is called, the DataAdapter is retrieved via the `GetDataAdapter` method, and the underlying DataAdapter's `Update(DataSet,TableName)` method is called to perform the update to the data source. Thus, it is the underlying DataAdapter that performs the ultimate update to the data source.

It is the DataAdapter's responsibility to throw an exception if it encounters an issue trying to handle a specific command. For example, if a record is removed from a DataTable in a DataSet but the DataAdapter has not been given enough information to perform a delete in the backend database, it is the DataAdapter's responsibility to throw or propagate an exception. The Data Access Application Block then propagates this exception back to the caller of the `UpdateDataSet` method.

A new enumeration, `UpdateBehavior`, has been added to this version of the Data Access Application Block. `UpdateBehavior` provides a caller of the `UpdateDataSet` method with more control over what should happen if an exception occurs during an update. For example, you can specify that all updates should be rolled back if an exception occurs or that updates that have already been successfully committed should be allowed to remain in the database. The following are the possible values for an `UpdateBehavior`.

- **Standard.** If an exception occurs, the updates stop. Updates that have already occurred will be allowed to remain; however, additional updates will not occur.

- **Continue.** If an exception occurs, the update will continue. The DataAdapter's `Update` command will try to update the remaining rows. This relies heavily on the existence of an event handler for the DataAdapter's `RowUpdated` method in the concrete database provider (e.g., `SqlDatabase`, `OracleDatabase`) class. The `RowUpdated` event is raised just after a DataAdapter updates a row. After a record is updated, the event handler checks to determine if any records were affected. If not, and an exception was raised, the error that occurred is specified in the `RowError` property for that row and the row is skipped.
- **Transactional.** If an exception occurs, all updated rows will be rolled back.

In Listing 3.16, a `CustomersDS` DataSet is populated by calling `LoadDataSet`. A change is then made to one of the `Customers` rows and a new `Customers` row is added to the `Customers` DataTable for this typed DataSet. The `UpdateDataSet` method is called to propagate these changes back to the database. Since no rows were removed, a null value (Nothing in VB.NET) is supplied for the `Delete` command in the call to the `UpdateDataSet` method. Also, because the `UpdateBehavior` is set to `Standard`, if an exception occurs during the update, all records that have been successfully added or modified will remain but no further updates will occur.

LISTING 3.16: Using `UpdateDataSet` to Update Data

```
[C#]
Database db = DatabaseFactory.CreateDatabase("PortalDatabase");

//Create a new CustomersDS typed DataSet
CustomersDS customerDataSet = new CustomersDS();

// Load the Customer DataTable in the typed DataSet
string[] tableNames = new string[1];
tableNames[0] = customerDataSet.Customers.TableName;
int divId = 1;
db.LoadDataSet("GetCustomers", customerDataSet, tableNames, divId);

// Establish the Insert and Update commands
DbCommandWrapper insertCommandWrapper =
            db.GetStoredProcCommandWrapperWithSourceColumns(
```

```
            "AddCustomer",
            new string[] {
                "DivisionId",
                "CompanyName",
                "CustomerName"}
            );

DbCommandWrapper updateCommandWrapper =
            db.GetStoredProcCommandWrapperWithSourceColumns(
            "UpdateCustomer",
            new string[] {
                "CustomerID",
                String.Empty,
                "CompanyName",
                "CustomerName"}
            );

// Need to explicitly set the value for the LastUpdate parameter
IDataParameter dbParam = (IDataParameter)
                         updateCommandWrapper.Parameters[1];

if (dbParam != null) dbParam.Value = DateTime.Now;

// Modify an existing customer
if (customerDataSet.Customers.Count > 0)
{
      customerDataSet.Customers[0].CustomerName = "Len Fenster";
}

// Add a new customer
CustomersDataRow customersRow =
            customersTable.AddCustomersRow(divId,
                                          "CompanyXYZ", "John Doe");

// Submit the DataSet, capturing the number of rows that were affected
int rowsAffected = db.UpdateDataSet(
                  customerDataSet, tableNames[0], insertCommandWrapper,
                  updateCommandWrapper, null, UpdateBehavior.Standard);

[Visual Basic]
Dim db As Database = DatabaseFactory.CreateDatabase("PortalDatabase")

'Create a new CustomersDS typed DataSet
Dim customerDataSet As CustomersDS = New CustomersDS()

' Load the Customer DataTable in the typed DataSet
Dim tableNames As String() = New String(0) {}
Dim tableNames(0) = customerDataSet.Customers.TableName
Dim divId As Integer = 1
db.LoadDataSet("GetCustomers", customerDataSet, tableNames, divId)
```

```
' Get the table that will be modified
Dim customersTable As CustomersDataTable = customerDataSet.Customers

' Establish the Insert and Update commands
Dim insertCommandWrapper As DbCommandWrapper = _
      db.GetStoredProcCommandWrapperWithSourceColumns( _
                        "AddCustomer", _
                        New String() { _
                              "DivisionId", _
                              "CompanyName", _
                              "CustomerName"})

Dim updateCommandWrapper As DbCommandWrapper = _
      db.GetStoredProcCommandWrapperWithSourceColumns( _
                        "UpdateCustomer", _
                        New String() { _
                              "CustomerID", _
                              String.Empty, _
                              "CompanyName", _
                              "CustomerName"})

' Need to explicitly set the value for the LastUpdate parameter
Dim dbParam As IDataParameter = CType( _
                              updateCommandWrapper.Parameters(1), _
                              IDataParameter)

If Not dbParam Is Nothing Then
      dbParam.Value = DateTime.Now
End If

' Modify an existing customer
If customerDataSet.Customers.Count > 0 Then
      customerDataSet.Customers(0).CustomerName = "Len Fenster"
End If

' Add a new customer
Dim customersRow As CustomersDataRow = _
            customersTable.AddCustomersRow(divId, _
                                    "CompanyXYZ", "John Doe")

' Submit the DataSet, capturing the number of rows that were affected
Dim rowsAffected As Integer = db.UpdateDataSet( _
            customerDataSet, tableNames(0), insertCommandWrapper, _
            updateCommandWrapper, Nothing, UpdateBehavior.Standard)
```

The `UpdateBehavior` enumeration is a welcome addition to this version of the Data Access Application Block. If you need a more granular level of control over what the `UpdateBehavior` enumeration provides, you can modify the code in the Data Access Application Block. One way to accomplish this is to handle the `RowUpdating` event in addition to the `RowUpdated` event that is already being handled. The `RowUpdating` event is raised just before a DataAdapter begins an update to a row. Additional overloads for the `UpdateDataSet` method must be added that will allow delegates to be passed in for the `RowUpdated` and `RowUpdating` events and can take action when they occur. The `RowUpdatedEventArgs` and `RowUpdatingEventArgs` objects carry properties that allow a consumer to check data like the `Command`, `StatementType`, `Status`, and `Errors`. The `Errors` property, for example, returns the exception that was generated by the .NET managed data provider when the command was executed.

This approach actually allows for more possibilities than just checking for exceptions. A consumer of a particular database provider could perform any custom action; that is, it isn't limited to checking for nulls and throwing exceptions. Listing 3.17, for example, shows how a `RowUpdating` event handler can be used to capture information about the records before they are updated at the data source.

LISTING 3.17: Adding a `RowUpdating` Event Handler

```
[C#]
protected static void OnRowUpdating(
            object sender,
            System.Data.Common.RowUpdatingEventArgs e)
{
      Debug.WriteLine("OnRowUpdating");
      Debug.WriteLine(String.Format("event args: (command = {0}
                        commandType = {1} status = {2}",
                        e.Command, e.StatementType, e.Status));
}

[Visual Basic]
Protected Shared Sub OnRowUpdating( _
            ByVal sender As Object, _
            ByVal e As System.Data.Common.RowUpdatingEventArgs)

      Debug.WriteLine("OnRowUpdating")
      Debug.WriteLine(String.Format("event args: (command = {0}" & _
                        "commandType = {1} status = {2}", _
                        e.Command, e.StatementType, e.Status))
End Sub
```

The `GetStoredProcCommandWrapperWithSourceColumns` method is another new function that is intended to be used in conjunction with the `UpdateDataSet` method. Prior to the advent of this method, dynamic parameter discovery could not be used with the `UpdateDataSet` method. There was no way to take advantage of dynamic parameter discovery and also specify that the values for the parameters of a stored procedure should come from the data contained in a DataSet. Rather, parameters had to be explicitly handled using the `AddInParameter` or `AddParameter` methods of a database command wrapper.

The `GetStoredProcCommandWrapperWithSourceColumns` method allows the names of DataFields in the DataTables of a DataSet to be specified as the source for the values of a stored procedure's parameters. It does this by iterating through the parameters that are dynamically discovered for the stored procedure and mapping the corresponding DataParameter's `SourceColumn` property to the name of a DataField. Listing 3.16 illustrated this. The stored procedure for adding new customer data to the database is named `AddCustomer` and it accepts three parameters: one that represents a company division ID, one that represents the company name for a customer, and one that represents the customer's name. The `GetStoredProcCommandWrapperWithSourceColumns` method was used to tell the Data Access Application Block that it should get the values for these parameters from the `DivisionId`, `CompanyName`, and `CustomerName` DataFields respectively.

This is straightforward if the data always comes only from the DataFields. There are often situations, however, where some data must come from a DataSet and other data must come from outside of a DataSet. For example, some stored procedures may require a `UserId` parameter to be present to determine if a user is authorized to modify order information. However, from an object-oriented perspective, it may not make sense to have a `UserId` DataField in the DataSet. Identification and authentication parameters that represent values like *SessionId, UserId,* or the current date and time often need to be explicitly set; they are elements of data that exist for data entitlement and auditing reasons, but they are more global in nature than the data that typically exists in a DataSet.

When using the `GetStoredProcCommandWrapperWithSourceColumns` method, the order in which the names of the DataFields are added dictates the order in which they will be mapped to the parameters of the stored procedure. Therefore, if some values are not to be mapped to DataFields in a DataSet, then an empty string should be set for that field. This will set that DataParameter's `SourceColumn` property to an empty string, which tells the DataAdapter not to map this parameter. This has the effect of "leaving room" for these explicit, non-DataSet parameters. After the database command wrapper has been created, but before the `UpdateDataSet` method is called, the parameter collection should be modified with the values for the explicit parameters.

An example of how to do this is also shown in Listing 3.16. The database command wrapper for the `Update` command is returned from the call to the `GetStoredProcCommandWrapperWithSourceColumns` method, and three of the four stored procedure parameters are mapped to DataFields in the DataSet. The second parameter, `LastUpdate`, is not mapped to a DataField. An empty string is substituted in place of the name of a DataField for this parameter.

After the database command wrapper is returned from the `GetStoredProcCommandWrapperWithSourceColumns` method, the value for this field can be explicitly set. In Listing 3.16, I have set the value for this parameter equal to the current `DateTime`. When the `UpdateDataSet` method is called, all parameter values have either been explicitly set or mapped to DataFields.

Transaction Support

Often an application will perform multiple database operations at one time and will require that either all operations are successfully committed or none of the operations are. This type of requirement is known as a **transaction,** and it is used to ensure the integrity of a database system's state. The Data Access Application Block supports the use of manual transactions for all database operations.[6] Every one of a database provider's methods that

6. Transactions can be manual or automatic. Manual transactions allow explicit control of the transaction boundary with instructions to begin and end the transaction. Manual transactions are often significantly faster than automatic transactions because they do not require any interprocess communication with the Microsoft Distributed Transaction Coordinator (DTC).

can be used to access or update data in a database is overloaded with a signature that accepts an object that implements the `IDbTransaction` interface.

The `IDbTransaction` interface is exposed from a .NET managed data provider and enables transactions by providing a set of objects that create a connection to the database, begin a transaction, commit or abort the transaction, and finally close the connection. To execute multiple database operations in a single transaction, an object that is specific to a particular database and that supports the `IDbTransaction` interface can be created by calling `BeginTransaction` on an open `Connection`. This object can then be passed to all of the methods that must exist in that transaction. Finally, the transaction can be committed or rolled back depending on factors like whether an exception occurred or not. Listing 3.18 provides a sample for performing multiple database operations in a single transaction. In this example, data must be added to both the Order and OrderDetails table or it must not be added to either of them.

LISTING 3.18: Performing Database Operations in a Transaction

```
[C#]
Database db = DatabaseFactory.CreateDatabase("PortalDatabase");

//Add records to the Orders and OrderDetails tables
int newOrderId = 101;
DbCommandWrapper dbAddOrderCommand =
      db.GetStoredProcCommandWrapper("AddOrder", newOrderId);

using (IDbConnection connection = db.GetConnection())
{
      connection.Open();
      IDbTransaction transaction =
            connection.BeginTransaction(eTransactionType);

      try
      {
            //Add the record to the Orders table
            db.ExecuteNonQuery(dbAddOrderCommand, transaction);

            //Add a record to the OrderDetails table
            DbCommandWrapper dbAddOrderDetail1Command =
                        db.GetStoredProcCommandWrapper("AddOrderDetail",
                        newOrderId, "Cheesy Garlic Monkey Bread");
            db.ExecuteNonQuery(dbAddOrderDetail1Command, transaction);
```

```
            //Add a second record to the OrderDetails table
            DbCommandWrapper dbAddOrderDetail2Command =
                        db.GetStoredProcCommandWrapper("AddOrderDetail",
                        newOrderId, " Luscious Homemade Calzones");
            db.ExecuteNonQuery(dbAddOrderDetail2Command, transaction);

            //Commit all changes
            transaction.Commit();
      }
      catch(Exception ex)
      {
            //An exception occurred, so roll back all changes
            transaction.Rollback();
      }
      finally
      {
            //Close the connection
            connection.Close();
      }
}

[Visual Basic]
Dim db As Database = DatabaseFactory.CreateDatabase("PortalDatabase")

'Add records to the Orders and OrderDetails tables
Dim newOrderId As Integer = 101
Dim dbAddOrderCommand As DbCommandWrapper = _
db.GetStoredProcCommandWrapper("AddOrder", newOrderId)

Dim connection As IDbConnection = db.GetConnection()
Try
      connection.Open()
      Dim transaction As IDbTransaction = _
            connection.BeginTransaction(eTransactionType)

      Try
            'Add the record to the Orders table
            db.ExecuteNonQuery(dbAddOrderCommand, transaction)

            'Add a record to the OrderDetails table
            Dim dbAddOrderDetail1Command As DbCommandWrapper = _
                  db.GetStoredProcCommandWrapper("AddOrderDetail", _
                  newOrderId, "Cheesy Garlic Monkey Bread")
            db.ExecuteNonQuery(dbAddOrderDetail1Command, transaction)

            'Add a second record to the OrderDetails table
            Dim dbAddOrderDetail2Command As DbCommandWrapper = _
                  db.GetStoredProcCommandWrapper("AddOrderDetail", _
                  newOrderId, " Luscious Homemade Calzones")
            db.ExecuteNonQuery(dbAddOrderDetail2Command, transaction)
```

```
            'Commit all changes
            transaction.Commit()
        Catch ex As Exception
            'An exception occurred, so roll back all changes
            transaction.Rollback()
        Finally
            'Close the connection
            connection.Close()
        End Try
    Finally
        If TypeOf connection Is IDisposable Then
            Dim disp As IDisposable = connection
            disp.Dispose()
        End If
    End Try
```

Data Access Logic Components

Earlier in this section I discussed how generic DataSets, typed DataSets, and custom business entity components can all be used as different ways to represent data in a distributed application. These classes, though, are meant as a way to represent data, not to access it. DataSets and custom entity classes should have no knowledge of the underlying database or how to access it. Unfortunately, too often the code to populate them is scattered throughout many different places in an application. It is not unusual to have to modify the logic that surrounds populating a DataSet with data; if the code to accomplish this is dispersed throughout an application, making such changes becomes tedious and error-prone.

A better design is to create separate classes, known as **data access logic components** (DALCs), which have the responsibility for populating the DataSets and entity classes with data and propagating the changes in them back to the database. Data access logic components are a recommended best practice for accessing business data, because they abstract the semantics of the underlying data store and data access technology and provide a simple programmatic interface for retrieving and performing operations on data. Data access logic components typically provide methods to perform Create, Retrieve, Update, and Delete (CRUD) operations relating to a specific business entity in an application (e.g., customers). Centralizing these types of operations allows for greater reuse not only in one application but among many. By maintaining this code in data access logic components, you can achieve reuse in different types of applications with different types of clients.

Data access logic components should *not* be designed to invoke other data access logic components. Avoiding such a design helps keep the path to data predictable, thereby improving application maintainability. They should also not initiate heterogeneous transactions. Each data access logic component should be designed to work with a single data source; therefore, there should not be a scenario in which a data access logic component is the root for a heterogeneous transaction. It is appropriate, however, for a data access logic component to control a transaction that involves multiple updates in a single data source.

The use of data access logic components does not negate the need for database providers; quite the contrary. They are complementary constructs. Most enterprise-level applications should contain multiple data access logic components, and they can benefit from a database provider's capability for managing database connections, executing commands, caching parameters, and so on.

Data access logic components provide the logic required to access specific business data, while database providers supply a centralized interface for data access development and data connection configuration. Figure 3.8 is from the patterns & practices publication *Architecture for .NET: Designing Applications and Services,*[7] and it illustrates how data access logic components should work together with database providers (these are referred to as data access helpers in this publication) to perform database operations.

Data access logic components can also implement business logic before and after using a database provider to control database operations. They should also be used to control the mappings that are needed between the business entity and the database. That is, the logic that was previously described for mapping the fields in a DataSet to the parameters in a stored procedure should be encapsulated in a data access logic component.

---

7. From http://msdn.microsoft.com/library/default.asp?url=/library/en-us/dnbda/html/distapp.asp.

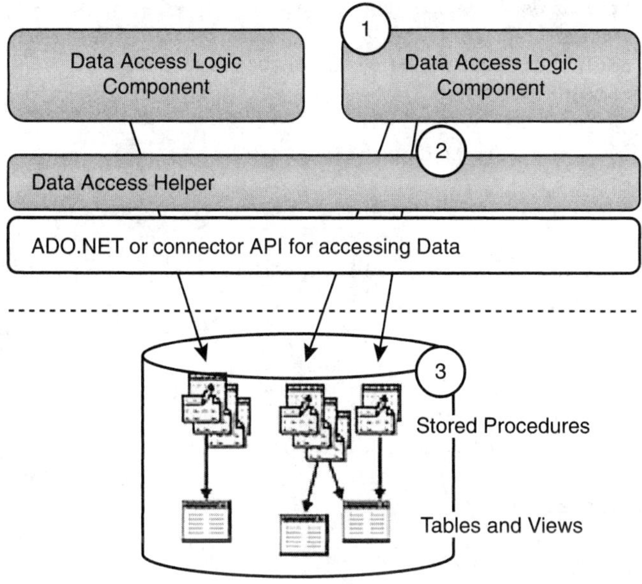

FIGURE 3.8: Data Access Logic Components

Listing 3.19 provides an example of a data access logic component, named `CustomersDALC`, which manages data related to customer information in a database. The data that is managed by this class is represented by a typed DataSet named `CustomersDS`. The methods shown in this listing use a database provider to return this DataSet and update changes to the customers in this database.

LISTING 3.19: Returning a Customer's DataSet from a Data Access Logic Component

```
[C#]
public class CustomersDALC
{
     public static CustomersDS GetCustomers(int divisionId)
     {
          Database db =
               DatabaseFactory.CreateDatabase("PortalDatabase");

          //Create a new CustomersDS typed DataSet
          CustomersDS customerDataSet = new CustomersDS();
```

```
        // Load the DataTables for this typed DataSet
        string[] tableNames = null;
        DataTableCollection dataTables = customersDataSet.Tables;
        if (dataTables.Count > 0)
        {
            tableNames = new string[dataTables.Count];
            int tableId  = 0;
            foreach(DataTable table in dataTables)
            {
                tableNames[tableId] = table.TableName;
                tableId++;
            }
        }

        db.LoadDataSet("GetCustomers",
            customerDataSet, tableNames, divisionId);

        return customerDataSet;
    }

    public static int UpdateCustomers(CustomersDS currentCustomers)
    {
        int rowsAffected = 0;
        if (currentCustomers != null)
        {
            // Establish the Update command
            DbCommandWrapper updateCommandWrapper =
                db.GetStoredProcCommandWrapperWithSourceColumns(
                    "UpdateCustomer",
                    new string[] {
                        "CustomerID",
                        String.Empty,
                        "CompanyName",
                        "CustomerName"}
                );

            // Need to explicitly set LastUpdate parameter
            IDataParameter dbParam = (IDataParameter)
                updateCommandWrapper.Parameters[1];

            if (dbParam != null) dbParam.Value = DateTime.Now;

            // Submit the DataSet
            rowsAffected = db.UpdateDataSet(
                        currentCustomers,
                        currentCustomers.Customers.TableName,
                        null, updateCommandWrapper, null,
                        UpdateBehavior.Standard);
        }
```

```
            return rowsAffected;
        }
    }

[Visual Basic]
Public Class CustomersDALC

     Public Shared Function GetCustomers(ByVal divisionId As Integer) _
               As CustomersDS

          Dim db As Database = _
               DatabaseFactory.CreateDatabase("PortalDatabase")

          'Create a new CustomersDS typed DataSet
          Dim customerDataSet As CustomersDS = New CustomersDS()

          ' Load the DataTables for this typed DataSet
          Dim tableNames As String() = Nothing
          Dim dataTables As DataTableCollection = _
               customersDataSet.Tables

          If dataTables.Count > 0 Then
               tableNames = New String(dataTables.Count - 1) {}
               Dim tableId As Integer = 0
               For Each table As DataTable In dataTables
                    tableNames(tableId) = table.TableName
                    tableId += 1
               Next table
          End If

          db.LoadDataSet("GetCustomers", customerDataSet, _
                         tableNames, divisionId)

          Return customerDataSet
     End Function

     Public Shared Function UpdateCustomers( _
                    ByVal currentCustomers As CustomersDS) _
                         As Integer

          Dim rowsAffected As Integer = 0
          If Not currentCustomers Is Nothing Then

               ' Establish the Update command
               Dim updateCommandWrapper As DbCommandWrapper = _
                    db.GetStoredProcCommandWrapperWithSourceColumns( _
                         "UpdateCustomer", _
                         New String() { "CustomerID", _
                                   String.Empty, _
                                   "CompanyName", _
```

```
                                    "CustomerName"})

            ' Need to explicitly set LastUpdate parameter
            Dim dbParam As IDataParameter = _
                CType(updateCommandWrapper.Parameters(1), _
                    IDataParameter)

            If Not dbParam Is Nothing Then
                dbParam.Value = DateTime.Now
            End If


            ' Submit the DataSet
            rowsAffected = db.UpdateDataSet(currentCustomers, _
                        currentCustomers.Customers.TableName, _
                        Nothing, updateCommandWrapper, Nothing, _
                        UpdateBehavior.Standard)
        End If

        Return rowsAffected
    End Function
End Class
```

One of the recommendations for designing data access logic components is to expose expected functionality that is common across all data access logic components in a separately defined interface or base class. However, if I go too far into how to design data access logic components in an application, I will quickly extend outside the scope of features that the Data Access Application Block is intended to provide.

This section on data access logic components is intended to convey the point that using database providers in a "utility" class is generally not an ideal design. This is especially true for distributed applications. Rather, data access logic components should be used that control database providers for accessing and updating data that is specific to a certain type of data (e.g., customers). Chapter 9 covers how to create a separate application block that adheres to the promoted best practices for designing data access logic components.

Summary

This chapter covered the design of Enterprise Library's Data Access Application Block and how to configure and develop an application to use it. It was very important to the Microsoft patterns & practices team that this application block remain very simple and straightforward to use for performing the most common database operations. It was also important that the block evolved to allow for a consistent interface regardless of the database that is being used by an application.

Database providers are at the core of the solution for this design and thus are a central part of this chapter. This chapter documented the general capabilities of each of the database providers that ship with Enterprise Library as well as specific differences that make one database provider different from another. It provided a sample database provider and detailed the steps that are needed to create a new database provider that extends the available data sources available to Enterprise Library's Data Access Application Block.

Like the other Enterprise Library application blocks, configuring the Data Access Application Block is more of an administrative detail than it is a development task. Still, since configuration information drives the behavior for this application block, it is important to know how database providers can be configured for an application. The chapter also discussed where and why the methods exposed by these database providers should be used, and how data access logic components should be used to control the database providers for a distributed application. This discussion highlighted the methods where a change to the configuration from one database provider to another would require some code changes. These methods are few, though, and typically changing the configuration for an application from one database provider to another can be done with little or no code changes.

4

The Caching Application Block

Many enterprise applications focus on moving data and presenting data to users in unique and interesting ways. Yet, all of this data does not necessarily need to be retrieved from a backend database for every request. Data that is semi-static, nontransactional, and consumed frequently or is expensive to create, obtain, or transform is ideal for caching. Caching helps not only reduce the amount of data that is transferred between processes and computers, but it also helps reduce the amount of data processing that occurs in a system and the number of disk access operations that must occur. Unfortunately, leveraging caching techniques to improve the performance and scalability metrics in enterprise applications is an important area that is too often overlooked.

For application architects, it is not good enough to design applications that solve specific business problems. An application that "does the job" but does not perform or scale well will eventually see little use. Even if users are attracted to the application at first, as performance degrades and the application is deemed unreliable, users will turn away. Unless thorough stress testing is performed, these types of problems rarely show themselves early on. It is the architect's responsibility to ensure that applications and systems are designed to meet performance, scalability, and availability needs.

It would be ideal to have service-level agreements in place that detail the metrics that need to be met for a specific application or system; however, reality does not always match ideology. It is often the case that systems and applications must be designed without specific information about how the application needs to perform or scale. This, however, is not an excuse to design a system that does not perform or scale well. Architects must strive for a design that overcomes these challenges. It is important to remember that caching isn't something that can typically be added to an application at any point in the development cycle; the application should be designed with caching in mind.

The Microsoft patterns & practices team has published a lot of excellent information on caching best practices, most notably the *Caching Architecture Guide for .NET Framework Applications.*[1] The section in the chapter that covers the design of the Caching Application Block details how the recommendations in this guide are core to the design of Enterprise Library's Caching Application Block. The chapter describes how the application block has been designed for extensibility and provides examples for how to extend it. It also shows how to configure and develop an application so that it can benefit from the features of the Caching Application Block.

Note that much of the information in this chapter is not new; rather, it is a combination of parts of the *Caching Architecture Guide for .NET Framework Applications* document and the Enterprise Library documentation for the Caching Application Block. Most of the new information in this chapter is where I show how to extend the Caching Application Block by way of a custom Cache Storage Provider, expiration policy, and callback. I don't repeat all the information found in these guides, but I focus on the parts that are specific to Enterprise Library's implementation for caching.

What Is the Caching Application Block?

The Enterprise Library's Caching Application Block is an implementation of the recommendations that are put forth in the *Caching Architecture Guide for .NET Framework Applications.* Its design contains all of the fundamental elements found in the Solution Blueprint suggested in this guide; namely,

1. Found at http://msdn.microsoft.com/library/default.asp?url=/library/en-us/dnbda/html/CachingArch.asp.

providing implementations for CacheManagers, a cache service, and cache storage. Furthermore, the design of the Caching Application Block provides extension points that allow an enterprise to add new implementations for certain critical areas.

For example, if the cache StorageProviders (aka BackingStores) that ship with the Caching Application Block are not sufficient for the needs of a particular enterprise, a new one can be developed and "plugged in" so that it is as easy to use as the ones that ship with the block. Additionally, a simple and consistent programming interface is exposed that allows the code for an application to be written so that it is agnostic as to the type of BackingStore that is used. This allows the code for an application to remain unchanged if a modification needs to be made to the BackingStore that is used for caching. Overall, the major objective for the Caching Application Block is to provide a set of classes and interfaces that make it easy for an application to cache data to help tune that application's performance, scalability, and availability.

Performance

By storing data as close as possible to the consumer of the data, repetitive data creation, processing of the data, and data retrieval can be avoided. Reference data like countries and states are excellent candidates for information that should be cached, because this type of information rarely changes. Therefore, it can be retrieved from the backend data source less frequently and cached on an application server or Web server. This reduces or eliminates the need to make multiple roundtrips to a database to retrieve this type of data as well the need to recreate the same data for each request. Eliminating these types of activities can dramatically improve an application's performance.

Scalability

Often the same data, business functionality, and user interface fragments are required by many users and processes in an application. For example, a combo box that lets users select a specific country in a form could be used by all the users of a Web application regardless of who that user is or even where they are in the Web application. If this information is processed for each request, valuable resources are wasted recreating the same output. Instead, the page fragment can be stored in the ASP.NET output cache and reused for each request. This improves the scalability of the application because as the user base increases, the demand for server resources for these tasks remains constant and the resources that would be used to render these results can now be used for other purposes. Furthermore, this helps scale the resources of the backend database server. By storing frequently used data in a cache, fewer database requests are made, meaning that more users can be served.

Availability

Sometimes the services that provide information to an application may be unavailable. This is very common, for example, in occasionally connected smart client systems. By storing that data in another place, an application may be able to survive system failures such as Web service problems or hardware failures. Of course, this depends a lot on the type and amount of the actual data that is cached and if the application has been designed to cache information specifically to handle availability issues.

It is atypical and often inadvisable to cache *all* the information for an application, especially if that data is not relatively static or is transactional in nature. One exception to this rule, however, is if the application must be designed to be available even when a backend data store is not available. For example, it may be reasonable for the application to cache all of its information because the data store has scheduled periods where it may be offline or connectivity to the data source is unreliable. Each time a user requests information from the data store while it is online, the information can be returned and cached, updating the cache on each request. When the data store becomes unavailable, requests can still be serviced using the cached data until the data store comes back online.

Why Not Use the ASP.NET Cache?

We should. The .NET Framework includes support for caching in Web applications and Web services with the `System.Web.Caching` namespace. It should still be used to cache information in a Web application, especially when it comes to page and page fragment caching. However, there are other scenarios in which a caching mechanism that is agnostic to the runtime environment would be a valuable addition to the application to increase performance and availability. The Caching Application Block is not a replacement for the ASP.NET cache; it should be used in situations where the ASP.NET cache is not an ideal fit. The Caching Application Block is a good choice for the following circumstances.

- For situations that require a consistent form of caching across different application environments. For example, it is a good idea to design the data layers or business layers of enterprise applications so that they can be used independently of the application environment in which they run; that is, the business or data layer can run just as well in a Windows application as it does in a Web service or Web application. Although it is possible to use the ASP.NET cache in non-Web scenarios,[2] it has not been tested and is not supported by Microsoft.
- For smart client applications, Windows Services, and console applications that use locally cached reference data to create requests and support offline operations or need a cache to improve performance.
- For situations that require a configurable and persistent BackingStore. The Caching Application Block supports both isolated storage and database BackingStores. This allows cached data to survive application restarts. Developers can create additional BackingStore providers and add them to the Caching Application Block using its configuration settings. The application block can also symmetrically encrypt a cache item's data before it is persisted to a BackingStore.
- For situations that need the cache to be highly configurable so that changes to the cache configuration settings will not require application source code changes. Developers first write the code that uses one or more named caches, and then system operators and develop-

2. This is true for the ASP.NET cache in .NET Framework 1.1. Microsoft has tested and does support using the ASP.NET cache for non-Web scenarios for .NET Framework 2.0.

ers can configure each of these named caches differently using the Enterprise Library Configuration Tool.

- When cache items require a combination of expiration settings for absolute time, sliding time, extended time format (e.g., every evening at midnight), file dependency, or never expired. The ASP.NET cache supports absolute time and sliding time expirations; however, it does not support setting both expirations at one time. Only one type of expiration can be set for a particular cache item. The CacheManager supports setting multiple types of cache item expirations at the same time.

The Previous Version of the Caching Application Block

There are some significant differences between the previous version of the Caching Application Block and the Enterprise Library version.

- First and foremost, Enterprise Library's Caching Application Block is thread-safe. The earlier version of the application block could return incorrect data when multiple threads accessed a single cache item in a short period of time.
- The earlier version supported multiple processes sharing a single cache by way of a Singleton object (via the `SingletonCacheStorage`). The Enterprise Library version supports using a cache in a single application domain only.
- The `ICacheStorage` interface has been replaced with the `IBackingStore` interface. Persistent storage in a database is provided through its dependency on the Data Access Application Block. Isolated storage is supported for persistent storage via the new `IsolatedStorageBackingStore`. The application block does not, however, include support for memory-mapped files.
- The earlier version included the scavenging algorithm as a pluggable provider. In the Enterprise Library version, you must modify the application block source code to change the scavenging algorithm.
- The earlier version included encryption as a pluggable provider. The encryption of cache item data in the Enterprise Library version is provided by the Cryptography Application Block.

The Design of the Caching Application Block

The design goals for a custom cache outlined in the *Caching Architecture Guide for .NET Framework Applications* are to:

- Decouple the front-end application interface from the internal implementation of the cache storage and management functions.
- Provide best practices for a high-performance, scalable caching solution.
- Offer support for cache-specific features, such as dependencies and expirations, and enable the use of custom expiration and dependency implementations.
- Allow for support of cache management features such as scavenging.
- Enable extension points for a custom cache storage solution by implementing the storage class interfaces provided.
- Allow the use of custom cache scavenging algorithms by implementing the classes and interfaces provided.

Except for the last bullet point, the design goals for the Caching Application Block are the same. Additionally, the design goals for the Caching Application Block include providing a caching API that is easy to use, easy to maintain, and easy to configure. Furthermore, the caching solution needs to perform efficiently and must be reliable by ensuring that the BackingStore remains intact if an exception occurs while the cache is being accessed.

One of the most important design goals with this version of the Caching Application Block was to ensure that the cache is thread safe, which helps to ensure that the states of the in-memory cache and the BackingStore remain synchronized. The following sections define the primary classes in the Caching Application Block and explain how they are used to accomplish these design goals. Figure 4.1 provides a high-level overview of many of these classes.

`CacheManager`, `CacheManagerFactory`, and `CacheFactory`

The `CacheManager` class lies at the core of the Caching Application Block and provides the application interface for a single cache. In the Caching

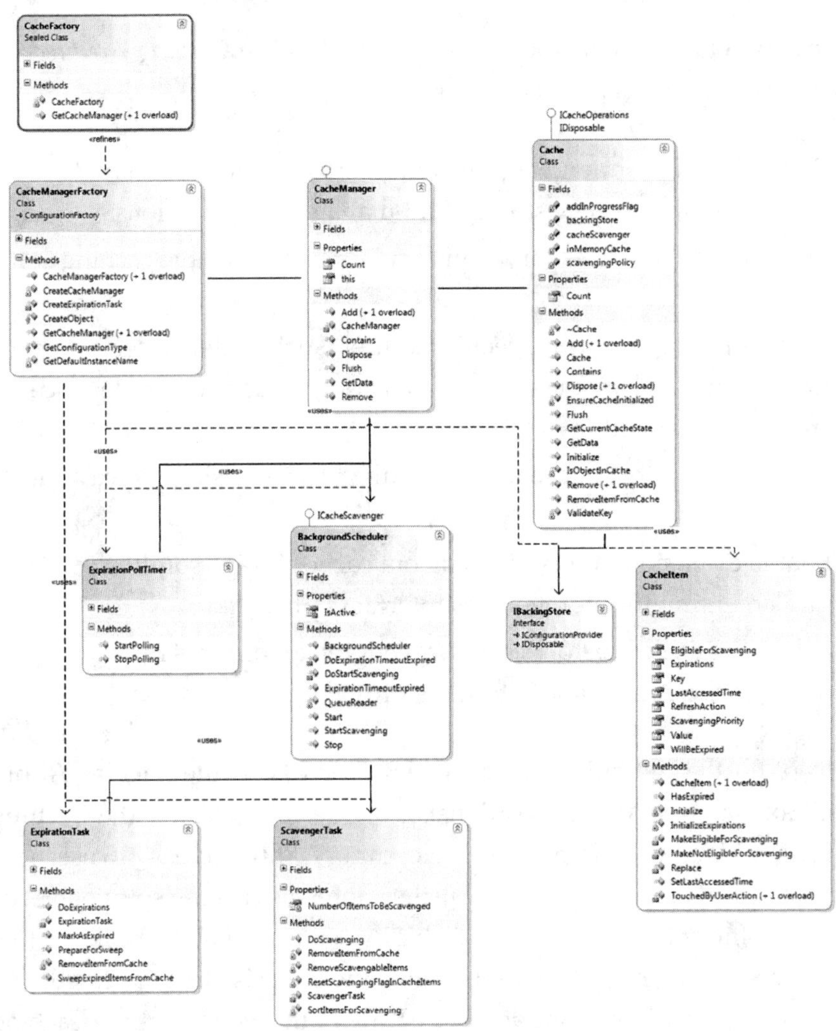

FIGURE 4.1: Design of Enterprise Library's Caching Application Block

Application Block, it is possible to configure and use multiple caches, and thus multiple CacheManagers, in a single application. This is another factor that differentiates the Caching Application Block from the ASP.NET cache; with ASP.NET there can be only one cache. However, it is recommended by the patterns & practices team that when different types of items (e.g., customer data, countries, zip codes, etc.) are being stored, it is best to store them in different caches—one cache for each type of item. This increases the efficiency of searching when retrieving an item because it reduces the number of items in each cache. In the Caching Application Block, all caching operations occur through the `CacheManager` class. The `CacheManager` class provides all the methods needed to add, retrieve, and remove items from the cache.

All of the Enterprise Library application blocks are designed using the factory design pattern. **Factories** are objects that exist solely to create other objects. In the Caching Application Block, the `CacheManagerFactory` is used to create an instance of a `CacheManager`. The `CacheManagerFactory` uses the features provided by the Configuration Application Block to retrieve configuration information and determine which `CacheManager` should be created. The `CacheManagerFactory` class has two overloads for its `GetCacheManager` method that are used to create a `CacheManager`: one overload takes the name of a `CacheManager` and the other one doesn't take any arguments. The overload that requires an argument will initialize the `CacheManager` with the name that is supplied. The overload that takes no arguments initializes the `CacheManager` that is configured as the `DefaultCacheManager` in the configuration data for this application block. In both cases, the private `CreateCacheManager` method is called to ultimately create the `CacheManager`.

In its `CreateCacheManager` method, the `CacheManagerFactory` first creates a `ScavengingPolicy` and `BackingStore` and uses the instances of these objects to construct the actual Cache object that the `CacheManager` will encapsulate. It then creates instances of the `ExpirationTask` and `ScavengingTask` and uses these instances to create a new `BackgroundScheduler`. The `BackgroundScheduler` is used to initialize the underlying cache.

An `ExpirationPollTimer` is also created, and both the `BackgroundScheduler` and the `ExpirationPollTimer` are started. The instances of the cache, `BackgroundScheduler`, and `ExpirationPollTimer` are passed into the `CacheManager`'s constructor to create the new instance. This new instance is then added to the `HashTable` of `CacheManagers` that the `CacheManagerFactory` manages. Therefore, the `CacheManager` is held in the scope of the application, and as such, its cache can be accessed from any class or thread concurrently without the need to recreate the `CacheManager` class multiple times.

It is important to note that the `CacheManager` does not hold any state and is simply a front-end interface to the cache. This design allows the `CacheManager` to provide the quickest possible response times to the cache client by performing any operations on the cache metadata after returning the control to the cache client. Because it is such a critical method, I have included the code for the `CreateCacheManager` in Listing 4.1.

LISTING 4.1: The `CreateCacheManager` Method

```
private CacheManager CreateCacheManager(string cacheManagerName)
{
     CacheManager cacheManager =
                    cacheManagers[cacheManagerName] as CacheManager;
     if (cacheManager != null)
     {
          return cacheManager;
     }

     CachingConfigurationView view =
          new CachingConfigurationView(ConfigurationContext);
     CacheManagerData cacheManagerData =
          view.GetCacheManagerData(cacheManagerName);
     CacheCapacityScavengingPolicy scavengingPolicy =
          new CacheCapacityScavengingPolicy(cacheManagerName, view);

     IBackingStore backingStore =
          backingStoreFactory.CreateBackingStore(cacheManagerName);
     Cache cache = new Cache(backingStore, scavengingPolicy);

     ExpirationPollTimer timer = new ExpirationPollTimer();
     ExpirationTask expirationTask = CreateExpirationTask(cache);
     ScavengerTask scavengerTask =
          new ScavengerTask(cacheManagerName, view,
                         scavengingPolicy, cache);
     BackgroundScheduler scheduler =
          new BackgroundScheduler(expirationTask, scavengerTask);
     cache.Initialize(scheduler);

     scheduler.Start();
     timer.StartPolling(new
          TimerCallback(scheduler.ExpirationTimeoutExpired),
          cacheManagerData.ExpirationPollFrequencyInSeconds * 1000);
```

```
        cacheManager = new CacheManager(cache, scheduler, timer);
        cacheManagers.Add(cacheManagerName, cacheManager);
        return cacheManager;
    }

[Visual Basic]
Private Function CreateCacheManager(ByVal cacheManagerName As String) _
                As CacheManager

    Dim cacheManager As CacheManager = _
        IIf(TypeOf cacheManagers(cacheManagerName) Is CacheManager,_
            CType(cacheManagers(cacheManagerName), CacheManager), _
            CType(Nothing, CacheManager))
        If Not cacheManager Is Nothing Then
            Return cacheManager
        End If

    Dim view As CachingConfigurationView = _
        New CachingConfigurationView(ConfigurationContext)
    Dim cacheManagerData As CacheManagerData = _
        view.GetCacheManagerData(cacheManagerName)
    Dim scavengingPolicy As CacheCapacityScavengingPolicy = _
        New CacheCapacityScavengingPolicy(cacheManagerName, view)

    Dim backingStore As IBackingStore = _
        backingStoreFactory.CreateBackingStore(cacheManagerName)
    Dim cache As Cache = New Cache(backingStore, scavengingPolicy)

    Dim timer As ExpirationPollTimer = New ExpirationPollTimer()
    Dim expirationTask As ExpirationTask = CreateExpirationTask(cache)
    Dim scavengerTask As ScavengerTask = _
        New ScavengerTask(cacheManagerName, view, _
                               scavengingPolicy, cache)
    Dim scheduler As BackgroundScheduler = _
        New BackgroundScheduler(expirationTask, scavengerTask)
    cache.Initialize(scheduler)

    scheduler.Start()
    timer.StartPolling(New TimerCallback( _
        AddressOf scheduler.ExpirationTimeoutExpired), _
        cacheManagerData.ExpirationPollFrequencyInSeconds * 1000)

    cacheManager = New CacheManager(cache, scheduler, timer)
    cacheManagers.Add(cacheManagerName, cacheManager)
    Return cacheManager
End Function
```

When the internal Cache object is constructed, all data in the BackingStore is loaded into an in-memory representation that is contained in the Cache object. This is the only time that the BackingStore is ever read—when an application makes changes to the cache, the changes are written to both the internal cache and the BackingStore. An application can make requests to the `CacheManager` object to retrieve cached data, add data to the cache, and remove data from the cache, and it should always be synchronized with the BackingStore. Table 4.1 describes the methods that the `CacheManager` class exposes for performing these functions.

Another class, `CacheFactory`, refines the `CacheManagerFactory` class with static methods that simply pass through to an instance of the `CacheManagerFactory` class. This provides a simpler interface for developers because it allows a `CacheManager` to be created without directly having to instantiate a factory class, and it just contains a single method: `GetCacheManager`. `GetCacheManager` contains two overloads: one overload accepts

TABLE 4.1: `CacheManager` **Class**

Method/Property	Description
`Add`	This overloaded method adds new `CacheItem` to cache. If another item already exists with the same key, that item is removed before the new item is added. The `Add` method enables adding items to the cache with or without metadata (expiration policies, scavenging priority, etc.). In the simplest case, the `Add` method just contains a key/value pair. If any failure occurs during this process, the cache will not contain the item being added.
`Count`	Returns the number of items currently in the cache.
`Flush`	Removes all items and metadata from the cache. If an error occurs during the removal, the cache is left unchanged.
`GetData`	Returns the value associated with the given key.
`Item`	Returns the item identified by the provided key.
`Remove`	Removes the given item and its metadata from the cache. If no item exists with that key, this method does nothing.

no arguments and wraps around the CacheManagerFactory's GetCacheManager method, and the other overload accepts a string and wraps around the CacheManagerFactory's GetCacheManager(string) method. Both the CacheManagerFactory and the CacheFactory class can be used to obtain a CacheManager.

Cache Objects

A **Cache object** receives requests from a CacheManager and implements all operations between the BackingStore and the in-memory representation of the cached data. A **cache** is simply a copy of the master data stored in memory or on disk. Therefore, a Cache object simply contains a hash table that holds the in-memory representation of the data; however, that item of data must first be packaged as a CacheItem object. A CacheItem includes the data itself, together with other information such as the item's key, its priority, a RefreshAction, and an array of expiration policies. (All of these classes are explained in detail in the following sections.) The Cache object uses a hash table as a lock to control access to the items in the cache, both from the application and from the BackgroundScheduler. It also provides thread safety for the entire Caching Application Block.

When an application adds an item to the cache by calling CacheManager's Add method, the CacheManager simply forwards the request to the Cache object. If there isn't an item in the in-memory hash table that matches the key for the item being added, the Cache object will first create a dummy cache item and add it to an in-memory hash table. Then, whether the item exists or not, it will use the item found for this key as a snapshot of the item before performing the insert. It then locks the cache item in the in-memory hash table, adds the item to BackingStore, and finally replaces the existing cache item in the in-memory hash table with the new cache item. (In the case where the item was not already in the in-memory hash table, it replaces the dummy item.)

If there is an exception while writing to the BackingStore, it removes the dummy item added to the in-memory hash table and does not continue. The Caching Application Block enforces a strong exception safety guarantee. This means that if an Add operation fails, the state of the cache rolls back to what it was before it tried to add the item. In other words, either an operation is completed successfully or the state of the cache remains unchanged. (This is also true for the `Remove` and `Flush` methods.)

If the number of cached items exceeds a predetermined limit when the item is added, the `BackgroundScheduler` object begins scavenging. When adding an item, the application can use an overload of the `Add` method to specify an array of expiration policies, the scavenging priority, and an object that implements the `ICacheItemRefreshAction` interface. As explained later in this chapter, a `RefreshAction` receives a notification when an item is removed from the cache.

When an application calls the `CacheManager's GetData` method to retrieve an item, the `CacheManager` object forwards the request to the Cache object. If the item is in the cache, it is returned from the Cache's in-memory representation. If it isn't in the cache, the request returns the value null (or Nothing in VB.NET). If the item is expired, the item also returns the value null (or Nothing in VB.NET).

`CacheService` Objects

As described in the section "Custom Cache Detailed Design" of the *Caching Architecture Guide* for .NET Framework Applications, a `CacheManager` object has references to both a `CacheStorage` and a `CacheService` object. The `CacheStorage` object is used for inserting, getting, and removing items from the cache storage. The Caching Application Block implements this design by way of the `BaseBackingStore` class (and classes that inherit from it). The `CacheService` object is designed to manage metadata that may be associated with `CacheItems`. This metadata may include items like expiration policies, priorities, and callbacks. While a single `CacheService` class does not exist in the Caching Application Block, the functionality that such a service is designed to implement does exist by way of the `BackgroundScheduler` and `ExpirationPollTimer` classes.

The `BackgroundScheduler` Class

The `BackgroundScheduler` class is designed to periodically monitor the lifetime of the items in the cache. It is responsible for expiring aging cache items and scavenging lower-priority cache items. When an item expires, the

BackgroundScheduler first removes it and then, optionally, notifies the application that the item was removed. At this point, it is the application's responsibility to refresh the cache as necessary.

The BackgroundScheduler operates in a worker thread. If a request is made to the BackgroundScheduler, the BackgroundScheduler packages the request as a message and puts it in a message queue instead of immediately executing the requested behavior. This all occurs in the caller's thread. From its own thread, the BackgroundScheduler sequentially removes messages from the queue and then executes the request. The advantage to performing operations serially on a single thread is that it guarantees that the code will run in a single-threaded environment. This makes both the code and its effects simpler to understand.

The ExpirationPollTimer Class

The ExpirationPollTimer triggers the expiration cycle and makes a call to the BackgroundScheduler. The frequency of the timer that regulates how often the BackgroundScheduler should check for expired items can be set through configuration. The unit is in seconds and is determined by the ExpirationPollFrequencyInSecond attribute in the configuration data.

Expiration Policies

An important aspect of caching state is the way in which it is kept consistent with the master data and other application resources. Expiration policies can be used to define the contents of a cache that are invalid based on the amount of time that the data has been in the cache or on notification from another resource. The first type of expiration policy is known as a **time-based expiration** and the second is known as a **notification-based expiration.**

The Caching Application Block's expiration process is performed by the BackgroundScheduler that periodically examines the CacheItems to see if any items have expired. The ExpirationPollFrequencyInSeconds setting for a CacheManager controls how frequently the expiration cycle occurs for that instance of the CacheManager. Expiration is a two-part process. The first part is known as **marking** and the second part is known as **sweeping.** The process is divided into separate tasks to avoid any conflicts that can occur if the application is using a cache item that the `BackgroundScheduler` is trying to expire.

- During marking, `BackgroundScheduler` makes a copy of the hash table and examines each cache item in it to see if it can be expired. It locks the item while it is doing this. If an item is eligible for expiration, the `BackgroundScheduler` sets a flag in the cache item.
- During sweeping, the `BackgroundScheduler` reexamines each flagged `CacheItem` to see if it has been accessed since it was flagged. If it has been accessed, the item is kept in the cache. If it hasn't been accessed, it is expired and removed from the cache. A Windows Management Instrumentation (WMI) event occurs when an item expires. WMI events publish management information, like performance counters, about an application so that management systems, like Microsoft Operations Manager, can better manage an application.

The Caching Application Block ships with four expiration policies; three are time-based expirations and one is a notification-based expiration. The time-based expirations are `AbsoluteTime`, `SlidingTime`, and `ExtendedFormatTime`. The notification-based expiration is `FileDependency`. Furthermore, the Caching Application Block provides the capability for adding a custom extension policy to the ones that already exist by creating a new class that implements the `ICacheItemExpiration` interface. This interface, as well as the expiration policies that ship with Enterprise Library, are shown in Figure 4.2.

Time-Based Expirations. Time-based expirations invalidate data based on either relative or absolute time periods. Use time-based expiration when volatile cache items, such as those that have regular data refreshes or those that are valid for only a set amount of time, are stored in a cache. Time-based expiration enables policies to be set that keep items in the cache only as long as their data remains current. For example, if an application displays product information that gets updated in the product catalog once a day at most, the product information can be cached for the time that those products remain constant in the catalog, that is, for a 24-hour period.

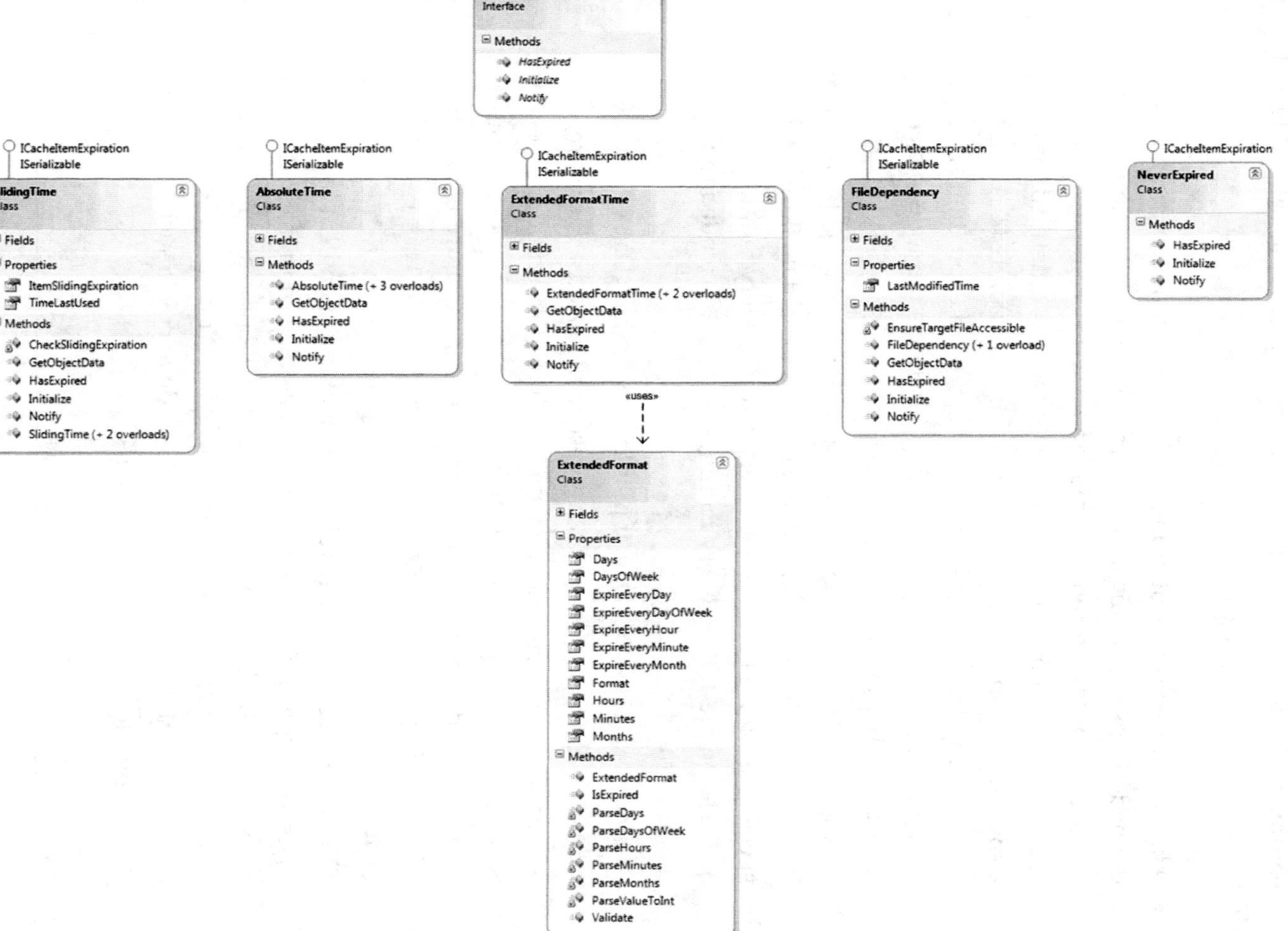

FIGURE 4.2: Expiration Policies in Enterprise Library's Caching Application Block

There are two categories of time-based expiration policies: **absolute** and **sliding.**

- **Absolute time expiration policies** allow the lifetime of an item to be defined by specifying the absolute time for an item to expire. They can use a simple or extended time format. With a simple format absolute time expiration, the lifetime of an item is defined by setting a specific date and time, for example, July 26, 2007 12:00 AM. The Caching Application Block refers to this type of expiration simply as an `AbsoluteTime` expiration. Listing 4.2 shows the code to create an `AbsoluteTime` expiration.

  Absolute time expirations can also be in an extended time format. With an extended time format, the lifetime of an item is defined by specifying expressions such as every minute, every Sunday, expire at 5:15 AM on the 15th of every month, and so on. Extended time format uses this format:

  <Minute> <Hour> <Day of month> <Month> <Day of week>

  where an asterisk (*) is used to represent all periods. Therefore, an expression to indicate that an item should expire at midnight every Saturday can be represented by the string `0 0 * * 6` (0 minutes, 0 hours, every day of the month, every month, on Saturday). Listing 4.3 shows the code to create this `ExtendedFormatTime` expiration expression.
- **Sliding expiration policies** allow the lifetime of an item to be defined by specifying an interval between the last time the item was accessed and the duration until it is expired. For example, it might be desirable to expire a particular cache item if it hasn't been accessed in the last five minutes. The code to create such a `SlidingTime` expiration is shown in Listing 4.4.

LISTING 4.2: Creating an `AbsoluteTime` Expiration

```
[C#]
DateTime expiryTime = new DateTime(2007, 7, 26, 0, 0, 0);
AbsoluteTime absExpiryTime = new AbsoluteTime(expiryTime);

[Visual Basic]
Dim expiryTime As DateTime = New DateTime(2007, 7, 26, 0, 0, 0)
Dim absExpiryTime As AbsoluteTime = New AbsoluteTime(expiryTime)
```

Listing 4.3: Creating an `ExtendedFormatTime` Expiration

```
[C#]
ExtendedFormatTime expireTime = new ExtendedFormatTime("0 0 * * 6");

[Visual Basic]
Dim expireTime As ExtendedFormatTime = _
     New ExtendedFormatTime("0 0 * * 6")
```

Listing 4.4: Creating a `SlidingTime` Expiration

```
[C#]
TimeSpan expiryTime = new TimeSpan(0, 5, 0);
SlidingTime slideExpireTime = new SlidingTime(expiryTime);

[Visual Basic]
Dim expiryTime As TimeSpan = New TimeSpan(0, 5, 0)
Dim slideExpireTime As SlidingTime = New SlidingTime(expiryTime)
```

Notification-Based Expirations. Notification-based expirations invalidate data based on instructions from an internal or external source. Notification-based expirations define the validity of a cached item based on the properties of an application resource, such as a file, a folder, or any other type of data source. If a dependency changes, the cached item is invalidated and removed from the cache.

The Caching Application Block ships with one notification-based expiration: the `FileDependency` expiration. With the `FileDependency` expiration, the item expires after a specific file has been modified. For example, a cache item can be set to expire if an XML file that contains product information has been modified. Listing 4.5 shows how to create a `FileDependency` expiration.

Listing 4.5: Creating a `FileDependency` Expiration

```
[C#]
FileDependency expireNotice = new FileDependency("ProductInfo.xml");
productsCache.Add(myProduct.ProductID, myProduct,
CacheItemPriority.Normal, null, expireNotice);

[Visual Basic]
Dim expireNotice As FileDependency = New FileDependency("Products.XML")
```

```
productsCache.Add(myProduct.ProductID, myProduct, _
CacheItemPriority.Normal, Nothing, expireNotice)
```

Creating a Custom Expiration Policy

More often than not, the master data source for an enterprise application is a database and not a file. Therefore, a useful notification-based expiration would be one that expires a cached item based on modifications that are made to a database table instead of a file. While no such notification-based expiration policy ships with Enterprise Library, there is an example of a similar type of expiration that extends the ASP.NET cache capabilities. It was developed by Rob Howard and can be found at www.gotdotnet.com/team/rhoward. It is called the `SqlDependency Expiration` and can be found under the example for ASP.NET Cache Invalidation on Database Change. I have taken the ideas behind this expiration policy and refactored it to not only work with Enterprise Library's Caching Application Block, but to also take advantage of the Data Access Application Block's data transparency features (explained in more detail in Chapter 3).

Fortunately, the designers of the Caching Application Block foresaw that there might be a need for other expiration policies other than the ones that shipped with Enterprise Library and allowed the addition of custom expiration policies as an extension point. All that is required of a custom expiration policy is to implement the `ICacheItemExpiration` interface. This interface contains three methods: `Initialize`, `HasExpired`, and `Notify`. Listing 4.6 shows the `HasExpired` method for a custom `DatabaseDependency` expiration policy. This is the most interesting part of this expiration policy, because it is the check to determine if any data in the table has been modified and signifies to the `BackgroundScheduler` that this item has expired if it has. The `Notify` and `Initialize` methods for this expiration policy do nothing.

LISTING 4.6: `HasExpired` Method for the `DatabaseDependency` Expiration Policy

```
[C#]
public bool HasExpired()
{
     bool bRetVal = false;
     try
```

```
    {
        DateTime currentLastWriteTime = DateTime.MinValue;
        Database db =
            DatabaseFactory.CreateDatabase
            (dependencyDatabaseInstance);

        IDataReader dataReader =
            db.ExecuteReader
            ("GetLastNotificationDate", dependencyTableName);

        if( dataReader.Read())
            currentLastWriteTime = dataReader.IsDBNull(0) ?
                                    DateTime.MinValue :
                                    dataReader.GetDateTime( 0 );
        dataReader.Close();
        if (lastModifiedTime.Equals(DateTime.MinValue))
        {
            lastModifiedTime = currentLastWriteTime;
        }

        if (lastModifiedTime.Equals(currentLastWriteTime) == false)
        {
            lastModifiedTime = currentLastWriteTime;
            bRetVal = true;
        }
    }
    catch (Exception e)
    {
        throw new ApplicationException(String.Format("{0}: {1}",
                SR.ExceptionInvalidDatabaseNotificationInfo
                (dependencyTableName),e.Message), e);
    }
    return bRetVal;

}

[Visual Basic]
Public Function HasExpired() As Boolean
    Dim bRetVal As Boolean = False
    Try
        Dim currentLastWriteTime As DateTime = DateTime.MinValue
        Dim db As Database = _
            DatabaseFactory.CreateDatabase _
                (dependencyDatabaseInstance)

        Dim dataReader As IDataReader = _
            db.ExecuteReader _
             ("GetLastNotificationDate", dependencyTableName)

        If dataReader.Read() Then
```

```
                currentLastWriteTime = IIf(dataReader.IsDBNull(0), _
                                          DateTime.MinValue, _
                                          dataReader.GetDateTime(0))
            End If
            dataReader.Close()
            If lastModifiedTime.Equals(DateTime.MinValue) Then
                lastModifiedTime = currentLastWriteTime
            End If

            If lastModifiedTime.Equals(currentLastWriteTime) = False Then
                lastModifiedTime = currentLastWriteTime
                bRetVal = True
            End If
        Catch e As Exception
            Throw New ApplicationException(String.Format("{0}: {1}", _
                    SR.ExceptionInvalidDatabaseNotificationInfo _
                    (dependencyTableName),e.Message), e)
        End Try
        Return bRetVal
    End Function
```

After the `DatabaseDependency` expiration policy has been created, using it with the Caching Application Block is just as easy as using the other expiration policies (see Listing 4.7).

LISTING 4.7: Setting a `DatabaseDependency` Expiration Policy for a `CacheItem`

```
[C#]
//Monitor the Products table in the Northwind DB instance.
DatabaseDependency expireNotice =
          new DatabaseDependency("Northwind", "Products");
productsCache.Add(myProduct.ProductID, myProduct,
          CacheItemPriority.Normal, null, expireNotice);

[Visual Basic]
'Monitor the Products table in the Northwind DB instance.
Dim expireNotice As DatabaseDependency = _
          New DatabaseDependency ("Northwind", "Products");
productsCache.Add(myProduct.ProductID, myProduct, _
          CacheItemPriority.Normal, Nothing, expireNotice)
```

The `ICacheItemRefreshAction` Interface (aka `CacheItemRemovedCallback`)

The `ICacheItemRefreshAction` is a bit of a misnomer. The Caching Application Block does an excellent job of keeping similar terminology and design to what it laid out in the *Caching Architecture Guide for .NET Frame-*

work Applications; however, it seems to deviate on this one item. The delegate that is described as the `CacheItemRemovedCallback` in the *Caching Architecture Guide for .NET Framework Applications* is known as the `ICacheItemRefreshAction` interface in the Caching Application Block.

During the development of the Caching Application Block, the responsibility for this delegate changed. Originally, callbacks were only designed for expirations, and the purpose of the callback was solely to allow the owner of that item to refresh it in the cache. However, as development progressed, the requirement surfaced that callbacks were needed for removals and scavengings too, but the name was never changed. So, even though the name implies that an implementation of this interface should *refresh* a cached item, it is not necessary to do so. Rather, the `ICacheItemRefreshAction` interface just defines the contract that must be implemented so that an object will be notified when an item is removed from cache. It is then up to that implementation to determine what action should occur.

It is important to note that the implementing class of an `ICacheItemRefreshAction` must be serializable. Take care when implementing this interface not to create an object that maintains too much state about its environment, because all portions of its environment will be serialized as well, possibly creating a huge object graph. Figure 4.3 illustrates the `ICacheItemRefreshAction` interface as well as the enumeration that is passed to the `Refresh` method, which lists the possible values for why an item may have

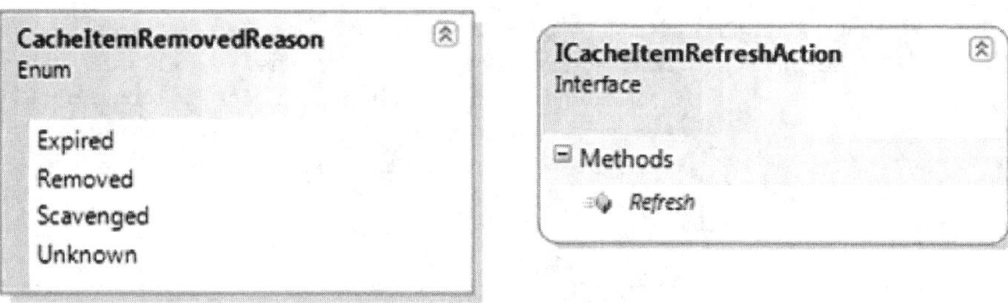

FIGURE 4.3: The `ICacheItemRefreshAction` Interface and Reasons for Removing an Item from Cache

been removed from the cache. This enumeration is named CacheItemRemovedReason.

As Figure 4.3 illustrates, there is only one method that must be developed to implement the ICacheItemRefreshAction interface. This is the Refresh method. Listing 4.8 provides an example of an implementation that does not refresh the cache, but instead leverages the Logging and Instrumentation Application Block to log the fact that an item was removed from the cache.

LISTING 4.8: Implementing the ICacheItemRefreshAction Interface

```
[C#]
public class LoggingRefreshAction : ICacheItemRefreshAction
{
    public void Refresh(string key,
                        object expiredValue,
                        CacheItemRemovedReason removalReason)
    {
        // Log that the item has been removed from cache.
        Logger.Write(String.Format("The {0} with the key {1} was
            removed from the cache for the following reason: {2}",
            expiredValue.GetType().Name, key,
            removalReason.ToString()), Category.General,
            Priority.Normal);
    }
}


[Visual Basic]
Public Class LoggingRefreshAction : Inherits ICacheItemRefreshAction
    Public Sub Refresh(ByVal key As String, _
                       ByVal expiredValue As Object, _
                       ByVal removalReason As CacheItemRemovedReason)

        'Log that the item has been removed from cache.
        Logger.Write(String.Format("The {0} with the key {1} was" & _
                       " removed from the cache for the following " & _
                       "reason: {2}", expiredValue.GetType().Name, key, _
                       removalReason.ToString()), Category.General, _
                       Priority.Normal)
    End Sub
End Class
```

CacheStorage

The *Caching Architecture Guide for .NET Framework Applications* defines the third major component of a custom cache triad to be CacheStorage. The CacheStorage implementation separates the cache functionality from the cache data store. The Caching Application Block implements this design and provides an extension point to the block with the IBackingStore interface and the BaseBackingStore abstract base class. This interface defines the contract that must be implemented by all BackingStores.

Implementers of this method are responsible for interacting with their underlying persistence mechanisms to store and retrieve CacheItems. All methods must guarantee Weak Exception Safety—that operations must complete entirely, or they must completely clean up from the failure and leave the cache in a consistent state. The mandatory cleanup process will remove all traces of the item that caused the failure, causing that item to be expunged from the cache entirely.

The abstract BaseBackingStore class, which implements the IBackingStore interface, is provided to facilitate the creation of BackingStores. This class contains implementations of common policies and utilities that can be used by all BackingStores. Table 4.2 lists the BaseBackingStore's methods and properties. All methods other than the Add, CurrentCacheManager, and Load methods are abstract and must therefore be overridden by a concrete BackingStore.

The concrete cache storage classes that are included with the Caching Application Block are the NullBackingStore, the IsolatedStorageBackingStore, and the DataBackingStore.

- The NullBackingStore class simply retains the cached items in memory.
- The IsolatedStorageBackingStore class stores cache items in domain-specific isolated storage and is configured to use a named isolated storage.
- The DataBackingStore class uses a database as its BackingStore and leverages the Data Access Application Block to connect to and perform database operations against a database.

TABLE 4.2: `BaseBackingStore` **Methods and Properties**

Method/Property	Description
`Add`	Is responsible for adding a `CacheItem` to the BackingStore. This operation must be successful even if an item with the same key already exists. This method must also meet the exception safety guarantee and make sure that all traces of the new or old item are gone if the add fails in any way.
`CurrentCacheManager`	Gets the current name of the `CacheManager` using this instance.
`Load`	Loads all `CacheItems` from the underlying database.
`AddNewItem`	A protected method that adds a new item to the persistence store.
`Count`	The number of objects stored in the BackingStore.
`Flush`	Flushes all `CacheItems` from the BackingStore. This method must meet the Strong Exception Safety guarantee.
`LoadDataFromStore`	A protected method that is responsible for loading items from the underlying persistence store.
`Remove`	An overloaded method that removes an item with the given key from the BackingStore.
`RemoveOldItem`	A protected method that removes existing items stored in the persistence store with the same key as the new item.
`UpdateLastAccessedTime`	An overloaded protected method that updates the last accessed time for a cache item referenced by this unique storage key.

The Caching Application Block communicates with all BackingStores through the `IBackingStore` interface. Figure 4.4 shows the relationship between the `IBackingStore`, `BaseBackingStore`, `DataBackingStore`, `IsolatedStorageBackingStore`, and `NullBackingStore` classes.

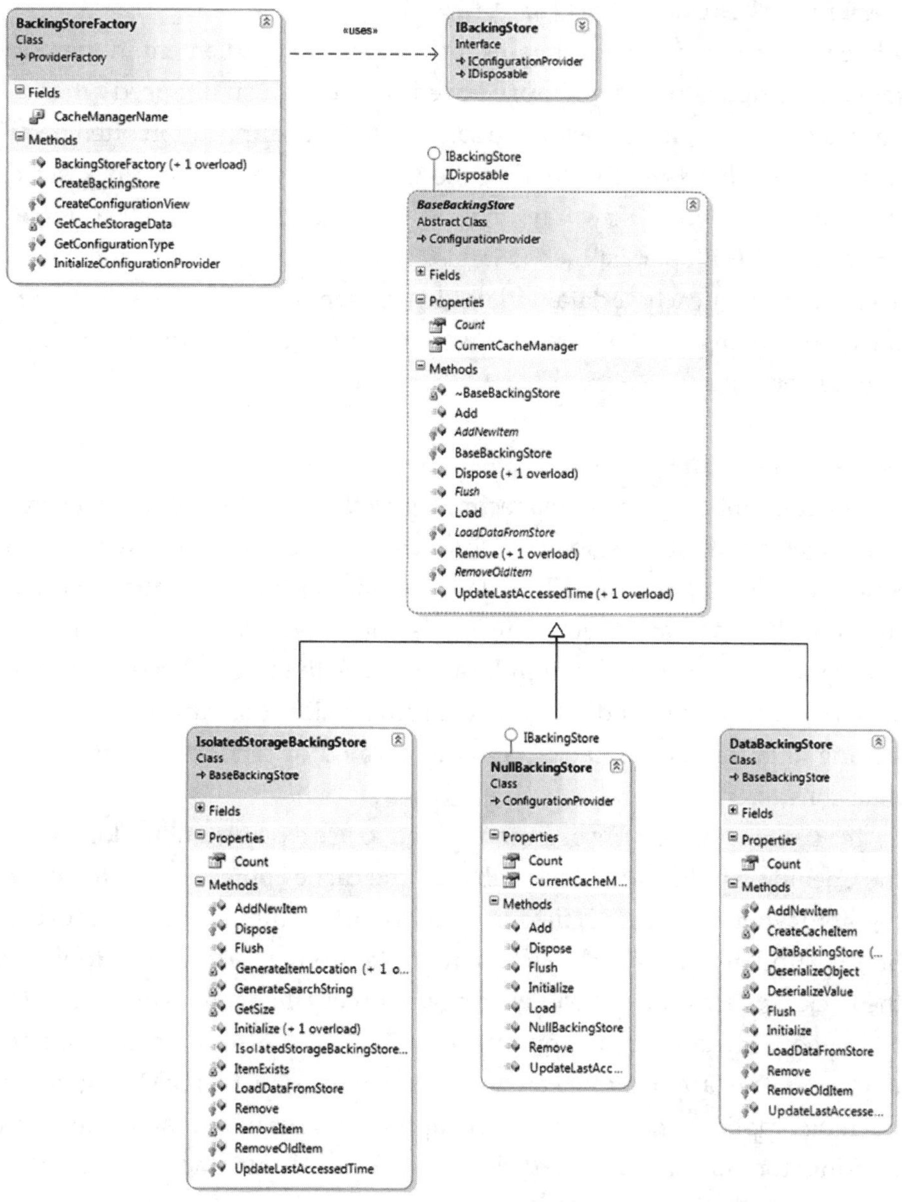

FIGURE 4.4: Available BackingStores in Enterprise Library's Caching Application Block

Memory-Resident Cache (`NullBackingStore`)

A memory-resident cache contains techniques that implement in-memory temporary data storage. Memory-based caching is usually used when an application is frequently using the same data or an application often needs to reacquire the data. By default, the Caching Application Block stores items only in memory by way of a `NullBackingStore`. The `NullBackingStore` doesn't persist cached items; cached data exists only in memory. This means that cached data will not live past application restarts; that is, the cached items will be refreshed from the original data source when the application restarts.

Disk-Resident Cache

A disk-resident cache contains technologies that use disk-based data storages, such as files or databases. Disk-based caching is useful when large amounts of data need to be handled, the data in the application services may not always be available for reacquisition, or the cached data must survive process recycles and computer reboots. Both the overhead associated with data processing and interprocess communications can be reduced by storing data that has already been transformed or rendered nearer to the data consumer.

If a `CacheManager` has been configured to use a persistent BackingStore, the Caching Application Block will load the cache contents from the BackingStore when the cache is first created. After the initial load, the BackingStore is updated after each operation on the in-memory cache. However, the BackingStore is never read from again (unless the cache is disposed and recreated, for example, on application restart). It is also important to note that while an application can use more than one CacheManager, the Caching Application Block does not support the use of the same persistent BackingStore location and partition name by multiple CacheManagers in an application. For example, configuring an application with two CacheManagers that both leverage isolated storage and have a partition name of *ProductCache* will most likely cause data corruption.

In its original state, the Caching Application Block supports two types of persistent BackingStores, each of which is suited to particular situations: isolated storage and data cache storage. Additionally, you can also extend the Caching Application Block to support additional types of BackingStores, including custom cache storage.

Isolated Storage. Isolated storage is a data storage mechanism that provides isolation and safety by defining standardized ways of associating code with saved data. When an application stores data in a file without leveraging isolated storage, the file name and storage location must be carefully chosen to minimize the possibility that the storage location will be known to another application and, therefore, vulnerable to corruption. Without a standard system in place to manage these problems, developing ad hoc techniques that minimize storage conflicts can be complex and the results can be unreliable.

With isolated storage, data is always isolated by user and by assembly. Credentials such as the origin or the strong name of the assembly determine assembly identity. Data can also be isolated by application domain using similar credentials. Because of the obstacles that must be overcome to isolate by user, isolated storage is rarely used for server applications; it is, however, a good choice for smart client applications.

When using isolated storage, you don't need to write any code to determine unique paths to specify safe locations in the file system, and data is protected from other applications that only have isolated storage access. "Hard-coded" information that indicates where an application's storage area is located is unnecessary.

When configured to use isolated storage, the Caching Application Block isolates the BackingStore by the cache instance name, the user name, the assembly, and the application domain. The data compartment is an abstraction, not a specific storage location; it consists of one or more isolated storage files, called **stores,** which contain the actual directory locations where data is stored. For example, a smart client application might have a data compartment associated with it, and a directory in the file system would implement the store that actually preserves the data for that application. For the developer, the location of the data compartment is transparent.[3]

---

3. Introductory formation about isolated storage is from http://msdn.microsoft.com/library/en-us/cpguide/html/cpconintroductiontoisolatedstorage.asp.

The decision whether or not to use isolated storage must be weighed very carefully. The general rule is that it usually makes sense for smart client applications where the cache needs to survive application restarts, but it does not generally make sense for server applications. The following are some other scenarios for using isolated storage.

- **Downloaded controls.** Managed code controls downloaded from the Internet are not allowed to write to the hard drive through normal I/O classes, but they can use isolated storage to persist users' settings and application states.
- **Persistent Web application storage.** Web applications are also prevented from using I/O classes. These programs can use isolated storage for the same purposes as downloaded components.
- **Shared component storage.** Components that are shared between applications can use isolated storage to provide controlled access to data stores.
- **Roaming.** Applications can also use isolated storage with roaming user profiles. This allows a user's isolated stores to roam with the profile.

Data Cache Storage. The data cache storage is a disk-resident storage mechanism that allows an application to leverage the Data Access Application Block to store cached data in a database. The Data Access Application Block BackingStore option is suitable for server applications where each application domain has its own cache and access to a database. Currently, the Caching Application Block includes a script to create the required database schema for Microsoft SQL Server and has only been tested against Microsoft SQL Server databases. Other database types, like Oracle and DB2, can certainly be used as BackingStores; however, you must first port the SQL script to support that database type.

It is important to note that each `CacheManager` object that is running in a single application domain must use a different portion of the database. A **partition** for a data cache store is defined as a combination of the application name and the cache instance name. Therefore, two separate and distinct applications cannot have the same application name and cache instance name where both leverage the same Data Access Application Block configuration. For example, two distinct applications that are both configured to use the `DataBackingStore`, both named Northwind, and both have `CacheManagers` named *ProductCache* will be seen as sharing a `CacheManager` across application domains and is not supported by the Caching Application Block. Rather, every application that leverages the data cache store should have its own instance and partition.

It is possible, however, to have the same application run in multiple processes (for example, the application is deployed on multiple computers in a Web farm). There are three possible ways to configure the Caching Application Block for this circumstance.

- **Partitioned caches.** All instances of the application use the same database instance, but each instance of the application uses a different database partition. In this scenario, each `CacheManager` operates independently. Although they share the same BackingStore database instance, each `CacheManager` persists the cache data to a different partition. In effect, there is one cache for each application instance. When an application restarts, each `CacheManager` loads its data from its own partition in the BackingStore.
- **Shared partition.** All instances of the application use the same database instance and the same database partition, and all `CacheManagers` can read from and write to the cache. Each instance of an application operates against a unique in-memory cache. When an application creates a `CacheManager`, the `CacheManager` populates the in-memory cache with the data in the BackingStore. This means that if an application creates a `CacheManager` when it starts, and if all of the application instances are started at the same time, each in-memory cache will be loaded with identical data. Because the applications are using the same partition, each application instance does not require additional storage in the BackingStore.

  After the `CacheManagers` are created, the in-memory cache contents are determined by the application instance using the cache. How an instance of the application uses the cache can vary from one instance to another as requests are routed to different servers. Different instances of an executing application can have in-memory caches with different contents. As an application adds and removes items, the contents of the in-memory cache change. The in-memory cache contents also change when the `CacheManager` removes or scavenges expired items.

As the in-memory cache changes, the `CacheManager` updates the BackingStore to reflect these changes. This is risky, though, because the BackingStore does not notify `CacheManager` instances when its contents have changed. Therefore, when one application instance changes the BackingStore contents, the other application instances will have in-memory caches that don't match the BackingStore data. This means that after an application restarts, the in-memory cache can have contents that are different from the contents it contained before the application restarted.

- **Single writer.** All instances of the application use the same database instance and the same database partition, and only one `CacheManager` can write to the cache. All `CacheManagers` can read from the cache. In this scenario, only one instance of the application writes to the cache. All other application instances can only read from the cache.

  The instance of the application that writes to the cache is the master. The in-memory cache of the master is always identical to the data in the BackingStore. The in-memory cache in each application instance is populated with data from the BackingStore at the time the `CacheManager` is created. The application instances that can only read data from the cache receive a snapshot of the data. However, this is rarely wise because the application instances don't have the ability to refresh their caches; therefore, their caches become stale and shrink as items expire.

Custom Cache Storage. As previously mentioned, Enterprise Library's Caching Application Block has been designed to allow another extension point by adding and using custom BackingStores in addition to the BackingStores that ship with the application block. There are two ways that the Caching Application Block can be extended with a BackingStore: by creating and adding a custom BackingStore, or by creating and adding a new BackingStore with all the design-time features as the ones that ship with the Caching Application Block.

The simplest approach from a development perspective is to simply create a new custom BackingStore that inherits from the abstract `BaseBackingStore` class. Be sure that the implementation guarantees the BackingStore will remain intact and functional if an exception occurs during any operation that accesses it. For example, if the application tries to add an item to the cache and there is already an item in the cache with the same name, an exception may be thrown. The implementation should remove the older item from both the BackingStore and the in-memory representation, and then it should throw an exception to the application.

Because of the way the Cache object operates, any BackingStore is guaranteed to be called in a single-threaded manner. This means that custom BackingStore implementations do not need to be overly concerned with thread safety. Furthermore, custom configuration information for a custom BackingStore can be retrieved through an `Extensions` collection that the Caching Application Block provides for all custom BackingStores. When the BackingStore is initialized, it can retrieve its necessary configuration information via this collection.

For example, imagine that a new BackingStore was needed in an enterprise that leveraged an XML file on the server instead of a database. A quick way to provide this type of functionality and use it with the Caching Application Block is to create a new class that derives from the `BaseBackingStore` class and overrides the abstract methods. This class would need to read configuration information to determine the name of the file that it should use as the BackingStore, and it might also need a partition name to avoid collisions between applications that might choose the same XML file name. Listing 4.9 illustrates how you can use the `Extensions` collection to get the configuration information for just such a custom BackingStore.

LISTING 4.9: `Initialize` Method for a Custom BackingStore

```
[C#]
public override void Initialize(ConfigurationView configurationView)
{
     ArgumentValidation.CheckForNullReference
          (configurationView, "configurationView");
     ArgumentValidation.CheckExpectedType
```

```
            (configurationView, typeof (CachingConfigurationView));

        CachingConfigurationView cachingConfigurationView =
            (CachingConfigurationView) configurationView;

        CustomCacheStorageData  customConfiguration =
            (CustomCacheStorageData)
                cachingConfigurationView.GetCacheStorageDataForCacheManager
                (CurrentCacheManager);

        partitionName = customConfiguration.Extensions["PartitionName"];
        xmlFileName = String.Format("{0}.{1}",
            customConfiguration.Extensions["XmlFileName"],partitionName);

        if (customConfiguration.StorageEncryption != null)
        {
            StorageEncryptionFactory encryptionFactory = new
                StorageEncryptionFactory
                (cachingConfigurationView.ConfigurationContext);

            encryptionProvider =
                encryptionFactory.CreateSymmetricProvider
                (CurrentCacheManager);
        }
    }

[Visual Basic]
Public Overrides Sub Initialize _
    (ByVal configurationView As ConfigurationView)

    ArgumentValidation.CheckForNullReference _
        (configurationView, "configurationView")
    ArgumentValidation.CheckExpectedType _
        (configurationView, GetType(CachingConfigurationView))

    Dim cachingConfigurationView As CachingConfigurationView = _
        CType(configurationView, CachingConfigurationView)

    Dim customConfiguration As CustomCacheStorageData = _
        (CustomCacheStorageData) _
        cachingConfigurationView.GetCacheStorageDataForCacheManager _
        (CurrentCacheManager)

    partitionName = customConfiguration.Extensions("PartitionName")
    xmlFileName = String.Format("{0}.{1}", _
        customConfiguration.Extensions("XmlFileName"),partitionName)

    If Not customConfiguration.StorageEncryption Is Nothing Then
        Dim encryptionFactory As StorageEncryptionFactory = _
```

```
            New StorageEncryptionFactory _
                (cachingConfigurationView.ConfigurationContext)

        encryptionProvider = _
            encryptionFactory.CreateSymmetricProvider _
            (CurrentCacheManager)
    End If
End Sub
```

Implementing this method as well as the abstract methods defined by the `BaseBackingStore` class makes it easy to create new custom BackingStores. This is a nice feature of the Caching Application Block because it does not tie an enterprise into just using the BackingStores that ship with the application block, and it doesn't require a massive amount of development to create a new one.

One of the worrisome aspects of using this approach, however, is that the configuration information will not be strongly typed. That is, there is a greater possibility that an error can be made when entering the configuration information for a custom BackingStore than there is when adding configuration information for one of the BackingStores that ship with the Caching Application Block. The Enterprise Library Configuration Tool will not perform any validation on the name or the values of the items that are stored in the `Extensions` collection. For example, an administrator may accidentally transpose some of the characters for the name of the `XmlFileName` item by accidentally typing *XlmFileName*. Such an error would not be caught at design time, but rather it would be caught at runtime when an attempt to retrieve the `XmlFileName` item takes place in the `Initialize` method.

To avoid these types of errors and provide a more user-friendly experience for configuring a custom BackingStore, a new BackingStore can be created and used that has all the design-time features as the ones that ship with the Caching Application Block. To create such a BackingStore, a few more steps are required than with the kind of custom BackingStore just discussed.

The first task is to create a data transfer object that is responsible for housing the configuration information needed by the new BackingStore. By expanding the previous example and creating a custom BackingStore that uses an XML file, the custom BackingStore will need to retain information about the name of the XML file and the partition name. Therefore, a data transfer object must be created that encapsulates this information. This object will be used by design-time classes for setting the configuration information, and it will be used by the custom BackingStore to initialize itself in its `Initialize` method. Listing 4.10 shows two properties of an `xmlFileCacheStorageData` class that let the file name and partition name be set and retrieved.

LISTING 4.10: Properties for the `XmlFileCacheStorageData` Class

```
[C#]
[XmlAttribute("xmlFileName")]
public string XmlFileName
{
     get { return xmlFileName; }
     set { xmlFileName = value; }
}

[XmlAttribute("partitionName")]
public string PartitionName
{
     get { return partitionName; }
     set { partitionName = value; }
}

[Visual Basic]
<XmlAttribute("xmlFileName")> _
Public Property XmlFileName() As String
     Get
          Return xmlFileName
     End Get
     Set
          xmlFileName = Value
     End Set
End Property

<XmlAttribute("partitionName")> _
Public Property PartitionName() As String
     Get
          Return partitionName
     End Get
     Set
          partitionName = Value
     End Set
End Property
```

The second task that must be completed is the same as the task that needed to be completed for the previous type of custom BackingStore; that is, to create a class that inherits from the abstract `BaseBackingStore` class and override the abstract methods. The only difference between this class and the one created for the previous type is that in this class' `Initialize` method, the data transfer object that was just created will be used instead of the `CustomCacheStorageData` class. Listing 4.11 shows what the revised `Initialize` method would look like.

LISTING 4.11: `Initialize` Method for the `XmlFileBackingStore`

```
[C#]
public override void Initialize(ConfigurationView configurationView)
{
     ArgumentValidation.CheckForNullReference
          (configurationView, "configurationView");
     ArgumentValidation.CheckExpectedType
          (configurationView, typeof (CachingConfigurationView));

     CachingConfigurationView cachingConfigurationView =
          (CachingConfigurationView) configurationView;

     xmlFileCacheStorageData xmlFileConfiguration =
               (xmlFileCacheStorageData)
               cachingConfigurationView.GetCacheStorageDataForCacheManager
               (CurrentCacheManager);

     partitionName = xmlFileConfiguration.PartitionName;
     xmlFileName = String.Format("{0}.{1}",
               xmlFileConfiguration.XmlFileName,
               xmlFileConfiguration.PartitionName);

     if (xmlFileConfiguration.StorageEncryption != null)
     {
          StorageEncryptionFactory encryptionFactory = new
               StorageEncryptionFactory
               (cachingConfigurationView.ConfigurationContext);

          encryptionProvider =
               encryptionFactory.CreateSymmetricProvider
               (CurrentCacheManager);
     }
}

[Visual Basic]
Public Overrides Sub Initialize _
```

```
    (ByVal configurationView As ConfigurationView)

    ArgumentValidation.CheckForNullReference _
         (configurationView, "configurationView")
    ArgumentValidation.CheckExpectedType _
         (configurationView, GetType(CachingConfigurationView))

    Dim cachingConfigurationView As CachingConfigurationView = _
         CType(configurationView, CachingConfigurationView)

    Dim xmlFileConfiguration As xmlFileCacheStorageData = CType _
         (cachingConfigurationView.GetCacheStorageDataForCacheManager _
         (CurrentCacheManager), xmlFileCacheStorageData)

    Dim partitionName = xmlFileConfiguration.PartitionName
    Dim xmlFileName = String.Format("{0}.{1}", _
         xmlFileConfiguration.XmlFileName, _
         xmlFileConfiguration.PartitionName)

    If Not xmlFileConfiguration.StorageEncryption Is Nothing Then
         Dim encryptionFactory As StorageEncryptionFactory = New _
              StorageEncryptionFactory _
               (cachingConfigurationView.ConfigurationContext)

         encryptionProvider = _
         encryptionFactory.CreateSymmetricProvider _
              (CurrentCacheManager)
    End If
End Sub
```

The last step is to create the design-time classes that allow the Enterprise Library Configuration Tool to present the user-friendly interface that makes configuring a new BackingStore easier and less error-prone. This step is not absolutely necessary; a new BackingStore can still be used even if design-time classes for it do not exist. In that case, however, the configuration information for it needs to be entered and modified manually, and the benefits with respect to validating configuration information will not be realized.

Three tasks must be performed to create the design-time classes needed to configure a new BackingStore.

1. Create a `ConfigurationNode` for the new BackingStore.
2. Create a `ConfigurationDesignManager` for the new BackingStore.

3. Modify the AssemblyInfo file so the Enterprise Library Configuration Tool can recognize the design-time features for the new BackingStore.

Chapter 2 provides much more detail about how and why these classes need to be created. The next few paragraphs document the specific steps needed to create the design-time interface for the `XmlFileBackingStore`.

The first task is to create a new `ConfigurationNode` that provides a user with the ability to add and modify the configuration properties of the `XmlFileBackingStore`. The specific properties that need to be exposed are the `FileName` and the `PartitionName`. The Caching Application Block's design-time assembly provides an abstract base class named `CacheStorageNode` that makes it easier to create a `ConfigurationNode` for a BackingStore. Listing 4.12 shows the `XmlFileCacheStorageNode` class that is derived from the `CacheStorageNode` base class.

LISTING 4.12: `XmlFileCacheStorageNode` Class

```
[C#]
public class XmlFileCacheStorageNode : CacheStorageNode
{
     xmlFileCacheStorageData xmlFileCacheStorageData;

     public XmlFileCacheStorageNode():
          this(new xmlFileCacheStorageData(SR.XmlFileCacheStorage))
     {
     }

     [Browsable(false)]
     public override string Type
     {
          get { return xmlFileCacheStorageData.TypeName; }
     }

     [Required]
     [SRDescription(SR.Keys.FileNameDescription)]
     [SRCategory(SR.Keys.CategoryGeneral)]
     public string FileName
     {
          get { return xmlFileCacheStorageData.XmlFileName; }
          set { xmlFileCacheStorageData.XmlFileName = value; }
     }
```

```
    [Required]
    [SRDescription(SR.Keys.FilePartitionNameDesciption)]
    [SRCategory(SR.Keys.CategoryGeneral)]
    public string PartitionName
    {
        get { return xmlFileCacheStorageData.PartitionName; }
        set { xmlFileCacheStorageData.PartitionName = value; }
    }
}

[Visual Basic]
Public Class XmlFileCacheStorageNode : Inherits CacheStorageNode
    Private xmlFileCacheStorageData As xmlFileCacheStorageData

    Public Sub New()
        Me.New(New xmlFileCacheStorageData(SR.XmlFileCacheStorage))
    End Sub

    <Browsable(False)> _
    Public Overrides ReadOnly Property Type() As String
        Get
            Return xmlFileCacheStorageData.TypeName
        End Get
    End Property

    <Required, _
        SRDescription(SR.Keys.FileNameDescription), _
        SRCategory(SR.Keys.CategoryGeneral)> _
    Public Property FileName() As String
        Get
            Return xmlFileCacheStorageData.XmlFileName
        End Get
        Set
            xmlFileCacheStorageData.XmlFileName = Value
        End Set
    End Property

    <Required, _
        SRDescription(SR.Keys.FilePartitionNameDesciption), _
        SRCategory(SR.Keys.CategoryGeneral)> _
    Public Property PartitionName() As String
        Get
            Return xmlFileCacheStorageData.PartitionName
        End Get
        Set
            xmlFileCacheStorageData.PartitionName = Value
        End Set
    End Property
End Class
```

A new class that implements the IConfigurationDesignManager interface is needed to register the new XmlFileCacheStorageNode and associate menu items and commands with it. An XmlIncludeType also needs to be added so the Configuration Application Block knows how to create the xmlFileCacheStorageData type. Listing 4.13 shows the RegisterIncludeTypes and RegisterNodeTypes methods that are called from the virtual Register method for the new xmlFileBackingStoreConfigurationDesignManager.

Listing 4.13: Registration Methods for the xmlFileBackingStoreConfigurationDesignManager

```
[C#]
private static void RegisterXmlIncludeTypes
     (IServiceProvider serviceProvider)
{
     IXmlIncludeTypeService xmlIncludeTypeService =
          serviceProvider.GetService(typeof(IXmlIncludeTypeService))
          as IXmlIncludeTypeService;

     xmlIncludeTypeService.AddXmlIncludeType
          (CacheManagerSettings.SectionName,
          typeof(xmlFileCacheStorageData));
}

private static void RegisterNodeTypes(IServiceProvider serviceProvider)
{
     INodeCreationService nodeCreationService =
          ServiceHelper.GetNodeCreationService(serviceProvider);

     Type nodeType = typeof(XmlFileCacheStorageNode);

     NodeCreationEntry entry =
          NodeCreationEntry.CreateNodeCreationEntryNoMultiples
          (new AddChildNodeCommand(serviceProvider, nodeType), nodeType,
          typeof(xmlFileCacheStorageData), SR.XmlFileCacheStorage);

          nodeCreationService.AddNodeCreationEntry(entry);
}

[Visual Basic]
Private Shared Sub RegisterXmlIncludeTypes _
      (ByVal serviceProvider As IServiceProvider)

     Dim xmlIncludeTypeService As IXmlIncludeTypeService = _
          IIf(TypeOf serviceProvider.GetService _
```

```
            (GetType(IXmlIncludeTypeService)) Is IXmlIncludeTypeService, _
            CType(serviceProvider.GetService _
             (GetType(IXmlIncludeTypeService)), IXmlIncludeTypeService), _
            CType(Nothing, IXmlIncludeTypeService))

        xmlIncludeTypeService.AddXmlIncludeType _
       (CacheManagerSettings.SectionName, GetType(xmlFileCacheStorageData))
End Sub

Private Shared Sub RegisterNodeTypes _
             (ByVal serviceProvider As IServiceProvider)

        Dim nodeCreationService As INodeCreationService = _
            ServiceHelper.GetNodeCreationService(serviceProvider)

        Dim nodeType As Type = GetType(XmlFileCacheStorageNode)

        Dim entry As NodeCreationEntry = _
            NodeCreationEntry.CreateNodeCreationEntryNoMultiples _
            (New AddChildNodeCommand(serviceProvider, nodeType), _
                nodeType, GetType(xmlFileCacheStorageData), _
                SR.XmlFileCacheStorage)

        nodeCreationService.AddNodeCreationEntry(entry)
End Sub
```

Lastly, a new assembly attribute needs to be added to the `AssemblyInfo.cs` (or `vb`) file because the Enterprise Library Configuration Tool looks for this to determine whether it should load a new `ConfigurationDesignManager`. Listing 4.14 shows the part of the `AssemblyInfo` file that sets the `ConfigurationDesignManagerAttribute` to the `xmlFileBackingStoreConfigurationDesignManager`.

LISTING 4.14: Assembly Attribute for the `xmlFileBackingStoreConfigurationDesignManager`

```
[C#]
[assembly :
    ConfigurationDesignManager(
    typeof(xmlFileBackingStoreConfigurationDesignManager))
]

[Visual Basic]
<assembly : _
    ConfigurationDesignManager( _
    GetType(xmlFileBackingStoreConfigurationDesignManager))
>
```

Once this assembly has been compiled and deployed so the Enterprise Library Configuration Tool can access it, you can add and configure the `XmlFileBackingStore` just as easily as any of the `BackingStores` that ship with Enterprise Library's Caching Application Block. (You'll see how to do this for all of the BackingStores a little later in the chapter.) Figure 4.5 shows the list of options for adding a `BackingStore` in the Enterprise Library Configuration Tool once this new assembly has been deployed.

Encrypting Cached Data

It is often important to ensure that data that must be secured in its original format is also secured when being transmitted to and from the cache and when stored inside the cache. Data that is stored in a cache may be accessed or altered by a process that isn't permitted access to the master data. The `DataBackingStore`, `IsolatedStorageBackingStore`, and custom BackingStores allow cache item data to be encrypted before it is persisted to storage; however, the `NullBackingStore` does not.

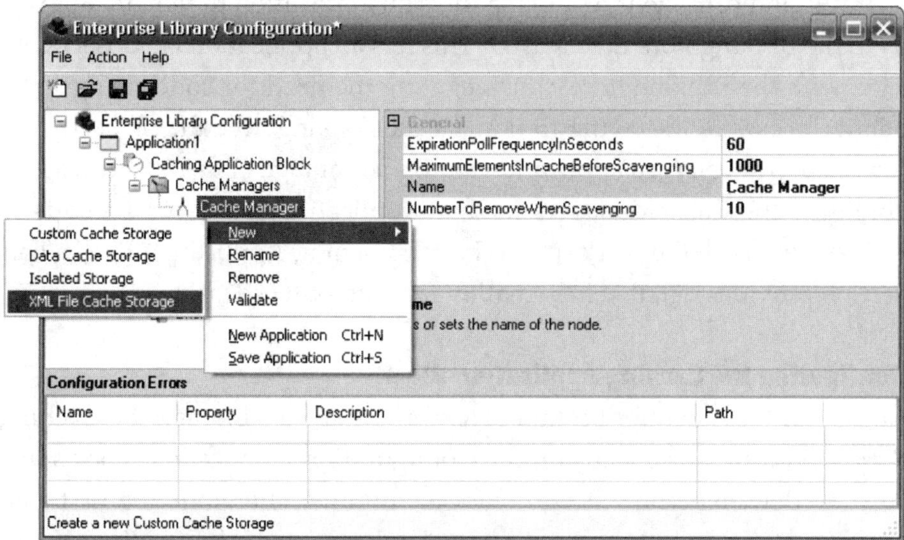

FIGURE 4.5: Available BackingStores Now Include the `XmlFileBackingStore`

Methods to prevent tampering of cache items usually include signing and verifying the items, and spoofing can be prevented by encrypting the cache items. The Caching Application Block does not offer any functionality in the way of signing data; however, it does offer the option to encrypt the cache data that is written to persistent storage. The Caching Application Block uses the Cryptography Application Block to create a symmetric encryption algorithm provider that you can use to encrypt cached data. You'll learn how to configure a BackingStore to use a symmetric encryption algorithm later in this chapter. More detailed information about using symmetric encryption algorithms in Enterprise Library can be found in Chapter 8.

Developing with the Caching Application Block

The previous section detailed the design of the Caching Application Block and showed that it met the design goals outlined in the *Caching Architecture Guide for .NET Framework Applications.* As you saw, the Caching Application Block has been designed for extensibility: It offers extension points for creating new expiration policies, `RefreshActions`, and BackingStores.

Another design goal for the Caching Application Block was to provide a simple and consistent API that allows an application to remain agnostic as to the BackingStore that is used. This lets an application be loosely coupled with the BackingStore, thus negating the need for code changes if a change occurs to the configuration for the BackingStore that is used. The first step to develop an application to take advantage of these features is to configure the CacheManagers for that application; the second step is to write code to call the API exposed by the Caching Application Block. This section provides detailed information for both of these tasks.

Configuring the Caching Application Block

Like all of the other application blocks in Enterprise Library, the Caching Application Block depends on the Configuration Application Block's features to determine how it will work at runtime. Therefore, the first step toward using the Caching Application Block is to add it by creating configuration information for it. The easiest and least error-prone way to do this is to use the Enterprise Library Configuration Tool (described in Chapter 2).

To add the Caching Application Block, open the application's domain configuration file in the Configuration Tool, right-click on the application node, and select *New > Caching Application Block.* Figure 4.6 shows the resulting configuration hierarchy. A new configuration section is added to the nodes underneath the settings for the Configuration Application Block, and a configuration hierarchy has been created to hold the settings for the Caching Application Block.

CacheManagers

In the previous version of the Caching Application Block, only one cache could exist per application domain. However, in Enterprise Library's version, many caches can be created and configured for an application. As described earlier in this chapter, there is a one-to-one relationship between a CacheManager and a cache.

To add a CacheManager to the configuration for an application, right-click the Cache Managers node and select *New > Cache Manager.* Since each instance of a CacheManager must have a unique name, it is advisable to rename the CacheManager with a name that is meaningful for the application (e.g., ReferenceDataCacheManager or CustomersCacheManager). The configuration information for each CacheManager is kept independent of the others. In addition to its `Name`, the other properties that can be configured for every CacheManager are `ExpirationPollFrequencyIn-Seconds`, `MaximumElementsInCacheBeforeScavenging`, and `Number-`

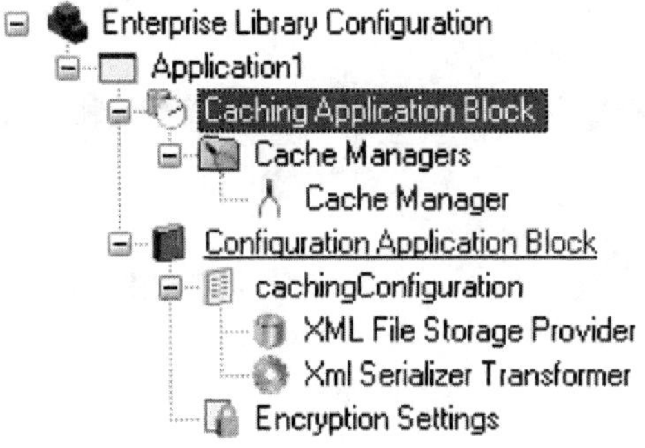

FIGURE 4.6: Hierarchy from Adding the Caching Application Block to an Application

ToRemoveWhenScavenging. Figure 4.7 shows the Property pane where these settings can be modified.

- The ExpirationPollFrequencyInSecond property determines how frequently the BackgroundScheduler checks for expired items. The unit is seconds; the minimum time is 1 second and the default time is 60 seconds. Modifying this value changes the frequency of the timer that regulates this BackgroundScheduler.
- The MaximumElementsInCacheBeforeScavenging is the maximum number of elements that can be held in the cache before scavenging begins. The default is 1,000 elements. To modify this value, simply change the number of elements for the property.
- The NumberToRemoveWhenScavenging is the number of elements that will be removed at one time from the cache after scavenging begins. The default is to remove 10 elements at a time. To modify this value, simply enter a different number for this property.

Additionally, the DefaultCacheManager property can be set for the Caching Application Block. The DefaultCacheManager property signifies the CacheManager that will be used if the name of a CacheManager is not supplied through the API. This can be set by selecting the Caching Application Block node and selecting an available CacheManager for the Default-CacheManager property. Figure 4.8 illustrates how to accomplish this.

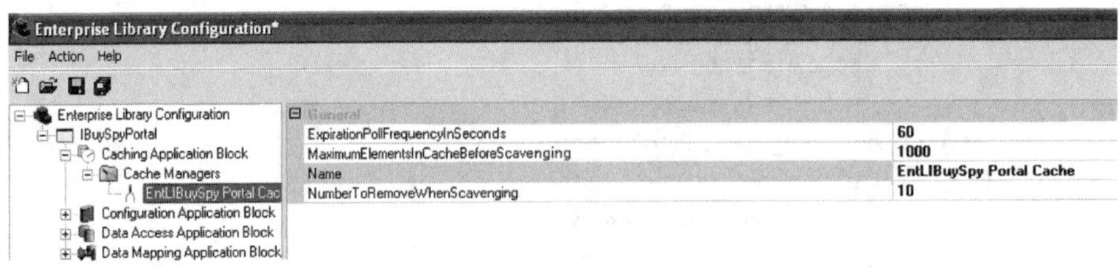

FIGURE 4.7: Setting Properties for a CacheManager

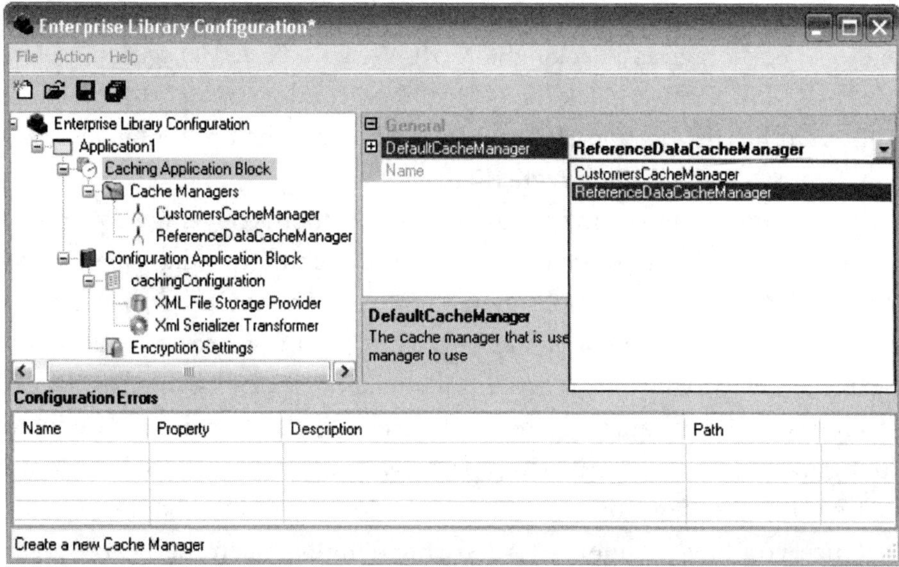

FIGURE 4.8: Setting the `DefaultCacheManager` Property

Cache Stores

In addition to selecting the data to be cached, another major consideration is where the data should be physically located if the cached data must survive application restarts. Each CacheManager can either be configured to store data only in memory or to store data both in memory and in persistent storage, also known as a **BackingStore.** Many caching implementations are available, all of which can be categorized as either a memory-resident cache or a disk-resident cache.

`NullBackingStore`. By default, the Caching Application Block stores items in memory by using the `NullBackingStore`. A CacheManager will use the `NullBackingStore` if no other BackingStore has been explicitly configured for it. If a BackingStore has been added and there is a need to switch back to the `NullBackingStore`, then the BackingStore that was added must be removed. This will allow the CacheManager to determine that there is no explicit BackingStore configured and cause it to use the `NullBackingStore`.

IsolatedStorageBackingStore. To configure an application to leverage isolated storage as a BackingStore, right-click a *CacheManager* and select *New > Isolated Storage.* Click the new subnode and enter a partition name. This identifies the portion of the isolated store that the CacheManager will use. Figure 4.9 illustrates how to do this.

DataBackingStore. To configure an application to leverage data cache storage as a BackingStore, you must add and configure the Data Access Application Block for the application. Right-click on the *Cache Manager* node and select *New > Data Cache Storage* to add the Data Access Application Block hierarchy to the overall configuration hierarchy. However, this doesn't configure the information for the Data Access Application Block. You must configure a `DatabaseInstance` separately. For information on how to do this, see the "Configuring a Database Provider" section in Chapter 3.

Once you have configured a `DatabaseInstance` in the Data Access Application Block, that `DatabaseInstance` can be selected from the drop-down list box for the data cache storage's `DatabaseInstance` property. Additionally, a partition name must be entered so two applications that point to the same `DatabaseInstance` don't corrupt each other's cached

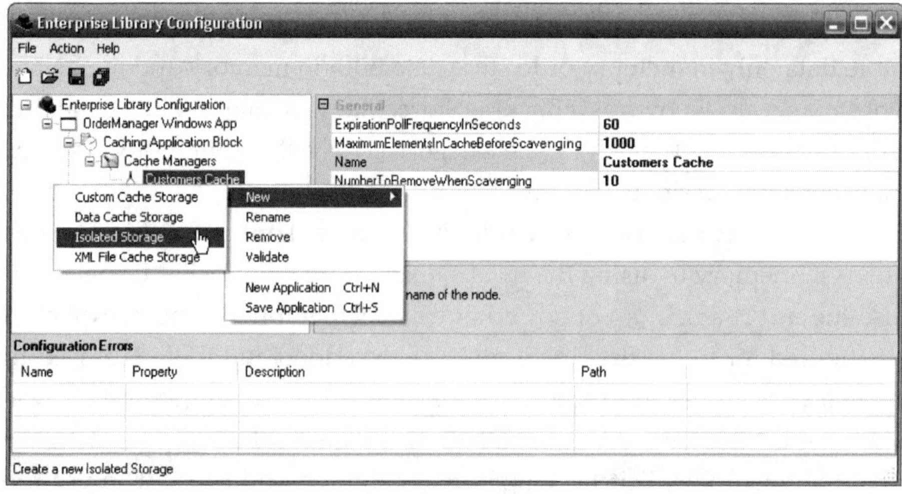

FIGURE 4.9: Configuring an Isolated Storage BackingStore

data. Figure 4.10 illustrates what the configuration for a data BackingStore might look like.

`Custom BackingStore.` Earlier in this chapter you saw how to create a custom BackingStore that is designed to work with the Caching Application Block. There are two kinds of BackingStores that can be created: a custom BackingStore and a new BackingStore that has the same design-time features as the ones that ship with the Caching Application Block.

To add the first type of custom BackingStore so that it can be used by a CacheManager, right-click on the *Cache Manager* node and select *New > Custom Cache Storage.* A new node will be created underneath the CacheManager node and three properties will be available to set the values for the `Name`, `Type`, and `Extensions` collection for the custom BackingStore.

The first property that you should configure is the `Type` property. Clicking the ellipses button for this property will display the Type Selector dialog. This dialog box only shows the classes that the tool recognizes as having implemented the `IBackingStore` interface. Figure 4.11 shows how to use this dialog box to select the `CustomXmlFileBackingStore` that was created earlier in this chapter.

Once the application has been configured with the type of the custom BackingStore, you can configure the `Extensions` collection to add any items that the BackingStore will need to initialize properly. Figure 4.12 shows how to add the `XmlFileName` and `PartitionName` items to the `Extensions` collection for this BackingStore. Setting these two properties correctly is crucial for a custom BackingStore to function properly.

If you took the additional steps to create a custom BackingStore that has the same design-time features as those provided by the Caching Applica-

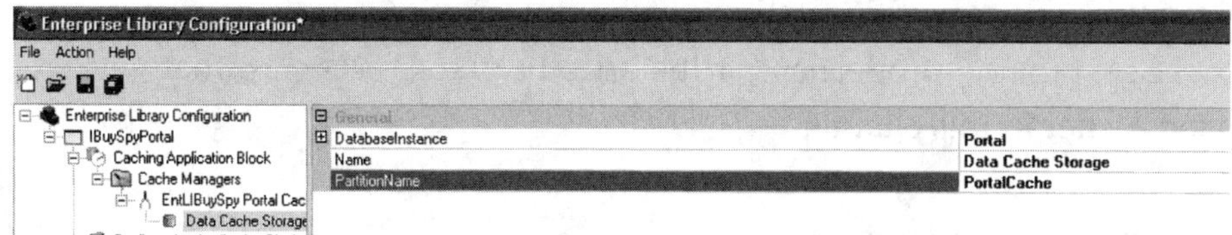

FIGURE 4.10: Configuring a Data BackingStore

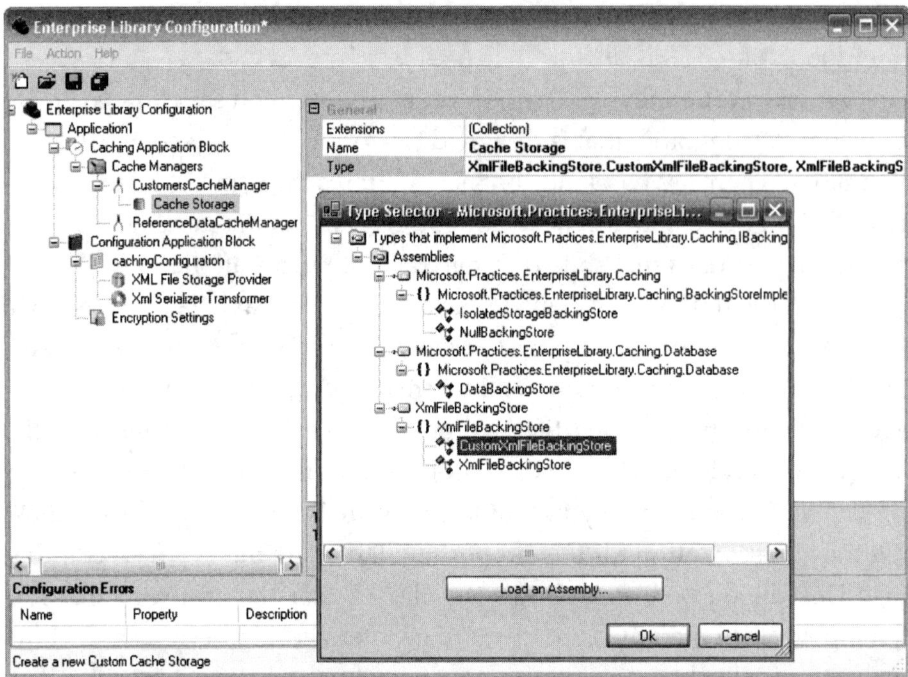

FIGURE 4.11: Selecting the Type for a Custom BackingStore

tion Block, then you don't need to set the `Type` and `Extensions` properties. Instead, the properties that are exposed by the new BackingStore will need to be set. A new menu option will appear for the CacheManager node that will let the new BackingStore be added for it (shown earlier in Figure 4.5). Once the new BackingStore has been added, its properties can be set in the same way that the properties for the IsloatedStorageBackingStore and DataBackingStore were set. Figure 4.13 shows how to set the `FileName` and `PartitionName` properties for the `XmlFileBackingStore` that was created earlier in this chapter.

Encrypting Cached Data

You can configure a BackingStore to leverage the features in the Cryptography Application Block to encrypt and decrypt cached data using a named symmetric encryption algorithm. To configure a BackingStore to use a symmetric encryption algorithm, right-click on the *BackingStore* node and select

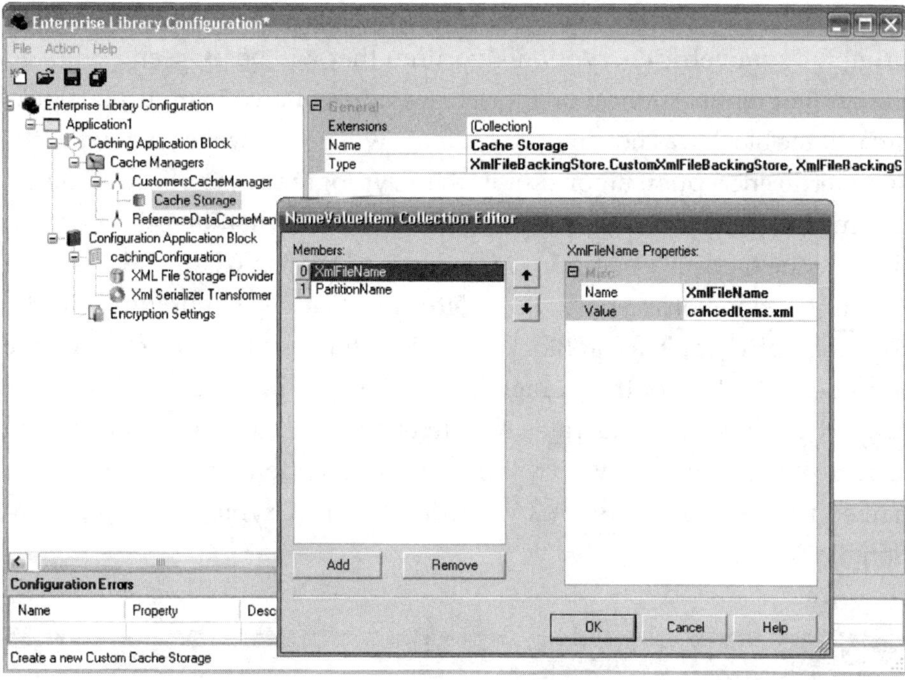

FIGURE 4.12: Adding Items to the `Extensions` Collection for a Custom BackingStore

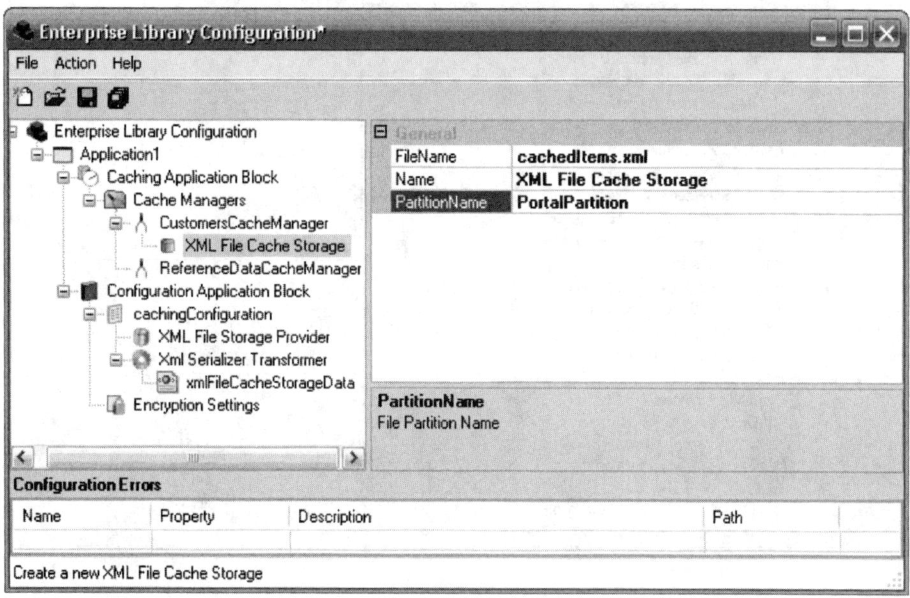

FIGURE 4.13: Configuring the New `XmlFileBackingStore`

New > Symmetric Storage Encryption. This will add a new node for configuring the symmetric encryption algorithm that will be used and will add the Cryptography Application Block to the application's configuration hierarchy if the block was not already added. It will not, however, configure the symmetric encryption algorithm in the Cryptography Application Block; this must be completed as a separate step. For information on how to do this, see the section "Encrypting/Decrypting Data" in Chapter 8.

Once a symmetric encryption algorithm has been configured in the Cryptography Application Block, that algorithm can be selected from the drop-down list box for the StorageEncryption node's `SymmetricProvider` property. Figure 4.14 illustrates how to enable encryption for the custom `XmlFileBackingStore` with a symmetric encryption algorithm provider named `RijndaelManaged` that was added to the Cryptography Application Block.

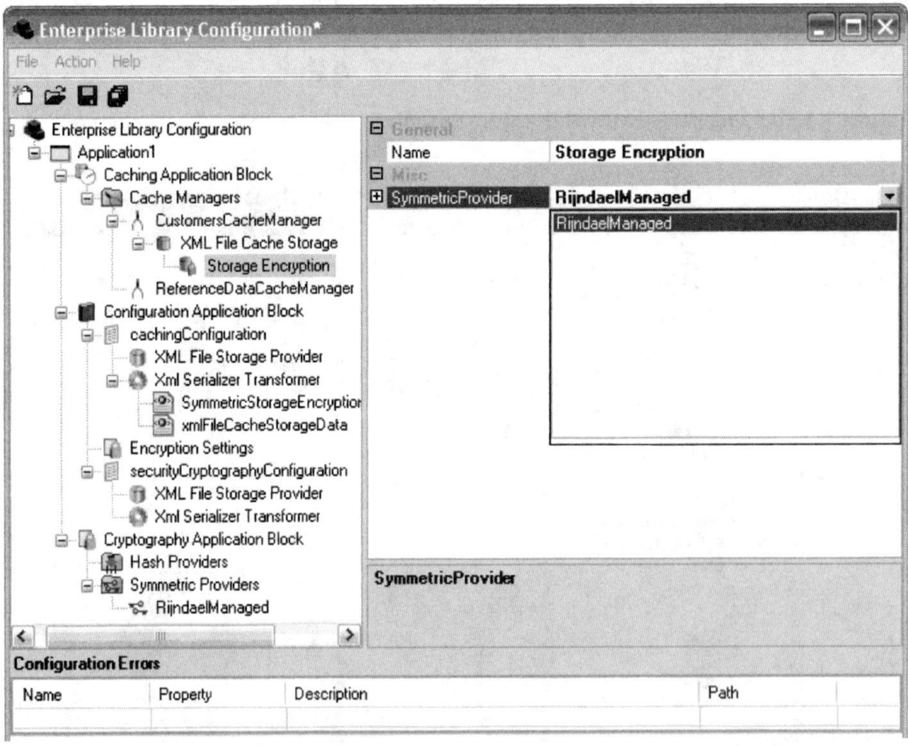

FIGURE 4.14: Configuring Encryption for the New `XmlFileBackingStore`

Using the Caching Application Block's API

Using the CacheFactory or CacheManagerFactory to obtain an instance of a CacheManager is the most probable starting point for performing any type of caching operation. The CacheFactory's overloaded GetCacheManager method will return the CacheManager that was configured as the DefaultCacheManager when the name of a CacheManager is not specified. Alternatively, a specific CacheManager can be obtained by supplying the name of the CacheManager as an argument to the GetCacheManager method. Listing 4.15 shows both methods for creating a CacheManager. The first line obtains the DefaultCacheManager and the second line obtains a CacheManager that has been configured with the name Products.

LISTING 4.15: Obtaining a CacheManager

```
[C#]
CacheManager myCache = CacheFactory.GetCacheManager();
CacheManager productsCache =
          CacheFactory.GetCacheManager("Products");

[Visual Basic]
Dim myCache As CacheManager = CacheFactory.GetCacheManager()
Dim productsCache As CacheManager = _
          CacheFactory.GetCacheManager("Products")
```

Adding Items to the Cache

A cache should be used to store items that are either expensive to create or expensive to transport and in which a degree of staleness is acceptable. This is typically semi-static, nontransactional data like reference data (e.g., countries, states, etc.) or customer information. With the Caching Application Block, there are several overloaded Add methods that make it possible to not only add an item to the cache, but also to set cache item expiration policies, priorities for the scavenging process, and cache item removal callbacks. The only caveat for adding an item to the cache is that the item must be remoting-serializable for it to work with any of the BackingStores that ship with the Caching Application Block. This is because the BackingStores serialize the object before storing it and deserialize it when the item is retrieved.

If the expiration policies, removal callback, or priority properties are not explicitly set in the Add method, then the Caching Application Block sets them to their default settings. The default setting for cache item expirations is `NeverExpire`; the default setting for the `CacheItemRefreshAction` is null (or Nothing in VB.NET), which indicates that no method will be notified when a `CacheItem` is removed; and the default setting for the scavenging priority is `Normal`.

Listing 4.16 shows the simplest way to call the `Add` method. It creates an object of type `Product` and then adds it to the cache, with the default scavenging priority (`Normal`), no callback to refresh the item if it expires, and no expiration policies.

LISTING 4.16: Adding an Item to the Cache with Default Settings

```
[C#]
Product product = new Product("Product1", "Pickled Peppers");
productsCache.Add(product.ProductID, product);


[Visual Basic]
Dim product As Product = New Product("Product1", "Pickled Peppers")
productsCache.Add(product.ProductID, product)
```

Expiration Policies. As mentioned earlier, the `CacheManager's Add` method is overloaded to allow expiration policies to be set for a cached item. The different types of expiration policies, as well as a step-by-step process for creating a new expiration policy, were discussed in detail earlier in this chapter.

There is no logical limit to the number of expiration policies that can be set for an item. If an item is added with multiple policies, the item will expire if any one of the expiration policy's criteria is met. Listing 4.17 adds a product to the product cache while setting several expiration policies, including the custom one created earlier in this chapter.

LISTING 4.17: Adding an Item to the Cache with Multiple Expiration Policies

```
[C#]
ICacheItemExpiration[2] cacheExpirys;
cacheExpirys[0] = new ExtendedFormatTime("0 0 * * 6");
TimeSpan expiryTime = new TimeSpan(0, 5, 0);
cacheExpirys[1] = new SlidingTime(expiryTime);
cacheExpirys[2] = new DatabaseDependency("Northwind", "Products");
productsCache.Add(myProduct.ProductID, myProduct,
                  CacheItemPriority.Normal, null, cacheExpirys);
```

```
[Visual Basic]
Dim cacheExpirys As ICacheItemExpiration(2)
Dim cacheExpirys(0) = New ExtendedFormatTime("0 0 * * 6")
Dim expiryTime As TimeSpan = New TimeSpan(0, 5, 0)
Dim cacheExpirys(1) = New SlidingTime(expiryTime)
Dim cacheExpirys(2) = New DatabaseDependency("Northwind", "Products")
productsCache.Add(myProduct.ProductID, myProduct, _
            CacheItemPriority.Normal, Nothing, cacheExpirys)
```

`CacheItemRemovedCallback` (aka `ICacheItemRefreshAction`). The `Add` method also gives you the ability to receive a callback after an item expires and is removed from the cache. Although it isn't mandatory, the application can refresh the item at this time. This might be useful for reducing the degree of staleness for a particular cached item, as the application can determine if the item was removed because of an external change and can refresh the cached item with fresh data if appropriate.

In the Caching Application Block, the interface that allows this capability is the `ICacheRefreshAction` interface. The `Add` method lets an object that implements the interface `ICacheItemRefreshAction` be specified. The object's `Refresh` method is called whenever this item is removed from the cache, providing the opportunity to refresh items in the cache. Earlier in this chapter you saw how to create a class that implements the `ICacheItemRefreshAction` interface. In Listing 4.18, an item is added to the cache and a `RefreshAction` is set that will be notified when the item is removed from the cache.

LISTING 4.18: Adding an Item to the Cache with a `RefreshAction`

```
 [C#]
productsCache.Add(product.ProductID, product, 2, new
          ProductCacheRefreshAction(),
          new SlidingTime(TimeSpan.FromMinutes(5)));

[Visual Basic]
productsCache.Add(product.ProductID, product, 2, _
          New ProductCacheRefreshAction, _
          New SlidingTime(TimeSpan.FromMinutes(5)))
```

Loading Items in the Cache. Before data can be retrieved from a cache, data must first be loaded into it. For example, in a retail application it may make sense to load data about various products, or all products, into the cache when the application initializes. You can use various methods to load data into a cache. When determining the data acquisition methods for a cache, it is important to consider how much data will need to be acquired and when it will need to be loaded. The two methods for loading data into the cache are proactive loading and reactive loading.

A **proactive loading method** retrieves required data for an application or process before it is requested and typically caches it for the lifetime of the application or the process. Proactively loading data into a cache usually occurs when the application or process starts. Proactive caching is recommended in the following situations.

- The static or semi-static state that will be cached has known update periods. In other scenarios, the state might expire before it is used.
- The state has a known lifetime.
- The state has a known size. Proactively caching data when the size of the data is unknown might exhaust system resources.
- Resources are problematic, such as a slow database, a slow network, or unreliable Web services. Proactively caching data allows an application to retrieve all of the state up front, cache it, and work against the cache as much as possible. This works well for occasionally connected applications like a smart client application too.

There are several advantages to proactively loading data into a cache.

- Because it can be guaranteed that the data has been loaded into the cache, in theory there is no need to check whether the state exists in the cache. It is wise, however, to always check whether an item exists in the cache before retrieving it, because the cache may have been flushed or individual items may have been removed for some reason.
- Application performance can be improved because cache operations are optimized when loading state into the cache proactively, and application response times improve because all of the data is cached. This is generally true as long as the cost for managing the cache is not higher than the cost for fetching the data.

Conversely, there are also a few disadvantages to proactively loading data into cache.

- Proactive loading may not result in the most optimized system because a large amount of the state is cached, and all of the state may not be needed. For example, an application may contain 100 processes, each of which may require a few items in the cache. If a user launches this application but activates only one process, hundreds of items are needlessly cached.
- Proactive caching may result in an implementation that is more complex than traditional techniques, in which each item is retrieved synchronously in a well-known program flow. Proactive caching can sometimes require working with several threads. Synchronizing these threads with the application main thread, keeping track of their status, and handling exceptions in an asynchronous programming model can be more difficult than may be necessary.

If proactive loading is not leveraged properly, applications may initialize slowly. When proactive caching is implemented, it is important to load as much state as needed when the application or process initializes. You should use an asynchronous programming model like asynchronous pull loading to load the state on a background thread.

Asynchronous pull loading is a proactive loading process that is based on expected, not actual, usage. When using asynchronous pull loading, none of the requests for data perform worse than any other because the state is retrieved into the cache proactively, not as a response to a specific request. Service agent caches are usually good candidates for asynchronous pull loading, especially if the data comes from many services and needs to be consolidated for consumption. Listing 4.19 shows how to implement asynchronous pull loading to populate a CacheManager with static employee information like an employee's photograph.

Listing 4.19: Asynchronous Pull Loading of Employee Information

```
[C#]
private void PopulateCache()
{
     CacheManager cache = CacheFactory.GetCacheManager();
     EmployeesDataSet dsEmployees = LoadContactDetails();

     foreach(EmployeesDataSet.EmployeesRow employee
               in dsEmployees.Employees)
     {
          if (!cache.Contains(employee.EmployeeID.ToString()))
          {
               EmployeeDataProvider dataProvider =
                    new EmployeeDataProvider();
               cache.Add(employee.EmployeeID.ToString(),
                  dataProvider.GetEmployeePhotoData(employee.EmployeeID));
          }
     }
}

private delegate void PopulateCacheDelegate();

public void BeginBackgroundLoad()
{
     if (!ConnectionManager.IsOnline)
          return;

     PopulateCacheDelegate mi = new PopulateCacheDelegate(PopulateCache);
     mi.BeginInvoke(null, null);
}

[Visual Basic]
Private Sub PopulateCache()
     Dim cache As CacheManager = CacheFactory.GetCacheManager()
     Dim dsEmployees As EmployeesDataSet = LoadContactDetails()

     Dim employee As EmployeesDataSet.EmployeesRow
     For Each employee In dsEmployees.Employees
          If Not cache.Contains(employee.EmployeeID.ToString()) Then
               Dim dataProvider As New EmployeeDataProvider
               cache.Add(employee.EmployeeID.ToString(), _
                   dataProvider.GetEmployeePhotoData(employee.EmployeeID))
          End If
     Next employee
End Sub

Delegate Sub PopulateCacheDelegate()

Public Sub BeginBackgroundLoad()
```

```
    If Not ConnectionManager.IsOnline Then
        Return
    End If

    Dim mi As New PopulateCacheDelegate(AddressOf PopulateCache)
   mi.BeginInvoke(Nothing, Nothing)
End Sub
```

A **reactive loading method** retrieves data when it is requested by the application and then caches it for future requests. Reactive caching is recommended in the following situations.

- Large amounts of state are used and adequate resources may not exist to cache all of the state for the entire application at once.
- Resources are reliable and responsive, such as a database, network, or Web service that will not impede application stability and performance.
- Data is not available at application or process initialization. For example, the data that should be cached is affected by user input such as common search queries.

There are several advantages to reactively loading data into a cache.

- Because large amounts of data are not loaded when the application initializes, system resources are not misused.
- Caching is optimized because only requested items are stored.

There are also a few disadvantages to reactively loading data into a cache.

- Performance might decrease when any piece of data is requested the first time because it must be loaded from the source, not retrieved from the cache.
- A check must be made against the cache as to whether an item exists in the cache before it can be used. Implementing this checking in every service agent can result in additional conditional logic in the code.

Reactive cache loading means that the state is loaded only when it is requested, and it is acquired using a synchronous programming model like

synchronous pull loading. With synchronous pull loading, the data is loaded into the cache when the application requires the data. When using synchronous pull loading, the first request for the data decreases performance because the data has to be retrieved from the application service. Therefore, synchronous pull loading is best used when a specific piece of state is needed rather than all of the state for the entire application or process.

It is relatively easy to implement synchronous pull loading, because all of the loading code is written in the application and none is needed in the underlying application services. However, the major problem that occurs when using pull loading is state staleness. If no mechanism exists to notify the cache of data changes in the underlying application services, data changes in the application services might not be reflected in the cached data. Listing 4.20 demonstrates the simplicity involved with synchronously pull loading static product information.

LISTING 4.20: Synchronous Pull Loading of Product Information

```
[C#]
Product product = (Product) productsCache.GetData(productID);

if (product == null)
{
    // Retrieve from the data provider and cache it for more requests.
    product = dataProvider.GetProductByID(productID);
    if (product != null)
    {
        productsCache.Add(productID, product);
    }
}

[Visual Basic]
Dim product As Product = CType(productsCache.GetData(productID), Product)

If product Is Nothing Then
    ' Retrieve from the data provider and cache it for more requests.
    product = dataProvider.GetProductByID(productID)

    If Not product Is Nothing Then
       productsCache.Add(productID, product)
    End If
End If
```

Retrieving Items from the Cache

The Caching Application Block is generic in that it supports the storage of many types of items (as long as they are remoting-serializable). You can make several different design choices when designing a generic cache. One possible design allows a cache to have multiple potential keys with a hash table for each identifier. However, doing so makes it harder to remove items from the cache because information is needed for all of the hash tables that refer to the cache item. The Caching Application Block design doesn't allow multiple keys; only one primary key or identifier is used to identify an item in the cache. Its API lets you load and retrieve cached items based on a single identifier, for example, a product ID.

When different types of items are being stored, it is best to create multiple CacheManagers—one CacheManager for each type of item. This increases the efficiency of data searching when retrieving an item because it reduces the number of items in each cache. The `GetData` method is used to retrieve items from a CacheManager. Because the CacheManager deals with its data in a generic fashion, the `GetData` cannot be aware what data type to return and therefore returns a data type of `object`. Consumers of this method must cast the `object` to the proper type. Furthermore, it is important to note that if an item doesn't exist in the cache for the requested key, the `GetData` method will return a null (or Nothing in VB.NET). Listing 4.21 shows how you can use the `GetData` method to retrieve an instance of the serializable `Product` object from a `ProductsCache`.

LISTING 4.21: Retrieving Items from the Cache

```
[C#]
//Read the item from the cache. If the item is not found
//in the cache, the return value will be null.
Product product = (Product) productsCache.GetData(productID);

[Visual Basic]
'Read the item from the cache. If the item is not found
'in the cache, the return value will be Nothing.
Dim product As Product = DirectCast _
     (productsCache.GetData(productID), Product)
```

Removing Items from the Cache

This chapter has already discussed how the Caching Application Block's scavenging and expiration processes automatically remove items from the cache according to the priorities and expiration policies of the items. Items can also be explicitly removed from the cache. For example, it may make sense to simply remove items from a cache when an update to an item occurs, so the item will be restored from its original data source the next time it is retrieved.

The `CacheManager`'s `Remove` method removes a specific item from a cache. Listing 4.22 shows how you can use the `Remove` method to remove a product from the `ProductsCache`.

LISTING 4.22: Removing an Item from the Cache

```
[C#]
productsCache.Remove(productID);

[Visual Basic]
productsCache.Remove(productID)
```

Flushing the Cache

Flushing lets the management of cached items ensure that storage, memory, and other resources are used efficiently. Flushing is different from expiration policies in that valid cache items may be removed to make space for more frequently used items, whereas expiration policies are used to remove invalid items.

There are two categories of flushing techniques: explicit flushing and scavenging. **Explicit flushing** requires that code be written not only to determine when the item should be flushed from cache but also to flush it. **Scavenging** can be implemented to flush items based on when they were last used, how often they have been used, or using priorities that were assigned in an application. With scavenging, an algorithm is used for the cache to determine what items can be flushed.

Explicit Flushing. Different scenarios require that cache stores be explicitly flushed by instructing the cache to clear its content. Explicit flushing can be implemented either manually or programmatically. For example, if cached data becomes obsolete or damaged, there may be an immediate need to clear the contents of the cache. In this situation, a system administrator must be able to explicitly flush the cache.

The CacheManager's Flush method removes all the items in a cache. If an error occurs, the cache does not change. Listing 4.23 shows how to flush the ProductsCache.

LISTING 4.23: Explicitly Flushing the Cache

```
[C#]
productsCache.Flush();

[Visual Basic]
productsCache.Flush()
```

Scavenging. You can use a scavenging algorithm to automatically remove seldom used or unimportant items from the cache when system memory or some other resource becomes scarce. Typically, scavenging is activated when storage resources become scarce, but it can also be activated to save computing resources—for example, to reduce the time and CPU cycles required to look up specific cached items.

The Caching Application Block's scavenging process is performed by the BackgroundScheduler. It checks the cache every time an item is added to see if the number of items in the cache has reached a predetermined limit. This is determined by the MaximumElementsInCacheBeforeScavenging property. The Caching Application Block also uses the value for a Cache-Manager's NumberToRemoveWhenScavenging property to determine how many items should be removed from the cache after scavenging begins. The earlier section about configuration showed how to configure both of these properties.

Unlike the expiration process, the scavenging process performs marking and sweeping in a single pass. When an item is added to the cache, it is given one of four priorities: Low, Normal, High, or Not Removable. The BackgroundScheduler determines which items should be scavenged by doing a major sort based on priority and a minor sort based on the last time the item was accessed. For example, an item with a Low priority that has just been used will be scavenged before something with a High priority that has not been accessed for three years. The default value is Normal. The NotRemovable priority is used when it is imperative that an item remain in the cache until it expires. However, the cache should not be the only location where such an item exists. A cache should be used to improve performance and scalability, but it should never be used as a form of permanent storage.

Summary

This chapter covered the design of Enterprise Library's Caching Application Block and how to configure and develop an application to use it. The design for this application block was based primarily on the Solution Blueprint that is documented in *Caching Architecture Guide for .NET Framework Applications.* Additionally, it was designed to allow an application to be decoupled from the type of BackingStore that may be used for persisting cached data between application restarts.

This chapter included a detailed analysis of the design for the Caching Application Block and compared the classes and interfaces in its design to the design suggested by the *Caching Architecture Guide for .NET Framework Applications* Solution Blueprint. It described how the Caching Application Block provides extension points by creating new expiration policies, item removal callbacks, and BackingStore providers. Lastly, it covered how to configure the Caching Application Block and how to develop an application to use the application programming interface that this block provides.

The two key points you should understand from this chapter are that the Caching Application Block is based on the suggested best practices for a custom cache design, and that it provides a simple interface that makes it easy for an application architect to design caching capabilities into an application in an effort to ensure that the application can be tuned for optimal performance, scalability, and availability.

5

The Exception Handling Application Block

I WAS ONCE BROUGHT into a company to help them diagnose an issue they were having with one of their applications that had already been deployed to production. The Web application was redirecting users to the home page for every request. It was causing users a great deal of pain and the company was losing a lot of business. Upon investigation, I observed that the code shown in Listing 5.1 was smattered throughout the application.

Listing 5.1: Bad Example of Exception Handling

```
Try
...
Catch ex As Exception
     Response.Redirect("welcome.aspx")
End Try
```

Exceptions were being caught and "swallowed" by the application. There was no notification or record of the actual issues that were occurring. The company lost several days of business while the application was malfunctioning, and the application frustrated many of the end users. I don't know how many dollars of business were lost; however, I do know that the consulting firm that developed the application was written off from ever doing business with that company again.

This is an example of what *not* to do when it comes to exception handling. Most developers understand that it is important to handle the exceptions that occur in an application; however, this example surfaces another point that may be less understood: It can often be worse to do exception handling wrong than not to do exception handling at all. The best solution is to handle exceptions in accordance with the best practices documented by the Microsoft patterns & practices team and highlighted in this chapter.

This chapter focuses on how to use Enterprise Library's Exception Handling Application Block (EHAB) so you can avoid scenarios like that shown in Listing 5.1. It describes how the design for the Exception Handling Application Block lets the way exceptions are handled and propagated through an application be expressed through configuration instead of code. It also shows how the application block has been designed for extensibility and provides examples for how to extend it.

The chapter goes into detail on how an enterprise can extend the Exception Handling Application Block with new `ExceptionFormatters` and `ExceptionHandlers`, because I believe it is important to understand that the Exception Handling Application Block does not constrain an enterprise from handling and formatting messages in the ways that best suit their needs. Lastly, it shows you how to configure and develop an application so you can benefit from the features provided by the Exception Handling Application Block.

What Is the Exception Handling Application Block?

Enterprise Library's Exception Handling Application Block is a policy-driven system that lets an administrator determine *how* specific exceptions are handled in an application and allows a developer to concentrate on *why* and *where* exceptions should be handled. The block is an implementation of the best practices promoted by the Microsoft patterns & practices team. Its design allows exception policies to be defined for an application so that many different types of exceptions can be handled by different kinds of exception handlers without the need to specify these relationships through code.

Furthermore, the design provides extension points for creating new exception handlers and exception formatters that can be used by the Exception Handling Application Block. For example, if the exception handlers that ship with the block don't meet the needs for your application, you can develop a new one that can be used just as easily as the ones that ship with the block. The design for this application block allows for an extremely simple programming interface so application developers don't need to be concerned how an exception gets handled. This lets the code for an application remain unchanged even if a change is made to the way an exception is handled or exception handlers are added or removed for a particular scenario.

Relationship to the Exception Management Application Block

A previous application block existed that was named the Exception Management Application Block (EMAB). The Exception Management Application Block served two different purposes. The first was to assist developers in subscribing to the published best practices for creating their own custom application exceptions. The second was to provide a method for publishing this exception information to particular locations while allowing the application to remain agnostic as to the ultimate destination for the exception. The default location to which exceptions were published was the Windows Event Log; however, if an application needed to publish exception information to a different location, a developer could create a custom `Publisher` that could write to another location. The custom `Publisher` could be developed outside of the actual application, and the application could simply be configured to use the new publisher. In other words, an `ExceptionPublisher` in the Exception Management Application Block could really have been thought of as a "handler" for exceptions.

That brings us back to the Exception Handling Application Block. There were a lot of best practices that the Exception Management Application Block promoted; namely, the use of a base application exception class for deriving any custom application exceptions. This does not change with the Exception Handling Application Block, although the Exception Handling Application Block doesn't mention how to create custom application exceptions. Rather, the focus of the Exception Handling Application Block is to pick up where the handling mechanisms in the Exception Management Application Block left off. The specific responsibility for "publishing" information to an event log, file, or database is now handled primarily by the Logging and Instrumentation Application Block. The Exception Handling Application Block introduces a policy-based approach to exception handling by expanding on several of the concepts introduced in the Exception Management Application Block. Of course, there are a few caveats/differences.

- There is no longer a default Exception Handling publisher that publishes its information to the Windows Event Log. Instead, the task of persisting exception information is handled specifically by the `LoggingExceptionHandler`, which formats the information and hands it off to the Logging and Instrumentation Application Block to publish.
- Exception handlers can be chained together.
- The Exception Management Application Block only operated on the original exception that was passed to it by the application and it could only log this exception information. The Exception Handling Application Block allows exceptions to be changed, suppressed, and have information added to it, and it replaces most of the code typically found in an application's `catch` statements.

Because there are some best practices mentioned in the Exception Management Application Block that are not mentioned in Exception Handling Application Block, the best practices that are promoted by both of these blocks should be aggregated together. These blocks are both implementations of guidance that has been published by Microsoft's patterns & practices team in the *Exception Management in .NET Architecture Guide.*[1] Similar to the approach in Chapter 4, I am not going to repeat all the information that can be found in that guide; I will focus on the parts of the guide that are specific to Enterprise Library's implementation of exception handling.

1. Found at http://msdn.microsoft.com/library/default.asp?url=/library/en-us/dnbda/html/exceptdotnet.asp.

Custom Exceptions and Exception Hierarchies

Before delving into the specific design of the Exception Handling Application Block, let's focus on the part of the Exception Management Application Block that is not directly addressed by the Exception Handling Application Block: the need to have a well-thought out and designed exception hierarchy.

The Microsoft .NET common language runtime provides a means for notifying programs of exceptions in a uniform way. The guidance found in the *Exception Management in .NET Architecture Guide* states that all application-specific exception classes should derive from the `ApplicationException` class. This class derives from the base `Exception` class but does not provide any extended functionality. Rather, it merely serves as a base class in the `Exception` class hierarchy from which all custom application exceptions should be derived.

This hierarchy is important as it allows an application to benefit from the following.

- Easier development, because properties and methods can be defined on a base application exception class and inherited by derived application exception classes.
- New exception classes created after an application has been deployed can derive from an existing exception type. Existing exception handling code that catches one of the base classes of the new exception object will catch the new exception without any modifications to existing code, interpreting it as one of the object's base classes.

Figure 5.1, which is from the *Exception Management in .NET Architecture Guide,* depicts the hierarchy recommended by the Microsoft patterns & practices team.

You should only create a new application exception class for an exception type that needs to be handled but is not already available in the application exception hierarchy or in the .NET Framework. Most application exception hierarchies are fairly flat, with groupings used for organizational purposes or to allow some set of application exceptions to inherit common properties or functionality. If it is valuable to include additional fields in the

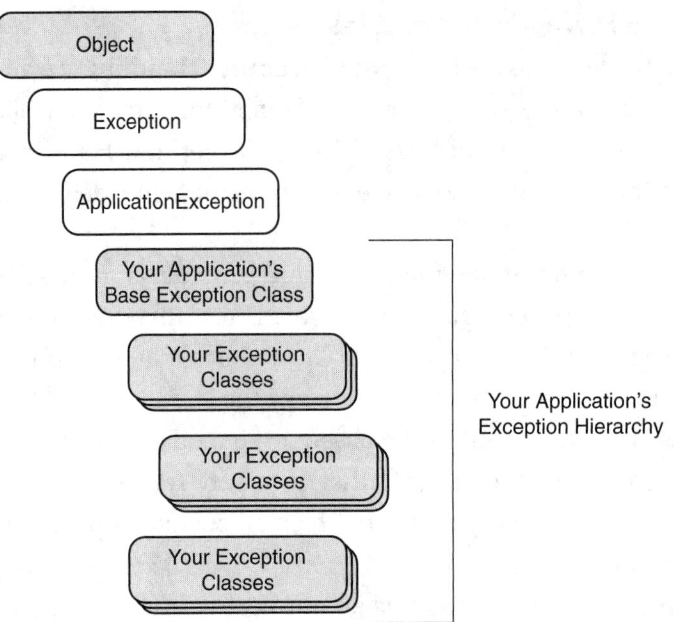

FIGURE 5.1: `ApplicationException` **Class Hierarchy**

exception (e.g., machine name) that are not in the .NET `ApplicationException` class, then the values for these fields can be persisted in the new exception's serialized data stream by overriding an exception's `GetObjectData` method.

These values can then be retrieved from the `SerializationInfo` object in the constructor of the custom exception object by using one of the `Get` methods of the `SerializationInfo` object (such as the `GetString` method). This is necessary, because if the exception is to be marshaled across remoting boundaries it must be serializable; therefore, the additional fields must be added to the serialized data stream. Although it doesn't add other fields to the serialized data stream, the `WrapperException` that is shown later in this chapter (see Listing 5.11) highlights the methods that need to be created to provide this capability.

The `BaseApplicationException` class that existed in the Exception Management Application Block made it easy for application developers to subscribe to the best practice of handling exceptions with a single base application exception class that derives from `ApplicationException`. This class served as the base class for all application exception classes. It contained fields that captured specific information like the date and time an exception occurred, the machine name on which an exception occurred, and so on. Rather than requiring every custom application exception to include these fields, these common exception details were encapsulated in this single base class and made available to any custom application exception class through inheritance.

The Exception Management Application Block provided the `BaseApplicationException`, but this isn't included in Enterprise Library's Exception Handling Application Block. If it is important to capture the exception information in the actual exception object itself, then it still makes sense to use a class like `BaseApplicationException` in an application. The Exception Handling Application Block provides an alternate method for obtaining the exception information that the `BaseApplicationException` encapsulated; however, it does not require the exception information to be added to the actual exception object. This construct is known as an `ExceptionFormatter`. (The `ExceptionFormatter` as well as how to extend the Exception Handling Application Block to use a new, custom `ExceptionFormatter` is covered with the `LoggingExceptionHandler` later in this chapter.)

Whether you use `ExceptionFormatters` explicitly or leverage a base application exception class, it is important that an application's exception hierarchy has been designed. It is this hierarchy that guides the behavior of how exceptions are handled both with the Exception Handling Application Block and the .NET runtime. Once this hierarchy has been designed, you can think more about how exceptions should be handled in an application. This is where the new Exception Handling Application Block really provides the most benefit.

The Design of the Exception Handling Application Block

Before the Exception Handling Application Block existed, developers could use the Exception Management Application Block to publish and log exceptions in their applications. Its capabilities let applications abstract away the underlying details of the publication (logging or notification) process. This was accomplished by using the `ExceptionManager`'s `Publish` method. The `ExceptionManager` class would retrieve its configuration information to determine how exceptions should be published. If no settings were found, the exception was published in the Windows Event Log by using the `DefaultPublisher` class. If the application had exception management settings configured, the publishers listed in the configuration file were used to publish the exception.

The Exception Handling Application Block has taken these concepts and combined them with a policy-based approach. Moreover, the Exception Handling Application Block does not constrain an application to just publish exception information. Logging exceptions (which uses the Logging and Instrumentation Application Block to determine where to log the information) is just one of the possible ways to handle an exception; Exception handlers also exist to wrap exceptions and replace exceptions. And just as custom exception publishers could be built for the Exception Management Application Block, so too can custom Exception Handlers be built for Exception Handling Application Block.

The design of the Exception Handling Application Block is focused on providing a simple interface that lets developers care less about *how* a particular exception is handled and concentrate more on *when* to handle an exception. The combination of the `ExceptionPolicyFactory`, the `ExceptionPolicy`, the `ExceptionHandlerFactory`, and exception handlers give the Exception Handling Application Block its flexibility. This section defines these classes and describes how they work together to achieve the design goals of the Exception Handling Application Block. It also demonstrates how to extend the application block by creating and configuring a new exception formatter and exception handler.

The `ExceptionPolicy` Class

With the Exception Handling Application Block, the code for how to handle a particular exception does not need to exist in the application itself. Rather, the exception handlers for the application can be centralized outside of the application and referenced via an exception policy. An exception policy has a name and a one-to-many relationship with the exception handlers that must execute when a particular exception type occurs. When an exception occurs in an application, the application just refers to the policy by its name and forwards the exception to the application block.

For example, let's say that it is very important to a company to understand when `SqlExceptions` occur in a particular application because there have been many instances where the connections to their SQL Servers have been broken. To understand when and why these exceptions are occurring, the company wants to log this information and notify someone in operations when it occurs. Traditionally, this would be accomplished by sticking some code into the application to log the message to a file or event log. There might also be code that would create a WMI event that a product like Microsoft Operation Manager could handle and notify someone in operations that the exception has occurred.

However, by employing exception policies and the Exception Handling Application Block, you don't need to write this code. Instead, you can define and configure an exception policy for `SqlExceptions` for the application. An exception policy has a name (e.g., `SqlPolicy`) and is configured to handle a set of exception types (e.g., `SqlException`).

Each exception type has a list of exception handlers that are executed sequentially when an exception occurs. This policy can be configured to both log an exception and send a WMI event. However, no code in the calling application actually performs either of these operations. Instead, the exception that occurred and the name of the policy that had been configured to handle this exception are forwarded to the Exception Handling Application Block, which then takes care of performing whatever actions it has been configured to perform. In this case, that is to call handlers that will log the exception and send a WMI event. Listing 5.2 shows the code that would need to be written in the application described.

LISTING 5.2: Handling a `SqlException` with the Exception Handling Application Block

```
[C#]
try
catch(SqlException ex)
{
     bool rethrow = ExceptionPolicy.HandleException(ex, "SqlPolicy");
     if (rethrow)
             throw;
```

```
}

[Visual Basic]
Catch ex As SqlException
     Dim rethrow As Boolean = ExceptionPolicy.HandleException _
          (ex, "SqlPolicy")

     If (rethrow) Then
          Throw
     End If
End Try
```

When you resolve the instability in this environment, it may be appropriate to change how a `SqlException` gets handled in this application. This particular exception handler could be removed or replaced with another one. If a change does occur for how to handle a particular exception, no code in the calling application has to change, because the application is decoupled from the actions that occur on exceptions.

The `ExceptionPolicy` class is vital to this decoupling. It serves as a simple service interface for the Exception Handling Application Block. It contains only one shared, public method: `HandleException`. Listing 5.2 demonstrates the intended use of the `HandleException` method; that is, to tell the Exception Handling Application Block that an exception has occurred and which policy needs to be executed to handle it.

The `HandleException` method expects the exception that occurred and the name of an exception policy that has been configured for the application. `HandleException` then calls its private `GetExceptionPolicy` method, which, in turn, uses the `ExceptionPolicyFactory` to create and return a specific instance of an `ExceptionPolicy` for the policy name. If no exception occurs, the private `Initialize` method is called to initialize and cache the exception policy with information about its configured exception handlers and exception types. Lastly, it passes control to this `ExceptionPolicy`'s private `HandleException(Exception)` method. Figure 5.2 shows the relationship between the `ExceptionPolicy` class and several of the classes it uses to help handle exceptions.

After the private `HandleException` method receives the exception, the Exception Handling Application Block attempts to locate an `ExceptionPolicyEntry` for the type of exception that occurred. For the example

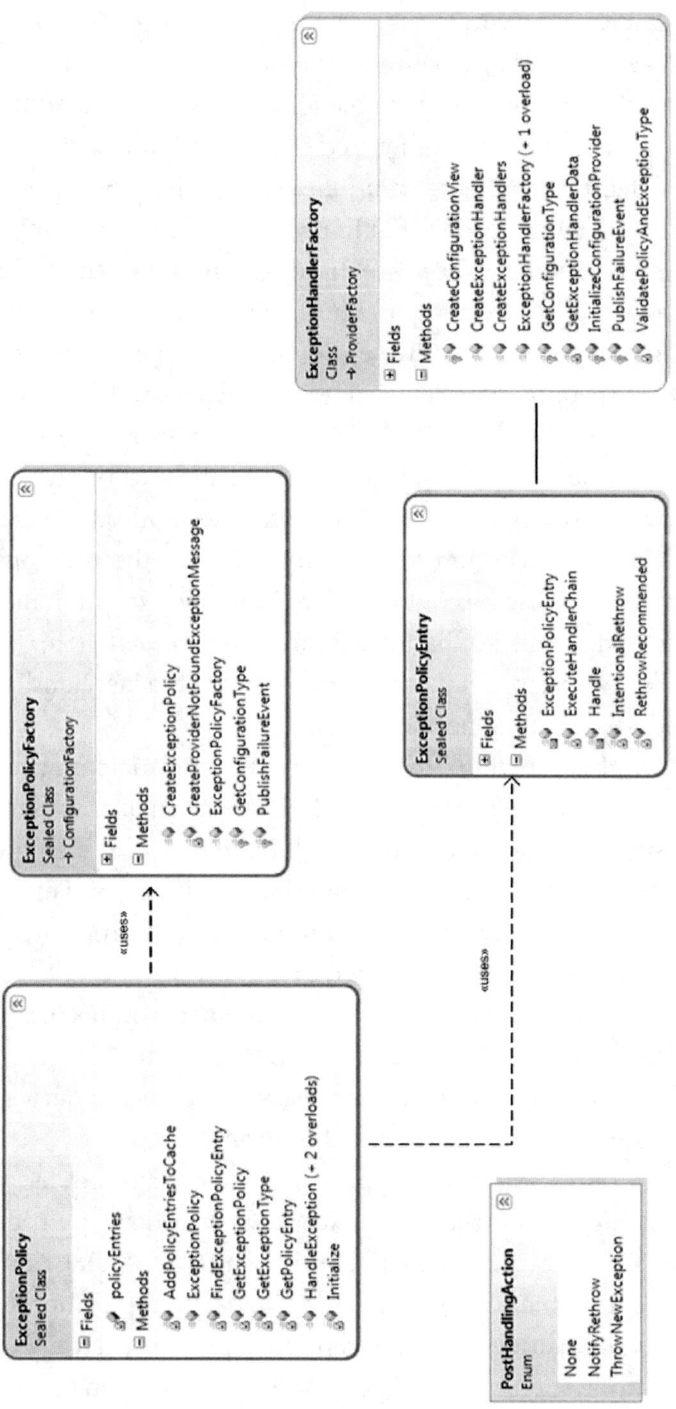

FIGURE 5.2: `ExceptionPolicy` **and Related Classes**

shown in Listing 5.2, it would try to locate an `ExceptionPolicyEntry` for a policy named `SqlPolicy` and an exception of type `SqlException`.

An `ExceptionPolicyEntry` is responsible for looping through all the `ExceptionHandlers` that have been configured for a policy and calling the `HandleException` methods with the same `HandlingInstanceID`. The `HandlingInstanceID` is a unique identifier that you can use to group multiple exception handlers together. These are discussed in more detail later in this chapter; for now it is just important to understand that an exception policy can be configured to chain multiple exception handlers together. When this occurs, the exception type can change as it gets passed from one handler to another. The first handler will always receive the original exception. However, any handler in the chain can change the exception (for example, by wrapping it or replacing it with another exception). Subsequent handlers receive the exception that is returned from the previous handler. An exception policy can be configured to throw the exception that is returned from the final exception handler (known as `ThrowNewException`); thus, it will be the exception that is returned from the last handler that will be returned to the calling application.

It is also important to understand that the algorithm for matching the exception object to a set of handlers mimics the .NET exception policy algorithm. That is, the specified exception object will be matched to a single `ExceptionPolicyEntry` by traversing its inheritance hierarchy. This is why it is very important to design an exception hierarchy appropriately. For example, if a `SqlException` is passed to the `HandleException` method and the exception type that the exception policy is configured to handle is `System.Exception` or `System.SystemException`, the event handlers for one of these would be invoked because `SqlException` derives from `SystemException`, which ultimately derives from `Exception`.

If, however, the only exception type that is configured is a `System.Data.DataException`, then no exception handlers will be invoked because `SqlException` does not fall underneath `DataException` anywhere in the exception hierarchy. This logic allows an application to take different actions depending on the exception type that occurs. For example, exception information can be logged and WMI events can be sent for all `SqlExceptions`, but only `SecurityException` may be replaced with another exception before being propagated back.

An exception policy must be configured with a PostHandlingAction for every type of exception that it has been configured to handle. The value for the PostHandlingAction determines what the return value for the HandleException method will be. As Listing 5.2 demonstrates, an application should always check the value that is returned from the HandleException method. If the value is true, then the application should rethrow the original exception. It is necessary for this to be completed in the calling application; it cannot be accomplished in the application block because if the original exception were thrown inside the block, the stack trace would be lost.

The possible values for the PostHandlingAction property are NotifyRethrow, None, and ThrowNewException. The default is NotifyRethrow. Each of these flags corresponds to the guidance outlined in the *Exception Management in .NET Architecture Guide* on exception propagation and are described in Table 5.1.

A value of true can also be returned from the HandleException method for another reason other than those specified in Table 5.1. If a policy entry

Table 5.1: PostHandlingAction Values

PostHandlingAction Value	Description
NotifyRethrow	The default. HandleException returns true to the calling application. This indicates that the application should catch and rethrow the exception. With this approach, an application catches and reacts to the exception and cleans up or performs any other required processing in the scope of the current method. If it cannot recover from the exception, it rethrows the same exception to the caller.
None	HandleException returns false to the application. This indicates that the application should not (re)throw an exception and the exception is effectively swallowed.
ThrowNewException	The application block throws the last exception to occur in the exception handling chain. This is recommended whenever the exception is manipulated inside an exception policy (i.e., the exception is wrapped or replaced, resulting in the creation of a new exception).

cannot be located, then `HandleException` will fire an `Exception-NotHandledEvent` and return true to indicate that a rethrow is recommended. This can also occur if an exception occurs during the exception handling process.

Figure 5.3 depicts an exception policy named `SqlException Policy`. It is configured to chain together two exception handlers—a `Logging-ExceptionHandler` and a `ReplaceHandler`—when an exception of type `SqlException` occurs. The `LoggingExceptionHandler` logs the exception information; the `ReplaceHandler` replaces the exception with an entirely new exception. The order in which the exception handlers are executed is the order in which they appear in the tree; therefore, the `Logging-ExceptionHandler` runs before the `ReplaceHandler`. The *SqlException Policy* has been configured to `ThrowNewException`; therefore, it is expected that the application block will throw the new exception that gets created by the `ReplaceHandler`.

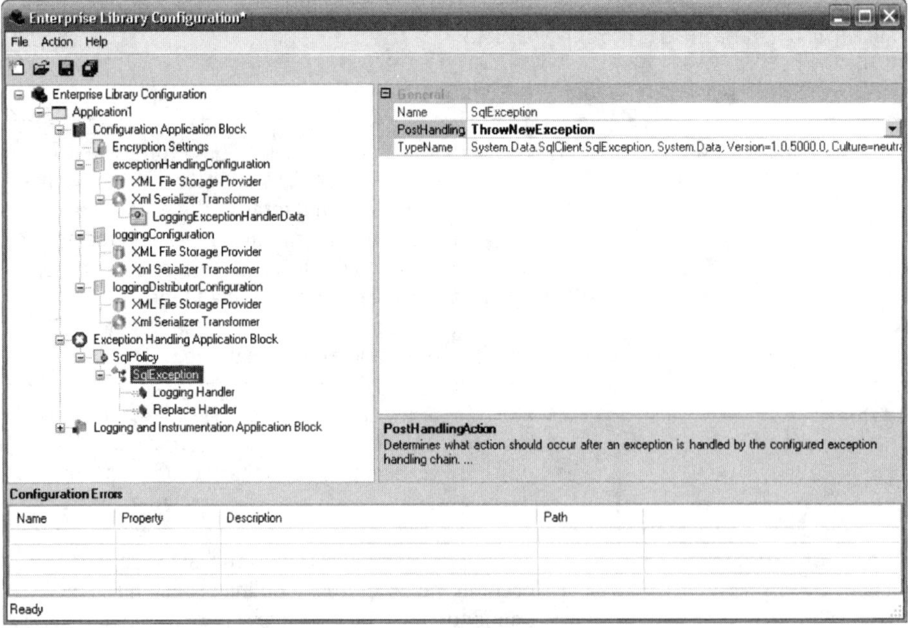

FIGURE 5.3: Configuration for the SqlException Policy

Exception Handlers

An **exception handler** performs an action based on the existence of a specific exception type. Typically, without the Exception Handling Application Block, these handlers are called directly in an application after a specific exception type has been caught (i.e., handled). For example, if a `SqlException` is detected, code might exist that calls a logging handler that accepts and logs the exception information. If the way to handle this particular exception needs to change, then the code would also need to change to call a different handler.

Keep in mind, however, that not all exceptions should be caught. Listing 5.1 showed an example of poor exception handling. The *Exception Management in .NET Architecture Guide* provides detailed guidance on why and how exceptions should be handled in an application. Catching and swallowing exceptions is generally not a recommended best practice. According to the *Exception Management in .NET Architecture Guide*, exceptions should only be caught when information needs to be gathered for logging, relevant information needs to be added to the exception (i.e., wrap the exception), or code needs to be executed to clean up or recover from the exception.

One more reason can be added that is not directly addressed in this guide: to replace the exception entirely. In today's environment, companies must be more sensitive to security issues than ever before. Therefore, it is often not good enough to simply wrap an exception in another exception. Many times an exception must be completely replaced with another exception so any sensitive information is protected from those who shouldn't see it. For example, if an exception occurs while connecting to a database in an enterprise, it is conceivable that the exception message might have information about the failed attempt. It may provide a message like `Cannot open database requested in login 'baddatabase'. Login fails. Login failed for user 'lfenster'.`

While this is good information for a person in operations to have, it is probably wise not to display information like the name of a database or a user ID to an end user or partner company. In this case, it would be wise to log the actual exception so that a person in operations can see it, replace the exception with a message that is more user friendly and contains less information about the data connection, and have some way to link the two messages together. The Exception Handling Application Block ships with exception handlers that can log, wrap, and replace exceptions. Additionally, the exception policy can link all of these activities together. These exception handlers, as well as the abstract base `ExceptionHandler` class from which they all derive, are displayed in Figure 5.4.

The exception handlers themselves are not responsible for determining when, where, or why an exception should be handled. Rather, they are responsible only for how to handle an exception type. For example, the `ReplaceHandler` that ships with the Exception Handling Application Block does not contain any logic for determining *when* an exception should be replaced. It is the responsibility of the exception policy to determine which exception types should call through the `ReplaceHandler`. Instead, the `ReplaceHandler` is only responsible for replacing one exception type with another. If more then one action needs to be taken upon detection of a specific exception type, then the exception policy can chain several exception handlers together; each exception handler is still only responsible for executing one action, though.

`WrapHandler` (Using `InnerException`)

Wrapping exceptions means creating a new exception, storing the handled exception in the `InnerException` property of this new exception, and propagating the new exception back in place of the original. You should do this when additional contextual information needs to be added to the exception message. The *Exception Management in .NET Architecture Guide* states that exceptions should *only* be wrapped "when there is a compelling reason to do so." The `WrapHandler` class allows an exception type to be configured so that it will be wrapped in another exception type and will contain a predefined string to use as the new exception message. The logic for accomplishing this is contained in two methods: `Initialize` and `HandleException`.

The `Initialize` method reads in the configuration information for this specific instance of the `WrapHandler`. In the case of the `WrapHandler` class, the configuration information contains the exception type and exception message to use for the new "outer" exception once the exception has been wrapped. The `HandleException` method creates and returns the new

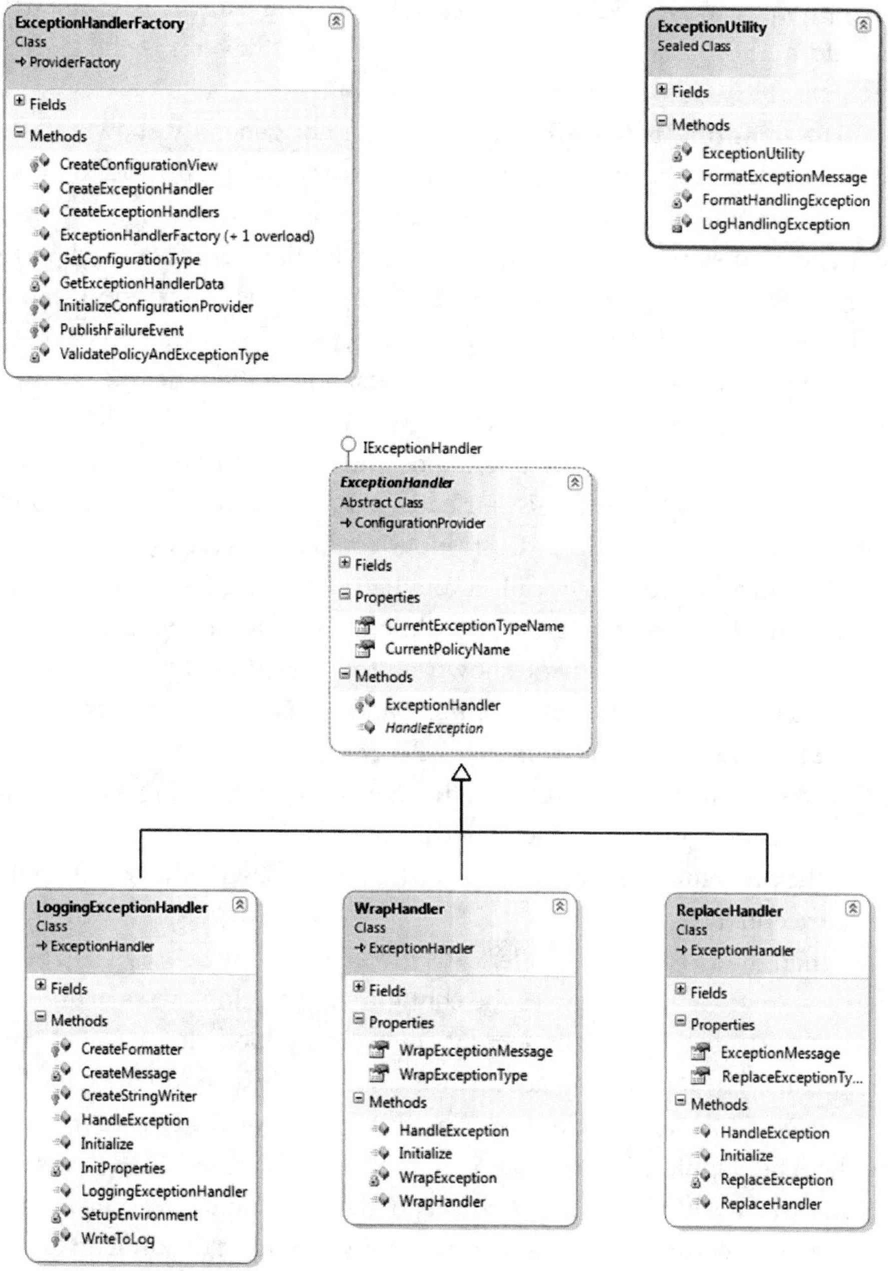

ExceptionHandlerFactory
Class
→ ProviderFactory

- Fields
- Methods
  - CreateConfigurationView
  - CreateExceptionHandler
  - CreateExceptionHandlers
  - ExceptionHandlerFactory (+ 1 overload)
  - GetConfigurationType
  - GetExceptionHandlerData
  - InitializeConfigurationProvider
  - PublishFailureEvent
  - ValidatePolicyAndExceptionType

ExceptionUtility
Sealed Class

- Fields
- Methods
  - ExceptionUtility
  - FormatExceptionMessage
  - FormatHandlingException
  - LogHandlingException

IExceptionHandler

ExceptionHandler
Abstract Class
→ ConfigurationProvider

- Fields
- Properties
  - CurrentExceptionTypeName
  - CurrentPolicyName
- Methods
  - ExceptionHandler
  - *HandleException*

LoggingExceptionHandler
Class
→ ExceptionHandler

- Fields
- Methods
  - CreateFormatter
  - CreateMessage
  - CreateStringWriter
  - HandleException
  - Initialize
  - InitProperties
  - LoggingExceptionHandler
  - SetupEnvironment
  - WriteToLog

WrapHandler
Class
→ ExceptionHandler

- Fields
- Properties
  - WrapExceptionMessage
  - WrapExceptionType
- Methods
  - HandleException
  - Initialize
  - WrapException
  - WrapHandler

ReplaceHandler
Class
→ ExceptionHandler

- Fields
- Properties
  - ExceptionMessage
  - ReplaceExceptionTy...
- Methods
  - HandleException
  - Initialize
  - ReplaceException
  - ReplaceHandler

FIGURE 5.4: ExceptionHandlers Provided by the Exception Handling Application Block

exception. However, before it creates the new outer exception, it first tries to add a `handlingInstanceID` to the message. It leverages the `ExceptionUtility` class to provide this functionality.

The handlingInstanceID. End users are not generally shown all the complex details that are contained in an exception log. Instead, they are usually shown a friendly error message. However, without some way of correlating the user-friendly error message with the more detailed descriptions in the error log, it can be difficult for operations and support staff to help resolve issues as they occur. This is where the `handlingInstanceID` plays a part. The `handlingInstanceID` is a unique identifier (i.e., a Guid) for each handled exception in an exception handling chain. The idea behind it is that a user can provide operations and support staff with the `handlingInstanceID`, and the user-friendly error message can then be correlated with the more detailed descriptions contained in the log.

How an exception policy calls through to each of the exception handlers for which it has been configured was described earlier in this chapter. This list of exception handlers is known as the **exception handling chain**. Because every handler in an exception handling chain gets the same `handlingInstanceID`, exceptions can be correlated. There is, however, one requirement that must exist to get the `handlingInstanceID` to show up in the exception message: the `{handlingInstanceID}` string must exist with the predefined exception message that will be used when creating the new exception.

When the Exception Handler calls the `ExceptionUtility`'s `FormatExceptionMessage`, it passes the configured exception message and the `HandlingInstanceID`. The `ExceptionUtility` looks for a `{handlingInstanceID}` token to replace in the message. Case *is* important. If the last character is a lowercase *d* instead of a capital *D*, the `handlingInstanceID` will not be populated in the exception message. If the `{handlingInstanceID}` token isn't found in the message, then the `handlingInstanceID` will not be inserted in the message and it will be much more difficult to correlate exception information.

After the exception message has been created (with or without the `handlingInstanceID`), the `WrapHandler` uses reflection to create the new exception as indicated by the `WrapExceptionTypeName` property and populates it with the handled exception as the inner exception and the new exception message. Listing 5.3 shows how the new exception gets created.

LISTING 5.3: How the `WrapHandler` Creates a New Outer Exception

```
[C#]
try
{
     object[] extraParameters = new object[2];
     extraParameters[0] = wrapExceptionMessage;
     extraParameters[1] = originalException;
     return (Exception)Activator.CreateInstance
           (wrapExceptionType, extraParameters);
}

[Visual Basic]
Try
     Dim extraParameters As Object() = New Object(1) {}
     extraParameters(0) = wrapExceptionMessage
     extraParameters(1) = originalException
     Return CType(Activator.CreateInstance _
           (wrapExceptionType, extraParameters), Exception)
End Try
```

Thus, if an exception policy is configured to use a `WrapHandler` when a `SqlException` is caught, and the exception message is configured to read `An exception was thrown in the data layer: {handlingInstanceID}`, the resulting exception information might look like:

```
An exception was thrown in the data layer: f1b4752a-
ab46-4a53-a867-0f9893c7c6e7
```

with an `InnerException` message of:

```
Cannot open database requested in login 'baddatabase'.
Login fails.\r\nLogin failed for user 'lfenster'.
```

`ReplaceHandler` (Hiding Exception Information)

The point of wrapping an exception is to provide additional relevant information. The original exception is preserved in the `InnerException` of the newly created message so that it remains possible to dive deeper into the details of how the outer exception may have originated.

Often, however, it will be important to *not* share these details with others. It's a fairly common practice for hackers to try to cause exceptions on a Web site in order to leverage the details of the exception. For example, hackers will often try to get a Web site to create incorrect SQL syntax in the hope that this will cause an exception to be thrown from the database and provide clues about how to break into the database. This type of exception should not be wrapped because the original exception will still be preserved. Rather, it should be replaced altogether with an exception that contains only the information that needs to be conveyed to the end user. Thus, the Exception Handling Application Block's `ReplaceHandler` was born.

The `ReplaceHandler` is no more complex that the `WrapHandler`. In fact, the only difference between the two is that the `ReplaceHandler` doesn't populate the inner exception with the exception that is being handled. Instead, it just creates a new exception as indicated by the `ReplaceExceptionTypeName` and populates it with the new `ExceptionMessage`.

If the exception policy that was shown for the `WrapHandler` example is configured to use a `ReplaceHandler` instead, then the resulting exception will simply contain the message `An exception was thrown in the data layer: f15b0a15.7a4d-44d7-abc3-d2d5f53651cf`, but it won't have an `InnerException`.

LoggingExceptionHandler

If the exception is only replaced and no other action is taken, valuable information will be lost that might help the operations staff determine what the original cause of the exception was. Therefore, it is often important to record the information from the original exception before it is replaced entirely. This is one reason for using the `LoggingExceptionHandler`. Another common reason is to log exception information so developers of the application have a record of the intricate details as to why a particular exception may have occurred.

Continuing with the example started with the `WrapHandler` and `ReplaceHandler`, the exception policy could be configured to chain together a `LoggingExceptionHandler` with the `ReplaceHandler`. This will result in the original exception being logged for the operations personnel before it is replaced and sent to the client.

Logging exceptions can be extremely useful. Figure 5.5, from the *Exception Management in .NET Architecture Guide*, suggests ways that exceptions can be logged before they are propagated. However, it doesn't specifically indicate where the exceptions should be logged, nor does it indicate whether exceptions should be written to the event log, a file, or a centralized database.

How and where the exceptions get logged is actually not the specific responsibility of the `LoggingExceptionHandler`. The `LoggingExceptionHandler` uses the Logging and Instrumentation Application Block to determine exactly *how* and *where* the exception will get logged. The Logging and Instrumentation Application Block is covered in depth in Chapter 6, but for now it is just important to understand that it isn't the `LoggingException-`

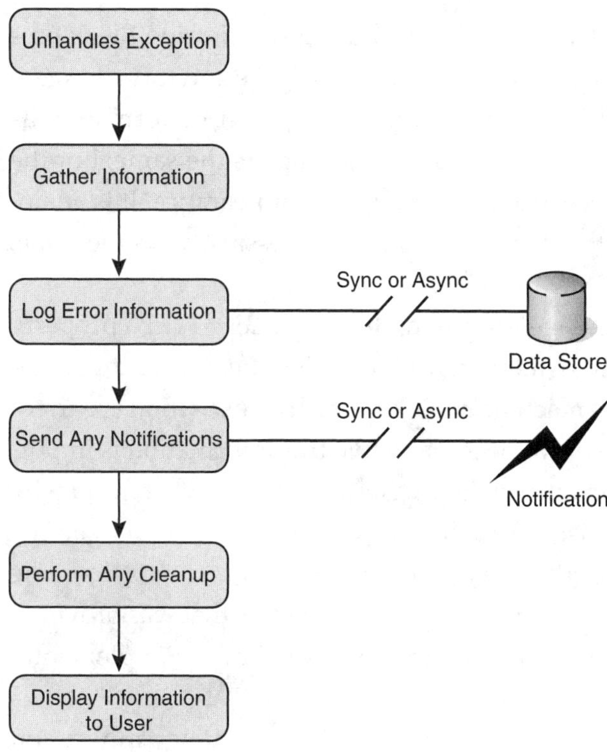

FIGURE 5.5: Logging Exception Information

Handler's responsibility to actually *log* the exception; instead, its responsibility is to pass the exception off to the Logging and Instrumentation Application Block. It is then that block's responsibility to log the exception.

The LoggingExceptionHandler is more complex than the other two exception handlers. One reason is that it needs a lot more information to work properly. When logging a message, the Logging and Instrumentation Application Block needs to have information like the log's category, severity, and priority. All of these settings are configurable. When the LoggingExceptionHandler gets initialized, it needs to obtain and make a copy of this configuration information so that it can pass it off to the Logging and Instrumentation Application Block. Another configurable setting for the LoggingExceptionHandler is the type of ExceptionFormatter that it will use when it writes the exception information. The LoggingExceptionHandler is unique in its ability to use different exception formatters.

ExceptionFormatters. The Exception Handling Application Block provides ExceptionFormatters as a flexible way to configure and format exception messages. For example, an exception message can be formatted as XML or just plain old text. The data for the message is the same, but the ExceptionFormatter that is used will modify its appearance. It is analogous to XSLT for XML in that the data in an XML message stays the same, but the XSLT will change how the XML appears.

When an exception message is created, the AdditionalInfo property for an ExceptionFormatter adds information like the date and time an exception occurred and the machine name on which an exception occurred. The nice thing about this approach is that while this information is important contextual information that can help determine when, where, and why the exception occurred, it isn't actually *part* of the exception per se. The information that results from using an ExceptionFormatter is the same as deriving from the BaseApplicationException class that was provided with the Exception Management Application Block, but the implementation is different.

When exceptions get handled in the Exception Handling Application Block, the ExceptionHandler calls an ExceptionFormatter's Format method to format the exception message. The Exception Handling Application Block ships with two ExceptionFormatters: the TextException-

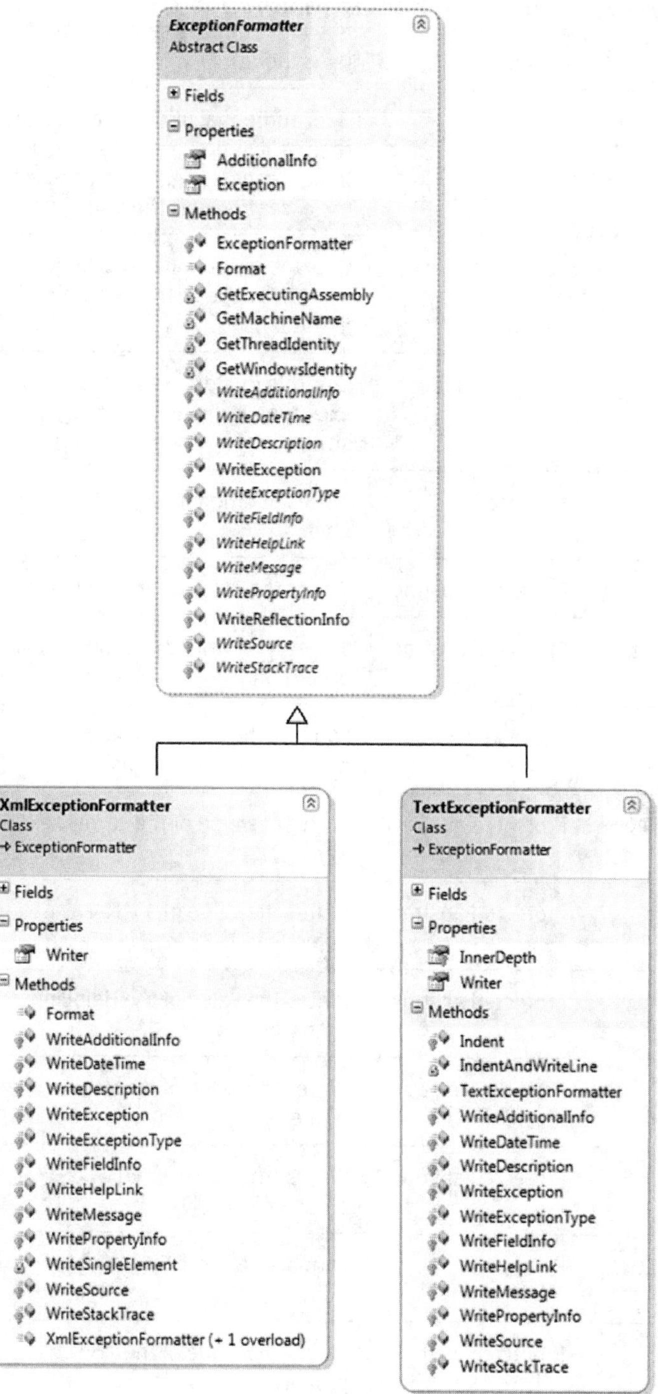

FIGURE 5.6: ExceptionFormatters in the Exception Handling Application Block

Table 5.2: `ExceptionFormatter`**'s Methods and Properties**

Method/Property	Access	Description
`AdditionalInfo`	Public	Gets additional information related to the exception but not stored in the exception (e.g., the time when the exception was thrown).
`Exception`	Public	Gets the exception object containing the exception that is being formatted.
`Format`	Public virtual	Controls the formatting of the exception into the underlying stream.
`WriteAdditionalInfo`	Protected	Writes additional properties if available.
`WriteDateTime`	Protected abstract	Writes the current time.
`WriteDescription`	Protected abstract	Writes a description of the caught exception.
`WriteException`	Protected virtual	Formats the exception and all nested inner exceptions.
`WriteExceptionType`	Protected abstract	Writes the type of the current exception.
`WriteFieldInfo`	Protected abstract	Writes the value of a `FieldInfo` object.
`WriteHelpLink`	Protected abstract	Writes the value of the HelpLink property.
`WriteMessage`	Protected abstract	Writes the value of the `Message` property.
`WritePropertyInfo`	Protected abstract	Writes the value of a `PropertyInfo` object.
`WriteReflectionInfo`	Protected	Formats an exception using reflection.
`WriteSource`	Protected abstract	Writes the value of the `Source` property.
`WriteStackTrace`	Protected abstract	Writes the value of the `StackTrace` property.

Formatter and the XmlExceptionFormatter. Both derive from the abstract ExceptionFormatter base class. Figure 5.6 displays this class hierarchy.

The ExceptionFormatter formats the message by writing the description of the exception's message, the current time, and then the exception. This order is determined in the ExceptionFormatter's virtual WriteException method. Because this method is virtual, the order can be changed in any derived class. In addition to the WriteException method, the Format method makes calls to several abstract methods. Therefore, a class that derives from the ExceptionFormatter base class must provide specific implementations for how it writes the exception information. Table 5.2 lists all of the ExceptionFormatter methods and properties.

TextExceptionFormatter. Since the ExceptionFormatter class is abstract, it cannot be created directly. Instead, one of its derived classes must be instantiated. The Exception Handling Application Block ships with the TextExceptionFormatter class for formatting exception objects as plaintext. The TextExceptionFormatter class writes each of the exception's data elements to a separate line and increments the indentation for each exception as it gets further down the stack.

Both the WrapHandler and the ReplaceHandler use the TextExceptionFormatter to format their exception messages. There's really little need for them to do otherwise as they aren't storing the exception information anywhere, but at most propagating the exception information back. On the other hand, the LoggingExceptionHandler is persisting the log information. Therefore, configuring which ExceptionFormatter it uses makes a lot more sense. Listing 5.4 shows an example of the output from a wrapped exception that uses the TextExceptionFormatter.

LISTING 5.4: Example of Output Using TextExceptionFormatter

```
An exception of type 'System.ApplicationException' occurred and was
caught.
-----------------------------------------
05/08/2006 19:55:13
Type : System.ApplicationException, mscorlib, Version=1.0.5000.0,
Culture=neutral, PublicKeyToken=b77a5c561934e089
Message : new exception message
Source :
Help link :
TargetSite :
```

```
Stack Trace : The stack trace is unavailable.
Additional Info:

MachineName : LFENSTERBOX
TimeStamp : 5/8/2006 7:55:13 PM
FullName : Microsoft.Practices.EnterpriseLibrary.ExceptionHandling,
Version=1.0.0.0, Culture=neutral, PublicKeyToken=null
AppDomainName :
ThreadIdentity :
WindowsIdentity :

     Inner Exception
     ---------
     Type :
Microsoft.Practices.EnterpriseLibrary.ExceptionHandling.Tests.MockEx-
ception, Microsoft.Practices.EnterpriseLibrary.ExceptionHandling,
Version=1.0.0.0, Culture=neutral, PublicKeyToken=null
     Message : Value cannot be null.
     Parameter name: MOCK EXCEPTION
     Source :
     Help link :
     PropertyString : MockPropertyString
     ParamName : MOCK EXCEPTION
     TargetSite :
     FieldString : MockFieldString
     Stack Trace : The stack trace is unavailable.
```

Because the `ExceptionFormatter` base class handles most of the needs for any `ExceptionFormatter`, a derived class like the `TextExceptionFormatter` only needs to implement the abstract methods that write data in the specific format which it represents. For example, Listing 5.5 shows how the `TextExceptionFormatter`'s `WriteDateTime` method formats the current date and time.

LISTING 5.5: The `TextExceptionFormatter`'s `WriteDataTime` Method

```
[C#]
protected override void WriteDateTime(DateTime utcNow)
{
     DateTime localTime = utcNow.ToLocalTime();
     string localTimeString = localTime.ToString
           ("G", DateTimeFormatInfo.InvariantInfo);
     this.Writer.WriteLine(localTimeString);
}

[Visual Basic]
Protected Overrides Sub WriteDateTime(ByVal utcNow As DateTime)
```

```
        Dim localTime As DateTime = utcNow.ToLocalTime()
        Dim localTimeString As String = localTime.ToString _
              ("G", DateTimeFormatInfo.InvariantInfo)
        Me.Writer.WriteLine(localTimeString)
    End Sub
```

Similar code exists for each of the ExceptionFormatter's abstract methods that the TextExceptionFormatter overrides. The TextExceptionFormatter also includes protected methods that assist in indenting the text for each exception in the call stack and for obtaining the instance of the TextWriter that it uses. Table 5.3 lists all of the methods and properties that the TextExceptionFormatter provides.

XmlExceptionFormatter. The XmlExceptionFormatter also derives from the ExceptionFormatter abstract base class and provides a different way to represent the exception information. It works exactly like the TextExceptionFormatter except that it uses an XmlTextWriter to format the message as XML instead of strings of indented text. This type of format is much more useful when the data from the message needs to be consumed and shared with others. Because the exception data is represented with name/value pairs, you can use XML tools to search, filter, and report the data. Listing 5.6 shows what the same exception message that was shown in Listing 5.5 would look like with the XmlExceptionFormatter.

LISTING 5.6: Sample Output Using an XmlExceptionFormatter

```
<Exception>
<Description>An exception of type 'System.ApplicationException'
                    occurred and was caught.</Description>
  <DateTime>2006-05-08 16:29:47Z</DateTime>
  <ExceptionType>System.ApplicationException, mscorlib,
                    Version=1.0.5000.0, Culture=neutral,
                    PublicKeyToken=b77a5c561934e089</ExceptionType>
  <Message>new exception message</Message>
  <Source />
  <HelpLink />
  <Property name="TargetSite"><undefined value></Property>
  <StackTrace />
  <additionalInfo>
       <info name="MachineName" value="LFENSTERBOX" />
       <info name="TimeStamp" value="5/8/2006 7:55:13 PM" />
       <info name="FullName"
                   value="Microsoft.Practices.EnterpriseLibrary.
                   ExceptionHandling, Version=1.0.0.0, Culture=neutral,
```

TABLE 5.3: `TextExceptionFormatter`'s Methods and Properties

Method/Property	Access	Description
`Writer`	Public	Gets the underlying TextWriter that the current formatter is writing to.
`InnerDepth`	Protected virtual	Gets a value that indicates the depth of the exception currently being written.
`Indent`	Protected virtual	Indents the underlying TextWriter based on the value of the InnerDepth property.
`WriteAdditionalInfo`	Protected override	Writes the additional properties to the underlying stream.
`WriteDateTime`	Protected override	Writes the current date and time to the underlying text stream.
`WriteDescription`	Protected override	Writes a generic description of the caught exception.
`WriteException`	Protected override	Controls the formatting of the specified exception and its inner exception if there is one.
`WriteExceptionType`	Protected override	Writes the value of the AssemblyQualifiedName property for the specified exception type to the underlying text stream.
`WriteFieldInfo`	Protected override	Writes the name and value of the specified field to the underlying text stream.
`WriteHelpLink`	Protected override	Writes the value of the HelpLink property.
`WriteMessage`	Protected override	Writes the value of the Message property to the underlying text stream.
`WritePropertyInfo`	Protected override	Writes the name and value of the specified property to the underlying text stream.
`WriteSource`	Protected override	Writes the value of the Source property.
`WriteStackTrace`	Protected override	Formats the stack trace.

```
                PublicKeyToken=null" />
        <info name="AppDomainName" value="" />
        <info name="ThreadIdentity" value="" />
        <info name="WindowsIdentity" value="" />
    </additionalInfo>
    <InnerException>
        <ExceptionType>Microsoft.Practices.EnterpriseLibrary.
                        ExceptionHandling.Tests.MockException,
                        Microsoft.Practices.EnterpriseLibrary.
                        ExceptionHandling, Version=1.0.0.0,
                        Culture=neutral,PublicKeyToken=null
        </ExceptionType>
        <Message>Value cannot be null.\r\nParameter name: MOCK
                EXCEPTION</Message>
        <Source />
        <HelpLink />
        <Property name="PropertyString">MockPropertyString</Property>
        <Property name="ParamName">MOCK EXCEPTION</Property>
        <Property name="TargetSite"><undefined value></Property>
        <Field name="FieldString">MockFieldString</Field>
        <StackTrace />
    </InnerException>
</Exception>
```

Creating a Custom Exception Formatter. Expressing the exception as XML is useful for many situations. However, the Exception Handling Application Block does not constrain you to only using the `TextExceptionFormatter` or `XmlExceptionFormatter`. If you need to express exception information in some other format, you can develop and use a custom `ExceptionFormatter` for the Exception Handling Application Block to express the exception in that format.

For example, if a company uses Microsoft Excel as a means to share information with its operations staff, it might be advantageous to express the exceptions in a comma-separated format. A `CsvExceptionFormatter` could be created to suit this purpose. Also, instead of displaying the additional information after the outermost exception, it might be more beneficial to have it written immediately before this exception. This would make it easy for the additional contextual information to appear at the top of an Excel worksheet. Thus, the exception information would appear in the following order.

1. The exception description
2. The exception date and time

3. Any additional information
4. A list of all exception records

To create such an `ExceptionFormatter`, the following two steps need to be completed.

1. Derive a custom `ExceptionFormatter` class from the `ExceptionFormatter` abstract base class and override all of its abstract methods so that the data is written out in comma-separated format.

   Listing 5.7 shows the `WriteAdditionalInfo` method for this class. This method calls the protected `WriteWithDelimiter` method, which writes a string with the predetermined delimiter. In this case, the delimiter is a comma.

LISTING 5.7: The `CsvExceptionFormatter`'s WriteAdditionalInfo Method

```
[C#]
protected override void WriteAdditionalInfo
     (NameValueCollection additionalInfo)
{
     StringBuilder sbAddInfo = new StringBuilder();
     foreach (string name in additionalInfo.AllKeys)
     {
          sbAddInfo.Append(name);
          sbAddInfo.Append(" : ");
          sbAddInfo.Append(additionalInfo[name]);
          sbAddInfo.Append("\n");
     }
     this.WriteWithDelimter(sbAddInfo.ToString());
}

protected virtual void WriteWithDelimter(string strValue)
{
     if (strValue == null)
          this.Writer.Write(Delimiter);
     else
     {
          string strFormat = "{0}{1}";
          char[] arrCheckDelims = new char[] {',','\n','\r'};
          if (strValue.IndexOfAny(arrCheckDelims) >= 0)
               strFormat = "\"{0}\"{1}";
          this.Writer.Write(strFormat,strValue,Delimiter);
     }
}
```

```
[Visual Basic]
Protected Overrides Sub WriteAdditionalInfo _
    (ByVal additionalInfo As NameValueCollection)

    Dim sbAddInfo As StringBuilder = New StringBuilder()
    For Each name As String In additionalInfo.AllKeys
        sbAddInfo.Append(name)
        sbAddInfo.Append(" : ")
        sbAddInfo.Append(additionalInfo(name))
        sbAddInfo.Append(Constants.vbLf)
    Next name
    Me.WriteWithDelimter(sbAddInfo.ToString())
End Sub

Protected Overridable Sub WriteWithDelimter(ByVal strValue As String)

    If strValue Is Nothing Then
        Me.Writer.Write(Delimiter)
    Else
        Dim strFormat As String = "{0}{1}"
        Dim arrCheckDelims As Char() = New Char() _
            {",",c,ControlChars.Lf,ControlChars.Cr}
        If strValue.IndexOfAny(arrCheckDelims) >= 0 Then
            strFormat = """{0}""{1}"
        End If
        Me.Writer.Write(strFormat,strValue,Delimiter)
    End If
End Sub
```

2. If only the abstract methods were overridden, this would still be a functioning `ExceptionFormatter`. However, there are additional requirements for the `CsvExceptionFormatter`. The header information must appear before any of the generic data that gets written, and the information for each exception message in the stack should be grouped under a second lower header. To meet these requirements, the virtual `Format` and `WriteException` methods must also be overridden.

   The base `ExceptionFormatter`'s `WriteException` method contains a call to the `WriteAdditionalInformation` method. For this implementation, this call will be moved from the `WriteException` method to the `Format` method. Calls to write the header information will also be added to the `Format` method. It is important to keep in mind that if there were no requirements about formatting the additional exception information *after* the outermost exception and there was no need to write headers for the columns, then this step would not be needed. Listing 5.8 shows how the virtual `Format` and `WriteException` methods have been overridden.

LISTING 5.8: `CsvExceptionFormatter` Format and `WriteException` Methods

```
[C#]
public override void Format()
{
     this.WriteHeader1();
     this.WriteDescription();
     this.WriteDateTime(DateTime.UtcNow);
     this.WriteAdditionalInfo(this.AdditionalInfo);
     this.WriteHeader2();
     this.WriteException(Exception, null);
}

protected override void WriteException
     (Exception e, Exception outerException)
{
     this.WriteExceptionType(e.GetType());
     this.WriteMessage(e.Message);
     this.WriteSource(e.Source);
     this.WriteHelpLink(e.HelpLink);
     this.Writer.Write('\"');
     this.WriteReflectionInfo(e);
     this.Writer.Write("\",");
     this.WriteStackTrace(e.StackTrace);
     this.Writer.WriteLine();

     Exception inner = e.InnerException;

     if (inner != null)
     {
          // Recursive call.
          this.WriteException(inner, e);
     }
}

[Visual Basic]
Public Overrides Sub Format()
     Me.WriteHeader1()
     Me.WriteDescription()
     Me.WriteDateTime(DateTime.UtcNow)
     Me.WriteAdditionalInfo(Me.AdditionalInfo)
     Me.WriteHeader2()
     Me.WriteException(Exception, Nothing)
```

```
End Sub

Protected Overrides Sub WriteException _
      (ByVal e As Exception, ByVal outerException As Exception)

     Me.WriteExceptionType(e.GetType())
     Me.WriteMessage(e.Message)
     Me.WriteSource(e.Source)
     Me.WriteHelpLink(e.HelpLink)
     Me.Writer.Write("""c)
     Me.WriteReflectionInfo(e)
     Me.Writer.Write(""",")
     Me.WriteStackTrace(e.StackTrace)
     Me.Writer.WriteLine()

     Dim inner As Exception = e.InnerException

     If Not inner Is Nothing Then
          ' Recursive call.
          Me.WriteException(inner, e)
     End If
End Sub
```

That's all you need to do to create the CsvExceptionFormatter. Now you can configure the CsvExceptionFormatter for use by the LoggingExceptionHandler, and instead of writing the exception information as indented text or XML, the information will be saved to a comma-delimited file. (You will learn how to configure the Formatter for the LoggingExceptionHandler later in this chapter.) Figure 5.7 shows what the comma-delimited file looks like in Microsoft Excel (with some slight formatting to highlight the headers).

Since the LoggingExceptionHandler uses an ExceptionFormatter to create the message, it does not allow for a predefined exception message through configuration. A side effect of this is that there is nowhere to set where the handlingInstanceID should appear in the message. Therefore, the LoggingExceptionHandler adds the handlingInstanceID to the beginning of the message before it calls the specific ExceptionFormatter to format the message.

After the exception message has been formatted, the LoggingExceptionHandler calls its private WriteToLog method. WriteToLog creates a LogEntry and calls LogWriter.Write to log the message. Both LogEntry and LogWriter are classes in the Logging and Instrumentation Application

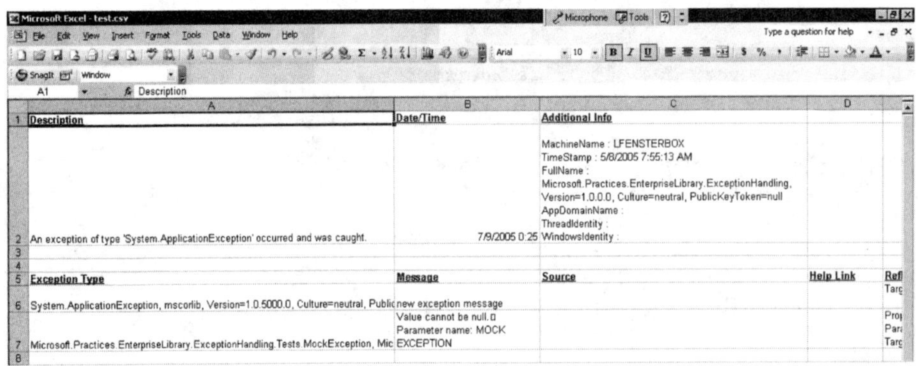

FIGURE 5.7: Results of `CsvExceptionFormatter`

Block. How and where this data gets logged is determined by the configuration in that block. This is covered in more detail in Chapter 6.

Listing 5.9 shows the results of using a `LoggingExceptionHandler` for the scenario described in Listing 5.2 and using an `XmlExceptionFormatter`.

LISTING 5.9: Sample Output Using a `LoggingExceptionHandler`

```
--------- Log Entry ---------
<EntLibLog>

<message>HandlingInstanceID: f15b0a15.7a4d-44d7-abc3-d2d5f53651cf

An exception of type 'System.Data.SqlClient.SqlException' occurred and
was caught.
-----------------------------------------
05/08/2006 09:33:52
Type : System.Data.SqlClient.SqlException, System.Data, Ver-
sion=1.0.5000.0, Culture=neutral, PublicKeyToken=b77a5c561934e089
Message : Cannot open database requested in login 'baddatabase'. Login
fails.
Login failed for user 'lfenster'.
Source : .Net SqlClient Data Provider
Help link :
Errors : System.Data.SqlClient.SqlErrorCollection
Class : 11
LineNumber : 0
Number : 4060
Procedure :
Server :
State : 1
```

```
TargetSite : System.Data.SqlClient.SqlInternalConnection
GetConnection(Boolean ByRef)
Stack Trace :    at
System.Data.SqlClient.ConnectionPool.GetConnection(Boolean&
isInTransaction)
   at
System.Data.SqlClient.SqlConnectionPoolManager.GetPooledConnection
(SqlConnectionString options, Boolean& isInTransaction)
   at System.Data.SqlClient.SqlConnection.Open()
   at
Microsoft.Practices.EnterpriseLibrary.ExceptionHandling.Logging.Tests.Log
gingExceptionHandlerFixture.LogHandlerSqlTest() in c:\program
files\microsoft enterprise
library\src\exceptionhandling\logging\tests\loggingexceptionhandlerfix-
ture.cs:line 63

Additional Info:

MachineName : LFENSTERBOX
TimeStamp : 5/8/2006 9:33:52 AM
FullName : Microsoft.Practices.EnterpriseLibrary.ExceptionHandling, Ver-
sion=1.0.0.0, Culture=neutral, PublicKeyToken=null
AppDomainName :
ThreadIdentity :
WindowsIdentity :
</message>
\t<timestamp>5/8/2006 9:33:52 AM </timestamp>
\t<title>TestTitle</title>
</EntLibLog>
----------- End -----------
```

This log becomes very valuable when the `LoggingExceptionHandler` and `ReplaceHandler` are chained together for an exception. The exception information in the log can then be correlated with a message that the end user receives. In this scenario, the end user can report receiving the exception `An exception was thrown in the data layer: f15b0a15.7a4d-44d7-abc3-d2d5f53651cfs`, which can be correlated to the log in Listing 5.9.

Custom Handler

The *Exception Management in .NET Architecture Guide* points out that "While logging is important in helping you understand what went wrong and what must be done to correct the problem, notification informs you about the condition in the first place. Without correct notification, exceptions can go undetected." Yet, a "notification handler" isn't shipped as part of the Exception Handling Application Block.

However, the documentation for this block does propose a solution for one, and the code for one is supplied by way of a Quick Start. This solution creates a custom `ExceptionHandler` to notify users when an exception has occurred. Custom `ExceptionHandlers` are an extension point to the Exception Handling Application Block. They can be developed to perform exception handling in ways other than what the out-of-the-box handlers provide. As the Quick Start details, such an exception handler can be created and used to display an exception message like that shown in Figure 5.8 to an end user.

The Quick Start solution was not shipped as part of the actual application block because it can easily be construed that this exception handler promotes the practice of providing end users with all the exception information about an exception that has occurred. As I pointed out earlier in this chapter in the discussion about the `ReplaceHandler`, it is generally not a best practice to do this. Thus, a "notification handler" like the one included in the Quick Start should usually be chained with a `ReplaceHandler`; this will let an end user be notified about the exception, but will prevent that user from seeing all the intricate details about the exception.

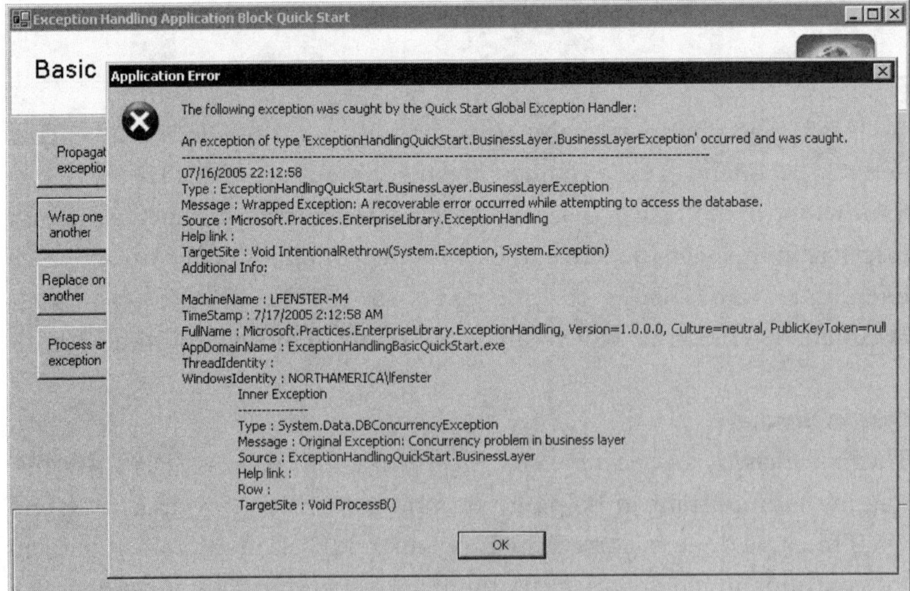

FIGURE 5.8: Exception Thrown with the `AppMessageExceptionHandler`

Like ExceptionFormatters, ExceptionHandlers are designed for simplicity. This makes it easy to create a new custom ExceptionHandler if you need one. In fact, if no configuration information needs to be obtained to handle an exception, then the HandleException method is the only method that needs to be overridden. The HandleException method determines how an exception handler will handle the exception that gets passed to it. This is exactly the case for the AppMessageExceptionHandler that is included with the Quick Start. Listing 5.10 shows the code that was written for its HandleException method.

LISTING 5.10: AppMessageExceptionHandler's HandleException Method

```
[C#]
public override Exception HandleException
      (Exception exception, string policyName,
Guid handlingInstanceId)
{
      DialogResult result = this.ShowThreadExceptionDialog(exception);
      return exception;
}

[Visual Basic]
Public Overrides Function HandleException _
      (ByVal e As Exception, ByVal policyName As String, _
       ByVal correlationID As Guid) As Exception

     Dim result As DialogResult = Me.ShowThreadExceptionDialog(e)
     Return e
End Function
```

The support that the Exception Handling Application Block provides to create and configure these types of ExceptionHandlers is nice because it makes it easy for you to create new ExceptionHandlers and configure them for an application without having to worry about any design-time requirements. When you create a custom ExceptionHandler, it uses the design-time properties that have been established for all custom ExceptionHandlers. Namely, these are the TypeName and Attributes properties. The Attributes property is a NameValueCollection of configuration items. If the ExceptionHandler needs to be initialized with configuration information, then the Initialize method will need to be overridden and it will need to access this configuration information from the Attributes property's NameValueCollection.

Sometimes, however, it may be desirable to create an `ExceptionHandler` that works more like the `WrapHandler`, `ReplaceHandler`, and `LoggingExceptionHandler`; that is, an exception handler that can use its own strongly typed set of design-time attributes.

For example, let's say that an organization wants to wrap exceptions a little bit differently than the `WrapHandler` does. The Enterprise Library's `WrapHandler` is sufficient for many situations; however, it cannot be used if context-sensitive information needs to be added to an exception message. The `WrapHandler` and `ReplaceHandler` are constrained by the fact that the exception messages they produce will always be the same (aside from the `handlingInstanceID`).

In the scenario examined earlier in this chapter for the `WrapHandler`, the new exception message was always `An exception was thrown in the data layer: {handlingInstanceID}`. There is no way to be more specific in the exception message. For example, for an enterprise portal application, there is no way for the exception message to return "`An exception was thrown in the data layer` **`trying to retrieve Announcements:`** `{handlingInstanceID}.`" when the exception is caught trying to retrieve *Announcements* data and produce "`An exception was thrown in the data layer` **`trying to retrieve Links`**`: {handlingInstanceID}.`" when the exception is caught trying to retrieve a *Links* data. This additional, contextual information can be extremely helpful in determining exactly where an exception occurred.

If the new exception message could be sent through the `ExceptionPolicy` interface, then a new exception handler would not need to be created. However, it cannot. The interaction with the Exception Handling Application Block is through the `ExceptionPolicy.HandleException` method. There is no argument for passing a new exception message. This is because the intent of the block is to completely decouple the exception handlers from the initiating code in the application. To truly decouple the code from the handling policies, the block only allows the exception that occurred and the name of the policy to handle it as arguments.[2]

---

2. In actuality, the `ConfigurationContext` which represents the configuration information for this application can also be passed to the block. However, it is not relevant to the scenario.

So if additional information that is not known until runtime needs to be passed to the Exception Handling Application Block, you can develop a new ExceptionHandler that "hacks" around the interface. The following are the steps you need to complete to create this specific custom ExceptionHandler.

1. Create a new exception type that wraps around the caught exception but lets a new exception message be created. Let's call this class WrapperException.
2. Create a data transfer object similar to the WrapHandler's WrapHandlerData class to hold the configuration information. This class will be called ContextualWrapData.
3. Create a new exception handler that derives from the WrapHandler but implements the functionality that I have just described. This exception handler will check to see if the exception it is handling is of the type WrapperException. If it isn't handling a WrapperException, it will just work the same way that its base WrapHandler class works. If it is handling a WrapperException, it will create the new exception the same way that the WrapHandler does, but it will set its exception message to the WrapperException's exception message, and it will set its InnerException equal to the WrapperException's InnerException. The result is that there will be no trace that the WrapperException was used to create the new exception message. Let's call this new exception handler ContextualWrapHandler.
4. Create the design-time classes that make it easier and less error-prone to configure this ExceptionHandler by allowing the Enterprise Library Configuration Tool to be used.

Before we dive too deep into the details for how to do this, I need to go on record as stating that this is *not* the ideal example for creating an ExceptionHandler. A more straightforward scenario would simply have been to show the steps needed to modify the AppMessageExceptionHandler (the one provided with the Quick Start) so that it could have its own design-time features instead of relying on the design-time for custom ExceptionHandlers. However, I have included this example primarily because I have seen many situations where there is a need to wrap exceptions and still allow the exception message to be determined at runtime. At the same time, it is also advantageous for the application to reap the benefits of being decoupled from how the exception is handled.

While this exception handler provides these benefits, there is, however, a drawback to this solution that would not exist for a typical custom ExceptionHandler. Because I am passing a different exception to the Exception Handling Application Block than the one that occurred, the exception policy needs to be configured to catch a WrapperException, ApplicationException, or Exception. If the policy is configured to just catch a SqlException, the handler will not get called.

Although this sample is a bit more complex than a typical ExceptionHandler would be, I am hopeful that it adequately communicates the steps that need to be completed to create a custom ExceptionHandler with its own design-time features. I will call out which tasks are only necessary for this scenario.

Step 1: Creating the WrapperException Class

This step is only needed for this specific scenario and would not be needed to create a typical custom ExceptionHandler. The WrapperException class is just an exception that serves as a container for the new exception message and InnerException. Nothing unusual needs to be performed when creating the WrapperException; it is created just as any other custom exception would be created. Listing 5.11 shows the WrapperException class.

LISTING 5.11: WrapperException **Class**

```
[C#]
[Serializable()]
public class WrapperException : ApplicationException
{
```

```
    // Default constructor.
    public WrapperException() {}

    // Constructor with exception message.
    public WrapperException(string message) : base(message)
    {}

    // Constructor with message and inner exception.
    public WrapperException(string message, Exception inner) :
        base(message, inner)
    {}

    // Protected constructor to deserialize data.
    public WrapperException
         (SerializationInfo info, StreamingContext context) :
            base(info,context)
    {}

    public override void GetObjectData
        (System.Runtime.Serialization.SerializationInfo info,
        System.Runtime.Serialization.StreamingContext context)
    {
        //Persist any values into the serialized data stream here
        //(e.g., info.AddValue("m_strMachineName", "My machine
        //name")).
        base.GetObjectData(info, context);
    }
}

[Visual Basic]
<Serializable()> _
Public Class WrapperException : Inherits ApplicationException

    ' Default constructor.
    Public Sub New()
    End Sub

    ' Constructor with exception message.
    Public Sub New(ByVal message As String)
    End Sub

    ' Constructor with message and inner exception.
    Public Sub New(ByVal message As String, ByVal inner As Exception)
    End Sub

    ' Protected constructor to deserialize data.
    Public Sub New(ByVal info As SerializationInfo, _
            ByVal context As StreamingContext)

        MyBase.New(info,context)
```

```
        MyBase.New(message, inner)
        MyBase.New(message)
    End Sub

    Public Overrides Sub GetObjectData _
          (ByVal info As _
           System.Runtime.Serialization.SerializationInfo, _
           ByVal context As _
           System.Runtime.Serialization.StreamingContext)

        'Persist any values into the serialized data stream here
        '(e.g., info.AddValue("m_strMachineName", _
        "My machine 'name"))

        MyBase.GetObjectData(info, context)
    End Sub
End Class
```

Step 2: Creating the `ContextualWrapData` Class

The `ContextualWrapHandler` needs a `ContextualWrapData` class in the same way that the `WrapHandler` class needed the `WrapHandlerData` to encapsulate the configuration information for it. It is needed because when the Exception Handling Application Block determines which handlers to create, it doesn't look for the type of the exception handler in an application's configuration information; instead, it looks for the type of data transfer object that will contain the configuration data for the `ExceptionHandler`.

The `ExceptionHandler` is ultimately determined by this class' `TypeName` property; that is, the value returned from this property is the type of the `ExceptionHandler` that should be created. For example, the `WrapHandlerData`'s `TypeName` property returns the `WrapHandler` type. Custom `ExceptionHandlers` like the `AppMessageExceptionHandler` work because the block creates a `CustomHandlerData` class and sets the value for its `TypeName` property to the value specified through configuration. This is also why additional strongly typed configuration information cannot be added for this type of `ExceptionHandler`.

Another important point to keep in mind when creating an `ExceptionHandler`'s data transfer object is that it must be attributed with `[XmlRoot("exceptionHandler", Namespace=ExceptionHandling-`

Settings.ConfigurationNamespace)]. If it isn't attributed this way, then a ConfigurationException will be thrown when the configuration data is being read. The reason is that the ExceptionType's ExceptionHandler property is attributed to be an array of ExceptionHandlerData with the namespace ExceptionHandlingSettings.ConfigurationNamespace.

Once you understand these facts, you can create an ExceptionHandler's data transfer object. Listing 5.12 shows the code for the ContextualWrapData class. The DefaultExceptionMessage property exists so a user can set a default exception message for this exception handler the same way that the WrapHandler allows.

LISTING 5.12: ContectualWrapData **Class**

```
[C#]
[XmlRoot("exceptionHandler", Namespace=ExceptionHandlingSettings.
ConfigurationNamespace)]
public class ContextualWrapData : WrapHandlerData
{
     public ContextualWrapData()
     {}

     public ContextualWrapData(string name) : base(name)
     {}

     public ContextualWrapData(string name, string exceptionMessage,
               string wrapExceptionTypeName) :
                    base(name, exceptionMessage,wrapExceptionTypeName)
     {}

     [XmlAttribute("defaultExceptionMessage")]
     public string DefaultExceptionMessage
     {
          get { return base.ExceptionMessage; }
          set { base.ExceptionMessage = value; }
     }

     [XmlIgnore]
     public override string TypeName
     {
          get
          {
             return typeof(ContextualWrapHandler).AssemblyQualifiedName;
          }
          set
```

```
            {
            }
        }
    }

[Visual Basic]
<XmlRoot("exceptionHandler", _
Namespace:=ExceptionHandlingSettings.ConfigurationNamespace)> _
Public Class ContextualWrapData : Inherits WrapHandlerData
     Public Sub New()
     End Sub

     Public Sub New(ByVal name As String)
          MyBase.New(name)
     End Sub

     Public Sub New(ByVal name As String, _
                    ByVal exceptionMessage As String, _
                    ByVal wrapExceptionTypeName As String)
          MyBase.New(name, exceptionMessage,wrapExceptionTypeName)
     End Sub

     <XmlAttribute("defaultExceptionMessage")> _
     Public Property DefaultExceptionMessage() As String
          Get
               Return MyBase.ExceptionMessage
          End Get
          Set
               MyBase.ExceptionMessage = Value
          End Set
     End Property

     <XmlIgnore> _
     Public Overrides Property TypeName() As String
         Get
          Return GetType(ContextualWrapHandler).AssemblyQualifiedName
         End Get
         Set
         End Set
     End Property
End Class
```

Step 3: Creating the `ContextualWrapHandler Class`

Creating the custom `ExceptionHandler` involves deriving a class from the `ExceptionHandler` base class and overriding the `Initialize` and `HandleException` methods. For this custom `ExceptionHandler`, the `Con-`

textualWrapData object will be populated in the Initialize method instead of a CustomHandlerData. Listing 5.13 shows that the exception is being checked to determine if it is of type WrapperException, and if so the HandleException method calls the private ContextualWrapException method, which sets the new exception message and InnerException. If not, it simply operates the same way the WrapHandler does.

LISTING 5.13: The ContextualWrapHandler's HandleException Method

```
[C#]
[ReflectionPermission(SecurityAction.Demand, MemberAccess=true)]
public override Exception HandleException
     (Exception exception, string policyName, Guid handlingInstanceId)
{
     if (! (exception is WrapperException))
          return base.HandleException
           (exception, policyName, handlingInstanceId);

     return ContextualWrapException(
          exception,
          WrapExceptionType,
          DefaultExceptionMessage,
          handlingInstanceId);
}

private Exception ContextualWrapException
     (Exception originalException, Type wrapExceptionType,
     string defaultExceptionMessage, Guid handlingInstanceId)
{
     string strNewExceptionMessage = originalException.Message;

     if ((strNewExceptionMessage == null) ||
          (strNewExceptionMessage.Equals(String.Empty)))
          strNewExceptionMessage = defaultExceptionMessage;

     if (strNewExceptionMessage == null)
          strNewExceptionMessage = String.Empty;

     strNewExceptionMessage = ExceptionUtility.FormatExceptionMessage
           (strNewExceptionMessage, handlingInstanceId);

     Exception innerException =
           (originalException.InnerException == null)? originalException
               : originalException.InnerException;

     try
     {
          object[] extraParameters = new object[2];
```

```
            extraParameters[0] = strNewExceptionMessage;
            extraParameters[1] = innerException;
                return (Exception)Activator.CreateInstance
                     (wrapExceptionType, extraParameters);
        }
        catch (Exception ex)
        {
            throw new ExceptionHandlingException
             (SR.ExceptionUnableToWrapException
                 (wrapExceptionType.Name), ex);
        }
}

[Visual Basic]
<ReflectionPermission(SecurityAction.Demand, MemberAccess:=True)> _
Public Overrides Function HandleException _
     (ByVal exception As Exception, ByVal policyName As String, _
      ByVal handlingInstanceId As Guid) As Exception

    If Not(TypeOf exception Is WrapperException) Then
        Return MyBase.HandleException _
         (exception, policyName, handlingInstanceId)
    End If

    Return ContextualWrapException _
         (exception, WrapExceptionType, DefaultExceptionMessage, _
            handlingInstanceId)
End Function

Private Function ContextualWrapException _
         (ByVal originalException As Exception, _
          ByVal wrapExceptionType As Type, _
          ByVal defaultExceptionMessage As String, _
          ByVal handlingInstanceId As Guid) As Exception

    Dim strNewExceptionMessage As String = originalException.Message

        If (strNewExceptionMessage Is Nothing) OrElse _
           (strNewExceptionMessage.Equals(String.Empty)) Then
             strNewExceptionMessage = defaultExceptionMessage
        End If

    If strNewExceptionMessage Is Nothing Then
        strNewExceptionMessage = String.Empty
    End If

    strNewExceptionMessage = _
        ExceptionUtility.FormatExceptionMessage _
        (strNewExceptionMessage, handlingInstanceId)
```

```
    Dim innerException As Exception = _
         IIf((originalException.InnerException Is Nothing), _
         originalException, originalException.InnerException)

    Try
         Dim extraParameters As Object() = New Object(1) {}
         extraParameters(0) = strNewExceptionMessage
         extraParameters(1) = innerException
              Return CType(Activator.CreateInstance _
               (wrapExceptionType, extraParameters), Exception)
    Catch ex As Exception
         Throw New ExceptionHandlingException _
              (SR.ExceptionUnableToWrapException _
              (wrapExceptionType.Name), ex)
    End Try
End Function
```

Step 4: Creating Design-Time Classes

The last step is to create the design-time classes that let the Enterprise Library Configuration Tool present a user-friendly interface which makes configuring an `ExceptionHandler` easier and less error-prone than configuring it manually. This step is not absolutely necessary, but without it the configuration information for an `ExceptionHandler` would need to be entered and modified manually, and the benefits with respect to validating configuration information for it will not be realized.

A `ConfigurationNode` that wraps around the `ContextualWrapData` class and a `ConfigurationDesignManager` class that registers and recognizes this node need to be created. Additionally, the AssemblyInfo file must be modified so the Enterprise Library Configuration Tool can recognize the design-time features for the `ContextualWrapHandler`. (Chapter 2 provides much more detail about how and why these classes need to be created.)

The source code for the design-time classes for the `ContextualWrapHandler` is on the book's Web site, so I will not show all the details for creating these classes. Once the design-time classes have been developed and deployed, you can add and modify the `ContextualWrapHandler` as easily as any of the ones that ship with Enterprise Library. Figure 5.9 displays the list of options for adding an `ExceptionHandler` in the Enterprise Library Configuration Tool once this new assembly has been deployed.

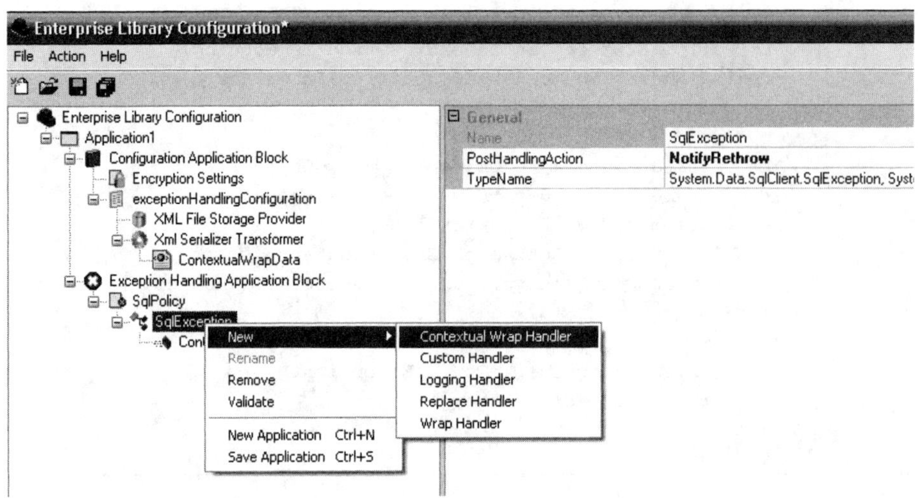

FIGURE 5.9: Adding a Contextual WrapHandler to an Application's Configuration

Once an application has been configured to use the `ContextualWrapHandler`, the Exception Handling Application Block can use it to wrap the exception with the original exception as the `InnerException` and with a message that is provided at runtime. Listing 5.14 uses a static function to create the `WrapperException` and pass it to the Exception Handling Application Block. This step is only needed for the scenario shown here because a different exception other than the one that originally occurred is being sent to the Exception Handling Application Block. Normally, `ExceptionPolicy.HandleException` would just be called the way it is called for all other exception handlers.

LISTING 5.14: Using the `WrapperException` Class with the `ContextualWrapHandler`

```
[C#]
private static bool HandleException(Exception ex,
                                    string strNewExceptionMessage,
                                    string strPolicy)
{
     return ExceptionPolicy.HandleException(new WrapperException
                   (strNewExceptionMessage, ex),strPolicy);
}

public Announcements GetAnnouncements(int moduleId)
```

```
{
     try
     {
          return (Announcements) GetObject(moduleId);
     }
     catch (Exception ex)
     {
          string strTestMessage = "An exception was thrown in the data
                         layer trying to retrieve Announcements:
                         {handlingInstanceID}";
           bool bRethrow = HandleException(ex,
                              strTestMessage, "Wrap Policy");

           if (bRethrow)
                     throw;
     }
}

[Visual Basic]
Private Shared Function HandleException(ByVal ex As Exception, _
               ByVal strNewExceptionMessage As String, _
               ByVal strPolicy As String) As Boolean

          Return ExceptionPolicy.HandleException( _
          New WrapperException (strNewExceptionMessage, ex),strPolicy)

End Function

Public Function GetAnnouncements(ByVal moduleId As Integer) _
                    As Announcements

     Try
          Return CType(GetObject(moduleId), Announcements)
     Catch ex As Exception
          Dim strTestMessage As String = "An exception was thrown" & _
                    "in the data layer trying to retrieve " & _
                    " Announcements: {handlingInstanceID}"

          Dim bRethrow As Boolean = HandleException( _
                    ex, strTestMessage, "Wrap Policy")

          If bRethrow Then
               Throw
          End If
     End Try
End Function
```

As Listings 5.15 and 5.16 show, this produces the desired result: a wrapped exception with the new, dynamic exception message and an `InnerExcep-`

tion that is equal to the exception that was caught and not the WrapperException.

LISTING 5.15: Resulting Message from Using the ContextualWrapHandler

```
An exception of type 'System.ApplicationException' occurred and was
caught.
Type : System.ApplicationException, mscorlib, Version=1.0.5000.0,
Culture=neutral, PublicKeyToken=b77a5c561934e089
Message : An exception was thrown in the data layer trying to retrieve
Announcements: 3518ef0c-ce23-4006-9736-df8251a740b7.
```

LISTING 5.16: Resulting InnerException from Using the ContextualWrapHandler

```
Type : System.Data.SqlClient.SqlException, System.Data, Ver-
sion=1.0.5000.0, Culture=neutral, PublicKeyToken=b77a5c561934e089
Message : Cannot open database requested in login 'baddb'. Login fails.
Login failed for user 'lfenster'.
     Source : .Net SqlClient Data Provider
...
```

Developing with the Exception Handling Application Block

The previous section covered the design of the Exception Handling Application Block and how it can be extended through custom ExceptionFormatters and ExceptionHandlers. I went into great detail to cover this, because I feel that it is important for you to know that you aren't constrained to only using the exception formatters and exception handlers that ship with the Exception Handling Application Block. However, if the exception formatters and exception handlers that ship with the block do serve all your needs, then you will have to write very little code to use the block.

Writing code to leverage the Exception Handling Application Block is trivial because most of the processes are handled by the ExceptionPolicy service. The bulk of the work that you need to do is configuring these exception policies, not coding them. This section details how to configure and develop an application to use the features of the Exception Handling Application Block.

Configuring the Exception Handling Application Block

The `ExceptionPolicy` class uses configuration data to create exception policies that handle predefined exception types with predefined `ExceptionHandlers`. As is the case with the other application blocks, the Enterprise Library Configuration Tool provides the easiest and least error-prone method for creating and modifying this configuration data.

To add the Exception Handling Application Block, open the application's domain configuration file in the tool, right-click on the application node, and select *New > Exception Handling Application Block*. Figure 5.10 shows the resulting configuration hierarchy. A new configuration section is added to the nodes underneath the settings for the Configuration Application Block, and a configuration hierarchy has been created to hold the settings for the Exception Handling Application Block.

After the block has been added, the next task is to create the exception policies. An **exception policy** defines how to handle a specific type of exception that may occur in an application. An application may be configured with many exception policies.

To add an exception policy to an application's configuration, right-click on the *Exception Handling Application Block* node and select *New > Exception Policy*. You can configure each exception policy to handle many types of exceptions. To add an exception type to an exception policy, right-click the exception policy node and select *New > Exception Type*. When you add an

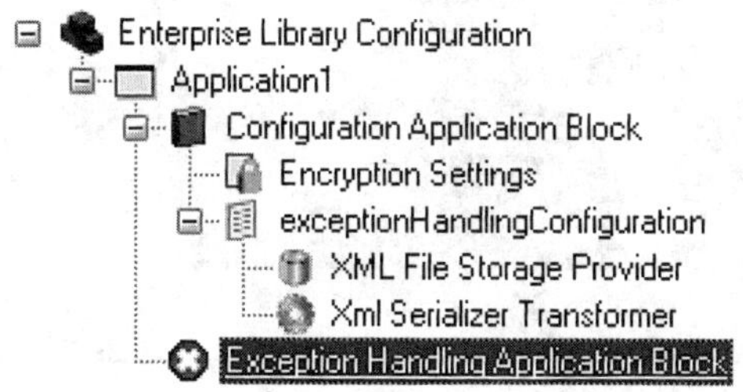

FIGURE 5.10: Hierarchy After Adding the Exception Handling Application Block

exception type to an exception policy, the Enterprise Library Configuration Tool displays the Type Selector dialog to make it easy to add an exception type to an exception policy. The Type Selector dialog will only let you select a class that derives either directly or indirectly from the base `Exception` class.

Figure 5.11 shows how the Type Selector dialog is used to add an exception type for the `System.Exception` to an exception policy. This will handle any exception that may occur, because `System.Exception` is the base class for all exceptions, and when the Exception Handling Application Block looks for a particular exception type, it will navigate up a class hierarchy until it finds a match.

Every exception type for an exception policy must be configured with a `PostHandlingAction`. Table 5.1 listed the values for the `PostHandlingAction` property. The default is `NotifyRethrow`. Because this exception

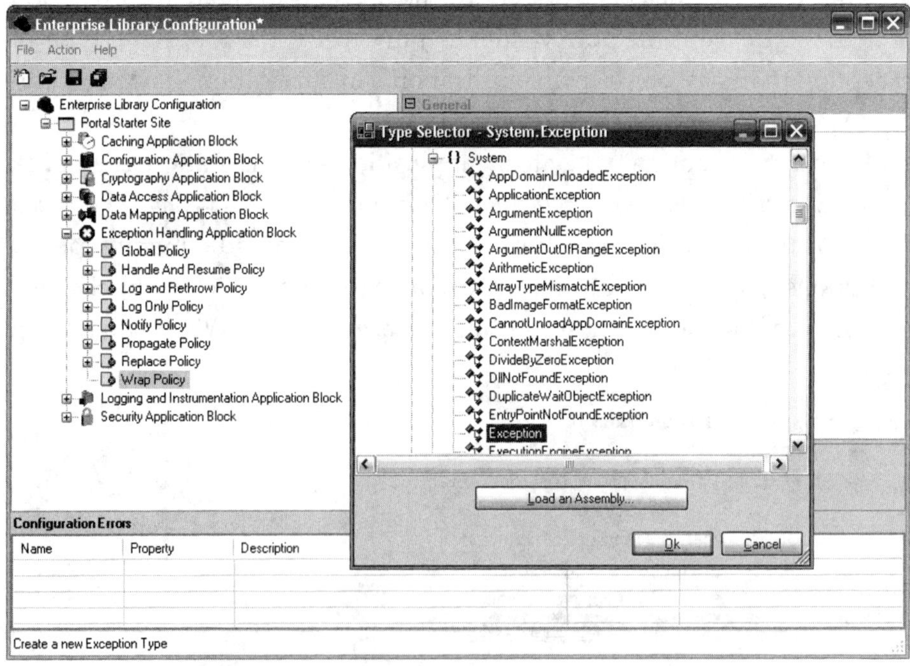

FIGURE 5.11: Adding an Exception Type to an Exception Policy

will eventually use a WrapHandler to create a new exception, I have changed the `PostHandlingAction` property to `ThrowNewException` so the Exception Handling Application Block will throw the new exception that is created by the WrapHandler and return true to the calling application. Figure 5.12 shows where this change is made.

For each exception type in an exception policy, you can configure many exception handlers to run. The combination of the exception handlers, exception types, and exception policies dictate how a specific exception is handled in an application. For example, let's say a distributed, multitiered application is being developed. There are a few different ways to handle any exceptions that might occur in this application. If an exception occurs in the data layer, it may be desirable to simply log the exception and propagate it to the business layer; exceptions at the business layer may be logged and then wrapped in a custom exception before being propagated to the UI layer; in the UI layer, exception messages may be replaced with a user-friendly message before notifying the user. An exception policy can be created for each of these scenarios in the application. Rather than writing

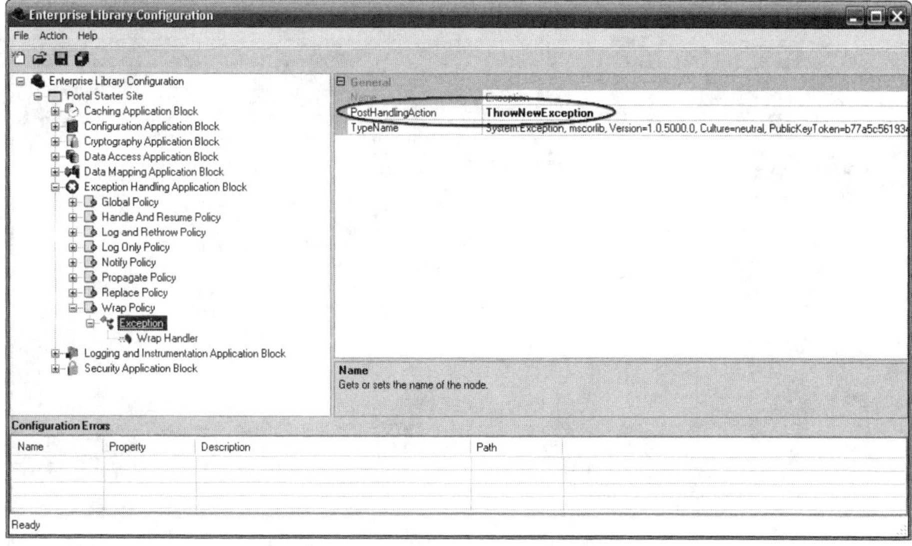

FIGURE 5.12: `PostHandlingAction` **for an Exception Type**

code to perform each of these specific tasks, the exception policies just need to be configured to handle specific exception types in specific ways.

Wrapping an Exception

To wrap one exception in another, an exception type should be configured with a WrapHandler. To do this, select the exception type for a particular exception policy, right-click on it, and select *New > Wrap Handler*. In Figure 5.13, an exception policy named *Wrap Policy* has been created and configured to wrap an exception with a new `System.ApplicationException`.

Clicking the ellipses button for the `WrapExceptionTypeName` property will open the same Type Selector dialog that was used to create the exception type (shown in Figure 5.11). In this case, you use the dialog to specify which type of exception should be created to wrap around the handled exception. The WrapHandler shown in Figure 5.13 will create a new `ApplicationException` with the original exception as its `InnerException` and the exception message `An exception has occurred and been wrapped inside this exception` when an exception of type `System.Exception` (or a class derived from it) is handled for the *Wrap Policy*.

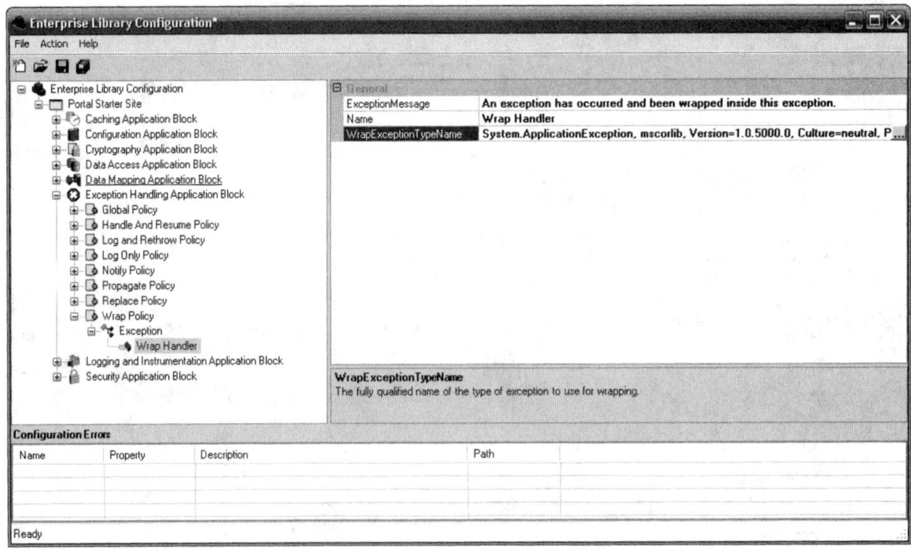

FIGURE 5.13: Configuration for a WrapHandler

Replacing an Exception

Replacing an exception is very similar to wrapping an exception, except that the `InnerException` is not populated with the original exception that is received. If this policy were changed to use a Replace Handler instead of a WrapHandler, the calling code would not change; it could remain completely untouched. To configure an exception type to use a Replace Handler, select the exception type for a particular exception policy, right-click on it, and select *New > Replace Handler.*

Logging an Exception

Logging an exception means that exception information is written to some type of storage. The Exception Handling Application Block relies on the Logging and Instrumentation Application Block to determine how and where to log the exception information. The only requirement from the Logging and Instrumentation Application Block is that it can obtain enough information to create an instance of a `LogEntry` class. Therefore, to configure an exception to use a logging handler, the configuration information listed in Table 5.4 needs to be set in the Exception Handling Application Block.

TABLE 5.4: Logging Handler Properties

Property	Description
`EventID`	An `Event` number or identifier.
`FormatterTypeName`	The type of ExceptionFormatter to use to format the exception information. (ExceptionFormatters were covered earlier in this chapter.)
`LogCategory`	The category name that is used to route the LogEntry to one or more log Sinks.
`Priority`	The importance of the log message. Only messages above the minimum priority are processed.
`Severity`	LogEntry severity enumeration: Unspecified, Information, Warning, or Error.
`Title`	Additional description of the LogEntry message.

This configuration information gives the Logging and Instrumentation Application Block all the information that it needs to create a `LogEntry`. To configure an exception type to use a logging handler, select the exception type for a particular exception policy, right-click on it, and select *New > Logging Handler*. When a logging handler is configured, the Logging and Instrumentation Application Block is automatically added to the available application blocks if it hasn't already been added.

In Figure 5.14, the *Log Only Policy* has been configured with a logging handler. The logging handler has been configured to log the exception infor-

FIGURE 5.14: Configuration for a Logging Handler (Including Configuration in the Logging and Instrumentation Application Block)

mation with a log Category of *Exceptions*. This Category has been configured in the Logging and Instrumentation Application Block to use a Flat File Sink, which has been configured to store its information in a file called exceptions.log. See Chapter 6 for more detail about log Categories and log Sinks.

Setting an `ExceptionFormatter`

Other than the FormatterTypeName property, all the properties that must get configured for the logging handler are used to create a `LogEntry` for the Logging and Instrumentation Application Block. You use the `FormatterTypeName` property to configure the `ExceptionFormatter` that the logging handler uses to write exception information. By default, the logging handler is configured to use the `TextExceptionFormatter` to write each of the exception's data elements onto a separate line, with the indentation incremented for each exception as it gets further down the stack.

You can change the type of exception formatter by clicking the ellipses for this property. This opens the Type Selector dialog again; however, this time it is only populated with classes that derive from the `ExceptionFormatter` base class. Choosing one of these classes changes the exception formatter that will be used for that Log Handler. Figure 5.15 shows how to select the custom `CsvExceptionFormatter` that was created earlier in this chapter.

It is important to note that as the configuration for a particular exception handler changes or an exception policy changes to use different exception handlers, the code to handle these exceptions remains unmodified. Even though the exception formatter for this exception has changed, the code that is needed to use it remains unchanged.

Simple Customized Exception Handling

This chapter has shown the different ways to create a custom exception handler so that it can be used by the Exception Handling Application Block. The first way is to develop a custom exception handler that derives from the `ExceptionHandler` base class and leverages the existing design-time features for all custom exception handlers. The second method expands upon this; however, instead of relying on the existing configuration and design-time features for a custom exception handler, a strongly typed one can be created.

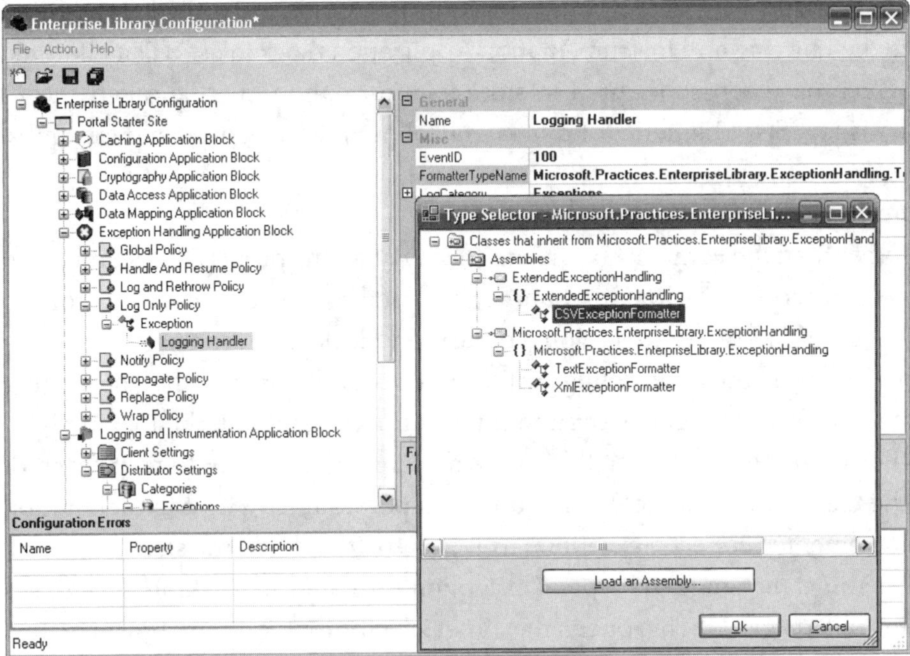

FIGURE 5.15: Changing the `ExceptionFormatter` for a Logging Handler

To add the first kind of custom exception handler to an exception type, select *New > Custom Handler*. Once the exception handler has been added, you must set its `TypeName` property to the type of exception handler that will handle this exception. The Type Selector dialog is used to make it easy for you to select the type of exception handler to use. The dialog box is only populated with classes that the Enterprise Library Configuration Tool knows to derive from the base `ExceptionHandler` class. Figure 5.16 shows how the `AppMessageExceptionHandler` class is added to the *Global Policy* exception policy for a `System.Exception` exception type for an application.

A custom handler can also use its `Attributes` property to retrieve additional configuration data. The `Attributes` property is a `NameValueCollection`. A custom handler can read the extra configuration data that it needs from this `NameValueCollection` instead of requiring the existence

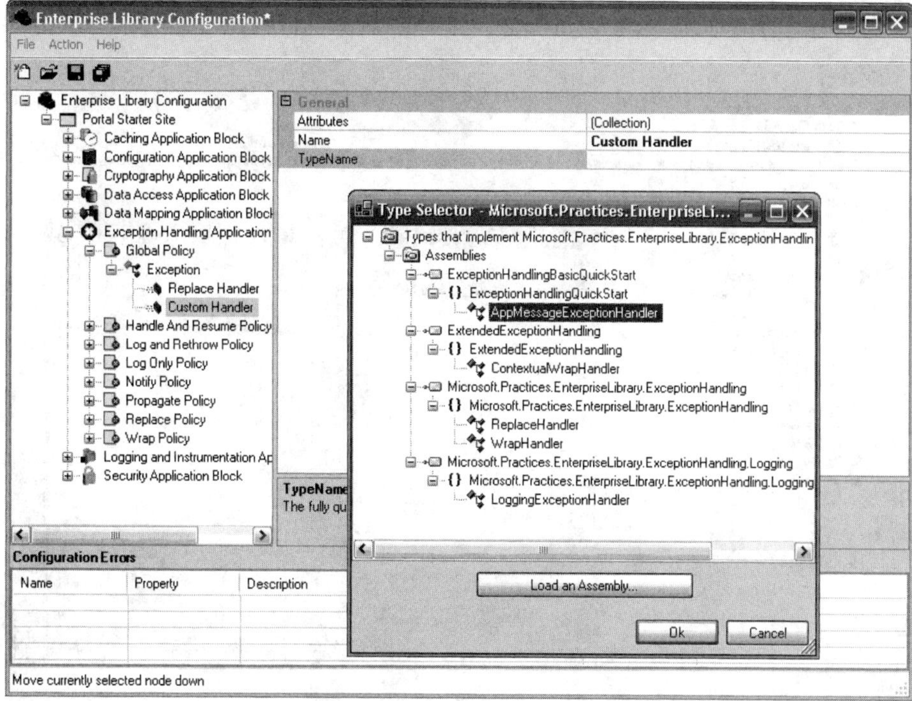

FIGURE 5.16: Setting the `TypeName` for a Custom Handler

of a strongly typed configuration schema. For example, the custom handler that is created in the Exception Handling Application Block Quick Start displays "`The following exception was caught by the Quick Start Global Exception Handler:`" to the end user when an unhandled exception has been caught. However, instead of hard-coding this string in the code, it could have been read from configuration and used via the `Attributes` property as shown in Listing 5.17.

LISTING 5.17: Resulting `InnerException` by Using the `ContextualWrapHandler`

```
[C#]
string errorMsg = handlerData.Attributes["ErrorMsg"];

[Visual Basic]
Dim errorMsg as String = handlerData.Attributes("ErrorMsg")
```

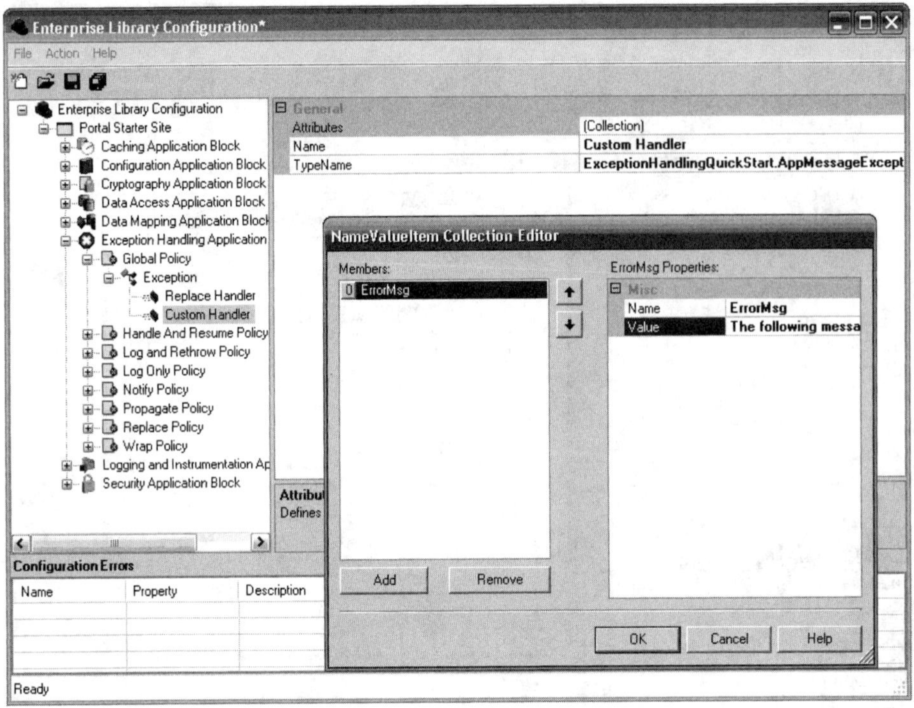

FIGURE 5.17: Setting Attributes for the `AppMessageExceptionHandler`

For this to work, the `Attributes` property would have to be populated with an item named *ErrorMsg*. The Enterprise Library Configuration Tool provides a NameValueItem Collection Editor to make adding and configuring NameValue items easy. Figure 5.17 shows how to use the NameValueItem Collection Editor to configure the `Attributes` property with the needed *ErrorMsg* item.

Advanced Customized Exception Handling

The drawback to using a `NameValueCollection` to specify configuration settings is that it is more error-prone because no validation can be done on the items contained in the collection when it is being configured. You won't know until runtime if an error has been made with the configuration data that is set through the `Attributes` property.

An alternative is to provide a more advanced custom exception handler that uses strongly typed configuration data and design-time classes that work the same way that the `WrapHandler`, `ReplaceHandler`, and `LoggingExceptionHandler` do. Adding and using an advanced custom exception handler is similar to adding and using any of the exception handlers that ship with the application block. Right-click on the exception type for an exception policy and select the new custom exception handler (refer back to Figure 5.9 for an example of creating a custom exception handler of this type).

Chaining Exceptions

Exception handlers can be chained together to perform multiple actions when an exception occurs. You do this by adding multiple exception handlers to an exception type. The order in which the handlers execute is the order in which the exception handlers occur in the configuration. For this reason, there are additional menu options to move an exception handler up and down in its hierarchy in the configuration. Figure 5.18 displays a *Global Policy* that chains together a Replace Handler and a custom handler named *Notification Handler*. Since it is generally a good idea to replace an exception before notifying end users about the exception, the Replace Handler should occur before the Notification Handler in the configuration hierarchy. Figure 5.18 shows how to move the Replace Handler up in the hierarchy.

As previously discussed, any handler in the chain can change the exception before it gets passed to another handler. Exception handlers receive the exception that is returned from the previous handler. The first handler in a chain will always receive the original exception, and the last handler in the chain will always produce the exception that may be returned to the application.

Using the Exception Handling Application Block's API

Writing code for an application so that it can use the Exception Handling Application Block is extremely straightforward. The only code you need to write is to call the `ExceptionPolicy`'s static `HandleException` method. This method expects the exception that was caught by the calling application and the name of an exception policy that has been configured to handle this exception.

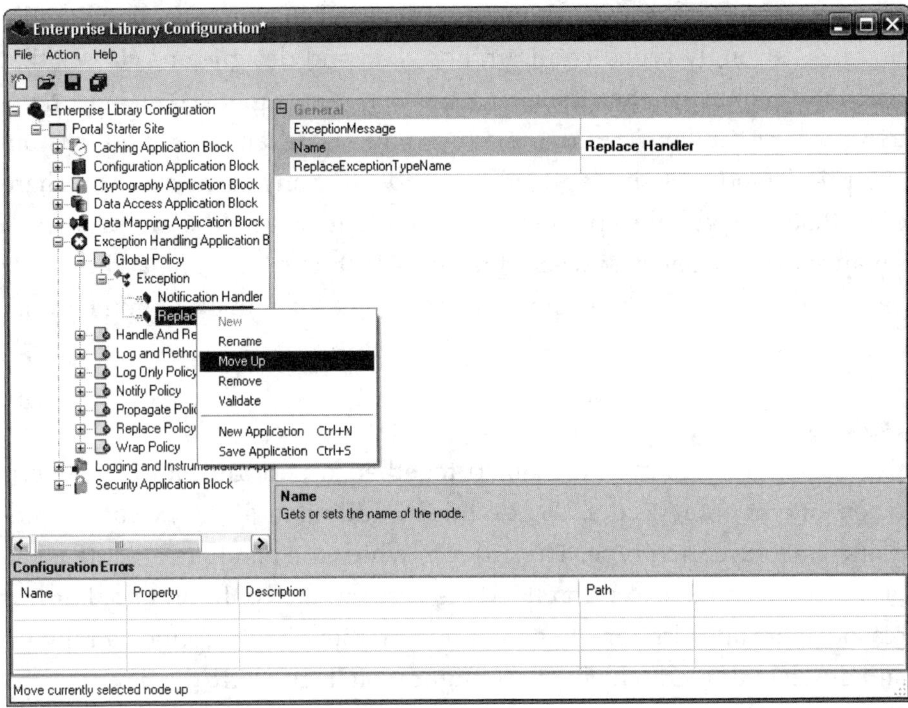

FIGURE 5.18: Moving a Handler Up in the Chain so It Is Executed First

For example, Listing 5.18 displays the kind of code you would need to write if you're not using the Exception Handling Application Block. In this example, a data access routine is used to populate and return a typed DataSet in an application's business layer. If an exception occurred during this process, code might have been written to wrap this exception before propagating it. When the exception gets propagated, some other code may display the exception to an end user or log the exception somewhere or both.

LISTING 5.18: Handling an Exception without the Exception Handling Application Block

```
[C#]
try
{
    return GetAnnouncements(moduleId);
}
catch (Exception ex)
```

```
{
     String formattedInfo = FormatException(ex);
     BusinessLayerException businessLayerException =
          new BusinessLayerException
          ("Failed to retrieve necessary data", ex);
     Throw(businessLayerException);
}

[Visual Basic]
Try
  Return GetAnnouncements(moduleID)
Catch ex As Exception
  Dim formattedInfo As String = FormatException(ex)
  Dim businessLayerException as BusinessLayerException = _
      new BusinessLayerException _
      (""Failed to retrieve necessary data", ex)
  Throw businessLayerException
End Try
```

This is not bad code. It is perfectly acceptable to handle exceptions this way. However, if it is likely that the behavior will change or the behavior could be reused in many places, externalizing the behavior via the Exception Handling Application Block can make a lot of sense. If you use the Exception Handling Application Block, you don't need to write any code to create and throw a particular exception. Instead, this responsibility can be delegated to the Exception Handling Application Block. Thus, the code in Listing 5.18 can be rewritten as shown in Listing 5.19 to notify the block which exception occurred and which policy should be executed.

LISTING 5.19: The Exception Handling Application Block Determines How to Handle Exceptions

```
[C#]
try
{
     return GetAnnouncements(moduleId);
}
catch (Exception ex)
{
     bool rethrow = ExceptionPolicy.HandleException
                      (ex, "Business Layer Policy");

     if (rethrow)
          throw;
}
```

```
[Visual Basic]
Try
       Return GetAnnouncements(moduleID)
Catch
     Dim rethrow As Boolean = ExceptionPolicy.HandleException _
                                   (ex, "Business Layer Policy")

     If (rethrow) Then
         Throw
     End If
 End Try
```

This has the distinct advantage that the way an exception is handled is separated from the code that initiates the exception handling process. If sometime later it is deemed necessary to change the behavior for how the exception is handled, then no code would need to be changed. For example, if this exception is currently being wrapped or replaced with another exception, but later it is decided that the exception also needs to be logged before it is replaced and then someone should be notified about the exception, no code would need to be changed. All the changes are made in the configuration data for the exception policy.

Summary

This chapter compared the features of the Enterprise Library Exception Handling Application Block to its predecessor, the Exception Management Application Block, covered the design of the application block, and described how to configure and develop an application to use it. The design for this application block is based in large part on the guidance found in the *Exception Management in .NET Architecture Guide.* The major principle that you should understand from this chapter is that the Exception Handling Application Block allows an application to decouple *when* it handles an exception from *how* it handles an exception.

The chapter reviewed the features that existed in the Exception Management Application Block that are not mentioned in the Exception Handling Application Block, and it highlighted where new functionality replaced some of the functionality that previously existed and which functionality was moved to the Logging and Instrumentation Application Block. It included a detailed analysis of the design for the `Exception-`

`Policy`, `ExceptionHandler`, and `ExceptionFormatter` classes and showed how the interfaces for the `ExceptionFormatter` and `ExceptionHandler` provide extension points that you can use to its advantage. It also covered how to configure the Exception Handling Application Block and how developing an application to use it only requires understanding an extremely simple interface with a single method. Emphasis was placed on the fact that very little code actually needs to be written to use the Exception Handling Application Block. As exception policies change over time, the code that initiates these exception policies does not; only the configuration for how these exception policies run needs to be modified.

6

The Logging and Instrumentation Application Block

THE LAST CHAPTER touched on the fact that it is very common for an application to have to log information. For example, it isn't unusual for an application to log exceptions that occur. I mentioned that, while handling exceptions is the responsibility of the Exception Handling Application Block, logging the exceptions is the responsibility of the Logging and Instrumentation Application Block. Unfortunately, like caching, logging is often an afterthought to the design of the application and only gets added to the application after it has already been deployed and issues start to arise. When this occurs, logging is often "slammed" into the application in a haphazard manner.

The Logging and Instrumentation Application Block is meant to make it easy to architect and develop a solution with very flexible logging capabilities. Regrettably, I have heard from many developers and architects that the Logging and Instrumentation Application Block appears to be too complex to fit their needs—they feel that it is just too much to deal with when all they need to do is log a message to a file or the event log. This is an unfortunate assessment.

In this chapter I will attempt to change this perception by first explaining the reasons for the classes that exist in the Logging and Instrumentation

Application Block. More importantly, however, I will attempt to show that any complexity that exists because of these classes is "hidden" from most developers who will use the block. If your only need is to write to a file or an event log, the only code that you may ever need to write is `Logger.Write(string)`. If your applications have more complex logging needs, the Logging and Instrumentation Application Block has been designed to accommodate those needs without causing an undue burden on those developers who don't need it. And best of all, the application is automatically indifferent to changes that may occur with respect to the final location for the log messages and how to get them there.

This chapter has a lot of code samples, but don't confuse this with the need to write a lot of code to take advantage of the features in the Logging and Instrumentation Application Block. Quite the opposite is true. The capabilities that this block provides in terms of its extensibility are the very reasons why the average developer who works with this block can be hidden from any complex logging needs. That is the main point of this chapter.

What Is the Logging and Instrumentation Application Block?

The Logging and Instrumentation Application Block provides a standard and consistent way to log messages. It is designed to make it easy for developers to incorporate logging and tracing functionality into an application. By allowing the destination for log messages to be determined through configuration instead of code, the Logging and Instrumentation Application Block allows an application to be completely decoupled from any particular logging store (e.g., e-mail, files, databases, etc.). Furthermore, configuration data can drive characteristics like the format for the log messages, which messages should be filtered out of a log, and even whether the distribution strategy for a log message should be synchronous or asynchronous.

The primary goal of the Logging and Instrumentation Application Block is to allow a developer to focus on when and why a message should get logged and to allow an administrator to determine how, where, and if the message gets logged. By removing the complexities that surround dynamically routing, formatting, and filtering logs in an application and making it a "no brainer," it is more likely that logging will be considered when designing an application instead of as an afterthought. Furthermore, just like the Exception Handling Application Block (discussed in Chapter 5), even after an application has been deployed and changes occur as to how and where messages should be logged, these changes can be handled through modifications to configuration settings and without the need to modify any code in the application.

Relationship to the Previous Version of the Logging Application Block and the EIF

Microsoft released the Enterprise Instrumentation Framework (EIF) in April 2003. The Enterprise Instrumentation Framework focused on logging and instrumentation tasks in an application. It supported raising and logging events to the WMI, the Windows event log, and a trace log.

Later that same year, Microsoft provided an extension to the Enterprise Instrumentation Framework with the Logging Application Block. The Logging Application Block added such features as Formatters, more Logging Sinks, centralized logging, asynchronous logging, configurable log levels, and a custom `Publisher` for the Exception Management Application Block. There's a complete document[1] produced by the Microsoft patterns & practices team that is dedicated to the design and development features for that version of the Logging Application Block, so this book won't go into great detail on those specific features. Besides, many of the features that were in the previous version still exist in some way in Enterprise Library's version, so they will be covered later in this chapter. It is important, however, to acknowledge the previous version of the Logging Application Block and the Enterprise Instrumentation Framework as the rightful ancestors to the Logging and Instrumentation Application Block that ships with Enterprise Library.

It seems that the process of natural selection doesn't apply only to organic creatures. To make it more useful, new features like templates, a flat

---

1. The document is included as part of the package when you download the block from microsoft.com/downloads/details.aspx?FamilyID=24f61845-e56c-42d6-bbd5-29f0d5cd7f65&DisplayLang=en.

file Sink, and an e-mail Sink have been introduced with the Enterprise Library version of the Logging and Instrumentation Application Block. Vestigial or overly complex techniques and constructs have been eliminated. One of these is the integration with the Enterprise Instrumentation Framework. Many developers who used the previous version of this application block felt that the Enterprise Instrumentation Framework was overly complex. It was too hard to configure and use. In the Enterprise Library version of the Logging and Instrumentation Application Block, the dependency on the Enterprise Instrumentation Framework has been completely removed; however, the features have not. Thus, you can think of the Enterprise Library Logging and Instrumentation Application Block as the successor to the Enterprise Instrumentation Framework and the Logging Application Block.

Design of the Logging and Instrumentation Application Block

The design goals for the Logging and Instrumentation Application Block were to make it easy for developers to accomplish the most common application logging and instrumentation tasks and to do so in a consistent manner. To meet this design goal, the block provides a high degree of configurability and leverages two service façades that determine which actions to take based upon the configuration information and not the code. This allows all logging and tracing decisions to be externalized through configuration and lets changes to the logging behavior occur without changes to an application's code.

While this makes it simple to accomplish the most common logging and instrumentation tasks, it does not preclude the ability to leverage many of the other classes that exist in the block. Furthermore, if you have logging needs that are not directly covered by the Logging and Instrumentation Application Block, its many extension points let you customize the block to fit your needs.

This section discusses the classes that exist in the block and the role they play in logging, not only to explain these extension points, but to also explain how logging in the Logging and Instrumentation Application Block works underneath the covers. To do so, this section reviews each class in the order that it comes into play as a message gets logged. I've broken this flow into several categories: log creation, filtering, log distribution, and routing (including Formatters and Sinks). This section concludes with a discussion of the design for tracing and how it relates to logging in this block.

Log Creation

The first step in logging information is to create the entry that will eventually be logged. One of the challenges in providing a generic solution that represents a log entry for any application is determining what information is needed for every log entry, what information is not mandatory but important enough to include in every log entry, and how to provide a solution that allows any application with the ability to include other extra information that may only be pertinent to that application. Another challenge that must be overcome involves designing a solution that is flexible enough to accommodate virtually any type of log information without being so complex that it is difficult to use or causes major performance issues in an application.

The primary classes that are involved in the log creation process are the `Logger`, `LogWriter`, `LogEntry`, `ContextItems`, and `ExtraInformationProviders`. Figure 6.1 shows the relationship between these classes except for `ExtraInformationProviders`, which will be discussed a bit later in this chapter.

Basic Logging

Like the other application blocks, the Logging and Instrumentation Application Block achieves its design goal of a simplified programming interface by exposing a service façade; in this case, it is the `Logger` class. The `Logger` interface only exposes one method for logging information—a static `Write` method. This method is overloaded ten times, so technically it is really more than one method. The point, however, is that to log information in an application, the only method that needs to be called is `Write`. The implementation for how and where to log information happens behind the `Logger` service façade.

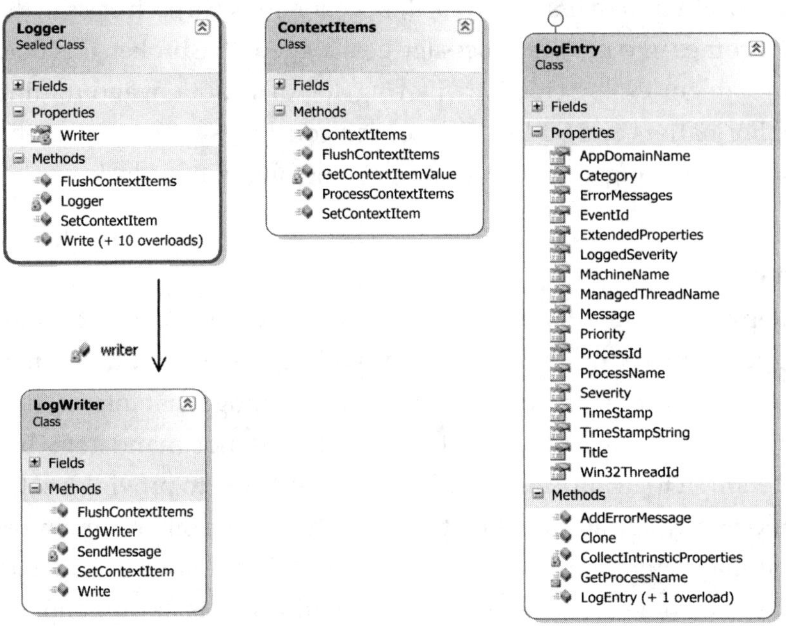

FIGURE 6.1: Primary Classes for Creating Logs

The Logging and Instrumentation Application Block is a message-based architecture. The `Logger` creates the message. This message is called the `LogEntry`. The `Logger` encapsulates a `LogWriter` object for publishing the message. The `LogWriter` filters the messages based on the Category and Priority of the `LogEntry` and, if it passes the filter, sends the `LogEntry` to the appropriate distribution strategy. This all happens in the process space of the running application. The distribution strategy then sends the message to a distributor, and the distributor determines how the message should be routed to a specific destination (also known as a *Sink*). Figure 6.2 illustrates how the Logging and Instrumentation Application Block works to synchronously distribute the logs that are created in different applications.

The overloads for the `Logger`'s `Write` method simply represent different ways to create an instance of a `LogEntry`. One overload accepts an instance of a `LogEntry` object; the other overloads accept various fields from which a `LogEntry` can be created. The simplest way to automatically

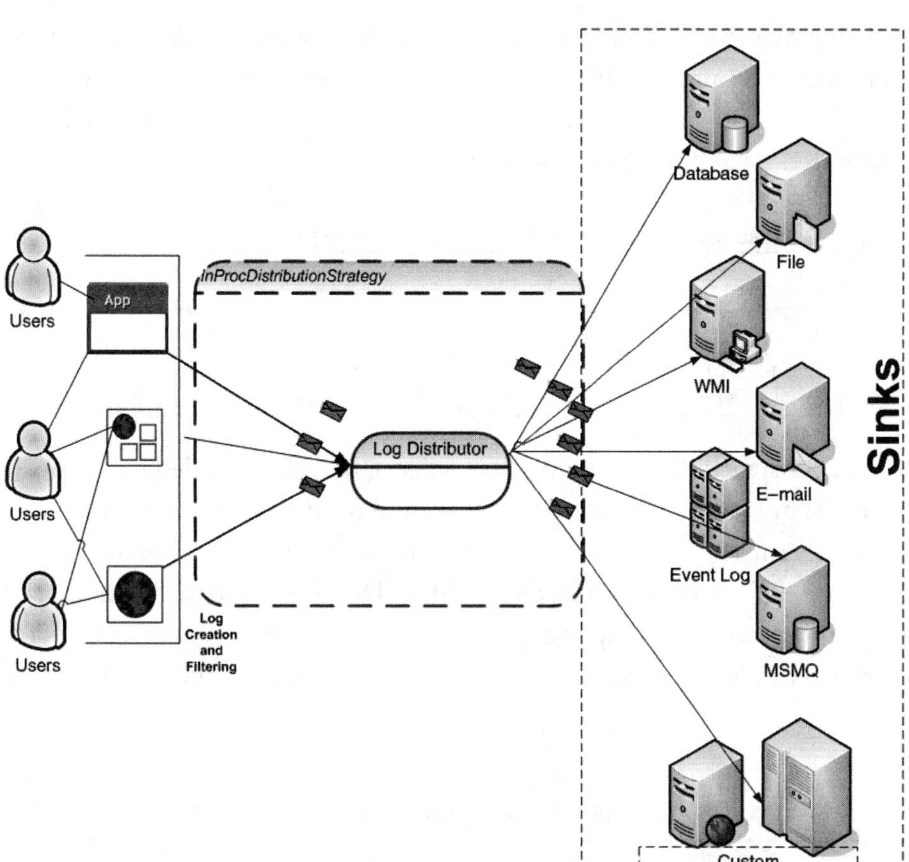

FIGURE 6.2: Synchronous Distribution of Logs

create a `LogEntry` is to call the `Write` method that takes a single string representing the `LogEntry`'s `Message` property. Listing 6.1 shows an example of this. The `Logger` class will use this string to create a `LogEntry` with default values for all of the other `LogEntry` properties.

LISTING 6.1: Creating a `LogEntry` with a Message

```
[C#]
Logger.Write("This is a log message");

[Visual Basic]
Logger.Write("This is a log message")
```

Other overloads allow different combinations of certain LogEntry properties to be populated. For example, Listing 6.2 creates the same LogEntry as Listing 6.1 but with the Category myCategory instead of the one that is configured to be the default Category.

LISTING 6.2: Creating a LogEntry with a Message and Category

```
[C#]
Logger.Write("This is a log message", "myCategory");

[Visual Basic]
Logger.Write("This is a log message" , "myCategory")
```

The constructor for the LogEntry expects the fields detailed in Table 6.1.

Thus, in Listing 6.1, default values were used for the Category, Priority, EventID, Title, Severity, and ExtendedProperties. In Listing 6.2, myCategory was used in place of the default Category. The ExtendedProperties field is especially interesting; it represents an instance of a class that implements the IDictionary interface and embodies additional

TABLE 6.1: Fields Expected for the LogEntry Constructor

Property	Description
Message	Represents the body of the message.
Category	Determines how the LogEntry should be routed.
Priority	Represents the significance of the LogEntry. LogEntries can be filtered based upon the priority.
EventID	Categorizes messages.
Title	Describes the LogEntry.
Severity	Specifies the severity of the message: Unspecified, Information, Warning, or Error.
ExtendedProperties	Represents name/value pairs of additional information to be logged.

name/value pairs to log that are not part of the `LogEntry` class. For example, Listing 6.3 could be used to log some characteristics about a user.

Listing 6.3: Creating a `LogEntry` with `ExtendedProperties`

```
[C#]
Hashtable userHash = new Hashtable();
IIdentity identity = Thread.CurrentPrincipal.Identity;
userHash["userName"] = identity.Name;
userHash["isAuthenticated"] = identity.IsAuthenticated;
Logger.Write("Some user info", userHash);

[Visual Basic]
Dim userHash As Hashtable = New Hashtable()
Dim identity As IIdentity = Thread.CurrentPrincipal.Identity
Dim userHash("userName") = identity.Name
Dim userHash("isAuthenticated") = identity.IsAuthenticated
Logger.Write("Some user info", userHash)
```

Extra Information

The `ExtendedProperties` field represents "extra information" to add to the log. As you can see in Listing 6.3, this dictionary can be populated with any (serializable) information that an application may need to add to the log. There are common sets of this extra information that many applications will need to add. It is not information that belongs in every log, but it is common enough to deserve an easy way to create it.

For example, it is very common to include user information like the kind added in Listing 6.3. To meet this need, the Logging and Instrumentation Application Block ships with additional classes that will obtain this information and populate an `IDictionary` with it. Of course, automatically obtaining and populating this information does not come without a performance cost; therefore, these classes should only be used as needed. The classes that ship with the Logging and Instrumentation Application Block are `ComPlusExtraInformationProvider`, `DebugInformationProvider`, `ManagedSecurityContextInformationProvider`, and `UnmanagedSecurityContextInformationProvider`. They are depicted in Figure 6.3.

`IExtraInformationProvider`. The `IExtraInformationProvider` interface defines a method to populate an `IDictionary` with extra informa-

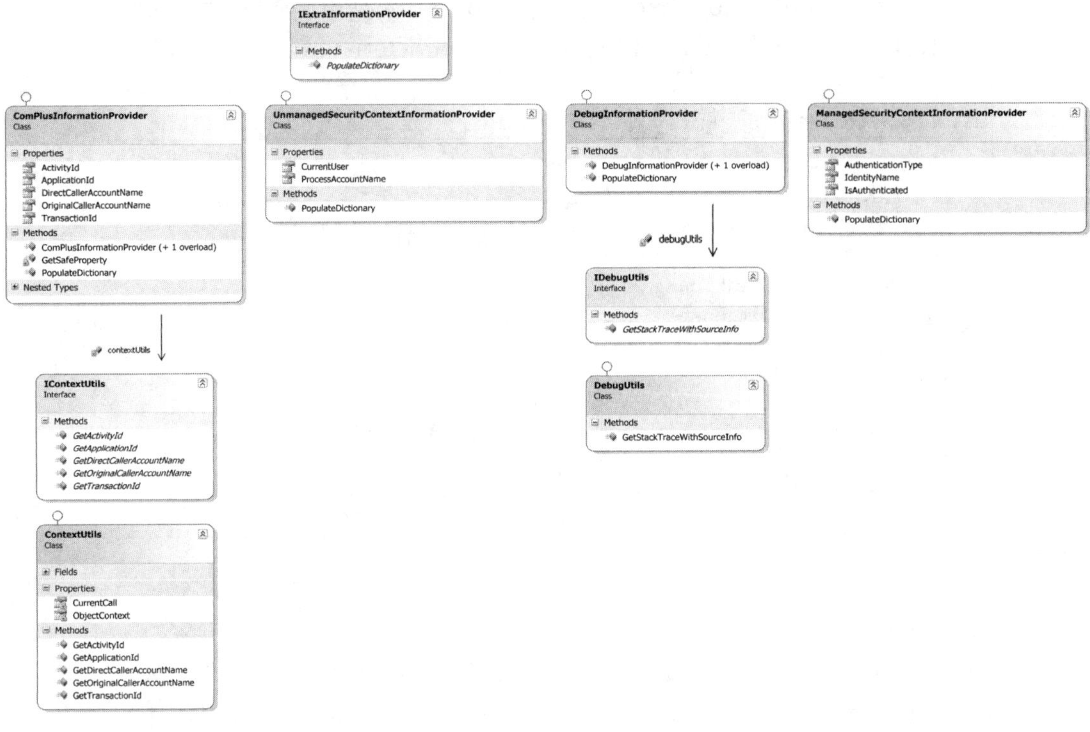

FIGURE 6.3: `ExtraInformationProvider` **Classes**

tion. It is not necessary to implement this interface to pass an `IDictionary` to the `LogEntry` class; however, this interface provides a neat method for hiding any complexities that might occur to populate a specific `IDictionary`. (A better name for the interface might have been *`IDictionaryPopulater`*.) The interface provides a method which returns an `IDictionary` that is aptly named `PopulateDictionary(IDictionary dict)`.

`ComPlusInformationProvider.` The `PopulateDictionary` method for the `ComPlusInformationProvider` fills the supplied `IDictionary` with common COM+ diagnostic information. To retrieve this information from COM+, the `ComPlusInformationProvider` encapsulates a `ContextUtils` object which in turn wraps around the `System.EnterpriseServices.ContextUtil` class. The `IDictionary` is filled with the key/values specified in Table 6.2.

`DebugInformationProvider.` It is very common to want to log information from the debugging subsystem when developing and testing an

TABLE 6.2: Keys and Values for the `ComPlusInformationProvider`

Key	Description
`ActivityId`	Returns the COM+ Activity ID.
`ApplicationId`	Returns the COM+ Application ID.
`DirectCallerAccountName`	Returns the COM+ Direct Caller Name.
`OriginalCallerAccountName`	Returns the COM+ Original Caller Account Name.
`TransactionId`	Returns the COM+ Transaction ID.

application. The `DebugInformationProvider` is intended to facilitate this task. The `PopulateDictionary` method for the `DebugInformationProvider` fills the supplied `IDictionary` with diagnostic information from the debug subsystem. To retrieve this information, the `DebugInformationProvider` encapsulates a `DebugUtils` object that retrieves the stack trace. The `IDictionary` contains a name/value pair named `StackTrace` that contains a value equal to the corresponding stack trace. Listing 6.4 shows code from the `DebugInformationProviderFixture` class, which is part of the application block's test project, to show how this works.

LISTING 6.4: Using `DebugInformationProvider` to Populate a Dictionary

```
[C#]
public void PopulateDictionaryFilledCorrectly()
{
     Hashtable dictionary = new Hashtable();
     provider = new DebugInformationProvider();
     provider.PopulateDictionary(dictionary);
}

[Visual Basic]
Public Sub PopulateDictionaryFilledCorrectly()
     Dim Hashtable dictionary = New Hashtable()
     provider = New DebugInformationProvider()
     provider.PopulateDictionary(dictionary)
End Sub
```

This produces a dictionary with one key named `StackTrace` and the value shown (and formatted for legibility purposes) in Listing 6.5.

LISTING 6.5: Results from Using the `DebugInformationProvider`

```
StackTrace -        at
Microsoft.Practices.EnterpriseLibrary.Logging.ExtraInformation.
DebugInformationProvider.PopulateDictionary(IDictionary dict)in
c:\program files\microsoft enterprise library\src\logging\
extrainformation\debuginformationprovider.cs:
line 54 at
     LoggingQuickStart.QuickStartForm.logExtraInformationButton_Click
     (Object sender, EventArgs e) in c:\program files\microsoft
     enterprise library\quickstarts\logging\cs\loggingquickstart
     \quickstartform.cs: line 379
          at System.Windows.Forms.Control.OnClick(EventArgs e)
          at System.Windows.Forms.Button.OnClick(EventArgs e)
          at System.Windows.Forms.Button.WndProc(Message& m)
          at System.Windows.Forms.ControlNativeWindow.OnMessage
                (Message& m)
          at System.Windows.Forms.ControlNativeWindow.WndProc
                (Message& m)
          at System.Windows.Forms.NativeWindow.Callback
                (IntPtr hWnd, Int32 msg, IntPtr wparam, IntPtr lparam)
          at System.Windows.Forms.UnsafeNativeMethods.SendMessage
               (HandleRef...
```

`ManagedSecurityContextInformationProvider.` Listing 6.3 created a hash table and populated it with user information from `Thread.CurrentPrincipal.Identity`. Obtaining and logging user information is a very common need for many applications. As such, the Logging and Instrumentation Application Block ships with the `ManagedSecurityContextInformationProvider` to facilitate this process. Listing 6.6 shows how to rewrite Listing 6.3 to use this class.

LISTING 6.6: Using `ManagedSecurityContextInformationProvider` **to Fill** `ExtendedProperties`

```
[C#]
Hashtable userHash = new Hashtable();
ManagedSecurityContextInformationProvider provider =
     new ManagedSecurityContextInformationProvider();
provider.PopulateDictionary(userHash);
Logger.Write("Some user info", userHash);

[Visual Basic]
Private userHash As Hashtable = New Hashtable()
Private provider As ManagedSecurityContextInformationProvider = _
```

```
        New ManagedSecurityContextInformationProvider()
    provider.PopulateDictionary(userHash)
    Logger.Write("Some user info", userHash)
```

TABLE 6.3: Keys and Values for the `ManagedSecurityContextInformationProvider`

Key	Description
`AuthenticationType`	The authentication type.
`IdentityName`	The identity's name.
`IsAuthenticated`	The `IsAuthenticated` flag.

Notice that there is no code that gets any information from the `CurrentPrincipal`'s `Identity`. Well, actually there is, but it is all in the `ManagedSecurityContextInformationProvider` class. This class retrieves the values listed in Table 6.3 from `Thread.CurrentPrincipal.Identity` and fills the supplied IDictionary with them.

`UnmanagedSecurityContextInformationProvider`. Unfortunately, not all applications today operate in the .NET managed environment. Yet, the need still exists to obtain and log valuable information about the current user. The `UnmanagedSecurityContextInformationProvider` gets the security context information from the unmanaged world and leverages a `NativeMethods` class that calls the native `GetUserNameEx` and `GetSecurityInfo` methods to populate its dictionary. The `IDictionary` is filled with the keys and values listed in Table 6.4.

Custom ExtraInformationProvider. As already mentioned, it isn't required to use an ExtraInformationProvider to supply an `IDictionary`

TABLE 6.4: Keys and Values for the `UnmanagedSecurityContextInformationProvider`

Key	Description
`CurrentUser`	Gets the current user.
`ProcessAccountName`	Gets the account name of the process.

to the `LogEntry` class. However, if there is common information that you continually want to log and this information is not represented by any of the ExtraInformationProviders that are supplied with the Logging and Instrumentation Application Block, it makes sense to encapsulate it with a custom ExtraInformationProvider. Creating such a provider is not complicated; the only task you need to implement for the `IExtraInformation-Provider` interface is the `PopulateDictionary` method.

For example, let's say you need to log the configuration information used by an application. As applications rely on configuration information to drive the runtime behavior, logging the configuration information can become as valuable as logging debugging information. To provide this functionality, I have created the `ELConfigurationContextInformation-Provider`. Listing 6.7 shows how its `PopulateDictionary` method populates the dictionary with an application's Enterprise Library configuration data (the complete source code is on the book's Web site).

Listing 6.7: `ELConfigurationContextInformationProvider`'s `Populate-Dictionary` Method

```
[C#]
public void PopulateDictionary(IDictionary dict)
{
     ConfigurationContext context = ConfigurationManager.GetCurrentCon-
text();
     ConfigurationSettings configSettings = context.GetMetaConfigura-
tion();

     dict.Add("ApplicationName",configSettings.ApplicationName);
     foreach (ConfigurationSectionData configSection in
                  configSettings.ConfigurationSections)
     {
          string sectionName = configSection.Name;

          //I don't want to just GetConfiguration b/c then I would be
          //deserializing just to reserialize. I want to just use the
          //StorageProvider to get the serialized object.
          Type storageProviderType = Type.GetType
                    (configSection.StorageProvider.TypeName);
          ConstructorInfo constructor =
                         storageProviderType.GetConstructor(new Type[]
{});
          object createdObject = constructor.Invoke(null);
          IStorageProviderReader storageProviderReader =
```

```
                    (IStorageProviderReader) createdObject;
          RuntimeConfigurationView view = new
                    RuntimeConfigurationView(context);
          storageProviderReader.ConfigurationName =
                    configSection.StorageProvider.Name;
          storageProviderReader.CurrentSectionName = sectionName;
          storageProviderReader.Initialize(view);
           object configSectionSettings = storageProviderReader.Read();

           //I need to tell it how I want the value written, so the
           //Serialize method will write out config.
           dict.Add(sectionName,Serialize(configSectionSettings));
     }
}


[Visual Basic]
Public Sub PopulateDictionary(ByVal dict As IDictionary)

     Dim context As ConfigurationContext = _
               ConfigurationManager.GetCurrentContext()
     Dim configSettings As ConfigurationSettings = _
               context.GetMetaConfiguration()

    dict.Add("ApplicationName",configSettings.ApplicationName)
     For Each configSection As ConfigurationSectionData In _
                    configSettings.ConfigurationSections
          Dim sectionName As String = configSection.Name

         'I don't want to just GetConfiguration b/c then I would be
          'deserializing just to reserialize. I want to just use the
          'StorageProvider to get the serialized object.
          Dim storageProviderType As Type = Type.GetType _
                    (configSection.StorageProvider.TypeName)
          Dim constructor As ConstructorInfo = _
               storageProviderType.GetConstructor(New Type() {})
          Dim createdObject As Object = constructor.Invoke(Nothing)
          Dim storageProviderReader As IStorageProviderReader = _
                    CType(createdObject, IStorageProviderReader)
          Dim view As RuntimeConfigurationView = _
                    New RuntimeConfigurationView(context)
          storageProviderReader.ConfigurationName = _
                    configSection.StorageProvider.Name
          storageProviderReader.CurrentSectionName = sectionName
          storageProviderReader.Initialize(view)
          Dim configSectionSettings As Object = _
          storageProviderReader.Read()

          'I need to tell it how I want the value written, so the
```

```
            'Serialize method will write out config.
            dict.Add(sectionName,Serialize(configSectionSettings))
        Next configSection
    End Sub
```

The log produced includes the configuration data for all of the application blocks that have been configured for that application. Listing 6.8 shows this output (truncated for brevity).

LISTING 6.8: Log Produced from Using `ELConfigurationContextInformation-Provider` **(Truncated)**

```
...
Message: EntLib Configuration Information

Extended Properties:
Key: ApplicationName              Value:
Key: dataConfiguration             Value:
<xmlSerializerSection type="System.Xml.XmlElement, System.Xml,
     Version=1.0.5000.0, Culture=neutral,
PublicKeyToken=b77a5c561934e089">
<xmlSerializerSection
          type="Microsoft.Practices.EnterpriseLibrary.Data.Configura-
          tion.

DatabaseSettings,Microsoft.Practices.EnterpriseLibrary.Data">
     <enterpriseLibrary.databaseSettings
               xmlns:xsd="http://www.w3.org/2001/XMLSchema"
               xmlns:xsi="http://www.w3.org/2001/XMLSchema-instance"
               xmlns="http://www.microsoft.com/practices/enterpriseli-
               brary/
                    08-31-2004/data" defaultInstance="Service_Dflt">
     <databaseTypes>
          <databaseType name="SqlServer"
               type="Microsoft.Practices.EnterpriseLibrary.Data.Sql.Sql-
               Database,
               Microsoft.Practices.EnterpriseLibrary.Data"/>
     </databaseTypes>
     <connectionStrings>
          <connectionString name="Northwind">
               <parameters>
                    <parameter name="server" value="localhost" />
                    <parameter name="database" value="Northwind" />
                    <parameter name="Integrated Security"
value="true"/>
               </parameters>
          </connectionString></connectionStrings>
     <connectionStrings>
```

```
            <connectionString name="LoggingConnection">
                <parameters>
                    <parameter name="server" value="localhost" />
                    <parameter name="database" value="Logging" />
                    <parameter name="Integrated Security" value="true"
                    />
                </parameters>
            </connectionString>
        </connectionStrings>
        <instances>
            <instance name="Service_Dflt"
                type="SqlServer" connectionString="Northwind" />
            <instance name="LoggingDb" type="SqlServer"
                connectionString="LoggingConnection" />
        </instances>
        </enterpriseLibrary.databaseSettings>
</xmlSerializerSection></xmlSerializerSection>
Key: loggingConfiguration            Value:
<xmlSerializerSection type="System.Xml.XmlElement, System.Xml,
    Version=1.0.5000.0, Culture=neutral, PublicKeyToken=b77a5c561934e089">
<xmlSerializerSection
        type="Microsoft.Practices.EnterpriseLibrary.Logging.
        Configuration.
        LoggingSettings,
        Microsoft.Practices.EnterpriseLibrary.Logging">
        <enterpriseLibrary.loggingSettings
            xmlns:xsd="http://www.w3.org/2001/XMLSchema"
            xmlns:xsi="http://www.w3.org/2001/XMLSchema-instance"
            xmlns="http://www.microsoft.com/practices/
            enterpriselibrary/
            08-31-2004/logging" loggingEnabled="true"
            tracingEnabled="true"
            minimumPriority="5" distributionStrategy="InProc"
            categoryFilterMode="AllowAllExceptDenied">
        <categoryFilters>
            <categoryFilter name="MyDeniedCategory" />
            <categoryFilter name="MyDeniedCategory2" />
            <categoryFilter name="MyDeniedCategory3" />
        </categoryFilters>
        <distributionStrategies>
            <distributionStrategy
                xsi:type="InProcDistributionStrategyData" name="InProc"
                />
            <distributionStrategy
                xsi:type="MsmqDistributionStrategyData"
                name="Msmq" queuePath=".\Private$\entlib" />
            <distributionStrategy
                xsi:type="CustomDistributionStrategyData" name="Mock-
                Strategy"
```

```
                type="Microsoft.Practices.EnterpriseLibrary.
                Logging.
                Distributor.Tests.MockDistributionStrategy,
                Microsoft.Practices.EnterpriseLibrary.Logging" />
        </distributionStrategies>
        </enterpriseLibrary.loggingSettings>
    </xmlSerializerSection></xmlSerializerSection>
    ...
```

More on `LogWriter` and `LogEntry`

It might seem that an obvious ExtraInformationProvider would be one that populates the `IDictionary` with certain machine and application-specific information like `MachineName` or `ProcessId`. Such an ExtraInformation-Provider isn't needed, however, because the `LogEntry` class contains several intrinsic properties that contain this system information. Table 6.5 lists these additional intrinsic properties.

Table 6.5: `LogEntry`'s Intrinsic Properties

Property	Description
`AppDomainName`	The `AppDomain` in which the application is running.
`LoggedSeverity`	Gets or sets the Int32 value of the `Severity` enumeration.
`MachineName`	The name of the computer.
`ManagedThreadName`	The name of the .NET thread.
`ProcessId`	The Win32 process ID for the current running process.
`ProcessName`	The name of the current running process.
`TimeStamp`	The date and time of the LogEntry message.
`TimeStampString`	A read-only property that returns the `TimeStamp` formatted using the current culture.
`Win32ThreadId`	The Win32 Thread ID for the current thread.

These intrinsic properties are automatically collected and populated when a LogEntry is created. Therefore, you don't need to write any other code for this additional information to be logged. Many of these properties can have their values overwritten if necessary. For example, if it were necessary to change the TimeStamp of a LogEntry to a time other than when it was created (perhaps to simulate a delay for testing), it is possible to do so. To do this, the LogEntry must first be created, the TimeStamp property must be set, and then the LogEntry must be passed to the Logger's Write method, which accepts an already created LogEntry. Listing 6.9 shows such an example.

LISTING 6.9: Setting Intrinsic Oroperties for a `LogEntry`

```
[C#]
LogEntry log = new LogEntry();
log.Category = "Logging Test Category";
log.Message = "A Message in a Bottle";
log.Title = "Some Title";
log.EventId = 25;
log.Severity = Severity.Warning;
log.Priority = loggingSettings.MinimumPriority;
log.TimeStamp = DateTime.Now;
Logger.Write(log);

[Visual Basic]
Dim log As LogEntry = New LogEntry()
Dim log.Category = "Logging Test Category"
Dim log.Message = "A Message in a Bottle"
Dim log.Title = "Some Title"
Dim log.EventId = 25
Dim log.Severity = Severity.Warning
Dim log.Priority = loggingSettings.MinimumPriority
Dim log.TimeStamp = DateTime.Now
Logger.Write(log)
```

Custom `LogEntry`. You can capture additional information in a LogEntry by creating a class that derives from the LogEntry class. The Logger's Write(LogEntry) method will accept an instance of the LogEntry class or any subclass thereof. This is a powerful feature because it allows a strongly typed object to be defined that can contain additional important information as an enterprise's *standard* log message.

For example, the Microsoft WS-I Basic Security Profile Sample Application[2] leverages Enterprise Library's configuration, data, exception handling, and logging blocks. The data that gets logged to the database for this application contains extra fields to capture information like the `ServiceId`. It's possible that a custom `LogEntry` like that shown in Listing 6.10 could have been used to automatically capture this information.

LISTING 6.10: Custom `LogEntry` for the WS-I Basic Security Profile Application Example

```
[C#]
[Serializable]
public class WSILogEntry : LogEntry
{
     public WSILogEntry() : base()
     {
     }

     public string ServiceId = string.Empty;
}

[Visual Basic]
<Serializable> _
Public Class WSILogEntry : Inherits LogEntry
     Private Function WSILogEntry() As Public
          MyBase.New()
     End Function

     Public ServiceId As String = String.Empty
End Class
```

The `WSILogEntry` could then be used to log all the information that the base `LogEntry` already logs—plus the `ServiceId`—by using code like that shown in Listing 6.11.

LISTING 6.11: Sample WS-I Basic Security Profile Application Log

```
[C#]
WSILogEntry wsiLog = new WSILogEntry();
wsiLog.Category = "WSICat";
wsiLog.EventId = "UC2-2-1";
wsiLog.Message = "WarehouseA will determine its ability to ship";
wsiLog.Title = "WSI Log Event";
wsiLog.ServiceId = "WarehouseA.ShipGoods";
```

2. The Microsoft WS-I Basic Security Profile Sample Application is at www.gotdotnet.com/codegallery/codegallery.aspx?id=0fecd2c7-b2b1-4d85-bd66-9d07a6ecbd86.

```
Logger.Write(wsiLog);

[Visual Basic]
Dim wsiLog As WSILogEntry = New WSILogEntry()
Dim wsiLog.Category = "WSICat"
Dim wsiLog.EventId = "UC2-2-1"
Dim wsiLog.Message = "WarehouseA will determine its ability to ship"
Dim wsiLog.Title = "WSI Log Event"
Dim wsiLog.ServiceId = "WarehouseA.ShipGoods"
Logger.Write(wsiLog)
```

However, as powerful as this is, there is a catch to using it. LogEntries are eventually written to their ultimate data store using the `Sink` and `Formatter` classes (described later in this chapter). Typically, a `Sink` uses a `Formatter` to format the LogEntry before persisting it; usually, this `Formatter` will be the `TextFormatter`. The `TextFormatter` doesn't know anything about any custom properties or fields that may exist in a subclassed `LogEntry`. Therefore, to persist a custom `LogEntry`, either a `Sink` or `Formatter` must be used that can account for these additional properties. The `WMISink`, which ships with Enterprise Library, works this way because the custom schema must be registered with WMI prior to its use and no formatting occurs on it.

`ContextItems`. Yet one last way to add information to a `LogEntry` is through the indirect use of an internal class named `ContextItems`, which wraps around the `System.Runtime.Remoting.Messaging.CallContext` class. This class is a specialized collection for method calls and provides data slots that are unique to each logical thread of execution. The `Logger` class exposes two additional static methods for modifying data on the `CallContext`. `SetContextItem` and `FlushContextItems`. `SetContextItem` adds a key/value pair to the `CallContext` dictionary. Context items will be recorded with every log entry. `FlushContextItems` empties the context items dictionary.

Because the `SetContextItem` method actually adds data to the thread's `CallContext`, every `LogEntry` that is written on the same thread after a `SetContextItem` method call will contain the additional data. This data is added to the `ExtendedProperties` dictionary. To flush the data from any future LogEntries for that thread, the `FlushContextItems` method must be called. Listing 6.12 adds the `AppVersion` identifier for all LogEntries written on a specific thread.

LISTING 6.12: Using `SetContextItem` and `FlushContextItems`

```
[C#]
Logger.SetContextItem("AppVersion", "1234");
LogEntry log = new LogEntry();
log.Message = "Message Number 1";
Logger.Write(log);
Logger.Write("Message Number 2");
Logger.FlushContextItems();

[Visual Basic]
Logger.SetContextItem("AppVersion", "1234")
Dim log As LogEntry = New LogEntry()
Dim log.Message = "Message Number 1"
Logger.Write(log)
Logger.Write("Message Number 2")
Logger.FlushContextItems()
```

So, even though the `SetContextItem` was only set before the first `LogEntry`, it applied to both. Listing 6.13 shows the results.

LISTING 6.13: Results from Using `SetContextItem`

```
Message: Message Number 1
Extended Properties:
Key: AppVersion               Value: 1234

Message: Message Number 2
Extended Properties:
Key: AppVersion               Value: 1234
```

The `Logger`'s static `Write`, `SetContextItem`, and `FlushContextItems` methods all pass control to an instance of the `LogWriter` class. The `LogWriter`'s `SetContextItem` and `FlushContextItems` methods just use the `ContextItems` class. The `Write` method, however, leverages the configuration data that is passed to it from the Configuration Application Block to determine whether the `LogEntry` should be filtered before it is sent. If the `LogEntry` passes the filter criteria, the `LogWriter` then leverages the configuration information passed to it so that it can determine which distribution strategy should be used for this `LogEntry`. It then sends the `LogEntry` via that distribution strategy.

Filtering

Filtering a `LogEntry` means that the `LogEntry` is not passed to a distribution strategy and therefore it is not forwarded onto its final endpoint. The

LogWriter delegates responsibility for filtering a LogEntry to the LogFilter class, which is an internal class dedicated solely to reading the filter information from the configuration data passed to it and determining whether the log should be filtered based on Category and Priority. It does this by examining all the filters that have been configured and comparing the log's Category and Priority. If any of the filter tests return false, then the LogFilter returns false to the LogWriter and the log is filtered. Otherwise, the LogWriter sends the LogEntry on its way. Figure 6.4 shows the classes involved in filtering a LogEntry. The following overview of Category and Priority filters will help you better understand how the log filtering process works.

Categories

A **Category** is a string that represents a collection of Destinations. A **Destination** holds information about how to format a LogEntry and where a LogEntry will be sent (see the sections on Formatters and Sinks later in this chapter). Many Categories can be defined in the configuration for the Logging and Instrumentation Application Block. The Category to which a LogEntry ultimately belongs is set at runtime when the LogEntry is created; if no Category is set, then the Category that is configured as the

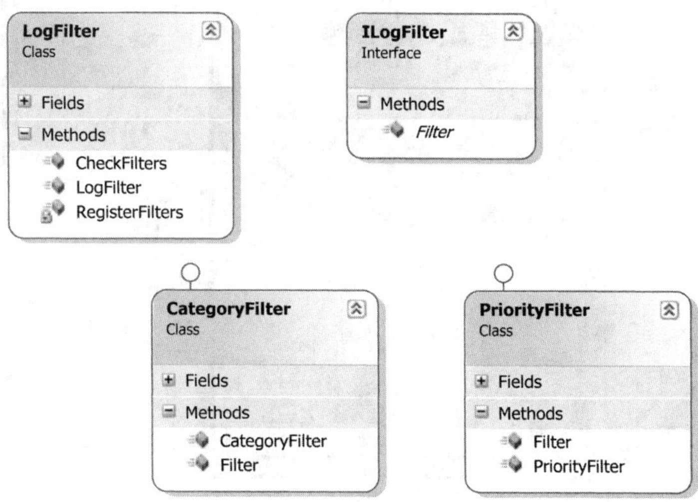

FIGURE 6.4: Classes Involved in Filtering

default Category will be assigned to the `LogEntry`. Examples of both of these scenarios were demonstrated in Listings 6.2 and 6.1 respectively.

Categories can be leveraged to filter LogEntries. For example, if three Categories—Category A, Category B, and Category C—were configured for an application, the application could be configured to deny all messages except those that belong to Category C and Category B. In this case, LogEntries that have their Category property set to Category A will not be logged. Conversely, the application could be configured to allow all messages except those that only belong to Category A. Figure 6.5 shows a configuration that allows all messages except for those that belong to Category A.

Whether an application is configured to exclude all Categories listed or to include all Categories listed, the final configuration for Category filters is represented by two constructs: a list of Categories and a flag that indicates whether the list is exclusive (*AllowAllExceptDenied*) or inclusive

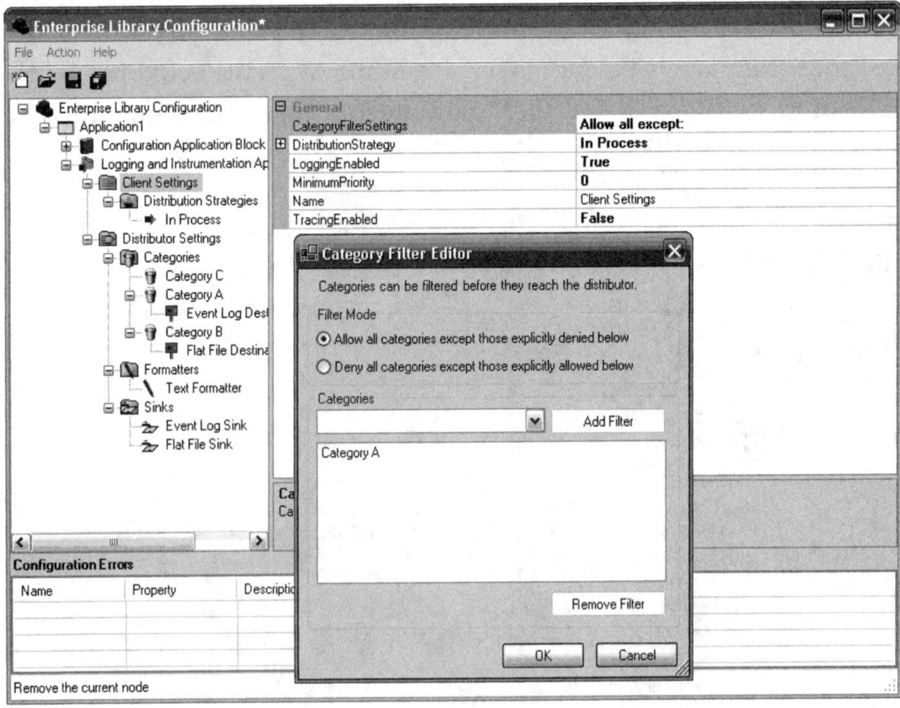

FIGURE 6.5: Filtering Out Category A

(*DenyAllExceptAllowed*). Either representation can equally define which Categories to allow and which Categories to deny. For example, in the scenario represented by Figure 6.5, {*Category A* and *AllowAllExceptDenied*} could also be represented as {(*Category B, Category C*) and *DenyAllExceptAllowed*}.

Since only these three Categories exist, they both mean the same thing; however, the first representation only requires one item to be listed, while the second requires two. That's not terribly significant for this scenario; however, it could get unwieldy if there were many Categories. So, the best representation for an application is the one that requires the least number of Categories to be listed.

The `LogFilter` class contains a hash table of filters that have been configured for the application. Filters must implement the `IFilter` interface; the Logging and Instrumentation Application Block only ships with two such filters: `CategoryFilter` and `PriorityFilter`. Although there is a well-defined interface for filters, they are not exposed as an extension point in the Logging and Instrumentation Application Block.

The `CategoryFilter` and `PriorityFilter` classes implement the `IFilter`'s `Filter` method. This method accepts a `LogEntry` and returns a `Boolean`. The `LogFilter` class calls all of its configured filters' `Filter` methods to determine if any of them return false, which would indicate that the `LogEntry` should be filtered.

The logic for the `CategoryFilter` is pretty straightforward. False is returned if either of the following two conditions is met.

- The `LogEntry`'s Category is not in the list of Categories and the mode is set to *DenyAllExceptAllowed*.
- The `LogEntry`'s Category is in the list of Categories and the mode is set to *AllowAllExceptDenied*.

To extend the previous scenario, if a LogEntry was written and its `Category` property was set as Category A, it would be filtered because the second condition would be met; Category A is in the list and the mode is set to *AllowAllExceptDenied*.

Priorities

LogEntries can also be filtered based upon Priority. **Priority** is an integer that represents the significance of the `LogEntry`. A higher number represents greater importance. Whereas Categories are not only used for filtering but also for setting the formatting and Destination for a `LogEntry`, Priorities are only used for filtering. If the Priority that is set for a `LogEntry` is below the configured `MinimumPriority` for the application, then the `LogEntry` will be filtered.

Log Distribution

If a LogEntry passes the filter criteria, the `LogWriter` checks the configuration information to determine which distribution strategy has been configured for the application to use. It then passes the `LogEntry` and all control of writing it to this distribution strategy. The `LogWriter`'s job is now complete; at this point it is the responsibility of the distribution strategy to get the LogEntry to a distributor that can take a single `LogEntry` and distribute it to all the necessary Destinations. Figure 6.6 highlights the primary classes that are related to log distribution.

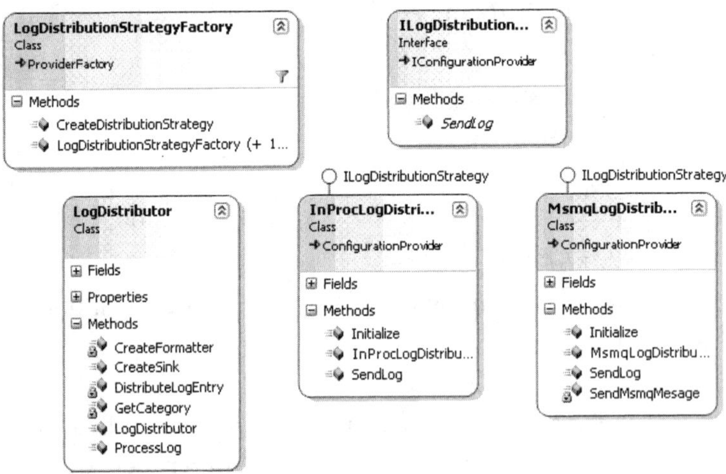

FIGURE 6.6: Log Distribution Classes

The `ILogDistributionStrategy` Interface

To qualify as a distribution strategy, the `ILogDistributionStrategy` interface needs to be implemented. This interface only contains a single method definition: `SendLog(LogEntrylog)`. Enterprise Library ships with two implementations of an `ILogDistributionStrategy`: a synchronous one named `InProcLogDistributionStrategy` and an asynchronous one named `MsmqLogDistributionStrategy`.

The `InProcLogDistributionStrategy` Class

The `InProcLogDistributionStrategy` class is a thin wrapper around the `LogDistributor` class. The `LogDistributor` class distributes the `LogEntry` to all Destinations for which it has been configured. As the name implies, this all occurs in-process. The `InProcLogDistributionStrategy` class just creates a new instance of the `LogDistributor` class and calls the `LogDistributor`'s `ProcessLog` method.

`MsmqLogDistributionStrategy`

The Logging and Instrumentation Application Block is also able to send messages asynchronously. The `MsmqDistributionStrategy` is the Logging and Instrumentation Application Block's solution for sending messages asynchronously. The `MsmqDistributionStrategy` serializes a received `LogEntry` message and stores it in a Microsoft Message Queuing (MSMQ) queue according to the `QueuePath` for which it is configured. At this point, an `MsmqLogDistributor` class is responsible for reading the LogEntries from the queue and distributing them to all Destinations for which it has been configured.

Whether an application is configured to use the `InProcLogDistributionStrategy` or the `MsmqLogDistributionStrategy`, the important concept to recognize is that both are responsible for getting the messages from the application that creates a LogEntry to a centralized distributor for all LogEntries. The objects covered up to this point are responsible for creating the message, determining whether the message should be sent, and publishing the message to a centralized distributor. They all run in an application's `AppDomain`, and from the Logging and Instrumentation Application Block's point of view they are considered to be the *client* side of logging.

The important point is that the publisher of the message—that is, the client that creates the `LogEntry`—is completely decoupled from any Destinations that have been configured to receive the message. It is the centralized distributor's responsibility to determine all the Destinations that need the message. This is considered to be the *distributor* side of logging. In fact, if desired, the distributor can be deployed to run on a completely separate process from the client application. That is exactly how the `MsmqLogDistributor` works.

If you're not very familiar with message-based design patterns (www.integrationpatterns.com is a great resource), perhaps a "real-world" example would help to clarify the concept. Think of this design working the same way that a beverage distributor works. A beverage manufacturer makes the product and packages it for delivery. However, the manufacturer does not deliver the product to every bar and restaurant that wants it. This would be very inefficient. Instead, it sends the product to beverage distributors, who then figure out how much and which type of product goes to each restaurant and bar and to deliver it there. Think of the `LogWriter` as the beverage manufacturer, the `LogEntry` as the product, the Distributors as the beverage distributor, and the Sinks (discussed later in this chapter) as the restaurants and bars that want the product.

`LogDistributor`. The `LogDistributor` is a base class that represents the centralized distributor. It combines its configuration information with the value of a `LogEntry`'s Category to determine all the Destinations to which a `LogEntry` should be sent. A Destination combines a **Sink**, which defines the data source to which a message can be persisted (e.g., e-mail, database, file, MSMQ, WMI), with a Formatter that defines how the message will look and what data it will contain.

For every Destination, the `LogDistributor` performs four tasks.

1. Creates an instance of the `Sink`.
2. Creates an instance of the `Formatter`.
3. Sets the `Sink`'s `Formatter` property to the `Formatter` created in step 2.
4. Calls the `Sink`'s `SendMessage(LogEntry log)` method.

The `Sink` then takes care of writing the message for its specific protocol. A high-level overview of this process was illustrated earlier in this chapter in Figure 6.2.

`DistributorService`. That all works great if the distribution strategy is the `InProcLogDistributionStrategy` and the `LogDistributor` is called directly. However, for asynchronous messaging with the `MsmqDistributionStrategy`, the `LogDistributor` never gets called. After the `MsmqDistributionStrategy` stores the `LogEntry` in the queue, something else needs to get the message from the queue to the `LogDistributor`. This function is fulfilled by the Distributor Service.

The **Distributor Service** is a Windows Service that polls a message queue to determine if any messages need to be sent. This design completely decouples any client that publishes messages from the "hub" that distributes the messages. The Distributor Service can be replaced by a different mechanism for routing messages to their Sinks (e.g., the Microsoft BizTalk Server), and none of the client applications will be any the wiser. Similarly, the Distributor Service is completely agnostic as to any changes made by client applications. As long as they still publish the messages to the message queue in the same way, the Distributor Service is happy.

Figure 6.7 illustrates the design for asynchronous publishing of `LogEntry` messages and the resultant decoupling between the client applications and the Distributor Service.

The Distributor Service, as shown in Figure 6.7, is really comprised of three separate classes. The first is the actual Windows Service, which is named `DistributorService`. This is the controlling member of the trio; it controls what occurs when the service is started, paused, or stopped. When the service is initialized, the `DistributorService` uses the information that is read from configuration to create a new instance of the `MsmqListener` class. When the `DistributorService` is started, the `DistributorService` tells the `MsmqListener` instance to start polling for messages from the configured MSMQ queue; on pause and stop it notifies the `MsmqListener` that it should stop polling for new messages. Figure 6.8 provides a closer look at the classes that are involved in the Distributor Service.

`MsmqListener`. The `MsmqListener` controls the polling of the queue for which the `DistributorService` is configured. When the `MsmqListener` is created, it creates an instance of the `MsmqLogDistributor`. When

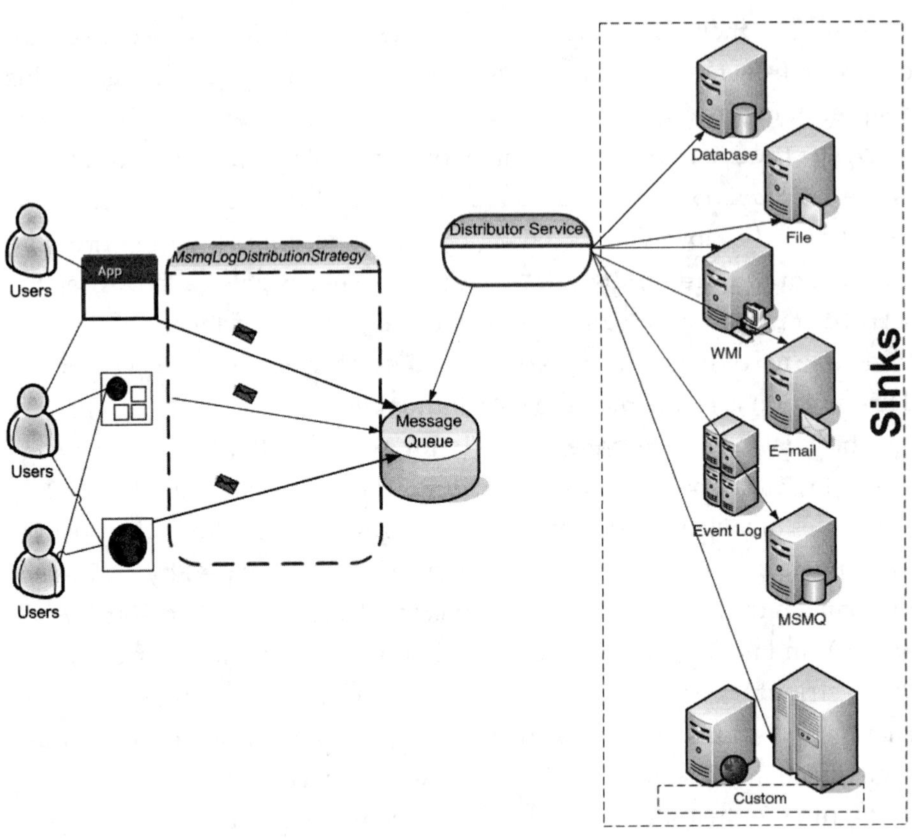

FIGURE 6.7: `MsmqLogDistributionStrategy` **and the Distributor Service**

the `MsmqListener` is started, it creates a new `Timer` and `EventHandler` that instructs the `MsmqLogDistributor` to check for new messages in the queue. When it is stopped, the `MsmqLogDistributor` is "wound down" so that any messages already queued up are allowed to complete their process, and then the `MsmqLogDistributor` is no longer instructed to look for new messages.

`MsmqLogDistributor`. The `MsmqLogDistributor` is a subclass of the `LogDistributor` class. It represents the centralized distributor for asynchronous log distribution. When the `MsmqListener` notifies this class to check the queue for messages, the `MsmqLogDistributor` loops through all

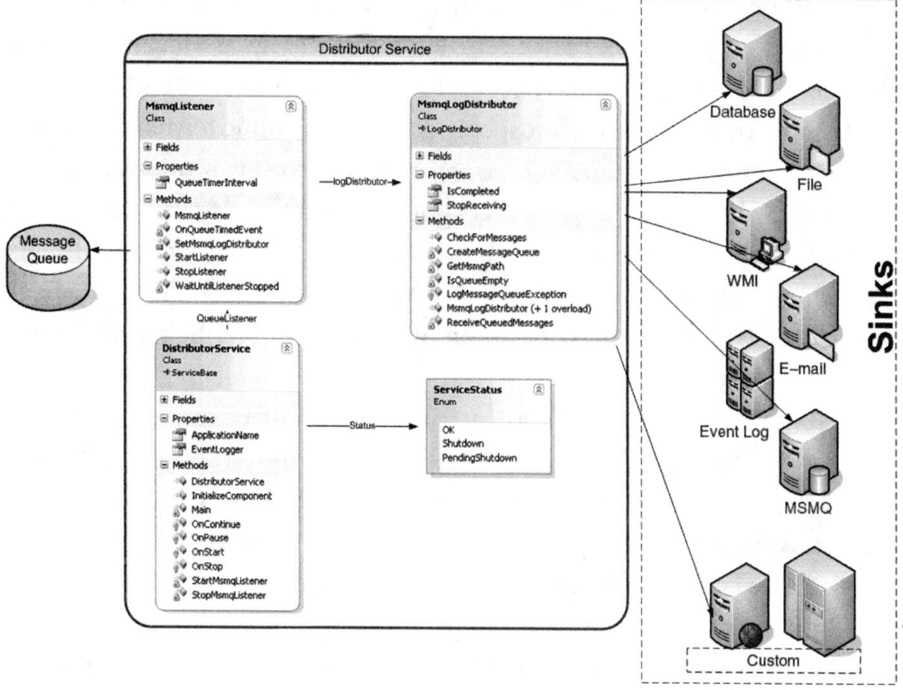

FIGURE 6.8: A Closer Look at the Distributor Service

`LogEntry` messages that exist in the queue, deserializes them, and calls the base `LogDistributor`'s `ProcessLog` method. `ProcessLog` then performs the four tasks outlined previously to format and route the `LogEntry` to every Destination for which it has been configured.

Custom Distribution Strategy

It is rare that you should ever have to write a custom distribution strategy or distributor. However, some exceptional situations exist where one may be needed. For example, some companies refuse to use MSMQ. Sometimes they just don't want it to exist on client machines; other times it is banned from server applications too. Many times this is more due to corporate governance policy than any technical reason. For example, it is not uncommon for a company to "standardize" on a queuing product like IBM MQ Series.

Any solution that leverages a queuing product other than this is not in line with corporate governance policies. Therefore, leveraging a technology like MSMQ in these organizations becomes a difficult political battle at best.

On the flipside, however, most corporations use some form of relational database in their applications. Thus, an alternative asynchronous distribution strategy that might appeal to corporations that don't promote the use of MSMQ might be one that leverages a relational database instead. In this way, a company can still reap the asynchronous logging benefits of the Logging and Instrumentation Application Block without sacrificing adherence to governance policies.

Fortunately, the Logging and Instrumentation Application Block provides an extension point for adding custom distribution strategies. Unfortunately, creating a custom, asynchronous, distribution strategy is probably one of the more complex types of extensions to undertake with Enterprise Library. This is because both a custom distribution strategy and a custom Distributor Service need to be developed. The custom Distributor Service is especially interesting. The following steps will walk you through creating a custom asynchronous distribution strategy and distributor. (The complete code sample is on the book's Web site.) This exercise is divided into two steps: the client (distribution strategy) and the distributor.

Creating the distribution strategy is the more straightforward part of this exercise. It isn't much different than any of the other extensions that have been shown in this book. To create a custom asynchronous distribution strategy, do the following three steps.

1. Define the runtime classes for holding the configuration data. For the Database Distribution strategy, this is the `DatabaseDistributionStrategyData` class. This class contains the member variables for the database instance and the stored procedure to use for storing LogEntries. For more information on creating runtime configuration classes, see Chapter 1.
2. Create the distribution strategy class by deriving a class from `ConfigurationProvider` and implementing the `ILogDistributionStrategy` interface. For the Database Distribution strategy, I have named this class `DatabaseDistributionStrategy`. This class seri-

alizes the LogEntry and uses it as the single parameter for the stored procedure that stores the LogEntry. The defining methods to this class are the SendLog method, which serializes the LogEntry, and the ExecuteStoredProc method, which writes the serialized LogEntry to the database. Listing 6.14 includes this method.

LISTING 6.14: The DatabaseDistributionStrategy's SendLog Method

```
[C#]
public void SendLog(LogEntry entry)
{
    SoapFormatter formatter = new SoapFormatter();
    string serializedEntry = String.Empty;
    using (MemoryStream ms = new MemoryStream())
    {
        formatter.Serialize(ms, entry);
        ms.Position = 0;
        byte[] buffer = new byte[ms.Length];
        ms.Read(buffer, 0, (int) ms.Length);
        serializedEntry = Encoding.UTF8.GetString(buffer);
    }

    ExecuteStoredProc(serializedEntry);

    LoggingLogDistributedEvent.Fire(serializedEntry);
}

private void ExecuteStoredProc(string serializedEntry)
{
     DatabaseProviderFactory factory = new
          DatabaseProviderFactory(configView.ConfigurationContext);

     Database db =
          (databaseDistributionStrategyData.DatabaseInstance.Equals
               (String.Empty))
                    ? factory.CreateDefaultDatabase()
                    : factory.CreateDatabase
                     (databaseDistributionStrategyData.DatabaseInstance);

     db.ExecuteNonQuery
          (databaseDistributionStrategyData.StoredProcedure,
          serializedEntry);
}

[Visual Basic]
Public Sub SendLog(ByVal entry As LogEntry)
     Dim formatter As SoapFormatter = New SoapFormatter()
     Dim serializedEntry As String = String.Empty
```

```
    Dim ms As MemoryStream = New MemoryStream()
    Try
        formatter.Serialize(ms, entry)
        ms.Position = 0
        Dim buffer As Byte() = New Byte(ms.Length - 1) {}
        ms.Read(buffer, 0, CInt(ms.Length))
        serializedEntry = Encoding.UTF8.GetString(buffer)
    Finally
        If TypeOf ms Is IDisposable Then
            Dim disp As IDisposable = ms
            disp.Dispose()
        End If
    End Try

    ExecuteStoredProc(serializedEntry)

    LoggingLogDistributedEvent.Fire(serializedEntry)
End Sub

Private Sub ExecuteStoredProc(ByVal serializedEntry As String)
    Dim factory As DatabaseProviderFactory = _
        New DatabaseProviderFactory(configView.ConfigurationContext)

        Dim db As Database
        If _
         (databaseDistributionStrategyData.DatabaseInstance.Equals _
         (String.Empty)) Then
                db = factory.CreateDefaultDatabase()
        Else
            db = factory.CreateDatabase _
                (databaseDistributionStrategyData.DatabaseInstance)
        End If

    db.ExecuteNonQuery _
        (databaseDistributionStrategyData.StoredProcedure, _
        serializedEntry)
End Sub
```

3. Create design-time classes that make it easy to configure the `DatabaseDistributionStrategy` class. The design-time classes needed for the `DatabaseDistributionStrategy` are the `DatabaseDistributionStrategyNode` and the `DatabaseDistributionStrategyDesignManager`. For more information on creating design-time configuration classes, see Chapter 2.

After the runtime and design-time classes have been created and the assemblies have been deployed properly, you can use the Enterprise Library Configuration Tool to choose a Database Distribution strategy as easily as the In-Process or MSMQ Distribution strategies. Leveraging this as the distribution strategy will result in LogEntries stored in the database instead of being sent directly to the `LogDistributor` or stored in an MSMQ queue. Figure 6.9 illustrates how the Database Distribution strategy can be added to an application's configuration as easily as any of the ones that ship with the Logging and Instrumentation Application Block.

But creating the distribution strategy is only half the battle. If a distributor doesn't exist that will read the LogEntries from the database and forward them to the appropriate Destination, the LogEntries will remain "in limbo" in the database. A custom Distributor Service must be created to fit this purpose.

Extending Enterprise Library with a custom Distributor Service is a little unorthodox from the way all other extensions are created. This is primarily because the `MsmqLogDistributor` cannot be used as a viable model to emulate because its configuration information is retrieved through a spe-

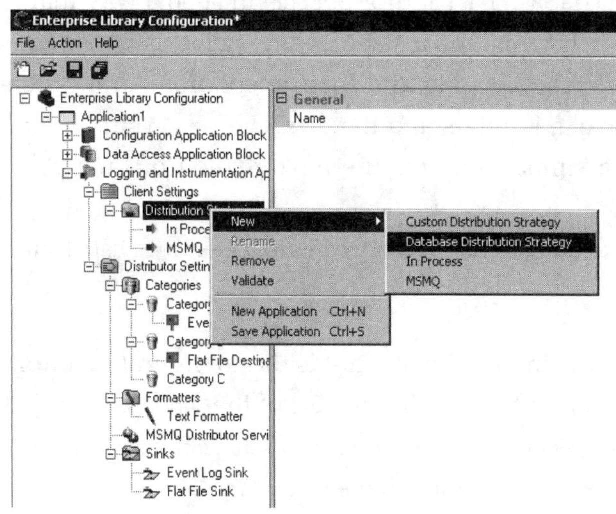

FIGURE 6.9: Selecting the Database Distribution Strategy

cific property in the `DistributorSettings` class. The DistributorService property of the `DistributorSettings` class returns an instance of the `MsmqDistributorServiceData` class. If instead a `DistributorService-Data` class existed that was returned from this property and served as the base class not only for the `MsmqDistributorServiceData` class but also for any custom Distributor Service data classes, then this model could be reused. But, alas, it doesn't exist, and any custom Distributors will not have the advantage of using this property in `DistributorSettings`. Therefore, the same design cannot be used.

As it turns out, though, there is another option. Keep in mind that the distribution strategy is completely decoupled from the distributor. Although both are needed for a LogEntry to make its way to its final Destination, the distributor does not need to know anything at all about the distribution strategy. In fact, in many ways, a Distributor Service can be thought of as just another application that uses the configuration features in Enterprise Library.

A Distributor Service needs to read and write its own configuration information in addition to leveraging the available configuration information about the Sinks to which it needs to send the LogEntries. Therefore, I have implemented the Database Distributor Service in such a way that it uses its own configuration information instead of having it exist in the configuration information for the Logging and Instrumentation Application Block. As luck would have it, I understand that the `MsmqLogDistributor` has been refactored in a similar way for the next version of Enterprise Library.

So, the following three steps were taken to create a custom Distributor Service.

1. Create a project with a single class that holds the configuration information for the Distributor Service. In the case of the `DatabaseDistributorService`, this is the `DatabaseDistributor.Configuration` project and it contains the `DatabaseDistributorSettings` class. The `DatabaseDistributorSettings` class contains information about the `DatabaseInstance`, the stored pro-

cedure used to read the LogEntries, and the timing interval used to poll for new messages.

The reason that an entire project needs to be dedicated to the runtime configuration information is that the consumer of this information, the `DatabaseDistributorService`, will be a Windows Service and thus be part of an .exe project and not a class library project. If the two classes were combined in the same project, then the design-time project that will be created next would not be able to reference it. See Chapter 1 for more information on creating runtime configuration classes.

2. Create the design-time classes that make it easy to configure the `DatabaseDistributorSettings` with the Enterprise Library Configuration Tool. Because the design-time is implemented with its own configuration section, the process for creating it is essentially the same as the process that is needed for creating the design-time for a custom application block. It is not very complex since only one node is needed. The `DatabaseDistributorNode` and `DatabaseDistributorConfigurationManager` are the important classes that need to be implemented in this scenario. For more information on how to extend the design-time experience with your application block settings, see Chapter 9.

   Once the design-time classes have been created and deployed properly, you can use the Enterprise Library Configuration Tool to set the configuration settings for the Database Distributor Service. Figure 6.10 shows how the Database Distributor Service exists at the same level as the other application blocks in the tool.

3. Now the Distributor Service can be created. I modeled the `DatabaseDistributor` after the `MsmqDistributor`. Therefore, the `DatabaseDistributorService` starts up a `DatabaseListener`. The `DatabaseListener` encapsulates a `DatabaseLogDistributor` class and Timer class and leverages the configuration information for the polling interval to determine when to tell the `DatabaseLogDistributor` to check for new messages. The `DatabaseLog-`

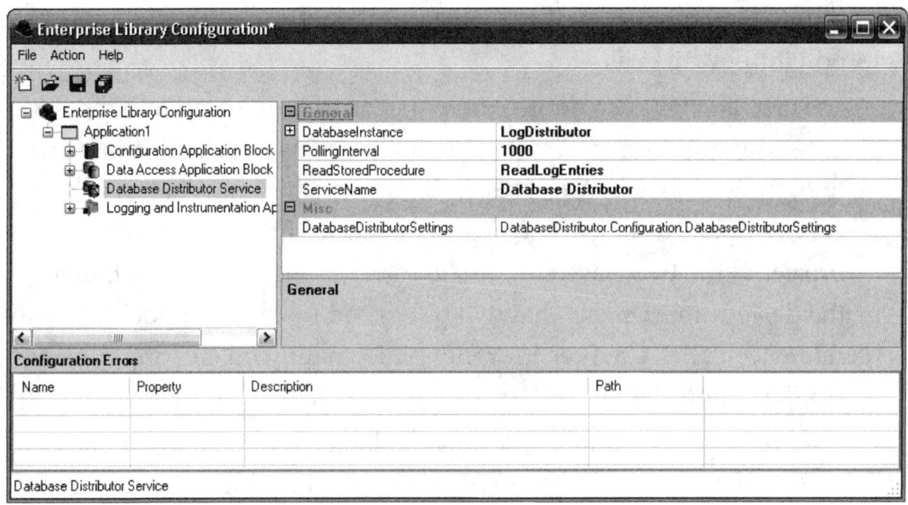

FIGURE 6.10: Configuring the Database Distributor Service

`Distributor` uses the configuration information about the `DatabaseInstance` and stored procedure name to check the database for new LogEntries.

Figure 6.10 depicts a Database Distributor that checks for new LogEntries every second and uses the `LogDistributor`'s `DatabaseInstance` (as configured in the Data Access Application Block) and the ReadLogEntries stored procedure to check for the LogEntries. When new LogEntries have been read, they are flagged as such in the database and sent to the appropriate Destinations.

Routing

A **Destination** is comprised of two components: a Sink and a Formatter. The Sink signifies the store where a LogEntry will be routed, and the Formatter is used to transform the LogEntry into its final format. Many Destinations can exist for each Category that is defined in a Logging and Instrumentation Block's distributor settings.

Sinks

A Sink represents the final resting place for a LogEntry. In many applications this may be the Event Log, a text file, or a database. It is also very common that LogEntries of certain Categories result in both an e-mail message and an entry into one of these data stores. In that case, two or more Logging Sinks could be set up as separate Destinations for a single Category. Each type of Logging Sink is responsible for saving the LogEntry into the specific data store for which it has been created. If you are familiar with integration products like Microsoft BizTalk Server, you will be familiar with this concept. In BizTalk terms, Sinks are analogous to Adapters. The Distributor acts as the messaging hub and routes the messages to all Sinks that "subscribe" to messages of certain Categories.

Enterprise Library ships with six Logging Sinks, and it provides an extension point for creating new ones. The six Sinks that come out of the box are the `EventLogSink`, `FlatFileSink`, `MsmqSink`, `WMILogSink`, `EmailSink`, and `DatabaseSink`. All these Sinks derive from an abstract base class named `LogSink`. Figure 6.11 depicts this class hierarchy.

`ILogSink` and `LogSink`. The `LogDistributor` doesn't know anything about any of the specific LogSinks that are available. Instead, it only knows that it may be configured to send LogEntries to many classes that have implemented the `ILogSink` interface. Therefore, new LogSinks can be created without any change to the distributor that sends the messages to the Sinks.

The `ILogSink` interface only contains one method and one property. The single method it defines is `SendMessage(LogEntry)`. This is used for the `LogDistributor` to send the `LogEntry` to the Sink. The single property is an accessor for getting and setting the Formatter that will be used to format the `LogEntry`. This makes it easy for the `LogDistributor` to format and distribute the LogEntries it has received. It simply loops through all the Destinations for the Category that is equal to the `LogEntry`'s `Category` property, sets the Formatter, and sends the message. The code in Listing 6.15 is at the heart of the `LogDistributor`'s `DistributeLogEntry` method.

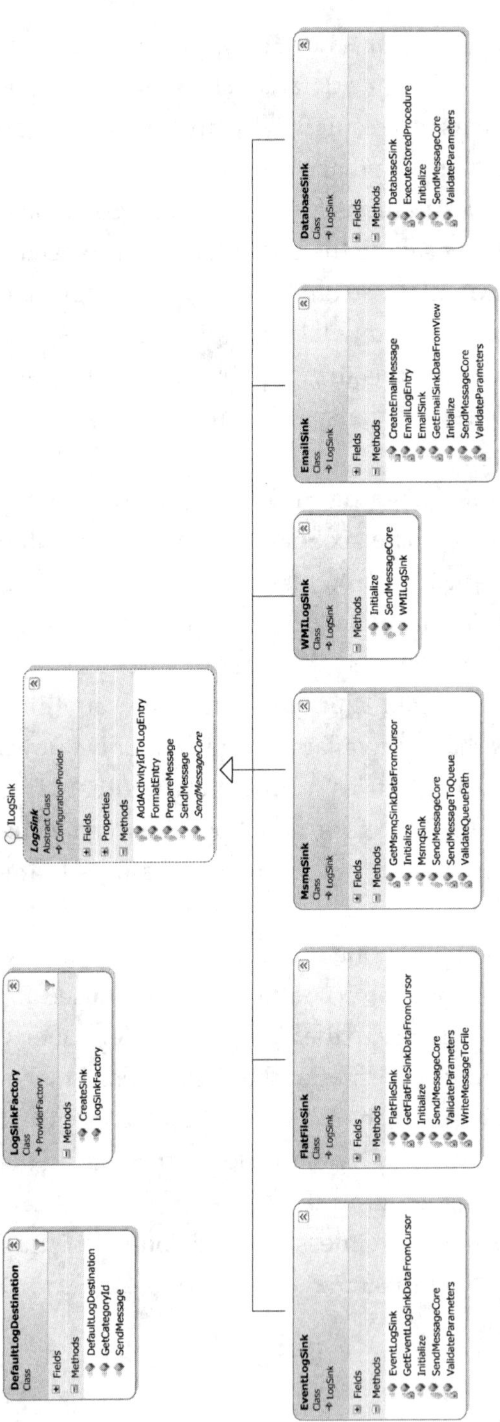

FIGURE 6.11: `LogSinks` in Enterprise Library

LISTING 6.15: How the `LogDistributor` Sends LogEntries to Sinks

```
[C#]
foreach (DestinationData destination in
     category.DestinationDataCollection)
{
    try
    {
          ILogSink sink = CreateSink(destination.Sink);
          sink.Formatter = CreateFormatter(destination.Format);
          sink.SendMessage(log);

          LoggingLogWrittenEvent.FireToPerfCounter();
    }
    catch (Exception ex)
    {
          this.events.LogSendingMessageException
               (ex, destination.Sink, log);
          this.defaulLogSink.SendMessage(log);
    }
}

[Visual Basic]
For Each destination As DestinationData In _
                         category.DestinationDataCollection
     Try
          Dim sink As ILogSink = CreateSink(destination.Sink)
          sink.Formatter = CreateFormatter(destination.Format)
          sink.SendMessage(log)

          LoggingLogWrittenEvent.FireToPerfCounter()
     Catch ex As Exception
          Me.events.LogSendingMessageException _
                    (ex, destination.Sink, log)
          Me.defaulLogSink.SendMessage(log)
     End Try
Next destination
```

The `LogSink` class is an abstract base class that implements the `ILogSink` interface. In addition to the public `SendMessage` method and `Formatter` property, the `LogSink` class contains the protected methods listed in Table 6.6.

The `SendMessage` method is implemented at this base class and simply calls the `PrepareMessage` and `SendMessageCore` methods. By default, the `PrepareMessage` method will call the `AddActivityIdToLogEntry` method. If a `Tracer` is being used, this method adds the `Tracer's Cur-`

TABLE 6.6: The LogSink's Protected Methods

Method	Description
AddActivityIdToLogEntry	Adds the current CurrentActivityId to the LogEntry's ExtendedProperties. The CurrentActivityId is a property of the Tracer class, which is discussed later in this chapter. This property is used to correlate Trace messages with Log messages.
FormatEntry	Formats a LogEntry using the configured Formatter.
PrepareMessage	Prepares a message for sending to the Sink. The base implementation calls the AddActivityIdToLogEntry method.
SendMessageCore	Defines the abstract method that must be overridden by a derived class and its specific message-sending mechanism for that class.

rentActivityId to the LogEntry's ExtendedProperties. The Tracer object will be covered later in this chapter.

The Formatter property is also implemented in this base class. The LogSink class will return the Formatter that has been configured for the specific Destination. If no Formatter has been configured, then the TextFormatter will be returned. Formatters are covered in the next section.

The abstract LogSink class makes it easier to create Sinks, because the only thing that needs to be implemented in a derived class is the SendMessageCore method. This method should determine how to store the LogEntry in the data store that the specific LogSink represents.

DatabaseSink. The DatabaseSink is a great example of this; it is a concrete class that overrides the SendMessageCore method to store messages in a relation database. The DatabaseSink stores LogEntries in a database by executing a stored procedure. Its implementation of the SendMessageCore method calls a private method to execute a stored procedure against the database for which it was configured. The formatted LogEntry and many of its properties—like `Title`, `Category`, `Severity`, and `TimeStamp`—are passed in as separate parameters to the stored procedure. Once the stored procedure has successfully run, the `LogEntry` rests in the database.

EmailSink. The `EmailSink`'s implementation of the `SendMessageCore` method leverages some private functions and an internal class to create and format an e-mail message[3] from the data contained in the `LogEntry` class. It uses its configuration information to populate a list of recipient e-mail addresses, the sender's e-mail address, a subject line prefix, and a subject line suffix. It then sends the e-mail message to the SMTP server for which it was configured.

EventLogSink. The `SendMessageCore` method for the `EventLogSink` creates an instance of a `System.Diagnostics.EventLog` object for the event log and event source that it reads from its configuration data. It then formats the `LogEntry` and stores the `LogEntry` in the Windows Event Log by calling the `System.Diagnostics.EventLog`'s `WriteEntry` method.

FlatFileSink. The `SendMessageCore` method for the `FlatFileSink` uses configuration information about the name of the file, header text to place at the beginning of a `LogEntry`, and footer text to place immediately after a `LogEntry` in order to write a `LogEntry` to a flat file. The `SendMessageCore` method calls a private `WriteMessageToFile` method that creates the directory for the file if it doesn't exist and writes the header (if configured), `LogEntry`, and footer (if configured) to the flat file.

MsmqSink. The `MsmqSink` writes a `LogEntry` to a Microsoft Message Queue. Its `SendMessageCore` method for the `MsmqSink` creates an instance of a `System.Messaging.MessageQueue` from the `QueuePath` that it reads from configuration. It formats the `LogEntry` and sets this as the body of a new `System.Messaging.Message`. It sets the message label to be the title of the `LogEntry` and the message priority equal to the priority of the `LogEntry`. Finally, it sets the appropriate value for `MessageQueueTransactionType` based upon whether the message queue is transactional and sends this new message to the `MessageQueue`.

---

3. Technically, it creates an instance of the System.Web.Mail.MailMessage class.

WMILogSink. The SendMessageCore method for the WMILogSink fires a LoggingWMISinkEvent with the LogEntry as the EventData. Because the LogEntry is attributed as an InstrumentationClass of InstrumentType.Event, a LogEntry or any subclass thereof can be published proactively to any WMI consumer that has subscribed to it. The only additional step that is required for custom LogEntry classes is to register the class schema with WMI.

For example, the WSILogEntry class shown in Listing 6.10 can be registered with WMI by running installutil.exe against its assembly. Once this has been completed, a WMI consumer can be created that listens for a WMILogEntry and can take appropriate actions once one has been received. Listing 6.16 sets a WMI consumer up so that it will asynchronously "listen" for the WSILogEntry event data. When a WSILogEntry is received, the watcher_EventArrived delegate will be called.

LISTING 6.16: Listening for a WSILogEntry Event

```
[C#]
ManagementScope scope = new ManagementScope(@"\\.\root\EnterpriseLibrary");
scope.Options.EnablePrivileges = true;

string query = "SELECT * FROM WSILogEntry";
EventQuery eq = new EventQuery(query);

ManagementEventWatcher watcher = new ManagementEventWatcher(scope, eq);
watcher.EventArrived +=
        new EventArrivedEventHandler(watcher_EventArrived);
watcher.Start();

[Visual Basic]
Dim scope As ManagementScope = _
        New ManagementScope("\\.\root\EnterpriseLibrary")
Dim scope.Options.EnablePrivileges = True

Dim query As String = "SELECT * FROM WSILogEntry"
Dim eq As EventQuery = New EventQuery(query)

Dim watcher As ManagementEventWatcher = _
        New ManagementEventWatcher(scope, eq)
Dim watcher.EventArrived += _
        New EventArrivedEventHandler(watcher_EventArrived)
watcher.Start()
```

Creating a Custom Logging Sink

The Sinks that ship with Enterprise Library represent a pretty good suite of logging Destinations. Sometimes, however, the provided Sinks just won't fit every need for every company. That's okay, though. Creating a custom Logging Sink is straightforward, and there are already quite a few that have been created and can be found at gotdotnet.com.[4]

The tasks needed to create a custom Sink are no different than the tasks that were needed to complete the Sinks that ship with Enterprise Library. A class must be derived from the `LogSink` base class and the `SendMessageCore` function must be overridden to accomplish the specific tasks needed for that `LogSink`. Enterprise Library ships with a Quick Start sample for creating a custom Sink.

The Quick Start outlines the steps needed to create the `DebugSink`, a Logging Sink that will send the debugging information to Visual Studio's Output window. The following are the steps to create this custom Sink (as taken from the Enterprise Library Quick Start documentation).

1. Create a new class, `DebugSink`, that derives from `LogSink`.
2. Implement the required constructors and the `Initialize` method.
3. Add the `SendMessageCore` method to your class, and then implement the behavior required when logging to the custom Sink. In Listing 6.17, the custom Logging Sink sends the message to the Visual Studio Output window.

LISTING 6.17: Creating a Custom `DebugSink` Class

```
[C#]
public class DebugSink : LogSink
{
     public DebugSink()
     {
     }

     public override void Initialize
            (ConfigurationView configurationView)
     {
     }
```

4. See www.gotdotnet.com/community/usersamples/Default.aspx?query=enterprise%20library.

```
    protected override void SendMessageCore(LogEntry logEntry)
    {
        try
        {
            System.Diagnostics.Debug.WriteLine(logEntry.Message));
        }
        catch (Exception e)
        {
            logEntry.AddMessage(e.ToString());
            this.defaultSink.SendMessage(logEntry);
        }
    }
}

[Visual Basic]
Public Class DebugSink
            Inherits LogSink

    Public Sub New()
    End Sub

    Public Overrides Sub Initialize _
             (ByVal configurationView As ConfigurationView)
    End Sub

    Protected Overrides Sub SendMessageCore(ByVal log As LogEntry)
        Try
            System.Diagnostics.Debug.WriteLine _
                 (SR.DebugSinkMessage(log.EventId, log.Message))
        Catch e As Exception
            log.AddMessage(SR.SinkFailureMessage(e.ToString()))
            Me.defaultSink.SendMessage(log)
        End Try
    End Sub
End Class
```

That's really all there is to it. To use new Logging Sink, it needs to be configured in an application as a custom Sink and the `DebugSink` type information needs to be specified for the `TypeName` property. Then the logging Categories simply need to be modified to use this new Sink.

This is a great example for using the out-of-the-box features for a custom Sink because it does not need to read any information in from configuration. However, it isn't hard to imagine that a custom Sink would need to leverage configuration information in the same way that the Sinks that ship with Enterprise Library do. There are two different ways to support this if a custom Sink had this requirement.

A custom Sink can use its `Attributes` `NameValueItemCollection` to read in and use additional information from configuration. For example, if it were desirable to have a header and footer available to surround the debugging information (like the `FlatFileSink`), this information could be added to the custom Sink by adding two new items to the custom Sink's `Attributes` collection. Figure 6.12 shows how to use the `Attributes` collection to add configuration data for a custom Sink.

The custom Sink would need to use the instance of the `CustomSinkData` object that can be obtained in the `Initialize` method and used in the `SendMessageCore`. Listing 6.18 demonstrates this.

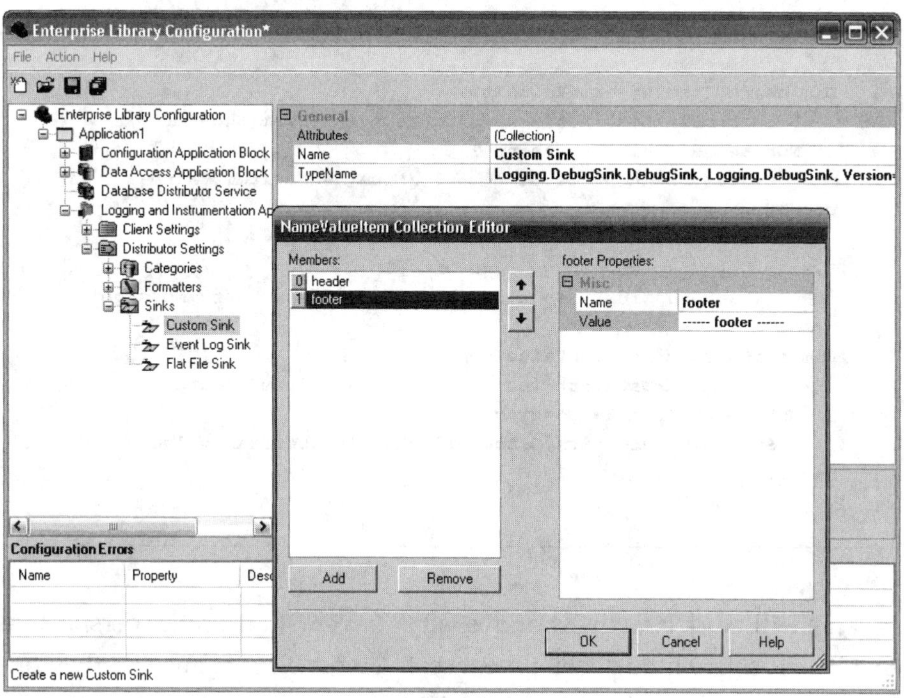

FIGURE 6.12: Adding Attributes to a Custom Sink

LISTING 6.18: Adding Code to the `Initialize` Method to Read Configuration Data from `Attributes`

```
[C#]
try
{
    NameValueItem headerItem =
        customSinkData.Attributes.GetNameValueItem("header");
    if (headerItem != null)
        System.Diagnostics.Debug.WriteLine(headerItem.Value);

    System.Diagnostics.Debug.WriteLine
        (SR.DebugSinkMessage(logEntry.EventId,logEntry.Message));

    NameValueItem footerItem =
        customSinkData.Attributes.GetNameValueItem("footer");
    if (footerItem != null)
        System.Diagnostics.Debug.WriteLine(footerItem.Value);
}
...


[Visual Basic]
Try
    Dim headerItem As NameValueItem = _
        customSinkData.Attributes.GetNameValueItem("header")
    If Not headerItem Is Nothing Then
        System.Diagnostics.Debug.WriteLine(headerItem.Value)
    End If

    System.Diagnostics.Debug.WriteLine _
        (SR.DebugSinkMessage(logEntry.EventId,logEntry.Message))

    Dim footerItem As NameValueItem = _
        customSinkData.Attributes.GetNameValueItem("footer")
    If Not footerItem Is Nothing Then
        System.Diagnostics.Debug.WriteLine(footerItem.Value)
    End If
End Try
...
```

This will work effectively and is very convenient from the perspective that it incurs very little development cost. A more elegant but slightly more costly approach is to provide a design-time interface for the `DebugSink` so the configuration information can be checked at design-time instead of run-time.

The first step to creating a design-time interface for the DebugSink is the creation of a new class that contains the runtime configuration data specific for the DebugSink class. I'll name this class DebugSinkData. It is very similar to the FlatFileSinkData except there is no need for a filename variable or property. For instructions on how to accomplish this, see Chapter 1 and the source code for this chapter on the book's Web site.

Secondly, a design-time node and configuration manager need to be created to allow an end user to configure an application to use the DebugSink. For instructions on how to accomplish this, see Chapter 2 and this chapter's accompanying source code.

Lastly, the DebugSink needs to use the DebugSinkData instead of the CustomSinkData. Listing 6.19 shows the changes that need to occur in the DebugSink's SendMessageCore method.

Listing 6.19: Changing the DebugSink's Initialize Method to use DebugSinkData

```
[C#]
try
{
    if (!debugSinkData.Header.Equals(String.Empty))
        System.Diagnostics.Debug.WriteLine(debugSinkData.Header);

    System.Diagnostics.Debug.WriteLine
         (SR.DebugSinkMessage(logEntry.EventId,logEntry.Message));

    if (!debugSinkData.Footer.Equals(String.Empty))
        System.Diagnostics.Debug.WriteLine(debugSinkData.Footer);
}
...

[Visual Basic]
Try
    If (Not debugSinkData.Header.Equals(String.Empty)) Then
        System.Diagnostics.Debug.WriteLine(debugSinkData.Header)
    End If

    System.Diagnostics.Debug.WriteLine _
         (SR.DebugSinkMessage(logEntry.EventId,logEntry.Message))

    If (Not debugSinkData.Footer.Equals(String.Empty)) Then
        System.Diagnostics.Debug.WriteLine(debugSinkData.Footer)
    End If
End Try
...
```

When these three steps have been completed, the `DebugSink` can be added as easily as any of the Sinks that ship with Enterprise Library. Figure 6.13 shows how to add the `DebugSink` to an application's configuration information.

Formatters

One half of a Destination's purpose is to facilitate the routing of the `LogEntry` to the appropriate endpoint. That is the Sink's role. The other half of a Destination's job is to format the `LogEntry` into its appropriate representation. This is the role of the Formatter. The Logging and Instrumentation Application Block ships with a single Formatter, the `TextFormatter`. This Formatter, as well as any custom Formatters that are created, must implement the `IFormatter` interface. Figure 6.14 illustrates this relationship, as well as some of the other classes that are used in the formatting process.

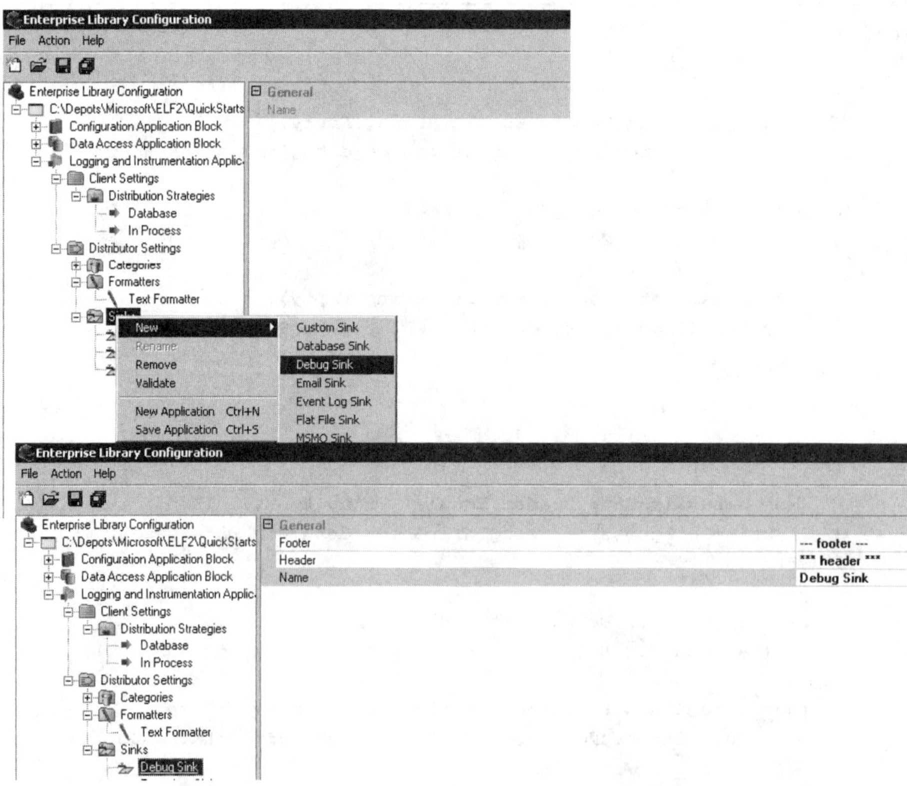

FIGURE 6.13: Configuring the `DebugSink`

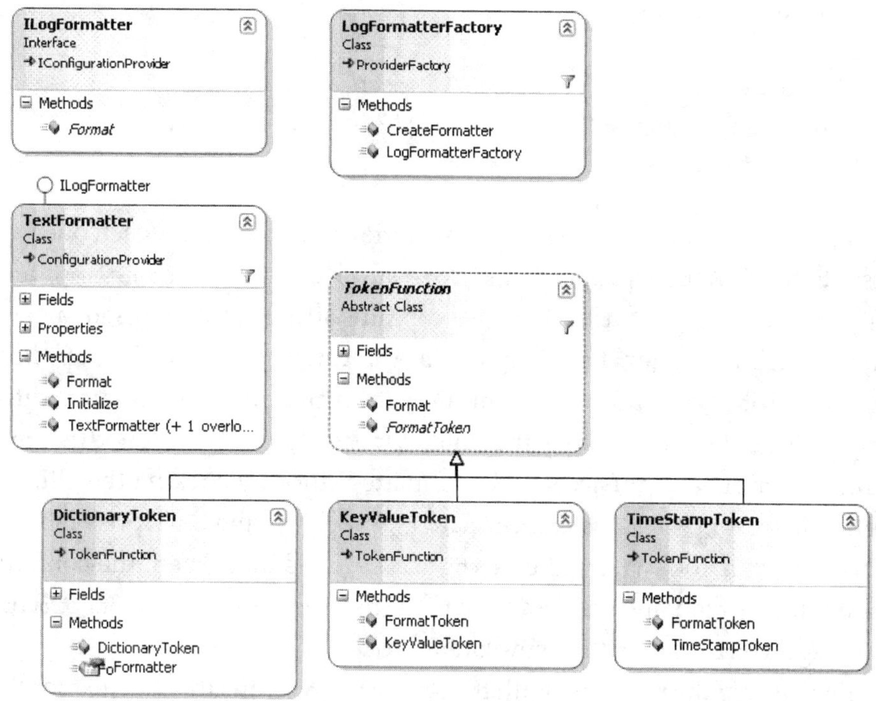

FIGURE 6.14: Classes Involved in Formatting

ILogFormatter. The `LogDistributor` reads configuration data to determine which instance of a class that implements the `ILogFormatter` interface must be created to use for transforming a `LogEntry`. The single method for this interface, `Format(LogEntry log)`, returns a string. Thus, any concrete Formatter must implement the `Format` method and return the LogEntry as a string.

TextFormatter. The `TextFormatter` combines a template and tokens to create a formatted string. The template is a string that represents the final text that the `Format` method will return plus placeholders (aka tokens) that represent specific values that will be inserted at runtime. For example, a simple template that returns a `Message`, `EventId`, `TimeStamp`, and `Severity` might look like:

```
The message '{message}' with an EventId of {eventid}
was logged at {timestamp} with a severity of {sever-
ity}. {newline}
```

This would return:

```
The message 'This is a test.' with an EventId of 123 was
logged at 05/06/2006 23:05:06 with a severity of
Unspecified.
```

The `TextFormatter` class contains static string constants; each one represents a `LogEntry` property like `Message`, `EventId`, `TimeStamp`, and `Severity`. The `TextFormatter` also contains strings that represent a newline and tab character. The template is stored with the rest of an application's distributor setting configuration information. A Template Editor ships with Enterprise Library that makes it easy to create and modify `Formatter` templates. You access the Template Editor by clicking the ellipses button for a `TextFormatter`'s `Template` property in the Enterprise Library Configuration Tool. When the `TextFormatter` is initialized, the configuration data is read and the template is "registered" with the `TextFormatter`. Figure 6.15 shows the Template Editor.

Registering the template with the `Formatter` means that the text for the template is used to create an internal `StringBuilder` object, and an `ArrayList` of TokenFunctions is created. The first thing the `Format`

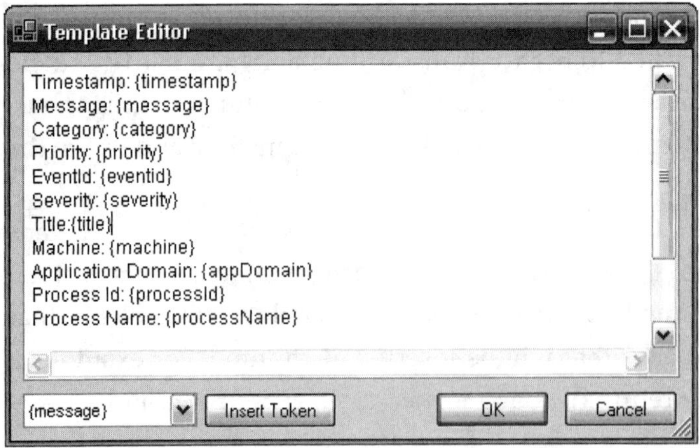

FIGURE 6.15: The Template Editor

method does is to replace all the tokens in the template with the actual data contained in the `LogEntry` object. For example, the `{message}` token is replaced with the value of the `LogEntry.Message` property, the `{eventid}` token is replaced with the value of the `LogEntry.EventId` property, and so on. Then, the `Format` method is called for each `TokenFunction`.

`TokenFunction`. You can think of a `TokenFunction` as a token that requires something other than simply being replaced with a `LogEntry` property. It requires some additional formatting to take place. For example, the timestamp for a `LogEntry` can be represented using many different date/time formats; two options are MM-dd-yyyy and dd-MM-yyyy. By leveraging a `TokenFunction` that supports this capability, this level of formatting can be supported.

An abstract `TokenFunction` class exists that is used to set up these special formatting needs. Table 6.7 lists the constructs used by a `TokenFunction` class to perform the necessary formatting.

TABLE 6.7: Constructs Needed by a `TokenFunction`

Construct	Description	TimeStampToken Example
Start Delimiter	Marks the beginning of the token—the starting text to find and replace in the template.	`{timestamp(`
End Delimiter	Marks the end of the token—the end of the text to find and replace in the template.	`)}`
Inner Template/ TokenTemplate	The text between the Start and End Delimiters. Can be overridden in a derived class.	`MM-dd-yyyy (for example)`
TokenToReplace	The combination of the Start Delimiter, the Inner Template, and the End Delimiter.	`{timestamp(MM-dd-yyyy)}`

To achieve these special formatting needs, a class must derive from the abstract `TokenFunction` class. The abstract `TokenFunction` class has protected constructors that allow the start and end delimiters to be set. The `TokenFunction` class contains a virtual `Format` method that searches the template for all instances of the `TokenToReplace` and replaces them with formatted values. Finally, the `TokenFunction` class contains one abstract method named `FormatToken`. This is the only method that must be implemented by any derived class and is the method that takes the `TokenToReplace` and formats the `LogEntry` data into its final form.

Figure 6.14 shows the `TokenFunction` classes that ship with Enterprise Library: `TimeStampToken`, `KeyValueToken`, and `DictionaryToken`.

`TimeStampToken`. The `TimeStampToken` class lets an end user dictate the date/time representation for the `LogEntry`'s `TimeStamp` property. For example, to format a timestamp using a date/time format of MM-dd-yyyy, the token `{timestamp(MM-dd-yyyy)}` can be used. The `TimeStampToken` performs `log.TimeStamp.ToString(tokenTemplate, CultureInfo.CurrentCulture)` on the `InnerTemplate` (aka `tokenTemplate`) that is passed to the `FormatToken` method.

Because the `TimeStampToken` does not override the default behavior for `InnerTemplate`, which is simply the text between the start and end delimiters, many different date/time formats can be used in a single template. As the `Format` method loops through the template replacing `TimeStampTokens`, it will pass a different `templateToken` to the `FormatToken` method each time. For example, suppose a template consisted of:

```
In the United States, this message was logged as {time-
stamp(MM-dd-yyyy)}, but in the United Kingdom it was
logged as {timestamp(dd-MM-yyyy)}
```

The first call to the `FormatToken` method would use MM-dd-yyyy as the `templateToken` and the second call would use dd-MM-yyyy. This would result in:

```
In United States, this message was logged as 12/7/2006,
but in the United Kingdom it was logged as 7/12/2006
```

KeyValueToken. The keyValueToken class lets an end user create a template that uses a specific value in a LogEntry's ExtendedProperties dictionary object. The KeyValueToken uses the templateToken that is passed to the FormatToken method as the key that needs to be located in the ExtendedProperties dictionary object. If the key does not exist in ExtendedProperties, an empty string is returned.

For example, let's say that a LogEntry's ExtendedProperties dictionary was populated with the results of the ManagedSecurityContextInformationProvider.PopulateDictionary method. This would populate the ExtendedProperties dictionary with key/value pairs where the keys are AuthenticationType, IdentityName, and IsAuthenticated. This information can be used in the template by leveraging the KeyValueToken class. So, a template that consists of the string:

```
This message was logged by
{keyvalue(IdentityName)}.{newline}
```

will return

```
This message was logged by AppDomain\TestUser.
```

when the name of the user logged into the application is TestUser in the AppDomain domain.

DictionaryToken. The DictionaryToken class iterates over *all* the key/value pairs in a LogEntry's ExtendedProperties dictionary and displays the data for both the keys and the values. The start delimiter for the DictionaryToken is {dictionary(and the tokenTemplate that is passed to the DictionaryToken's FormatToken method contains an additional template that dictates the string representation for these key/value pairs. It substitutes the {key} token with the name of the key and substitutes the {value} token with the value of the item.

Let's use the same example as with the KeyValueToken: a LogEntry's ExtendedProperties dictionary is populated with the results of the ManagedSecurityContextInformationProvider.PopulateDictionary method. However, let's add the DictionaryToken to the template to change it to:

```
This message was logged by
{keyvalue(IdentityName)}.{newline}. Extended
Properties are:
{dictionary({key} has a value of {value}.{newline})}
```

This will return a formatted `LogEntry` of:

```
This message was logged by AppDomain\TestUser.
Extended Properties are:
IdentityName has a value of AppDomain\TestUser.
AuthenticationType has a value of NTLM.
IsAuthenticated has a value of True.
```

Because the regular tokens get replaced before any `TokenFunctions`, the `{newline}` token was replaced with a newline character before the `DictionaryToken` was replaced. Similarly, if the template for the `DictionaryToken` included other tokens, like the `{message}` or `{severity}`, those would also get replaced before any `TokenFunction` replacement.

Revisiting the `DebugSink` (a Custom Sink)

Upon examining the output that is produced by the `DebugSink`, it becomes apparent that the output that is produced is not the string that is expected as a result of using the `TextFormatter`. Instead, it is a string with only the `EventId` and the message. This is because the code shown so far for the `DebugSink` does not take into account the `Formatter` that may have been set for it. Instead, it simply wrote the `EventId` and `Message`. For a Logging Sink and Formatter to work together properly, the Logging Sink must use the Formatter in its `SendMessageCore` method. Thus, changing the line of code in the `DebugSink` `SendMessageCore` function from this:

```
Diagnostics.Debug.WriteLine(SR.DebugSinkMessage(logEntry.Ev
entId,logEntry.Message))
```

to this:

```
Diagnostics.Debug.WriteLine(FormatEntry(logEntry)
```

results in the expected formatted output.

Creating a Custom Token and Formatter

When I provided the code sample for the custom ExtraInformationProvider in Listing 6.7, I left out one step. For this custom ExtraInformationProvider to work, both a custom `TokenFunction` and Formatter are needed. This is because the data that is replacing the token actually contains the token that is being replaced. Because the `TextFormatter` loops through the template and replaces the tokens with the entries in the dictionary, using the `DictionaryToken` with `TextFormatter` results in an infinite loop when replacing the tokens.

To better demonstrate the scenario, let's concentrate on the token and the data. The template contains the `DictionaryToken` as `{dictionary(Key: {key}{tab}{tab}Value: {value}`. Because the actual configuration data that contains the template is being logged, the data that gets logged will also contain `{dictionary(Key: {key}{tab}{tab}Value: {value}`. After the first instance of this token is replaced, the code looks for the next instance of the token. If the starting position to search for the token is *before* the start of the data that just replaced the token, the token will be found in the newly entered data and the configuration data will be replaced here again. This process will continue infinitely (or until the machine runs out of memory). The `DictionaryToken`'s `Format` method works this way.

So, to log the application blocks' configuration data for an application, I created a new token named `ELDictionaryToken` that is a subclass of `DictionaryToken` and overrides the `Format` method, so the start position for the next token search is *after* the last character of the newly entered data. Because the `TextFormatter` is coded to just register the `TimeStampToken`, `KeyValueToken`, and `DictionaryToken`, a new custom Formatter needed to be created that registers the `ELDictionaryToken` instead of the `DictionaryToken`. Therefore, I created a custom Formatter that derives from the `TextFormatter` to suit this purpose. Listing 6.20 shows the `ELDictionaryToken`'s `Format` method.

LISTING 6.20: `ELDictionaryToken`'s `Format` Method

```
[C#]
public override void Format(StringBuilder messageBuilder, LogEntry log)
{
     if (this.startDelimiter.Length == 0)
     {
```

```
        return;
    }

    int pos = 0;
    while (pos < messageBuilder.Length)
    {
        string messageString = messageBuilder.ToString();
        if (messageString.IndexOf(this.startDelimiter) == -1)
        {
            break;
        }

         string tokenTemplate = GetInnerTemplate(pos, messageString);
         string tokenToReplace = this.startDelimiter + tokenTemplate
                  + this.endDelimiter;
         pos = messageBuilder.ToString().IndexOf(tokenToReplace);

         string tokenValue = FormatToken(tokenTemplate, log);

         messageBuilder.Replace(tokenToReplace, tokenValue);

        //Skip past the token we just entered so we don't get into
        //an infinite loop if the token is part of the value.
         pos += tokenValue.Length;
    }
}

[Visual Basic]
Public Overrides Sub Format _
          (ByVal messageBuilder As StringBuilder, ByVal log As LogEntry)
     If Me.startDelimiter.Length = 0 Then
          Return
     End If

     Dim pos As Integer = 0
     Do While pos < messageBuilder.Length
         Dim messageString As String = messageBuilder.ToString()
         If messageString.IndexOf(Me.startDelimiter) = -1 Then
              Exit Do
         End If

         Dim tokenTemplate As String = _
                  GetInnerTemplate(pos, messageString)
         Dim tokenToReplace As String = _
                  Me.startDelimiter + tokenTemplate + Me.endDelimiter
          pos = messageBuilder.ToString().IndexOf(tokenToReplace)

         Dim tokenValue As String = FormatToken(tokenTemplate, log)

         messageBuilder.Replace(tokenToReplace, tokenValue)
```

```
        'Skip past the token we just entered so we don't get into
        'an infinite loop if the token is part of the value.
       pos += tokenValue.Length
    Loop
End Sub
```

The only differences between the new `TextFormatterWithELDictionary` that I created and the `TextFormatter` that ships with Enterprise Library are in the `Initialize` and `RegisterTokenFunctions` methods. Listing 6.21 shows these methods.

LISTING 6.21: `TextFormatterWithELDictionary`

```
[C#]
public override void Initialize(ConfigurationView configurationView)
{
     ArgumentValidation.CheckForNullReference
          (configurationView, "configurationView");
     ArgumentValidation.CheckExpectedType
          (configurationView, typeof(LoggingConfigurationView));

     LoggingConfigurationView loggingConfigurationView =
          (LoggingConfigurationView)configurationView;
     FormatterData formatterData =
          loggingConfigurationView.GetFormatterData(ConfigurationName);
     ArgumentValidation.CheckExpectedType
          (customFormatterData, typeof(ELTextFormatterData));

     customFormatterData = (ELTextFormatterData)formatterData;
     RegisterTemplate();
}

private void RegisterTokenFunctions()
{
     tokenFunctions = new ArrayList();
     tokenFunctions.Add(new ELDictionaryToken());
     tokenFunctions.Add(new KeyValueToken());
     tokenFunctions.Add(new TimeStampToken());
}

[Visual Basic]
Public Overrides Sub Initialize _
          (ByVal configurationView As ConfigurationView)
     ArgumentValidation.CheckForNullReference _
          (configurationView, "configurationView")
     ArgumentValidation.CheckExpectedType _
          (configurationView, GetType(LoggingConfigurationView))
```

```
        Dim loggingConfigurationView As LoggingConfigurationView = _
            CType(configurationView, LoggingConfigurationView)
        Dim formatterData As FormatterData = _
            loggingConfigurationView.GetFormatterData(ConfigurationName)
        ArgumentValidation.CheckExpectedType _
            (customFormatterData, GetType(ELTextFormatterData))

        customFormatterData = CType(formatterData, ELTextFormatterData)
        RegisterTemplate()
    End Sub

    Private Sub RegisterTokenFunctions()
        tokenFunctions = New ArrayList()
        tokenFunctions.Add(New ELDictionaryToken())
        tokenFunctions.Add(New KeyValueToken())
        tokenFunctions.Add(New TimeStampToken())
    End Sub
```

The normal procedure for adding a design-time interface on top of the `TextFormatterWithELDictionary` can be taken to configure it through the Enterprise Library Configuration Tool (see Chapter 2). The complete source code is on the book's Web site.

Tracing

Tracing is considered to be related—but different—from logging in the Logging and Instrumentation Application Block. Whereas logging is the act of publishing a `LogEntry` message to one or more endpoints, **tracing** is concerned with "telling a story" by logging and correlating multiple messages that occur in a particular activity in an application.

Examples help to differentiate the two. Let's say that a Web application exists for taking online orders. It would be typical to "log" events like receiving a request via a Web service or storing data in a database. It is also typical to "trace" the activity of a process throughout the entire application from start to finish. That is, it wouldn't be atypical to trace when the UI process started, when the business process started, when the data process started and finished, when the business process finished, and, finally, when the UI process finished. This would represent an entire activity in an application with several subactivities along the way. The "logs" occur in the tracing for this process. Figure 6.16 illustrates this scenario.

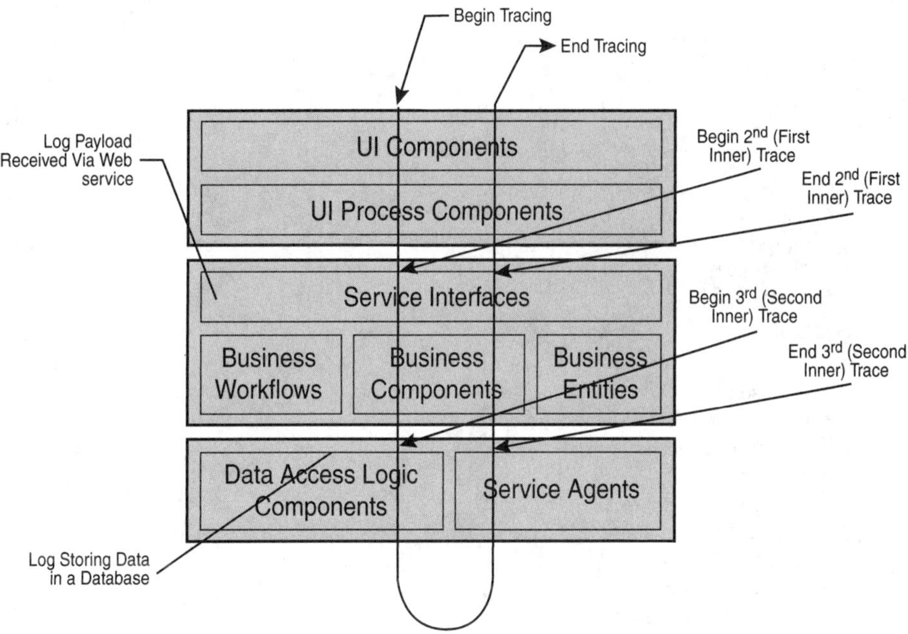

FIGURE 6.16: Tracing and Logging in an Application

The design goal for the Logging and Instrumentation Application Block is to make it as easy to trace processes in an application as it is to log when specific events occur. To this end, the `Tracer` service façade exists. `Tracer` is the object that is used to trace processes in an application. The public interface that is exposed to accomplish this is simple: constructors are used to create and start the tracing process, and a `Dispose` method is exposed to clean up and end the tracing process.

When an instance of a `Tracer` object is created, a `Start Trace: Activity '<ActivityId>' in method '<MethodName>' at <NumberOfTicks> ticks` message is logged. The `ActivityId` is used to correlate the log messages, the `MethodName` is the name of the method where this `Tracer` was created, and the `NumberOfTicks` represents the time this instance was created as obtained from the native Win32 `QueryPerformanceCounter` function.[5]

5. See the article "How To: Time Managed Code Using QueryPerformanceCounter and QueryPerformanceFrequency" at http://msdn.microsoft.com/library/default.asp?url=/library/en-us/dnpag/html/scalenethowto09.asp) for more detailed information on leveraging these native Win32 functions to time the execution of managed code.

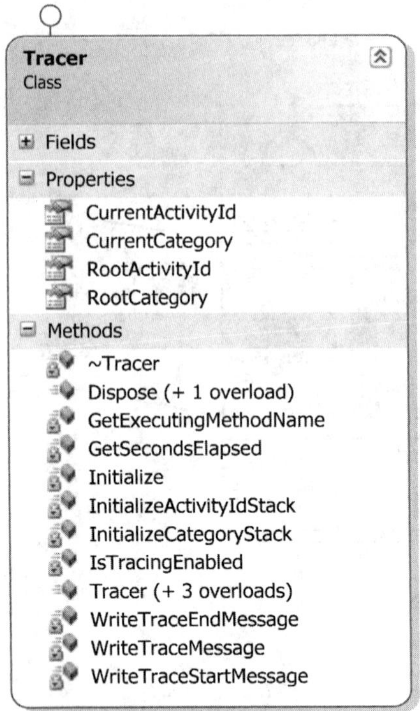

FIGURE 6.17: The `Tracer` Class

When the `Dispose` method is called, an `End Trace: Activity '<ActivityId>' in method '<MethodName>' at <NumberOfTicks> ticks (elapsed time: <Seconds> seconds)` message is logged. If using VB.NET, the `Dispose` method must be explicitly called to release the `Tracer` object and generate the `End Trace` message. This happens automatically when using the `using` keyword in C#. Figure 6.17 depicts how the `Tracer` class contains a constructor, `Dispose` method, and four properties.

For example, in Figure 6.16 the first `Tracer` object was created in the UI layer. This represents the outer Trace for all other Traces that may occur in this activity. The code to perform this Trace could be as simple as that in Listing 6.22.

LISTING 6.22: Creating the Trace in the UI Layer

```
[C#]
private void UIButton_Click(object sender, EventArgs e)
{
     using (new Tracer("UI Layer"))
     {
       //Get some information from the form and call the business layer.
       //Display the results to the user.
     }
}

[Visual Basic]
Private Sub UIButton_Click(ByVal sender As Object, ByVal e As EventArgs)
     Dim newTracer As New Tracer("UI Layer")

     'Get some information from the form and call the business layer.
     'Display the results to the user.

     newTracer.Dispose()
End Sub
```

The two log messages that result from just using the `Tracer` in this way are shown in Listing 6.23.

LISTING 6.23: Results from Using the `Tracer` in the UI Layer

```
Timestamp: 7/8/2006 11:59:18 AM
Message: Start Trace: Activity '6b773efc-5598-4406.b94d-d539f2400a7d'
in method 'UIButton_Click' at 34886400658 ticks
Category: UI Layer
Priority: 5
EventId: 1
Severity: Information
Title:TracerEnter
Machine: TESTMACHINE
Application Domain: MyApp.exe
Process Id: 5864
Process Name: C:\TestApp\bin\Debug\MyApp.exe
Win32 Thread Id: 4696
Thread Name:
Extended Properties:
TracerActivityId has a value of 6b773efc-5598-4406.b94d-d539f2400a7d.


Timestamp: 7/8/2006 11:59:18 AM
Message: End Trace: Activity '6b773efc-5598-4406.b94d-d539f2400a7d' in
method 'UIButton_Click' at 34898308490 ticks (elapsed time: 3.326633
seconds)
```

```
Category: UI Layer
Priority: 5
EventId: 1
Severity: Information
Title:TracerExit
Machine: TESTMACHINE
Application Domain: MyApp.exe
Process Id: 5864
Process Name: C:\TestApp\bin\Debug\MyApp.exe
Win32 Thread Id: 4696
Thread Name:
Extended Properties:
TracerActivityId has a value of 6b773efc-5598-4406.b94d-d539f2400a7d.
```

Because the `ActivityId` is not specified in the `Tracer`'s constructor, its value is automatically set equal to a new `Guid`.

Activity Identifiers

`ActivityIds` are used to correlate different trace messages that occur in a single activity in an application. The previous scenario illustrated the entire process of entering data into a UI form, sending it through the different layers in the application, and returning the results in the UI. This can be thought of as a single activity, and showed how a unique activity identifier can be automatically generated and used to correlate all traces and logs that occur in this activity.

Sometimes, however, it may be beneficial to override a particular activity identifier for some of the messages logged during a component's execution. Nonetheless, callers to this component shouldn't have to be concerned with whether the activity identifier is being changed or not. Therefore, the `Tracer` object uses an Activity Identifier Stack to ensure that the activity identifier returned from any component has the same value that it had before the component was called. Each time a new `Tracer` object is created, the application block pushes an activity identifier to the top of the stack. When `Dispose` is called, the activity identifier is popped from the stack. The value for the activity identifier is determined according to the following rules.

1. If no activity identifier is specified and there is no current activity identifier (the stack is empty), the application block generates a new activity identifier as a `Guid`. This activity identifier is pushed onto

the stack. Creating the `Tracer` object this way ensures that every user of an application has unique activity identifiers in the log. This was illustrated in Listing 6.22.

2. If a value for the activity identifier is specified as the second parameter in the `Tracer`'s constructor, that value is pushed onto the stack. For the most part, when the `Tracer` object is created this way, the logs for all users of an application will contain the same `ActivityId` because the `Tracer` won't append the `ActivityId` with any type of information that would make it unique for a user.

   For example, if the code in Listing 6.23 was modified so the constructor for the `Tracer` object was *`new Tracer("UI Layer", "Activity Id 1")`*, then all messages logged in this activity, independent of user, would be logged with the `ActivityID` of *`Activity Id 1`*. Listing 6.24 shows how the results shown in Listing 6.23 would change if `Tracer` were passed this `ActivityID`.

LISTING 6.24: Results from Using `Tracer` with `ActivityId` of `Activity Id 1`

```
Timestamp: 7/8/2006 11:59:18 AM
Message: Start Trace: Activity 'Activity Id 1' in method
'UIButton_Click' at 34886400658 ticks
...

Message: End Trace: Activity ' Activity Id 1' in method
'UIButton_Click' at 34898308490 ticks (elapsed time: 3.326633
seconds)
...
```

   The exception to this rule is if the string that is passed to the `Tracer` constructor is dynamically created for each user. For example, if `Guid.NewGuid().ToString()` was used for the `ActivityId` parameter, then the activity identifier would remain unique for each user.

3. If no value is specified but a current activity identifier exists, the value of the current activity identifier is pushed onto the stack again. So, if Listing 6-22 was modified so that one `Tracer` object was nested in another, then the second (inner) `Tracer` object would use the activity identifier that was created from the first (outer) `Tracer` object because the same `ActivityId` would be pushed onto the stack again. Listing 6.25 depicts one `Tracer` nested in another.

LISTING 6.25: Nested Tracers using the Same `ActivityId`

```
[C#]
private void UIButton_Click(object sender, EventArgs e)
{
     using (new Tracer("UI Layer"))
     {
          //Get some information from the form.

          using (new Tracer("Bus Layer"))
          {
               // Call the business layer.
     }

     //Display the results to the user.
     }
}

[Visual Basic]
Private Sub UIButton_Click(ByVal sender As Object, ByVal e As EventArgs)
     Dim newTracer As New Tracer("UI Layer")
     'Get some information from the form.

     Dim innerTracer As New Tracer("Bus Layer")
     'Call the business layer.
     innerTracer.Dispose()

     'Display the results to the user.
     newTracer.Dispose()
End Sub
```

Listing 6.26 shows how all log messages have the same activity identifier.

LISTING 6.26: Results of Nested Tracers with the Same `ActivityId`

```
Timestamp: 7/8/2006 11:59:18 AM
Message: Start Trace: Activity '6b773efc-5598-4406.b94d-d539f2400a7d'
in method 'UIButton_Click' at 103207729815 ticks
Category: UI Layer
Priority: 5
EventId: 1
Severity: Information
Title:TracerEnter
Machine: TESTMACHINE
Application Domain: MyApp.exe
Process Id: 5864
Process Name: C:\TestApp\bin\Debug\MyApp.exe
Win32 Thread Id: 4696
```

```
Thread Name:
Extended Properties:
TracerActivityId has a value of 6b773efc-5598-4406.b94d-d539f2400a7d.

Timestamp: 7/8/2006 11:59:18 AM
Message: Start Trace: Activity '6b773efc-5598-4406.b94d-d539f2400a7d'
in method 'UIButton_Click' at 103218953050 ticks
Category: Bus Layer
Priority: 5
EventId: 1
Severity: Information
Title:TracerEnter
Machine: TESTMACHINE
Application Domain: MyApp.exe
Process Id: 5864
Process Name: C:\TestApp\bin\Debug\MyApp.exe
Win32 Thread Id: 4696
Thread Name:
Extended Properties:
TracerActivityId has a value of 6b773efc-5598-4406.b94d-d539f2400a7d.

Timestamp: 7/8/2006 11:59:21 AM
Message: End Trace: Activity '6b773efc-5598-4406.b94d-d539f2400a7d' in
method 'UIButton_Click' at 103218997011 ticks (elapsed time: 0.012281
seconds)
Category: Bus Layer
Priority: 5
EventId: 1
Severity: Information
Title:TracerExit
Machine: TESTMACHINE
Application Domain: MyApp.exe
Process Id: 5864
Process Name: C:\TestApp\bin\Debug\MyApp.exe
Win32 Thread Id: 4696
Thread Name:
Extended Properties:
TracerActivityId has a value of 6b773efc-5598-4406.b94d-d539f2400a7d

Timestamp: 7/8/2006 11:59:21 AM
Message: End Trace: Activity '6b773efc-5598-4406.b94d-d539f2400a7d' in
method 'UIButton_Click' at 103219008621 ticks (elapsed time: 3.150905
seconds)
Category: UI Layer
Priority: 5
EventId: 1
Severity: Information
Title:TracerExit
Machine: TESTMACHINE
Application Domain: MyApp.exe
```

```
Process Id: 5864
Process Name: C:\TestApp\bin\Debug\MyApp.exe
Win32 Thread Id: 4696
Thread Name:
Extended Properties:
TracerActivityId has a value of 6b773efc-5598-4406.b94d-d539f2400a7d.
```

This is true whether the nesting occurs in the same method or not. For example, the same result would occur if the second `Tracer` object was created in a method in a business object instead of in the `UIButton_Click` method. The only difference in the log would be the value for the `MethodName` that is displayed as the *Start* and *End* Log messages. In other words, the same result can be achieved from the code shown in Listing 6.27.

LISTING 6.27: Nested Traces in Multiple Methods

```
[C#]
public class BusinessObject
{
     public static void DoSomething()
     {
          using (new Tracer("Bus Layer"))
          {
          }
     }
}
...
private void UIButton_Click(object sender, EventArgs e)
{
     using (new Tracer("UI Layer"))
     {
          //Get some information from the form.

          // Call the business layer.
          BusinessObject.DoSomething();

          //Display the results to the user.
     }
}

[Visual Basic]
Public Class BusinessObject
     Public Shared Sub DoSomething()
          Dim newTracer As New Tracer("Bus Layer")
          newTracer.Dispose()
     End Sub
End Class
```

```
Private Sub UIButton_Click(ByVal sender As Object, ByVal e As EventArgs)
     Dim newTracer As New Tracer("UI Layer")
     'Get some information from the form.

     'Call the business layer.
     BusinessObject.DoSomething()

     'Display the results to the user.

     newTracer.Dispose()
End Sub
```

The `Tracer` object exposes two static properties that can help you determine the activity identifiers that are in use. The `CurrentActivityId` property returns the current activity identifier, and the `RootActivityId` property returns the root (or outermost) activity identifier.

Category Stack

In addition to maintaining a stack for the activity identifiers, the `Tracer` object maintains a stack for the Categories. Since the `Category` is a required argument in the `Tracer`'s constructor, it must always be supplied; therefore, the `Category` is always pushed onto the stack when the `Tracer` is created. When the `Tracer` is disposed, the `Category` is always popped from the stack.

It can be useful for you to ascertain the current and root Categories that exist when tracing an activity. For that reason, the `Tracer` object exposes two static properties similar to the properties exposed for the `ActivityId` stack. The `CurrentCategory` property returns the current Category, and the `RootCategory` property returns the root (or outermost) Category that was used when the initial Tracer was created.

Logging While Tracing

Any logging that is performed in the scope of a `Tracer` object will automatically have the value of the `Tracer.CurrentActivityId` added to its `ExtendedProperties` with a key of `TracerActivityId`. This `ActivityId` is added by the abstract base `LogSink` class when it prepares the message to be sent. This occurs in the `LogSink`'s virtual `PrepareMessage` method that is called right before `SendMessageCore`.

This is an important point to understand if a custom Sink needs to be created that must perform some additional logic to prepare the message before calling `SendMessageCore`. This logic belongs in the `PrepareMessage` method; if this method is overridden, it is important to remember that either the `base.PrepareMessage` method or the `AddActivityIdToLogEntry` method should be called. Failure to do this will result in the absence of the `ActivityId` in a `LogEntry`'s `ExtendedProperties` when logging in the scope of a Trace. All results from the code examples in this section resulted in the existence of this additional extended property.

Developing with the Logging and Instrumentation Application Block

The previous section covered the design of the Logging and Instrumentation Application Block and how it can be extended. Admittedly, there's a lot of code that accompanies that section, but that code is solely for the purpose of adding new features to the block. The major design goal for the block—and for Enterprise Library in general—is to make it very simple to create enterprise-level applications. That is the reason why the `Logger` and `Tracer` façades exist.

If you just plan on using the ExtraInformationProviders, distribution strategies, Distributors, Formatters, and Sinks that ship with this block, you will need to write very little code. And the good news is that the components that ship with the block cover the majority of the situations that you may ever encounter. The intent of the extensions shown in the previous section is simply to show that there are options available if none of the components fit your particular needs.

Whether you use the out-of-the-box assets or develop extensions for the Logging and Instrumentation Application Block, it is important to understand that writing code to leverage these assets is very straightforward. The bulk of the work that needs to be done is configuring them, not coding against them.

Configuring the Logging and Instrumentation Application Block

There are two parts to the Logging and Instrumentation Application Block: the client side and the distributor side. The client side is responsible for creating the log or trace messages, filtering them as needed, and sending the messages to a distributor via a specific distribution strategy. The distributor receives the log/trace messages and determines how to format and route each message based on its Category. In an asynchronous model, the client and distributor can actually exist on separate physical machines. As such, there are actually two separate configuration sections that get created for the Logging and Instrumentation Application Block: one for the client side and one for the distributor side. Let's start with how to create the client side configuration.

Client Settings

The client settings themselves can be broken down further into two major areas: configuring filters and configuring the distribution strategies.

Configuring Filters. LogEntry messages get filtered based on their `Category` and `Priority` (the Filtering section earlier in this chapter discussed how this works). These filters get configured on the Client Settings node.

- The `CategoryFilterSettings` property provides the capability to either filter all Categories except for specific ones *or* to include all Categories except for specific ones—but not both.
- The `MinimumPriority` property is used to set the minimum priority that a `LogEntry` must have to be passed to the `Distributor`. If the `Priority` that is set for a `LogEntry` is below the configured `MinimumPriority`, the `LogEntry` will be filtered.

There is one more kind of filter that can be configured on the Client Settings node: the enabling of logging or tracing for all messages. Disabling one of these essentially has the effect of "filtering" all messages for that type of log (i.e., a log message or a trace). The `LoggingEnabled` and `TracingEnabled` properties can be used to enable or disable Logging or Tracing respectively. Figure 6.18 highlights the different ways to set filtering criteria in the Logging and Instrumentation Application Block.

Configuring the Distribution Strategy. The other decision that needs to be made for the client side of logging is whether the log messages should be distributed synchronously or asynchronously. The default is synchronous

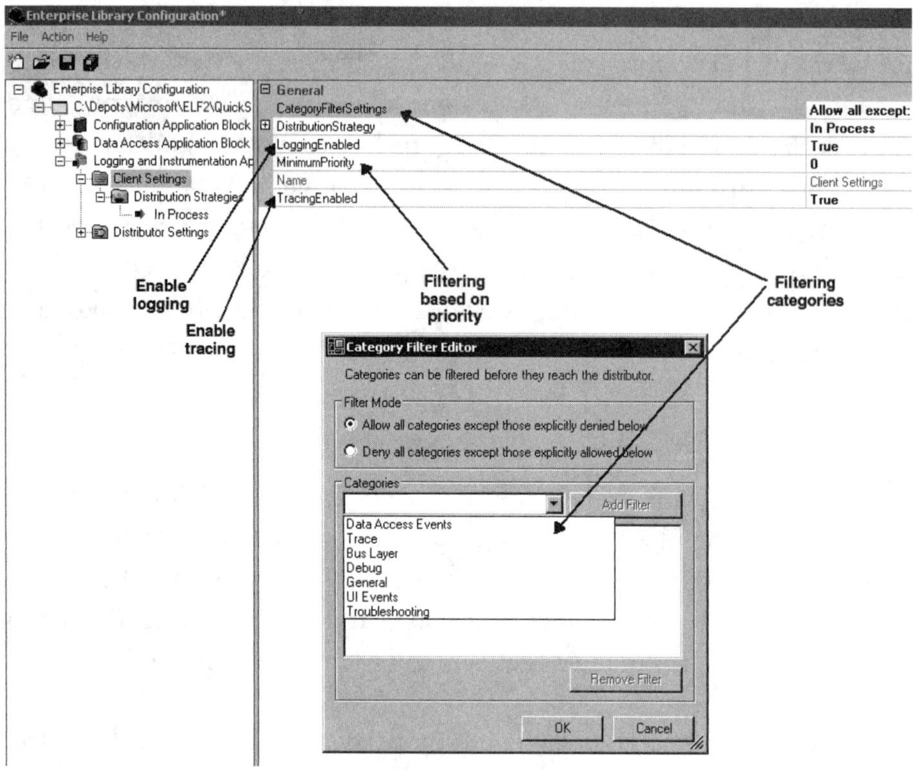

FIGURE 6.18: Configuring Filters

processing, which uses the `InProcLogDistributionStrategy`. If the default is chosen, then the client and distributor must remain on the same machine because the distribution of log messages is completed in-process.

Enterprise Library ships with the `MsmqLogDistributionStrategy` as a means for accomplishing asynchronous log distribution. To configure an application to use the `MsmqLogDistributionStrategy`, the `MsmqDistributionStrategyNode` first needs to be added as a valid distribution strategy. To add this node, right-click on the *Distribution Strategies* node in the Enterprise Library Configuration Tool and select *New > MSMQ*. Then configure the new `MsmqDistributionStrategyNode` with the location for the queue to which the distribution strategy will write and the `Distributor` will read. The default is .\Private$\myQueue.

Two distribution strategies will now exist under the Distribution Strategies node. The block isn't configured to use the new `MsmqLogDistributionStrategy` until this distribution strategy is configured as the current one in the Property pane for the Client Settings. Figure 6.19 shows the three steps that are needed to configure the Logging and Instrumentation Application Block to distribute logs asynchronously.

If you've compiled and deployed the Database Distribution Strategy code that accompanies this chapter, you can use that to distribute log messages asynchronously too. The prerequisite to using it is that the Data Access Application Block has already been configured to point to the database where the LogEntries will be stored. The process for configuring the Database Distribution Strategy is outlined earlier in this chapter in the Custom Distribution Strategy section.

Distributor Settings

That is all that is needed to configure the client settings. The `Distributor` is responsible for formatting and routing the messages that it receives to the

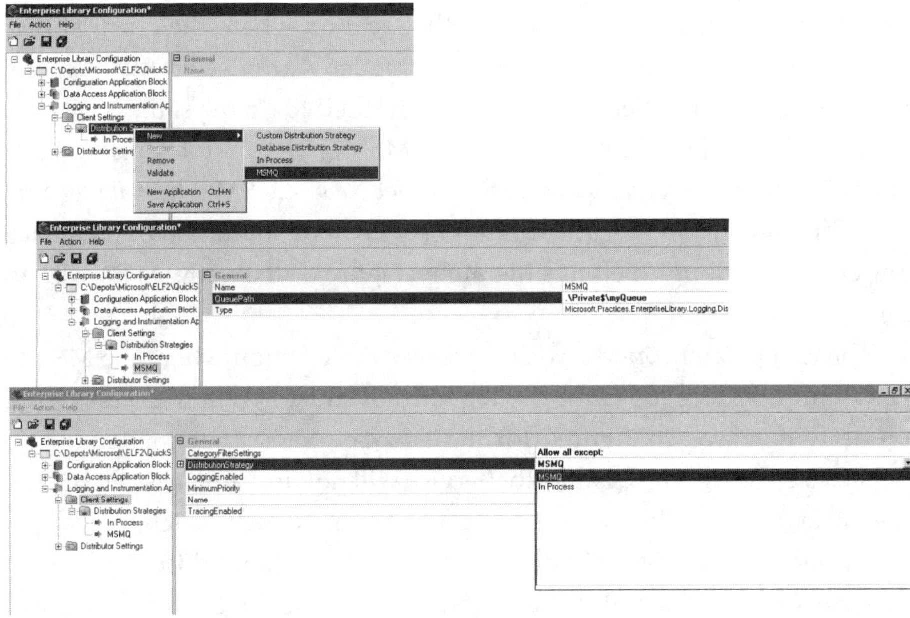

FIGURE 6.19: Configuring Asynchronous Log Distribution

Sinks that have been configured to accept them. This equates to the following configuration settings.

- The Distributor may need to be configured to match the distribution strategy.
- The Formatters may need to be configured.
- The Sinks will need to be configured.
- Destinations in Categories need to be configured. The Destinations determine how the log messages will be formatted and routed.
- The default Category and default Formatter must be set.

Configuring the Distributor. If the In-Process distribution strategy (the default setting) was left to distribute the log messages to the endpoints, then no configuration needs to be completed for the Distributor. However, if an asynchronous log distribution strategy was selected, the Distributor Service must be configured to match the distribution strategy. That is, if the `MsmqLogDistributionStrategy` was selected as the distribution strategy in the client settings, then the MSMQ Distributor Service must be configured to receive the LogEntries from the location where the client stored them. If the `DatabaseDistributionStrategy` was selected, then the Database Distributor Service must be configured to do the same.

To configure the Distributor to use the MSMQ Distributor Service, right-click the *Distributor Settings* node and select *New > MSMQ Distributor Service*. This adds the MSMQ Distributor Service node to the rest of the nodes under the Distributor Settings hierarchy. Figure 6.20 illustrates how to do this.

The `MsmqPath` property, which denotes the location where the MSMQ Distributor Service looks for the log entries, must match the `QueuePath` property that was configured for the `MsmqLogDistributionStrategy`. Otherwise, the MSMQ Distributor Service will not find any messages in the queue. Figure 6.21 illustrates how the two settings must match.

By default, the MSMQ Distributor Service is configured to poll for new messages every 1,000 milliseconds (one second); however, this setting can be changed by setting a different value for the `QueueTimeInterval` property.

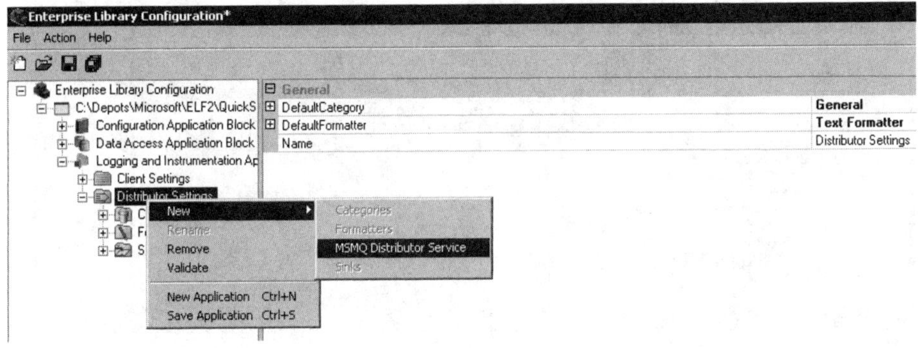

FIGURE 6.20: Selecting the MSMQ Distributor Service

If the client settings were configured to use the Database Distribution Strategy included with this chapter, then the Database Distributor Service must also be configured to match the settings of the Database Distribution Strategy. The specifics about configuring the Database Distributor Service are outlined in the Custom Distribution Strategy section earlier in this chapter.

Configuring Formatters

By default, the Logging and Instrumentation Application Block is configured with a single `TextFormatter` whose template will format a `LogEntry` as:

```
Timestamp: {timestamp}
Message: {message}
Category: {category}
Priority: {priority}
EventId: {eventid}
Severity: {severity}
Title:{title}
Machine: {machine}
Application Domain: {appDomain}
Process Id: {processId}
Process Name: {processName}
```

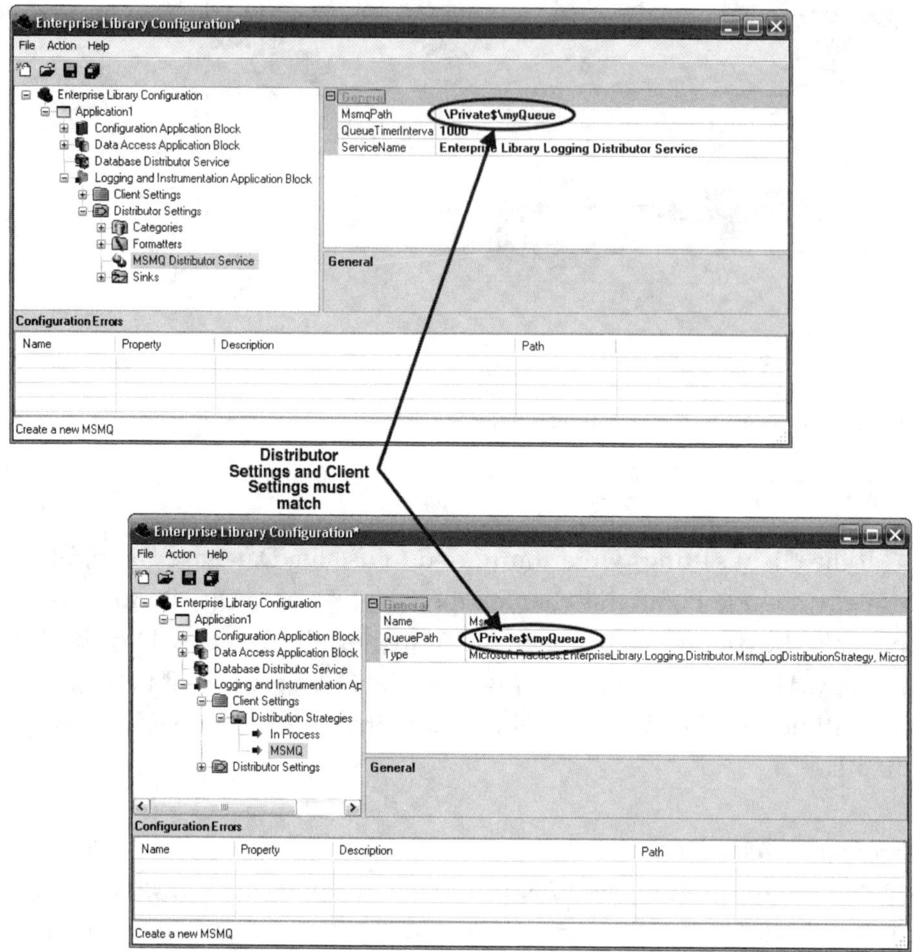

FIGURE 6.21: Configuring Asynchronous Distributor Settings to Match Client Distribution Strategy Settings

```
Win32 Thread Id: {win32ThreadId}
Thread Name: {threadName}
Extended Properties: {dictionary({key} - {value}
)}
```

If this template suits the needs for all the LogEntries for your application, you don't need to do any further configuration for Formatters. However, if you need to modify this template or add new templates or Formatters, then read on.

Figure 6.15 showed the Template Editor in the discussion about the design of the `TextFormatter`. Modifying a template involves editing the text that exists with the Template Editor's text box. It is this text that is saved in the configuration file with the rest of the Distributor Settings configuration. For your convenience, the Template Editor also provides a drop-down box with a list of available tokens. This is intended to make it easy to add tokens to a template.

If you need more than one template because it is necessary to have some LogEntries formatted differently than others, then you need to add a new `TextFormatter` (or another class that implements that `ILogFormatter` interface and supports templates) to the configuration settings. To add a new Formatter, and therefore a new template, right-click on the *Formatters* node and select *New > Text Formatter*. Figure 6.22 shows how to accomplish this.

Configuring Sinks

Sinks represent the place where the LogEntries will finally reside. Each Sink needs its own unique set of configuration data to determine where the LogEntry will reside. The `FlatFileSink`, for example, requires a filename,

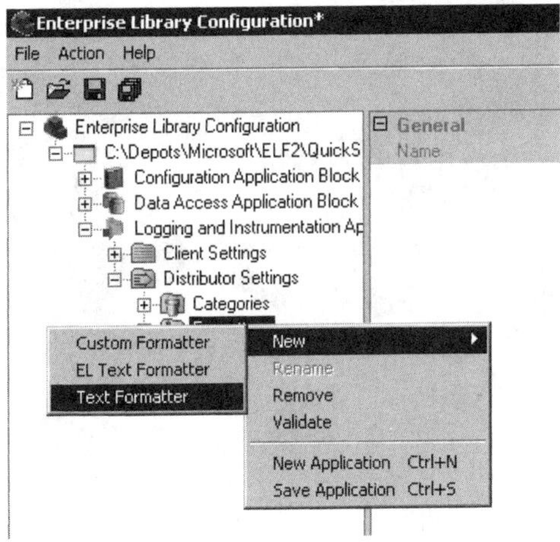

FIGURE 6.22: Adding a New `TextFormatter`

the EmailSink requires the name of an SMTP server, and the DatabaseSink requires the name of a DatabaseInstance. Table 6.8 details how to configure each of the Sinks that ship with Enterprise Library.

To add a Logging Sink to the configuration information for an application, follow these steps.

1. Right-click on the *Sinks* node, select *New*, and select the type of Sink that you want to add.
2. Configure the properties for that Sink (see Table 6.8).

The following example shows how to add and configure an EmailSink.

1. Add the Sink to the configuration (see Figure 6.23).
2. Configure the SmtpServer, ToAddress, and ForAddress properties. In Figure 6.24:

- The SmtpServer has been configured as *mysmtpserver.*
- The ToAddress has been configured as importantperson@example.com;operationaladmin@example.com.
- The FromAddress has been configured as someone@example.com.

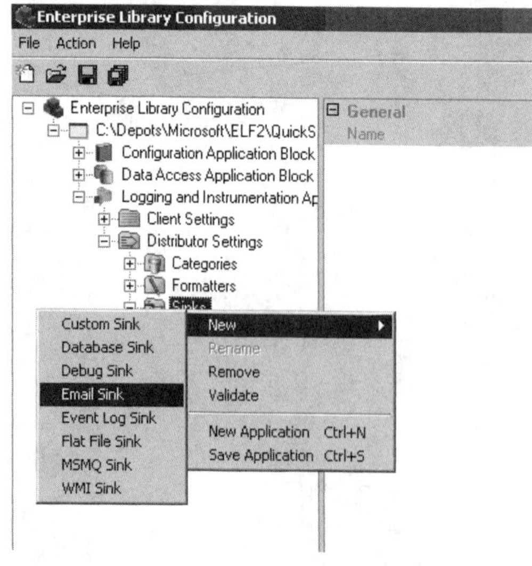

FIGURE 6.23: Adding an EmailSink

Table 6.8: Configuration Properties for the Logging Sinks

Sink	Property	Description
Database	`DatabaseInstanceName`	The name of a `DatabaseInstance` that specifies where the LogEntry should be stored. The `DatabaseInstance` must already have been configured under the Data Access Application Block settings. The Logging and Instrumentation Application Block includes a SQL script that you can use to create this database.
	`StoredProcName`	The name of the stored procedure to be used to write the LogEntry to the database. If not specified, this defaults to `WriteLog`.
Email	`SmtpServer`	The name of the SMTP server to be used to send the e-mail.
	`ToAddress`	A semi-colon delimited list of e-mail addresses to be used for the recipients.
	`FromAddress`	The e-mail address that will appear as the sender's e-mail address.
	`SubjectLineStarter` (optional)	The text to appear at the beginning of the subject line.
	`SubjectLineEnder` (optional)	The text to be added at the end of the subject line.
EventLog	`EventLogName` (optional)	The name of the event log. If not specified, it defaults to `Application` log.
	`EventSourceName`	Represents the `SourceColumn` in the `EventLog`.
FlatFile	`Filename`	The name of the file where the event information will be written. If a path isn't specified, it will default to the application's current directory.

(continued)

TABLE 6.8: Configuration Properties for the Logging Sinks (*continued*)

Sink	Property	Description
FlatFile	`Header` (optional)	A line of text to appear before each LogEntry.
	`Footer` (optional)	A line of text to appear after each LogEntry.
Msmq	`QueuePath`	The path of the private or public message queue. The path is specified in the format <servername>\private$\<queuename>, where "." may be used to specify the servername of the local server.
WMI	---	The `WMISink` does not need any additional information from configuration.

Optionally, the `SubjectLineStarter` and `SubjectLineEnder` properties can be configured so that the text on the subject lines can be customized. The `SubjectLineStarter` property has been config-

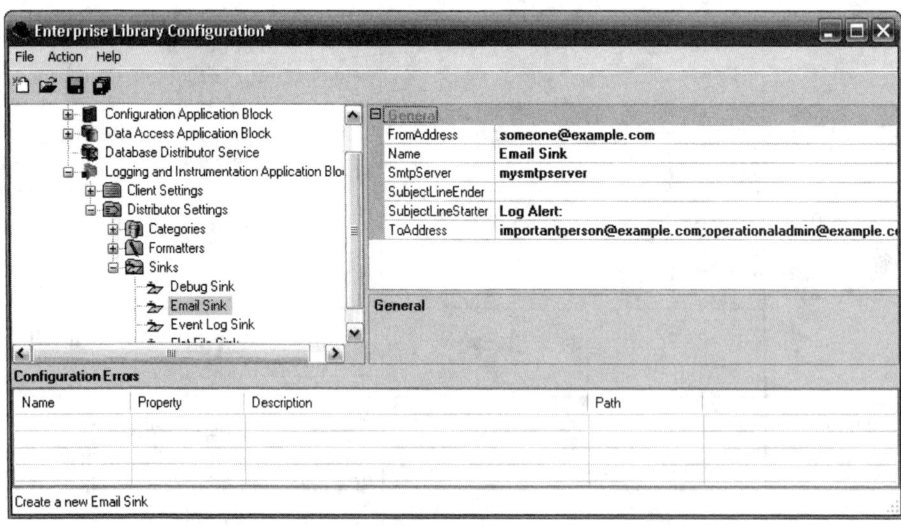

FIGURE 6.24: Configuring an `EmailSink`

ured to *Log Alert:* so that every e-mail that gets sent from this Sink will start with a subject line of *Log Alert:*.

Configuring Categories and Destinations

Last but certainly not least are the details for configuring Categories. The configuration for Categories determines how all LogEntries will be formatted and to which Sinks they will be routed.

Each Category has a name. For most of the constructs in Enterprise Library, the `Name` property isn't too important; it is usually just meant to signify a unique way to identify a node in configuration. Category names, however, are more important. It is this name that gets matched to the LogEntry's Category; thus, it ultimately decides which Destinations a LogEntry will be routed to. If no match is made between a LogEntry's Category and one of the configured Category names, the LogEntry will be assigned to the default Category. Changing the name of a Category that is used in an application can easily cause LogEntries to be assigned to the default Category simply because the value for their Category property no longer matches an existing one.

To add a Category to an application's configuration information, right-click the *Categories* node and select *New > Category*. Add the name for the

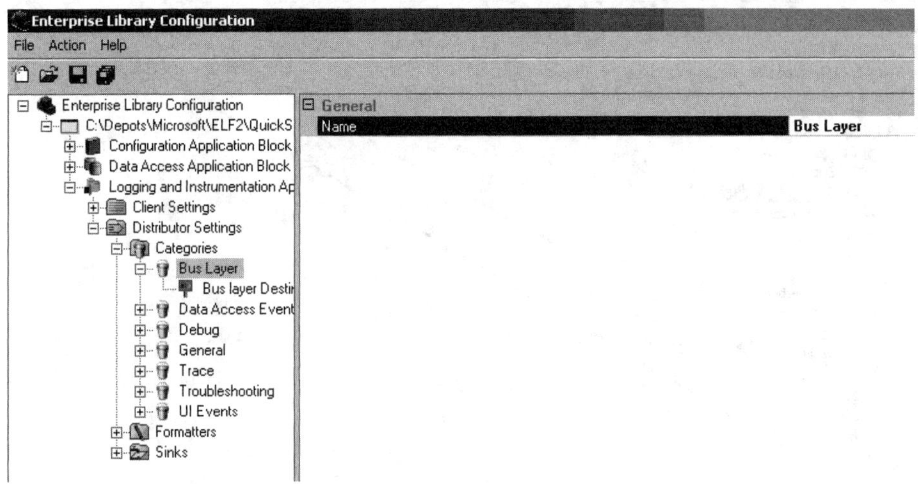

FIGURE 6.25: Adding a New Category

Category that matches the name of one of the Categories that will be used to log messages. In Figure 6.25, the name of the Category is *Bus Layer*. Any LogEntries written as `Logger.Write("log message", "Bus Layer")` will be routed to the Destinations configured for this Category.

In addition to a name, every Category can be configured with zero or more Destinations. Of course, configuring a Category with no Destinations is not usually very beneficial because the LogEntries won't go anywhere. Therefore, it is a good idea to add at least one Destination. As mentioned before, a Destination is a pairing of a Formatter and a Sink.

Consequently, before a Destination can be configured for a Category, you must have already configured the Formatter and Sink that will be used for that Destination. All that is left after that point is to add the Destination node by right-clicking on the *Category* node and selecting *New > Destination* and then selecting a Formatter and Sink. Figure 6.26 shows how to configure a Destination with a Formatter and Sink.

Defaults

It is possible to configure a Destination without pointing to a Formatter; only the Sink is a required field. It is also possible for a LogEntry to be pub-

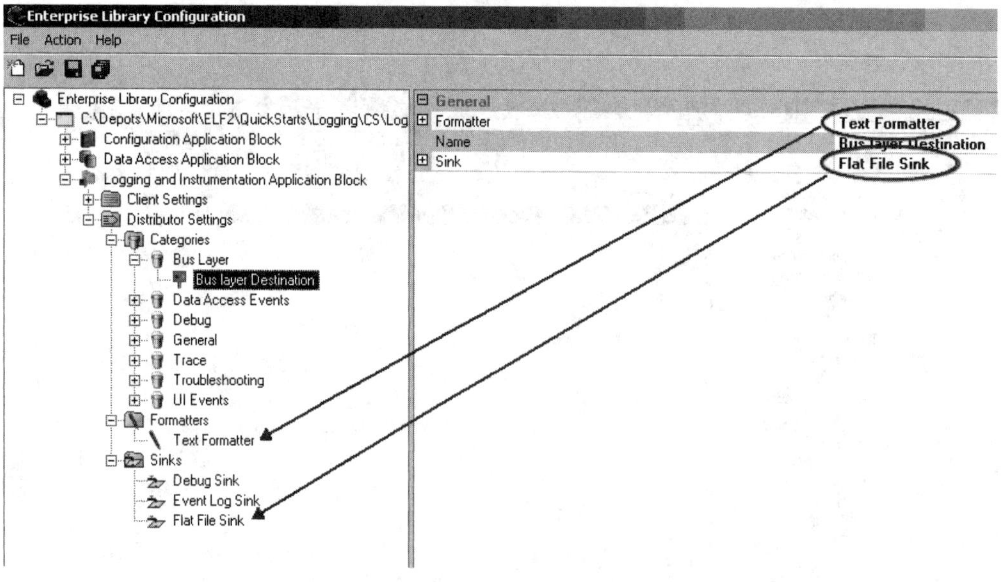

FIGURE 6.26: Configuring the Formatter and Sink for a Destination

lished with a Category name that doesn't match one of the Categories defined in configuration for that application. The question, then, is what should the Logging and Instrumentation Application Block do when one of these scenarios is encountered? The answer is that it uses the default values for these constructs.

The root node for the Distributor Settings allows default values to be specified to let the Logging and Instrumentation Application Block continue functioning when it encounters a Destination without a Formatter or a LogEntry that does not match one of the predefined Categories.

The last task that remains to be completed for configuring the Logging and Instrumentation Application Block is to set the default Formatter and Category by selecting the *Distributor Settings* node and setting the properties accordingly. Each property will provide a drop-down box from which one of the available Formatters and Categories can be selected. Figure 6.27 illustrates this.

Using the Logging and Instrumentation Application Block's API

A detailed analysis of the logging and tracing features were covered at the beginning of this chapter. This section is meant as a review of this block's API to make logging and tracing messages very straightforward. For more detailed information about how it works beneath the covers, please refer

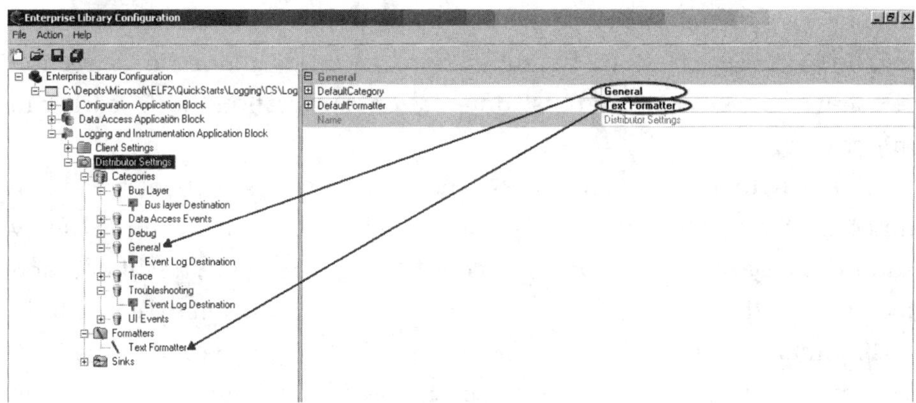

FIGURE 6.27: Setting the Default Formatter and Category

back to the section "Design of the Logging and Instrumentation Application Block" earlier in this chapter.

Logging

When it comes to developing an application that uses the Logging and Instrumentation Application Block, configuring the application is actually the most complex part. The primary design goal for this block was to make it very simple to develop against it. Therefore, two service façades exist to serve this need. The first is the `Logger` class. Its principal method for use is its static `Write` method.

For most situations, the overloads for the `Write` method will provide all the functionality that is needed to log a message. Table 6.9 shows the different signatures for the `Write` method.

The method that you will probably use the most is the second one, `Write(object,string)`. It is easy to use in that it only takes two parameters (usually just two strings) and robust enough to ensure that the message will get logged to the proper Sink because it includes the name of the Category. The point to remember is that `Logger.Write` may be the only method that you will have to use to accomplish all the logging needs for an application.

Should you need to add more application-specific information to a LogEntry, you can extend the log message in many ways. The most straightforward technique is to add items to the LogEntry's `ExtendedProperties` dictionary. For more advanced techniques (namely subclassing the `LogEntry` class), see the subsection Custom `LogEntry` in the section "Design of the Logging and Instrumentation Application Block" earlier in this chapter.

One way to add items to the `ExtendedProperties` dictionary is illustrated by the last four overloads listed in Table 6.9. These samples show adding items to an object that implement `IDictionary` (e.g., Hashtable) and then setting the `LogEntry`'s `ExtendedProperties` dictionary equal to it.

Another way is to use the Logger's static `SetContextItem` method. This method was covered in detail in the section "Design of the Logging and Instrumentation Application Block" of this chapter; however, here's a quick recap. Every `LogEntry` that is written on the same thread after the

TABLE 6.9: Logger Write Overloads and Examples

Overload/Description	Example
(object): Writes a new LogEntry to the default Category using the value of the object's `ToString()` method as the message.	`Logger.Write("My log message");`
(object,string): Same as `Write (object)` but allows a Category to be specified.	`Logger.Write("My log message", "My Category");`
(object,string,int): Same as `Write (object, string)` but also includes Priority.	`Logger.Write("My log message", "My Category",100);`
(object,string,int,int): Same as `Write (object, string, int)` but also includes the event ID.	`Logger.Write("My log message", "My Category", 100, 123);`
(object,string,int,int,Severity): Same as `Write (object, string, int, int)` but also includes Severity.	`Logger.Write("My log message", "My Category", 100, 123, Severity.Error);`
(object,string,int,int,Severity, string): Same as `Write (object, string, int, int, Severity)` but also includes Title.	`Logger.Write("My log message", "My Category", 100, 123, Severity.Error, "LogEntry Title");`

(LogEntry): Writes a new LogEntry using an already created LogEntry object.	`LogEntry log = new LogEntry();`
	`log.Category = "My Category";`
	`log.Message = "My log message";`
	`log.Severity = Severity.Error;`
	`log.Priority = 100;`
	`Logger.Write(log);`

(object,IDictionary): Same as `Write (object)` but also includes ExtendedProperties.	`Hashtable hash = new Hashtable();`
	`hash["item1"] = "my item";`
	`Logger.Write("My log message",hash);`

(object,string,IDictionary): Same as `Write (object, string)` but also includes ExtendedProperties.	`Hashtable hash = new Hashtable();`
	`hash["item1"] = "my item";`
	`Logger.Write("My log message", "My Category",hash);`

(continued)

TABLE 6.9: Logger Write Overloads and Examples (*continued*)

Overload/Description	Example

(object,string,int,IDictionary): Same as `Write (object, string, int)` but includes ExtendedProperties.	`Hashtable hash = new Hashtable();`
	`hash["item1"] = "my item";`
	`Logger.Write("My log message",`
	`"My Category",100,hash);`

(object,string,int,int,Severity, string,IDictionary): Same as `Write (object, string, int, int, Severity, string)` but includes ExtendedProperties.	`Hashtable hash = new Hashtable();`
	`hash["item1"] = "my item";`
	`Logger.Write("My log message",`
	`"My Category",`
	`100, 123, Severity.Error, "LogEntry`
	`Title", hash);`

`SetContextItem` method call will contain the additional data that is passed to it. This data is added to every `LogEntry`'s `ExtendedProperties` dictionary. To flush the data from any future LogEntries for that thread, the `FlushContextItems` method must be called. Listing 6.28 adds the `AppVersion` identifier for two LogEntries.

LISTING 6.28: Adding Contextual Information with `SetContext`

```
[C#]
Logger.SetContextItem("AppVersion", "1234");
LogEntry log = new LogEntry();
log.Message = "Message Number 1";
Logger.Write(log);
Logger.Write("Message Number 2");
Logger.FlushContextItems();

[Visual Basic]
Logger.SetContextItem("AppVersion", "1234")
Dim log As LogEntry = New LogEntry()
Dim log.Message = "Message Number 1"
Logger.Write(log)
Logger.Write("Message Number 2")
Logger.FlushContextItems()
```

Using the `Tracer` *Object*

Tracing entails correlating multiple messages that occur in a particular activity in an application. From a technical perspective, tracing involves logging an initial LogEntry, a final LogEntry, and adding an `ActivityId` to every LogEntry that occurs between the two. This activity ID allows all of these LogEntries to be grouped as one "activity."

Adding tracing to an application is even more straightforward than logging. The constructor for the `Tracer` object creates and sends the initial LogEntry and, if an `ActivityId` has not already been created, creates a new `Guid` that represents it. The `Tracer`'s `Dispose` method creates and sends the final LogEntry. The `ActivityId` is pushed onto an internal stack and every LogEntry that occurs between the constructor and the `Dispose` method has the `ActivityId` added as an item to its `ExtendedProperties`. The bottom line is that the only methods that you need to be concerned about are the constructor and `Dispose` method.

Table 6.10 lists the public constructors for the `Tracer` object.

TABLE 6.10: Tracer Constructors

Overload	Description	Example

()	Default constructor. Will use the current `ActivityId` if one exists or create a new `Guid` to represent one if it does not. Will log trace messages to the default Category.	`using (new Tracer())`
		`{`
		`}`

(string)	Same as the default constructor except that it will log trace messages to the Category specified by the supplied string.	`using (new Tracer(`
		`"My Category"))`
		`{`
		`}`

(string,string)	Logs trace message to the Category using the first supplied string and pushes the value of the second supplied string to the top of the stack, setting and using it as the current `ActivityId`.	`using (new Tracer(`
		`"My Category",`
		`"MyNewActID"))`
		`{`
		`}`

That's all that you need to know to add tracing to an application. If you're using Visual Basic, you won't be able to leverage the `using` statement, so you'll need to explicitly call the `Dispose` method when you're done tracing.[6]

The `Tracer` object also exposes four public static properties to help you determine what the current activity identifier is, what the root (outermost) activity identifier is, what the current Tracer's Category is, and what the root Tracer's Category is. These property names, aptly enough, are `CurrentActivityId`, `RootActivityId`, `CurrentCategory`, and `RootCategory` respectively.

Summary

This chapter covered the design of Enterprise Library's Logging and Instrumentation Application Block and how to configure and develop an application to use it. The description of the design of this block explained the purpose of each class that is involved in getting a log message from its sender to its final endpoints. This was broken down into two main areas: the client and the distributor.

The client side is responsible for the logging, ExtraInformationProviders, filtering, and distribution strategies. Formatters, Sinks, Categories, and Destinations were explained for the distributor. Examples showed how to leverage the extension points that exist for these elements. The chapter also included an analysis of the design for tracing in the Logging and Instrumentation Application Block and how it differs from pure logging.

The final section of this chapter represents the "how to" for the Logging and Instrumentation Application Block. If you only want to know how to log to a file or event log, this may be the only section that you will need to read. It showed how to configure the application block and how to write code to use it.

---

6. While the `using` statement does not exist for the .NET Framework 1.1, it has been introduced into the language in the .NET Framework 2.0.

It is my hope that I have been able to convey that the Logging and Instrumentation Application Block is not difficult to use. It has been designed to abstract an application away from needing to know where LogEntries will be stored and how to get them there. The intent is to let you focus on simply logging a message at the proper point. Moreover, because the code for an application can be indifferent as to the Destination for its log messages, if the Destinations change, no code in the application needs to; only the application's configuration does.

7

The Security Application Block

WITH ALL OF the viruses, worms, and theft that appears to be rampant in cyberspace today, securing applications has been thrust to the forefront of application design. Software architects cannot ignore the threats that exist to an application and the data that drive it. These concerns are especially true for enterprise applications that will live on the corporate network and most probably will leverage the Internet in some way. Additionally, government legislation is demanding that enterprise applications either meet certain security criteria or cease to exist. I have been in more than one company that feared it would have to "turn off" production applications because of new, more rigorous security audits.

Architects and developers can use a helping hand as the pressures rise for designing and developing applications that answer the call of this strict legislation and the ever increasing security risks. The Security Application Block is intended to help. While it isn't intended to solve every security issue that might arise in an application, it is designed to help in five main areas that deal with user data and the tasks those users are entitled to perform. Specifically, the Security Application Block has been designed to address the following areas.

- Authentication
- Caching profile information and security-related credentials
- Authorization

- Role management
- Profile management

Typically, this type of data about the users of an application exists in a variety of data stores. Very often, relational databases are used to store some of this information. In many enterprises, some form of LDAP user store like Microsoft Active Directory or Active Directory Application Mode (ADAM) is used. Authorization information might be contained in code, files, databases, or products like Authorization Manager. The Security Application Block allows developers of an application to be indifferent as to where the data for user information is stored. Thus, you can concentrate on ensuring that applications are authenticating and authorizing users at appropriate points in an application and not *how* or *where* that authentication or authorization occurs.

This chapter discusses how the features in the Security Application Block work and how any one of them can be extended if your needs are different than the out-of-the-box functionality. The Security Application Block is a bit different from the other application blocks in that there are many disparate providers and none of the providers rely on any of the others to accomplish their functionality.

There is a dependency in the block, though; the `DbAuthenticationProvider`, `DbRoleProvider`, and `DbProfileProvider` rely on the existence of a specific database schema to function properly. Therefore, the chapter begins with the design of the Security Application Block and details the purpose and use of the Security Database. It then shows the design for authentication, the Security Cache, authorization, role management, and profile management. Each of these sections describes how the relevant providers in the Security Application Block work and gives examples of how to extend the functionality if you need to.

The chapter ends with a description of how to configure and develop against each of the different providers included in the Security Application Block. If an application only needs to access users, roles, and profiles from a database, and can use the AuthorizationRuleProvider that ships with this block for its authorization needs, you don't need to develop any custom extensions. The point of the custom extensions is merely to show that the capability exists should you need it.

What Is the Security Application Block?

The primary design goals for the Security Application Block were to make an application more flexible by allowing it to abstract itself away from needing to know where this information is maintained. Each type of data is accompanied by a respective provider that handles the most common tasks associated with that data. For example, AuthenticationProviders exist that let you write an application that determines whether a user can be authenticated without the need for you to know where the authentication information is stored or how the determination of authentication is performed. At the same time as providing this flexibility, the Security Application Block is designed to be as simple as possible—the only method that you need to learn to authenticate a user is `Authenticate`.

By subscribing to the Provider pattern, yet another benefit is realized. An application is not tied to any specific user store for accessing the necessary information. If user information is moved from one store to another, you don't need to change any application code; you just have to modify the configuration for that application.

Relationship to the Authorization and Profile Application Block

Microsoft released a subset of the features of the Security Application Block as the Authorization and Profile Application Block in January 2004. There are some important differences to keep in mind if you need to migrate from the previous application block to Enterprise Library's Security Application Block.

- The previous block only focused on two of the five features that exist in the current Enterprise Library block: authorization and profile management. Authentication, Authorization, Roles, Profiles, and Security Caches all have separate provider interfaces in the current incarnation.

- There is no need to use an extended principal with additional methods in the Security Application Block.
- Cryptography functionality has been migrated to the Cryptography Application Block (covered in Chapter 8).
- Some of the features of the AuthorizationManagerProvider (AzManProvider) don't exist in the current providers. Features like the `CheckAccess` method that supports passing dynamic business rule parameters and values as well the `GetRoles` method for acquiring a collection of roles for a given identity are no longer included. The latter isn't too big a deal though—I'll show how to add your own RolesProvider to `GetRoles` from AzMan.

Design of the Security Application Block

The Security Application Block has several providers to make it easier for you to accomplish the tasks of authenticating users for an application, authorizing users for operations and tasks in an application, managing the list of roles to which a user belongs in an application, obtaining and persisting profile information for a user, and caching security and profile information for users in an application. The tasks that each provider accomplishes are defined by its interface. The interesting thing about each provider is which system it interfaces with. The block ships with providers for common systems, but it's expected that you will want to create your own to interface with your own systems. Each provider is intended to not only provide a level of flexibility for the application by abstracting it away from a particular security system, but to make it easy for you to accomplish the necessary tasks.

Unlike the Logging and Instrumentation Application Block, where many features existed that were dependent on the others, the Security Application Block has many features that can work completely independently of one another. The authentication features can be used regardless of whether or not the authorization, role, or profile features are used. Likewise, the authorization features can be used without using the AuthenticationProvider, RolesProvider, or ProfileProvider. However, while the providers are not dependent on each other, they are closely related. Thus, although it isn't necessary to use the AuthenticationProvider with the AuthorizationProvider, an application can reap many advantages by using both together. To help you understand this better, I will detail the design for each of the different areas covered by Enterprise Library's Security Application Block.

The Security Database

Before diving right into the specific design of the Security Application Block and how it provides capabilities to facilitate authentication, authorization, role management, profile management, and security credential caching in an enterprise application, it is a worthwhile exercise to learn about the features of the Security Database that ship with Enterprise Library. The reason for this is that many of the providers that ship with the Security Application Block depend on the existence of this database. Figure 7.1 illustrates the data model for the Security Database.

It is common for applications to maintain at least some security-related information in a relational database. Very often, this information is specific to the users who have been authorized for an application, the roles for those users, and profile information for those users. The Security Database is provided with tables for storing all of this data. Enterprise Library ships with an AuthenticationProvider, RolesProvider, and ProfileProvider that rely on the existence of this database. The Security Application Block includes a

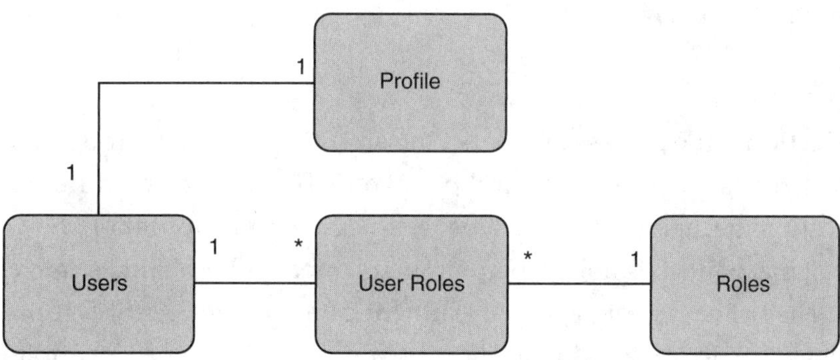

FIGURE 7.1: The Security Database

SQL script, SecurityDatabase.sql, that installs the necessary schema to a database named *Security*. You can change the name of the database where this exists or even install the schema in an existing database, but if you do, you will need to modify the configuration for the Security Database Administration Console so that it points to the proper database.

The Security Database Administration Console

Enterprise Library also ships with a tool for managing the data contained in this database. This tool, the Security Database Administration Console, lets an administrator create user identities and roles in the Security Database. It also allows the credentials for the users to be modified and for users to be associated with specific roles. Details on how to use and configure the Security Database Administration Console are covered later in the chapter in the section "Developing with the Security Application Block."

The `UserRoleManager` Class

The Security Database Administration Tool uses a utility class that ships with the Security Application Block for managing the Security Database. This class, `UserRoleManager`, encapsulates the stored procedures that perform activities like adding users, adding roles, and adding users to roles. It is really this class that has the dependency on Security Database schema and the fact that the Users and Roles tables must exist in the same database. More information about best practices and using `UserRoleManager` in your application is in the "Developing with the Security Application Block" section of this chapter.

Authentication

Authentication is the process of identifying an entity, typically through the use of credentials like user name and password. There are many different authentication mechanisms that can be leveraged for an application; however, if that mechanism is not properly implemented, vulnerabilities can be exposed. The primary design goal for authentication in the Security Application Block was to abstract an application away from the need to implement these particular authentication mechanics. Instead, the specifics behind any one authentication technology are handled by an AuthenticationProvider for that technology. Therefore, you can create applications to be indifferent as to the technology that is used to authenticate and instead concentrate on ensuring that authentication occurs at the proper places in the application. Figure 7.2 depicts the primary classes that the Enterprise Library uses for authentication.

The `AuthenticationProviderFactory` Class and the `IAuthenticationProvider` Interface

The `IAuthenticationProvider` interface is the means by which this abstraction occurs. When an application needs to authenticate an entity, it does so by calling the `Authenticate` method of an `AuthenticationProvider`. If the authentication technology that is used needs to be changed, you can simply reconfigure the application with a different `AuthenticationProvider`.

Two constructs exist to help an application achieve this level of abstraction: the `AuthenticationProviderFactory` class and the `IAuthenticationProvider` interface. The `AuthenticationProviderFactory` class uses its configuration information to create an instance of an `AuthenticationProvider`. An `AuthenticationFactory` class (no "Provider" in the name) also exists that provides static methods that wrap around the public methods of the `AuthenticationProviderFactory` class. Either class can be used to obtain either a named instance of an `AuthenticationProvider` or one that is configured as the default `AuthenticationProvider`.

Both the `AuthenticationFactory` and `AuthenticationProviderFactory` classes expose a method named `GetAuthenticationProvider` that returns an instance of an `AuthenticationProvider`. An `AuthenticationProvider` is a class that implements the `IAuthenticationProvider` interface. The `GetAuthenticationProvider` method is overloaded two times: one overload expects a string that represents the name of an `AuthenticationProvider` that has been configured for the application, and the other overload does not expect any arguments. The first overload returns the named `AuthenticationProvider`, and the second returns the `AuthenticationProvider` that has been configured as the default `AuthenticationProvider` for the application.

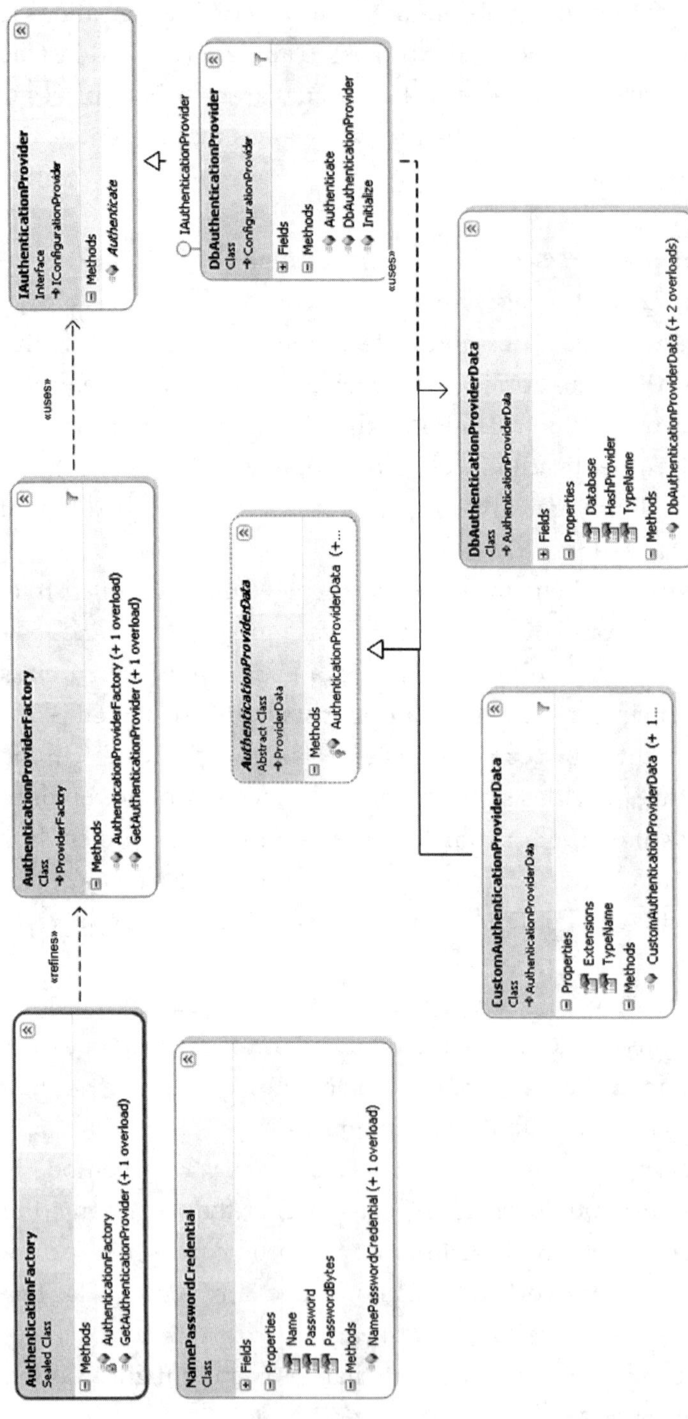

FIGURE 7.2: Authentication in the Security Application Block

The only method that a class must implement to support the `IAuthenticationProvider` interface is `Authenticate`. This method accepts an object that represents an entity's credentials (like `NamePasswordCredentials`) and, if the credentials are valid, will return a value of true for the method and an object that implements `IIdentity` as an output parameter.

An `Identity` object encapsulates information about the entity being authenticated. `Identity` objects contain the name of the entity, the authentication status, and an authentication type. The .NET Framework contains two `Identity` classes: `WindowsIdentity` and `GenericIdentity`. The `Name` property is the name of a Windows account for a `WindowsIdentity` and is typically the logged in user's name for a `GenericIdentity`. Custom `Identity` objects can be created; typically this is accomplished by subclassing the `GenericIdentity`.

The `DbAuthenticationProvider` Class

Enterprise Library provides an implementation of an AuthenticationProvider by way of the `DbAuthenticationProvider`. This class is used to authenticate a user based on the information stored in the Security Database that is provided with Enterprise Library. The `DbAuthenticationProvider` expects a `NamePasswordCredentials` instance and validates that the password for this user matches the password stored in the Users table for this user.

For security reasons, the passwords are stored as hashes in the database. This provider leverages the Data Access Application Block to connect to the proper database and the Cryptography Application Block to compare the hashed passwords. If the passwords match, a new `GenericIdentity` is created for the user with the `AuthenticationType` equal to the fully qualified name for the `DbAuthenticationProvider` + "." + the name of the AuthenticationProvider that was used. For example, if the name of the AuthenticationProvider was `AuthProvider`, the Identity returned would be this `AuthenticationType`:

```
Microsoft.Practices.EnterpriseLibrary.Security.Database.
Authentication.DbAuthenticationProvider.AuthProvider
```

NOTE

Because identity is verified by comparing the hash of the password stored in the database, it is imperative that the Hash provider configured for an application's `DbAuthenticationProvider` matches the Hash provider that is used to store the user passwords in the database. If the Security Database Manager is used to configure the users and roles, the out-of-the-box setting is SHA1Managed. If the hashing algorithms do not match, then all authentication attempts will fail.

The `NamePasswordCredential` Class

Although it can also be used for other purposes, the `NamePasswordCredential` class is intended to facilitate passing a user name and password to the `DbAuthenticationProvider`. This class is very much like the `System.Net.NetworkCredential` class except that it doesn't have a field to represent the `Domain` to which a user might belong, and it possesses properties to represent a string as a byte array (a security best practice). The class has two constructors: one accepts the password as a string and the other accepts the password as a byte array. It also has three properties: `Name`, `Password`, and `PasswordBytes`.

Creating a Custom AuthenticationProvider

The Security Application Block is a little different than the other application blocks in Enterprise Library. While I have shown how to create custom providers for the other application blocks, you may never need to actually leverage them. The other application blocks are intended to supply the providers needed for most enterprise-level applications. I posit that although the Security Application Block provides many useful providers, it is fully expected that developers will need to create new providers to fit the needs of many enterprise applications.

It is possible that many enterprise applications will authenticate users by validating their credentials against a relational database. However, it is my experience that most enterprises use a different technology for authenticating users; most often users are stored in some type of LDAP store like Microsoft Active Directory.

The beauty of the Security Application Block is that it is provider based. While there is no issue with using the `DbAuthenticate-Provider` if that fits your scenario, you can simply use a different provider if it does not. Like the other custom providers that have been created in this book, there are two different ways to add a custom AuthenticationProvider. One way takes advantage of the `CustomAuthenticationProviderData` class and the hooks that exist for adding a class that implements the `IAuthenticationProvider` interface; the other way is to create a full-blown AuthenticationProvider with its own set of design-time features.

I ran into a situation where a custom AuthenticationProvider for Microsoft Active Directory would have been beneficial. Normally, most applications would not require such a provider because users can "automatically" authenticate to Active Directory for Windows Form applications when logging on to their machines or for Web applications using Integrated Windows Authentication in Internet Information Services (IIS). However, one company where I consulted needed to allow users to log into a Web application using HTML Forms authentication and authenticate the users against Active Directory. Integrated Windows Authentication could not be used because partners needed to log into the sites and there was little control over how a user would log into the client machine. To solve this problem, an AuthenticationProvider for Active Directory was created. The following steps show how to create this AuthenticationProvider for Microsoft Active Directory.

To create a custom AuthenticationProvider that takes advantage of the `CustomAuthenticationProviderData` class, the only thing you need to do is to create the AuthenticationProvider so that it implements the `IAuthenticationProvider` interface. The `Initialize` method can be used to read any configuration data that is needed; this configuration data will be contained in the `CustomAuthenticationProviderData` class.

The `CustomAuthenticationProviderData` class contains a `Dictionary` object named `Extensions` that can hold key/value pairs for the configuration data. Any specific data that is needed must be stored in this collection. The `Authenticate` method for this particular custom provider uses a private `Login` method that handles the specifics of dealing with

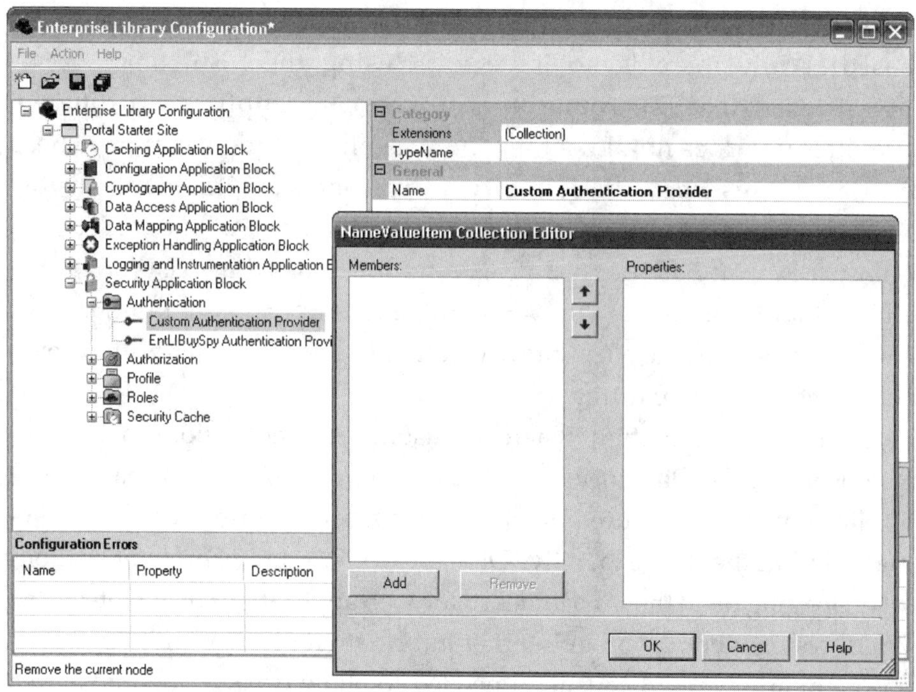

FIGURE 7.3: Adding a Custom AuthenticationProvider

Microsoft Active Directory. The full source code for this implementation is on this book's Web site.

When you have completed this, you can add the AuthenticationProvider as a custom AuthenticationProvider as shown in Figure 7.3.

To design an AuthenticationProvider complete with a design-time interface, three more steps are needed. The `CustomAuthenticationProviderData` class won't be of use; a class that will hold the strongly typed configuration information necessary to leverage the specific authentication technology (in this case, Microsoft Active Directory) will be needed. Creating the data class for this specific provider is simple because I am using serverless binding and the RootDSE[1] to locate an Active Directory Server and authenticate against it. Therefore, no extra data beyond the user's

1. See http://msdn.microsoft.com/library/default.asp?url=/library/en-us/ad/ad/serverless_binding_and_rootdse.asp for information on serverless binding and the RootDSE.

name and password is needed. I have added the ADAuthentication-ProviderData class for consistency, though. For complete information on how to create runtime configuration classes, see Chapter 1 and its accompanying source code.

The second step is to create a class that implements the IAuthenticationProvider interface and leverages the ADAuthenticationProvider-Data class. This new provider class is the same class that needs to be created using the previous method for creating a custom Authentication-Provider. Listing 7.1 is the core method used by the Authenticate method for determining whether an entity can be authenticated using the supplied user name and password. The full source code is on the book's Web site.

Listing 7.1: Login Method for the `ADAuthenticationProvider`

```
[C#]
private bool Login(string userName, string password)
{
     bool result = false;

     //Bind to rootDSE to get the Domain Name.
     DirectoryEntry rootDSE = new DirectoryEntry("LDAP://RootDSE");
     string domainName =
          Convert.ToString
          (rootDSE.Properties["defaultNamingContext"].Value);
     rootDSE.Dispose();

     //Bind to the domain root.
     DirectoryEntry domainRoot =
          new DirectoryEntry("LDAP://" + domainName);
     string path = domainRoot.Path;

     //Create the searcher, bound to the domain root.
     DirectorySearcher dirSearch = new DirectorySearcher(domainRoot);
     domainRoot.Dispose();

     //Retrieve the 'cn' and adspath, which is returned by default.
     dirSearch.PropertiesToLoad.Add("cn");

     dirSearch.Filter = String.Format
     ("(& (samaccountname={0})
           (objectCategory=person)(objectClass=user))",userName);
     SearchResult searchResult = dirSearch.FindOne();
     if (searchResult == null)
     {
          return false;
     }
```

```
        dirSearch.Dispose();

        string adsPathToUser =
             Convert.ToString(searchResult.Properties["adspath"][0]);
        DirectoryEntry userEntry;

        //'userName' is the sAMaccountName.
        userEntry = new DirectoryEntry(adsPathToUser, userName, password);
        if (userEntry != null)
        {
             try
             {
                  string commonName =
                       Convert.ToString(userEntry.Properties["cn"].Value);
                  if ( (commonName != null)
                       && (! commonName.Equals(String.Empty)))
                  {
                       result = true;
                  }
             }
             catch (Exception ex)
             {
                  string thisError = ex.ToString();
                  result = false;
             }
             finally
             {
                  userEntry.Dispose();
             }
        }

        return result;
   }

   [Visual Basic]
   Private Function Login(ByVal userName As String, _
                         ByVal password As String) As Boolean
        Dim result As Boolean = False

        'Bind to rootDSE to get the Domain Name.
        Dim rootDSE As DirectoryEntry = _
             New DirectoryEntry("LDAP://RootDSE")
        Dim domainName As String = Convert.ToString(rootDSE.Properties _
             ("defaultNamingContext").Value)
        rootDSE.Dispose()

        'Bind to the domain root.
        Dim domainRoot As DirectoryEntry = _
             New DirectoryEntry("LDAP://" + domainName)
        Dim path As String = domainRoot.Path
```

```
    'Create the searcher, bound to the domain root.
    Dim dirSearch As DirectorySearcher = _
        New DirectorySearcher(domainRoot)
    domainRoot.Dispose()

    'Retrieve the 'cn' and adspath, which is returned by default.
    dirSearch.PropertiesToLoad.Add("cn")

    dirSearch.Filter = String.Format _
        ("(& (samaccountname={0}) _
        (objectCategory=person)(objectClass=user))",userName)
    Dim searchResult As SearchResult = dirSearch.FindOne()
    If searchResult Is Nothing Then
        Return False
    End If
    dirSearch.Dispose()

    Dim adsPathToUser As String = _
        Convert.ToString(searchResult.Properties("adspath")(0))
    Dim userEntry As DirectoryEntry

    'userName' is the sAMaccountName.
    userEntry = New DirectoryEntry(adsPathToUser, userName, password)
    If Not userEntry Is Nothing Then
        Try
            Dim commonName As String = _
                Convert.ToString _
                    (userEntry.Properties("cn").Value)
            If (Not commonName Is Nothing) AndAlso _
                ((Not commonName.Equals(String.Empty))) Then
                result = True
            End If
        Catch ex As Exception
            Dim thisError As String = ex.ToString()
            result = False
        Finally
            userEntry.Dispose()
        End Try
    End If

    Return result
End Function
```

The third step is to add the design-time classes for the `ADAuthenticationProvider` to make it easy to add and configure the provider in the Enterprise Library Configuration Tool. This step is not absolutely necessary; the XML can be modified directly in the configuration file (or other

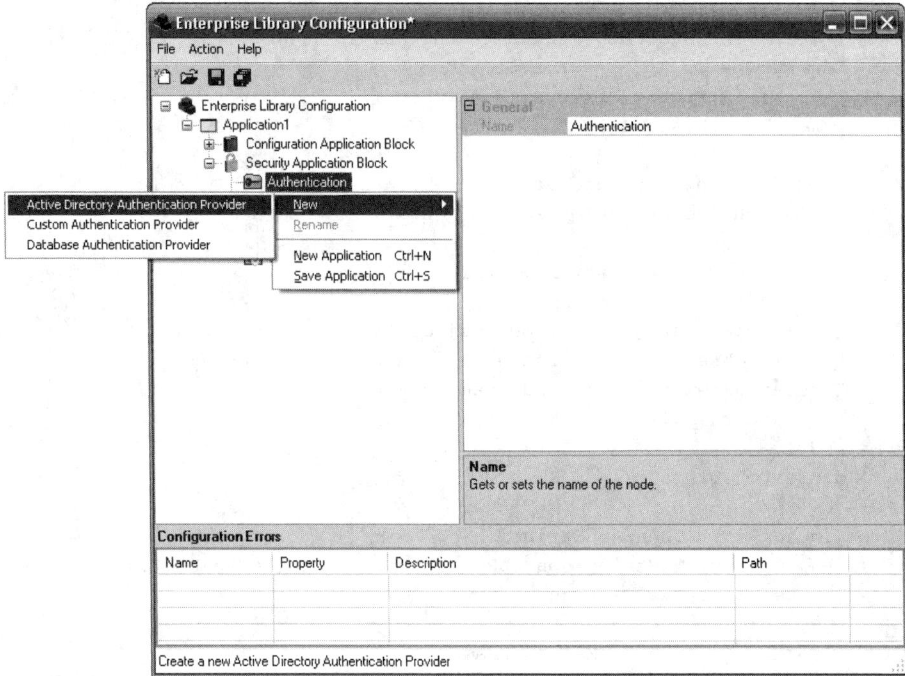

FIGURE 7.4: Adding the Active Directory AuthenticationProvider

StorageProvider); however, creating design-time features for this class allows the Enterprise Library Configuration Tool to be used to easily configure this provider with the rest of the application settings. (For more information about creating design-time configuration classes with Enterprise Library, see Chapter 2.) The full source code for the `ADAuthenticationProvider` design-time classes is on the book's Web site. Figure 7.4 shows the ability to add the new AuthenticationProvider in the Enterprise Library Configuration Tool.[2]

Caching Security Credentials

Many applications will not authenticate an entity for every request because it often carries too large of a performance overhead. Rather, authentication will often occur once and, for a period of time, any requests that require

2. Thanks go to Steven Case for collaborating with me on the details for using RootDSE and serverless binding to authenticate against Active Directory.

authentication will leverage the credentials used during the entity's original authentication. While this approach is less secure than authenticating for every request,[3] it greatly improves the performance of an application. A cost/benefits analysis of whether caching security credentials is appropriate as well as a determination of how long those credentials should stay in cache should be made on an application-by-application basis.

While the Security Application Block can't help an organization make those determinations, it can help with the implementation. The Security Application Block ships with a Security Cache that can cache the security credentials used for authentication. The SecurityCacheProvider that comes with Enterprise Library leverages the Caching Application Block; therefore, that block must be configured for an application before this provider can be used.

Once an entity has been authenticated, the identity/principal for that entity can be cached. A token (typically a `Guid)` is returned as the identifier for that entity. That token can then be used for any future authentication request and the cache can be checked to validate identity instead of hitting the user store. Figure 7.5 highlights the primary classes that provide the Security Cache implementation.

The `SecurityCacheFactory` Class and the `ISecurityCacheProvider` Interface

The Security Cache's design is flexible enough to let you implement a different SecurityCacheProvider if you don't want to use the one that comes with Enterprise Library. To accomplish this you must develop a class that implements the `ISecurityCacheProvider` interface. The `SecurityCacheProviderFactory` serves as the public interface for retrieving an instance of one of these classes. And just as the `AuthenticationFactory` makes static methods available for retrieving `AuthenticationProviders` by encapsulating the `AuthenticationProviderFactory` class, so too does the `SecurityCacheFactory` provide static methods for retrieving `ISecurityCacheProviders`. You can use either the `SecurityCacheFactory` or the `SecurityCacheProviderFactory` class to obtain either the default or a named instance of a `SecurityCacheProvider`.

---

3. *Improving Web Application Security*, p. 171, found at http://msdn.microsoft.com/library/default.asp?url=/library/en-us/dnnetsec/html/ThreatCounter.asp.

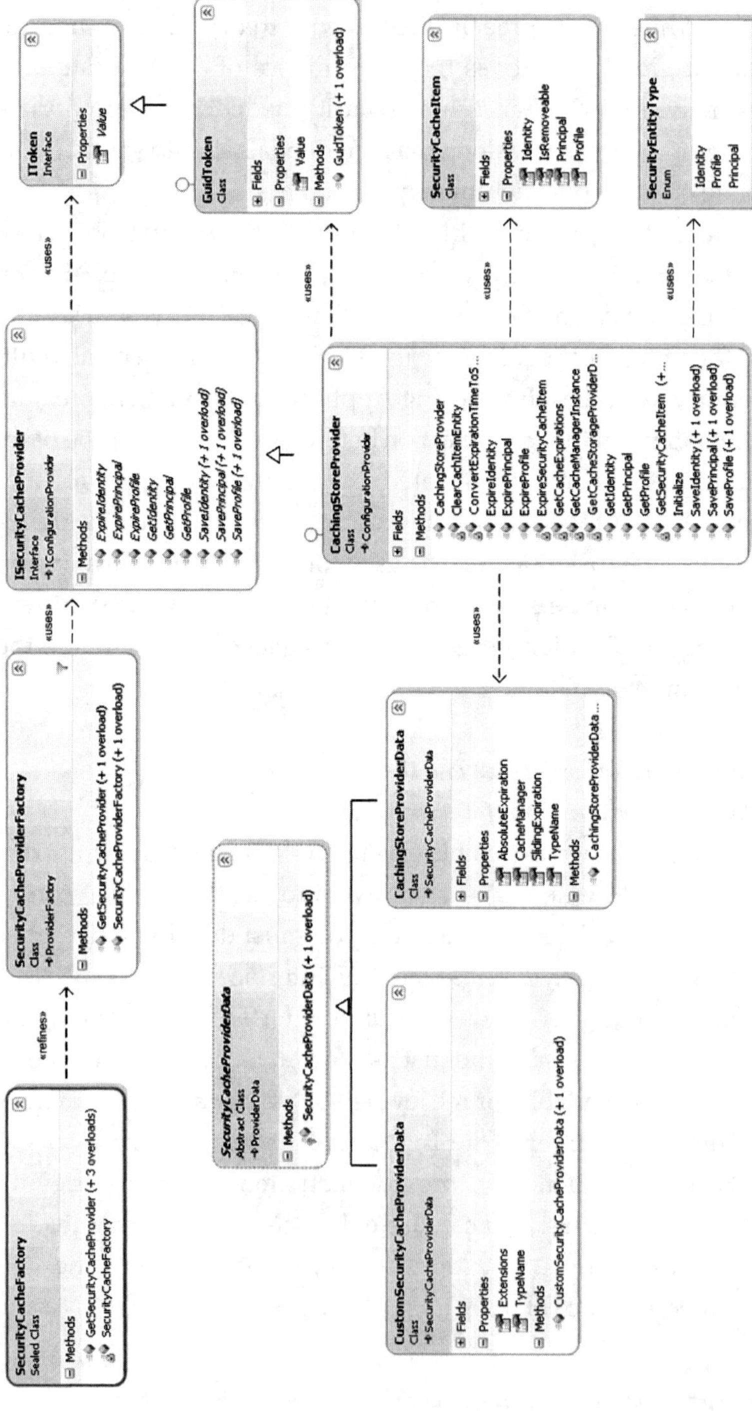

FIGURE 7.5: The Security Application Block's Security Cache Design

Both the SecurityCacheFactory and the SecurityCacheProvider-Factory class expose a method named GetSecurityCacheProvider that returns an instance of a SecurityCacheProvider. A SecurityCache-Provider is a class that implements the ISecurityCacheProvider interface. The GetSecurityCacheProvider method is overloaded two times: one overload expects a string that represents the name of a Security-CacheProvider that has been configured for the application, and the other overload does not expect any arguments. The first overload returns the named SecurityCacheProvider and the second returns the Security-CacheProvider that has been configured as the default SecurityCache-Provider for the application.

The ISecurityCacheProvider interface defines methods that allow caching, retrieval, and expiration of identities, principals, and profiles. (For information on principals, see the section Authorization; for information on profiles, see the section Profile Management.) Table 7.1 lists the methods defined by the ISecurityCacheProvider interface.

TABLE 7.1: ISecurityCacheProvider's Interface Methods

Method	Description
GetIdentity	Gets an Identity object from the cache.
SaveIdentity	Caches an authenticated Identity object using an existing token.
ExpireIdentity	Deletes an Identity object from the cache.
GetPrincipal	Gets an existing Principal from the cache.
SavePrincipal	Caches an authenticated Principal object using an existing token.
ExpirePrincipal	Deletes an existing Principal object from the cache.
GetProfile	Gets an existing Profile object from the cache.
SaveProfile	Caches a Profile for an authenticated user using an existing token.
ExpireProfile	Deletes an existing Profile object from the cache.

All SaveXXX methods have two overloads: one takes just the object being cached, and the other takes the object and a Token. For example, the SaveIdentity method has two overloads: SaveIdentity(IIdentity) and SaveIdentity(IIdentity, Token).

The CachingStoreProvider Class

The CachingStoreProvider is Enterprise Library's implementation of the ISecurityCacheProvider interface. The CachingStoreProvider uses Enterprise Library's Caching Application Block by storing the security credentials in a CacheManager. (For information about Cache Managers and the Caching Application Block, see Chapter 4.)

Although three different facets for an entity can be cached, only one CacheManager is used. This is accomplished by encapsulating the Identity, Principal, and Profile information for a single entity in a SecurityCacheItem object. Thus, a single token can be used to represent an entity with any combination of the Identity, Principal, and/or Profile stored for that entity.

When any of the CachingStoreProvider's methods are called, the SecurityCacheItem is retrieved from the cache. If the item doesn't exist and the method is a Save, then a new SecurityCacheItem is created, added to the cache, and the appropriate property is set. If the item doesn't exist and the method is a Get, then null is returned; if it is an Expire method, then nothing happens.

When the item does exist, the Save, Get, and Expire methods do what you would expect them to do—they store, retrieve, or remove the value for the appropriate SecurityCacheItem property. SaveIdentity, for example, will store the Identity value supplied to the Identity property for the proper instance of a SecurityCacheItem. GetIdentity will retrieve that property's value, and ExpireIdentity will set it equal to null. Additionally, any of the Expire methods will completely remove a SecurityCacheItem from the cache if all three of the Identity, Principal, and Profile properties have been set to null.

The IToken Interface

Tokens are used to uniquely identify an entity. The Security Application Block does not enforce any specific type of token; however, a good token is one that is guaranteed to be unique. The only property you must implement to support the `IToken` interface is `Value`, which can return any string that can be used to uniquely identify an entity.

A fairly obvious implementation for such a token is the `GuidToken`. `GuidToken` is supplied by the Security Application Block, and this token implementation simply maintains a private `Guid` member variable. The default constructor will create a new `Guid`, and there is also a constructor that will set the internal variable equal to the `Guid` that is passed to it. The `Value` property simply returns `Guid.ToString()`. The `CachingStoreProvider` uses a `GuidToken` to uniquely identify a `SecurityCacheItem` object.

Creating a Custom `SecurityCacheProvider`

It is important to keep in mind that the Caching Application Block does not encrypt the data it stores when it caches in memory. If the Security Cache is configured to use a `CacheManager` that leverages the default backing store (`NullBackingStore`), an attacker that compromises the computer and accesses the memory of this process can access information stored in the cache.

You could create a Security Cache that encrypts the Security Cache items before adding them into the cache (one is on the book's Web site for this chapter). However, it is important to realize that you don't even need to use Enterprise Library's Caching Application Block to cache the security information if you're not a fan of that block.

The SecurityCacheProvider is an extension point in Enterprise Library's Security Application Block that allows alternative providers to be created and configured in an application. As an alternative to the provider that ships with Enterprise Library, I will create a SecurityCacheProvider that relies on the `HttpRuntime.Cache` and encrypts the Security Cache items before adding them to the cache.

If you've been with me from the beginning, this is going to seem like old hat by now. The first step that is needed to create any custom provider is to create the class that will hold the configuration data. For this provider, I have named that class `HttpCachingStoreProviderData`. The items needed to configure this provider are the sliding time expiration, absolute time expiration, and the name of the symmetric algorithm provider that is configured in the Cryptography Application Block. Unlike the Cache Manager in the Caching Application Block, the `HttpRuntime.Cache` cannot set both an absolute time and sliding time expiration for a single cache item. Therefore, logic exists in the provider to use the sliding time expiration if its value is greater than zero; otherwise, it uses the absolute time expiration. (For complete information on how to create runtime configuration data classes, see Chapter 1 and the source code that accompanies that chapter.)

The second step is to create a class that implements the `ISecurityCacheProvider` interface and leverages the data class created in the previous step. This is where the "real" work is. It is in this class that the implementation for how to implement the `Get-`, `Save-`, and `Expire-Identity`, `Principal`, and `Profile` take place. The logic in this class differs from the `CachingStoreProvider` that ships with Enterprise Library in two ways.

- It encrypts and decrypts the data as it inserts and gets the items from the cache.
- It uses the `HttpRuntime.Cache` as its cache.

The majority of the code for this class is similar to the `CachingStoreProvider` code except for the two items just mentioned. In Listing 7.2, the `HttpCachingStoreProvider` class takes an item that has already been encrypted and stores it in the `HttpRuntime.Cache`.

LISTING 7.2: Inserting a Cache Item with the `HttpCachingStoreProvider`

```
 [C#]
private void InsertIntoCache(string key, byte[] item)
{
     HttpCachingStoreProviderData cacheStorageProviderData =
               GetCacheStorageProviderData();

     //Can't set both absolute time and sliding time on same item for
     //HttpCache, so if sliding time exists, we'll pick that;
     //otherwise, we'll use absolute.
     DateTime setAbsoluteTime;
     TimeSpan setSlidingTime;
     int absoluteTime = cacheStorageProviderData.AbsoluteExpiration;
     int slidingTime = cacheStorageProviderData.SlidingExpiration;
     if (slidingTime > 0)
     {
          setSlidingTime = new TimeSpan
          (0, 0, ConvertExpirationTimeToSeconds(slidingTime));
          setAbsoluteTime = DateTime.MaxValue;
```

```
        }
        else
        {
             setSlidingTime = TimeSpan.Zero;
             setAbsoluteTime = DateTime.Now.AddMinutes(absoluteTime);
        }

        WebCache.Cache cache = GetCache();
        cache.Insert(key, item, null, setAbsoluteTime, setSlidingTime);
   }

   [Visual Basic]
   Private Sub InsertIntoCache(ByVal key As String, ByVal item As Byte())
        Dim cacheStorageProviderData As HttpCachingStoreProviderData = _
                  GetCacheStorageProviderData()

        'Can't set both absolute time and sliding time on same item for
        'HttpCache, so if sliding time exists, we'll pick that;
        'otherwise, we'll use absolute.
        Dim setAbsoluteTime As DateTime
        Dim setSlidingTime As TimeSpan
        Dim absoluteTime As Integer = _
                  cacheStorageProviderData.AbsoluteExpiration
        Dim slidingTime As Integer = _
                  cacheStorageProviderData.SlidingExpiration
        If slidingTime > 0 Then
             setSlidingTime = New TimeSpan _
             (0, 0, ConvertExpirationTimeToSeconds(slidingTime))
             setAbsoluteTime = DateTime.MaxValue
        Else
             setSlidingTime = TimeSpan.Zero
             setAbsoluteTime = DateTime.Now.AddMinutes(absoluteTime)
        End If

        Dim cache As WebCache.Cache = GetCache()
        cache.Insert(key, item, Nothing, setAbsoluteTime, setSlidingTime)
   End Sub
```

Lastly, add the design-time classes for the `HttpCachingStoreProvider` to make it easy to add and configure. There is nothing too special about how to do this: derive the `HttpCachingStoreProviderNode` from the `SecurityCacheProviderNode` and add properties for the symmetric algorithm provider, absolute time, and sliding time. (For more information about creating design-time configuration classes with Enterprise Library, see Chapter 2.)

The full source code for the `HttpCachingStoreProvider` design-time classes accompanies this chapter on the book's Web site. Figure 7. 6 shows the result of adding the `HttpCachingStoreProvider` in the Enterprise Library Configuration Tool.

Authorization

Authorization is the process that an application uses to control access to resources and operations for an authenticated entity. Two methods of authorization are used in the Windows operating systems: access control list (ACL)-based authorization and role-based authorization.

For ACL-based authorization, discretionary access control lists (DACLs) can be attached to securable objects like files, directories, and registry keys. Authorization decisions are made by comparing the group memberships in a token to the contents of the ACL. The ACL model is great for dealing with static objects like files and registry keys, but it is difficult to use when well-defined persistent objects do not exist or business logic is needed to make an authorization decision.

For these situations, role-based authorization is preferred. Roles are associated with the actions and resources needed to perform specific activities. Administrators can then specify authority to those actions based on organizational structure—the roles or groups to which a user belongs. The

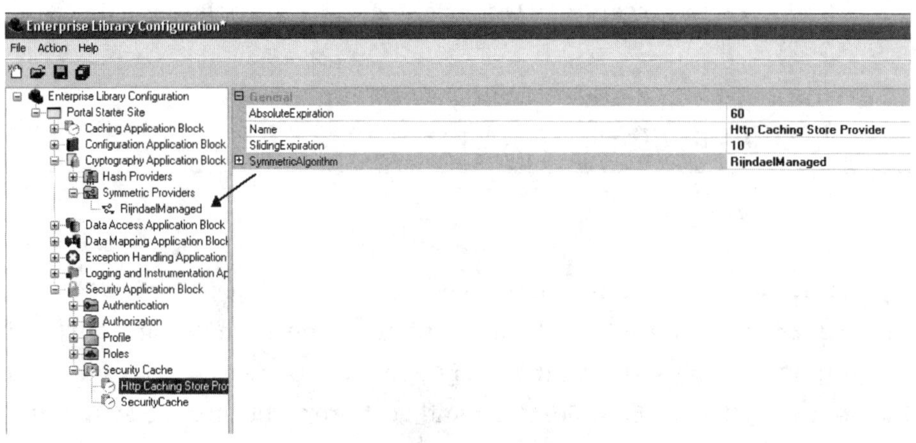

FIGURE 7.6: Configuring the `HttpCachingStoreProvider`

concept behind role-based authorization is that users or groups are associated with specific roles that allow them to perform their jobs effectively. When a user or group is added to a role, it automatically inherits the security permissions for that role.

For example, let's assume that a portal site exists where different types of users have different levels of authorization. Let's also assume that business users can only read content; content administrators can read, add, or edit content; and site administrators have the same permissions as content administrators but they can also add, edit, and remove users as well as add, edit, and remove roles and assign users to roles.

Users will have different experiences when they visit the site based on their roles. Business users will have a read-only version of the site. Content administrators will have the ability to add content to the site, edit content on the site, and remove content from the site. Site administrators will have additional pages available that will include functionality for user and role management for the site. These kinds of rules are often hard-coded into applications. Having a role-based authorization system that is independent of the application makes the application more flexible because the authorization rules can be updated independently of the application. Because the portal site and database represent a single system in this enterprise, this example represents single-system (or simple) role-based authorization. Figure 7.7 depicts the varying experiences for the different types of users.

If, however, resources from another system were exposed through the portal site, then multisystem role-based authorization might be necessary. The upper right side of the portal site in Figure 7.7 has a table that shows a kind of sales dashboard. It is conceivable that this data could have come from a different system in the organization. If this were the case, then users of the portal site would need to be authorized for multiple systems: the portal site itself and other systems in the enterprise where pertinent data resides.

This scenario is complicated further when authorization needs must be more granular than simply accessing the system. Often authorization is specific as to the functions that a user is entitled to perform. For example, while all users may be authorized to view this dashboard, another role may exist that has permission to edit it. Furthermore, it is not unusual to have

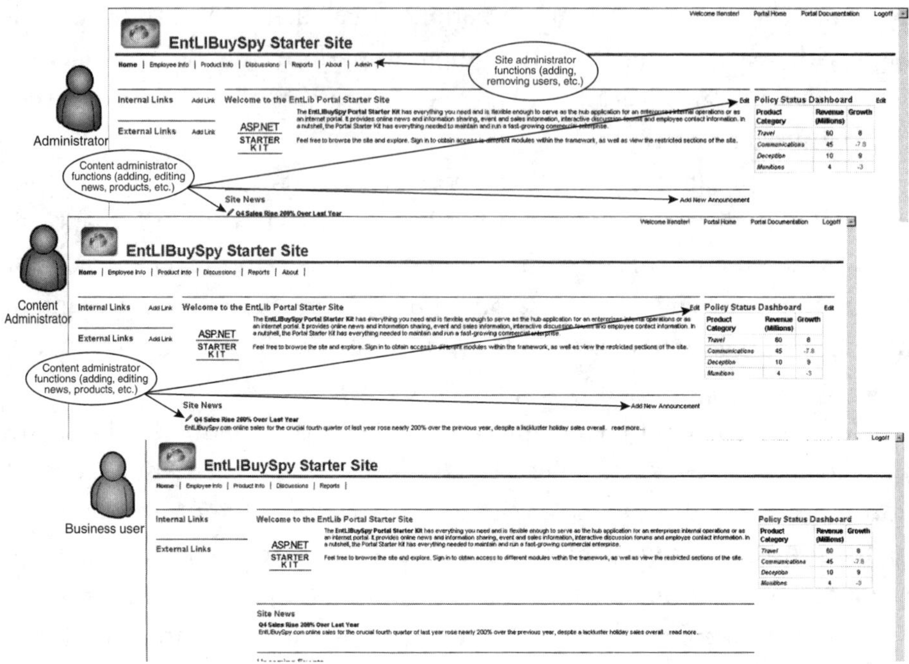

FIGURE 7.7: Role-Based Authorization Example

to temporarily grant "work on behalf" authorization to a user who does not exist in an authorized role or to allow a user a bit more permission than her role might allow.

A typical example, continuing the previous scenario, is when the site administrator goes on vacation. One possibility is for a different user to be temporarily assigned the role of site administrator during the vacation. However, if the site administrator has a lot of responsibilities, a common feature request is for those responsibilities to be divvied up to allow different users to perform the different operations. This type of multisystem authorization can get pretty complicated as role-based authorization is circumvented for direct operational-based authorization.

The authorization features in the Security Application Block will not make all complexities regarding authorization go away. In complex scenarios, issues still exist regarding the data a user is entitled to read or edit. While the Security Application Block doesn't address data entitlement, it does help with functional entitlement. Because the specific authorization rules are encapsulated by the AuthorizationProvider, you don't need to worry about the logic that is needed to authorize an entity for an operation.

For a simple version of this scenario, a provider that reads authorization rules from a database or file may be sufficient; for the most complex scenario, a provider that leverages Authorization Manager is probably needed. It doesn't matter to a developer, though; you can just call the AuthorizationProvider. Moreover, as authoritative rules change (like temporarily authorizing a user for an operation), only the configuration information needs to change; the application code does not. Figure 7.8 highlights the primary classes that create AuthorizationProviders in the Security Application Block.

The `AuthorizationProviderFactory` Class and the `IAuthorizationProvider` Interface

Once again, factories and providers are the pattern that is used to make this abstraction available. When an application needs to authorize an entity for an operation, it does so by calling the `Authorize` method of an `AuthorizationProvider`. If the authorization store needs to be changed, you simply need to reconfigure the application with a different `AuthorizationProvider`.

The `AuthorizationProviderFactory` class uses its configuration information to create an instance of an `AuthorizationProvider`. An AuthorizationProvider is any class that implements the `IAuthorizationProvider` interface. Furthermore, in a similar way that `AuthenticationFactory` refines the `AuthenticationProviderFactory` with public static methods, the `AuthorizationFactory` refines the `AuthorizationProviderFactory` class. Either class can be used to obtain either a named instance of an `AuthorizationProvider` or one that is configured as the default `AuthorizationProvider` via the `GetAuthorizationProvider` method.

The `GetAuthorizationProvider` method is overloaded two times: one overload expects a string that represents the name of an `AuthorizationProvider` that has been configured for the application, and the other overload does not expect any arguments. The first overload returns the

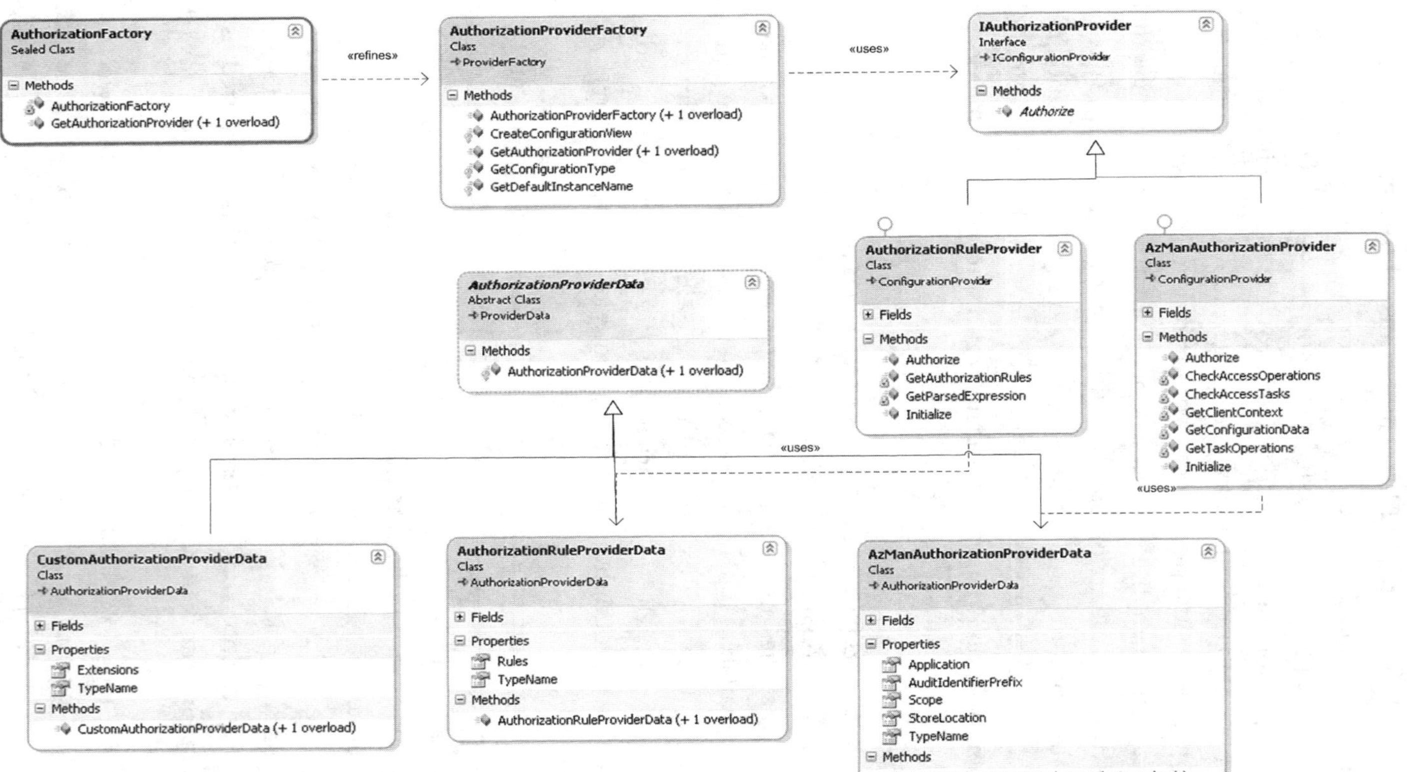

FIGURE 7.8: Authorization in the Security Application Block

named AuthorizationProvider, and the second returns the AuthorizationProvider that has been configured as the default AuthorizationProvider for the application.

There is only one method that a class must implement to support the IAuthorizationProvider interface: Authorize. The Authorize method is designed to take advantage of Principals to determine if an entity passes an authorization check.

A Principal represents the security context the code is running under. It is really a combination of an Identity (discussed earlier in the Authentication section) and a list of roles to which an entity belongs. The Authorize method expects a Principal object as its first parameter and a string that represents the name of the authorization rule to check as its second. The identity and role information contained in the Principal is run against the authorization rule, and if this information passes the authorization check, the method returns true. Otherwise, false is returned.

For example, let's assume the existence of an authorization rule named *AdminFunctions* that checks whether administrative functions in a site can be performed. The authorization rule could be expressed as simply as:

```
if (IsInRole("admins") ) then true else false;
```

If user Bob exists in the "admins" role but user Sally does not, then the Authorize(currentPrincipal, "AdminFunctions") method will return true for Bob and false for Sally. Consequently, Bob will be given access to administrative functions and Sally will not.

The AuthorizationRuleProvider Class

Enterprise Library ships with an AuthorizationProvider that allows easy creation and checking of rules. The AuthorizationRuleProvider uses a specialized grammar to evaluate expressions using the roles and Identity that exist in the Principal object that is passed to it. For example, the rule given in the previous example would be expressed as R:admins for the AuthorizationRuleProvider. The provider will interpret this rule expression as IsInRole("admins"). Authorization rules for the AuthorizationRuleProvider are kept in the configured StorageProvider with the rest of the settings for the Security Application Block.

Figure 7.9 highlights the classes used to implement the specialized grammar for `AuthorizationRuleProvider`.

Rule Expressions

The AuthorizationRuleProvider uses rule expressions to determine whether an entity is authorized to perform a specific operation. A **rule expression** is the aggregate of different Boolean expressions and returns a single Boolean result. To achieve this, the AuthorizationRuleProvider leverages the many subclasses of the abstract `BooleanExpression` base class. Figure 7.9 shows these classes.

A `BooleanExpression` class represents an operator, operand, or expression that returns a Boolean value. All of the expression classes used by `AuthorizationRuleProvider` must derive either directly or indirectly from this class. `BooleanExpression` defines a single method that must be overridden:

```
bool Evaluate(IPrincipal principal)
```

Table 7.2 lists the available operators and expressions.

An example of a complete authorization rule expression for "Joe or anyone who is part of the Admin group and not part of the Managers group and not Sally (because she will be let go next week)" would be expressed as:

```
I:Joe OR (R:Admins AND (NOT R:Managers) AND (NOT I:Sally))
```

This works because the `AuthorizationRuleProvider` is able to apply an entity's `Principal` against any representation using this grammar and arrive at a single Boolean value that indicates whether authorization is successful or not. It does this by first parsing the expression into representative tokens using the token syntax listed in Table 7.2. The lexical analyzer used to match the tokens also tokenizes the left and right parentheses characters, a quoted string, invalid characters, and the end of file.

All lexical analyzers are made up of finite state machines, and the Security Application Block's lexical analyzer is no different. If the rule in the previous example were run for Sally, the `Parser` would break the expression into the nineteen tokens {I:, Joe, OR, (, R:, Admins, AND, (, NOT, R:, Managers,), AND, (, NOT, I:, Sally,), and)}, and it would be evaluated using the

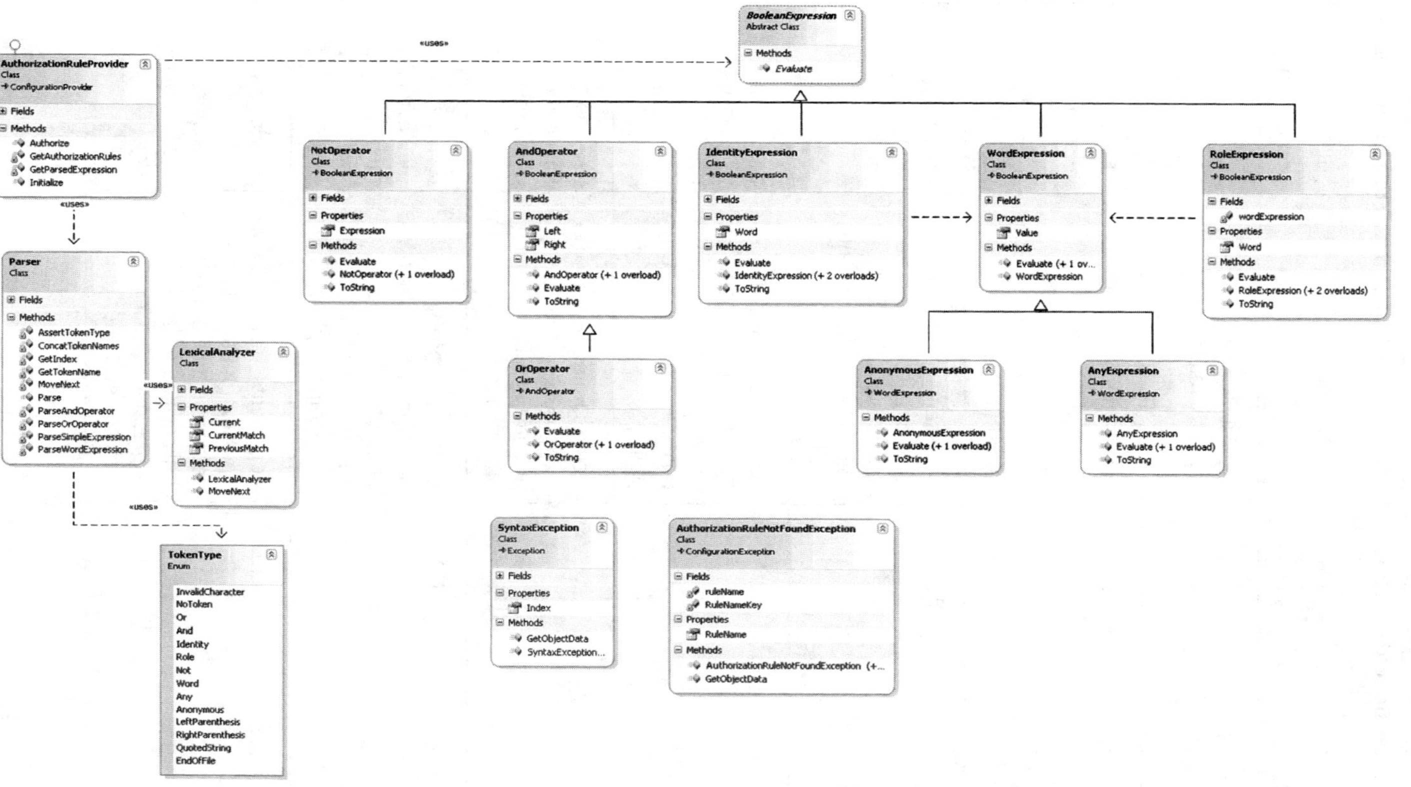

FIGURE 7.9: Classes Used for the AuthorizationRuleProvider

Table 7.2: Classes Derived from `BooleanExpression` for Use by the Lexical Analyzer

`BooleanExpression` Subclass	Token Syntax	Description	Example (and Translation)
`WordExpression`	--	Represents a word value such as a role name or identity name.	`Joe`
`IdentityExpression`	I:	Represents an expression that contains the name of an `IIdentity`. Uses a `WordExpression` for the value of the `Identity`.	`I:Joe` (Identity is Joe)
`RoleExpression`	R:	Represents an expression that contains the name of a role. Uses a `WordExpression` for the value of the role.	`R:Admins` (is in Admins Role)
`AnonymousExpression`	?	Derives from `WordExpression` and returns the negation of an IIdentity object's `IsAuthenticated` property.	`I:?` (is anonymous user)
`AnyExpression`	*	Derives from `WordExpression` and evaluates to true for any specified role or `Identity`.	`R:* OR I:*` (in any role or any Identity)
`NotOperator`	NOT	Represents the logical negation operator that negates its operand. Returns true if and only if its operand is false.	`NOT R:Admins` (not in Admins role)
`AndOperator`	AND	Represents the logical AND operator for its contained left and right expressions. Only evaluates its second expression if the first expression evaluates to true.	`R:Admins AND I:Joe` (in Admins role and Identity is Joe)

BooleanExpression Subclass	Token Syntax	Description	Example (and Translation)
OrOperator	OR	Derives from AndOperator. Represents the logical -OR operator for its contained left and right expressions. Only evaluates its second expression if the first expression evaluates to false.	R:Admins OR I:Joe (in Admins role or Identity is Joe)

finite state machine depicted in Figure 7.10. The final result would be false and Sally would not be granted access.

Enterprise Library's Authorization Manager Provider

The AuthorizationRuleProvider is very useful for specifying functional entitlement (that is, what operations certain entities are allowed to perform) in an application. If an application can express all its authorization rules

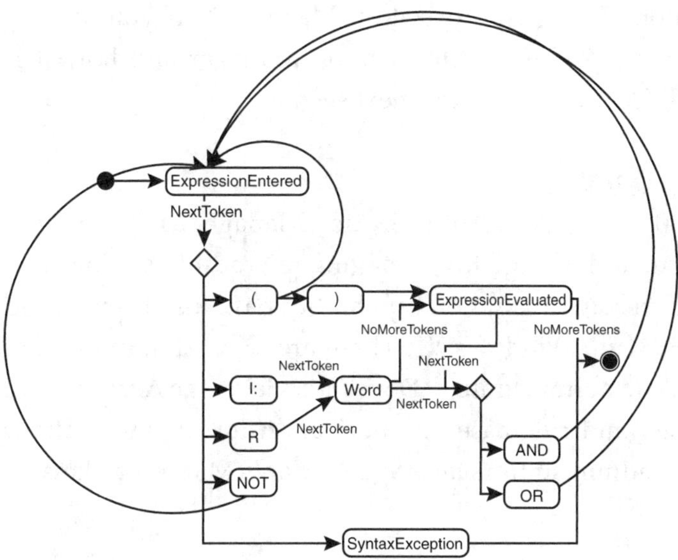

FIGURE 7.10: AuthorizationRuleProvider **Finite State Machine**

using the grammar shown in the previous section, then the AuthorizationRuleProvider should be sufficient. However, very often authorization to perform an activity cannot be based solely on identities and roles; often more complex relationships that exist between the roles, users, and activities must be considered for an authorization request. Additionally, it is very common for authorization decisions to consider data that is not known until runtime. The Microsoft Authorization Manager (aka AzMan) has been designed to not only consider the complex, hierarchical relationships that can exist between groups, roles, users, and tasks, but to also take the results of VBScript or Jscript into account, thereby allowing it to incorporate data entitlement (that is, what data an entity is entitled to view, change, or delete) as well as functional entitlement.

I am not going to describe Authorization Manager in depth. To do so would require at least another chapter and I probably wouldn't do it justice at that. I will, however, try to provide enough information for you to understand what Authorization Manager is, how it works, and how Enterprise Library's `AzManAuthorizationManager` uses it. For a more in-depth look at Authorization Manager, read the information about it on Microsoft TechNet[4] and Dave McPherson's article entitled "Role-Based Access Control for Multi-tier Applications Using Authorization Manager."[5] If you already understand the concepts behind Authorization Manager and how it is intended to be used, feel free to skip this next section.

Authorization Manager (AzMan)

Windows Server 2003 introduced Authorization Manager as a new capability for applications to leverage for managing and administering role-base authorization. The administration capabilities have also been ported to Windows 2000 SP4 and Windows XP. There are two primary users of AzMan: developers and administrators. Developers leverage AzMan's API to provide role-based and rule-based authorization for the applications they are developing; administrators leverage AzMan's Microsoft Manage-

---

4. Found at www.microsoft.com/technet/prodtechnol/windowsserver2003/ library/ServerHelp/1b4de9c6-4df9-4b5a-83e9-fb8d49772378.mspx.

5. Found at www.microsoft.com/technet/prodtechnol/windowsserver2003/technologies/management/athmanwp.mspx.

ment Console (MMC) snap-in to configure the various constructs that make up these roles and rules. The authorization information can be stored in either Microsoft Active Directory or an XML file; however, the developer does not need to be aware of the location for the authorization store. This is simply an administrative decision that needs to be made. It is important, however, for both developers and administrators to understand the various concepts in AzMan and how these concepts can be used to provide flexible authorization policies.

There are several constructs that define authorization policies in Authorization Manager. Two of these constructs, operations and tasks, fall into the category of functions that can be performed by an entity. Operations are more developer-centric because they are very granular and often times equate to specific functions that may exist in code. Tasks are more administrative-centric as they are the aggregation of multiple operations and other tasks into a unit of work.

For example, in the portal site scenario used earlier in this chapter, certain users are allowed to view a dashboard control while other users are not. Viewing the dashboard can be thought of as the task `ViewDashboard`. This task consists of several operations: `GetDashboardInfo`, `RenderDashboardInfo`, and `SetDashboardEditControls`. Furthermore, higher-level tasks can also exist that might leverage the other tasks. For instance, a task might exist to show the administrative tab and functions in the site; this task might be the combination of all the tasks that are considered to be administrative tasks, such as manage user accounts, remove accounts, assign users to roles, and so on.

Tasks are also extremely powerful because of the ability to associate a VBScript or Jscript with the task. This authorization script can take advantage of runtime parameters and values to determine whether permission to do the task should be granted. This allows tasks in Authorization Manager to reach beyond static, functional entitlement rules into the realm of dynamic, functional data entitlement. For example, an employee portal site might contain an authorization rule such that an employee can only create a purchase order if the amount is less than $1,000. The amount of the purchase order that contributes to this authorization check is dynamic; its value is not known until the application is running. The VBScript in Listing 7.3 is an example of such an authorization rule.

LISTING 7.3: Sample Authorization Rule in Authorization Manager

```
Dim poAmount
AzBizRuleContext.BusinessRuleResult = FALSE
Amount = AzBizRuleContext.GetParameter("POAmount")
if poAmount < 1000 then AzBizRuleContext.BusinessRuleResult = TRUE
```

Other concepts in Authorization Manager are associated with the entities that have access to the application, the relationship the entities have with one another, and the relationship those entities have with the tasks and operations they can perform. Table 7.3 defines the terminology used

TABLE 7.3: Authorization Manager Terminology

Responsibility	Term	Definition
Functional and Data Entitlement	Operation	A low-level permission used to identify access permission to a specific method. Several operations may be required to perform a meaningful task and are therefore often not exposed or meaningful to administrators.
	Task	A collection of operations. The purpose of the task is to determine which operations are required to do some unit of work that is meaningful to administrators.
	Authorization Script	Scripts that are attached to a task object that is run at the time of the access request. It can use information that is only available at runtime, such as "dollar amount," to make an authorization decision.
Grouping Entities and Resources	Role	The set of permissions that users must have to be able to do their job.
	Scope	A collection of objects or resources with a distinct authorization policy. Applications can use the scope as necessary to group resources.
	Application Group	Groups that are applicable only to an authorization store, an application in an authorization store, or a scope in an application.

when working with AzMan and categorizes which are related to entitlement and which are related to grouping entities and resources.

As you might expect, the concept of a role exists in Authorization Manager. **Roles** are used to group users together into categories that reflect the permissions those users need to do their jobs. A role definition consists of the tasks and operations that users in that role can perform as well as other, lower-level roles. For example, business users in the portal site may have very limited permissions; they may only be able to view the site in read-only mode and may not be able to view all controls that exist. A content administrator will probably have all the permissions that a business user has plus additional permissions to add, edit, and remove content.

Figure 7.11 illustrates the definition for the content administrator with the business user as a lower-level role and permission to execute an additional `ViewDashboard` task. The site administrator can be defined with the content administrator as a lower-level role and a permission to execute additional tasks and operations. This allows for a hierarchical model of roles and eases the burden of assigning multiple tasks to every role in the hierarchy.

Authorization Manager also has the concept of **scope**, which allows application resources to be grouped together so that different authorization policies can be specified per collection. Scope is very useful when there are specific areas in an application that must have specialized permission. For example, registering as a "member" for a business-to-consumer site will grant authorization for special areas in a Web site that nonmembers are not allowed. This membership area can often be represented as a subsite (e.g., http://myb2csite/membersonly) or a directory (e.g., C:\myb2csite\membersonly). A scope can be used to represent this membership area and tasks, operations, and roles that were defined at a global level for the application.

The configuration in Figure 7.11 includes two scopes: *Members Only Area* and *Work on behalf of Joe*. This second scope is meant to include tasks so a user can perform work on behalf of Joe. In this scenario, Joe is a site administrator. When Joe takes a vacation, the functions that Joe performs still need to continue—the site cannot be allowed to become dormant just because Joe is on vacation. So, a separate scope exists that allows roles to be defined that contain a subset of the work that Joe needs to perform as site administrator. When Joe goes on vacation, users can be added to these roles

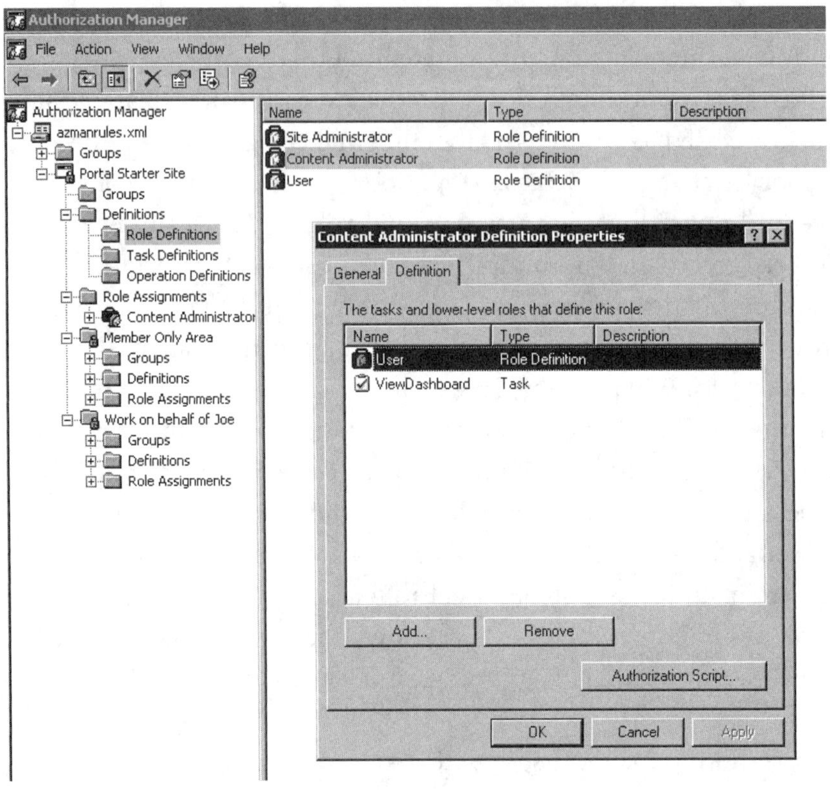

FIGURE 7.11: Authorization Manager Role Definition Example

to "work on behalf of Joe" while he is gone. When Joe returns from vacation, the users can be removed from these roles.

The last Authorization Manager concept that I will mention is that of application groups. **Application groups** work like Windows security groups except that they not only contain a list of members in the group, but they also have a list of nonmembers. The nonmembers list takes precedence over the members list. If a user appears in both lists, that user will not be granted membership. Application groups can also be assigned as members in a role. Because application groups can either be global throughout the entire authorization store or defined in a specific scope, they can be assigned to any role for any application in the authorization store.

Developing Against Authorization Manager. Authorization Manager is a set of COM-based runtime interfaces. The interop assembly, `Microsoft.Interop.Security.AzRoles.dll`, can be used to access the COM-based interfaces through managed code.[6] These interfaces are used to obtain a connection to the authorization store, to obtain roles, and to determine permission for a given operation.

The `AzAuthorizationStoreClass`' `Initialize` method must be called to initialize the Authorization Manager store. After this, the `AzAuthorizationStoreClass`' `OpenApplication` method can be called to bind to a specific application in the AzMan store. An AzMan context must be created for a client to connect to an application. The best and fastest method for accomplishing this is via the `IAzApplication`'s `InitializeContextFromToken` method. Once the client context is created, role and authorization information can be retrieved.

To obtain role information, the `IAzClientContext`'s `GetRoles` methods can be called. To obtain authorization information for an operation, first the scope in which the user is making the request must be determined. Then `IAzClientContext`'s `AccessCheck` can be called with an identifier to be used for auditing purposes, the relevant scope, the operations for which authorization is being requested, and the authorization script parameters and values. All of the arguments are evaluated against the information stored in AzMan, and an array of integers (signifying Boolean values) is returned. Each item in the array indicates whether authorization for a particular operation is granted.

`AzManAuthorizationProvider`. Most of these steps to obtain role information are the same steps taken when Enterprise Library's `AzManAuthorizationProvider` is used. Since the `AzManAuthorizationProvider` subscribes to the Provider pattern and implements the `IAuthorizationProvider` interface, you only need to understand one method to use it: `Authorize`.

That is a good thing for all the reasons that the Provider pattern is good. For example, if an application that subscribes to this pattern needs to switch

6. It is important to remember that the `AzManAuthorizationProvider` uses this interop assembly, because it is necessary to deploy the interop assembly when leveraging `AzManAuthorizationProvider` in an application and to ensure that the Enterprise Library Configuration Tool can access the assembly when configuring the `AzManAuthorizationProvider`.

from the AuthorizationRuleProvider to the AzManAuthorizationProvider, no code needs to change—at least in theory. In reality, there is a caveat that must be understood for this to actually be true. The caveat is that the *authorization function name*[7] must begin with an *O:* (the letter *O* and a colon) for an Authorization Manager operation. If the rule does not begin with an *O:*, then the AzManAuthorizationProvider will assume the request to be for an Authorization Manager task.

Regardless of whether the authorization request is for an operation or a task, an **audit identifier** is always created from a combination of the AuditIdentifierPrefix that is set through configuration, the Identity.Name of the principal for whom the authorization request is intended, and the name of the authorization function. Using the configuration shown in Figure 7.12, the auditIdentifier of an authorization request for Joe to access the operation named GetDashboardInfo would be *pssAuditId-Joe:O:GetDashboardInfo*.

When the AzManAuthorizationProvider checks access for an operation, it first gets the client context via the IAzApplication's InitializeContextFromToken method. It then obtains the scope for which the AzManAuthorizationProvider has been configured. In Figure 7.12, no scope was configured, so the value for the scope parameter would be null. These values, along with the auditIdentifier and the name of the authorization function (the OperationID) are passed to the IAzClientContext's AccessCheck method to determine authorization.

A similar process occurs when the AzManAuthorizationProvider checks access for a task. The primary difference is that an array of OperationIDs for the operations that make up a task are first retrieved by leveraging the Authorization Manager API. This array of OperationIDs is used instead of the single OperationID in the call to the IAzClientContext's AccessCheck method.

Notice that no script parameters or dynamic, runtime values are passed to the AccessCheck method. The AzManAuthorizationProvider doesn't

7. What I am calling an *authorization function name* is actually the value for the parameter named context in the Authorize method. To avoid confusion with Authorization Manager's client context, it seemed appropriate to refer to it as *authorization function name*.

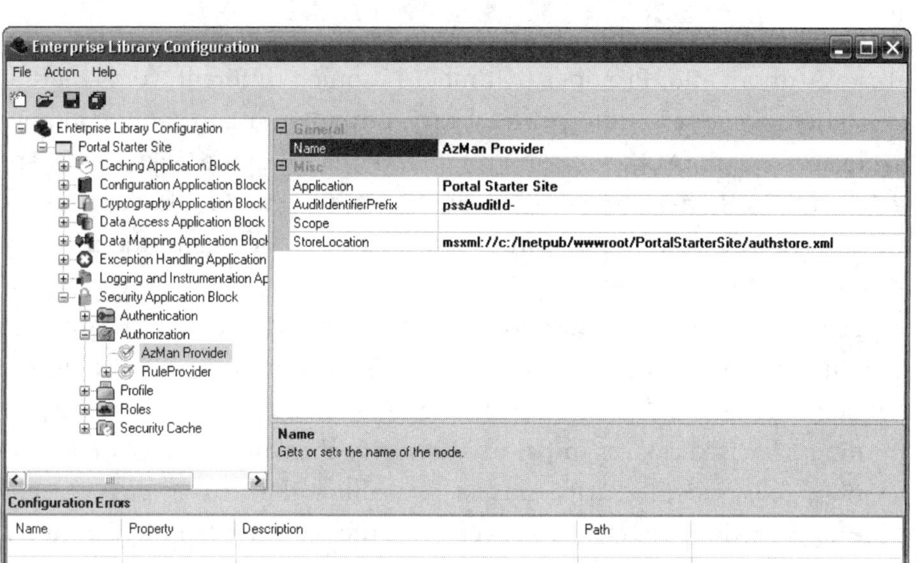

FIGURE 7.12: Enterprise Library's `AzManAuthorizationProvider`

support it. However, the `AzManProvider` in the previous Authorization and Profile Application Block supported this via the `CheckAccess` method. To support passing runtime values, the `Authorize` method would need to accept additional parameters to hold these values or the `AzManAuthorizationProvider` would need to provide another method for setting them. I can see that providing this functionality would be meaningless to the `AuthorizationRuleProvider`; however, the argument could be made that adding the ability for the `AuthorizationRuleProvider` to consider runtime values and parameters would be an excellent enhancement. It is a shame that the support for this feature was lost because it is extremely powerful.

Extending the AuthorizationProvider

AuthorizationProviders allow for another extension point in the Security Application Block. Custom AuthorizationProviders can be created to authorize against different authorization stores and in different ways than the AuthorizationRuleProvider and the AzManAuthorizationProvider.

Because there isn't anything too different about what you need to do to create an AuthorizationProvider that makes it much different from creating any other provider in Enterprise Library, I'm not going to show you how to create a custom AuthorizationProvider. (For a list of the tasks, see Chapters 1 and 2.) Rather, I'm going to show another way to add support for authorization by adding declarative security capabilities to the Security Application Block.

Using an AuthorizationProvider with Enterprise Library means that eventually there needs to be code that calls the AuthorizationProvider's `Authorize` method. When you write code to call `Authorize`, you are performing what is known as **imperative security checks**, which is akin to performing role-based security checks by calling the `Principal` object's `IsInRole` method directly. However, attributes can be decorated around a method to perform this check on your behalf. Instead of explicitly calling `principal.IsInRole("Manager")` in a method, the method could be decorated with a `PrincipalPermission` like that shown in Listing 7.4.

LISTING 7.4: Example of Declarative Security

```
[C#]
[PrincipalPermission (SecurityAction.Demand, Role = "Managers")]
public static void MyMethod()
{
     //Do some stuff.
}

[Visual Basic]
<PrincipalPermission (SecurityAction.Demand, Role := "Managers")> _
Public Shared Sub MyMethod()
     'Do some stuff.
End Sub
```

Because this method is attributed with the `PrincipalPermissionAttribute`, a security check will automatically be performed to determine whether the current user is in the Managers role. If the user is not, a `SecurityException` will be thrown; otherwise, access will be granted and the code will be allowed to execute.

Just because AuthorizationProviders are used to perform authorization with the Security Application Block does not mean that support for declarative security cannot be provided. However, it will take some extra code to allow for it. This section shows you how to create custom attributes to allow for declarative security against AuthorizationProviders. However, there are a couple of caveats that you should know about first.

- To create a custom attribute so that it can be leveraged by multiple applications, the assembly must be strongly named. By itself, this is not too big a deal; however, for an assembly to be strongly named, every assembly on which it depends must also be strongly named. For the custom attribute created in Listing 7.5 and shown in Listing 7.7, that includes the assemblies for the security, configuration, and common blocks.
- The assembly for the custom attribute must be installed in the Global Assembly Cache (GAC) for other applications to use it.

Okay, now that you're aware of these caveats, let's get started. The first step is to create a class that implements `IPermission` and keeps track of three main properties: whether the user is already authenticated, the name of the AuthorizationProvider, and the rule to use to determine authorization. The most interesting method in this class is the `Demand` method, because this is where the determination is made as to whether the user is authorized against the supplied rule or not.

LISTING 7.5: `Demand` Method for the Custom `Permission` Class

```
[C#]
public void Demand()
{
     IPrincipal principal = Thread.CurrentPrincipal;
     if (principal == null)
     {
          throw new
          SecurityException("Security_AuthProviderPermission",
               base.GetType(), this.ToXml().ToString());
     }
     if (this.arrProviderInfo != null)
     {
          int num = this.arrProviderInfo.Length;
          bool flag = false;
          for (int num2 = 0; num2 < num; num2++)
          {
               if (this.arrProviderInfo[num2].authenticated)
               {
```

```
                IAuthorizationProvider authorizationProvider;
                if ((this.arrProviderInfo[num2].providerName == null)
                     || (this.arrProviderInfo[num2].providerName.Equals
                          (String.Empty)))
                authorizationProvider =
                     AuthorizationFactory.GetAuthorizationProvider();
                else
                     authorizationProvider =
                          AuthorizationFactory.GetAuthorizationProvider
                          (this.arrProviderInfo[num2].providerName);

                     if ((this.arrProviderInfo[num2].rule != null) &&
                          !authorizationProvider.Authorize
                          (principal,this.arrProviderInfo[num2].rule))
                     {
                          throw new SecurityException
                           ("Security_AuthProviderPermission",
                               typeof(AuthorizationProviderPermission));
                     }
                     flag = true;
                     break;
                }
                flag = true;
                break;
           }
           if (!flag)
           {
                throw new SecurityException
                      ("Security_AuthProviderPermission",
                          typeof(AuthorizationProviderPermission));
           }
      }
}

[Visual Basic]
Public Sub Demand()
     Dim principal As IPrincipal = Thread.CurrentPrincipal
     If principal Is Nothing Then _
          Throw New _
               SecurityException _
                    ("Security_AuthorizationProviderPermission",_
                    MyBase.GetType(), Me.ToXml().ToString())
     End If
     If Not Me.arrProviderInfo Is Nothing Then
          Dim num As Integer = Me.arrProviderInfo.Length
          Dim flag As Boolean = False
          For num2 As Integer = 0 To num - 1
               If Me.arrProviderInfo(num2).authenticated Then
                    Dim authorizationProvider As _
                         IAuthorizationProvider
```

```
                If (Me.arrProviderInfo(num2).providerName Is _
                Nothing) OrElse _
               (Me.arrProviderInfo(num2).providerName.Equals _
               (String.Empty)) Then
                     authorizationProvider = _
                     AuthorizationFactory.GetAuthorizationProvider()
                Else
                     authorizationProvider = _
                     AuthorizationFactory.GetAuthorizationProvider _
                          (Me.arrProviderInfo(num2).providerName)
                End If

                If (Not Me.arrProviderInfo(num2).rule Is Nothing) _
                AndAlso (Not authorizationProvider.Authorize _
               (principal,Me.arrProviderInfo(num2).rule)) Then
                     Throw New SecurityException _
                     ("Security_AuthorizationProviderPermission", _
                     GetType(AuthorizationProviderPermission))
                End If
                flag = True
                Exit For
           End If
           flag = True
           Exit For
      Next num2
      If (Not flag) Then
           Throw New SecurityException _
           ("Security_AuthorizationProviderPermission", _
           GetType(AuthorizationProviderPermission))
      End If
   End If
End Sub
```

The full source code for the `AuthorizationProviderPermission` class is on the book's Web site.

After the Permission class is created, the `Attribute` class must be created. This class is easier to implement; it is more of a wrapper on top of the `Permission` class. It is just a matter of creating a single constructor that accepts a `SecurityAction`, a `CreatePermission` method that creates a new instance of the class highlighted in the previous step, and the three properties that contain the information that will need to be set: `Authenticated`, `ProviderName`, and `Rule`.

When this attribute has been successfully compiled, unit-tested, strong-named, and installed in the GAC, it is ready for use. Code that previously looked like Listing 7.6 can instead be written as Listing 7.7.

LISTING 7.6: Imperative Security Using AuthorizationProviders

```
[C#]
public static void MyMethod()
{
     bool bAuthorized = false;
     IAuthorizationProvider authProvider =
          AuthorizationFactory.GetAuthorizationProvider();
     bAuthorized =
     authProvider.Authorize(HttpContext.Current.User,"ViewDashboard");
     if (bAuthorized)
          //Do some stuff.
}


[Visual Basic]
Public Shared Sub MyMethod()
     Dim bAuthorized As Boolean = False
     Dim authProvider As IAuthorizationProvider = _
          AuthorizationFactory.GetAuthorizationProvider()
     bAuthorized = _
     authProvider.Authorize(HttpContext.Current.User, "ViewDashboard")
     If (bAuthorized) Then
          'Do some stuff.
End Sub
```

LISTING 7.7: Declarative Security Using AuthorizationProviders

```
[C#]
[AuthorizationProviderPermission
(SecurityAction.Demand, Rule = "ViewDashboard")]
public static void MyMethod()
{
     //Do some stuff.
}

[Visual Basic]
<AuthorizationProviderPermission _
(SecurityAction.Demand, Rule = "ViewDashboard")> _
Public Shared Sub MyMethod()
     'Do some stuff.
End Sub
```

Role Management

The previous section detailed that Enterprise Library applies roles and identities against predefined rules to determine if an entity is authorized to perform an operation. Enterprise Library's authorization features do not, however, include managing the roles in any way. An application must first get the roles for an entity before it is able to authorize that entity for an operation. This is the responsibility of the `RolesProviderFactory` and `IRolesProvider`. Figure 7.13 depicts the classes used to provide role management with the Security Application Block.

The `RolesProviderFactory` and the `IRolesProvider` Interface

The `RolesProviderFactory` class uses its configuration information to create an instance of a class that implements the `IRolesProvider` interface. By now you're probably getting the gist that for every `ProviderFactory` in Enterprise Library there is a corresponding `Factory` class that provides static methods to wrap around it. For the `RolesProviderFactory`, that class is the `RolesFactory`. Either class can be used to obtain a named instance of an `IRolesProvider` or the one that is configured as the default.

The `GetRolesProvider` method is exposed by both of these classes and is overloaded two times: one overload expects a string that represents the name of a `RolesProvider` that has been configured for the application, and the other overload does not expect any arguments. The first overload returns the named `RolesProvider` and the second returns the `RolesProvider` that has been configured as the default `RolesProvider` for the application.

There is a single method that a class must implement to support the `IRolesProvider` interface: `GetRoles`. The `GetRoles` method accepts an object that implements `IIdentity` and returns an `IPrincipal`. Typically, the `Identity` will be the same one that was retrieved from an AuthenticationProvider's `Authenticate` method and the `Principal` will be passed to an AuthorizationProvider's `Authorize` method.

The `SecurityRolesProvider` Class

The `SecurityRolesProvider` is an abstract base class that is intended to make it easier for developers to create `RolesProvider`. The `SecurityRolesProvider` implements the `IRolesProvider` interface and creates and returns a `GenericPrincipal` for the `GetRoles` method. It uses an

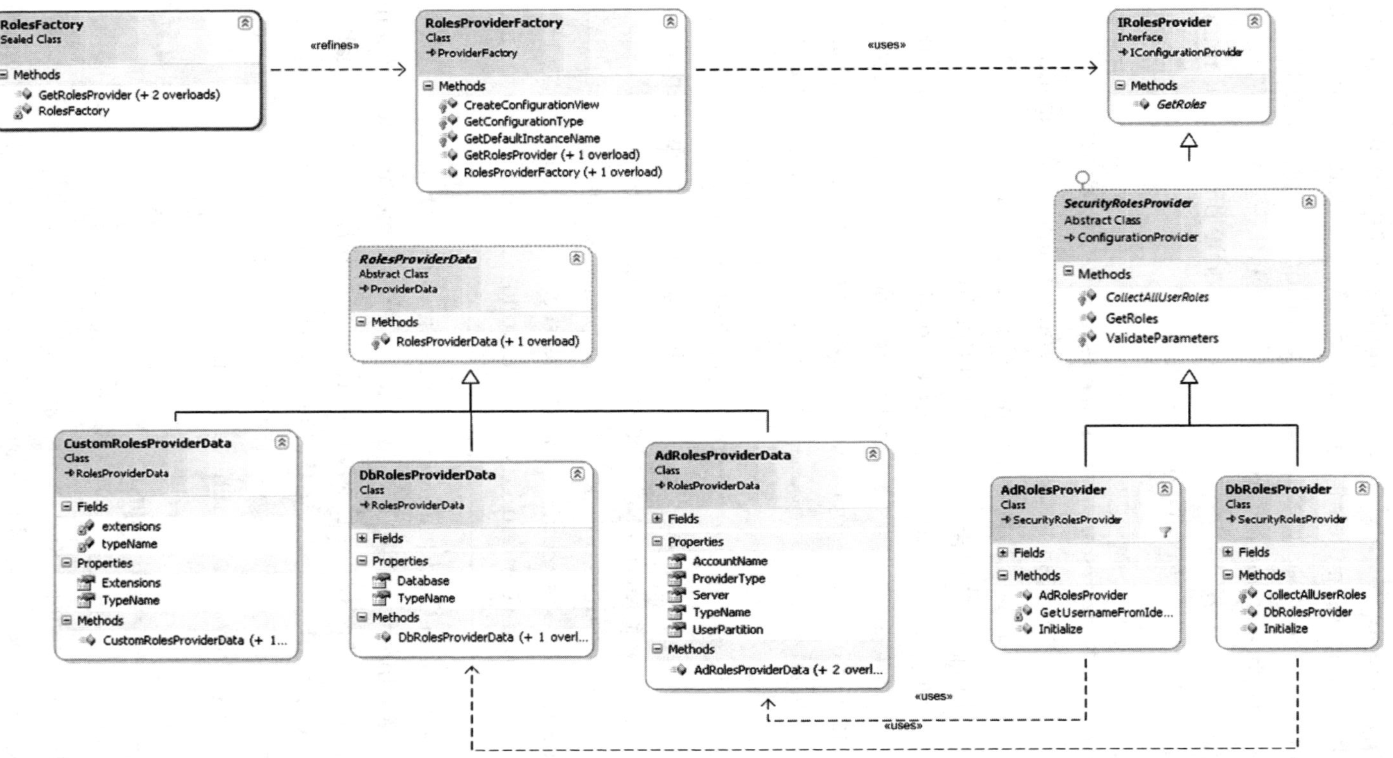

FIGURE 7.13: Role Management in the Security Application Block

abstract method named `CollectAllUserRoles` that must return an array of strings to represent the roles for the specified `Identity`. Thus, a concrete `RolesProvider` only needs to subclass the `SecurityRolesProvider` class and override the `CollectAllUserRoles` with the code needed for the user store it represents. The Security Application Block ships with two such providers: the `DbRolesProvider` and `AdRolesProvider`.

The `DbRolesProvider` retrieves the roles for a user from the Security Database that comes with the Security Application Block. The `DbRolesProvider` gets the name of the `DatabaseInstance` from the configuration data that is stored for the Security Application Block. It uses this in its `CollectAllUserRoles` method to create a `UserRoleManager`. It calls `UserRoleManager`'s `GetUserRoles` method to retrieve the roles; since `GetUserRoles` returns a DataSet, the `DbRolesProvider` first converts the DataSet to an array of strings before returning to the caller.

Enterprise Library also supplies the `AdRolesProvider` for getting an entity's roles from Active Directory. Its inner workings are a bit more complex than `DbRolesProvider`, but this complexity is mostly hidden from those applications consuming it. The `AdRolesProvider` must be configured with the name of the server hosting the Active Directory Service (*Server*), the provider type name for Active Directory (*ProviderType*), the partition in the Active Directory that contains the user objects/data (*UserPartition*), and the name of a field in the schema that can be used to find the current account name (*AccountName*).

It uses the first three values to bind to Active Directory and the last one to determine which field to use to search for the user. For example, if the value for this data is:

MyServer:389", "LDAP", "CN=CompanyUsers,O=OrgDept,C=US", and *"CN"*

the `AdRolesProvider` will bind to Active Directory with

LDAP://MyServer:389/CN=CompanyUsers,O=OrgDept,C=US

and search for the entry where *CN*=<name of Identity>. The `AdRolesProvider` then uses the names of the groups to which the user belongs for the list of roles that it returns.

Creating a Custom RolesProvider

If you used the previous Authorization and Profile Application Block and leveraged the AzManProvider, you may have also used its ability to get the roles that existed in Authorization Manager. Unfortunately, that feature did not make its way into Enterprise Library's Security Application Block. Roles and authorization were split into two separate providers, and an `AzManRolesProvider` does not exist. This may be, however, an important RolesProvider to have if you are using the AzMan AuthorizationProvider for authorization. It is useful to be able to get the roles for the users of an application from the same store that is used to authorize those users.

Therefore, I have migrated this feature from the previous Authorization and Profile Application Block and created a custom RolesProvider for getting the roles from Authorization Manager. First, I created a class that holds the configuration data. This class, the `AzManRolesProviderData` class, contains member variables to maintain information like the location of the AzMan authorization store, the name of the application, and the scope in the application (if any).

Then I created the actual RolesProvider, `AzManRolesProvider`, so that it derives from the `SecurityRolesProvider` base class. The base class does most of the work for returning the roles to the consumers of this provider; I only needed to create two methods: `Initialize` and `CollectAllUserRoles`. The `Initialize` method is needed to read the configuration settings; the `CollectAllUserRoles` method does the work of getting the roles from the specific user store and returning them as a string collection. Listing 7.8 shows the `CollectAllUserRoles` method for the AzManRolesProvider.

LISTING 7.8: `AzManRolesProvider`'s `CollectAllUserRoles` Method

```
[C#]
protected override string[] CollectAllUserRoles(IIdentity userIdentity)
{
     AzManRolesProviderData azManRolesData = (AzManRolesProviderData)
          securityConfigurationView.GetRolesProviderData
          (ConfigurationName);

     string applicationName = azManRolesData.Application;
     try
     {
```

```
            IAzApplication azApp = null;
            IAzClientContext clientCtx = GetClientContext(azManRolesData,
                                              userIdentity,
                                              applicationName,
                                              out azApp);
            IAzScopes scopes = azApp.Scopes;
            StringCollection rolesCollection = new StringCollection();

            // Get the application's roles.
            Array varRoles =
                 clientCtx.GetRoles(azManRolesData.Scope) as Array;
            Debug.Assert(varRoles != null);
            for(Int32 index =0; index < varRoles.Length; index++)
            {
                 rolesCollection.Add((String)varRoles.GetValue(index));
            }

            string[] arrRoles = new string[rolesCollection.Count];
            rolesCollection.CopyTo(arrRoles,0);
            return  arrRoles;
       }
       catch (COMException comEx)
       {
            throw new SecurityException(comEx.Message, comEx);
       }
}

[Visual Basic]
Protected Overrides Function CollectAllUserRoles _
                (ByVal userIdentity As IIdentity) As String()
     Dim azManRolesData As AzManRolesProviderData = _
           (AzManRolesProviderData) _
           securityConfigurationView.GetRolesProviderData _
           (ConfigurationName)

     Dim applicationName As String = azManRolesData.Application
     Try
          Dim azApp As IAzApplication = Nothing
          Dim clientCtx As IAzClientContext = GetClientContext( _
                                                  azManRolesData, _
                                                  userIdentity, _
                                                  applicationName, _
                                                  azApp)
          Dim scopes As IAzScopes = azApp.Scopes
          Dim rolesCollection As StringCollection = _
               New StringCollection()

          ' Get the application's roles.
          Dim varRoles As Array = IIf(TypeOf _
               clientCtx.GetRoles(azManRolesData.Scope) Is Array, _
```

```
                CType(clientCtx.GetRoles(azManRolesData.Scope), Array), _
                CType(Nothing, Array))
            Debug.Assert(Not varRoles Is Nothing)
            For index As Int32 = 0 To varRoles.Length - 1
                 rolesCollection.Add _
                 (CType(varRoles.GetValue(index), String))
            Next index

            Dim arrRoles As String() =  _
                New String(rolesCollection.Count - 1) {}
            rolesCollection.CopyTo(arrRoles,0)
            Return arrRoles
        Catch comEx As COMException
            Throw New SecurityException(comEx.Message, comEx)
        End Try
    End Function
End
```

Finally, I added the design-time classes needed to configure this provider with the Enterprise Library Configuration Tool. I derived my `AzManRolesProviderNode` from the `RolesProviderNode` and added properties for the store location, application name, and scope. (For more information about creating providers with Enterprise Library, see Chapters 1 and 2.) The full source code for the `AzManRolesProvider` is on this book's Web site. Figure 7.14 is the result of adding and configuring the `AzManRolesProvider` to an application's configuration data.

Profile Management

Authenticating and authorizing a user through the use of identities, roles, and rules is necessary to secure an application. Combining these three constructs also allows a level of personalization in an application, as one user may have a completely different experience than another user based on the way these constructs are configured in the application. The Authorization section showed how a business user, content administrator, and site administrator can all have different experiences when navigating a portal site because of their access to different features. True personalization, however, usually accounts for more than this; it must usually consider other attributes that are associated with a user's profile.

A profile can consist of anything that an application deems important enough to tie to an entity. Many times this information is kept permanently

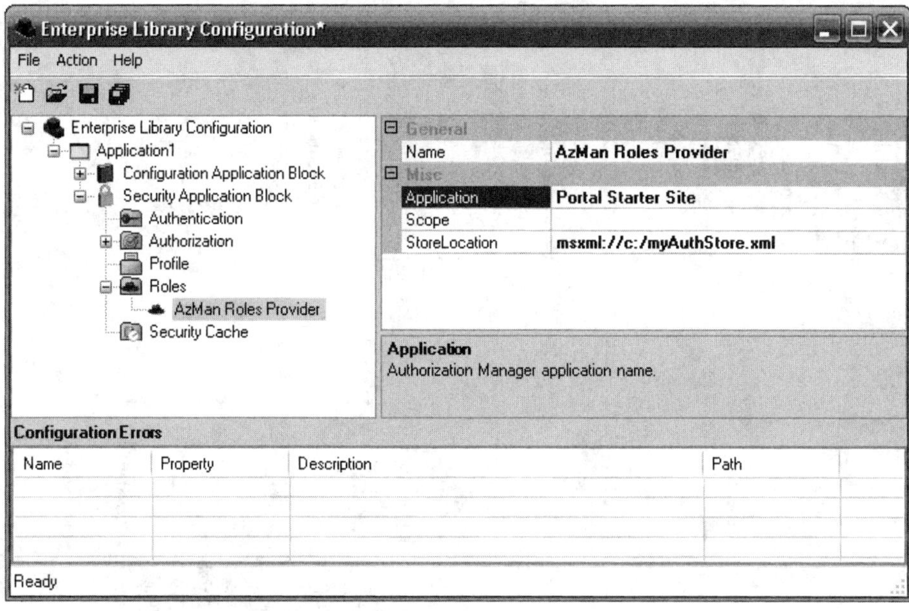

FIGURE 7.14: Configuring the `AzManRolesProvider`

for a user. Common examples are a user's address and preferences (like favorite color and stock symbols). However, profiles can also be used to store information related to a specific session. For example, items in a user's shopping cart from a consumer site or a list of documents to download from a portal site can often be kept in a user's profile.

While managing profiles isn't exactly related to security, it is related to user management. Its inclusion in the Security Application Block is a matter of convenience since other aspects of user management, like managing a user's identity, roles, and authorization also exist in this block. Figure 7.15 illustrates the primary classes that provide profile management features in the Security Application Block.

The `ProfileProviderFactory` Class and the `IProfileProvider` Interface

The `ProfileProviderFactory` class uses its configuration information to create an instance of a class that implements the `IProfileProvider` interface. The `ProfileFactory` provides public static methods that wrap around

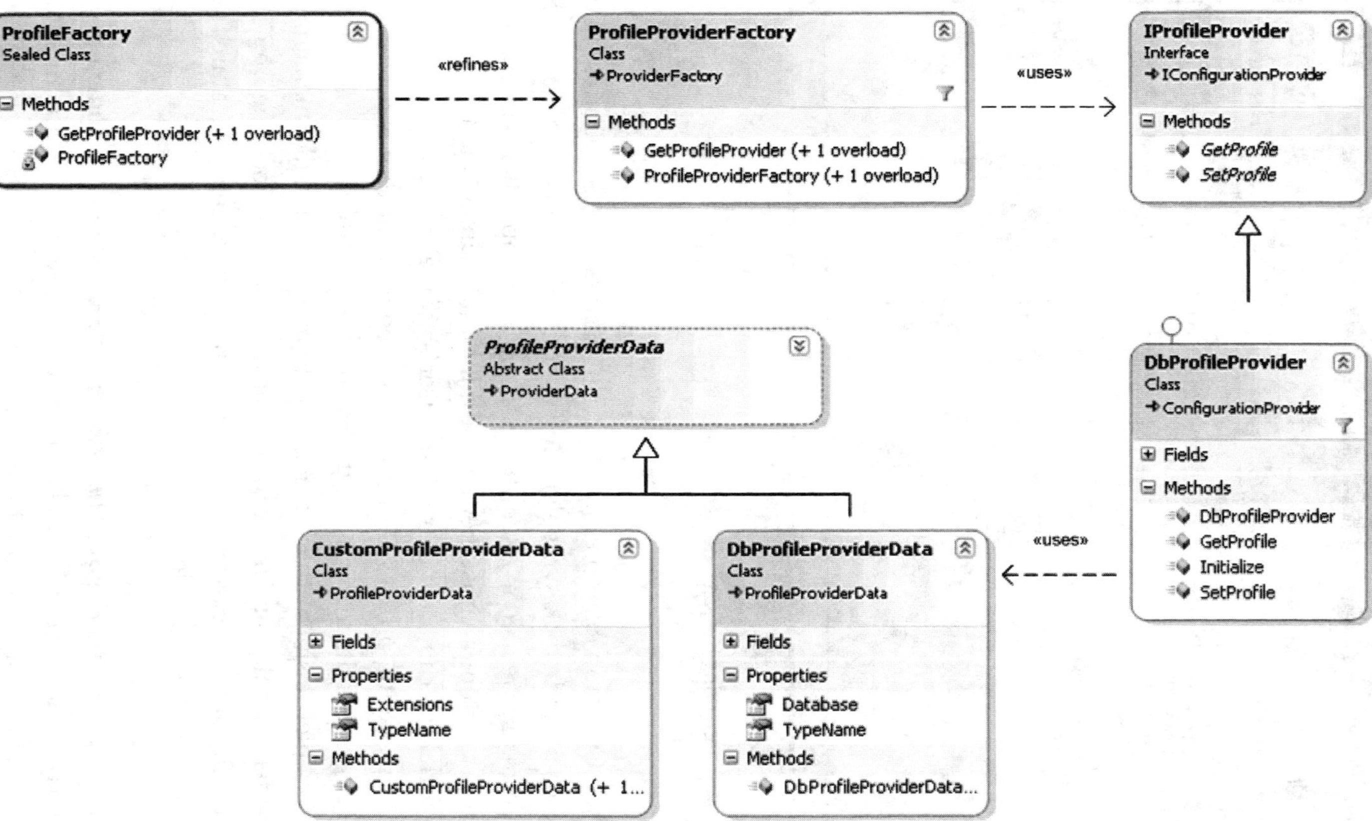

FIGURE 7.15: Profile Management in the Security Application Block

the ProfileProviderFactory methods. Either class can be used to obtain a named instance of an `IProfileProvider` or the one that is configured as the default.

The `GetProfileProvider` method is exposed by both of these classes and is overloaded two times: one overload expects a string that represents the name of a `ProfileProvider` that has been configured for the application, and the other overload does not expect any arguments. The first overload returns the named `ProfileProvider`, and the second returns the `ProfileProvider` that has been configured as the default `ProfileProvider` for the application.

There are two methods that a class must implement to support the `IProfileProvider` interface: `GetProfile` and `SetProfile`. The `GetProfile` method accepts an object that implements `IIdentity` and returns an object that represents the profile. `SetProfile` takes both an `IIdentity` object and an object that represents a profile and sets the profile for this Identity.

Note that the profile is just represented as an object for these methods; that is, there is no specific *`Profile`* object that needs to be passed into or returned from these methods. This gives you complete freedom to create your own representation of a profile. As long as your *`Profile`* object is serializable, it should be able to be stored by the ProfileProvider. It is the ProfileProvider's responsibility to serialize the object for the `SetProfile` method and deserialize it for `GetProfile`.

The `DbProfileProvider`

And that is exactly what the `DbProfileProvider` does. Enterprise Library ships with a ProfileProvider that stores and fetches the Profile information from the Security Database described earlier in this chapter. The `DbProfileProvider` gets the name of the `DatabaseInstance` from the configuration data that is stored for the Security Application Block. When `SetProfile` is called, the `DbProfileProvider` uses a `BinaryFormatter` to serialize the object and then calls two stored procedures—one to delete the profile if it already exists and another to insert the profile that was just serialized. Both are executed in the scope of a transaction. When `GetProfile` is called, the opposite occurs: the `GetProfile` stored procedure is called and the profile is deserialized and returned to the caller.

Creating a Custom ProfileProvider

The `DbProfileProvider` is very effective for storing profile information in the Security Database. Because it is indifferent to the specific type of object that is being stored, it serializes the Profile information and stores it in the database as binary. Therefore, the only requirement for using it is to ensure that the object that represents the Profile information is serializable.

There are, however, a few consequences associated with storing the Profile information as a single binary field.

- The actual Profile information cannot be queried or updated without an application that will deserialize the Profile information first. For example, if the Profile information contains data that represents a user's favorite Web links, there is no way to simply run a database query to determine how many users have specific links (e.g., How many users have a link to www.msn.com?). To perform this type of query, code needs to be written that deserializes the profile data.
- Additionally, there is no way to update specific fields in a profile. To update profile information, the `DbProfileProvider` actually removes the entire record that stores profile information for a user and adds a new record to the database. It performs this activity in the scope of a `DbTransaction` to ensure that either both actions succeed or that neither does. This could be less than optimal if there is a lot of profile information and only one bit of information needs to be updated.

I am not implying that the `DbProfileProvider` is ineffective. I think it is a very good provider and serves its purpose very well. There aren't many other ways to create a provider so that it doesn't require knowledge about the type of data that it is storing.

However, in *your* enterprise applications, you may know what type of profile information needs to be stored. There may not be the same requirement for the ProfileProvider to be so generic with respect to the type of data. Additionally, you may need to be able to query, update, and run reports against some of this profile information. If this requirement exists, then a custom ProfileProvider may be your answer. You can create a ProfileProvider that knows how to store the specific data that makes up the profile. The following steps show how I created just such a provider named `PortalProfileProvider`, for an enterprise portal site.

Creating the Data Access Logic Component

First, I needed to represent the data that I want to use to represent the profiles for users of the enterprise portal. Because the data will not be stored as binary in the database but will be broken down into its pertinent fields, it is not necessary to make the representation of the profile serializable. Furthermore, since the data will be stored as separate fields and not one big chunk, there is no size constraint for the amount of data the profile can contain. Therefore, I can pretty much use whatever mechanism makes sense to me to represent the profile information; there are very few constraints.

I've represented the `PortalProfile` information as a typed DataSet. For this example, the profile will contain information about the different URLs in which a user is interested. It's a pretty simple representation, but it does not need to be. Your profile can be much more complex if need be. Figure 7.16 shows the typed DataSet as it appears in the Visual Studio XSD Editor.

I've also created a table in the Portal database to contain this information and related it to the Users data table. The table is normalized so that there is a field for every item shown in the DataSet in Figure 7.16. I then created two stored procedures: one to insert and update records in the table and the other to retrieve the profile records given a user name.

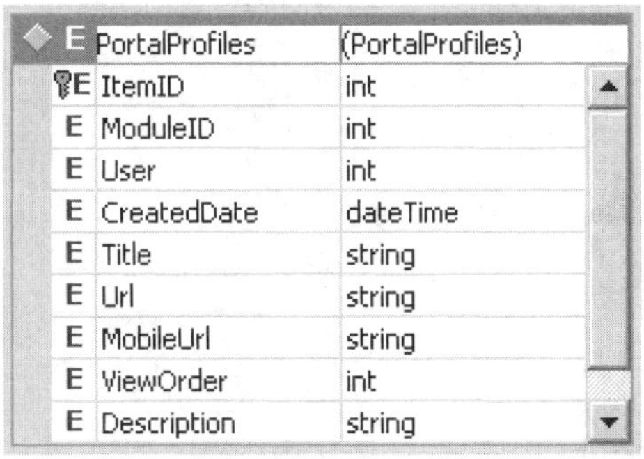

E	PortalProfiles	(PortalProfiles)
E	ItemID	int
E	ModuleID	int
E	User	int
E	CreatedDate	dateTime
E	Title	string
E	Url	string
E	MobileUrl	string
E	ViewOrder	int
E	Description	string

FIGURE 7.16: A PortalProfile Typed DataSet

Before I start the task of creating the ProfileProvider, I need to determine how I am going to retrieve the data from the database. I could have used the Data Access Application Block and hard-coded the ProfileProvider to map the fields in the DataSet to the parameters of the stored procedures. However, I created a Data Mapping Application Block (described in Chapter 9 and Appendix A) specifically to avoid hard-coding this type of "configuration data." Therefore, I have designed the `PortalProfileProvider` to leverage the Data Mapping Application Block instead of directly using the Data Access Application Block. If you're not a fan of the Data Mapping Application Block, you can use the Data Access Application Block instead and code the mapping of `SourceColumns` to stored procedure parameter names in the provider. Listing 7.9 shows the code for creating the `PortalProfileMapper`.

LISTING 7.9: `PortalProfileMapper`

```
[C#]
public class PortalProfileMapper : DataMapper
{
     protected override System.Data.DataSet DataSetType()
     {
          return new PortalProfile();
     }

     public PortalProfile GetProfile(string userName)
     {
          return (PortalProfile)base.GetObject(userName);
     }

     public void SetProfile(string userName, PortalProfile profile)
     {
          ListDictionary explicitParams = new ListDictionary();
          explicitParams.Add("@userName",userName);
          this.set_ExplicitParameters
               (profile.PortalProfiles.TableName,explicitParams);
          base.PutObject(profile);
     }
}

[Visual Basic]
Public Class PortalProfileMapper : Inherits DataMapper
     Protected Overrides Function DataSetType() As System.Data.DataSet
          Return New PortalProfile()
     End Function
```

```
        Public Function GetProfile(ByVal userName As String) _
                                 As PortalProfile
            Return CType(MyBase.GetObject(userName), PortalProfile)
        End Function

        Public Sub SetProfile(ByVal userName As String, _
                                 ByVal profile As PortalProfile)
            Dim explicitParams As ListDictionary = New ListDictionary()
            explicitParams.Add("@userName",userName)
            Me.set_ExplicitParameters _
                (profile.PortalProfiles.TableName,explicitParams)
            MyBase.PutObject(profile)
        End Sub
    End Class
```

Creating the `PortalProfileProvider`

Now that I have determined how to represent the Profile information and have confirmed that I can create, read, and update the information from the database, it is time to create the `PortalProfileProvider`. The `PortalProfileProvider` will use only the `PortalProfileMapper`.

Just like the other providers that have been created in this book, the first step is to create the runtime data class that will hold the configuration data needed. In this case, I just need to know which `DataSetMapping` will be used to map the `DataFields` to the stored procedure parameters. Therefore, the `PortalProfileProviderData` class contains a string that represents this `DataMapper`.

Once the data class has been created, the actual ProfileProvider can be created. The `GetProfile` and `SetProfile` methods will leverage the `PortalProfileMapper` to send and retrieve profile information to and from the database. Listing 7.10 shows the `SetProfile` and `GetProfile` methods. The full source code is on the book's Web site.

LISTING 7.10: `PortalProfileProvider`**'s** `SetProfile` **and** `GetProfile` **Methods**

```
[C#]
public void SetProfile(IIdentity identity, object profile)
{
     ArgumentValidation.CheckForNullReference(identity, "identity");
     ArgumentValidation.CheckForNullReference(profile, "profile");
     ArgumentValidation.CheckExpectedType
          (profile,typeof(PortalProfile));
```

```
        PortalProfile thisProfile = profile as PortalProfile;

        portalProfileMapper.SetProfile(identity.Name, thisProfile);

        SecurityProfileSaveEvent.Fire(identity.Name);
    }

    public object GetProfile(IIdentity identity)
    {
        ArgumentValidation.CheckForNullReference(identity, "identity");

        PortalProfile dsPortalProfile =
            portalProfileMapper.GetProfile(identity.Name);
        if (dsPortalProfile != null)
            ArgumentValidation.CheckExpectedType
            (dsPortalProfile,typeof(PortalProfile));

        PortalProfile profile = dsPortalProfile as PortalProfile;
        SecurityProfileLoadEvent.Fire(identity.Name);

        return profile;
    }

    [Visual Basic]
    Public Sub SetProfile(ByVal identity As IIdentity, _
                          ByVal profile As Object)
        ArgumentValidation.CheckForNullReference(identity, "identity")
        ArgumentValidation.CheckForNullReference(profile, "profile")
        ArgumentValidation.CheckExpectedType(profile, _
                GetType(PortalProfile))

        Dim thisProfile As PortalProfile = _
            IIf(TypeOf profile Is PortalProfile, _
            CType(profile, PortalProfile), _
            CType(Nothing, PortalProfile))

        portalProfileMapper.SetProfile(identity.Name, thisProfile)
        SecurityProfileSaveEvent.Fire(identity.Name)
    End Sub

    Public Function GetProfile(ByVal identity As IIdentity) As Object
        ArgumentValidation.CheckForNullReference(identity, "identity")

        Dim dsPortalProfile As PortalProfile = _
            portalProfileMapper.GetProfile(identity.Name)
        If Not dsPortalProfile Is Nothing Then
            ArgumentValidation.CheckExpectedType _
            (dsPortalProfile,GetType(PortalProfile))
        End If
```

```
        Dim profile As PortalProfile = _
            IIf(TypeOf dsPortalProfile Is PortalProfile, _
            CType(dsPortalProfile, PortalProfile), _
            CType(Nothing, PortalProfile))
        SecurityProfileLoadEvent.Fire(identity.Name)

        Return profile
    End Function
```

That's it for the runtime part of the provider. The provider can now be leveraged to store the data for a profile into the specific database fields that have been created to represent it. At this point, the configuration information in the Security Application Block would need to be manually modified to leverage this provider. The better alternative, however, is to configure this provider with the Enterprise Library Configuration Tool. Therefore, I derived the `PortalProfileProviderNode` from the `ProfileProviderNode` and added a property for the `DataMapper`. This property was created in such a way that it provides a list of the available `DataMappers` that exist in the application's configuration. For more details on how to accomplish this, read Chapter 2. The full source code for the `PortalProfileProvider` is on this book's Web site. Figure 7.17 shows how to configure the `PortalProfileProvider` by pointing it at the `DataMapper` shown in Listing 7.9.

Developing with the Security Application Block

The previous section covered the Security Application Block's various design features and how each of these features can be extended. Of all the application blocks, the Security Application Block probably has the most features that can be used in isolation of other features in a block. For example, using an AuthorizationProvider does not require that an AuthorizationProvider, RoleProvider, or ProfileProvider be used. Likewise, using any of the other providers does not require the AuthenticationProvider.

Using these providers is straightforward—that was the primary design goal for the Security Application Block. The previous section showed how the features of the Security Application Block work "under the covers" and how they have been designed for easy extension. This section details how

FIGURE 7.17: Configuring the PortalProfileProvider

to use those features by configuring and developing against the Security Application Block.

The Security Database Administration Console

The `DbAuthenticationProvider`, `DbRolesProvider`, and `DbProfileProvider` depend on the existence of the Security Application Block's Security Database. These providers aren't of much use if there is no data in the database for them to retrieve. The Security Database Administration Console is provided with Enterprise Library to facilitate the creation, modification, and removal of users and roles from the Security Database.

Sometimes you will need to modify the configuration of the Security Database Administration Console because it must use different databases, database servers, or hashing algorithms. For example, the default configuration for the Security Database Administration Console is to look for the Security Database on the local computer. However, this is typically not how it will be used in an enterprise environment. You can use the Enterprise Library Configuration Tool to configure the Security Database Administration Console just like any other application that uses Enterprise Library.

You modify the database information by changing the properties for the `DatabaseInstance` for which the relevant `DbAuthenticationProvider` is configured. Figure 7.18 shows how this `DbAuthenticationProvider`

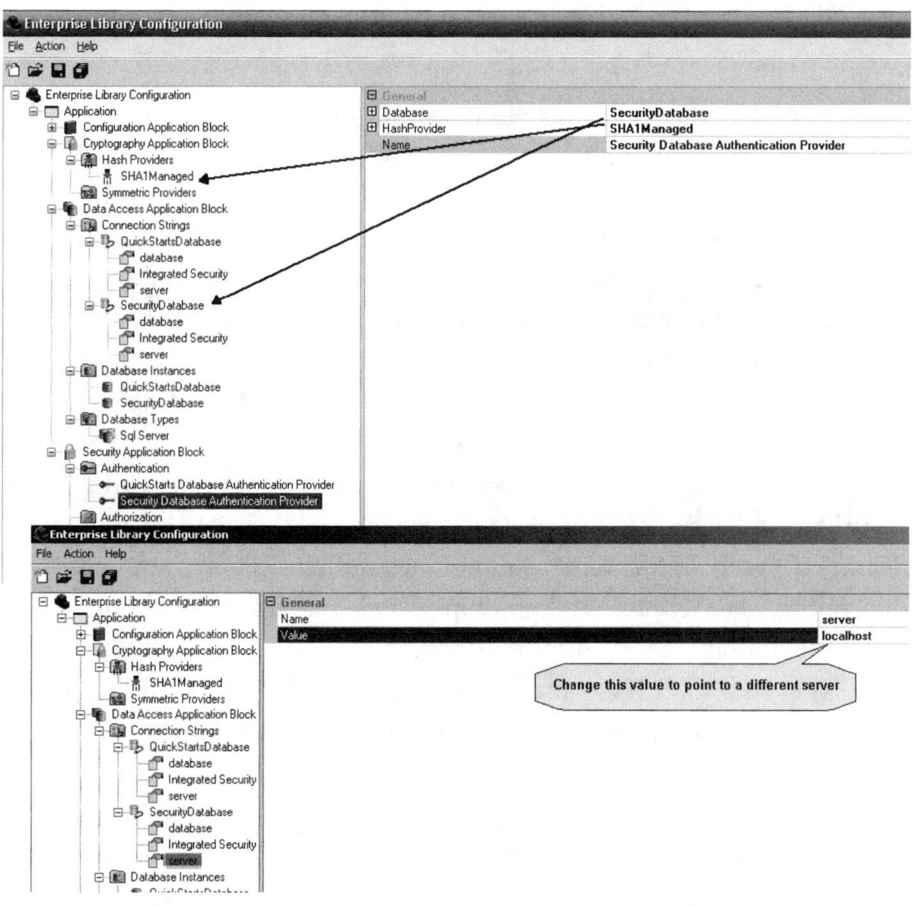

FIGURE 7.18: Configuration for the Security Database Administration Console

relates to a hash provider in the Cryptography Application Block and a `DatabaseInstance` in the Data Access Application Block. It also shows that changing the server for the database that is used for this provider equates to changing the value for the *server* parameter in the Data Access Application Block.

Note that Figure 7.18 does not contain any defined RoleProviders. Another important point about the Security Database Administration Console is that it assumes the Users and Roles tables will exist in the same database. Therefore, the tool uses the database connection information obtained from the `DatabaseInstance` defined for the AuthenticationProvider to get information about roles. Because both users and roles are assumed to be in the same database, the tool cannot be used to manage users in one database and roles in another. If this need exists in your organization, you will need to modify the tool (or create your own).

After the AuthenticationProvider for the Security Database Administration Console is pointing at the proper database, the tool can be used to manage users and roles in the Security Database. The first task when managing the users and roles is to select the AuthenticationProvider that will be used. The details for the AuthenticationProvider are core to the way this tool will store information about the users. Not only is its `DatabaseInstance` used to determine which database to use to store the user and role information, but its `HashProvider` is also used to hash the passwords for the users in the database. This is extremely important, because an application that uses the `DbAuthenticationProvider` configured for this same Security Database must also be configured to use the same hashing algorithm. Failure to do this will result in failed authentication for all users.

Adding, modifying, and removing roles and users is accomplished using the buttons at the bottom of the tool—New Role, Edit Role, Delete Role, New User, Edit User, and Delete User. Creating or modifying a user involves creating or modifying the password for that user, respectively. The arrow buttons in the middle of the tool are used to add users to and remove users from a role.

To add a user to a role, select the role from the *Roles* drop-down box, select the user to add in the list box on the right, and click the top button (<<<). To remove a user from a role, select the user in the list box on the left

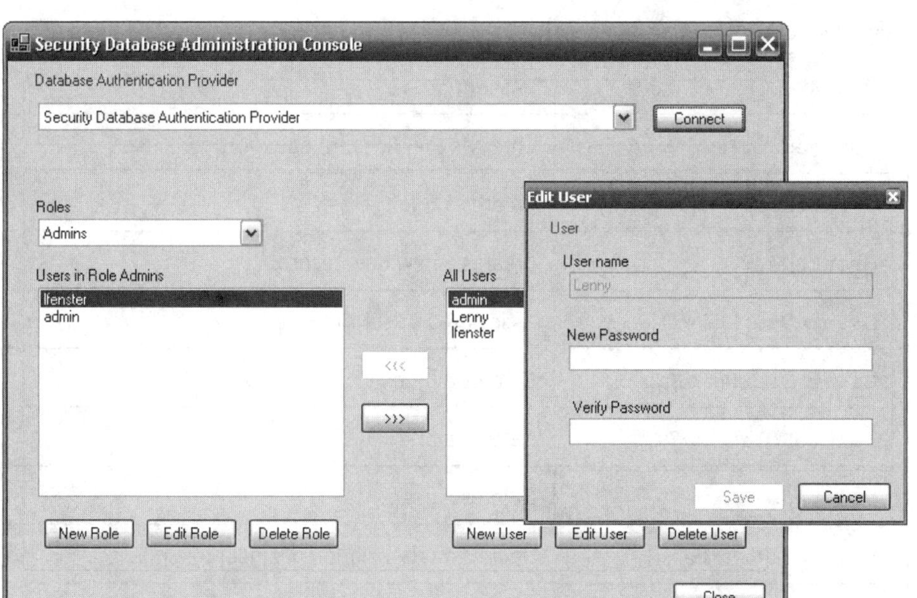

FIGURE 7.19: The Security Database Administration Console

and click the bottom button (>>>). Figure 7.19 shows this tool and how the password for a user can be modified using this tool.

The Security Database Administration Tool uses the `UserRoleManager` class to accomplish these administrative activities. Because of this, the `UserRoleManager` contains many administrative functions that parallel the features of the Security Database Administration Tool. Table 7.4 lists these methods.

This class is available to applications outside of the Security Database Administration Tool. It is a public class that ships with the Security Application Block and can be used in any application to perform the same type of administrative functionality. However, unlike most of the other classes that are covered in this book, this class does *not* subscribe to the Provider pattern. If this class is used in an application, that application will be coupled to the Security Database schema in the same way that the Security Database Administration Tool is. Therefore, a best practice for using this

TABLE 7.4: `UserRoleManager` **Methods**

Method	Description
`ChangeUserPassword`	Changes the (hashed) password for a user.
`CreateRole`	Creates a role.
`CreateUser`	Creates a new user record.
`CreateUserRole`	Associates a user to a role.
`CreateUserRoleBatch`	Creates a batch of user roles.
`DeleteRole`	Deletes a role.
`DeleteUser`	Deletes a user.
`DeleteUserRole`	Deletes an association of a user to a role.
`DeleteUserRoleBatch`	Deletes a batch of user roles.
`GetAllRoles`	Gets all roles.
`GetAllUsers`	Gets a list of users.
`GetPassword`	Gets the (hashed) password for a user.
`GetRoleIdFromRoleName`	Gets the role ID from a role's name.
`GetRoleUsers`	Gets the users associated with a role.
`GetUserIdFromUserName`	Gets a user's ID from the user name.
`GetUserRoles`	Gets all roles.
`RenameRole`	Renames a role.
`UserExists`	Checks to see if a user exists.

class is to create a façade that hides its specific use. In this way, if this `UserRoleManager` must be replaced by a different class, only the code in the façade needs to change. For example, in a portal application that includes administrative functions for adding users, roles, and so on, such a class might begin like the code shown in Listing 7.11.

LISTING 7.11: Sample Code for Creating a Façade Around the UserRoleManager class

```
[C#]
public class PortalSecurity
{

     private static UserRoleManager GetUserRoleManager
     {
          get
          {
               return new UserRoleManager("Portal",
                    ConfigurationManager.GetCurrentContext());
          }
     }

     public static bool UserExists(string strUserName)
     {
          return GetUserRoleManager.UserExists(strUserName);
     }

     public static DataSet GetUsers()
     {
          UserRoleManager mgrUserRoles = GetUserRoleManager;
          return mgrUserRoles.GetAllUsers();
     }

     public static DataSet GetUsers(string strRoleName)
     {
          UserRoleManager mgrUserRoles = GetUserRoleManager;
          return mgrUserRoles.GetRoleUsers(strRoleName);
     }
...

[Visual Basic]
Public Class PortalSecurity

     Private Shared ReadOnly Property GetUserRoleManager() _
                         As UserRoleManager
          Get
               Return New UserRoleManager("Portal", _
                    ConfigurationManager.GetCurrentContext())
          End Get
     End Property

     Public Shared Function UserExists(ByVal strUserName As String) _
                         As Boolean
          Return GetUserRoleManager.UserExists(strUserName)
     End Function

     Public Shared Function GetUsers() As DataSet
```

```
            Dim mgrUserRoles As UserRoleManager = GetUserRoleManager
            Return mgrUserRoles.GetAllUsers()
        End Function

        Public Shared Function GetUsers(ByVal strRoleName As String) _
                                    As DataSet
            Dim mgrUserRoles As UserRoleManager = GetUserRoleManager
            Return mgrUserRoles.GetRoleUsers(strRoleName)
        End Function
    ...
```

Authentication

Configuring an AuthenticationProvider starts with right-clicking on the *Authentication* node, selecting *New*, and then selecting the Authentication-Provider. As illustrated in Figure 7.20, Enterprise Library ships with the Custom AuthenticationProvider and Database AuthenticationProvider. (You'll also see that the custom Active Directory AuthenticationProvider created earlier in this chapter also exists in Figure 7.20; I deployed this provider to the same directory as the Configuration Tool when I created it.)

Figure 7.18 illustrated how the properties for a `DbAuthentication-Provider` relate back to settings in the Data Access Application Block and

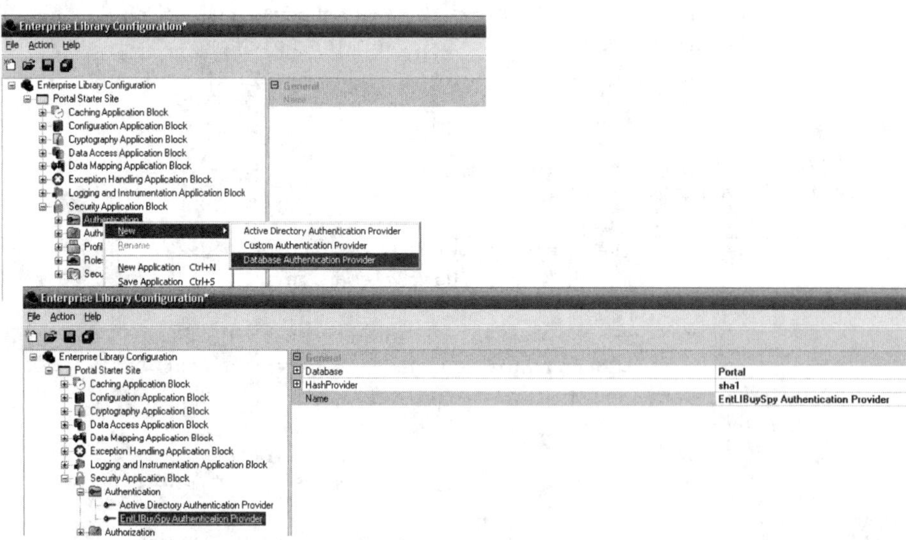

FIGURE 7.20: Configuring a Database AuthenticationProvider

the Cryptography Application Block. The Data Access Application Block and Cryptography Application Block should be added to the configuration prior to configuring the Database AuthenticationProvider. A `DatabaseInstance` should be configured in the Data Access Application Block for the database where the user information will be kept. Often this will be the Security Database; however, in Figure 7.20 the Portal database was used.

To accomplish this, the SQL script that creates the Security Database was simply modified to point to the Portal database so that the user and role information can be kept with the other application data for this Portal application. A HashProvider was also added and configured in the Cryptography Application Block so the Database AuthenticationProvider can compare password hashes when authenticating a user. (For more information about creating and configuring `DatabaseInstances` and HashProviders, see Chapters 1 and 8, respectively.)

Configuring any of the custom providers consists of selecting the type of provider for the `TypeName` property and adding any necessary items to the `Extensions` dictionary property. For example, if a custom AuthenticationProvider existed that needed information like an `AccountName` to authenticate a user, that information would have to be added to the `Extensions Dictionary` and referenced from that same dictionary in the provider implementation. Figure 7.21 shows how to add configuration data to the *Extensions* property for a custom AuthenticationProvider.

The first step to authenticating an entity with the Security Application Block involves using the `AuthenticationFactory` to create an AuthenticationProvider. There are two ways to retrieve an AuthenticationProvider: retrieve the default AuthenticationProvider or retrieve one by name.

To retrieve the default AuthenticationProvider, call the `AuthenticationFactory`'s static `GetAuthenticationProvider` method with no arguments. To retrieve a specific AuthenticationProvider, the name of the provider must be supplied to the `GetAuthenticationProvider` method. Using the same methods for an instance of the `AuthenticationProviderFactory` is an alternative to the static methods of the `AuthenticationFactory`, since the `AuthenticationFactory` just passes through to an instance of the `AuthenticationProviderFactory`.

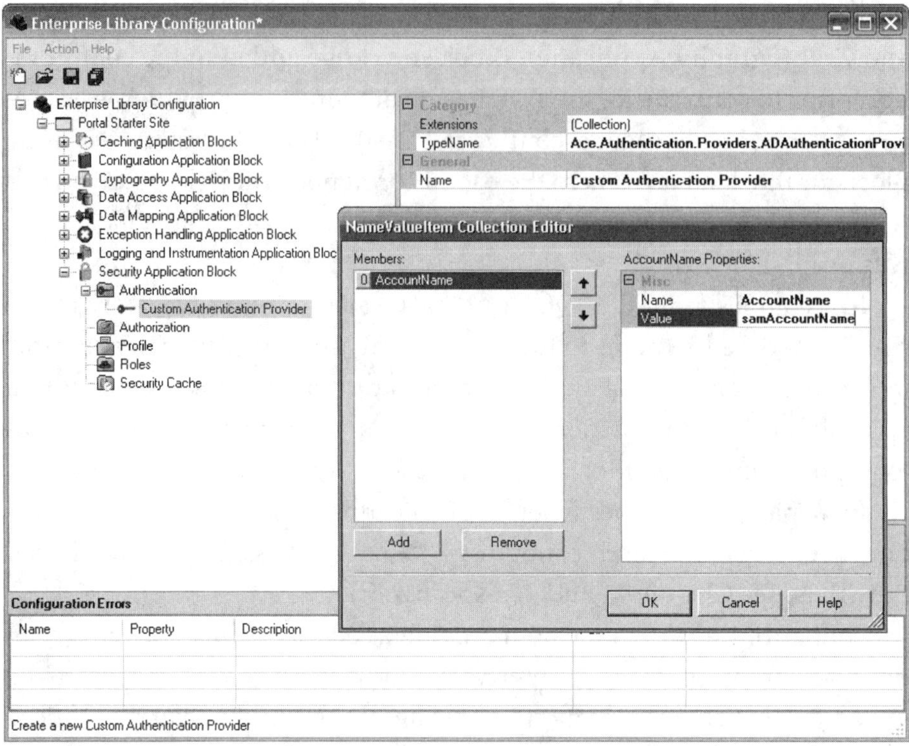

FIGURE 7.21: Configuring a Custom AuthenticationProvider

Once an AuthenticationProvider has been obtained, the only method that needs to be called to accomplish authentication is `Authenticate`. `Authenticate` accepts two parameters: the first one is an object like `NamePasswordCredential` that contains the information the provider needs to authenticate the user. Note that it accepts an `object` and not a specific type of credential. This was intentional. The type of credential that is used is an unenforced part of the AuthenticationProvider's contract. It was made an `object` to support other types of credentials, but the cost of this is a weaker interface that won't guarantee portability. The second parameter, an `out` parameter, is used to obtain the `Identity` for the user when the `Authenticate` method succeeds. Listing 7.12 populates the `NamePasswordCredential` class that is included as part of the Security Application Block with the name and password for a user who has logged onto the Portal site and then passes this to the `Authenticate` method of the default AuthenticationProvider.

LISTING 7.12: Using the `Authenticate` Method

```
[C#]
public static bool Authenticate(
                    string username,
                    string password,
                    out IIdentity identity)
{
     bool result = false;
     byte[] passwordByteArray =
               System.Text.ASCIIEncoding.ASCII.GetBytes(password);
     NamePasswordCredential credentials =
               new NamePasswordCredential(username, passwordByteArray);
     IAuthenticationProvider authProvider =
               AuthenticationFactory.GetAuthenticationProvider();

     result = authProvider.Authenticate(credentials, out identity);
     return result;
}

[Visual Basic]
Public Shared Function Authenticate( _
                         ByVal username As String, _
                         ByVal password As String, _
                         <System.Runtime.InteropServices.Out()> _
                         ByRef identity As IIdentity) As Boolean
     Dim result As Boolean = False
     Dim passwordByteArray As Byte() = _
          System.Text.ASCIIEncoding.ASCII.GetBytes(password)
     Dim credentials As NamePasswordCredential = _
          New NamePasswordCredential(username, passwordByteArray)
     Dim authProvider As IAuthenticationProvider = _
          AuthenticationFactory.GetAuthenticationProvider()

     result = authProvider.Authenticate(credentials, identity)
     Return result
End Function
```

The Security Cache

Once an entity has been authenticated, its `Identity`, `Profile`, and `Principal` can be cached so the application does not need to go back to the authentication store for every authentication request. The Security Application Block supplies an interface for caching security information and a provider, the `CachingStoreProvider` (refer back to Figure 7.5), which implements this interface by leveraging the Caching Application Block for its cache. To use this provider, you must first configure the Caching Application Block for an application. Figure 7.22 shows a CachingStoreProvider that has been added as a Security Cache to the configuration for the Portal site, and its cache has been set equal to the CredentialCache, which was already created in the Caching Application Block's configuration.

A token (typically a `Guid)` is returned when an Identity, Principal, or Profile are saved in the Security Cache. The token is the key for the items in the cache and can be used to keep an entity's identity, principal, and profile information together. The `ISecurityCacheProvider` interface provides methods that make it straightforward to save, retrieve, and remove Identities, Principals, and Profiles from the cache.

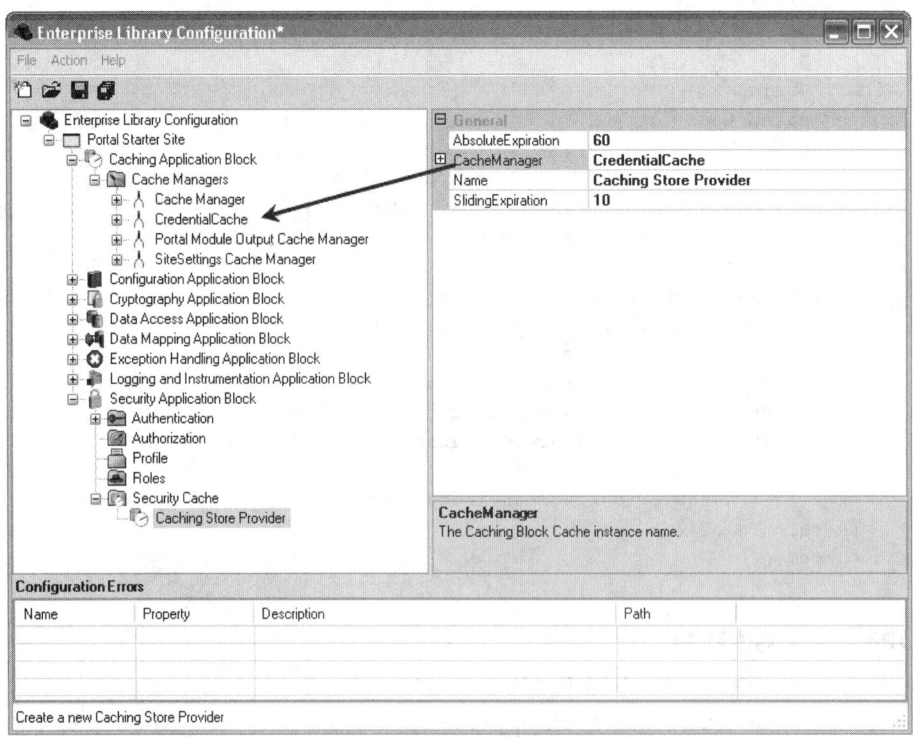

FIGURE 7.22: Configuring the Security Cache

The `SaveIdentity` Method

The `SaveIdentity` method allows the `IIdentity` for an authenticated user to be saved to the Security Cache and represented by a temporary security token. The SecurityCacheProvider that Enterprise Library ships with the `CachingStoreProvider` represents the token as a `Guid`; however, a custom SecurityCacheProvider can return tokens that are not `Guids`. Storing an `IIdentity` in cache involves obtaining the SecurityCache-Provider and calling its `SaveIdentity` method. Listing 7.13 shows this.

LISTING 7.13: Calling `SecurityCacheProvider.SaveIdentity`

```
[C#]
ISecurityCacheProvider securityCache =
          SecurityCacheFactory.GetSecurityCacheProvider();
this.token = securityCache.SaveIdentity(this.identity);

[Visual Basic]
Dim securityCache As ISecurityCacheProvider = _
          SecurityCacheFactory.GetSecurityCacheProvider()
Me.token = securityCache.SaveIdentity(Me.identity)
```

When no token is supplied to the `SaveIdentity` method, the Security-CacheProvider must create a token. Alternatively, a token can be supplied with the `Identity` when it is being saved, as shown in Listing 7.14.

LISTING 7.14: Supplying a Token with the `SaveIdentity` Method

```
[C#]
ISecurityCacheProvider securityCache =
          SecurityCacheFactory.GetSecurityCacheProvider();
this.token = Guid.NewGuid();
securityCache.SaveIdentity(this.identity, this.token);

[Visual Basic]
Dim securityCache As ISecurityCacheProvider = _
          SecurityCacheFactory.GetSecurityCacheProvider()
Me.token = Guid.NewGuid()
securityCache.SaveIdentity(Me.identity, Me.token)
```

The `GetIdentity` Method

Once an identity has been stored in the Security Cache, the token that represents that user can be employed for any future authentication requests instead of requiring the authentication against the user store every time. The `IIdentity` can be retrieved by calling `GetIdentity` on the SecurityCacheProvider. You can use the `IIdentity`'s `IsAuthenticated` property to determine whether the user has been authenticated. Listing 7.15 shows how to call the `GetIdentity` method.

LISTING 7.15: Calling `SecurityCacheProvider.GetIdentity`

```
[C#]
ISecurityCacheProvider securityCache =
        SecurityCacheFactory.GetSecurityCacheProvider();
IIdentity userIdentity = securityCache.GetIdentity(this.token);
If (userIdentity != null)
        bool bIsAuthenticated = userIdentity.IsAuthenticated;

[Visual Basic]
Dim securityCache As ISecurityCacheProvider = _
        SecurityCacheFactory.GetSecurityCacheProvider()
Dim userIdentity As IIdentity = securityCache.GetIdentity(Me.token)
If (Not userIdentity Is Nothing)
        Dim bIsAuthenticated As Boolean = userIdentity.IsAuthenticated
```

The `ExpireIdentity` Method

Under normal conditions, the items (`Identity` in this case) in the cache will expire according to the sliding time or absolute time expirations that are set. Figure 7.22 shows an absolute expiration of 60 minutes and a sliding time expiration of 10 minutes. In this example, if the identity is not explicitly expired from the cache, it will be expired after 60 minutes or if there is no activity for 10 minutes. However, in cases where a user logs off from a site or exits the application, it is probable that the identity should be explicitly expired from the cache. In such a case, the `ExpireIdentity` can be called with the token that represents the user to expire from the Security Cache. Listing 7.16 shows how to call the `ExpireIdentity` method.

LISTING 7.16: Calling `SecurityCacheProvider.ExpireIdentity`

```
[C#]
ISecurityCacheProvider securityCache =
        SecurityCacheFactory.GetSecurityCacheProvider();
securityCache.ExpireIdentity(this.token);
```

```
[Visual Basic]
Dim securityCache As ISecurityCacheProvider = _
          SecurityCacheFactory.GetSecurityCacheProvider()
securityCache.ExpireIdentity(Me.token)
```

The `SavePrincipal` Method

The `SavePrincipal` method is similar to the `SaveIdentity` method except that it allows the user's `IPrincipal` to be stored instead of the `IIdentity`. If the token from a previous `SaveIdentity` method is also passed to the `SavePrincipal` method, the `CachingStoreProvider` will keep the Identity and the Principal together as one item. Listing 7.17 gets a user's Principal from a RolesProvider (via the `PortalSecurity` façade) and saves it in the Security Cache.

Listing 7.17: Calling `SecurityCacheProvider.SavePrincipal`

```
[C#]
IPrincipal principal =
PortalSecurity.GetPrincipal(User.Identity.Name);
token = securityCache.SavePrincipal(principal);

[Visual Basic]
Dim principal As IPrincipal = _
          PortalSecurity.GetPrincipal(User.Identity.Name)
token = securityCache.SavePrincipal(principal)
```

The `GetPrincipal` Method

The `GetPrincipal` method is similar to the `GetIdentity` method except that it returns an `IPrincipal` instead of an `IIdentity`. The code in Listing 7.18 sets the `IPrincipal` for the current user on a portal site from the Security Cache.

Listing 7.18: Calling `SecurityCacheProvider.GetPrincipal`

```
[C#]
Context.User = securityCache.GetPrincipal(token);

[Visual Basic]
Context.User = securityCache.GetPrincipal(token)
```

The `ExpirePrincipal` Method

Expiring a Principal from the Security Cache can be useful for all the same reasons that expiring an `Identity` makes sense. You can use the `ExpirePrincipal` method to remove a Principal from the Security Cache. Listing 7.19 shows how to expire a Principal from the cache.

LISTING 7.19: Calling `SecurityCacheProvider.ExpirePrincipal`

```
[C#]
securityCache.ExpirePrincipal(token);

[Visual Basic]
securityCache.ExpirePrincipal(token)
```

The `SaveProfile` Method

You can use the `SaveProfile` method to store profile information in the cache. It can be stored by itself, or a previously acquired token from a `SaveIdentity` or `SavePrincipal` call can be used to keep the Profile information with the Identity or Principal. The `SaveProfile` method expects a serializable object as the Profile information.

Listing 7.20 expands on the code for the `SavePrincipal` method in Listing 7.17 by saving the Profile information with the Principal in the Security Cache. The Profile information is retrieved from a ProfileProvider (via the `PortalSecurity` façade) and passed to the CachingStoreProvider using the token from the `SavePrincipal` call.

LISTING 7.20: Calling `SecurityCacheProvider.SaveProfile`

```
[C#]
IPrincipal principal = PortalSecurity.GetPrincipal(User.Identity.Name);
token = securityCache.SavePrincipal(principal);
PortalProfile profile = PortalSecurity.Profile;
securityCache.SaveProfile(profile,token);

[Visual Basic]
Dim principal As IPrincipal = _
          PortalSecurity.GetPrincipal(User.Identity.Name)
token = securityCache.SavePrincipal(principal)
Dim profile As PortalProfile = PortalSecurity.Profile
securityCache.SaveProfile(profile,token)
```

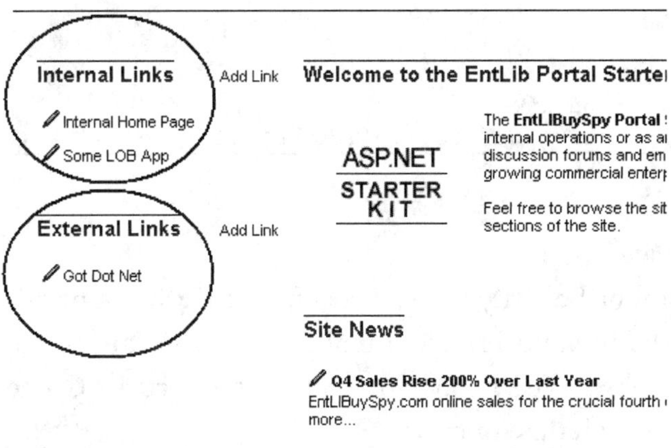

FIGURE 7.23: Using Profiles to Personalize a Portal Site

For this to be successful, the `PortalProfile` object must be serializable. In Listing 7.10, I created a `PortalProfile` object that was represented as a typed DataSet. This works because DataSets are serializable. An example of some profile information may be maintaining separate sets of favorite hyperlinks for internal sites and external sites in an enterprise portal application, like that shown in Figure 7.23.

The `GetProfile` Method

The `GetProfile` method is most beneficial because you can get a significant improvement in performance when obtaining an object from cache instead of accessing and deserializing an object from a database. The `GetProfile` method uses the token for which the Profile was saved to retrieve it from the Security Cache. Listing 7.21 gets the Profile from the Security Cache and sets it as the Profile for the current user.

Listing 7.21: Getting the Profile from Cache

```
[C#]
Context.Items["profile"] =
     (PortalProfile)securityCache.GetProfile(token);

[Visual Basic]
Private Context.Items("profile") =
     CType(securityCache.GetProfile(token), PortalProfile)
```

The `ExpireProfile` Method

Removing a Profile from the Security Cache is useful for all the same reasons that expiring an Identity and Principal make sense. You can use the `ExpireProfile` method to remove a `Profile` object from the Security Cache. Listing 7.22 shows how to call this function.

Listing 7.22: Removing a Profile from Cache

```
[C#]
securityCache.ExpireProfile(token);

[Visual Basic]
securityCache.ExpireProfile(token)
```

Authorization

To configure an AuthorizationProvider, right-click on the *Authorization* node, select *New*, and then select an AuthorizationProvider. Enterprise Library ships with three AuthorizationProviders: AuthorizationRuleProvider, AzManProvider (the Authorization Manager Provider), and a custom AuthorizationProvider. You may not see the AzManProvider show up on your installation. This is because it is not a certainty that every desktop will be running Authorization Manager. If you are running Authorization Manager and want to use the AzManProvider, you will need to complete a few tasks.

1. Build the AzMan runtime and design-time projects that are found under the source for the Security Application Block solution.
2. Deploy the resulting assemblies to a location where the Enterprise Library Configuration Tool can locate them.

3. Deploy the interop assembly to this location, because the AzManProvider depends on the interop assembly to leverage the Authorization Manager COM-based API.

Each AuthorizationProvider has a unique set of properties that are specific to the needs of that provider. The AzManProvider's properties, as illustrated earlier in the chapter, indicate where the authorization store is located, what the name of the application is in the store, an AuditIdentifierPrefix to use when making authorization requests, and the scope, if any, in the application to narrow down the authorization request. Figure 7.24 shows how to configure the AzManProvider.

Configuring the AuthorizationRuleProvider, however, is much different. The AuthorizationRuleProvider maintains the information about its authorization rules with the rest of the configuration data for the Security Application Block. You can add authorization rules to use with this provider by right-clicking on the *AuthorizationRulesProvider* node and selecting *New Rule*. The name for a rule is kept in the `Name` property, and this is the value that is passed to the `Authorize` method when referring to the rule in code.

Enterprise Library has a Rule Expression Editor to facilitate creating and maintaining rule expressions. It includes buttons that will automatically insert the corresponding token and a feature to test roles and identities against the configured rule expression. This is especially helpful for complex rules to ensure that the expression has been specified correctly. In Figure 7.25, the Rule Expression Editor has been configured for the rule expression example used in the first part of this chapter (i.e., `I:Joe OR (R:Admins AND (NOT R:Managers) AND (NOT I:Sally))`) and tested with an authenticated user with an identity of Sally that exists in the

General	
Name	AzMan Provider
Misc	
Application	Portal Starter Site
AuditIdentifierPrefix	pssAuditId-
Scope	
StoreLocation	msxml://c:/Inetpub/wwwroot/PortalStarterSite/authstore.xml

FIGURE 7.24: Properties for Configuring the AzManProvider

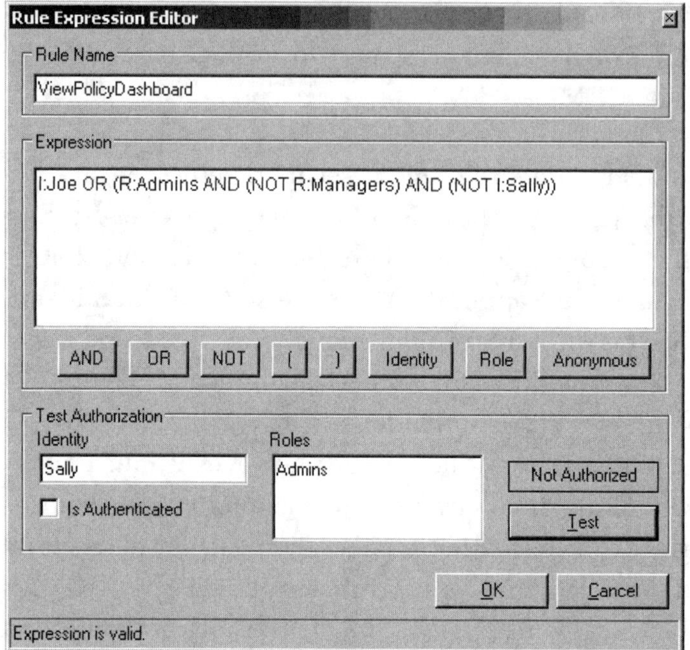

FIGURE 7.25: The Rule Expression Editor

Admins role. As expected, this user would not be authorized against this rule because of the last part of the expression: `(NOT I:Sally)`. If a syntax problem existed with the rule expression, an error message would be displayed instead.

Configuring the custom AuthorizationProvider is just like configuring a custom AuthenticationProvider except that the `TypeName` property must be of a class that implements the `IAuthorizationProvider` interface.

The `Authorize` Method

The complexities of adding and modifying the relationships between users, roles, and rules to determine permission for tasks and operations is best left to the administrators of an application. The details that need to be agreed upon, however, are the names for the rules that will be created. There is only one method, `Authorize`, which is used to determine authorization for a specific operation or task. `Authorize` accepts two parameters: the Principal of the entity for which permission is being ascertained and the name of the rule that signifies the operation in question.

Listing 7.23 passes the Principal for a user of the portal site and a name of a rule to the default AuthorizationProvider's `Authorize` method to determine if the user is authorized to execute the operation in question.

LISTING 7.23: Calling the `Authorize` Method

```
[C#]
bool bAuthorized = false;
IAuthorizationProvider authProvider =
     AuthorizationFactory.GetAuthorizationProvider();
bAuthorized = authProvider.Authorize(HttpContext.Current.User,rule);
if (!bAuthorized)
     LogEntries.Log(LogEntries.FailedAuthorization,rule);
return bAuthorized;


[Visual Basic]
Dim bAuthorized As Boolean = False
Dim authProvider As IAuthorizationProvider = _
     AuthorizationFactory.GetAuthorizationProvider()
bAuthorized = authProvider.Authorize(HttpContext.Current.User,rule)
If (Not bAuthorized) Then
     LogEntries.Log(LogEntries.FailedAuthorization,rule)
End If
Return bAuthorized
```

Configuring and Using RolesProviders

Before an authorization request can be made for a particular operation or task, the user's Principal first needs to be obtained. It is this Principal that gets passed with the name of the rule to an AuthorizationProvider's `Authorize` method. The `RolesFactory`, `RolesProviderFactory`, and RolesProviders exist so that an application can be abstracted away from the location for the roles. Two RolesProviders are supplied with Enterprise Library: the DatabaseRolesProvider and the ActiveDirectoryRolesProvider.

Configuring the DatabaseRolesProvider is similar to configuring the DatabaseAuthenticationProvider. Before a DatabaseRolesProvider can be properly configured, a `DatabaseInstance` must exist that is configured to point to the database where the role information is kept. Typically this will be the Security Database that comes with Enterprise Library or a database that was modified by running the Security Database script. Once the database information has been configured in the Data Access Application Block, the DatabaseRolesProvider can be added and configured to point to this `DatabaseInstance`. Figure 7.26 illustrates a DatabaseRolesProvider that has been configured to leverage the Portal database instance.

The ActiveDirectoryRolesProvider has no such dependency. When configuring the ActiveDirectoryRolesProvider, the provider needs information to allow it to properly access Active Directory to obtain the roles. This includes the name of the server hosting the Active Directory Service (*Server*), the provider type name for Active Directory (*ProviderType*), the partition in the Active Directory that contains the user objects/data (*UserPartition*), and the name of the field in the schema to use to find the current account name (*AccountName*).

In the sample configuration shown in Figure 7.27, the ActiveDirectoryRolesProvider will bind to Active Directory with *LDAP://MyServer:389/*

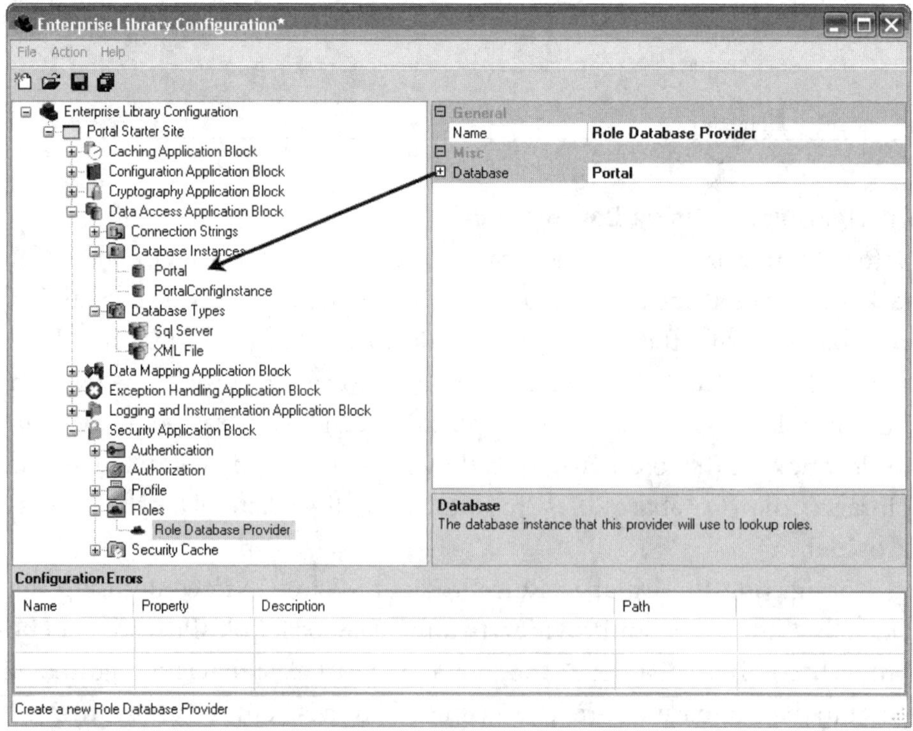

FIGURE 7.26: Configuring the DatabaseRolesProvider

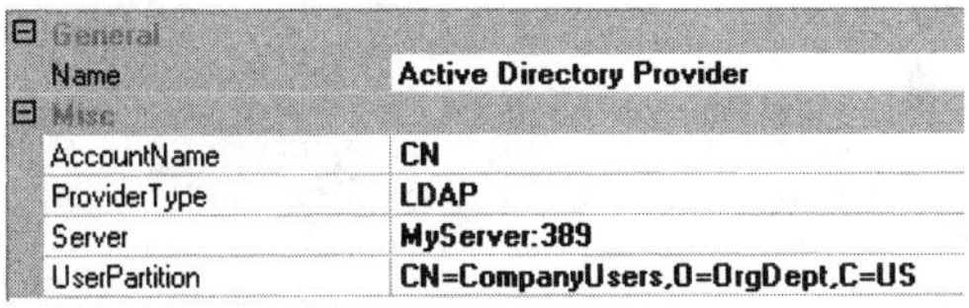

General	
Name	Active Directory Provider
Misc	
AccountName	CN
ProviderType	LDAP
Server	MyServer:389
UserPartition	CN=CompanyUsers,O=OrgDept,C=US

FIGURE 7.27: Properties for the ActiveDirectoryRolesProvider

CN=CompanyUsers,O=OrgDept,C=US and search for the entry where *CN=*<name of Identity>. The `AdRolesProvider` then uses the names of the groups to which the user belongs as the list of roles to populate in the Principal before it returns.

The `GetRoles` Method

The design goals of simplicity and flexibility are accomplished by way of the single method for any RolesProvider: `GetRoles`. A class that implements the `IRolesProvider` interface can be obtained by using either the `RolesProviderFactory` class directly or the wrapper `RolesFactory` class. Both classes allow for the default RolesProvider or a named RolesProvider to be obtained via the `GetRolesProvider` method. Once a RoleProvider is obtained, acquiring the Principal for a user is a matter of calling the `GetRoles` method with that user's `IIdentity`. Typically, the Identity will be the same one that was retrieved from an AuthenticationProvider's `Authenticate` method. The code sample in Listing 7.24 gets the Principal for a user from his or her identity.

LISTING 7.24: Obtaining Roles for a User

```
[C#]
public static IPrincipal GetPrincipal(IIdentity identity)
{
    IRolesProvider rolesProvider =
        RolesFactory.GetRolesProvider();
    IPrincipal principal =
        rolesProvider.GetRoles(new GenericIdentity(identity));
    return principal;
}

[Visual Basic]
Public Shared Function GetPrincipal(ByVal identity As IIdentity) _
```

```
        As IPrincipal
Dim rolesProvider As IRolesProvider = RolesFactory.GetRolesProvider()
Dim principal As IPrincipal = _
        rolesProvider.GetRoles(New GenericIdentity(identity))
    Return principal
End Function
```

Configuring and Using the ProfileProviders

You have already seen much of the Security Application Block's profile management capabilities in the `GetProfile`, `SaveProfile`, and `ExpireProfile` methods for the Security Cache. Before profiles can be saved in the Security Cache, though, a profile needs to be retrieved from its permanent storage facility.

The purpose of the `ProfileProviderFactory`, `ProfileFactory`, and ProfileProvider is to abstract an application away from needing to know where the profile data is kept for an application. Enterprise Library ships with the DatabaseProfileProvider, which serializes the profile data to store it in the Security Database and deserializes it when retrieving it from the Security Database.

You configure the DatabaseProfileProvider the same way as configuring the DatabaseRolesProvider and the DatabaseAuthenticationProvider. This involves configuring a `DatabaseInstance` in the Data Access Application Block so that it points to the database where the Profile information will be kept. Then the DatabaseProfilesProvider can be added and configured to point to this `DatabaseInstance`. Figure 7.28 illustrates a DatabaseProfilesProvider that has been configured to leverage the Portal database instance.

Creating a `Profile` Object

It is important to ensure that the class that is responsible for maintaining the Profile information is serializable. The DatabaseProfileProvider serializes the `Profile` object to binary before storing it as a Binary Large Object (BLOb) in the database. This brings up another important point to consider. By default, the field that stores the Profile information in the Security Database can hold a maximum of 4MB of data. This should be considered when

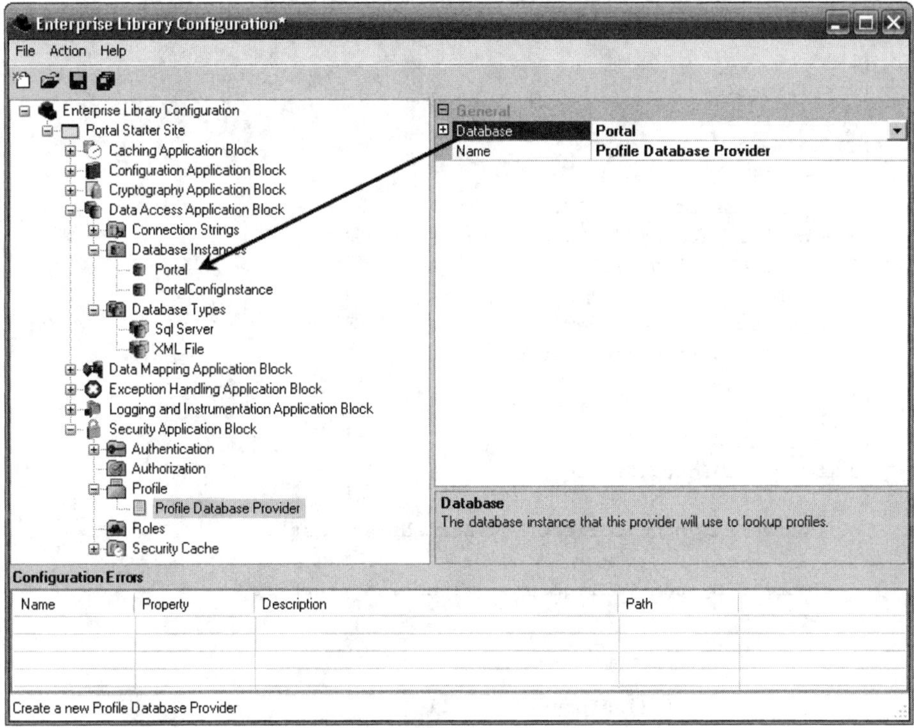

FIGURE 7.28: Configuring the DatabaseProfileProvider

designing the class that will hold the Profile information so that it doesn't store too much data.

Because of this size limitation, I have created an alternate way to represent the `PortalProfile` information shown earlier in this chapter. Although `DataSets` are serializable, they also take up a lot of space when they are serialized. Therefore, I've created a `PortalProfile` class that is serializable and that maintains a list of serializable objects that contain information about hyperlinks in which the user is interested. By maintaining a list of lists, the user can have multiple lists for different types of hyperlinks and can store more data before reaching the size limitation. Listing 7.25 shows this `PortalProfile` class.

LISTING 7.25: `PortalProfile` **Class**

```
[C#]
[Serializable]
public class Link
{
     public int itemId;
     public string userId;
     public DateTime createdDate;
     public string title;
     public string url;
     public int viewOrder;
     public string description;
}

[Serializable]
public class PortalProfile
{
     private System.Collections.SortedList listLinks;

     public System.Collections.SortedList LinkList
     {
          get
          {
               if (listLinks == null)
                    listLinks = new SortedList();
               return listLinks;
          }
     }
}

[Visual Basic]
<Serializable> _
Public Class Link
     Public itemId As Integer
     Public userId As String
     Public createdDate As DateTime
     Public title As String
     Public url As String
     Public viewOrder As Integer
     Public description As String
End Class

<Serializable> _
Public Class PortalProfile
     Private listLinks As System.Collections.SortedList

     Public ReadOnly Property LinkList() _
               As System.Collections.SortedList
          Get
```

```
            If listLinks Is Nothing Then
                listLinks = New SortedList()
            End If
            Return listLinks
        End Get
    End Property
End Class
```

The `SetProfile` Method

After you create Profile information in an application, you can use the ProfileProvider's `SetProfile` method to store the Profile information in the backend store. The `SetProfile` method accepts two arguments: the identity of the user for which the Profile information should be associated and the actual Profile information. In Listing 7.26, the Profile information is being stored for the current user on the portal site.

LISTING 7.26: Storing Profiles for the Current User

```
[C#]
public static void SaveProfile(PortalProfile profile)
{
    IProfileProvider profileProvider =
        ProfileFactory.GetProfileProvider();
    profileProvider.SetProfile
        (HttpContext.Current.User.Identity,profile);
}

[Visual Basic]
Public Shared Sub SaveProfile(ByVal profile As PortalProfile)
    Dim profileProvider As IProfileProvider = _
        ProfileFactory.GetProfileProvider()
    profileProvider.SetProfile _
        (HttpContext.Current.User.Identity,profile)
End Sub
```

The `GetProfile` Method

Saving the Profile information isn't of much use if there is no way to retrieve it. The `GetProfile` method is the obvious counterpart to the `SetProfile` method and is used to obtain Profile information for a user as specified by an `IIdentity`. For the DatabaseProfileProvider, the Profile data is retrieved from the database where the name of the user is equal to the `Name` property for the `IIdentity` that is passed into this call, and the data is deserialized back to an object instance. Listing 7.27 calls the `GetProfile` method for the default ProfileProvider and casts it back to a `PortalProfile` object.

LISTING 7.27: Obtaining Profile information

```
[C#]
IProfileProvider profileProvider = ProfileFactory.GetProfileProvider();
PortalProfile retProfile =
      (PortalProfile)profileProvider.GetProfile
      (HttpContext.Current.User.Identity);


[Visual Basic]
Dim profileProvider As IProfileProvider = _
     ProfileFactory.GetProfileProvider()
Dim retProfile As PortalProfile = _
     CType(profileProvider.GetProfile _
     (HttpContext.Current.User.Identity), PortalProfile)
```

Defaults

Defaults can be set for all of the providers detailed in this chapter. These defaults will be used when a name is not provided in the call to get a specific provider. For example, in the `GetAuthenticationProvider()` call, the name of the AuthenticationProvider is not passed. In this case, the default AuthenticationProvider will be returned. The defaults for each of the security features can be configured in the Property pane of the main Security Application Block node. Figure 7.29 shows how the defaults can be set for each of the providers in the Security Application Block.

Summary

The Security Application Block has quite a few different providers. However, each of the providers has a distinct purpose, and developing an application to leverage any one of them is fairly straightforward. It is advantageous to leverage the providers together. For example, the `Identity` obtained from the AuthenticationProvider can easily serve as one of the arguments for obtaining Profile information. Likewise, the `Principal`

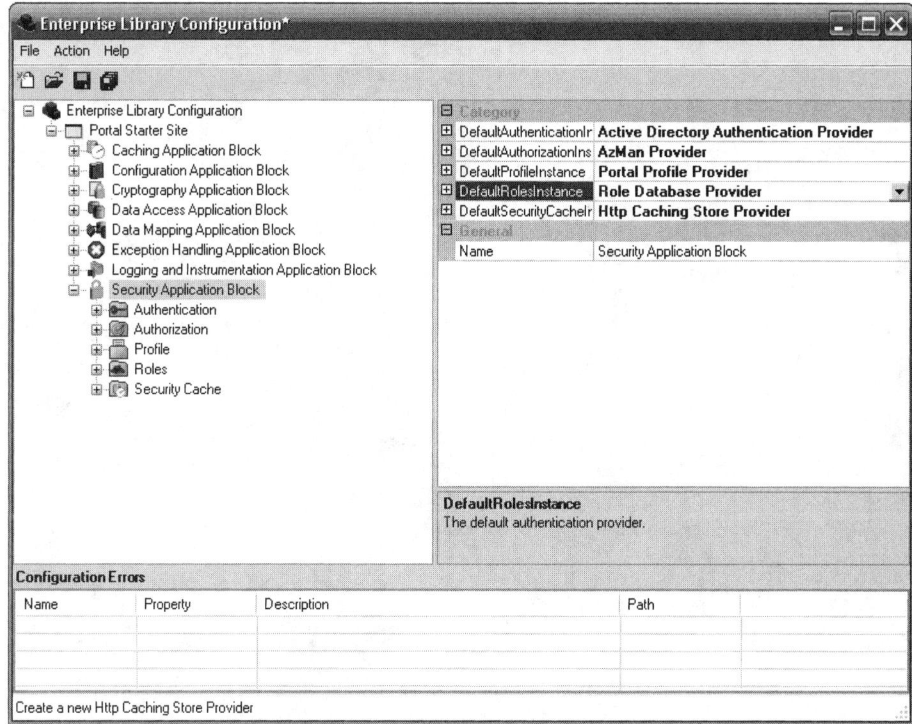

FIGURE 7.29: Configuring the Security Application Block's Default Providers

object that is retrieved by calling `GetRoles` on a RolesProvider can be passed to an AuthorizationProvider to determine entitlement for a specific task or operation.

Most importantly, I hope that you have seen that the Security Application Block has realized its design goals with a simple but flexible suite of providers. By leveraging the Security Application Block, an application can be abstracted away from the idiosyncrasies associated with any specific user or authorization store and can instead concentrate on developing the logic to solve the business needs at hand. Furthermore, the code for the application is isolated from changes if user information is moved from one store to another; rather than modifying any code, you only need to change the configuration data.

8

The Cryptography Application Block

NOT LONG AGO, few applications were coded with security in mind, let alone coded so that security was a central design concept. In the mid-1990s, for instance, few developers outside of niche areas such as finance or defense even addressed security in any substantive way. However, each time a new virus made the headlines or a security breach happened, security moved into the public awareness. Today, it is irresponsible for developers and architects to ignore security. Cryptography is one tool that developers have at their disposal to secure their applications. Cryptography is primarily used to ensure that data:

- Remains private (data privacy)
- Is protected from modification (data integrity)
- Originates from the party from which it is supposed to originate (authentication)

Data privacy is used to hide an application's secret information; in other words, "to keep secrets secret." Data privacy is often achieved by encrypting data. For example, if you log into Gmail or search for an item on Amazon.com, you'll often see a string of unfamiliar characters in the query string. These characters are usually information that is specific to your account, but it's encrypted so that it's unintelligible to the human eye.

Encryption's main purpose is to ensure that if unauthorized people see your information, they won't be able to understand it (or even know what it is).

Data integrity is typically implemented by means of computing mathematical "hash" values, which, in turn, allow you to verify that the information you are viewing has not been tampered with. If the values are intact, then the hash will compute correctly; otherwise, the hash will not match. This notion is commonly referred to as *nonrepudiation* and is critical to e-commerce, for instance.

The final facet of security is known as **authentication**—namely, proving that entities are who they say they are. For example, if Person A calls Person B on the phone, Person B typically relies on auditory familiarity to confirm that Person A is who he says he is. But if someone from your bank called and asked you for some sensitive information, you'd typically be suspicious. One way you'd address this is to call the bank back. This provides a level of authentication. Digital certificates are used in a similar way to prove that the entities on the other end are who they say they are.

This chapter describes how the Cryptography Application Block has been designed to make it easier for developers to mitigate data privacy and data integrity threats in their applications. Throughout the chapter I compare the design and code that exists in the Cryptography Application Block to the methods and samples in Chapters 8 and 9 of *Writing Secure Code*, Second Edition, by Michael Howard and David C. LeBlanc (Microsoft Press, 2003). I discuss how the code in this block leverages the best practices outlined in that book and how this results in an extremely simple interface for using this application block.

What Is the Cryptography Application Block?

Developing applications that meet strict security standards is not for the faint of heart. Without really knowing what is happening not only in the code that is written in an application but also in the code that is called, an application could easily be opened up for attack. The .NET Cryptography API can help; however, even when the .NET Cryptography API is properly used, there is still a fair amount of work that needs to be completed to get the job done.

This is where the Cryptography Application Block comes into the picture. The Cryptography Application Block makes it easier for you to add functionality to your applications for encrypting data, decrypting data, and creating and comparing hashes. At its core, the methods exposed by the Cryptography Application Block use many of the assets that exist in the .NET Cryptography API, while also eliminating some of the complexities of using it. The Cryptography Application Block does not, however, provide any functionality that facilitates the use of digital certificates or asymmetric encryption. Like many of the other application blocks in Enterprise Library, the Cryptography Application Block achieves its simplicity by exposing a service façade, often requiring you to write only a single line of code.

.NET Cryptography

The Cryptography Application Block is a wrapper for the `System.Security.Cryptography` namespace that is provided by the .NET Framework. The `System.Security.Cryptography` namespace provides functionality to encrypt data, decrypt data, hash data, generate random numbers, and authenticate messages. As such, it provides implementations for several symmetric, asymmetric, and hash algorithms. Table 8.1 shows the algorithms that exist in the `System.Security.Cryptography` namespace.

TABLE 8.1: Cryptography Algorithms in the .NET `System.Security.Cryptography` Namespace

Symmetric Algorithm	Asymmetric Algorithm	Hash Algorithm
• DES (Data Encryption Standard) • Triple DES (Triple Data Encryption Standard), also known as 3DES • Rijndael • RC2	• DSA (Digital Signature Algorithm) • RSA	• HMAC SHA1 (Hash-based Message Authentication Code using the SHA1 hash algorithm) • MAC Triple DES (Message Authentication Code using Triple DES) • MD5 • SHA1, SHA256, SHA384, and SHA512 (Secure Hash Algorithm using various hash sizes)

Symmetric and Asymmetric Algorithms

Symmetric and asymmetric algorithms are used to ensure data remains private (or confidential) by encrypting the data. The same `algorithm` used to convert cleartext into ciphertext can be used to convert the ciphertext back to cleartext. These algorithms are not just limited to encrypting and decrypting text, though. For example, a byte array created from a .JPG image can be encrypted too. The difference between symmetric and asymmetric algorithms lies in the keys that are used. **Symmetric algorithms** (or private-key algorithms) use the same key to encrypt and decrypt data. **Asymmetric algorithms** (or public-key algorithms) use two mathematically related but different keys to encrypt and decrypt data.

Both symmetric and asymmetric algorithms are **block ciphers**, because they encrypt and decrypt data a block at a time rather than as one continuous stream (which is known as a **stream cipher**). Blocks are usually 64 bits or 128 bits in size, although some may be larger. The Rijndael algorithm, for example, is 256 bits. The blocks are of a fixed size and encryption is accomplished by iterative rearrangement and substitution on successive blocks. The decision of what algorithm and what type of encryption to use for an application cannot be taken lightly—the cost of being wrong can be very high. If the algorithm is not strong enough, the private information can be compromised, but if it is too strong, an application may be so sluggish that it becomes unusable.

Symmetric encryption is preferred when performance is an issue and when the party encrypting the data can share the key with the party who is decrypting the data. Since both parties must share the same key, either both parties must know this information up front or one of them must be able to generate the information and securely send it to the other. Often this means that the two parties are actually the same.

Asymmetric encryption is preferred when the encrypted information needs to be sent over an insecure medium and when the sending and receiving parties cannot share the same key. A key pair must exist in this case. One key is a public key and is distributed to the world. The other is a private key that must be protected. Data that is encrypted using the private key can only be decrypted with the corresponding public key, and information encrypted with the public key can only be decrypted with the corresponding private key.

The goal for this version of Enterprise Library's Cryptography Application Block is to facilitate the encryption and decryption of data in a single application. It accomplishes this by wrapping around the symmetric algorithms and DPAPI (explained later) provided by the .NET Framework and listed in the first column of Table 8.1. This version of the Cryptography Application Block has not been designed to take advantage of the asymmetric algorithms in the .NET Framework.

Hash Algorithms

Hashing is used to ensure the integrity of the data; that is, to ensure that the data has not been accidentally or maliciously modified. Hash values are used to verify the integrity of data sent through insecure channels. A **hash value** is a unique, fixed-length value derived from a sequence of the data. Depending on the algorithm that is used, the hash value is usually 128 or 160 bits. Verification is accomplished by creating a hash of the data when the data is received and comparing it with the hash that is attached to the received data. Table 8.1 lists the hash algorithms provided by the .NET Framework.

Technically, hashes can be compromised by an attacker who changes the data, recalculates the hash, and then attaches the new hash to the data stream. If this occurs, it is very difficult to determine whether the data was modified or not. Keyed hashes (and digital signatures) address this issue. The HMAC SHA1 and MAC Triple DES are keyed hash algorithms.

Keyed hashes contain a secret key that is known only to the sender and the recipient of the data. The hash is usually created by concatenating the cleartext data and secret key. Without knowing the secret key, the proper hash cannot be calculated. According to Howard and LeBlanc (*Writing Secure Code*, Second Edition, pp. 291–294), developers often make many mistakes when creating keyed hashes, including

- Forgetting to use a key
- Using the same key to encrypt data and key-hash data
- Basing the key-hash key on the encryption key

"Salting" a hash can also make an attacker's job more difficult. A **salt value** is a cryptographically generated random number that is added to the hash data to defend against dictionary attacks. (A **dictionary attack** is an attack where every possible secret key is used to decrypt the encrypted data.) Salting provides entropy (a degree of disorder) to the algorithm. Howard and LeBlanc (pp. 302–303) provide a managed code fragment that can be used to create a salted hash. In this code fragment, the hash and salt are both created and their bytes are combined to create one salted hash. Interestingly, this is the same technique that the Cryptography Application Block uses when salting a hash.

Design of the Cryptography Application Block

The design goals for the Cryptography Application Block were to make it easy for you to accomplish the most common cryptography tasks without incurring significant performance degradation. Additionally, like all the other application blocks, the Cryptography Application Block contains extension points to provide consumers of the block with the ability to create and use their own providers. In short, the primary goal for this block was to provide you with the capability to forgo writing the same, often complex, code to perform cryptographic functions in your applications. The Cryptography Application Block provides a programming interface that supports encryption and hashing by letting you take advantage of configuration data and a service façade.

The `Cryptographer` Class

The Cryptography Application Block achieves its design goal of a simplified application programming interface (API) through the `Cryptographer` class. The `Cryptographer` is a service façade that leverages the `HashProviderFactory` and classes that implement the `IHashProvider` interface to provide hashing functionality, and the `SymmetricCryptoProviderFactory` and classes that implement the `ISymmetricCryptoProvider` interface to supply encryption/decryption functionality. The `Cryptographer` supports the static public methods listed in Table 8.2.

Each of the methods in Table 8.2 are overloaded with a function that takes strings for the cleartext, hashtext, and ciphertext arguments and another function that takes byte arrays. The string overloads are nice because they make it easy for you to support hashing and encryption calls

TABLE 8.2: The `Cryptographer` Class' Methods

Method	Description
`CompareHash`	Compares cleartext input with a computed hash.
`CreateHash`	Computes the hash value of cleartext.
`DecryptSymmetric`	Decrypts ciphertext using a specified SymmetricCryptographyProvider.
`EncryptSymmetric`	Encrypts a secret using a specified SymmetricCryptographyProvider.

without requiring the need to convert everything to byte arrays. Instead, the string overloads convert the contents of the string to the byte array, call the overloaded method that accepts the byte arrays, and fill the byte array with a cryptographically strong random set of bytes when the function is complete. This is an important point. In the .NET Framework 1.1, strings are immutable and cannot be overridden.[1] The byte arrays that hold the secrets are not left populated in memory in an effort to minimize an attack.

In addition to the cleartext, hashtext, or ciphertext, each of these methods also expects a string that represents the cryptography instance. For example, if an application were configured to use an SHA1 hashing algorithm named *SHA1Managed*, the `Cryptographer` would expect the call `CreateHash("SHA1Managed", "myStringToHash")`[2] to create a hash for *myStringToHash*.

1. *Writing Secure Code,* Howard and LeBlanc, Second Edition, p. 335.

2. Actually, the call would be `CreateHash(SR.SHA1Managed, SR.myStringToHash)`, where each of the properties for the `SR` class equates to the appropriate string. The `SR` class can be automatically created using the String Resource Tool, which is in the Downloads section of the Enterprise Library workspace at http://practices.gotdotnet.com/projects/entlib (you need to join but it's free).

The String Resource Tool is used extensively throughout Enterprise Library as a way of creating and managing the string resources in a particular project. I did not use the *SR.stringname* notation so as not to distract you from the primary point, which is that the `CreateHash` method expects two strings: the name of a hashing algorithm and the name of a cryptography instance.

For the CompareHash and CreateHash functions, the Cryptographer passes the string that represents the algorithm name to the HashProviderFactory so that an instance of a class that implements the IHashProvider interface can be created through reflection. Then the Cryptographer calls the newly created class' CreateHash method and passes it to the *myStringToHash* string. Similarly, for the DecryptSymmetric and EncryptSymmetric methods, the Cryptographer passes a string that represents the name of the SymmetricAlgorithmProvider to the SymmetricCryptoProviderFactory in order to create an instance of a class that implements the ISymmetricCryptoProvider interface. It then passes the rest of the arguments to the newly created class to encrypt and decrypt data. Figure 8.1 shows how the Cryptographer class uses the HashProviderFactory and SymmetricCryptoProviderFactory to create the providers it needs.

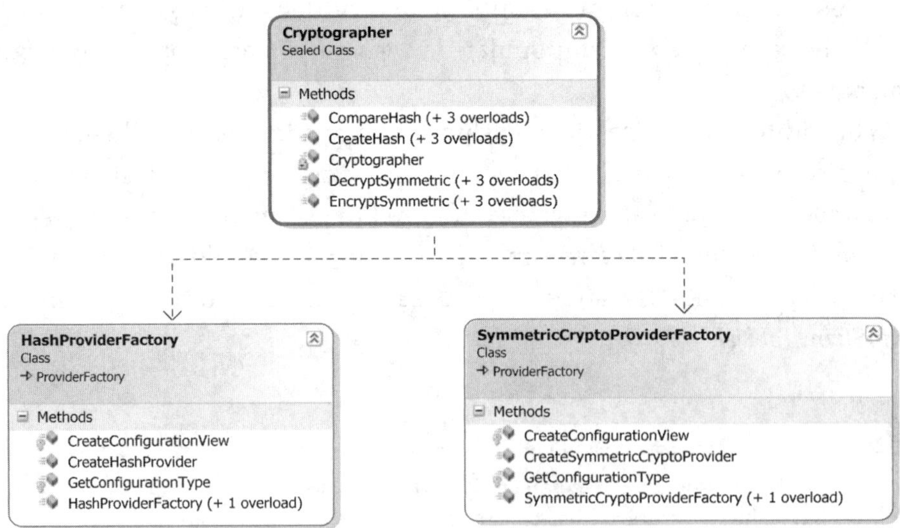

FIGURE 8.1: Cryptographer, HashProviderFactory, and SymmetricCryptoProviderFactory

The `SymmetricProviderFactory` and `HashProviderFactory` Classes

There's nothing very complicated about the `SymmetricProviderFactory` or the `HashProviderFactory`. These classes simply use the names of the providers that are passed to them to look up and create the proper provider from configuration. Once the type of the provider is found in the configuration information, it is created via reflection.

SymmetricProviders

All SymmetricProviders created via the `SymmetricProviderFactory` must implement the `ISymmetricCryptoProvider` interface. The `ISymmetricCryptoProvider` interface contains two methods: `Encrypt(byte[])` and `Decrypt(byte[])`. The Cryptography Application Block includes two implementations: the DpapiSymmetricCryptographyProvider and the SymmetricAlgorithmProvider. The DpapiSymmetricCryptographyProvider uses DPAPI to provide cryptography services, while the SymmetricAlgorithmProvider lets you use any symmetric algorithm that is derived from `System.Security.Cryptography.SymmetricAlgorithm`.

In addition to the `Initialize` method for initializing its data from configuration data, each of these providers must support the public `Encrypt` and `Decrypt` methods to implement the `ISymmetricCryptoProvider` interface. Figure 8.2 shows the classes the Cryptography Application Block uses to provide support for symmetric cryptography algorithms. However, before going too far into explaining how these providers work, let's discuss DPAPI.

What's DPAPI?

The Data Protection API (DPAPI) is a Win32 application programming interface that uses Windows-generated keys that are tied to a specific machine or user account to protect the data. Currently, this is considered the best way to protect secrets. The `CryptProtectData` method is used to encrypt the data and the `CryptUnprotectData` method is used to decrypt the data. You can use DPAPI to protect files in situations where other security measures cannot. For example, if someone mounts a disk remotely, access control lists (ACLs) cannot protect the file, but DPAPI can.

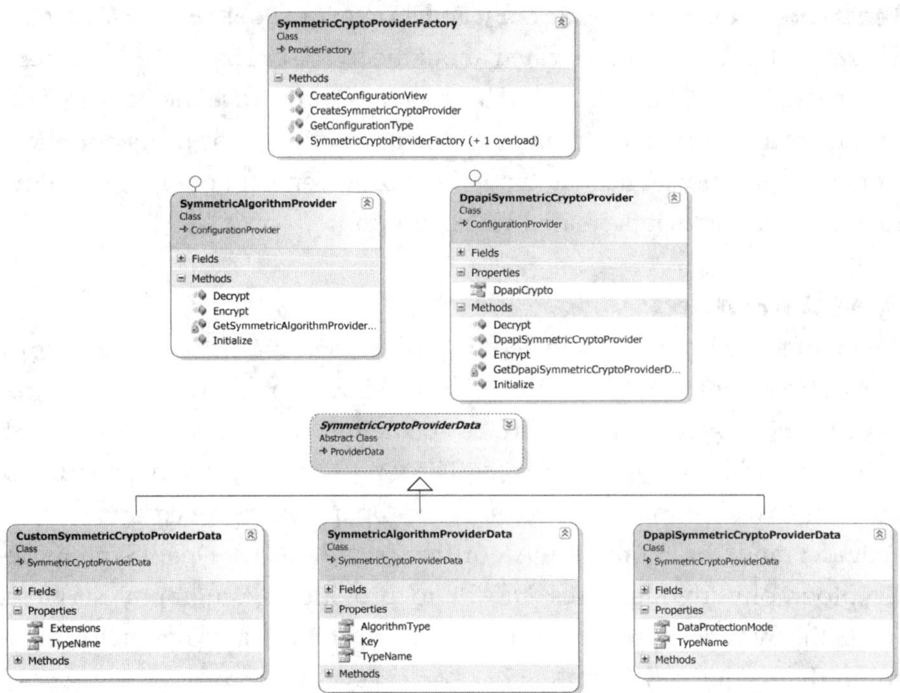

FIGURE 8.2: Classes Used for Providing Support for Symmetric Algorithms

DPAPI operates in either user or machine mode. In user mode, the ability to decrypt the file is restricted to the account of the user who was logged in when the file was encrypted. Machine mode restricts the ability to decrypt the file to the computer used when the file was encrypted. This means that any user with an account on that computer can decrypt the file. There exist additional mechanisms to further protect data when encrypted in machine mode, though. For example, the file (or registry) in which the data is stored can be further protected with ACLs. This ensures that an application must be running with an account that has been granted permission to the data in the file (or registry) in order to access it.

Using ACLs, however, does not prevent other applications that might also be running under that same account from accessing the data. Fortunately, the `CryptProtectData` method does allow for further protection by letting an additional password or random number be applied when the data is encrypted. This password is known as the *entropy*, and if it is used when encrypting the data, it must also be used when the `CryptUnpro-`

`tectData` method is called to decrypt the data. The entropy can be used to further protect the data when DPAPI is used in machine mode. In fact, the entropy is required by the Cryptography Application Block when using DPAPI in machine mode.

Machine mode must be used with caution. It is imperative that any ciphertext that is encrypted using machine mode be backed up. Otherwise, if the machine fails and must be rebuilt or replaced, the key that was used to encrypt the data is lost, and thus the data itself will also be lost. Also, by using machine mode, the data protection is tied to a single machine. This means that it cannot be used for applications that are intended to be distributed to multiple different machines where it is possible that data can be encrypted on one machine and decrypted on another.

The DpapiSymmetricCryptoProvider and the `DpapiCryptographer` Class

The DpapiSymmetricCryptoProvider takes advantage of the Data Protection API to protect secret information. The DpapiSymmetricCryptoProvider is initialized with data read from configuration. It uses this information to populate and pass to the `DpapiCryptographer` class. The `DpapiCryptographer` class is actually part of Enterprise Library's `Common` namespace and not officially in the `Cryptography` namespace. This enables its use by the Configuration Application Block to encrypt the configuration information for all of the application blocks (if enabled). The `Common` namespace contains helper and utility classes for use by all application blocks.

The `DpapiCryptographer` class is where the "real" encrypting and decrypting is accomplished. In the `DpapiCryptographer`'s `EncryptInternal` method, the cleartext and entropy are converted to a series of bytes, aggregated, and the `CryptProtectData` method is called to protect the data using DPAPI. Similarly, in the `DecryptInternal` method, the entropy is converted to a series of bytes, the `CryptUnprotectData` method is called, and the byte array that represents the cleartext secret is returned.

The SymmetricAlgorithmProvider and the `SymmetricCryptographer` Class

It's not always necessary (or even desirable) to encrypt *all* application data using DPAPI. Doing so may bind all data to a particular user or machine. Rather, it is often better to simply encrypt a single master key using DPAPI and leverage the other symmetric or asymmetric algorithms to encrypt the application data. Like the `DpapiSymmetricCryptoProvider`, the `SymmetricAlgorithmProvider` passes control to a separate cryptographer class that is part of the `Common` namespace. In this case, it is the `SymmetricCryptographer`. The `SymmetricCryptographer` creates an instance of the algorithm provider for which it is configured via reflection. It then uses this algorithm provider to encrypt and decrypt the data.

Custom Symmetric Algorithms

When the algorithm is created in the `SymmetricCryptographer` class, it is cast to the `System.Security.Cryptography.SymmetricAlgorithm` type. You can configure the Cryptography Application Block to use any algorithm that is derived either directly or indirectly from this abstract base class. Therefore, creating a cryptographic algorithm that works with the Cryptography Application Block means deriving a class from the `SymmetricAlgorithm` abstract base class or a class derived from it. While it is certainly possible to create such a class, this type of endeavor should really be avoided. To quote Howard and LeBlanc:

> Producing good cryptographic algorithms is a difficult task, one that should be undertaken only by those who well understand how to create such algorithms... The best way to use encryption is to use tried and trusted encryption algorithms defined in libraries such as CryptoAPI included with Windows.[3]

Still, if you don't want to heed this advice and absolutely feel that you *must* create your own custom symmetric algorithm to use in your applications, you should feel confident that the Cryptography Application Block can use it. There are three steps you must take.

1. Create a class that is derived from the `SymmetricAlgorithm` class.
2. Override all abstract methods.
3. Deploy the assembly.

---

3. *Writing Secure Code*, Second Edition, pp. 281-282.

Listing 8.1 shows such an implementation, named `DontTryThisSymmAlgorithm`. The implementation does not do any encryption or decryption; rather, it is included simply to show that it is possible to add a symmetric algorithm and have it used by the Cryptography Application Block.

LISTING 8.1: Custom Symmetric Algorithm

```
[C#]
public class DontTryThisSymmAlgorithm : SymmetricAlgorithm
{
    // Properties.
    private RNGCryptoServiceProvider RNG
    {
        get
        {
            if (this._rng == null)
            {
                this._rng = new RNGCryptoServiceProvider();
            }
            return this._rng;
        }
    }

    // Fields.
    private RNGCryptoServiceProvider _rng;
    public DontTryThisSymmAlgorithm()
    {
    }

    public override ICryptoTransform CreateDecryptor
        (byte[] rgbKey, byte[] rgbIV)
    {
        // TODO:  Add CreateDecryptor implementation.
        return null;
    }

    public override ICryptoTransform CreateDecryptor()
    {
        // TODO:  Add CreateDecryptor implementation.
        return base.CreateDecryptor ();
    }

    public override ICryptoTransform CreateEncryptor
        (byte[] rgbKey, byte[] rgbIV)
    {
        // TODO:  Add CreateEncryptor implementation.
        return null;
```

```
    }

    public override ICryptoTransform CreateEncryptor()
    {
        // TODO:  Add CreateEncryptor implementation.
        return base.CreateEncryptor ();
    }

    public override void GenerateIV()
    {
        // TODO:  Add GenerateIV implementation.
        this.IVValue = new byte[this.BlockSizeValue / 8];
        this.RNG.GetBytes(this.IVValue);
    }

    public override void GenerateKey()
    {
        // TODO:  Add GenerateKey implementation.
        this.KeyValue = new byte[this.KeySizeValue / 8];
        this.RNG.GetBytes(this.KeyValue);
    }
}

[Visual Basic]
Public Class DontTryThisSymmAlgorithm : Inherits SymmetricAlgorithm

    ' Properties.
    Private ReadOnly Property RNG() As RNGCryptoServiceProvider
        Get
            If Me._rng Is Nothing Then
                Me._rng = New RNGCryptoServiceProvider()
            End If
            Return Me._rng
        End Get
    End Property

    ' Fields.
    Private _rng As RNGCryptoServiceProvider
    Public Sub New()
    End Sub

    Public Overrides Function CreateDecryptor _
        (ByVal rgbKey As Byte(), ByVal rgbIV As Byte()) _
        As ICryptoTransform

        ' TODO:  Add CreateDecryptor implementation.
        Return Nothing
    End Function
```

```
        Public Overrides Function CreateDecryptor() As ICryptoTransform
            ' TODO:  Add CreateDecryptor implementation.
            Return MyBase.CreateDecryptor ()
        End Function

        Public Overrides Function CreateEncryptor _
            (ByVal rgbKey As Byte(), ByVal rgbIV As Byte()) _
            As ICryptoTransform
            ' TODO:  Add CreateEncryptor implementation.
            Return Nothing
        End Function

        Public Overrides Function CreateEncryptor() As ICryptoTransform
            ' TODO:  Add CreateEncryptor implementation.
            Return MyBase.CreateEncryptor ()
        End Function

        Public Overrides Sub GenerateIV()
            ' TODO:  Add GenerateIV implementation.
            Me.IVValue = New Byte(Me.BlockSizeValue / 8 - 1) {}
            Me.RNG.GetBytes(Me.IVValue)
        End Sub

        Public Overrides Sub GenerateKey()
            ' TODO:  Add GenerateKey implementation.
            Me.KeyValue = New Byte(Me.KeySizeValue / 8 - 1) {}
            Me.RNG.GetBytes(Me.KeyValue)
        End Sub
    End Class
```

When this class has been deployed so the Enterprise Library Configuration Tool recognizes it, it becomes as easy to support this algorithm as it is for any of the ones that are supported by default. Figure 8.3 displays the Type Selector dialog that is used to select a symmetric algorithm in the Configuration Tool. It illustrates how the new symmetric algorithm can be selected for use in an application.

Hash Providers

SymmetricAlgorithmProviders are included with the Cryptography Application Block to facilitate encrypting and decrypting data. Even encrypted data, however, is vulnerable to data tampering. Therefore, in addition to symmetric providers, hashing providers are included in the Cryptography Application Block to make it easier to validate the integrity of the data in an application.

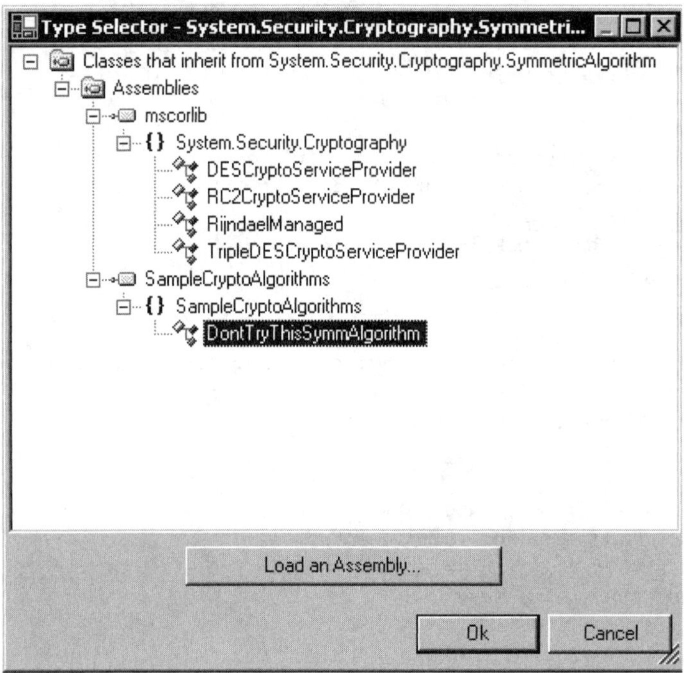

FIGURE 8.3: Using a Custom Symmetric Algorithm with the Cryptography Application Block

Some of the most common uses for such a need revolve around password validation. It is often necessary for an application to verify that a user knows his or her password; however, to do this, the application may not actually need to store and use the password itself. Instead, a hash for that data can be stored. When the user enters his or her password, a hash for the entered information is compared against the hash that is stored. If the two hashes are equal, then the application can verify that the password has been properly entered.

The Cryptography Application Block includes two implementations of hash providers: the HashAlgorithmProvider and the KeyedHashAlgorithmProvider. As the names imply, the HashAlgorithmProvider allows hash algorithms that do not require a key to be selected and configured, while the KeyedHashAlgorithmProvider is for hash algorithms that require a key. Both providers allow a salt value to be generated and prepended to the data before it is hashed. Figure 8.4 shows the classes used to support hashing in the Cryptography Application Block.

The `HashAlgorithmProvider` and `HashCryptographer` Classes

Just as all symmetric providers need to implement the `ISymmetricCryptoProvider` interface, all hash algorithm providers created via the `HashProviderFactory` must implement the `IHashProvider` interface. The `IHashProvider` interface contains two methods: `CreateHash(byte[])` and `CompareHash(byte[], byte[])`. The `CompareHash` method compares two hashes and determines if they are equal. Many people incorrectly assume that if the results of two `CreateHash` methods with the same byte array are equal, then the hashes are equal. However, this is not always true if salt is used. The `CompareHash` method takes the salt into account when comparing the hashes.

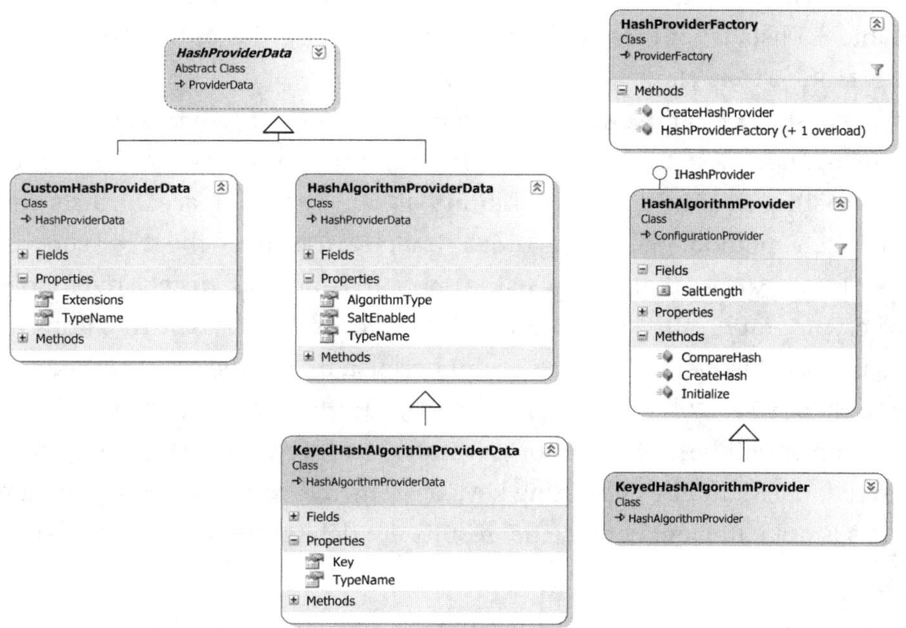

FIGURE 8.4: Classes Used for Providing Support for Hashing Algorithms

Table 8.3: Public Methods and Properties for the `HashAlgorithmProvider` Class

Method/Property	Description
`CompareHash`	Compares cleartext input with a computed hash.
`CreateHash`	Computes the hash value of cleartext.
`Initialize`	Initializes the provider with a CryptographyConfigurationView.
`SaltLength`	Returns the salt length used by the provider. This is a static property.

As Figure 8.4 shows, the `HashAlgorithmProvider` not only implements the `IHashProvider` interface, but it also derives from the `ConfigurationProvider` class. Therefore, the `HashAlgorithmProvider` class is a `ConfigurationProvider` that implements the `CreateHash` and `CompareHash` methods. As a `ConfigurationProvider`, it initializes the data that it will use from configuration data. It uses this data to determine the appropriate hash algorithm to use and to determine if the hash should be salted. Table 8.3 lists all of the public methods and properties of the `HashAlgorithmProvider` class.

Like the `SymmetricAlgorithmProvider` and `DpapiSymmetricCryptoProvider`, the `HashAlgorithmProvider` uses many of the helper classes that exist in Enterprise Library's `Common` namespace. In the `CreateHash` method, the `HashAlgorithmProvider` uses the `CryptographyUtility` class that resides in the `Common` namespace to get a byte array of cryptographically strong random data to use as the salt (if salting is enabled). This method is very useful because it uses the `RNGCryptoServiceProvider.Create().GetBytes(bytes)` to create this array. This is a recommended best practice for generating cryptographically strong random data.[4] Manually generating keys or using `System.Random` to generate keys is not sufficient because the results are deterministic and repeatable.

4. *Writing Secure Code*, Second Edition, pp. 268–269.

The HashAlgorithmProvider then uses the same CryptographyUtility class to combine the bytes for the salt with the bytes for the cleartext. A HashCryptographer, which also resides in the Common namespace, is then used to compute the actual hash. The HashCryptographer uses the algorithm for which the HashAlgorithmProvider has been configured to compute this hash. Then the bytes for the salt are combined once again, this time with the actual hashed value.

When comparing hashes, the HashAlgorithmProvider first extracts the salt from the hashed text. It then uses this salt to create a hash value for the plaintext to which it is comparing the hash. Then the CryptographyUtility class is used to compare the bytes of the two hashes. Finally, the CryptographyUtility class is used to zero out the bytes in memory for the salt value.

The `KeyedHashAlgorithmProvider` Class

The KeyedHashAlgorithmProvider class derives from the HashAlgorithmProvider class. The only difference between the two classes is how the HashCryptographer class gets created. When the KeyedHashAlgorithmProvider class creates the HashCryptographer class, it passes a key into the constructor. If the algorithm that is being used to hash the data is a keyed hash algorithm, for example, HMAC SHA1 or MAC Triple DES, then the key is read from the configuration data and used to set the key value for the actual underlying algorithm.

Custom Hash Algorithms

The HashCryptographer class first casts the algorithm that it creates to a System.Security.Cryptography.HashAlgorithm. After this step, it then attempts to cast it to a System.Security.Cryptography.KeyedHashAlgorithm to determine if the class is a KeyedHashAlgorithm or not. If the cast is successful, and therefore the object is not equal to null, then it is assumed to be a KeyedHashAlgorithm and its key is set. Otherwise, it is assumed to be a nonkeyed hash algorithm. Listing 8.2 shows the code for the HashCryptographer's GetHashAlgorithm method. The algorithm that is returned is then used to compute and compare hashes.

LISTING 8.2: How the `HashCryptographer` Sets the Key for a `KeyedHashAlgorithm`

```
[C#]
try
{
     Type type = Type.GetType(algorithmType);
     algorithm = Activator.CreateInstance(type, true) as HashAlgorithm;
     KeyedHashAlgorithm keyedHashAlgorithm =
          algorithm as KeyedHashAlgorithm;
     if ((null != keyedHashAlgorithm) && (key != null))
     {
          keyedHashAlgorithm.Key = key;
     }
}

[Visual Basic]
Try
     Dim type As Type = Type.GetType(algorithmType)
     algorithm = IIf(TypeOf Activator.CreateInstance(type, True) _
                    Is HashAlgorithm, _
                    CType(Activator.CreateInstance(type, True), _
                    HashAlgorithm), CType(Nothing, HashAlgorithm))

     Dim keyedHashAlgorithm As KeyedHashAlgorithm = _
          IIf(TypeOf algorithm Is KeyedHashAlgorithm, _
          CType(algorithm, KeyedHashAlgorithm), _
          CType(Nothing, KeyedHashAlgorithm))

          If (Not Nothing Is keyedHashAlgorithm) AndAlso _
          (Not key Is Nothing) Then
               keyedHashAlgorithm.Key = key
          End If
End Try
```

Custom hash algorithms use the same method that custom symmetric algorithms use; the only difference is that the abstract base class from which the custom class must derive is the `System.Security.Cryptography.HashAlgorithm` (or `System.Security.Cryptography.KeyedHashAlgorithm`) class. The same caveats apply as they did for the custom symmetric algorithm (see the section Custom Symmetric Algorithms earlier in this chapter). You must do the following three steps.

1. Create a class that is derived from the `HashAlgorithm` or `KeyedHashAlgorithm` class.
2. Override all abstract methods.
3. Deploy the assembly.

Listing 8.3 shows an implementation named `DontTryThisHashAlgorithm`. The implementation is intended to just show that it is possible to add a hash algorithm and have it used by the Cryptography Application Block.

LISTING 8.3: Custom Hashing Algorithm

```
[C#]
public class DontTryThisHashAlgorithm : HashAlgorithm
{
     public DontTryThisHashAlgorithm()
     {
     }

     protected override void HashCore
          (byte[] array, int ibStart, int cbSize)
     {
          // TODO:  Add HashCore implementation.
     }

     public override void Initialize()
     {
          // TODO:  Add Initialize implementation.
     }

     protected override byte[] HashFinal()
     {
          // TODO:  Add HashFinal implementation.
          return null;
     }
}

[Visual Basic]
Public Class DontTryThisHashAlgorithm : Inherits HashAlgorithm

     Public Sub New()
     End Sub

     Protected Overrides Sub HashCore _
          (ByVal array As Byte(), ByVal ibStart As Integer, _
          ByVal cbSize As Integer)

          ' TODO:  Add HashCore implementation.
     End Sub
```

```
        Public Overrides Sub Initialize()
             ' TODO:  Add Initialize implementation.
        End Sub

        Protected Overrides Function HashFinal() As Byte()
             ' TODO:  Add HashFinal implementation.
             Return Nothing
        End Function
    End Class
```

After the class has been deployed, the Enterprise Library Configuration Tool can recognize and support this hashing algorithm just like any of the ones that are a part of the .NET Framework. Figure 8.5 displays the Type Selector dialog that is used to select a hashing algorithm in the Configuration Tool.

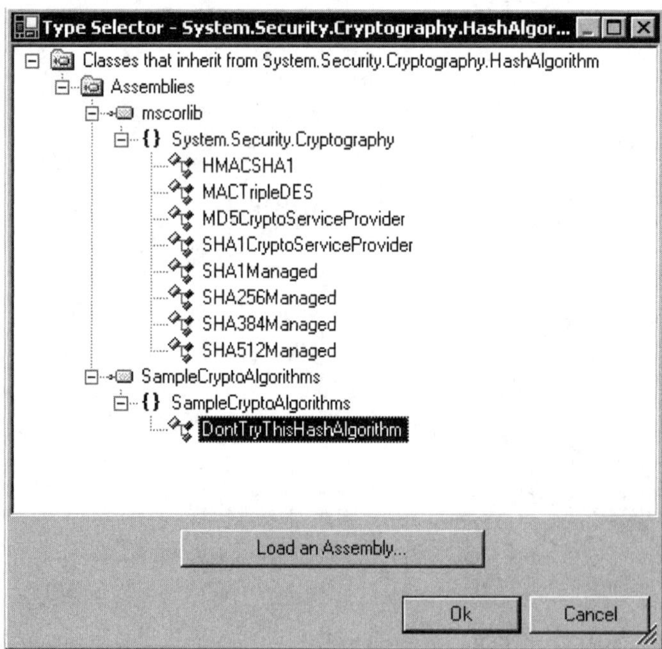

FIGURE 8.5: Using a Custom Hash Algorithm with the Cryptography Application Block

Developing with the Cryptography Application Block

The previous sections described the technologies used in the Cryptography Application Block and how it has been designed to subscribe to cryptography best practices. You also saw that, even though it is rarely wise to do so, custom symmetric and hashing algorithms can be created and used by the Cryptography Application Block. This section details how to configure and develop an application to take advantage of the Cryptography Application Block.

Adding the Cryptography Application Block

The first step to using the Cryptography Application Block is to add it to the configuration sections in an application. The easiest and least error-prone way to accomplish this is to add a new Cryptography Application Block in the Enterprise Library Configuration Tool.

In the Configuration Tool, right-click on the application node and select *New > Cryptography Application Block*. This generates a Cryptography Application Block subtree with further subtrees for HashProviders and SymmetricProviders. It also creates a configuration node named *securityCryptographyConfiguration* in the Configuration Application Block. Figure 8.6 depicts the resulting hierarchy.

Encrypting/Decrypting Data

At least one SymmetricProvider must be configured to use the Cryptography Application Block to encrypt and decrypt data. To add a Symmet-

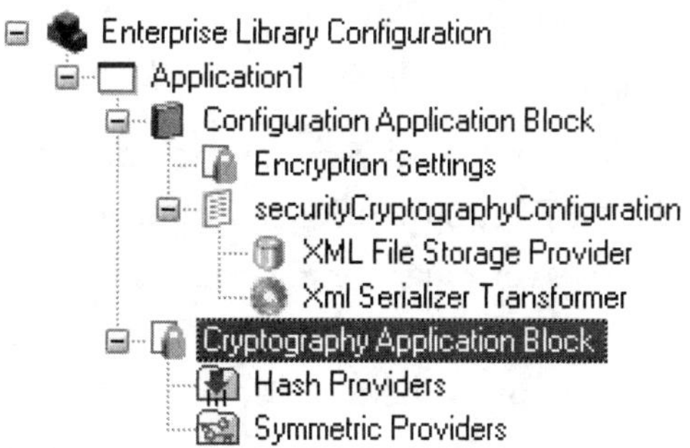

FIGURE 8.6: Hierarchy of the Cryptography Application Block

ricProvider, right-click on the *Symmetric Providers* node and select one of the providers: *Custom Symmetric Cryptography Provider, DPAPI SymmetricCryptographyProvider,* or *SymmetricAlgorithmProvider*. The option to create a custom symmetric provider is for enterprises that have applications that may need to do something other than leverage the underlying symmetric algorithm or DPAPI to encrypt and decrypt data. I have not seen this used anywhere, so I will focus on how to configure the DPAPI Symmetric Cryptography and SymmetricAlgorithmProviders that come with Enterprise Library.

The DpapiSymmetricCryptographyProvider

When you add a DpapiSymmetricCryptographyProvider to an application's configuration data, the Enterprise Library Configuration Tool displays the Data Protection Configuration dialog. This eases the process for configuring the DpapiSymmetricCryptographyProvider. This dialog lets you select the DPAPI mode as either user or machine. If you select machine mode, the dialog automatically adds the entropy to be used for its calls to `CryptProtectData` and `CryptUnprotectData`.

Figure 8.7 shows how to use the Data Protection Configuration dialog to set the DPAPI mode to machine mode and generate an entropy value. This value for the entropy is editable, so you can change it when it is created or at a later date by selecting the `DataProtectionMode` property for the DpapiSymmetricCryptographyProvider. However, if any data is encrypted before this setting is modified, it will not be able to be decrypted. So, unless there is a really good reason for modifying this value, it is probably better to accept the entropy that is automatically generated.

SymmetricAlgorithmProvider Configuration

The Enterprise Library Configuration Tool also makes it easy to configure an application to use with one of the .NET Framework's symmetric algorithms (or one that derives from `System.Security.Cryptography.SymmetricAlgorithm`). A wizard guides you through the process of selecting a symmetric algorithm and corresponding key. When you select one of the SymmetricAlgorithmProviders that exists, the Enterprise Library Configuration Tool displays the Type Selector dialog. This dialog displays a list of all classes that it knows derive from the `SymmetricAlgorithm` class.

FIGURE 8.7: Configuring a DpapiSymmetricCryptographyProvider

If you are not sure which algorithm to choose, the RijndaelManaged algorithm is usually a pretty good choice because it possesses the greatest key length of all the available providers. It is also the Advanced Encryption Standard accepted by the United States Federal Government in 2001 (the previous standard was DES). Figure 8.8 shows how to use the Type Selector dialog to select a SymmetricAlgorithmProvider.

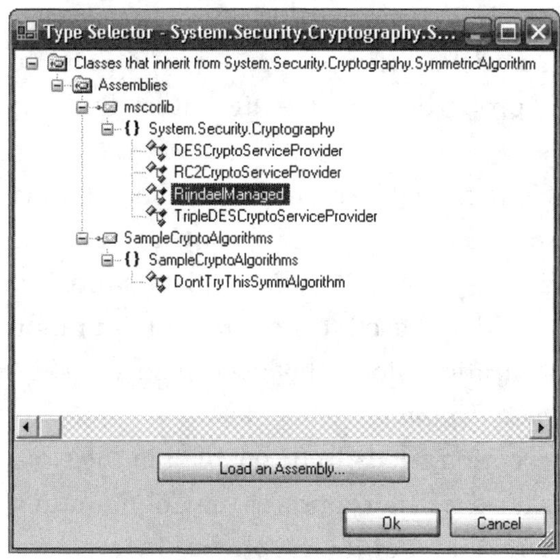

FIGURE 8.8: Selecting the RijndaelManaged SymmetricAlgorithmProvider

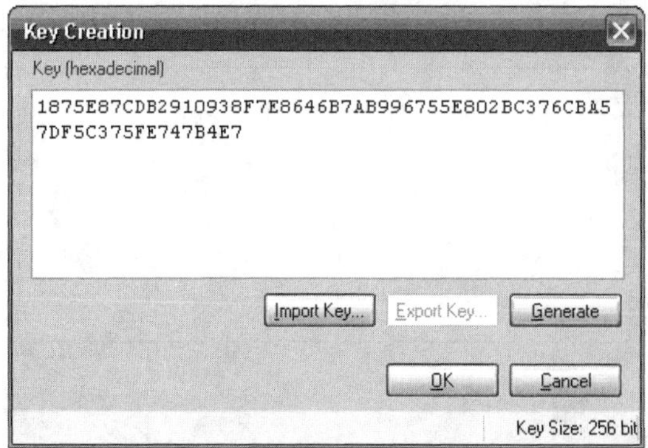

FIGURE 8.9: Adding a Key for the SymmetricAlgorithmProvider

Next you create an encryption key for the algorithm provider to use. The dialog lets a key either be imported or automatically generated by leveraging the helper methods in the `CryptographyUtility` class for generating cryptographically strong keys. Figure 8.9 shows the Key Creation dialog that is used to accomplish this.

After the key has been created, it is hidden in the Enterprise Library Configuration Tool for security reasons. That is, it cannot be edited with the tool. To modify the key with the tool, a new instance of the algorithm provider has to be created to use in place of the existing one. Alternatively, the key can be exported to a file that can be password protected. Figure 8.10 shows that by clicking on the `Key` property in the Configuration Tool, the encryption key can be exported.

This is not to say that the key value cannot be modified at all or to imply that it is extremely secured. It can be modified, and it is not secured. The key value is stored in cleartext in the StorageProvider's data store. For example, if the XMLFileStorageProvider is used to store the configuration settings for the Cryptography Application Block, the key can generally be located in the *securityCryptographyConfiguration.config* file.

To encrypt this key value, encryption needs to be enabled in the Configuration Application Block. This need for encryption in the Configuration Application Block is the reason why many of the cryptography methods that are used by the Cryptography Application Block actually reside in the

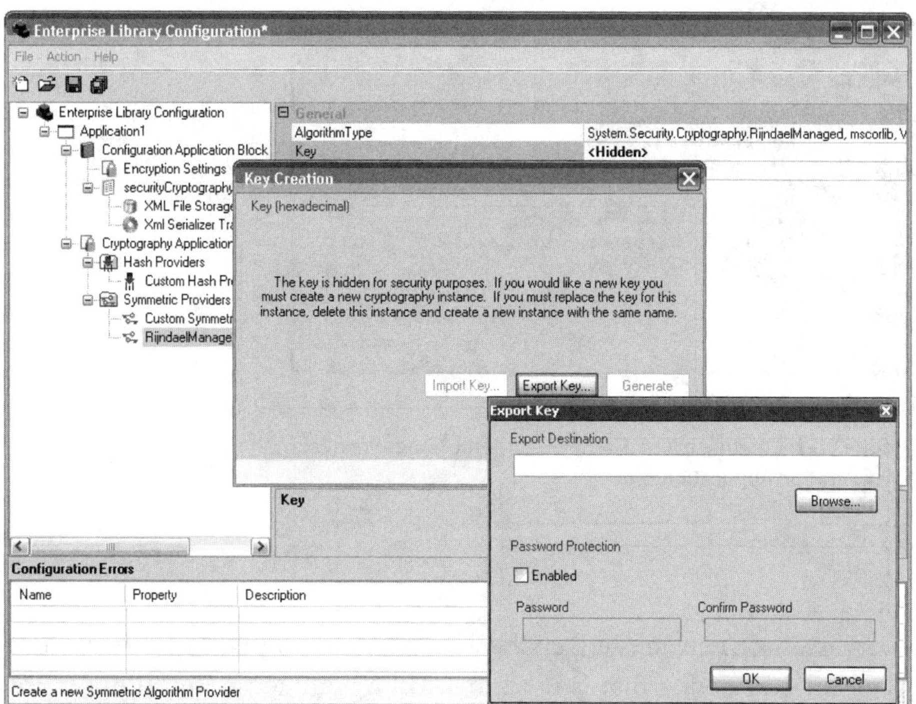

FIGURE 8.10: Key Modification Options

`Common` namespace. A circular dependency would occur if the Configuration Application Block depended on the Cryptography Application Block for cryptographic functions, while the Cryptography Application Block depended on the Configuration Application Block to get its configuration data.

To enable the encryption of configuration data, a Key Algorithm StorageProvider needs to be added to the Configuration Application Block. Enterprise Library ships with a FileKeyAlgorithmStorageProvider that lets you specify a single algorithm and key (i.e., a master key) for encrypting all configuration data. You add this key by right-clicking on the *Encryption Settings* configuration node in the Configuration Application Block and selecting a new FileKeyAlgorithmStorageProvider. Then, as depicted in Figure 8.11, a wizard will guide you through the process of either loading an existing key-algorithm pair or creating a new one.

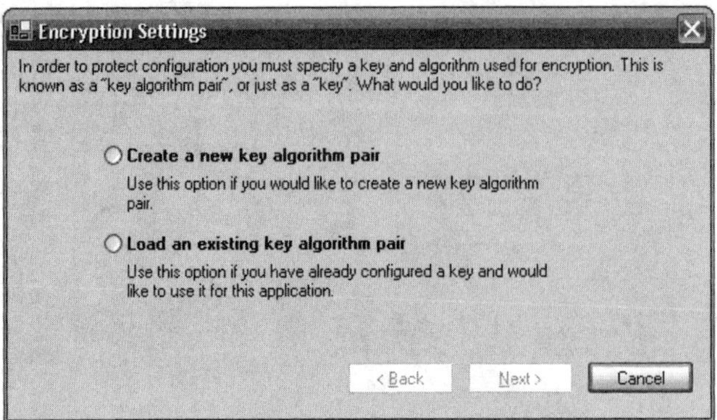

FIGURE 8.11: Creating a New FileKeyAlgorithmStorageProvider in the Configuration Application Block

If creating a new master key, the wizard next prompts you with the same Type Selector dialog that is used to select a Symmetric Algorithm in the Cryptography Application Block. After you select the algorithm provider, the wizard prompts you to select a file to use for saving this key-algorithm pair and provides the opportunity to protect the file using DPAPI. Figure 8.12 shows this dialog. If you choose to load the master key from an existing file instead of creating a new one, the wizard skips over the Type Selector dialog and goes right to the step shown in Figure 8-12. The master key is stored in the file that is created or selected in cleartext.

This may make you wonder whether the problem has not really been solved but just moved to a different file. From one perspective, the problem has just been moved because the master key exists as cleartext. However, because this single key file can now be used to encrypt *all* of the configuration data for an application, DPAPI can be used to help protect it. This is the first step toward better key management. Key management is the most challenging part of cryptography. Howard and LeBlanc devote a great deal of time to this subject.[5]

5. *Writing Secure Code,* Second Edition, pp. 272–281.

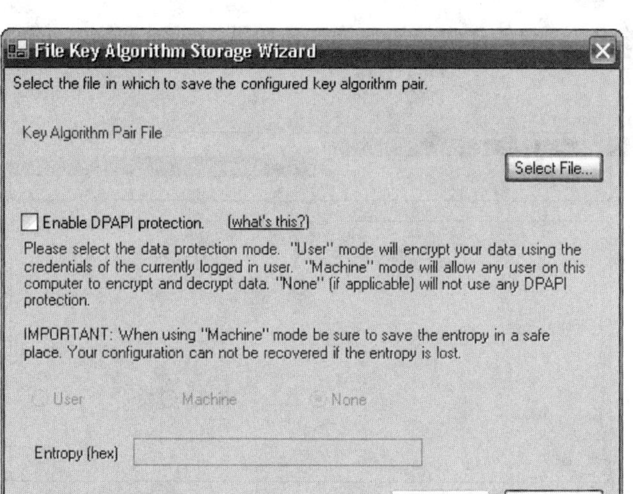

FIGURE 8.12: Saving the Master Key

Combining DPAPI (described earlier in this chapter) with ACLs could protect the single master key, while all other keys and data remain protected using the symmetric algorithm used when the FileKeyAlgorithmStorageProvider was configured. If the part of the application that uses the master key must be distributed to multiple machines, then straight ACLs might have to do. Another option available in Windows 2000 and later is the Encrypted File System (EFS), which encrypts and provides tamper detection for files.

Once the master key has been created, all configuration data for all blocks can be encrypted very easily. To encrypt the configuration data for a block, the `Encrypt` property for that application block's configuration settings needs to be set to true. Figure 8.13 shows how to switch the `Encrypt` flag to true for the Cryptography Application Block.

After the configuration data for the application block has been set to encrypted, the data is no longer stored in cleartext. For example, encrypting the settings shown in Figure 8.13 turns the cleartext shown in Listing 8.4 into the output shown in Listing 8.5.

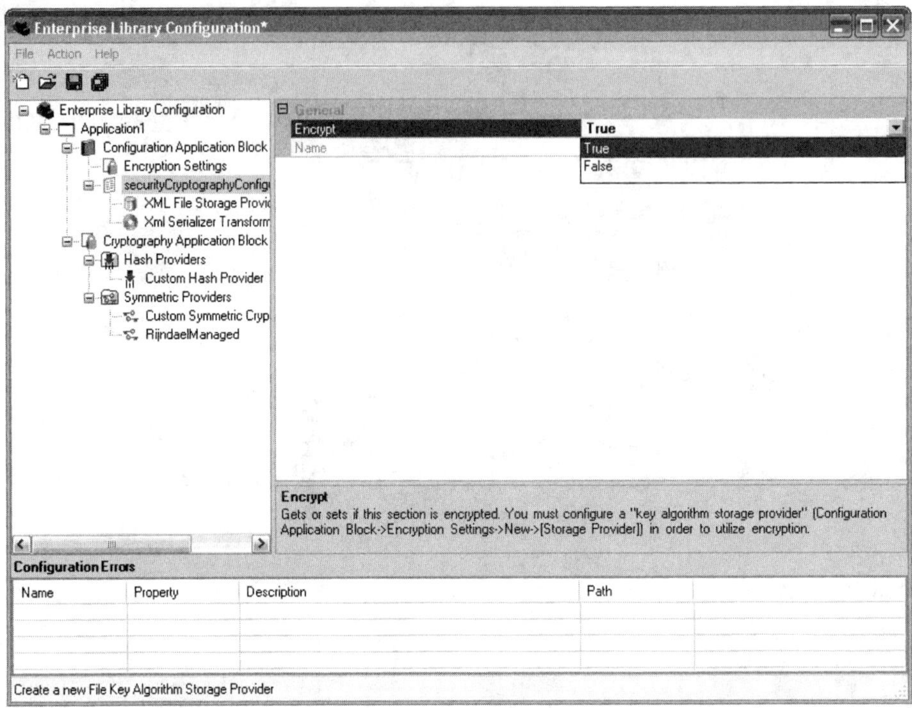

FIGURE 8.13: Turning Encryption On for an Application Block

Because this is a setting in the configuration for an application block and not dependent in any way on the use of the Cryptography Application Block, configuration data for any application block can be encrypted. That is, the capability to encrypt the configuration data is not isolated to cryptographic keys; it can and should be used for any configuration data for any application block.

The `EncryptSymmetric` Method

Once a symmetric algorithm has been configured for an application, encrypting data becomes simple. You can use the `Cryptographer`'s static `EncryptSymmetric` method to encrypt data by passing in the name of the SymmetricAlgorithmProvider and either a base64-encoded string or byte array to encrypt. In the first instance, the `EncryptSymmetric` method returns a base64-encoded string that represents the ciphertext; in the second instance it returns an array of bytes that represent the ciphertext. Listing 8.6

Listing 8.4: Configuration Data in Cleartext

```
<?xml version="1.0" encoding="utf-8"?>
<securityCryptographyConfiguration>
  <xmlSerializerSection type="Microsoft.Practices.EnterpriseLibrary.Security.Cryptography.Configuration.CryptographySettings, Microsoft.Practices.EnterpriseLibrary.Secu
    <enterpriseLibrary.securityCryptographySettings xmlns:xsd="http://www.w3.org/2001/XMLSchema" xmlns:xsi="http://www.w3.org/2001/XMLSchema-instance" xmlns="http://www
      <hashProviders />
      <symmetricCryptoProviders>
        <symmetricCryptoProvider xsi:type="DpapiSymmetricCryptoProviderData" name="DPAPI Symmetric Cryptography Provider">
          <dpapiSettings mode="Machine" entropy="YMO4qnQbcGR6OuD4kW2zKg==" />
        </symmetricCryptoProvider>
        <symmetricCryptoProvider xsi:type="SymmetricAlgorithmProviderData" name="RijndaelManaged" algorithmType="System.Security.Cryptography.RijndaelManaged, mscorlib,
      </symmetricCryptoProviders>
    </enterpriseLibrary.securityCryptographySettings>
  </xmlSerializerSection>
</securityCryptographyConfiguration>
```

Listing 8.5: Encrypted Configuration Data


```
�□<2ΦY!□□�□Ø  E)I□`8cL�:1���g#Y□�NT`□a�[��□5�A((�z_□L.i>v□□□5□$<1□��^FE�V̄&�v��OH��Cs)�_C�□����□����C□�d□J  �□"5:�z੫P"M9��?□�r�Q��R��pa�¿□□�□´av
:bg~□□7�I�□□���B□�9"/c*EL�!�=��@□"ú4�f�kw�>�
cC�□C~QhY;�□D��TE
�-8�-�`�8□□N(□�i□AXn�G/��Й\T�,"#□á*8□~>S�□k�^�(d�cEú�r�
;�□�B#�s�8D^�□�<�□□(8C�S�eF□t$□s□����2�N�]`8����`�_��C~)b□��nqz\�`kZj�/�□□´□�U��□□�*?□c�□�E��v�T7MU□�(�.□�ó.��w□J�
x4(E1�)¬�k□��|�N□b_�S*�[1û�ZM5�<X□w�\\Rx□2�□�o�[Ra�E�Cx�?�B#�:□��□�z�.1��□=□F/� □□aM�%□.�v□[��g����*~□
D$����\~i�oy�□se�□�+e[���o��w-T□"���Y0R�□�?��I9   ��M���<�(1`�µV_�`L��[��X�4�!Et7J□)1-|)(��$Z�sTÂ8ęQ"v(E□)y5��□��3w�n-y��0□S~*F5a`I□□��-��(��
��1□P□�CY�  ��3q��"□□x□fN��.z�=□KH��qd□�f�(□□□□�c�c□   h>dl
�e�0��¥"□�?)�)¥G�oX□�?S��R|~C□+�|□2�1?H□□'I"�g��Qq1Td2�□?�J□�□
3k�□�Im�gYE�*□�□□r�k□AI���*+=;j0�6□�E$|���P��/K□+5□□tO□*�□m���□�3:?,!Er□a�w�!�J(□R�
-vB�    j□��!�e�□(�uj��□��.5E.□:�g�□�j)K□(
,�
```

shows how to use the RinjdaelManaged provider that was configured in the previous section to encrypt a string of data that represents a Social Security Number. The remaining examples in this chapter (Listings 8.6 to 8.13) used the String Resource Tool[6] to create a class called `SR` that creates properties that represent the values of the strings used in an application.

LISTING 8.6: Encrypting Data with the `EncryptSymmetric` Method and a String

```
[C#]
string cipherText = Cryptographer.EncryptSymmetric
      (SR.RinjdaelManaged, "123-45-6789");

[Visual Basic]
Dim cipherText As String = Cryptographer.EncryptSymmetric _
     (SR.RinjdaelManaged, "123-45-6789")
```

Alternatively, as Listing 8.7 shows, the same result can be achieved by using the method that accepts a byte array.

Listing 8.7: Encrypting Data with the `EncryptSymmetric` Method and a Byte Array

```
[C#]
byte[] valueToEncrypt = new byte[]
     {49, 0, 50, 0, 51, 0, 45, 0, 52, 0, 53, 0, 45, 0, 54, 0, 55,
      0, 56, 0, 57, 0}
byte[] cipherContents = Cryptographer.EncryptSymmetric
(SR.RinjdaelManaged, valueToEncrypt);
Array.Clear(valueToEncrypt, 0, valueToEncrypt.Length);

[Visual Basic]
Dim valueToEncrypt As Byte() = New Byte() _
     {49, 0, 50, 0, 51, 0, 45, 0, 52, 0, 53, 0, 45, 0, 54, 0, 55, _
      0, 56, 0, 57, 0}
Dim cipherContents As Byte() = _
     Cryptographer.EncryptSymmetric(SR.RinjdaelManaged, valueToEncrypt)
Array.Clear(valueToEncrypt, 0, valueToEncrypt.Length)
```

Even though using a byte array is more secure than using strings, the byte array should still be cleared as soon as possible because having unencrypted data in memory can be a security risk.

---

6. As mentioned earlier, the String Resource Tool can be found in the Downloads section of the Enterprise Library workspace at http://practices.gotdotnet.com/projects/entlib.

The `DecryptSymmetric` Method

Decrypting data that has been encrypted with a configured symmetric provider is also straightforward. The static `DecryptSymmetric` method is overloaded to match its counterpart, the `EncryptSymmetric` method. Listing 8.8 provides a sample that decrypts the base64-encoded `cipherText` string that was encrypted in Listings 8.6 and 8.7.

LISTING 8.8: Decrypting data with `DecryptSymmetric` and a base64-encoded string

```
[C#]
string cleartext =
     Cryptographer.DecryptSymmetric(SR.RinjdaelManaged, cipherText);

[Visual Basic]
Dim cleartext As String = _
     Cryptographer.DecryptSymmetric(SR.RinjdaelManaged, cipherText)
```

And just as a byte array can be used to encrypt the data, it can also be used to decrypt it, as shown in Listing 8.9.

LISTING 8.9: Decrypting data with `DecryptSymmetric` and a byte array

```
[C#]
byte[] decryptedContents = Cryptographer.DecryptSymmetric
      (SR.RinjdaelManaged, cipherContents);

[Visual Basic]
Dim decryptedContents As Byte() = Cryptographer.DecryptSymmetric _
     (SR.RinjdaelManaged, cipherContents)
```

It is important to use the same provider to encrypt and decrypt the data. Notice that the same RinjdaelManaged provider was used to both encrypt and decrypt the data in Listings 8.6 through 8.9.

Creating and Comparing Hashes

It is better to hash secret data, like passwords, than it is to encrypt them using a symmetric key. Using a symmetric key to encrypt and store password data runs the risk of every password being compromised if the key is compromised. However, if the password is hashed, and only the hash is stored, the actual passwords themselves do not become compromised. When a user enters a password, the password gets hashed in the same manner as the hash that is stored and the two are compared. If the hashes match, the password has been entered correctly.

Hash Provider Configuration

At least one hash provider must be configured for an application for it to use the Cryptography Application Block to create and compare hashes. To add a hash provider, right-click on the *Hash Providers* folder and select *Custom Hash Provider* or *HashAlgorithm Provider*. There is no menu item for configuring a KeyedHashAlgorithmProvider. Instead, the block will automatically determine whether further configuration for a KeyedHashAlgorithmProvider needs to occur based on whether the hash algorithm that is selected is a keyed hash algorithm. Figure 8.14 demonstrates how to add a nonkeyed hash algorithm like SHA1Managed to the Cryptography Application Block.

Since this hash algorithm is not keyed, this is all you need to do to configure it. You can change the name or disable salting; however, it is not necessary.

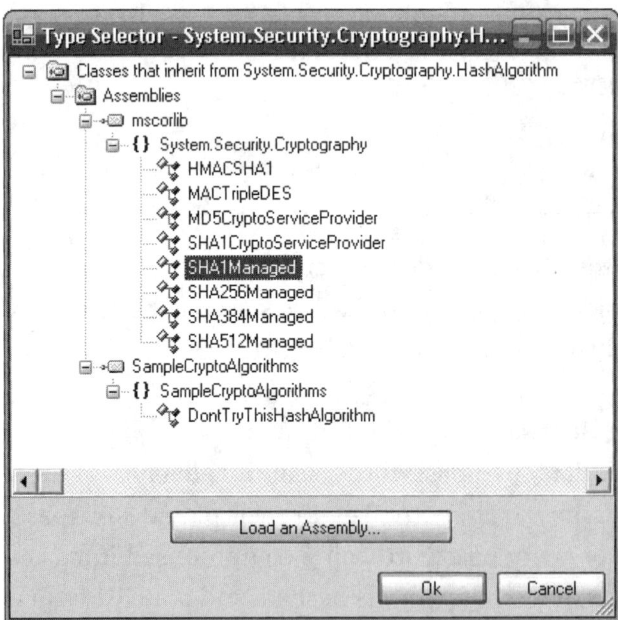

FIGURE 8.14: Adding the SHA1Managed HashAlgorithmProvider

If you select the keyed hashing algorithm instead of the nonkeyed hashing algorithm, an additional dialog will display that lets you enter a key. This is the same Key Creation dialog that was shown in Figure 8.9 for configuring a symmetric key. This key is configured in exactly the same way as the symmetric keys. For details on how to encrypt the configuration information for this key and further protect the master key, see the earlier section SymmetricAlgorithmProvider Configuration.

After the hashing algorithm has been created, you can set whether the algorithm should be salted or not. By default, the Cryptography Application Block enables salting for all hashing algorithms in an effort to reduce the risk of a dictionary attack. You can disable salting for a hashing algorithm by changing the `SaltEnabled` value to false. Figure 8.15 shows how to change the `SaltEnabled` value in the Enterprise Library Configuration Tool.

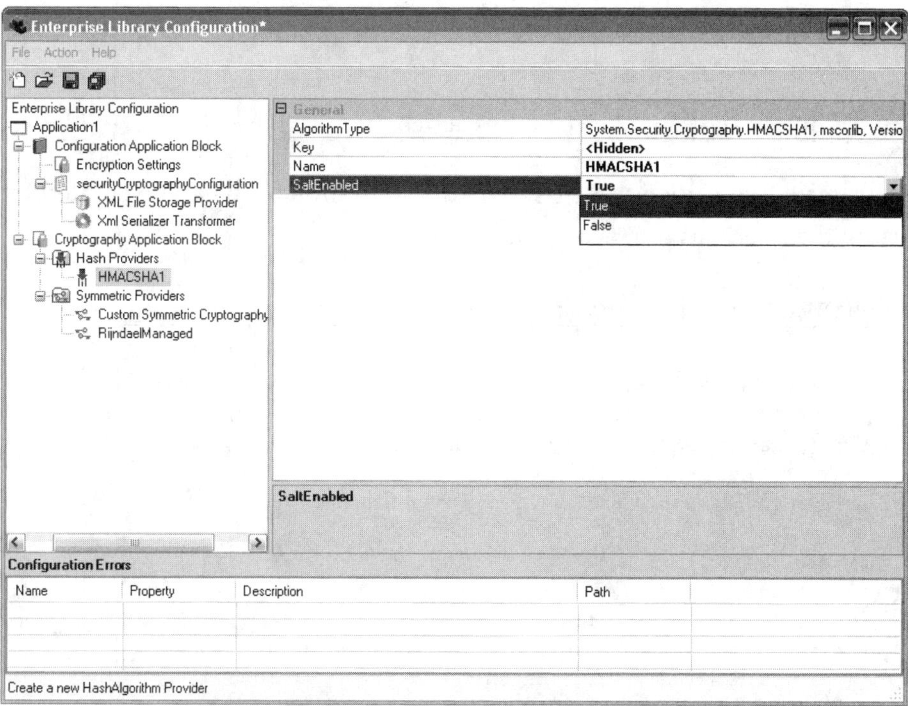

FIGURE 8.15: Changing the `SaltEnabled` Value for a Hash Provider

The `CreateHash` Method

After a hash algorithm provider has been configured, creating hashes is pretty trivial. You can use the `Cryptographer`'s static `CreateHash` method to create a hash by passing in the name of the hash provider and either a base64-encoded string or byte array to encrypt. In the first instance, the `CreateHash` method returns a base64-encoded string that represents the hash; in the second instance it returns an array of bytes that represent the hash. Listing 8.10 shows how to use the HMACSHA1 provider that was configured in Figure 8.15 to create a hash for a password. As in the examples for encrypting and decrypting data in Listings 8.6 through 8.9, the String Resource Tool is used to create a class called with properties that represent the values of the strings used in an application.

LISTING 8.10: Creating a Hash from a String

```
[C#]
string hashText =
    Cryptographer.CreateHash(SR.HMACSHA1, "p@ssw0rd");

[Visual Basic]
Dim hashText As String = _
    Cryptographer.CreateHash(SR.HMACSHA1, "p@ssw0rd")
```

Alternatively, Listing 8.11 shows that the same hash can be created by using the overload that accepts a byte array.

LISTING 8.11: Creating a Hash from a Byte Array

```
[C#]
byte[]valueToHash = new byte[]
    {112, 0, 115, 0, 115, 0, 119, 0, 48, 0, 114, 0, 100, 0}
byte[] generatedHash = Cryptographer.CreateHash
     (SR.HMACSHA1, valueToHash);
Array.Clear(valueToHash, 0, valueToHash.Length);

[Visual Basic]
Dim valueToHash As Byte() = New Byte() _
    {112, 0, 115, 0, 115, 0, 119, 0, 48, 0, 114, 0, 100, 0}
Dim generatedHash As Byte() = Cryptographer.CreateHash _
     (SR.HMACSHA1, valueToHash)
Array.Clear(valueToHash, 0, valueToHash.Length)
```

By only storing this hash and not the actual password, the password can only be verified; it cannot be decrypted.

The `CompareHash` Method

Creating a hash is only one half of the puzzle. The ability to create hashes is of little use if the hash cannot be used to verify that the proper data had been received and that the data has not been modified in transit. You can use the `Cryptographer`'s static `CompareHash` method to compare the received data against the hash that was created with the `CreateHash` method. As mentioned earlier in this chapter, many people assume that if the results of two `CreateHash` methods with the same byte array are equal, then the hashes are equal. However, this is not always true if salt is used. The `CompareHash` method takes the salt into account when comparing the hashes.

The `CompareHash` method is overloaded to accept three strings or to accept a string and two byte arrays. The data types must match between the received data and the original hash; therefore, if the original hash is stored as a string, then the first overload must be used; if it is stored as a byte array, then the second overload must be used. If the received data is not of the same data type as the stored hash, then one of them must be converted. Both overloads return a Boolean value that indicates whether the hashes are equal or not.

Listing 8.12 shows how to use the HMACSHA1 provider to compare the received data against the hash that was created in Listing 8.10.

LISTING 8.12: Comparing Hashes Using Strings

```
[C#]
bool bValid =
     Cryptographer.CompareHash(SR.HMACSHA1,"p@ssw0rd",hashText);

[Visual Basic]
Dim bValid As Boolean = _
     Cryptographer.CompareHash(SR.HMACSHA1,"p@ssw0rd",hashText)
```

Alternatively, the comparison could be done using byte arrays, as shown in Listing 8.13.

LISTING 8.13: Comparing Hashes Using Byte Arrays

```
[C#]
byte[] stringToCompare = new byte[]
     {112, 0, 115, 0, 115, 0, 119, 0, 48, 0, 114, 0, 100, 0}
bool bValid =
```

```
    Cryptographer.CompareHash(SR.HMACSHA1, stringToCompare, hashText);
```

```
[Visual Basic]
Dim stringToCompare As Byte() = New Byte() _
     {112, 0, 115, 0, 115, 0, 119, 0, 48, 0, 114, 0, 100, 0}
Dim bValid As Boolean = _
     Cryptographer.CompareHash(SR.HMACSHA1, stringToCompare, hashText)
```

Summary

The major point of this chapter is how the Cryptography Application Block not only makes it easier to perform cryptographic tasks that would otherwise take a lot of skill and effort, but also how the block performs these functions according to the best practices documented in Chapters 8 and 9 of the book *Writing Secure Code*, Second Edition, by Michael Howard and David C. LeBlanc. After the basic concepts of cryptography and the Microsoft .NET Framework were explored, the chapter continued with a detailed examination of the design of the Cryptography Application Block and how this design makes it easy for you to accomplish the most common cryptography tasks without incurring significant performance degradation. This chapter examined the design and functions of the `Cryptographer`, the DpapiSymmetricCryptoProvider, the SymmetricAlgorithmProvider, the HashAlgorithmProvider, and the KeyedHashAlgorithmProvider and the use of these providers' cryptographic utility classes that reside in the `Common` namespace.

The chapter concluded with demonstrations of how to configure the different providers with the Enterprise Library Configuration Tool and how to code against these providers. It showed how to configure the SymmetricAlgorithmProviders and how to code an application to use these providers for encrypting and decrypting data, and how the symmetric key can be protected by using the related cryptographic capabilities of Enterprise Library's Configuration Application Block. This chapter also reviewed how to configure hash providers and code against these providers to create and compare hashes. Throughout the chapter, emphasis was placed on the fact that, by using the Cryptography Application Block, very little code needs to be written to adhere to the best practices for cryptography.

9 Building an Application Block

THE PREVIOUS CHAPTERS have described the design for each of the application blocks that ship with Enterprise Library, how to configure them, and how to develop an application so that it can benefit from the application blocks. They have emphasized how the design of each block is not only an implementation of the best practices as promoted by the Microsoft patterns & practices team, but that special attention was paid to ensure the block was simple to use and extensible to fit the needs of many enterprises.

You saw how each application block can be extended so that you can *mold* them to fit your needs if your application requirements don't perfectly match the providers that ship with Enterprise Library. For example, Chapter 6 showed how the Logging and Instrumentation Application Block can be extended with a new distribution strategy and Distributor Service for enterprises that may not have standardized or do not promote the use of MSMQ.

The extensibility of Enterprise Library does not end with the ability to extend each application block. If you have a particular need that is not addressed by any of the application blocks that ship with Enterprise Library, you can develop a new application block that has the same design-time and configuration-driven capabilities as the application blocks that ship with Enterprise Library. This chapter walks you through the steps that are needed to create a new application block that can serve as a peer to the application blocks that ship with Enterprise Library.

To fully appreciate this chapter, I highly recommend that you first read Chapters 1 and 2. Understanding the contents of those chapters is important because all application blocks, including the one that is created in this chapter, depend on the Configuration Application Block for reading and writing its configuration information and enabling its design-time features. While this chapter recaps some of the important points detailed in those two chapters, it doesn't go into the depth that those chapters do.

Additionally, I recommend having read Chapters 3 and 4. While these aren't required reading to understand the concepts for how to build an application block, the block that I create in this chapter makes extensive use of the Data Access Application Block and the Caching Application Block by encapsulating and extending their functionality. Therefore, understanding those application blocks will help you understand the application block created in this chapter.

Vision and Design Goals

Designing an application block should not be approached any differently than designing any other software developed in an enterprise. As such, the first step to designing the application block should be determining what the vision and design goals for the application block are. If you read through the documentation that is provided for any of the application blocks that ship with Enterprise Library, you will see that one of the first details that are documented is the design goals for that block. This should not be any different for an application block that you create.

In this chapter I am going to create an application block that subscribes to the best practices published by the Microsoft patterns & practices team with respect to data access logic components. In some sense, this application block can be thought of as a level of abstraction above what the Data Access Application Block provides. If you read Chapter 3, you should understand that it is an implementation for simplifying the use of database providers (also known as data access helper components) in the data layer of an application. The Data Access Application Block implements the recommendations for database providers as published by Microsoft's patterns & practices group.

While database providers are extremely useful, they do not address all of the areas of guidance for designing the data layer of a distributed application. Unfortunately, the code that uses database providers is often scattered throughout many different places in an application, embedded in the actual business entity, or "utility" classes are created in an application that retrieve and update data regardless of the type of data (e.g., user information, reference data, transactional business data) with which it is working.

As mentioned at the end of the Chapter 3, a recommended design for an application is to create data access logic components (DALCs) that have the responsibility for populating business entity classes or DataSets with data and propagating changes in them back to the database. Data access logic components are a recommended best practice for accessing business data because they provide a simple programmatic interface for retrieving and performing operations on specific types of data. Data access logic components typically provide methods to perform Create, Retrieve, Update, and Delete operations relating to a specific business entity in an application (e.g., customers). Additionally, the logic for how the fields (e.g., customerID, customerName, etc.) in a particular business entity or DataSet map to a stored procedure's parameters or columns in a database table can be encapsulated by a data access logic component. By encapsulating this logic in data access logic components, you can achieve greater reuse throughout different types of applications with different types of clients.

The following sections walk you through the steps for developing and testing an application block that subscribes to the best practices for supporting data access logic components in an application. A major feature of this block is that it allows the DataFields in a typed DataSet to be mapped to the parameters for a stored procedure, thus making it possible for the in-memory objects to need no knowledge of the database schema or that a database is even present. Martin Fowler defines such an object as a *Data Mapper*[1]; therefore, I have named this application block as the Data Mapping Application Block. Its design goals are to provide:

---

1. Martin Fowler, *Patterns of Enterprise Application Architecture,* p. 165. Addison-Wesley, 2002.

- The ability to eliminate code that couples stored procedure parameters to the DataFields in a typed DataSet
- Capabilities to map stored procedure parameters to values that are not known to the system until runtime
- Support for performing database operations against multiple database tables in the scope of a database transaction
- Ability to cache business data in a data access logic component
- Support for setting command properties (e.g., command timeout) through configuration instead of code

In short, the design goals for the Data Mapping Application Block are to provide an interface that simplifies the creation of data access logic components while still subscribing to the best practices as detailed in the *Application Architecture for .NET: Designing Applications and Services* publication.[2] For example, this application block should make it easy to ensure that database operations occur in the scope of a transaction or specify whether business data should be cached by the data access logic component. The vision for this block is that using this application block will free developers from having to deal with such operational issues and instead allow them to concentrate on adding business logic.

Many classes exist in this application block to address the design goals and vision. There are too many to cover in a chapter that also addresses how to build an application block. Therefore, this chapter highlights the salient tasks that I needed to undertake to build this block so that you can understand what is involved with building your own custom application blocks. For detailed information on the design of the Data Mapping Application Block and how to configure and develop an application to take advantage of it, please read Appendix A and visit the book's Web site or the workspace that I created for this application block on www.gotdotnet.com.

---

2. Found at http://msdn.microsoft.com/library/default.asp?url=/library/en-us/dnbda/html/distapp.asp.

Core Functionality

An application block typically provides an implementation for solving a problem that is not solved by the .NET Framework or for which there is no alternate solution that is both simple to use and extensible for adaptability. Core functionality—code that provides the base functionality that implements best practices for solving that particular problem—must exist for any application block. The core functionality for a block is the functionality that is *not* intended to be extended through providers, because it must be consistent independent of the functionality that any one provider offers.

For example, in the Caching Application Block, `CacheManagers` are not an extension point; they are exposed as a class but are not extensible. Additionally, cached data is always stored in an internal hashtable when it is read from a BackingStore or items are added to the cache at runtime. The hashtable is not exposed and another mechanism for caching this data is not provided as an extension point. All application blocks have core functionality that is fundamental to the solution that it is providing. When creating an application block, some thought must be given to what functionality should be core to the block and what should be "pluggable" and extensible.

Three major classes are used to provide the core functionality for the Data Mapping Application Block: `DatabaseWrapper`, `DataCacheSettings`, and `DataMapper`. The `DatabaseWrapper` acts as a service layer that encapsulates the Data Access Application Block. This service layer primarily takes advantage of the Data Access Application Block's support for retrieving typed DataSets and propagating the changes in those DataSets to the backend database. It has the additional benefit of respecting any complex relationships that may exist between the tables in the DataSet and allows the transaction level to be set through configuration so an update can occur in the scope of a transaction.

The `DataCacheSettings` class contains information about how a particular typed DataSet should be cached after it is obtained via the `DatabaseWrapper`. Lastly, the `DataMapper` class is an abstract base class that subscribes to the best practice for exposing expected functionality that is common across all data access logic components. The best practice states that such functionality should be exposed in a separately defined interface or base class. This class uses both the `DataCacheSettings` and DatabaseWrapper to obtain typed DataSets, cache them, set transactions for them, and propagate the changes made to them back to the data store. The `DataMapper` is designed to make it easy to develop business data access logic components that contain functionality for managing "entities" through Create, Retrieve, Update, and Delete operations.

Figure 9.1 shows the primary classes that provide this core functionality. These classes are not exposed as extension points; that is, other classes cannot be plugged in to provide different implementations. For example, the `DatabaseWrapper` cannot be replaced by another class that retrieves and updates data from a data source in a way that is different from the methods used in the `DatabaseWrapper`. To do so would require modification of the code base provided with the application block. You can find more information about the specific features and design of these classes in Appendix A.

Pluggable Providers

There is a fine line between what should be core functionality and what should be "pluggable." Providers let flex points in an application block ensure that the core functionality is still applicable even when something outside of that core functionality changes. Throughout this book I have described and created many providers for all of the application blocks that ship with Enterprise Library. For example, Chapter 3 described the database providers (SqlDatabase, OracleDatabase, and Db2Database) that ship with the Data Access Application Block and showed how to create a new database provider that can be used to access other databases. Chapter 7 discussed the AuthenticationProvider that ships with the Security Application Block for authenticating users against a database and showed how to create a new AuthenticationProvider to authenticate users against a Microsoft Active Directory. Providers allow an application block to be adaptable so

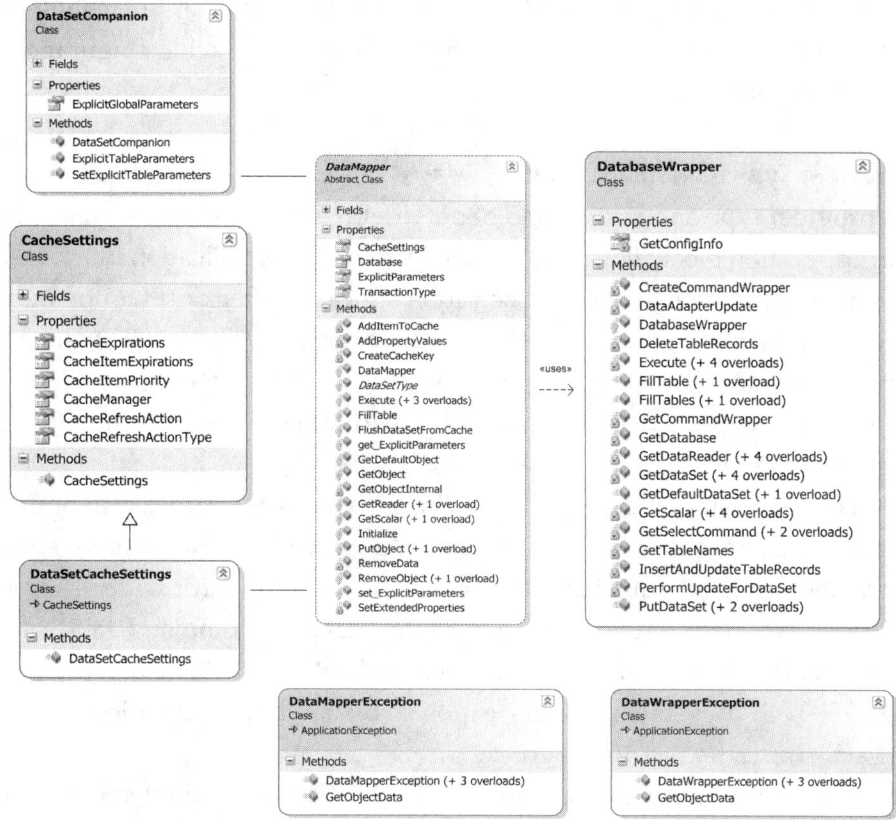

FIGURE 9.1: Classes Representing Core Functionality for the Data Mapping Application Block

that it can fit into an environment where the needs may be different than what Enterprise Library allows out-of-the-box.

There are several characteristics that define how an application block should be designed to use providers.

- An application block should provide at least one specific implementation of a provider type that demonstrates how the application block can be used.
- The application block should be developed so that its core functionality is decoupled from any specific provider implementation.

- It is almost always a good idea to ensure that providers are configurable; that is, that they can initialize themselves with configuration data that specifies how they should execute.

Provider Type Implementation

A **provider type** defines the kind of provider that is expected to be used by an application block. For example, the Data Access Application Block uses database providers, while the Security Application Block uses authentication, authorization, security cache, role management, and profile management providers. Every application block must determine which type of providers it expects to use and should provide at least one implementation of such a provider.

The Data Mapping Application Block expects to use DataMappingProviders. I have defined the `IDataMappingProvider` interface to represent the expected functionality that any DataMappingProvider should possess. When the `DatabaseWrapper` maps database command, table, and field information to the properties and fields of an "entity" (e.g., a typed DataSet), it uses the methods exposed by an implementation of the `IDataMappingProvider` interface.

The `DatabaseWrapper` can use any class that implements the `IDataMappingProvider` interface to map database constructs to the corresponding construct for that provider. The DataSetMappingProvider is provided with the application block as an implementation of the DataMappingProvider type and is intended to be used to map typed DataSets to database commands and command parameters. Figure 9.2 shows how the `DataSetMappingProvider` implements the `IDataMappingProvider` interface to serve as a provider type implementation for the DataMappingProvider type.

Decoupling from the Core Functionality

By developing the block so that it uses the interface exposed by the provider type and not any one specific provider, the application block is decoupled from any single provider's implementation. This helps to achieve the following goals.

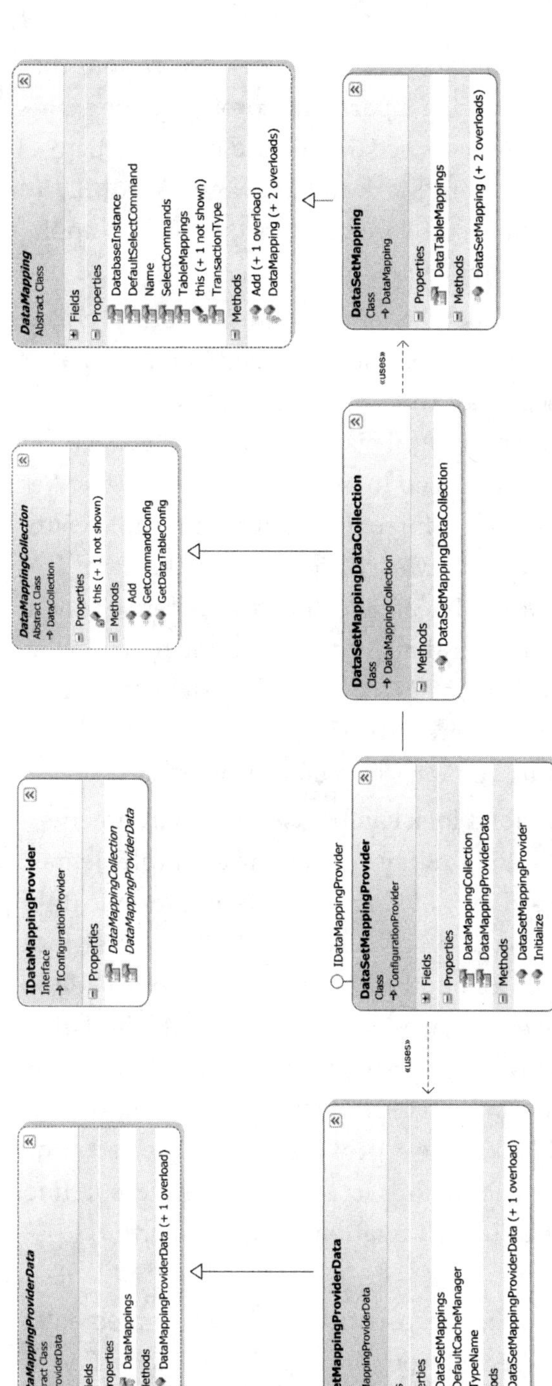

FIGURE 9.2: Primary Classes Used for DataSetMappingProvider Implementation

- **Variability.** Developers and architects can choose from various different implementations for solving a particular problem. For example, I once had to design a Web service that would convert Microsoft Word 2003 documents from Word Markup Language (WordML) to PDF format. There were many software vendors that offered application interfaces to allow for this type of functionality.

  To choose the vendor that met the requirements the best, I created a Document Conversion Application Block with an interface that met the requirements needed for this service. Then I developed a provider for each vendor's offering. This let me switch between vendors with ease and without the need to modify any code in the Web service or the application block. Moreover, it allowed me to create unit and load tests to compare how each solution matched the requirements for the service. If I need to evaluate another vendor, I simply created another provider that encapsulated the functionality for that vendor. There was a great deal of variety in determining which vendor best met the requirements for the service while not tying the service to any one vendor's implementation.
- **Extensibility.** An application block can be used in environments where a specific capability might have a mandatory implementation with which the block does not ship. There is an example of this in Chapter 6 in the discussion of the extensibility for distribution strategies and distributors in the Logging and Instrumentation Application Block. Some enterprises will not use MSMQ in their corporate environment, but this doesn't eliminate the ability to use the asynchronous distribution strategy in the Logging and Instrumentation Application Block. A new provider can be created and used with the block to distribute logs in a way that is more in line with the corporate strategy (e.g., a relational database or MQSeries).
- **Encapsulation.** Each provider encapsulates the way it implements the functionality that is expected from the application block. For example, the `SqlDatabase` provider encapsulates the logic needed to perform database operations against a Microsoft SQL Server database; the `OracleDatabase` provider does the same for Oracle data-

bases. These implementations are in the providers and not in the application block that the provider supports.

Additionally, this allows functionality that is not a part of the application block's core functionality to be replaced or upgraded without affecting other areas of the application block. For example, if a new database provider were created that worked more efficiently to perform database operations against a Microsoft SQL Server 2005 database, that provider could be used by the Data Access Application Block without the need for code changes in the block itself.

- **Minimized coupling between application blocks.** Application blocks that are dependent on other application blocks may encapsulate this dependency into a provider. This means that the application block is less vulnerable to revisions in the application block on which it depends. For example, the Exception Handling Application Block includes the `LoggingExceptionHandler`. This handler is dependent on the Logging Application Block and is included as a provider. A new version of the Logging Application Block would require only a new logging handler provider; the rest of the Exception Handling Application Block can remain unchanged.

Not only does Figure 9.2 show how the `IDataMappingProvider` interface exposed specific functionality that was implemented by the `DataSetMappingProvider` class, but it also showed the use of several abstract base classes that complement the `IDataMappingProvider`. The Data Mapping Application Block takes advantage of these classes to remain completely decoupled from any one provider's implementation. The `DatabaseWrapper` accesses a `DataMappingCollection` from the provider that it is configured to use and accesses all of the settings for mapping entities from the `DataMapping` objects contained in this collection.

The `DataMappingCollection` class and the `DataMapping` class are both abstract; an implementation of a DataMappingProvider must supply the specific way that it intends to map database fields to entities. The `DataSetMappingProvider` supplies this by way of the derived `DataSetMapping` class; however, the Data Mapping Application Block knows nothing of this derived class. It just expects to retrieve a class that is derived from the `DataMappingCollection` class and use it to access classes that must derive from the `DataMapping` class.

Listing 9.1 shows the code that illustrates how the `DatabaseWrapper` is decoupled from any one provider's implementation. In this method, the `DatabaseWrapper` is not referencing any classes that are used in the `DataSetMappingProvider` implementation; it only references the `IDataMappingProvider` interface and the abstract base classes shown in Figure 9.2.

LISTING 9.1: Binding Only to the `IDataMappingProvider` Interface

```
[C#]
private static DataMappingCollection GetConfigInfo
{
     get
     {
          DataMappingCollection configDataMappings = null;
          try
          {
               IDataMappingProvider mappingProvider =
                    DataMappingsFactory.GetDataMappingProvider ();
               configDataMappings =
                    mappingProvider.DataMappingCollection;
          }
          catch (Exception ex)
          {
               throw new DataWrapperException
                    ("Cannot obtain configuration information: " +
                       ex.Message, ex);
          }
          return configDataMappings;
     }
}

[Visual Basic]
Private Shared ReadOnly Property GetConfigInfo() _
               As DataMappingCollection

     Get
          Dim configDataMappings As DataMappingCollection = Nothing
          Try
               Dim mappingProvider As IDataMappingProvider = _
                    DataMappingsFactory.GetDataMappingProvider ()
```

```
                configDataMappings = _
                     mappingProvider.DataMappingCollection
           Catch ex As Exception
                Throw New DataWrapperException _
                      ("Cannot obtain configuration information: " & _
                         ex.Message, ex)
           End Try
           Return configDataMappings
      End Get
   End Property
```

Configurable

As I created new providers in the previous chapters, I described the benefit that can be achieved by enabling each provider to initialize itself with the configuration information that it needs to run properly. For example, for the `XMLFileDatabase` database provider to run properly, it needs to obtain configuration information about which file to use to store and retrieve data. Therefore, in Chapter 3, I designed the `XMLFileDatabase` database provider so that it could initialize itself with information about which XML file to use. The configuration data for a provider is generally stored with the rest of the configuration data for an application block and is specified in configuration by its type information and a name.

As discussed in Chapter 1, the abstract `ConfigurationProvider` base class defines the contract for initializing a provider with configuration information. A provider is afforded the ability to initialize itself with configuration data by deriving from this abstract base class and implementing the `Initialize` method. The `Initialize` method accepts an object containing the current `ConfigurationView` and uses it to obtain the provider's runtime configuration data. When building a provider for an application block, it is important to derive that provider either directly or indirectly from the `ConfigurationProvider` class so that it can initialize itself with configuration data. The `DataSetMappingProvider`, for example, implements the `IDataMappingProvider` interface and derives from the `ConfigurationProvider` class.

Additionally, the runtime configuration data for a provider is typically contained in a class that derives from the `ProviderData` class. In the case of the `DataSetMappingProvider`, the runtime configuration data is contained in a class named DataSetMappingProviderData. DataSetMappingProviderData derives from an abstract DataMappingProviderData class that derives from ProviderData. The DataMappingProviderData class contains runtime configuration information that would be common for all DataMappingProviders. The DataSetMappingProviderData class just adds configuration information that is specific to its implementation.

Listing 9.2 has a property for accessing the CacheManager that is used to cache typed DataSets and a property for returning the DataMappingCollection. This listing also demonstrates how each of these properties is decorated with attributes that allow the XmlSerializer to be used to serialize and deserialize the class. That is how the Configuration Application Block creates the provider classes (or any classes, for that matter) from the configuration data. You can read more about the ConfigurationProvider, ConfigurationView, and the other configuration runtime classes in Chapter 1.

Listing 9.2: Representing the Configuration Data for the DataSetMappingProvider

```
[C#]
public class DataSetMappingProviderData : DataMappingProviderData
{
    private string cacheManager;
    public DataSetMappingProviderData() : this(string.Empty)
    {
    }

    public DataSetMappingProviderData(string name) : base(name)
    {
        cacheManager = String.Empty;
        dataMappingCollection = new DataSetMappingDataCollection();
    }

    [XmlAttribute("cacheManager")]
    public string CacheManager
    {
        get {return cacheManager;}
        set {cacheManager= value;}
    }

    [XmlArray("DataSetMappings")]
    [XmlArrayItem(Type=typeof(DataSetMapping))]
    public override DataMappingCollection DataMappings
    {
        get { return base.DataMappings; }
    }
```

```
    [XmlIgnore]
    public override string TypeName
    {
        get
        {
            return
            typeof(DataSetMappingProvider).AssemblyQualifiedName;
        }
        set {}
    }
}

[Visual Basic]
Public Class DataSetMappingProviderData : _
            Inherits DataMappingProviderData

Private cacheManager As String
    Public Sub New()
        Me.New(String.Empty)
    End Sub

    Public Sub New(ByVal name As String)
        MyBase.New(name)
        cacheManager = String.Empty
        dataMappingCollection = New DataSetMappingDataCollection()
    End Sub

    <XmlAttribute("cacheManager")> _
    Public Property CacheManager() As String
        Get
            Return cacheManager
        End Get
        Set
            cacheManager = Value
        End Set
    End Property

    <XmlArray("DataSetMappings"), _
    XmlArrayItem(Type:=GetType(DataSetMapping))> _
    Public Overrides ReadOnly Property DataMappings() _
            As DataMappingCollection
        Get
            Return MyBase.DataMappings
        End Get
    End Property

    <XmlIgnore> _
    Public Overrides Property TypeName() As String
        Get
            Return _
```

```
                GetType(DataSetMappingProvider).AssemblyQualifiedName
            End Get
            Set
            End Set
        End Property
    End Class
```

Factories

Providers are just one of the two constructs that are used to allow an application block to be decoupled from any specific implementation. To truly be decoupled from a provider's implementation, a software factory should exist in the application block so that it allows providers to be created and used in a way that a consumer of the core functionality needs to know very little, if anything, about a particular provider. Listing 9.1 showed an example of this; a `DataMappingsFactory` was used to create and return a class that implemented the `IDataMappingProvider` interface. If the application block did not use the factory, but instead just initialized an instance of a class that implements the `IDataMappingProvider` interface, then the application block would be tightly coupled to that provider. The combination of the factory and the providers are what give an application block its ability to be decoupled from any single implementation.

The factories in the Enterprise Library application blocks subscribe to the *Plugin*[3] design pattern to create providers. By using this design pattern, neither applications nor application blocks require specific implementation information about the provider. Furthermore, specific implementations for each provider are constructed according to the configuration settings for that provider.

The Configuration Application Block contains an abstract base class named `ProviderFactory` that is intended to serve as the base class for any specific application block's provider factories. The `ProviderFactory` takes most of the hard work out of creating a factory to instantiate configurable providers away from any derived class.

---

3. Martin Fowler, *Patterns of Enterprise Application Architecture*, pp. 499–503. Addison-Wesley, 2002.

Each of the previous chapters have shown how an application block uses its provider factory to create a specific implementation of a provider. Most of the application blocks actually included two factory classes; one was the provider factory that creates a specific provider, and the other was a class that wrapped around the provider factory with static methods so a consumer doesn't need to directly instantiate a provider factory to obtain a provider. Also, each of the provider factories discussed generally contained two methods for creating a provider: one for creating the default provider as specified by the configuration settings and one for creating a named provider.

Listing 9.3 shows the code for the `DataMappingsProviderFactory`.

LISTING 9.3: The `DataMappingsProviderFactory` Class

```
[C#]
public class DataMappingsProviderFactory : ProviderFactory
{
     public DataMappingsProviderFactory() :
          this(ConfigurationManager.GetCurrentContext())
     {
     }

     public DataMappingsProviderFactory(ConfigurationContext context):
          base("DataMappings Factory", context,
          typeof(IDataMappingProvider))
     {
     }

     public IDataMappingProvider GetDataMappingProvider(string name)
     {
          return (IDataMappingProvider)base.CreateInstance(name);
     }

     public IDataMappingProvider GetDataMappingProvider()
     {
          return (IDataMappingProvider)base.CreateDefaultInstance();
     }

     protected override string GetDefaultInstanceName()
      {
          DataMappingsConfigurationView view =
               (DataMappingsConfigurationView)
               CreateConfigurationView();
          return view.GetDefaultDataMappingProviderDataName();
      }
```

```
        protected override ConfigurationView CreateConfigurationView()
        {
            return new
                DataMappingsConfigurationView(ConfigurationContext);
        }

        protected override Type GetConfigurationType(string instanceName)
        {
            DataMappingsConfigurationView view =
                (DataMappingsConfigurationView)
                CreateConfigurationView();
            DataMappingProviderData dataMappingProviderData =
                view.GetDataMappingProviderData(instanceName);
            return GetType(dataMappingProviderData.TypeName);
        }
}

[Visual Basic]
Public Class DataMappingsProviderFactory : Inherits ProviderFactory

    Public Sub New()
        Me.New(ConfigurationManager.GetCurrentContext())
    End Sub

    Public Sub New(ByVal context As ConfigurationContext)
        MyBase.New("DataMappings Factory", context, _
            GetType(IDataMappingProvider))
    End Sub

    Public Function GetDataMappingProvider(ByVal name As String) _
            As IDataMappingProvider
        Return CType(MyBase.CreateInstance(name), _
            IDataMappingProvider)
    End Function

    Public Function GetDataMappingProvider() As IDataMappingProvider
        Return CType(MyBase.CreateDefaultInstance(), _
            IDataMappingProvider)
    End Function

    Protected Overrides Function GetDefaultInstanceName() As String
            Dim view As DataMappingsConfigurationView = _
                CType(CreateConfigurationView(), _
                DataMappingsConfigurationView)
            Return view.GetDefaultDataMappingProviderDataName()
    End Function

    Protected Overrides Function CreateConfigurationView() _
                As ConfigurationView
            Return New _
```

```
            DataMappingsConfigurationView(ConfigurationContext)
    End Function

    Protected Overrides Function GetConfigurationType _
                (ByVal instanceName As String) As Type
            Dim view As DataMappingsConfigurationView = _
                CType(CreateConfigurationView(), _
                DataMappingsConfigurationView)
            Dim dataMappingProviderData As _
                DataMappingProviderData = _
                view.GetDataMappingProviderData(instanceName)

            Return GetType(dataMappingProviderData.TypeName)
    End Function
End Class
```

The important point to understand from this listing is that by deriving from the abstract `ProviderFactory` class, a concrete provider factory doesn't need to contain any code for reading configuration data and creating providers via reflection. This is accomplished in the base class. The concrete provider factory only needs to be able to return a `ConfigurationView` that contains the configuration settings for the provider and supplies methods for returning the providers to a consumer of the factory. Once the provider factory has been developed, the other factory can be written to encapsulate the provider factory and supply static methods for creating the default provider and a named provider.

In the Enterprise Library application blocks, this factory generally has the same name as the provider factory but without the word *Provider* in it. Thus, I have created a `DataMappingsFactory` that encapsulates the `DataMappingsProviderFactory` and exposes an overloaded method for obtaining either the default DataMappingProvider or a named DataMappingProvider. Figure 9.3 shows the relationship between these two factory classes and the `DataMappingsConfigurationView`.

Runtime Configuration

If you have perused even a few of the previous chapters, it should be fairly obvious that all application blocks are driven by their configuration information. The configuration information for an application block defines how

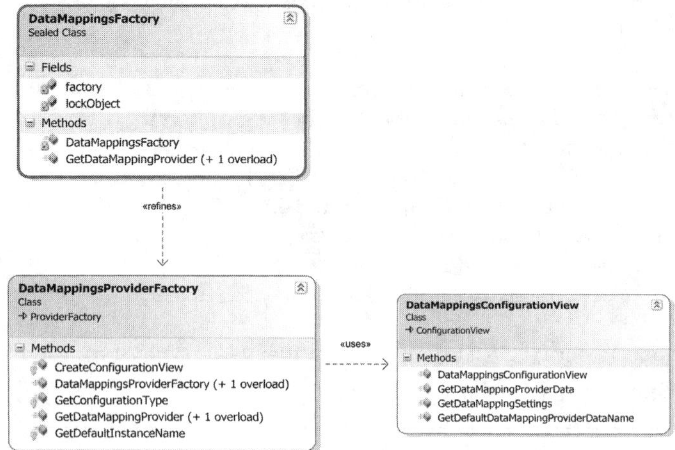

FIGURE 9.3: Factory Classes in the Data Mapping Application Block

the block and its providers will get the information they need to initialize, validate, and determine if any cross-block relationships exist. This provides several benefits.

- It provides the application block's flexibility and extensibility. An application block can be more easily adapted to meet the needs of different enterprise scenarios by allowing its runtime behavior to be configurable.
- Characteristics of an application block can be configured by different people at different times in the application's life cycle.
- The application block can be incrementally adapted for increasingly complex situations.
- The Configuration Tool provided with Enterprise Library makes it easy to create and edit configuration settings for an application block and its providers. Additionally, this tool makes it easy to specify cross-block relationships.

However, there is one detriment to being so configuration driven. It is sometimes more difficult to debug an issue in an application if it involves the way an application block or provider is configured. Developers are used to stepping through code if an issue occurs in an application, but unfortunately there is no way to step through the configuration data that drives the runtime behavior for an application block or provider. That is one reason why it is so important to use a tool like the Enterprise Library Configuration Tool for configuring an application block and its providers. While it will not catch every possible issue that can occur, it can catch many of them.

Specifying how the runtime configuration information for an application block will be represented entails designing and developing the set of objects that are needed to contain the configuration settings for that application block. For example, for the Data Access Application Block to function properly, the block needs to obtain information about the connection string to use for connecting to a database and the type of database that an application is configured to use (e.g., SQL Server, Oracle, or DB2). Therefore, it contains runtime configuration objects for representing the connection string and database type.

The Configuration Application Block reads settings from storage and returns the objects to the application block. Because all of the StorageProviders that ship with the Configuration Application Block require an object to be XML-serializable, the runtime configuration objects for a custom application block must also be XML-serializable. Therefore, in all of the runtime configuration objects in Enterprise Library and many of the code samples that you will see in the rest of this chapter, you will notice that the properties exposed by an object will be attributed with certain XML attributes like `XmlIgnore`, `XmlAttribute`, and `XmlArray`. These attributes allow the XmlSerializer to recognize how the values for these properties should be serialized and deserialized. For example, `XmlIgnore` indicates that the XmlSerializer should not attempt to serialize the value returned by that property. `XmlAttribute` signifies that the XmlSerializer should write the values out as an XML attribute and should read the values for this property out from this XML attribute when deserializing the object.

Figure 9.4 depicts the runtime configuration objects that are needed for the Data Mapping Application Block and the `DataSetMappingProvider` that ships with it. I won't provide the code for every class that is shown in

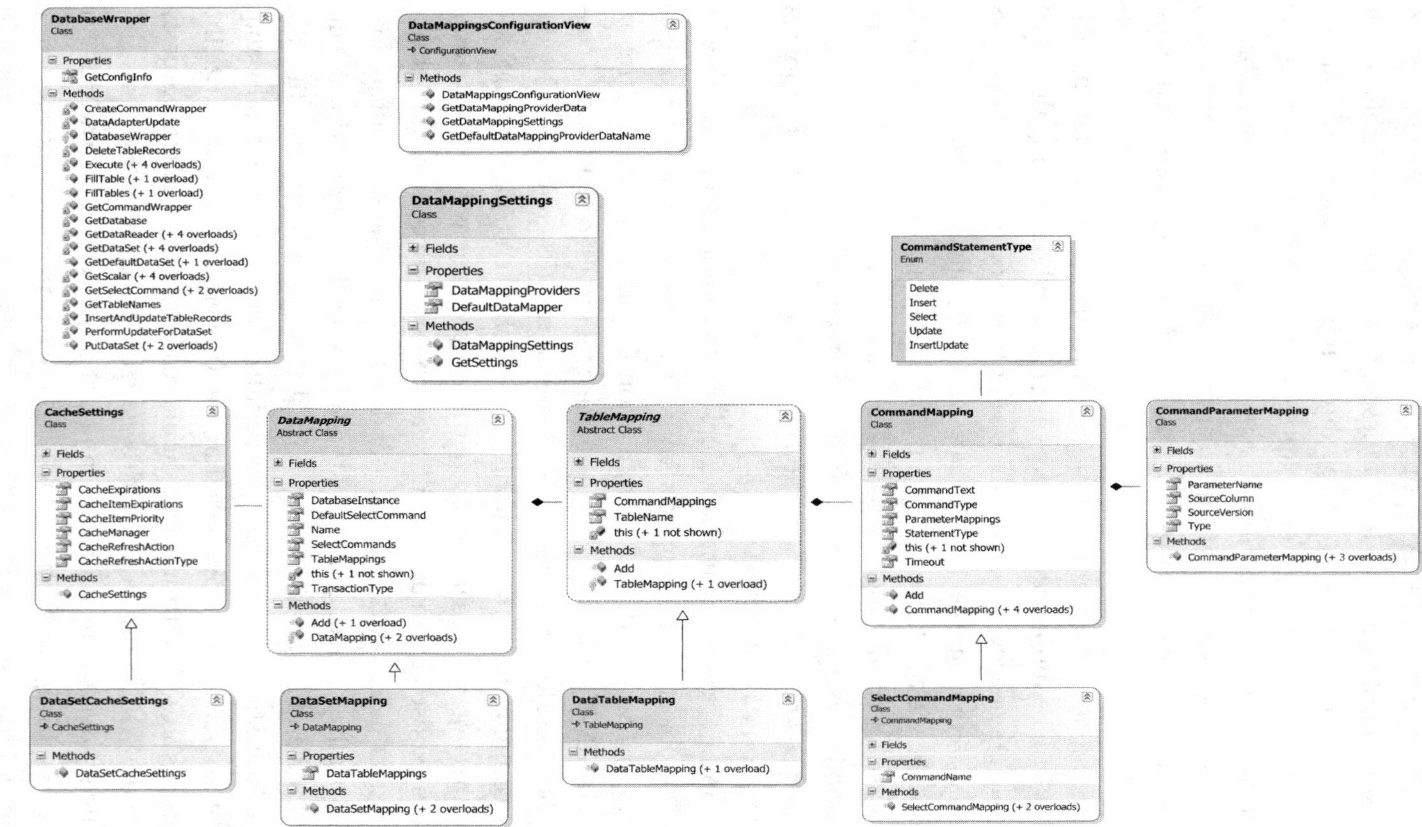

FIGURE 9.4: Runtime Configuration Object Graph for the Data Mapping Application Block

Figure 9.4 because much of the code that is created for each class is similar in its intent; the classes primarily differ only in the specific properties that they expose. I will, however, provide code samples for the classes where there is a significant difference in the way the class needs to be created or the purpose it serves. This should provide enough detailed information for you to be able to design and develop the objects that represent the runtime configuration for your own application blocks. All of the code for this application block is on this book's Web site if you want to review the code for all of the configuration objects.

The first runtime configuration class that needs to be created for an application block is the one that will hold the configuration information for the entire block. Typically this class is named according to the name of the application block and suffixed with *Settings* (e.g., `DatabaseSettings`, `ExceptionHandlingSettings`, `LoggingSettings`, etc.). For the Data Mapping Application Block I have named this class `DataMappingSettings`. In this class, the section name that identifies the section that the metaconfiguration data for this block will exist in must be specified. The Configuration Application Block looks for the metaconfiguration data in this section in the application's domain configuration file (i.e., app.config or web.config) and also uses the section name as the default file name for the configuration file (when using the `XmlFileStorageProvider`). Because the section name in the application's domain configuration file must be unique, the string that represents this application block must also be unique among all application blocks.

Listing 9.4 shows the code for the `DataMappingSettings` class. This class contains properties that return the name of the default `DataMappingProvider` that has been set through configuration, as well as a property that returns a collection of objects that contain the configuration data for the `DataMappingProviders` that have been configured for an application. Additionally, the section name is set to *DataMappings*. This means that the Configuration Application Block will read and write the metaconfiguration data for this application block in a section named *DataMappings*, and if the `XmlFileStorageProvider` is used to store the configuration data for this application block, that configuration data will be serialized to a file named *DataMappings.config* by default.

LISTING 9.4: The `DataMappingSettings` Class

```
[C#]
[XmlRoot("dataMappingSettings")]
public class DataMappingSettings
{
     public const string SectionName = "DataMappings";
     private DataMappingProviderDataCollection dataMappingProviders;
     private string defaultDataMapper;

     public const string ConfigurationNamespace =
          "http://www.example.com/eaf/datamappings";

     public DataMappingSettings()
     {
          dataMappingProviders = new
               DataMappingProviderDataCollection();
     }

     [XmlAttribute("defaultDataMapper")]
     public string DefaultDataMapper
     {
          get {return defaultDataMapper;}
          set {defaultDataMapper = value;}
     }

     [XmlArray(ElementName="dataMappingProviders")]
     [XmlArrayItem(Type=typeof(DataMappingProviderData))]
     public DataMappingProviderDataCollection DataMappingProviders
     {
          get { return dataMappingProviders; }
     }

     public static DataMappingSettings
          GetSettings(ConfigurationContext context)
     {
          return (DataMappingSettings)
               context.GetConfiguration(SectionName);
     }
}

[Visual Basic]
<XmlRoot("dataMappingSettings")> _
Public Class DataMappingSettings

     Public Const SectionName As String = "DataMappings"
     Private dataMappingProviders As DataMappingProviderDataCollection
     Private defaultDataMapper As String

     Public Const ConfigurationNamespace As String = _
```

```
        "http://www.example.com/eaf/datamappings"

    Public Sub New()
        dataMappingProviders = _
            New DataMappingProviderDataCollection()
    End Sub

    <XmlAttribute("defaultDataMapper")> _
    Public Property DefaultDataMapper() As String
        Get
            Return defaultDataMapper
        End Get
        Set
            defaultDataMapper = Value
        End Set
    End Property

    <XmlArray(ElementName:="dataMappingProviders"), _
    XmlArrayItem(Type:=GetType(DataMappingProviderData))> _
    Public ReadOnly Property DataMappingProviders() _
        As DataMappingProviderDataCollection
        Get
            Return dataMappingProviders
        End Get
    End Property

    Public Shared Function GetSettings _
        (ByVal context As ConfigurationContext) _
        As DataMappingSettings
        Return CType(context.GetConfiguration _
         (SectionName), DataMappingSettings)
    End Function
End Class
```

The rest of the runtime configuration objects that need to be created are to represent the configuration data for the `DataSetMappingProvider` and not the core functionality for the Data Mapping Application Block. Often the configuration data for a provider can be represented by an object or two. However, the configuration data for the `DataSetMappingProvider` is a bit more complex. At the lowest level I need to map DataFields in a DataTable to the parameters for stored procedures. So, I need an object to represent that mapping. I named this object `CommandParameterMapping`, and it holds the state for the name of the parameter and the source column (i.e., the name of the DataField) for the parameter. If the source column is left blank, the Data Mapping Application Block will assume that there is no mapping and that the value for the parameter will be set at runtime. This is to allow for non-DataSet parameters. (For information on the `UpdateDataSet` method, see the section Updating Data in Chapter 3.)

Furthermore, it is perfectly normal that different stored procedures may need to be called depending on the type of change that occurs in a DataTable in a DataSet. One stored procedure will generally need to be called to retrieve the data that is used to populate the DataTable; a different stored procedure is typically used when data is deleted from the table. Still another stored procedure is called when inserting or updating records in the DataTable. Often the same stored procedure will be called to handle both inserts and updates by determining if a database record already exists for the data that was modified in the DataTable: if a record does not exist, then the stored procedure performs an insert; otherwise, it updates the record that already exists.

I needed to create a configuration object that couples the name of the stored procedure that needs to be called for a specific operation for a DataTable with the collection of parameter mappings for that stored procedure. This class is named `CommandMapping`. The `CommandMapping` contains a collection of `CommandParameterMappings`, the command text (i.e., the stored procedure name), the command timeout, and an enumeration that represents the type of operation that it represents. The enumeration, `CommandStatementType`, contains values for `Select`, `Insert`, `Update`, `Delete`, and `InsertUpdate`. `InsertUpdate` is used to specify that the Data Mapping Application Block should call the same stored procedure for both inserts and updates that occur in the DataTable. This way, administrators who configure the Data Mapping Application Block do not need to replicate the same set of configuration data for two different `CommandMappings` just because they differ in the type of operations that they handle.

I have also created a specialized `CommandMapping`, named `SelectCommandMapping`, which derives from the `CommandMapping` class. This class has its `CommandStatementType` preset to `Select`. This type of command is used a bit differently than the other types because, in addition to setting a `SelectCommand` for a DataTable, an application may need to set multiple `SelectCommands` for the DataSet itself. One of the `SelectCommands` must be configured as the `DefaultSelectCommand` that will be used to retrieve the data for the entire DataSet; however, other SelectCommands can be used to return DataReaders and to call ExecuteNonQuery commands.

Since many DataTables can exist in one DataSet, I also needed to be able to signify the CommandMappings that are configured for each DataTable in the DataSet. The DataTableMapping object holds the state for the name of the DataTable and the CommandMappings for each of the types of operations that can occur for a DataTable.

Lastly, I needed to create the DataSetMapping to hold the collection of DataTableMappings and a collection of SelectCommandMappings. In addition to these collections, the DataSetMapping also keeps state about the name of the DataSet, the default SelectCommand (if one exists) for populating all the DataTables in the DataSet, the DatabaseInstance that is used to access the Database object from the Data Access Application Block, and a transaction's IsolationLevel so operations on the entire DataSet can be wrapped in the scope of a single database transaction. Because some of this same functionality must exist whether or not DataSets are used to map the relational database information to an object representation, many of its properties are actually defined in the DataMapping base class from which the DataSetMapping class derives.

As mentioned previously, I am not going to show all the code for all of these classes. Instead, the code for just the CommandMapping configuration object is provided in Listing 9.5. The code for the other configuration objects is very similar, differing only in the types of properties they expose.

LISTING 9.5: The CommandMapping Class

```
[C#]
[XmlInclude(typeof(CommandParameterMapping))]
public class CommandMapping
{
     private CommandStatementType commandStatementType;
     private string commandText;
     private int commandTimeout;
     private CommandParameterMappingDataCollection
               parameterMappingDataCollection;

     public CommandMapping()     {}

     public CommandMapping(CommandStatementType commandStatementType,
               string commandText) : this()
     {
```

```
        CommandType = commandStatementType;
        CommandText = commandText;
    }

    public CommandMapping(CommandStatementType commandStatementType,
            string commandText, int commandTimeout) :
            this(commandStatementType, commandText)
    {
        Timeout = commandTimeout;
    }

    [XmlAttribute]
    public CommandStatementType CommandType
    {
        get { return commandStatementType; }
        set { commandStatementType = value;}
    }

    [XmlAttribute]
    public string CommandText
    {
        get { return commandText; }
        set { commandText = value;}
    }

    [XmlAttribute]
    public int Timeout
    {
        get { return commandTimeout; }
        set { commandTimeout = value; }
    }

    [XmlArrayItem("ParameterMapping")]
    public CommandParameterMappingDataCollection ParameterMappings
    {
        get { return parameterMappingDataCollection; }
        set { parameterMappingDataCollection = value;}
    }

    [XmlIgnore()]
    public CommandParameterMapping this[int index]
    {
        get { return (parameterMappingDataCollection == null)? null
                    : parameterMappingDataCollection[index];}
        set
        {
            if (parameterMappingDataCollection == null)
            {
                parameterMappingDataCollection = new
                    CommandParameterMappingDataCollection();
```

```
                Add(value);
            }
            else
                parameterMappingDataCollection[index] = value;
        }
    }

    [XmlIgnore()]
    public CommandParameterMapping this[string name]
    {
        get { return (parameterMappingDataCollection == null)? null
                    : parameterMappingDataCollection[name];}
        set
        {
            if (parameterMappingDataCollection == null)
            {
                parameterMappingDataCollection = new
                    CommandParameterMappingDataCollection();

                Add(value);
            }
            else
                parameterMappingDataCollection[name] = value;
        }
    }

    public void Add(CommandParameterMapping mappingData)
    {
        if (parameterMappingDataCollection == null)
            parameterMappingDataCollection = new
                CommandParameterMappingDataCollection();
        parameterMappingDataCollection.Add(mappingData);
    }
}

[Visual Basic]
<XmlInclude(GetType(CommandParameterMapping))> _
Public Class CommandMapping
    Private commandStatementType As CommandStatementType
    Private _commandText As String
    Private commandTimeout As Integer
    Private parameterMappingDataCollection As _
            CommandParameterMappingDataCollection

    Public Sub New()
    End Sub

    Public Sub New(ByVal commandStatementType As _
            CommandStatementType, ByVal _commandText As String)
        Me.New()
```

```
        CommandType = commandStatementType
        CommandText = _commandText
    End Sub

    Public Sub New(ByVal commandStatementType As _
            CommandStatementType, ByVal _commandText As String, _
            ByVal commandTimeout As Integer)
        Me.New(commandStatementType, _commandText)
        Timeout = commandTimeout
    End Sub

    <XmlAttribute> _
    Public Property CommandType() As CommandStatementType
        Get
            Return commandStatementType
        End Get
        Set
            commandStatementType = Value
        End Set
    End Property

    <XmlAttribute> _
    Public Property CommandText() As String
        Get
            Return _commandText
        End Get
        Set
            _commandText = Value
        End Set
    End Property

    <XmlAttribute> _
    Public Property Timeout() As Integer
        Get
            Return commandTimeout
        End Get
        Set
            commandTimeout = Value
        End Set
    End Property

    <XmlArrayItem("ParameterMapping")> _
    Public Property ParameterMappings() _
            As CommandParameterMappingDataCollection
        Get
            Return parameterMappingDataCollection
        End Get
        Set
            parameterMappingDataCollection = Value
        End Set
```

```
        End Property

        <XmlIgnore()> _
        Public Default Property Item(ByVal index As Integer) _
                As CommandParameterMapping

            Get
                Return IIf((parameterMappingDataCollection Is _
                        Nothing), Nothing, _
                        parameterMappingDataCollection(index))
            End Get
            Set
                If parameterMappingDataCollection Is Nothing Then
                        parameterMappingDataCollection = New _
                        CommandParameterMappingDataCollection()
                    Add(Value)
                Else
                    parameterMappingDataCollection(index) = Value
                End If
            End Set
        End Property

        <XmlIgnore()> _
        Public Default Property Item(ByVal name As String) _
                As CommandParameterMapping

            Get
                Return IIf((parameterMappingDataCollection Is _
                    Nothing), Nothing, _
                    parameterMappingDataCollection(name))
            End Get
            Set
                If parameterMappingDataCollection Is Nothing Then
                    parameterMappingDataCollection = New _
                        CommandParameterMappingDataCollection()
                    Add(Value)
                Else
                    parameterMappingDataCollection(name) = Value
                End If
            End Set
        End Property

        Public Sub Add(ByVal mappingData As CommandParameterMapping)
            If parameterMappingDataCollection Is Nothing Then
                parameterMappingDataCollection = New _
                    CommandParameterMappingDataCollection()
            End If
            parameterMappingDataCollection.Add(mappingData)
        End Sub
    End Class
```

Once the core functionality, providers, factories, and runtime configuration objects have been created for an application block and its provider implementations, the application block can be used in an application. However, to do so requires manually creating the configuration data for the application block and manually modifying it whenever a change occurs. Because of the deep configuration hierarchy that is needed by this application block, manually creating and modifying the configuration data are exercises that are very prone to error. Besides that, while an application block is certainly usable without any design-time capabilities, it just doesn't *feel* like an application block that is on par with the application blocks that ship with Enterprise Library. To make it an application block that can be used in the Enterprise Library Configuration Tool as easily as the application blocks that ship with Enterprise Library, the design-time features must be added to the application block.

Design-Time Configuration

My goal is to make the process for creating, modifying, and validating the configuration settings for the Data Mapping Application Block very familiar to you if you have configured any of the application blocks that ship with Enterprise Library. This can be accomplished by adding design-time capabilities to the Data Mapping Application Block. Chapter 2 covered the Configuration Application Block's design-time capabilities in great depth, and you have seen how to provide design-time capabilities for custom providers in the previous chapters.

The process for adding design-time capabilities to an application block is not terribly different than it is for adding design-time capabilities for a custom provider to an existing application block. The primary difference is that you may need to create more configuration nodes to represent the runtime configuration classes for the application block and you may need to write additional code to consider the relationships between these classes. Thus, creating the design-time components for an application block can be broken down into three high-level steps.

1. Create configuration nodes that map to runtime configuration classes and consider the relationships between other configuration nodes.
2. Implement the `IConfigurationDesignManager` interface for the application block.
3. Add a `ConfigurationDesignManager` attribute to the AssemblyInfo file for the assembly that contains the design-time classes.

Creating the Configuration Nodes

The first step in adding design-time behavior to an application block is to develop the configuration nodes that represent the information contained in the runtime configuration classes. The runtime classes should be designed so that they are optimized for containing the configuration information; the design-time classes should be designed so that they make adding and modifying configuration data easy and natural for an end user. While there is no rule that mandates a one-to-one relationship must exist between a configuration node and a runtime object, it is very common for configuration nodes to be designed this way.

The ability to add and modify configuration information for the Data Mapping Application Block must exist for each of the runtime configuration classes outlined in the previous section. Figure 9.5 depicts the configuration nodes that I have created for the Data Mapping Application Block: `DataMappingSettingsNode`, `DataSetMappingProviderNode`, `DataSetMappingNode`, `DataTableMappingNode`, `CommandMappingNode`, `SelectCommandMappingNode`, `CommandParameterMappingNode`, and `DataSetCacheSettingsNode`. Because most of these nodes simply wrap around the runtime classes that they represent, which is the same way that configuration nodes work for all the custom providers created so far in this book, I will not show the code for every design-time configuration class. There is, however, an exceptional difference in the way some of these classes needed to be written that wasn't covered in previous chapters.

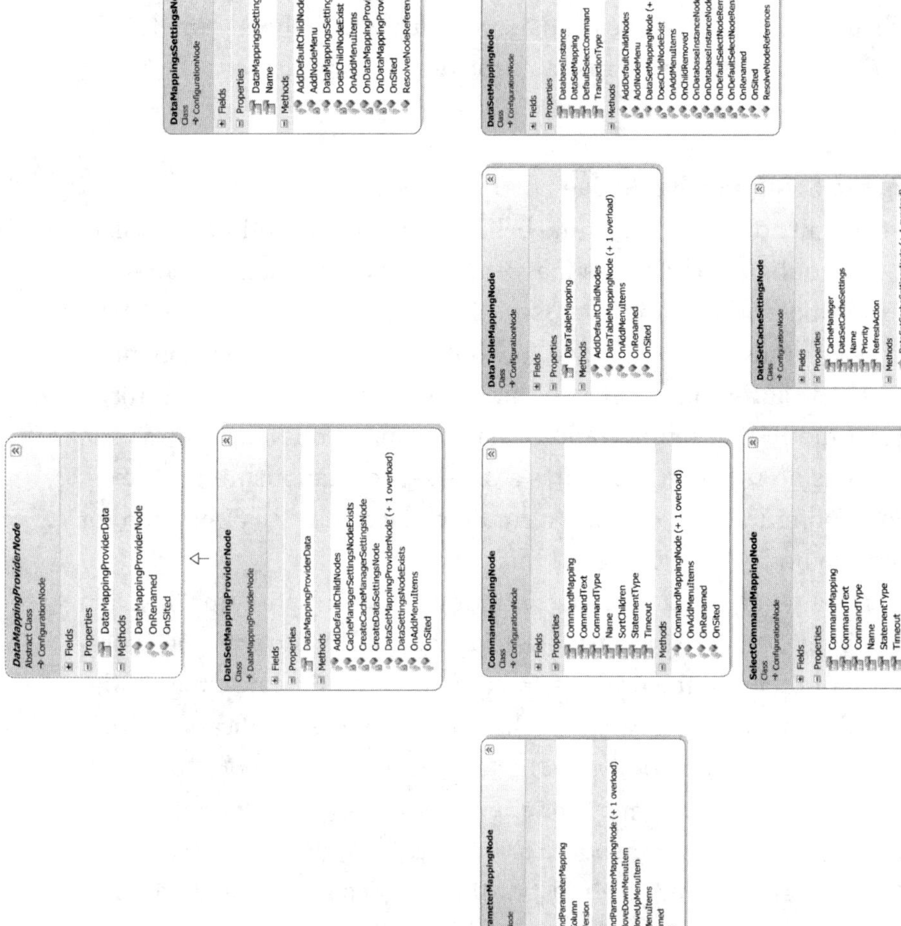

FIGURE 9.5: Data Mapping Application Block's Design-Time Objects

The major difference with these configuration nodes that didn't need to be considered for any of the other extensions provided earlier in this book is how to represent the hierarchical relationship among the configuration nodes during the design-time experience. When a user creates a new DataSetMapping, I need to allow the user to create DataTableMappings and SelectCommandMappings as subnodes to the DataSetMappingNode. Likewise, I need to enable the user so that CommandMappings can be added underneath DataTableMappings, and CommandParameterMappings can be added underneath CommandMappings. I also need to ensure that this hierarchical representation can be saved and loaded properly in the Enterprise Library Configuration Tool.

The key to providing menu items and commands so that a child configuration node can be added to a parent configuration node lies in the OnAddMenuItems method. When every configuration node is added in the Enterprise Library Configuration Tool, its OnAddMenuItems method is called. It is the responsibility for every node in the configuration hierarchy to add menu items that will allow its child nodes to be added underneath it. To add a menu item, the base ConfigurationNode's AddMenuItem method can be called. Listing 9.6 shows how the DataSetMappingProviderNode calls the AddMenuItem method to add a menu item for adding a DataSetMappingNode as a child node in the hierarchy.

LISTING 9.6: Adding Menu Items for the DataSetMappingProvider

```
[C#]
protected override void OnAddMenuItems()
{
     base.OnAddMenuItems ();
     AddMenuItem(new ConfigurationMenuItem(SR.DataMappingMenuText,
               new AddChildNodeCommand(Site,
               typeof(DataSetMappingNode)), this, Shortcut.None,
               SR.DataMappingStatusText, InsertionPoint.New));
}

[Visual Basic]
Protected Overrides Sub OnAddMenuItems()
     MyBase.OnAddMenuItems ()
     AddMenuItem(New ConfigurationMenuItem(SR.DataMappingMenuText, New _
               AddChildNodeCommand(Site, _
               GetType(DataSetMappingNode)), Me, Shortcut.None, _
               SR.DataMappingStatusText, InsertionPoint.New))
End Sub
```

Alternatively, rather than creating a new `ConfigurationMenuItem` and calling `AddMenuItem`, the base class' `CreateDynamicMenuItems` method can be used to dynamically create menu items for adding child nodes under a particular configuration node. For example, instead of creating a new `ConfigurationMenuItem` for a `DataTableMappingNode` and calling the `AddMenuItem` with it in the `OnAddMenuItems` for the `DataSetMappingNode`, `CreateDynamicMenuItems` can simply be called by passing in the `DataTableMappingNode` type. This will create the menu item for creating the `DataTableMappingNode` on behalf of the `DataSetMappingNode` as long as the child `DataTableMappingNode` nodes have been registered and configured properly. If they have not, then an exception will be thrown. This method determines valid child nodes that can be created by evaluating the `XmlIncludeAttributes` for the runtime configuration class that the configuration node wraps around.

For example, the runtime configuration class for the `DataSetMappingNode` is the `DataSetMapping`. The `DataSetMapping` class is attributed with an `XmlIncludeAttribute` with a value of `DataTableMapping`. For the purposes of creating dynamic menu items, this indicates that the `DataTableMapping` is a valid child of `DataSetMapping`. As long as the `DataTableMappingNode` is registered with the `ConfigurationDesignManager` as being linked to the `DataTableMapping` configuration class, then the Configuration Application Block will be able to create the menu items for creating the child nodes. Listing 9.7 shows how the `CreateDynamicMenuItems` method is used in the `OnAddMenuItems` method for the `DataSetMappingNode`.

LISTING 9.7: Dynamically Adding Menu Items

```
[C#]
protected override void OnAddMenuItems()
{
     base.OnAddMenuItems ();
     base.CreateDynamicMenuItems(typeof(DataTableMappingNode));
     base.CreateDynamicMenuItems(typeof(SelectCommandMappingNode));

     //Use AddNodeMenu (which checks DoesChildNodeExist) so that
     //we can only create one DataMappingProvider.
     AddNodeMenu(typeof(DataSetCacheSettingsNode),
          SR.DefaultDataSetCacheNodeName,SR.DataSetCacheStatusText);
}
```

```
[Visual Basic]
Protected Overrides Sub OnAddMenuItems()

     MyBase.OnAddMenuItems ()
     MyBase.CreateDynamicMenuItems(GetType(DataTableMappingNode))
     MyBase.CreateDynamicMenuItems(GetType(SelectCommandMappingNode))

     'Use AddNodeMenu (which checks DoesChildNodeExist) so that
     'we can only create one DataMappingProvider.
     AddNodeMenu(GetType(DataSetCacheSettingsNode), _
          SR.DefaultDataSetCacheNodeName,SR.DataSetCacheStatusText)
End Sub
```

Configuration nodes often contain nonbrowsable properties that return the runtime configuration class around which they wrap. For example, the `DatabaseStorageProviderNode` contains a property that returns the `DatabaseStorageProviderData` class. Similarly, the `DataSetMappingProviderNode` contains a property that returns a `DataSetMappingProviderData` class. These properties are used by the `ConfigurationDesignManager` when saving the configuration information for an application block or provider.

The `ConfigurationDesignManager` does not iterate down the configuration hierarchy for every node that exists when it is saving the configuration data for those nodes. Instead, it uses this property for every *provider* that has been registered with it. If the provider has a deep hierarchy of configuration nodes, then it is the provider's responsibility to iterate through the list of nodes to set the configuration data contained in them. Because the configuration hierarchy underneath the `DataSetMappingProviderNode` is very deep, the code in its `DataSetMappingProviderData` property is pretty large and contains many loops in loops. Listing 9.8 shows the first few loops.

Listing 9.8: DataSetMappingProvider's `DataMappingProviderData` Property

```
[C#]
public override DataMappingProviderData DataMappingProviderData
{
     get
     {
          DataSetMappingDataCollection mappings =
               this.dataSetMappingProviderData.DataSetMappings;
```

```
// Empty the collection of runtime configuration data for
// datamappings and reconstruct it from the current
// configuration data represented by the nodes.
mappings.Clear();

// Loop through all the DataMappingNodes and
// add their configuration data to the collection.
foreach (ConfigurationNode node in Nodes)
{
     DataSetMappingNode dataSetMappingNode =
          node as DataSetMappingNode;
if (dataSetMappingNode != null)
{
     DataSetMapping mapping =
          dataSetMappingNode.DataSetMapping;
     if (mapping.DataTableMappings != null)
          mapping.DataTableMappings.Clear();
     if (mapping.SelectCommands != null)
          mapping.SelectCommands.Clear();
     foreach (ConfigurationNode childNode in
          dataSetMappingNode.Nodes)
     {
          if (childNode != null)
          {
               if (childNode is SelectCommandMappingNode)
               {
                    SelectCommandMappingNode
                    selectCommandNode = childNode as
                         SelectCommandMappingNode;
                    mapping.SelectCommands.Add
                         (selectCommandNode.CommandMapping);
          }
          else if (childNode is
                         DataSetCacheSettingsNode)
          {
               DataSetCacheSettingsNode cacheNode =
                    childNode as
                    DataSetCacheSettingsNode;

...

          }
          else
          {
               DataTableMappingNode tableNode =
                    childNode as DataTableMappingNode;
               DataTableMapping dtMapping =
                    tableNode.DataTableMapping;
               dtMapping.CommandMappings.Clear();
               foreach (ConfigurationNode dtChildNode in
```

```
                                 tableNode.Nodes)
                            {
                                 ...
                            }
                            mapping.Add(dtMapping);
                       } //end else
                    } //end if
               }
               mappings.Add(mapping);
               }
             }
       return this.dataSetMappingProviderData;
       }
}

[Visual Basic]
Public Overrides ReadOnly Property DataMappingProviderData() _
               As DataMappingProviderData
Get
     Dim mappings As DataSetMappingDataCollection = _
          Me.dataSetMappingProviderData.DataSetMappings

     ' Empty the collection of runtime configuration data for
     ' datamappings and reconstruct it from the current
     ' configuration data represented by the nodes.
     mappings.Clear()

     ' Loop through all the DataMappingNodes and
     ' add their configuration data to the collection.
     For Each node As ConfigurationNode In Nodes
          Dim dataSetMappingNode As DataSetMappingNode = _
               IIf(TypeOf node Is DataSetMappingNode, _
                    CType(node, DataSetMappingNode), _
                    CType(Nothing, DataSetMappingNode))
          If Not dataSetMappingNode Is Nothing Then
            Dim mapping As DataSetMapping = _
               dataSetMappingNode.DataSetMapping
               If Not mapping.DataTableMappings Is Nothing Then
                    mapping.DataTableMappings.Clear()
               End If
               If Not mapping.SelectCommands Is Nothing Then
                    mapping.SelectCommands.Clear()
               End If
               For Each childNode As ConfigurationNode In _
                    dataSetMappingNode.Nodes

                    If Not childNode Is Nothing Then
                         If TypeOf childNode Is _
                              SelectCommandMappingNode Then
```

```
                    Dim selectCommandNode As _
                         SelectCommandMappingNode = _
                         IIf(TypeOf childNode Is _
                         SelectCommandMappingNode, _
                         CType(childNode, _
                         SelectCommandMappingNode), _
                         CType(Nothing, _
                         SelectCommandMappingNode))
                    mapping.SelectCommands.Add _
                         (selectCommandNode.CommandMapping)
               Else If TypeOf childNode Is _
                    DataSetCacheSettingsNode Then

                    Dim cacheNode As DataSetCacheSettingsNode _
                         = IIf(TypeOf childNode Is _
                              DataSetCacheSettingsNode, _
                              CType(childNode, _
                              DataSetCacheSettingsNode), _
                              CType(Nothing, _
                              DataSetCacheSettingsNode))

                              ...
                 Else
                     Dim tableNode As DataTableMappingNode = _
                              IIf(TypeOf childNode Is _
                              DataTableMappingNode, _
                              CType(childNode, _
                              DataTableMappingNode), _
                              CType(Nothing, _
                              DataTableMappingNode))
                    Dim dtMapping As DataTableMapping = _
                         tableNode.DataTableMapping
                    dtMapping.CommandMappings.Clear()
                   For Each dtChildNode As ConfigurationNode _
                         In tableNode.Nodes

                         ...

                   Next dtChildNode
                   mapping.Add(dtMapping)
                 End If 'end else
            End If 'end if
       Next childNode
       mappings.Add(mapping)
     End If
   Next node
   Return Me.dataSetMappingProviderData
End Get
End Property
```

On the reverse side, the configuration nodes for an application block or provider will get loaded starting from the root of the configuration data's hierarchy. To accomplish this, each node in the hierarchy is responsible for creating its child nodes. At startup, the Enterprise Library Configuration Tool creates a container, `ConfigurationDesignHost`, to host all configuration nodes. When a node is added to the configuration hierarchy, the Configuration Application Block adds the node to the `ConfigurationDesignHost` container and calls the node's `OnSited` method. This is the name of the node's `Site` property, which also appears as the name of the node in the configuration tree. Since the `OnSited` method always gets called when a node is added to the configuration hierarchy, it makes sense that this method should also be responsible for notifying the Configuration Application Block about its child nodes that also need to be added to the configuration hierarchy.

For example, when the `OnSited` method gets called in the `DataSetMappingProvider`, it creates a child `DataSetMappingNode` for every `DataSetMapping` that is contained in the configuration data. When each `DataSetMappingNode`'s `OnSited` method is called, it tells the Configuration Application Block to add `SelectCommandMappingNodes` and `DataTableMappingNodes` for every `SelectCommandMapping` and `DataTableMapping` that is configured for that `DataSetMapping`. This process continues down the configuration hierarchy until all of the `ConfigurationParameterMappingNodes` are created and the nodes for all the configuration data in the hierarchy have been created. Listing 9.9 shows the code for the `DataSetMappingProviderNode`'s `OnSited` method.

LISTING 9.9: DataSetMappingProvider's `OnSited` Method

```
[C#]
protected override void OnSited()
{
      base.OnSited();
      Site.Name = this.dataSetMappingProviderData.Name;

      // If this node represents a provider whose configuration is
      // being loaded from storage, then it may have existing data
      // mappings. Loop through the configuration data and
      // create child nodes for any existing data mappings.
      foreach (DataSetMapping dataSetMapping in
                this.dataSetMappingProviderData.DataSetMappings)
```

```
        {
          Nodes.Add(new DataSetMappingNode(dataSetMapping));
        }
}

[Visual Basic]
Protected Overrides Sub OnSited()
       MyBase.OnSited()
       Site.Name = Me.dataSetMappingProviderData.Name

       ' If this node represents a provider whose configuration is
       ' being loaded from storage, then it may have existing data
       ' mappings. Loop through the configuration data and
       ' create child nodes for any existing data mappings.
       For Each dataSetMapping As DataSetMapping In _
               Me.dataSetMappingProviderData.DataSetMappings

          Nodes.Add(New DataSetMappingNode(dataSetMapping))

       Next dataSetMapping
End Sub
```

Rather than explicitly looping through the configuration data that represents all the child elements for a node and calling `Node.Add`, the `CreateDynamicNodes` method can be used to dynamically create child nodes for a configuration node. This works similarly to the way `CreateDynamicMenuItems` works. As long as the child node is registered with the `ConfigurationDesignManager`, its parent node has been developed so that it signifies this child node to be valid, and the child node is linked properly to its runtime configuration object, the Configuration Application Block will be able to create the child nodes. Listing 9.10 shows how the `CreateDynamicNodes` method can be used to automatically create all child `DataTableMappingNodes` and `SelectCommandMappingNodes` for the `DataSetMappingNode`.

Listing 9.10: Dynamically Creating Child Nodes

```
[C#]
protected override void OnSited()
{
     base.OnSited();
     Site.Name = this.dataSetMapping.Name;

     if (dataSetMapping.CacheSettings != null)
          Nodes.Add(new DataSetCacheSettingsNode
```

```
            (dataSetMapping.CacheSettings));

        base.CreateDynamicNodes(this.dataSetMapping.DataTableMappings);
        base.CreateDynamicNodes(this.dataSetMapping.SelectCommands);
}

[Visual Basic]
Protected Overrides Sub OnSited()
    MyBase.OnSited()
    Site.Name = Me.dataSetMapping.Name

    If Not dataSetMapping.CacheSettings Is Nothing Then
        Nodes.Add(New DataSetCacheSettingsNode _
            (dataSetMapping.CacheSettings))
    End If

    MyBase.CreateDynamicNodes(Me.dataSetMapping.DataTableMappings)
    MyBase.CreateDynamicNodes(Me.dataSetMapping.SelectCommands)
End Sub
```

Implementing the `ConfigurationDesignManager`

Failure to register the runtime data types for configuration node types will cause an exception to be thrown on a call to `CreateDynamicNodes` or `CreateDynamicMenuItems`. Registration of these nodes occurs in the `Register` method for the specific `ConfigurationDesignManager` for an application block or provider. Every application block must contain a class that implements the `IConfigurationDesignManager` interface for the design-time classes to operate in the Enterprise Library Configuration Tool. This class provides the entry point to an application block's design-time configuration capabilities. The `DataMappingConfigurationDesign` is the implementation of this interface for the Data Mapping Application Block and is depicted in Figure 9.6.

Chapter 2 covered the `IConfigurationManager` interface and the base `ConfigurationDesignManager` class, so I won't repeat all the same information here. One of the things that makes the `DataMappingConfigurationDesignManager` a bit different from all the others created in the previous chapters is how the configuration nodes are registered such that the `CreateDynamicNodes` and `CreateDynamicMenuItems` methods can be used to create child nodes underneath another node in the configuration hierarchy. The code for this registration occurs in the private `Register-`

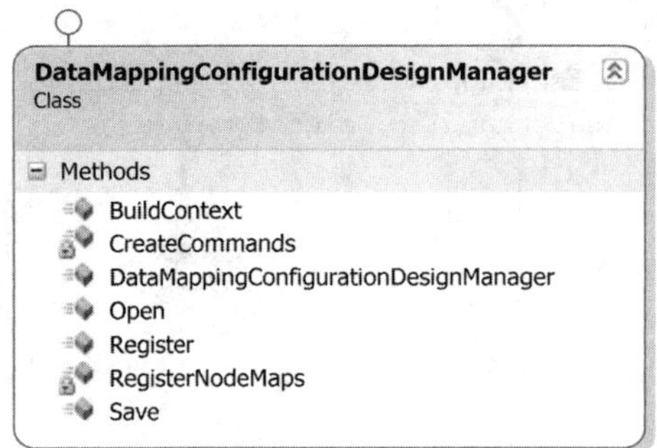

FIGURE 9.6: The `DataMappingConfigurationDesignManager` **Class**

NodeMaps method which is called from the public virtual Register method. Listing 9.11 shows this code.

LISTING 9.11: Registering Configuration Nodes in the `ConfigurationDesignManager`

```
[C#]
private static void RegisterNodeMaps(IServiceProvider serviceProvider)
{
    // Retrieve the INodeCreationService, which associates node
    // types with runtime configuration data types.
    INodeCreationService nodeCreationService =
        serviceProvider.GetService(typeof(INodeCreationService)) as
        INodeCreationService;

    // Associate the nodes for providers with their respective
    // runtime configuration data types. Once associated, provider
    // nodes can be created from their runtime configuration
    // data types.
    Type nodeType = typeof(DataSetMappingProviderNode);
    NodeCreationEntry entry =
        NodeCreationEntry.CreateNodeCreationEntryWithMultiples
        (new AddChildNodeCommand(serviceProvider, nodeType),
        nodeType, typeof(DataSetMappingProviderData),
        SR.DefaultDataSetMappingProviderNodeName);
    nodeCreationService.AddNodeCreationEntry(entry);

    nodeType = typeof(DataTableMappingNode);
    entry =
        NodeCreationEntry.CreateNodeCreationEntryWithMultiples
        (new AddChildNodeCommand(serviceProvider, nodeType),
```

```
            nodeType, typeof(DataTableMapping),
            SR.DefaultDataTableMappingProviderNodeName);
        nodeCreationService.AddNodeCreationEntry(entry);

        nodeType = typeof(CommandMappingNode);
        entry =
            NodeCreationEntry.CreateNodeCreationEntryWithMultiples
            (new AddChildNodeCommand(serviceProvider, nodeType),
            nodeType, typeof(CommandMapping),
        SR.DefaultCommandMappingProviderNodeName);
        nodeCreationService.AddNodeCreationEntry(entry);

        nodeType = typeof(SelectCommandMappingNode);
        entry =
            NodeCreationEntry.CreateNodeCreationEntryWithMultiples
            (new AddChildNodeCommand(serviceProvider, nodeType),
            nodeType, typeof(SelectCommandMapping),
            SR.DefaultSelectCommandMappingProviderNodeName);
        nodeCreationService.AddNodeCreationEntry(entry);

        nodeType = typeof(CommandParameterMappingNode);
        entry =
            NodeCreationEntry.CreateNodeCreationEntryWithMultiples
            (new AddChildNodeCommand(serviceProvider, nodeType),
            nodeType, typeof(CommandParameterMapping),
            SR.DefaultCommandParameterMappingProviderNodeName);
        nodeCreationService.AddNodeCreationEntry(entry);
}

[Visual Basic]
Private Shared Sub RegisterNodeMaps _
           (ByVal serviceProvider As IServiceProvider)

        ' Retrieve the INodeCreationService, which associates node
        ' types with runtime configuration data types.
        Dim nodeCreationService As INodeCreationService = _
            IIf(TypeOf serviceProvider.GetService _
            (GetType(INodeCreationService)) Is INodeCreationService, _
            CType(serviceProvider.GetService _
            (GetType(INodeCreationService)), INodeCreationService), _
            CType(Nothing, INodeCreationService))

        ' Associate the nodes for providers with their respective
        ' runtime configuration data types. Once associated, provider
        ' nodes can be created from their runtime configuration
        ' data types.
        Dim nodeType As Type = GetType(DataSetMappingProviderNode)
        Dim entry As NodeCreationEntry = _
            NodeCreationEntry.CreateNodeCreationEntryWithMultiples _
            (New AddChildNodeCommand(serviceProvider, nodeType), _
```

```
            nodeType, GetType(DataSetMappingProviderData), _
            SR.DefaultDataSetMappingProviderNodeName)
        nodeCreationService.AddNodeCreationEntry(entry)

        nodeType = GetType(DataTableMappingNode)
        entry = NodeCreationEntry.CreateNodeCreationEntryWithMultiples _
            (New AddChildNodeCommand(serviceProvider, nodeType), _
            nodeType, GetType(DataTableMapping), _
            SR.DefaultDataTableMappingProviderNodeName)
        nodeCreationService.AddNodeCreationEntry(entry)

        nodeType = GetType(CommandMappingNode)
        entry = NodeCreationEntry.CreateNodeCreationEntryWithMultiples _
            (New AddChildNodeCommand(serviceProvider, nodeType), _
            nodeType, GetType(CommandMapping), _
            SR.DefaultCommandMappingProviderNodeName)
        nodeCreationService.AddNodeCreationEntry(entry)

        nodeType = GetType(SelectCommandMappingNode)
        entry = NodeCreationEntry.CreateNodeCreationEntryWithMultiples _
            (New AddChildNodeCommand(serviceProvider, nodeType), _
            nodeType, GetType(CommandMapping), _
            SR.DefaultSelectCommandMappingProviderNodeName)
        nodeCreationService.AddNodeCreationEntry(entry)

        nodeType = GetType(CommandParameterMappingNode)
        entry = NodeCreationEntry.CreateNodeCreationEntryWithMultiples _
            (New AddChildNodeCommand(serviceProvider, nodeType), _
            nodeType, GetType(CommandMapping), _
            SR.DefaultCommandParameterMappingProviderNodeName)
        nodeCreationService.AddNodeCreationEntry(entry)
    End Sub
```

Another important point to understand that wasn't obvious from the `ConfigurationDesignManager`'s that were created in the previous chapters is what occurs when an application's configuration is saved. When an application's configuration is saved, the Configuration Application Block saves the metaconfiguration data about the application block's configuration sections to the application's domain configuration file. It then calls the `Save` method for every application block that the tool knows about, regardless of whether or not the application has been configured to use that application block.

In a similar way, it calls the `Open` method for every application block that the tool knows about when loading the configuration data for an application. Therefore, it is important to determine whether the configuration settings actually need to be loaded or saved to prevent unnecessary reads and writes from and to the configured StorageProvider. The check and subsequent save to storage occurs in the `DataMappingConfigurationDesignManager`'s `Save` method, which is shown in Listing 9.12. Similar checks exist for the `Open` method.

LISTING 9.12: `DataMappingConfigurationDesignManager`'s Save Method

```
[C#]
public void Save(IServiceProvider serviceProvider)
{
     ConfigurationContext builder =
          ServiceHelper.GetCurrentConfigurationContext
          (serviceProvider);

     // Verify that the application has been configured to use
     // the Data Mapping Application Block.
     if (builder.IsValidSection(DataMappingSettings.SectionName))
     {
          DataMappingsSettingsNode dataMappingsSettingsNode = null;
          try
          {
               // Attempt to retrieve the node that has the
               // DataMappingSettings.
               IUIHierarchy hierarchy =
                    ServiceHelper.GetCurrentHierarchy
                     (serviceProvider);
               dataMappingsSettingsNode =
                    hierarchy.FindNodeByType(typeof
                    (DataMappingsSettingsNode)) as
                    DataMappingsSettingsNode;

               // If application isn't configured to use the block
               // the node won't be found.
               if (dataMappingsSettingsNode == null)
               {
                    return;
               }

               // Save the settings to storage.
               DataMappingSettings dataMappingSettings =
               dataMappingsSettingsNode.DataMappingsSettings;

               builder.WriteConfiguration
               (DataMappingSettings.SectionName, dataMappingSettings);
          }
          catch (ConfigurationException e)
          {
```

```
                ServiceHelper.LogError
                (serviceProvider, dataMappingsSettingsNode, e);
            }
            catch (InvalidOperationException e)
            {
                ServiceHelper.LogError
                (serviceProvider, dataMappingsSettingsNode, e);
            }
        }
    }

[Visual Basic]
Public Sub Save(ByVal serviceProvider As IServiceProvider)
    Dim builder As ConfigurationContext = _
        ServiceHelper.GetCurrentConfigurationContext _
        (serviceProvider)

    ' Verify that the application has been configured to use
    ' the Data Mapping Application Block.
    If builder.IsValidSection(DataMappingSettings.SectionName) Then
        Dim dataMappingsSettingsNode As DataMappingsSettingsNode = _
            Nothing
        Try
            ' Attempt to retrieve the node that has the
            ' DataMappingSettings.
            Dim hierarchy As IUIHierarchy = _
                ServiceHelper.GetCurrentHierarchy _
                (serviceProvider)
            dataMappingsSettingsNode = IIf(TypeOf _
                hierarchy.FindNodeByType _
                (GetType(DataMappingsSettingsNode)) Is _
                DataMappingsSettingsNode, _
                CType(hierarchy.FindNodeByType _
                (GetType(DataMappingsSettingsNode)), _
                DataMappingsSettingsNode), _
                CType(Nothing, DataMappingsSettingsNode))

            ' If application isn't configured to use the block
            ' the node won't be found.
            If dataMappingsSettingsNode Is Nothing Then
                Return
            End If

            ' Save the settings to storage.
            Dim dataMappingSettings As DataMappingSettings = _
                dataMappingsSettingsNode.DataMappingsSettings

            builder.WriteConfiguration _
            (DataMappingSettings.SectionName, _
                dataMappingSettings)
```

```
            Catch e As ConfigurationException
                 ServiceHelper.LogError _
                       (serviceProvider, dataMappingsSettingsNode, e)
            Catch e As InvalidOperationException
                 ServiceHelper.LogError _
                      (serviceProvider, dataMappingsSettingsNode, e)
            End Try
       End If
  End Sub
```

Adding the `ConfigurationDesignManager` Attribute

After the configuration nodes and `ConfigurationDesignManager` have been developed, the coding for the application block is complete. However, one more task still needs to be completed. If the assemblies that contain the runtime and design-time classes for the application block are placed in the same directory as the Enterprise Library Configuration Tool, there still won't be a way to create the application block. This is because the tool does not recognize the assembly unless an assembly attribute with the type of the `ConfigurationDesignManager` that provides the entry point for this application block has been added to the assembly's AssemblyInfo file.

Listing 9.13 shows how to add this attribute to the AssemblyInfo file for the Data Mapping Application Block. Once this attribute has been added and the assemblies have been compiled and deployed to the same directory as the Enterprise Library Configuration Tool, a menu item will appear in the tool for adding the Data Mapping Application Block.

LISTING 9.13: Adding the `ConfigurationDesignManager` Attribute to the AssemblyInfo File

```
[C#]
[assembly: ConfigurationDesignManager(
     typeof(DataMappingConfigurationDesignManager))]

[Visual Basic]
<Assembly: ConfigurationDesignManager(
     GetType(DataMappingConfigurationDesignManager))>
```

Figure 9.7 illustrates what the configuration hierarchy might look like in the Enterprise Library Configuration Tool for an application that has been configured to use the Data Mapping Application Block.

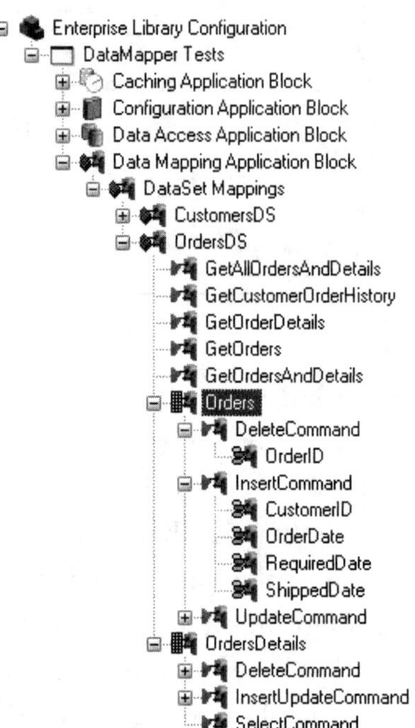

FIGURE 9.7: Configuration Hierarchy for the Data Mapping Application Block

Unit Tests

With the core functionality, providers, factories, runtime configuration classes, and design-time capabilities in place, the application block is now able to be used by developers and administrators in the same way that all the other application blocks that ship with Enterprise Library can be. There are, however, some additional best practices that the Microsoft patterns & practices team recommends when building and deploying an application block.

At the top of this list is the creation and use of unit tests. This is important for several reasons. First, it validates that the block works the way it is supposed to work. Second, it provides a method for ensuring that the same functionality can be provided as new providers need to be created for a particular block; the tests can help to ensure that the new provider can supply the required functionality while adhering to the interfaces contained in a particular block. Enterprise Library was developed using Test-Driven Development (TDD) methods. The unit tests are seen as extremely important to verify the functionality of application blocks and to verify that modifications to application blocks have not caused regression during the development of the blocks. The unit tests also have the additional benefit of providing sample code to developers on how certain functions should behave in the application block.

For example, the Data Mapping Application Block includes unit tests for testing virtually all aspects of the application block. These tests were extremely valuable during the development of the application block because as changes needed to be worked into the code (and changes always do), the unit tests could be run to ensure that these changes did not adversely affect the behavior of the application block. Listing 9.14 shows a couple of the unit tests that exist for the `DatabaseWrapper` class.

LISTING 9.14: `DatabaseWrapper` Unit Tests

```
[C#]
[Test]
[ExpectedException(typeof(DataWrapperException))]
public void InvalidSelectCommandThrowsException()
{
     IDataReader dataReader =
          DatabaseWrapper.GetDataReader(typeof(CustomersDS),
          SR.TestCustomersForException);
     dataReader.Close();
     Assert.IsNotNull(dataReader);
}

[Test]
public void GetNamedDataReaderWithNoParameters()
{
     IDataReader dataReader =
               DatabaseWrapper.GetDataReader(typeof(CustomersDS),
               SR.TestCustomers);
     dataReader.Close();
     Assert.IsNotNull(dataReader);
}

[Visual Basic]
<Test, ExpectedException(GetType(DataWrapperException))> _
Public Sub InvalidSelectCommandThrowsException()
     Dim dataReader As IDataReader = _
```

```
            DatabaseWrapper.GetDataReader(GetType(CustomersDS), _
            SR.TestCustomersForException)
        dataReader.Close()
        Assert.IsNotNull(dataReader)
    End Sub

    <Test> _
    Public Sub GetNamedDataReaderWithNoParameters()
        Dim dataReader As IDataReader = _
            DatabaseWrapper.GetDataReader(GetType(CustomersDS), _
            SR.TestCustomers)
        dataReader.Close()
        Assert.IsNotNull(dataReader)
    End Sub
```

Quick Start Application

For every application block that ships with Enterprise Library, a Quick Start application accompanies it to help people learn more about the block by using it. The Quick Starts are meant to demonstrate the common scenarios of the application block usage, display output that indicates what happens "under the covers" of the application block, and detect common errors (e.g., a user didn't perform the required setup) by displaying useful information.

The goal for the Quick Start is that a developer can select the *Start* command in Visual Studio and doesn't just see how a sample application uses the application block, but can also debug the application block to get more detail about what the application block is doing. I have provided a small Windows Forms application to accompany the Data Mapping Application Block that is intended to serve as a Quick Start for the application block. Figure 9.8 shows a screenshot of this Windows Forms application, the *Order Manager Administrator* application.

Summary

This chapter showed the steps that are involved in extending Enterprise Library by creating an entirely new application block and adding it to the design-time experience that is supported by the Enterprise Library Configuration Tool. In previous chapters, I showed how to extend Enterprise Library to fit in different enterprise environments by creating custom

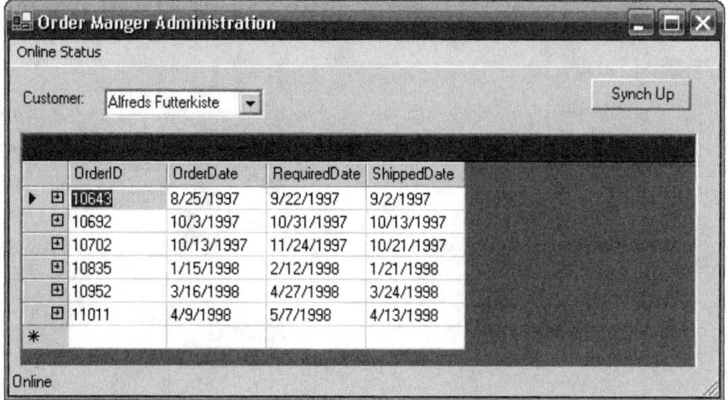

FIGURE 9.8: The Order Manager Administrator's Quick Start Application

providers. This chapter demonstrated that the extensibility features of Enterprise Library are not limited to creating providers; Enterprise Library can be extended in many ways, up to and including the creation of entirely new application blocks.

The chapter began by describing the primary tasks that are involved with creating a new application block and discussed how some thought needs to be given to what the core functionality of the block is and what should be designed for extensibility through the use of custom providers. It provided some details about the benefits that providers bring to an application block and how they should be designed to easily plug into an application block.

It also described software factories and how they are used in all the application blocks to aid in decoupling the core functionality provided by an application block from the implementation of any single provider, and discussed how some of the capabilities needed by the runtime and design-time configuration for an application block *may* differ from those that were needed for custom providers. The chapter reviewed some of the recommended accompaniments for an application block, namely unit tests, Quick Starts, and reference documentation and guidance. This chapter has presented a complete picture for how the benefits from Enterprise Library can be gained even if it is missing an application block that might be important to your organization.

A

The Data Mapping Application Block

THE END OF Chapter 3 began to discuss how it is a generally accepted best practice that database providers are called from data access logic components. The Microsoft patterns & practices team lists several goals to strive toward when designing data access logic components in a distributed application.[1] One of the recommended best practices is for the design to expose expected functionality that is common across all data access logic components in a separately defined interface or base class. This is the fundamental principal for the Data Mapping Application Block and more specifically for its abstract `DataMapper` base class. Martin Fowler defines a Data Mapper as:

> ...a layer of software that separates the in-memory objects from the database. Its responsibility is to transfer data between the two ends to isolate them from each other. With Data Mapper the in-memory objects needn't know even that there's a database present; they need no SQL interface code, and certainly no knowledge of the database schema.[2]

The `DataMapper` is intended to make it easy for developers of business data access logic components to create common functionality that relates to

1. *Application Architecture for .NET: Designing Applications and Services* at http://msdn.microsoft.com/library/default.asp?url=/library/en-us/dnbda/html/distapp.asp.

2. Martin Fowler, *Patterns of Enterprise Application Architecture*, p. 165. Addison-Wesley, 2002.

managing their "entities" with Create, Retrieve, Update, and Delete operations. Additionally, the `DataMapper` promotes the use of stored procedures as a best practice, facilitates the use of transactions when needed in an operation, makes it possible to configure specific command attributes like the command's timeout, and makes the ability to cache data in a data access logic component configurable. This appendix discusses how the design of the Data Mapping Application Block created in Chapter 9 is intended to satisfy the guidance promoted by the Microsoft patterns & practices team, and how to configure and develop an application to use this application block.

Design of the Data Mapping Application Block

The design goals for the Data Mapping Application Block were to:

- Provide best practices for developing data access logic components.
- Decouple the mapping of stored procedure parameters to the properties of an entity class (like a DataSet's DataFields) from the business logic that needs to be implemented for a specific operation.
- Provide capabilities to map stored procedure parameters to values that are not known to the system until runtime.
- Provide support for Insert, Update, and Delete transactions against multiple tables in an entity class or DataSet.
- Provide support for caching business entities in a Data Access Logic Component.
- Facilitate setting command properties like command timeouts and transaction levels through configuration instead of code.

In short, the design goals for the Data Mapping Application Block were to provide an API that makes it easy to create data access logic components that subscribe to the best practices as promoted by the Microsoft patterns & practices team and to make those data access logic components highly configurable. Examples of configurable properties include whether or not database operations should occur in the scope of a transaction, whether the business data should be cached by the data access logic component, and which stored procedure parameters map to which fields in the business entity.

The vision is that this will free developers up to concentrate on adding business logic instead of worrying about operational issues. It is not to say that you don't need to be concerned about such matters; rather, it is to say that this should be extremely easy for you to configure and modify and should not necessitate the need to recode if changes occur. Figure A.1 shows the primary classes that are responsible for providing the core functionality for the Data Mapping Application Block.

The `DatabaseWrapper` Class

The `DatabaseWrapper` acts as a service layer that encapsulates the Data Access Application Block. This service layer takes advantage of the Data Access Application Block's support for obtaining typed DataSets and propagating the changes in those DataSets to the backend database. The `Data-`

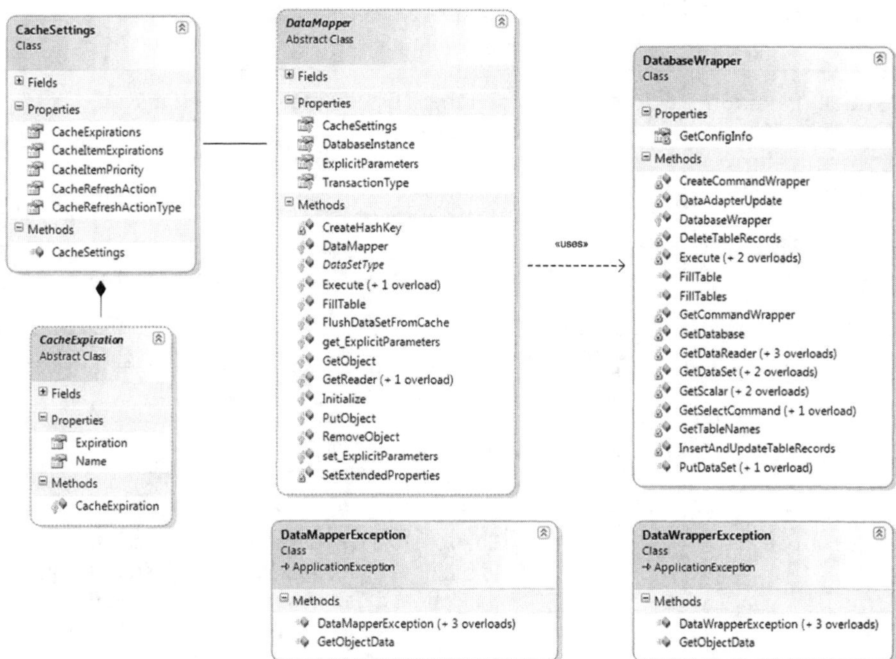

FIGURE A.1: Design of the Data Mapping Application Block

baseWrapper is core to the functionality of the Data Mapping Application block because it is in this class that configuration information is used to determine how to map stored procedure parameters to DataFields (that is, perform the *data mapping*), determine the value for a CommandTimeout, and obtain and use information relative to the database transaction isolation level.

The idea behind the DatabaseWrapper is simply to make it easy to retrieve typed DataSets from a data source and update a data source given the typed DataSet. It hides any complexities about creating the configured database provider, setting TableMappings for the DataSet properly, mapping DataColumns and non-DataSet columns to stored procedure parameters, and handling transactions. Table A.1 lists the public methods and properties for the DatabaseWrapper class.

TABLE A.1: DatabaseWrapper's Methods and Properties

Method/Property	Access	Description
GetDataSet	Public static	Returns a typed DataSet and uses it to load a typed DataSet.
GetDataReader	Public static	Returns a typed DataSet and returns a DataReader.
GetScalar	Public static	Returns a typed DataSet and performs an ExecuteScalar.
Execute	Public static	Returns a typed DataSet and performs an ExecuteNonQuery.
FillTable	Public static	Returns a typed DataSet and leverages it to load the DataTable for the DataSet.
FillTables	Public static	Performs the FillTable operation for multiple tables in a DataSet.
PutDataSet	Public static	Changes to a typed DataSet are passed through to the underlying data source by instantiating the correct database provider, mapping DataTable columns and non-DataSet columns to stored procedure parameters, and invoking transactions for DataTables if necessary. In short, it updates a DataSet while respecting all relationships among the tables in the DataSet.

The value that the `DatabaseWrapper` provides is most evident when it is used to propagate the changes that occur in a typed DataSet back to the data source from where it originated. Chapter 3 provided a fair amount of detail about the `UpdateDataSet` method that is used for updating a DataSet. And while the `UpdateDataSet` method is very powerful, it could be easier to use if it were able to use information that it read from configuration to determine which tables to call and which fields map to specific stored procedure parameters.

For example, in Chapter 3, Listing 3.16 illustrated using the `UpdateDataSet` method to propagate a single insert and update a typed DataSet back to the database. There was a bit of code that was specific to the name of the stored procedure that should be called for an insert, the name of the stored procedure to call for an update, and the name of the DataFields in the DataSet that should be mapped to the stored procedure's parameters. Such information can certainly be viewed as configuration information, and by placing the retrieval of this information behind the data service layer, Listing 3.16 could be simplified to look more like the code shown in Listing A.1. The `DatabaseWrapper` class contains a method named `PutDataSet` that will read the configuration information that is set for a particular typed DataSet and perform the various methods that must be called to update the DataSet by using the Data Access Application Block.

LISTING A.1: Using `PutDataSet` with the `DatabaseWrapper` Class

```
[C#]
//Create a new CustomersDS typed DataSet.
CustomersDS customerDataSet = new CustomersDS();

// Load the Customer DataTable in the typed DataSet.
int divId = 1;
DatabaseWrapper.GetDataSet(customerDataSet, divId);

//Explicitly set the value for the LastUpdate parameter
//to a value not known until runtime.
customerDataSet.Customers.ExtendedProperties.Add
      ("LastUpdate", DateTime.Now);

// Modify an existing customer.
if (customerDataSet.Customers.Count > 0)
{
      customerDataSet.Customers[0].CustomerName = "Len Fenster";
}
```

```
// Add a new customer.
CustomersDataRow customersRow = customersTable.AddCustomersRow
      (divId, "CompanyXYZ", "John Doe");

// Submit the DataSet, capturing the number of rows affected.
int rowsAffected = DatabaseWrapper.PutDataSet(customerDataSet);


[Visual Basic]
'Create a new CustomersDS typed DataSet.
Private customerDataSet As CustomersDS = New CustomersDS()

' Load the Customer DataTable in the typed DataSet.
Private divId As Integer = 1
DatabaseWrapper.GetDataSet(customerDataSet, divId)

'Explicitly set the value for the LastUpdate parameter
'to a value not known until runtime.
customerDataSet.Customers.ExtendedProperties.Add _
      ("LastUpdate", DateTime.Now)

' Modify an existing customer.
If customerDataSet.Customers.Count > 0 Then
     customerDataSet.Customers(0).CustomerName = "Len Fenster"
End If

' Add a new customer.
Dim customersRow As CustomersDataRow = customersTable.AddCustomersRow _
      (divId, "CompanyXYZ", "John Doe")

' Submit the DataSet, capturing the number of rows affected.
Dim rowsAffected As Integer =DatabaseWrapper.PutDataSet(customerDataSet)
```

This becomes even more important when two-sweeps operations and transaction support are needed when performing the database operation.

Two-Sweeps Operations

When a DataSet contains multiple tables and foreign-key relationships between those tables, determining the order in which Create, Update, and Delete operations need to be performed on the DataTables can get fairly complicated. It is important to update in the proper sequence to reduce the chance of violating referential integrity constraints. To prevent data integrity errors from being raised, the best practice is to update the data source in the following sequence.

1. Delete records in child tables.
2. Delete records in the parent table.
3. Insert and update records in the parent table.
4. Insert and update records in the child tables.

For example, suppose you have developed an application that lets you modify both the Order and the OrderDetail information. One DataSet can be used that contains an Orders table and an OrderDetails table, and the DataSet would either have a parent-child relationship or hierarchical relationship between the tables. When updating this dataset, it will be important to follow this sequence.

1. Delete records in the OrderDetails table.
2. Delete records in the Orders table.
3. Insert and update records in the Orders table.
4. Insert and update records in the OrderDetails table.

This process is called a **two-sweeps** update procedure. The Data Access Application Block does not implement a two-sweeps update procedure when `UpdateDataSet` is called. Currently the Data Access Application Block allows for update, insert, and delete commands for each table as it is updated; however, to support a two-sweep update, the block would need to have information about the commands for *all* tables prior to the update of any one table.

The Data Mapping Application Block contains this kind of information about all the tables in a DataSet in its configuration data. The `DatabaseWrapper` recursively navigates down through the child tables in a DataSet to perform the proper command and perform a two-sweeps as long as there is no circular relationship between the tables.

Transaction Support

A common requirement when an application executes multiple operations against a database is that all of the operations must succeed or the database must roll back to its state before the operations began. This all-or-nothing requirement is called a **transaction**. Transactions ensure the integrity of a database system's state.

In most circumstances, the root of the transaction is the business process rather than a data access logic component or a business entity component. The reason is that business processes typically require transactions that span multiple business entities, not just a single business entity. However, situations can arise where transactional operations may be needed on a single business entity without the assistance of a higher-level business process. If such requirements are needed and there is no possibility that the operation will be part of a larger business process that will initiate the transaction, then manual transactions are an acceptable solution. **Manual transactions** allow explicit control of the transaction boundary with explicit instructions to begin and end the transaction. When manual transactions are implemented in data access logic components, the following recommendations need to be considered.

- Where possible, transaction processing should be performed in stored procedures using statements like BEGIN TRANSACTION, END TRANSACTION, and ROLLBACK TRANSACTION.
- If stored procedures cannot be used and the data access logic components will not be called from a business process, ADO.NET can be used to control transactions programmatically. This is less efficient than using explicit transactions in stored procedures because manual transactions in ADO.NET take at least as many round trips to the data store as there are operations to execute in the transaction, in addition to trips that begin and end the transaction.

The Data Access Application Block supports the use of transactions through overloaded methods that accept a class that has implemented the `IDbTransaction` interface. The Data Mapping Application Block takes advantage of this functionality by creating an `IDbTransaction`, beginning the transaction, and passing it into a call to the Data Access Application Block when the particular database operation is configured to be wrapped in a transaction. A rollback or commit is performed depending on whether any exceptions were thrown during the execution of the operation.

Thus, the code needed to wrap database operations in a transaction for a specific database operation does not need to be written in a data access logic component. The transaction level can be configured at the DataSet level, and when a database operation is performed for that DataSet, it will be in the scope of a transaction.

The `DataMapper` Class

The `DataMapper` class is at the core of the Data Mapping Application Block. It is an abstract base class whose intent is to make it easy for developers to create data access logic components for managing Create, Retrieve, Update, and Delete (CRUD) operations on the business entities for an application. Data access logic components are recommended for accessing business data because they abstract the semantics of the underlying data store and data access technology, and they provide a simple programmatic interface for retrieving and performing operations on business entities.

Data access logic components provide the logic required to access specific business data, while generic database providers (also known as data access helper components) centralize the data access API development and data connection configuration, and help to reduce code duplication. Implementing data access logic components allows all the data access logic for a given business entity to be encapsulated in a single central location, making the application easier to maintain or extend. Data access logic components should

- Expose methods for inserting, deleting, updating, and retrieving data.
- Use a database provider to centralize connection management and all code that deals with a specific data source.
- Implement queries and data operations as stored procedures (if supported by the data source) to enhance performance and maintainability.

One of the largest uses of data access logic components is to perform the mappings and transformations needed between business entities and a relational data store. The primary intent of the Data Mapping Application Block is to move this mapping from being code driven to configuration driven.

With the Data Mapping Application Block, you create a business data access logic component by deriving a class from the abstract `DataMapper` base class and overriding the abstract `DataSetType` function. As the base class, the `DataMapper` is responsible for managing the mappings, transactions, and caching for the business data. As an application block, it takes advantage of Enterprise Library configuration capabilities to read its settings from configuration, thus letting you reap the benefits of mapping, transactions, and caching in a "codeless" manner. Listing A.2 demonstrates how to create a data access logic component for working with a Customers DataSet.

Listing A.2: Creating a Customers Data Access Logic Component

```
[C#]
public class CustomersMapper : DataMapper
{
     protected override DataSet DataSetType()
     {
          return new CustomersDS();
     }

     public CustomersDS GetCustomers()
     {
          return (CustomersDS)GetObject();
     }
}

[Visual Basic]
Public Class CustomersMapper : Inherits DataMapper

     Protected Overrides Function DataSetType() As DataSet
          Return New CustomersDS()
     End Function

     Public Function GetCustomers() As CustomersDS
          Return CType(GetObject(), CustomersDS)
     End Function
End Class
```

You'll notice that there is no code for setting transactions, caching, or mapping fields to parameters. As you will see later, this is as true for inserts, updates, and deletes as it is for reads from the data source. The base `DataMapper` class does this work for the derived class.

Table A.2 lists the methods and properties for the `DataMapper` class.

TABLE A.2: `DataMapper`'s Methods and Properties

Method/Property	Access	Description
`DataSetType`	Protected, Abstract	Needs to be overridden. Must return a new strongly typed DataSet for the proper type. This property gets called by the base `DataMapper` class to instantiate and return the proper typed (or generic) Dataset.
`Initialize`	Protected	Performs initialization logic for a derived `DataMapper`.
`ExplicitParameters`	Protected	Helper function that gets and sets the `ExplicitParameters` for all DataTables in a DataSet.
`get_ExplicitParameters`	Protected	Helper function that gets the `ExplicitParameters` for a specific DataTable in a DataSet.
`set_ExplicitParameters`	Protected	Helper function that sets the ExplicitParameters for a specific DataTable in a DataSet
`GetObject`	Protected	Returns a new typed DataSet as defined by the `DataSetType` property and filled with data from the appropriate data source.
`PutObject`	Protected	Inserts, updates, and deletes rows in the data source with the changes made to the typed DataSet.
`RemoveObject`	Protected	Removes an entire typed DataSet. Iterates through every row of every table and calls Delete, which will not cause AcceptChanges to occur on the DataSet.
`GetReader`	Protected	Based on the configured information for that DataSet, the correct database provider is created and returns a DataReader

(continued)

TABLE A.2: `DataMapper`**'s Methods and Properties (*continued*)**

Method/Property	Access	Description
`GetScalar`	Protected	Based on the configured information for that DataSet, the correct database provider is created and performs an `ExecuteScalar`.
`Execute`	Protected	Based on the configured information for that DataSet, the correct database provider is created and performs an `ExecuteNonQuery`.
`FillTable`	Protected	Allows for lazy loading by allowing `DataTables` to be populated independently of the entire DataSet.
`TransactionType`	Protected	Gets and sets the type of transaction. The default is IsolationLevel.Unspecified, which is interpreted as no transaction.
`CacheSettings`	Protected	Property that gets the current `CacheSettings` for the derived `DataMapper` and allows them to be programmatically overridden.
`FlushDataSetFromCache`	Protected	Flushes the DataSet from the cache (if any). Useful if the DataSet is being cached but operations are performed that do not automatically keep the cache in synch (e.g., `Execute`).

Caching Data

The guidance documented in the section Caching in the Data Services Layer in Chapter 3 of the *Caching Architecture Guide for .NET Framework Application*[3] states that because of the relatively high performance costs of opening a connection to a database and querying the data stored in it, data elements are excellent caching candidates and are commonly cached. Additionally, DataSets are excellent caching candidates because:

3. Found at http://msdn.microsoft.com/library/default.asp?url=/library/en-us/dnbda/html/CachingArch.asp.

- They are serializable and as such can be stored in caches either in the same process or in another process.
- They can be updated without needing to reinsert them into the cache. Because a reference to a DataSet can be cached, an application can update the data without the reference in the cache needing to change.
- They store formatted data that is easily read and parsed by the client. Caching frequently used DataSet objects in an application often results in improved performance.

A design goal for the Data Mapping Application Block in Chapter 9 was to provide the ability to cache data in a data access logic component and to allow the caching of data to be a configurable setting. By providing this capability, it also became important to allow for the configuration of multiple expiration policies for a data access logic component so that cached data can expire per the settings needed by an application, and that `CacheItemRefreshActions` can be set so that actions could be taken in the application when data expired. The classes shown in Figure A.2 highlight the design for caching in the Data Mapping Application Block.

The `CacheSettings` object contains information that allows the `DataMapper` to know whether it should cache its data. The `CacheSettings` object also encapsulates a collection of `CacheExpirationPolicies` and a `CacheRefreshAction` (aka `CacheRemovalCallback`).

To let users set properties for the `CacheExpirationPolicies` at deployment time, I needed to create a wrapper class around each of the existing implementations of an `ICacheItemExpiration` because a node based solely on an interface cannot be instantiated. Therefore, I created an abstract base class named `CacheExpiration` that encapsulates an `ICacheItemExpiration`, and all `CacheItemExpirationPolicies` derive from this class. When configuration data is read in for use by the `DataMapper`, it will contain data that indicates whether the `DataMapper` should cache its data, and if so, with which expiration policies and `RefreshAction`.

If a `DataMapper` is configured to cache its data, it will check the cache first to ascertain whether data exists. The key for caching the data is a com-

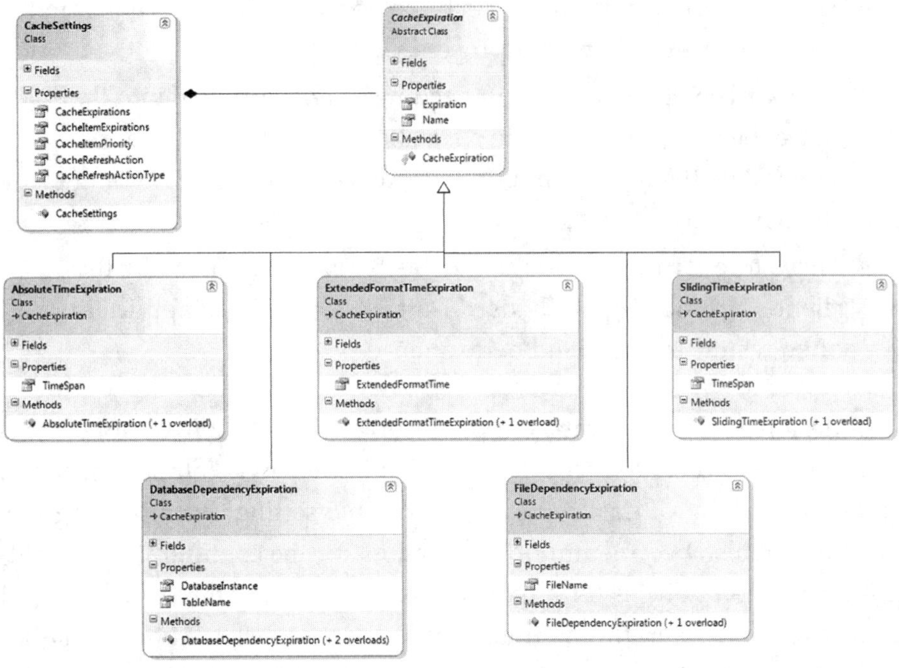

FIGURE A.2: Classes Used to Provide Caching Support in the Data Mapping Application Block

bination of the DataSet's name and the list of parameters that were used to retrieve it. This allows a separate copy of all the different variances that can occur for the retrieval of this data to be cached. If the data exists in the cache, it is returned. Otherwise, it is retrieved from the data source. If caching is enabled, the retrieved data is added to the cache with the appropriate expiration policies and `RefreshAction` as per the configuration settings. The data is then returned.

The guidance from the patterns & practices team suggests that you think about which data should be cached. The guidance states that only non-transactional data that is static or semi-static should be cached. Caching too much data or the wrong type of data can sometimes be worse than not caching any data at all. The semi-static data is the most interesting because a design needs to be applied for how to handle cached data that gets updated, inserted, or deleted. I have chosen to take the safest route by ensuring the least amount of data "staleness." I remove cached data if it is modified in any way. Another approach would be to update both the cache and data source as data is updated, inserted, and deleted.

The `DataMappingProviderFactory` Class and the `IDataMappingProvider` Interface

As previously stated, when data mapping needs to be performed in a data access logic component, a developer only needs to derive a class from the base `DataMapper` class. Underneath the covers, the `DataMapper` calls the `DatabaseWrapper` that uses a `DataMappingFactory` to obtain a `DataMappingCollection` from a data mapping provider. Although developers are abstracted away from needing to call the `DataMappingFactory` directly in their data access logic components, they can still use it if there are situations where information about the data mappings of one data access logic component are needed from another.

For example, if there were a circumstance where the information about the data mappings for an Orders data access logic component needed to be known when performing an operation in a Customers data access logic component, the `DataMappingFactory` can be used to obtain the `DataMappingCollection` that contains the mapping information for all data access logic components.

All data mapping providers should implement the `IDataMappingProvider` interface to provide support for the `DataMappingCollection`. The `DataMappingProviderFactory` class uses configuration information to create an instance of an `IDataMappingProvider`. Like the application blocks that ship with Enterprise Library, a factory also exists that provides static methods that wrap around the public methods of the `DataMappingProviderFactory` class. This factory is named `DataMappingFactory` (no *Provider* in the name). Either class can be used to obtain either a named instance of a `DataMappingProvider` or one that is configured as the default `DataMappingProvider`.

Both the `DataMappingFactory` and the `DataMappingProviderFactory` class expose a method named `GetDataMappingProvider` that returns an instance of a `DataMappingProvider`. The `GetDataMappingProvider` method is overloaded two times: one overload expects a string

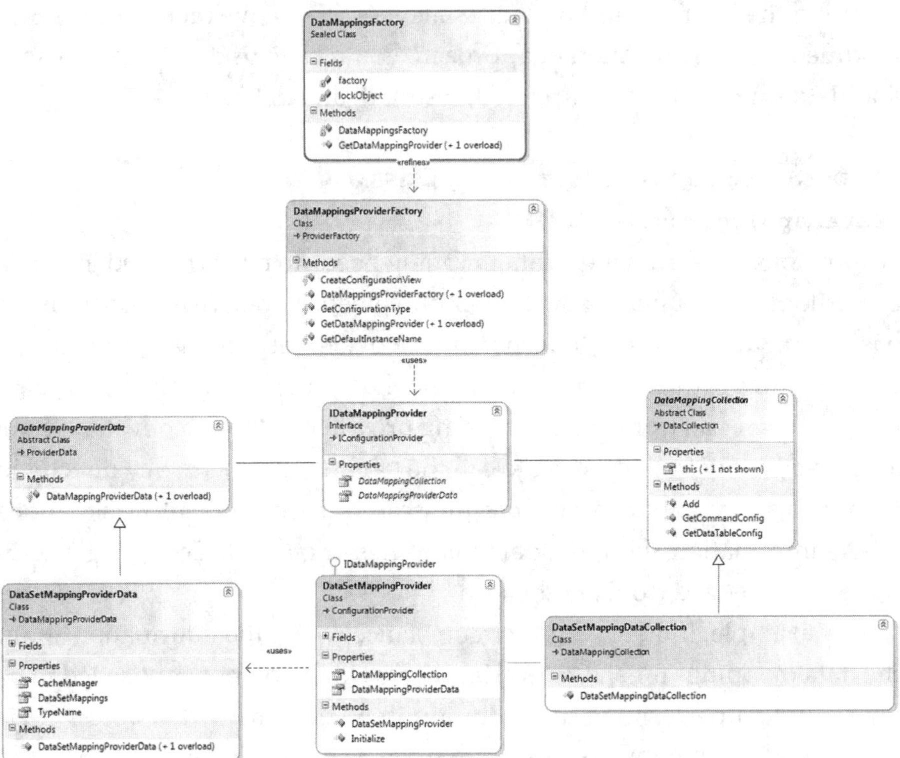

FIGURE A.3: `DataMapping` **Factories and Providers in the Data Mapping Application Block**

that represents the name of a `DataMappingProvider` that has been configured for the application, and the other overload does not expect any arguments. The first overload returns the named `DataMappingProvider`, and the second returns the `DataMappingProvider` that has been configured as the default `DataMappingProvider` for the application. Figure A.3 shows the relationship between the `DataMappingFactory`, the `DataMappingProviderFactory`, the `IDataMappingProvider` interface, and the `DataMappingCollection` class. The Data Mapping Application Block includes an implementation of the `IDataMappingProvider` interface by way of the `DataSetMappingProvider`.

The DataSetMappingProvider

The Data Mapping Application Block includes a data mapping provider named `DataSetMappingProvider` that lets it use configuration data maintained on the various different classes in a DataSet to aid in its data mapping. The configuration data for this provider is contained in an object named the `DataSetMappingDataCollection`, which is hierarchical in nature and is intentionally meant to resemble the hierarchy of a collection of DataSets. Figure A.4 depicts the hierarchy for the objects contained in the `DataSetMappingDataCollection`.

The `DataSetMappingCollection`'s root level contains a collection of `DataSetMapping` objects. A `DataSetMapping` object represents mapping information for a strongly typed DataSet. It contains information about the `DatabaseInstance` to which it is bound, the transaction IsolationLevel for wrapping transactions around data commands, a `CacheSettings` object that holds information about how the DataSet may be cached, a DataCollection of `DataTableMappings`, and a DataCollection of `SelectCommandMappings`.

The `CacheSettings` object represents the settings to use for caching a DataSet. It contains a `CacheItemRefreshAction`, a DataCollection of `CacheItemExpirations`, and a `CacheItemPriority` setting. These settings allow a concrete `DataMapper` to pass the arguments it needs to the Caching Application Block and have the appropriate refresh, expirations, and priorities set.

`DataTableMappings` simply contain a DataCollection of `CommandMappings` and a table name. `CommandMappings` contain information about the type of CommandStatement (Select, Insert, Update, Delete, or InsertUpdate) it uses, the name of the stored procedure to which it is bound, what the CommandTimeout period is (if any), and a DataCollection of `CommandParameterMappings`. `CommandParameterMappings` simply contain the name of a stored procedure parameter and the SourceColumn from the DataTable to which it should be mapped (if any).

Developing with the Data Mapping Application Block

The previous section covered the design of the Data Mapping Application Block. The primary design goal for the Data Mapping Application Block was to make it easy for developers to create data access logic components without having to worry about writing code to map stored procedure parameters to DataFields in DataTables. After the DataSets and stored pro-

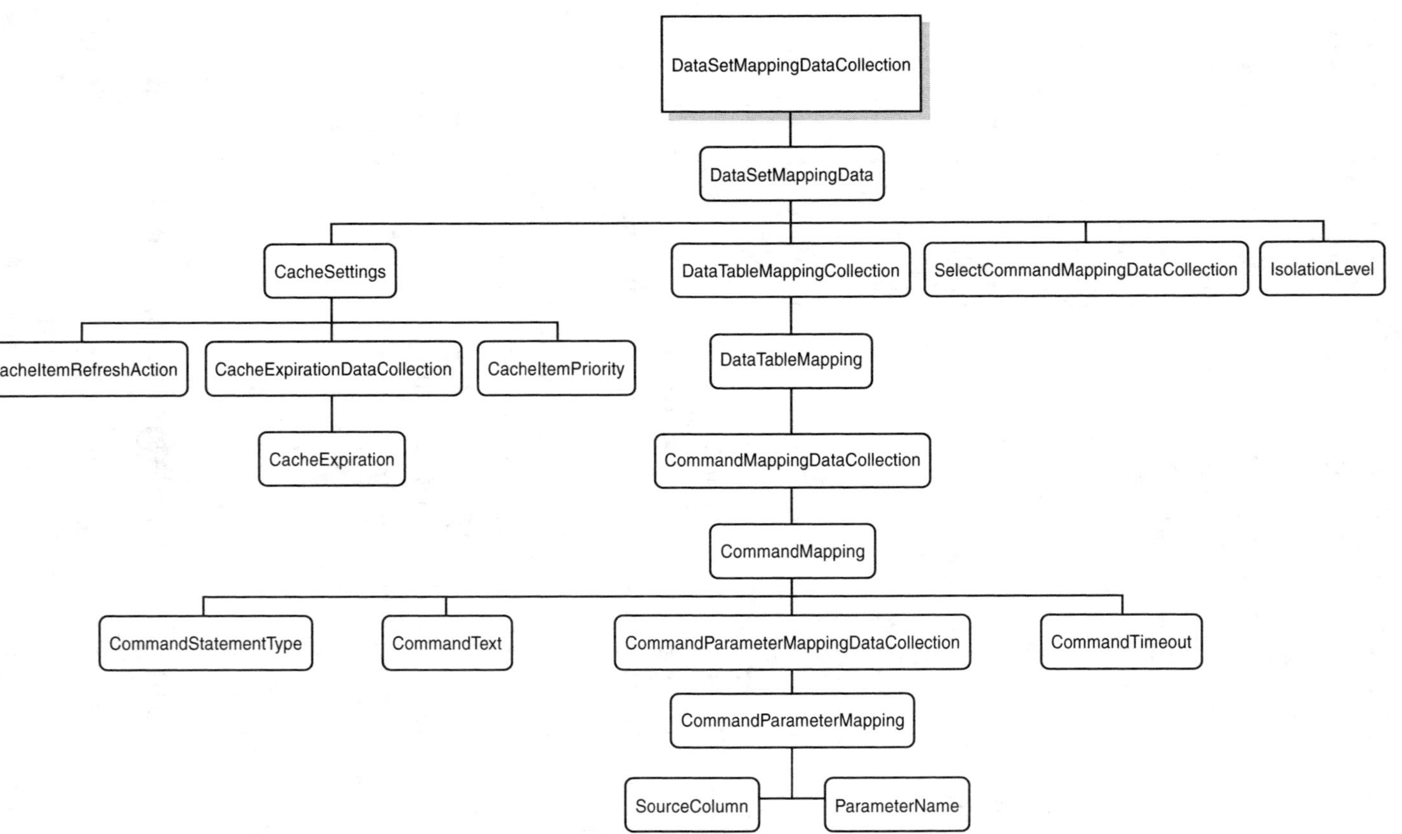

FIGURE A.4: `DataSetMappingDataCollection` **Object Hierarchy**

cedures have been created for an application, the next step is to create a class that is derived from the `DataMapper` base class and configure the application block so the new concrete `DataMapper` can use it. This section details how to use the features described in the previous section to configure and develop an application to use the Data Mapping Application Block.

Creating DataSets and Stored Procedures

Before you can develop and test a data access logic component, you must create the typed DataSet or business entity that it will manage as well as the stored procedures to which it will be mapped. There are many tools you can use to create stored procedures and typed DataSets. One of them is Visual Studio. You can easily create a typed DataSet in Visual Studio by dragging stored procedures or tables from Server Explorer onto the design-time surface for its XML Schema Definition (XSD) tool. Figure A.5 shows the results of dragging a stored procedure named *GetCustomers* onto this surface and renaming the element to *Customers*.

The process for creating the stored procedures and DataSets and configuring them to map to one another could be automated by making it wizard driven. It is possible that a complement to the Data Mapping Application Block could be developed that steps a developer through the

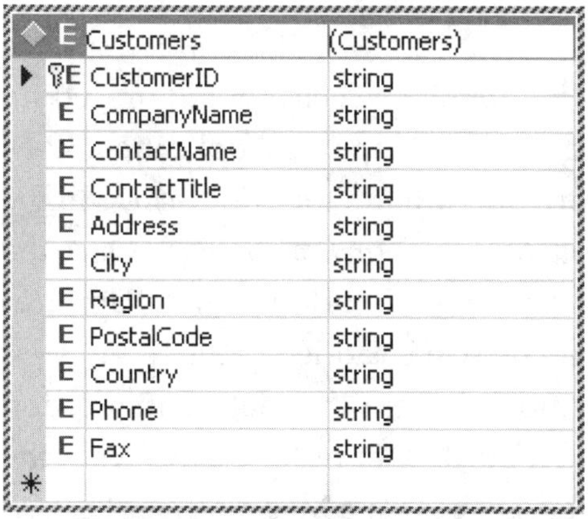

E	Customers	(Customers)
E	CustomerID	string
E	CompanyName	string
E	ContactName	string
E	ContactTitle	string
E	Address	string
E	City	string
E	Region	string
E	PostalCode	string
E	Country	string
E	Phone	string
E	Fax	string
*		

FIGURE A.4: Creating a Simple Strongly Typed DataSet in Visual Studio.NET process of creating a stored procedure and a corresponding strongly typed DataSet. It could produce output for the stored procedure, a strongly typed DataSet, configuration data that maps them together, and starting code for the derived `DataMapper`. This would make the setup needed before configuring and developing against the application block a more automated process.

Configuration and Development

The flexibility provided by the Data Mapping Application Block comes in its capacity to use configuration data to determine how to map stored procedure parameters to DataFields, determine the transaction IsolationLevel for database operations, decide how to cache and expire from cache the data returned from database operations, and set command properties like the command's Timeout. This not only drastically reduces the need to spend development cycles coding this logic in a data access logic component, but it also allows the data access logic to more easily adapt to changes in the environment. For example, if the names of stored procedure parameters change or entirely different stored procedures need to be called to perform specific database operations, no code needs to change. Only the configuration for a data access logic component in the Data Mapping Application Block would need to be modified. This section shows you how to configure the Data Mapping Application Block.

Adding the Application Block

The first step to configuring any data mapping between a stored procedure and a strongly typed DataSet is to add the Data Mapping Application Block to an application's configuration information. To do this, right-click on the application node and select *New > Data Mapping Application Block*. Once the block has been added, a subnode will be created underneath the application node and a new configuration section will be added to the settings for the Configuration Application Block to represent the metaconfiguration data for the Data Mapping Application Block. Figure A.6 shows what the new configuration hierarchy looks like once the Data Mapping Application Block has been added.

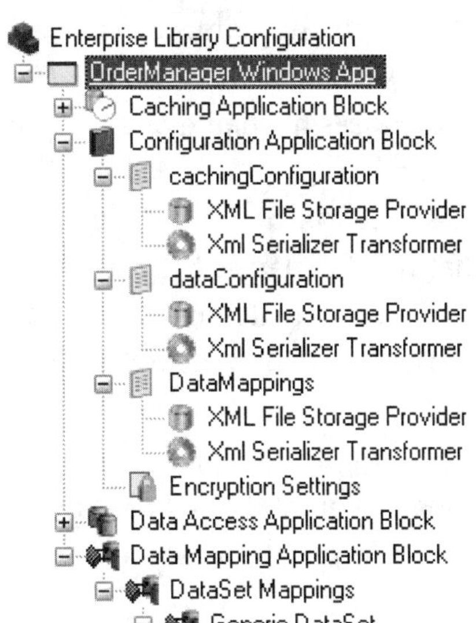

FIGURE A.6: Configuration Hierarchy After Adding the Data Mapping Application Block

Since the Data Mapping Application Block has a dependency on the Data Access Application Block and, if planning to cache data, a dependency on the Caching Application Block, those blocks are automatically added to the configuration hierarchy if they did not already exist. For more information on configuring the Data Access Application Block and the Caching Application Block, please see Chapters 3 and 4, respectively.

`DataSetMapping`

Once the block has been added to an application's configuration, a new, blank `DataSetMapping` will already have been added to the configuration hierarchy for the Data Mapping Application Block. New `DataSetMappings` can be added by right-clicking the *DataSet Mappings* node for the Data Mapping Application Block and selecting *New > DataSet Mapping*. The name for a `DataSetMapping` must be changed to the same name as the DataSet to which it is intended to map stored procedure parameters. For example, if a data access logic component is going to manage the operations for the

Customers DataSet shown in Figure A.5, then the name of the `DataSetMapping` must be *CustomersDS*, because that is the name that I gave to the DataSet. The `DataSetMappingProvider` uses the name of the DataSet to match the DataSet to its mapping information.

Additionally, the `DatabaseInstance` needs to be set to point to the database where the stored procedure that will be mapped to this DataSet exists. The `DatabaseInstance` is configured the way it normally would be with the Data Access Application Block. The Property pane for `DataSetMapping` provides a drop-down list box so that an existing `DatabaseInstance` can be selected. Figure A.7 shows how to use the configuration properties for a `DataSetMapping` to change to point it at a `DatabaseInstance` that is configured in the Data Access Application Block.

SelectCommandMapping

In order to retrieve data from the data source that is represented by the `DatabaseInstance` property, a `SelectCommandMapping` must be added to

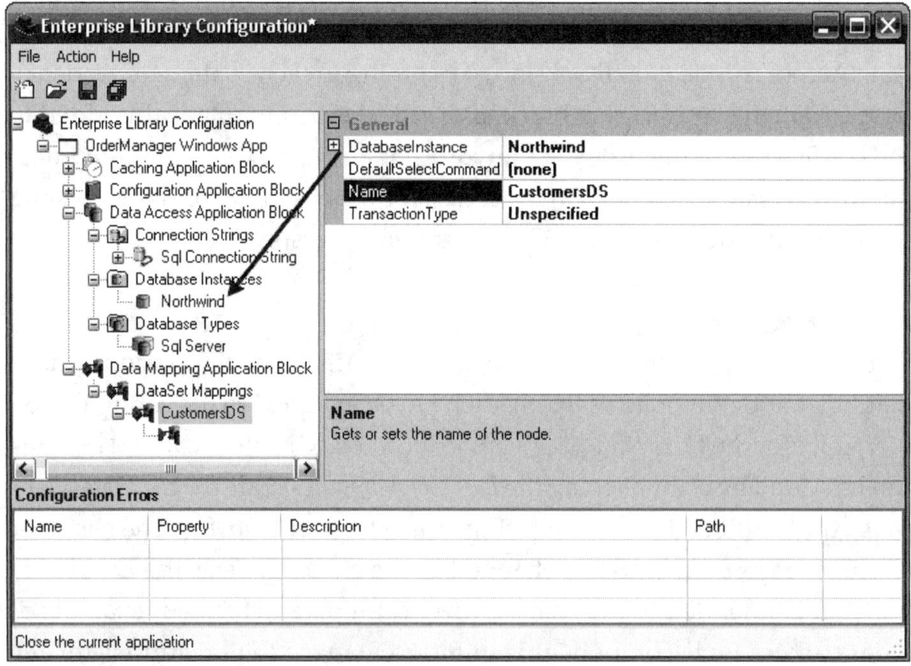

FIGURE A.7: Renaming the `DataSetMapping` and Setting the `DatabaseInstance`

the DataSetMapping. A SelectCommandMapping is a special type of CommandMapping that is preset for operations that do not require a mapping from DataFields to stored procedure parameters. For the most part, it is used for Retrieve operations; however, SelectCommandMappings can also be used to execute nonqueries because the parameters that get passed to this method do not require any mapping.

A DataSetMapping can have multiple SelectCommandMappings. One of the SelectCommandMappings must be used to fill the DataSet, while the others can be used to return DataReaders, scalar values, and to execute nonqueries. To add a SelectCommandMapping to a DataSetMapping, right-click the *DataSet Mappings* node and select *New > SelectCommand Mapping*. A new SelectCommandMapping node will be added as a subnode under the DataSetMapping node.

To configure which stored procedure this SelectCommandMapping represents, set the CommandText property to the name of the stored procedure. Additionally, the name for the SelectCommandMapping should be changed to something meaningful for this mapping. The CommandTimeout property can also be optionally set to any long value; the default value for the CommandTimeout is 30 seconds. In Figure A.8, a SelectCommandMapping has

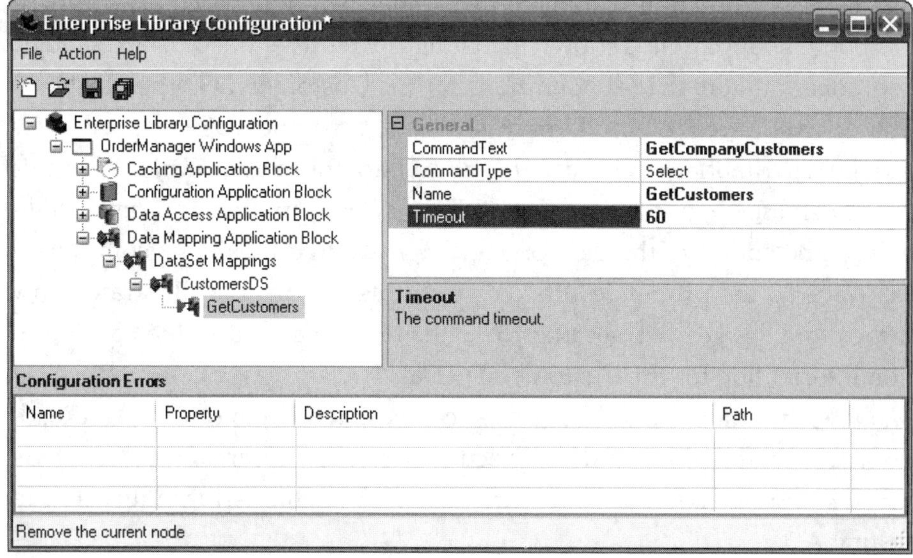

FIGURE A.8: Configuring a SelectCommandMapping

been added to the *CustomersDS* `DataSetMapping`. The name of the `SelectCommandMapping` has been changed to *GetCustomers* and maps to the stored procedure named *GetCompanyCustomers*. Also, the timeout for this command has been extended to 60 seconds.

After `SelectCommandMappings` have been created and configured, database operations can be executed that return results as strongly typed DataSets, DataReaders, scalar values, and values in output parameters (by executing nonqueries). One of the `SelectCommandMappings` should be selected as the `DefaultSelectCommand`. This is the `SelectCommandMapping` that represents the command that will be used to fill the DataSet. The `DefaultSelectCommand` is a property that can be configured for the `DataSetMapping` node. Figure A.7 shows the drop-down list box where an existing `SelectCommandMapping` can be selected as the `DefaultSelectCommand`.

Creating the Data Access Logic Component

A data access logic component needs to be created before any values can be returned in an application. To create a data access logic component, derive a class from the abstract `DataMapper` class and override the abstract `DataSetType` function so that it returns a new strongly typed DataSet. The `CustomersMapper` class shown in Listing A.2 represents a data access logic component that manages operations for the CustomersDS typed DataSet. The `DataSetType` method returns a new CustomersDS DataSet. New `SelectCommandMappings` can be added to the configuration for this `DataSetMapping` in the Enterprise Library Configuration Tool, and methods can be added to the `CustomersMapper` data access logic component that returns the proper results. For example, Figure A.9 illustrates how three more `SelectCommandMappings` have been added to the configuration information for the CustomersDS DataSet.

Now, the `CustomersMapper` class can be extended to return DataReaders and scalar values and to execute nonquery commands. The `CustomersMapper` class has been extended with methods to do just that in Listing A.3.

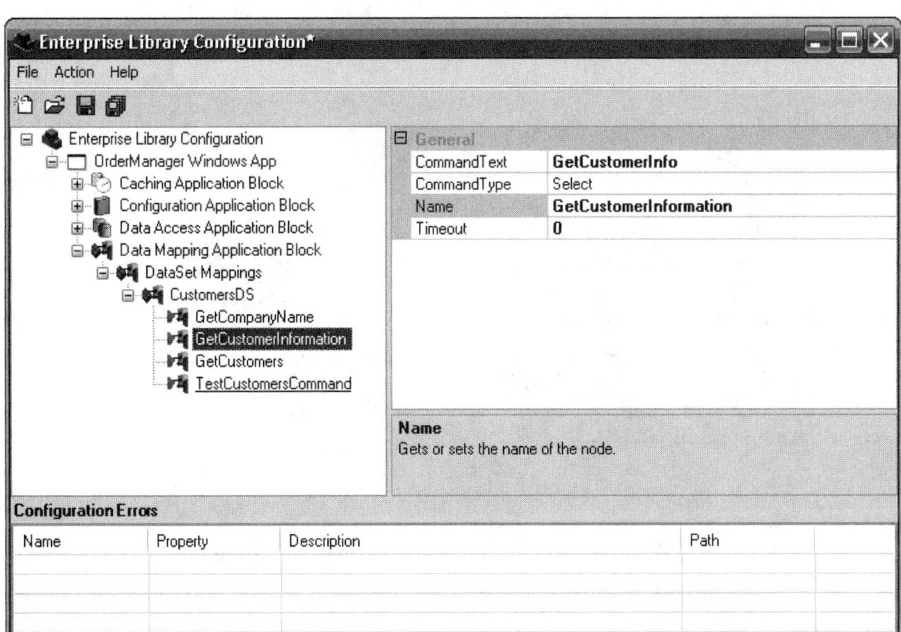

FIGURE A.9: Adding More `SelectCommandMapping`s

LISTING A.3: Extended `CustomersMapper` Data Access Logic Component

```
[C#]
public class CustomersMapper : DataMapper
{
     protected override DataSet DataSetType()
     {
          return new CustomersDS();
     }

     public CustomersDS GetCustomers()
     {
          return (CustomersDS)GetObject();
     }

     public string GetCompanyNameForCustomer(string customerID)
     {
          return GetScalar(SR.GetCompanyName,customerID)as string;
     }
```

```
        public IDataReader GetCustomersReader()
        {
            return GetReader();
        }
    }

[Visual Basic]
Public Class CustomersMapper : Inherits DataMapper
    Protected Overrides Function DataSetType() As DataSet
        Return New CustomersDS()
    End Function

    Public Function GetCustomers() As CustomersDS
        Return CType(GetObject(), CustomersDS)
    End Function

    Public Function GetCompanyNameForCustomer _
         (ByVal customerID As String) As String
        Return (Type(Get Scalar(SR.GetCompanyName,customerID), String)
    End Function

    Public Function GetCustomersReader() As IDataReader
        Return GetReader()
    End Function
End Class
```

Caching

One of the best practices with respect to designing data access logic components in a distributed application is to consider caching data that is nontransactional, expensive to create or transform, and is static or semi-static. Thus, another design goal for the Data Mapping Application Block was to provide configurable caching capabilities in data access logic components by encapsulating many of the features of the Caching Application Block. Configuration data is used to determine whether or not to cache data for a DataSet. If a DataSet is configured so that it is cached, additional configuration information is used to set multiple `CacheItemExpirations` and a `CacheItemRefreshAction` to control the expiration behavior for the cached data.

Caching is enabled for a data access logic component by right-clicking on a *DataSetMapping* node and selecting *New > Cache Settings*. The inclusion of this node indicates to the Data Mapping Application Block that it should cache the data for this data access logic component. The guidance around caching data in data access logic components is to have separate caches for each type of data. For example, if an application needs to cache orders data and customers data, it should use a different CacheManager for each of these. When the `CacheSettings` are added to the Data Mapping Application Block, a CacheManager that has already been configured in the Caching Application Block's settings must be selected (see Chapter 4 for more information on how to create a CacheManager).

If no other settings are added for caching this data, then the data will exist in cache until it is scavenged. This determination is made by the configuration that has been set for the CacheManager in the Caching Application Block. Figure A.10 shows how the *Customers* data access logic component has been configured to cache its data in the *Customers Cache* CacheManager.

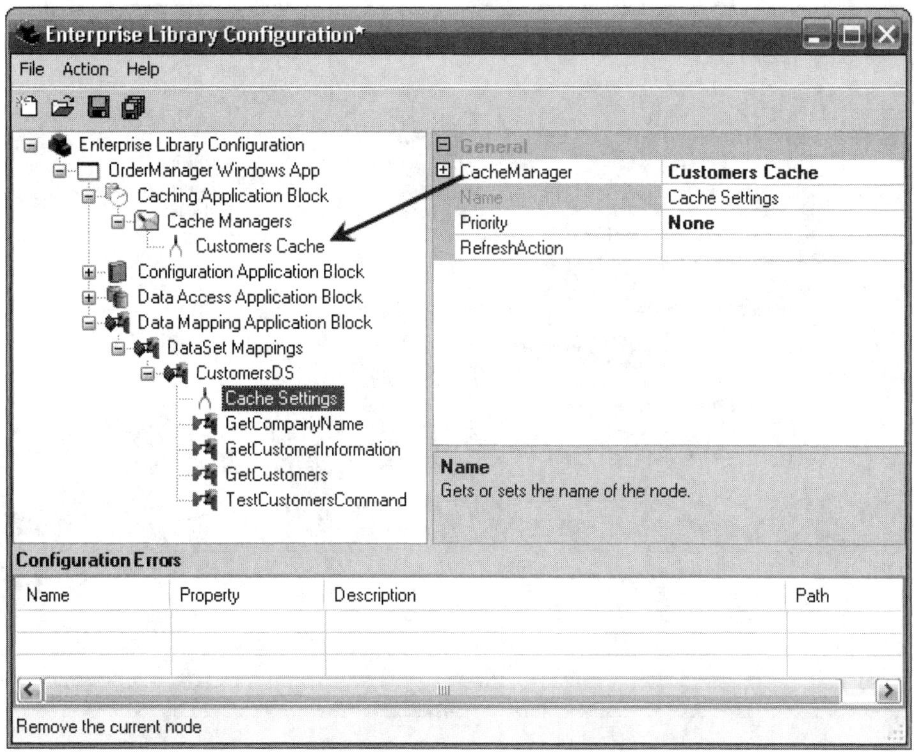

FIGURE A.10: Enabling Caching and Setting the CacheManager

Adding a CacheItemExpiration. It will often be necessary to expire data from the cache after a certain period of time has passed or a change has been made to some dependency, like a file or database table. For example, it may be desirable to expire the data from the cache if either the database table from which the cached data originated has been modified (i.e., a `DatabaseDependencyExpiration`) or if more than five minutes has passed since the last time this data was accessed (i.e., a `SlidingTimeExpiration`). Many expiration policies can be configured for a data access logic component; if any of them occurs, the item will be expired from cache. To create a `CacheItemExpiration`, right-click on the *Cache Settings* node, select *New*, and the type of expiration to add. Then configure the properties that are specific for that type of expiration policy. In Figure A.11, a database dependency expiration policy has been added to the cache settings for

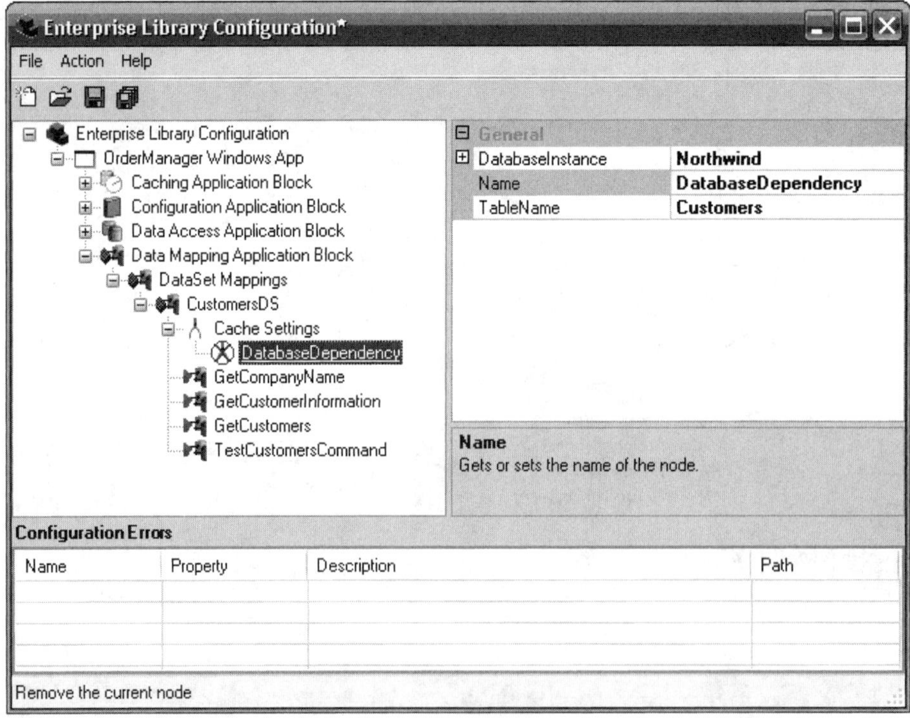

FIGURE A.11: Configuring a `DatabaseDependencyExpirationNode`

the *Customers* data access logic component and configured to remove cached data when a change occurs in the Customers table in the Northwind database. For more information about the properties that are available for each type of expiration policy, see Chapter 4.

Adding a RefreshAction. It is sometimes necessary to take some action when an item is removed from the cache. For example, sometimes it will be important to refetch the expired data and add it back to the cache, while other times it may simply be necessary to log the fact that an item was removed. The `CacheItemRefreshAction` serves this purpose. `CacheItemRefreshActions` can be powerful because they are completely decoupled from the data access logic component or the running application that references them. It is entirely possible to reconfigure a data access logic component to use a new `CacheItemRefreshAction` to perform a specific action (e.g., log information about why an item was expired from the cache) without modifying the application code in any way.

To add and configure a `CacheItemRefreshAction`, select the ellipses button for the `RefreshAction` property for the Cache Settings node. The Enterprise Library Configuration Tool will display the Type Selector dialog, and the tool will automatically try to find all implementations of the `ICacheItemRefreshAction` interface that it knows about. Selecting one of these implementations will cause that `CacheItemRefreshAction` to be notified as items are expired from that particular CacheManager. Figure A.12 shows how to add the `DataSetRefreshAction` to the configuration data for the CustomersDS cache settings information.

DataTableMappings

So far I haven't shown how to map stored procedure parameters to DataFields in the DataTables of a DataSet. That is because `SelectCommands` simply pass through the arguments that they are given. The Data Access Application Block handles mapping the values for these arguments to the parameters that it discovers for the stored procedure. It does not, however, do any mapping for Insert, Update, and Delete operations.

When using DataSets to contain the data that needs to be propagated to the database, data mapping entails setting the values that get passed into stored procedures to the values for DataFields in the DataTables of a

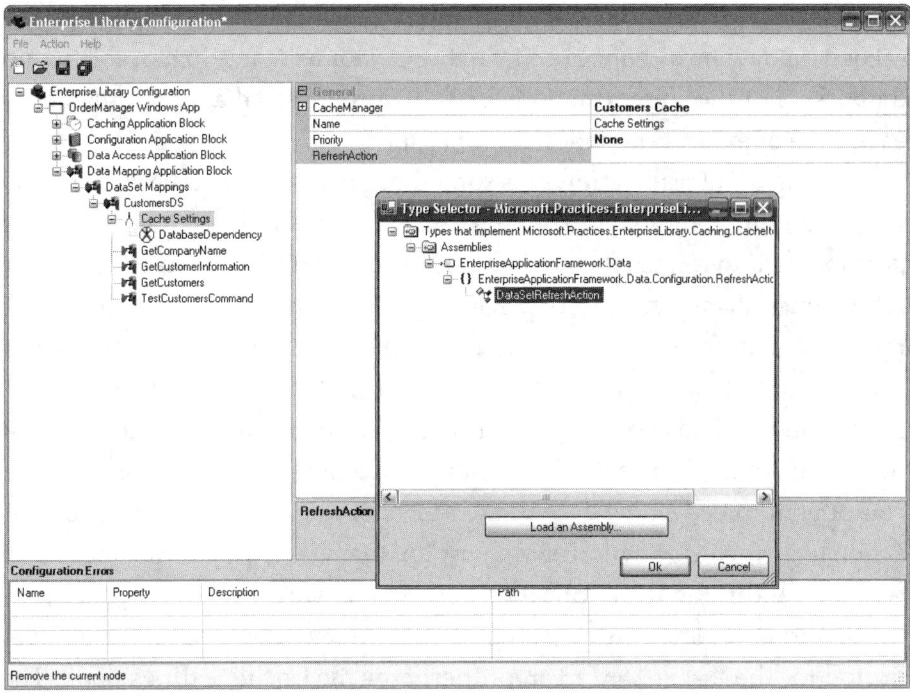

FIGURE A.12: Adding a `RefreshAction`

DataSet. To begin mapping these fields, a `DataTableMapping` needs to be added for a `DataSetMapping`. To add a `DataTableMapping`, right-click on the *DataSetMapping* node and select *New > DataTable Mapping*. The name for the `DataTableMapping` must be the same as the name of the DataTable to which it is being mapped. Figure A.13 shows the results of adding a `DataTableMapping` for the Customers DataTable in the CustomersDS DataSet.

CommandMappings

A `DataTableMapping` contains a collection of `CommandMappings`. After the `DataTableMapping` has been created, at least one `CommandMapping` should be added to insert, update, and/or delete data from the data source. Since it doesn't really make much sense to have a `DataTableMapping` without a `CommandMapping`, a `CommandMapping` is automatically added as a subnode to the `DataTableMapping` when the `DataTableMapping` node is created. Its `CommandType` is set to *Select* by default; however, this can be changed in

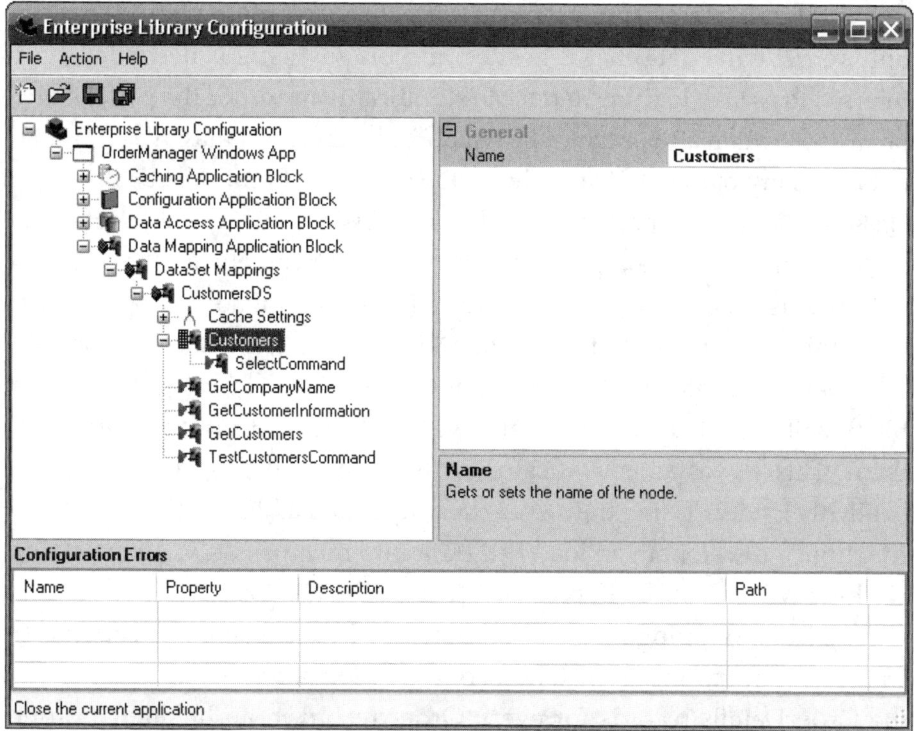

FIGURE A.13: Adding a `DataTableMapping`

the Property pane for the `CommandMapping` node. Before changing it however, it is important to understand what `SelectCommandMappings` mean in the context of a `DataTableMapping`.

SelectCommand: Lazy Loading. `SelectCommandMappings` for a DataTable work differently than `SelectCommandMappings` do for the entire DataSet. One of the benefits of loading a DataSet into memory is that all tables can get loaded into memory at the same time. For example, given a hierarchical DataSet where there is a parent Orders table and a child OrderDetails table, not only can the parent Orders table be loaded with data, but the child OrderDetails table can as well. However, loading all the data for a DataSet with a complex hierarchy or a tremendous amount of data can incur considerable performance costs. This is especially detrimental if some DataTables never need to be populated with data or all of the data that is loaded is not needed.

A best practice concerning the use of data access logic components is to only retrieve the data that is needed and only when it is needed.[4] This is referred to as **lazy loading** and it can significantly improve the performance of an application and enhance its scalability if there is a massive amount of data or many objects to load. The `FillTable` function in the `DataMapper` class can be used to perform lazy loading. Using the `DataMapper`'s `GetObject` function, a data access logic component can ensure that only the data that is required is retrieved during the initial load. The `FillTable` function can then be used to fill the DataTables in the DataSet as needed.

When the DataSet is originally filled, the Data Mapping Application Block will not fill DataTables that have a `SelectCommand` associated with them. This serves as an indicator to the block that this table should be explicitly loaded. Using the `SelectCommand` for a table and the `FillTable` function, a developer can load this data into memory only when needed. Caching will still apply if it has been set for the DataSet.

The Data Mapping Application Block will keep a separate copy of the DataSet for every unique instance. For example, rather than retrieving all of the OrderDetails records for every Order record in an hierarchal orders DataSet, only the Orders table can be initially populated and the OrderDetails records can be retrieved as needed. When the OrderDetails records are needed for a specific order, those records can be retrieved, cached, and returned by the Data Mapping Application Block. Listing A.4 demonstrates how to accomplish this by using the `FillTable` method to lazy load the data for the OrderDetails table for a specific Order record.

Listing A.4: Lazy Loading the `OrderDetails` Data

```
[C#]
public bool GetOrderDetails(ref OrdersDS orders, int iOrderID)
{
     return FillTable(orders,orders.OrdersDetails.TableName,
                      iOrderID);
}

[Visual Basic]
Public Function GetOrderDetails _
```

4. Except when data will definitely be used, like reference data that is proactively loaded and cached.

```
    (ByRef orders As OrdersDS, ByVal iOrderID As Integer) As Boolean
   Return FillTable(orders,orders.OrdersDetails.TableName, iOrderID)

End Function
```

Insert, Update, and Delete Commands. Configuring a `DataTableMapping` with its update operations is where the data mapping process actually begins. The difference between retrieval operations and update operations is that update operations contain zero or more `CommandParameterMappings` and retrieval operations do not. The first step in configuring an update operation is to change the CommandType for a `CommandMapping` to `Insert`, `Update`, `Delete`, or `InsertUpdate`. The `InsertUpdate` value is meant to be used for both insert and update operations. Often one stored procedure will exist that handles both insert and update operations by checking to see if a record exists (update) or not (insert). Rather than creating two separate `CommandMappings` with the same collection of `CommandParameterMappings`, the `InsertUpdate CommandType` allows one `CommandMapping` to be used for both operations.

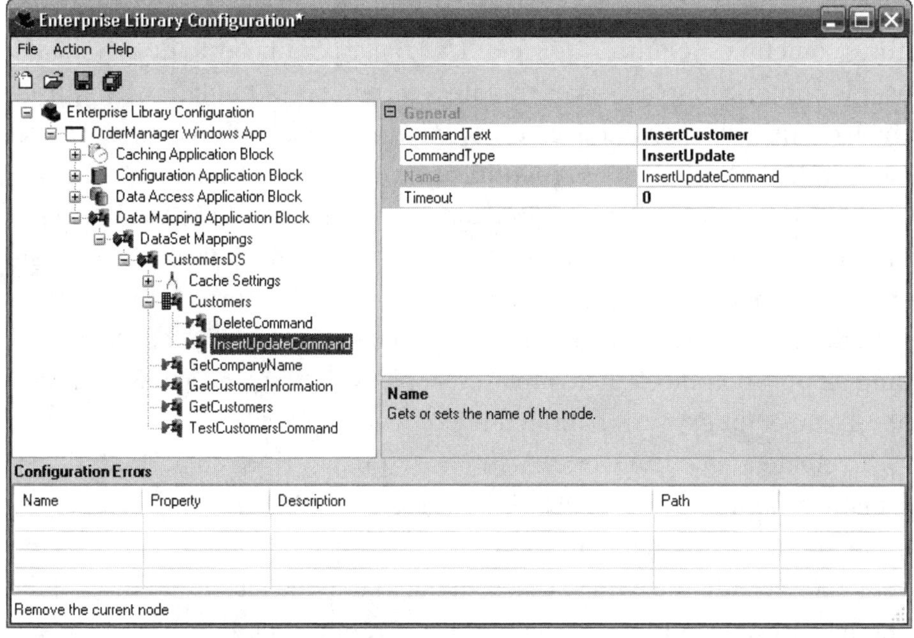

FIGURE A.14: Creating a New `CommandMapping` for a `DataTable`

To create a new `CommandMapping`, right-click on the *DataTableMapping* node and select *New > Command Mapping*. Then change the CommandType to either `Select`, `Insert`, `Update`, `Delete`, or `InsertUpdate`. Figure A.14 shows how the configuration for the `CustomersMapper` data access logic component has been extended with a `DeleteCommand` and `InsertUpdateCommand` for its Customers DataTable.

CommandParameterMappings

The details for the data mapping between a stored procedure's parameters and a DataSet's DataFields occur at the lowest level of the configuration hierarchy. `CommandParameterMappings` allow the DataFields in the DataTables of a DataSet to map to the parameters for a stored procedure. A `CommandParameterMapping` simply holds the state for the name of the parameter and the source column (i.e., name of the DataField) in the DataSet. If the source column is left blank, the block assumes that there is no DataField mapping and that the value for the parameter must be explicitly set at runtime. This is to allow for non-DataSet (or explicit) parameters.

There may be situations where it may not make sense to include all stored procedure parameters as DataFields. For example, stored procedures sometimes require a *UserId* or *UserName* parameter to determine if a user is authorized to access or update a certain set of data; however, from an object-oriented perspective, it may not make sense to have a user ID element in the typed DataSet. Identification/authentication fields like *SessionId*, *UserId*, or even *Current Date and Time* often need to be explicitly set; they are elements of data that need to be passed to the data source for data entitlement and auditing reasons. However, they are more global in nature than the data that typically exists in any specific DataSet. In the Data Mapping Application Block, fields that must be explicitly set are referred to as non-DataSet (or explicit) parameters.

To create a new `CommandParameterMapping`, right-click on the *CommandMapping* node and select *New > CommandParameterMapping*. Set the `Name` property to the name of the stored procedure parameter and `SourceColumn` to the name of the DataField to which it should map. If the parameter is meant to be explicitly set at runtime, then the `SourceColumn` property must be left blank. It is also important that the `CommandParameterMappings` are listed in the order in which they appear in the stored procedure, because the Data Access Application Block's `GetStoredProcCommandWrapperWithSourceColumns` method expects the `CommandParameters` to be in the order that they exist in the stored procedure. If the `CommandParameterMappings` are added in the wrong order, the order can

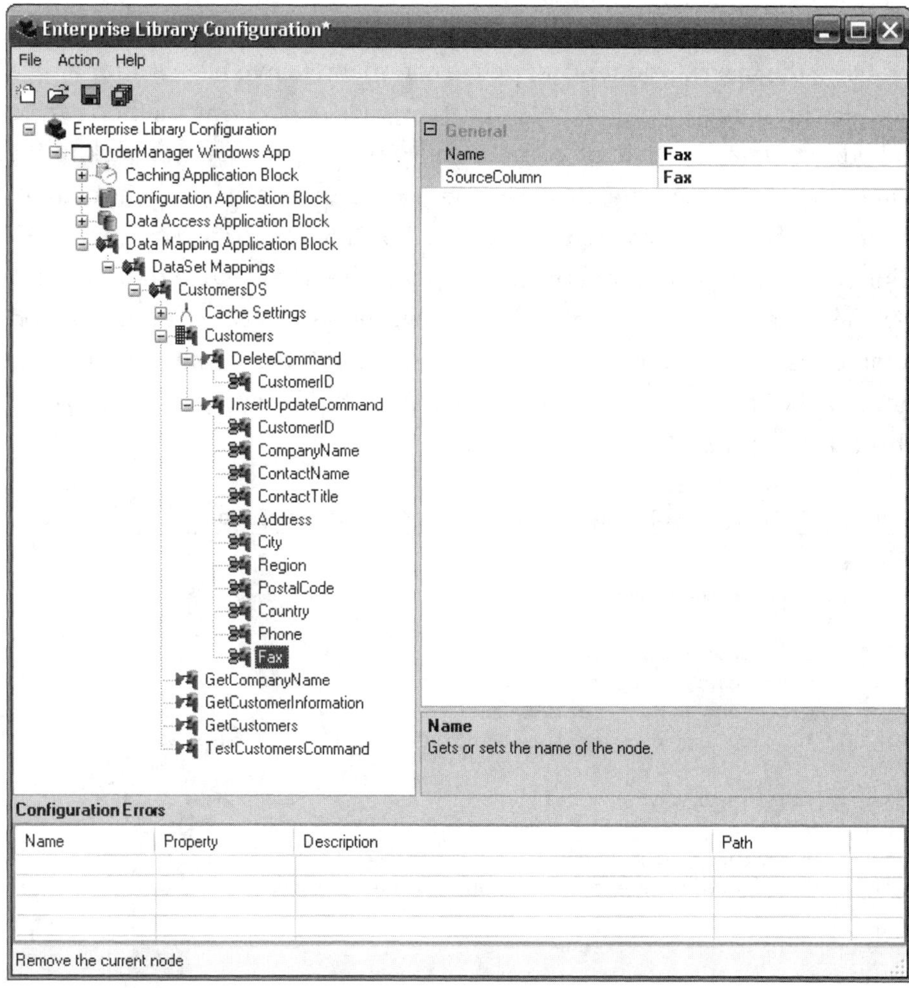

FIGURE A.15: Adding `CommandParameterMappings` for a Command

be changed by right-clicking on a *CommandParameterMapping* node and selecting either *Move Up* or *Move Down*.

Figure A.15 shows how the configuration for the *Customers* DataTable has been completed by adding the `CommandParameterMappings` to the two `CommandMappings`. The delete command accepts one parameter, and the value for this parameter is retrieved from the `CustomerID` field in the Customers DataTable. The insert and update commands accept the following parameters: `CustomerID`, `CompanyName`, `ContactName`, `ContactTitle`, `Address`, `City`, `Region`, `PostalCode`, `Country`, `Phone`, and `Fax`.

Once the insert, update, and delete commands have been set for a data access logic component, the base `DataMapper`'s `PutObject` method can be called in a data access logic component to propagate changes back to the data source. For example, the `CustomersMapper` data access logic component may have a `RemoveCustomer` method that accepts a customer ID. Since the mapping of stored procedure parameters to DataFields is handled by the Data Mapping Application Block, the `RemoveCustomer` method should just remove the appropriate record from the Customers DataTable and call the base `DataMapper`'s `PutObject` method. Listing A.5 shows how this is accomplished.

LISTING A.5: Calling `PutObject` to Propagate Changes to the Data Source

```
[C#]
public int RemoveCustomer(string customerID)
{
     int recordsAffected = 0;
     CustomersDS customers = GetCustomers();
     CustomersDS.CustomersRow customerRow =
          customers.Customers.FindByCustomerID(customerID);

     if (customerRow != null)
     {
          customerRow.Delete();
          recordsAffected = PutObject(customers);
     }
     return recordsAffected;
}

[Visual Basic]
Public Function RemoveCustomer(ByVal customerID As String) As Integer
     Dim recordsAffected As Integer = 0
     Dim customers As CustomersDS = GetCustomers()
```

```
    Dim customerRow As CustomersDS.CustomersRow = _
         customers.Customers.FindByCustomerID(customerID)

    If Not customerRow Is Nothing Then
         customerRow.Delete()
         recordsAffected = PutObject(customers)
    End If
    Return recordsAffected
End Function
```

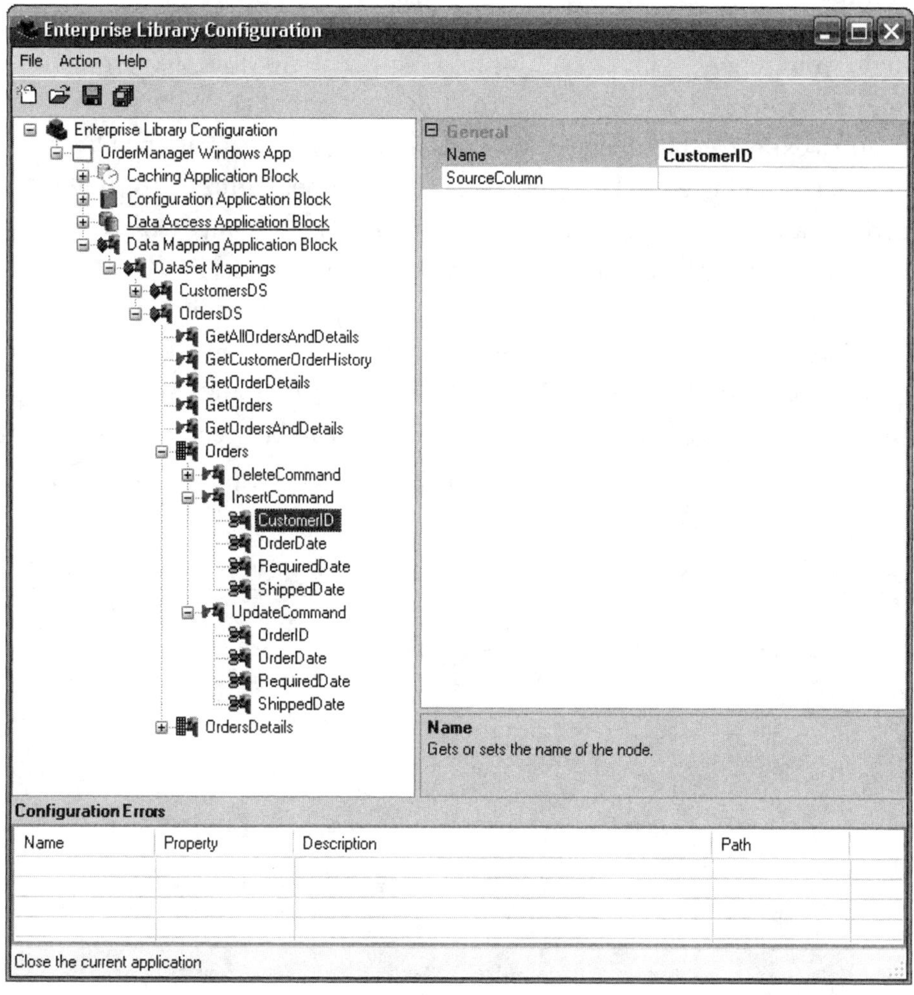

FIGURE A.16: Setting Explicit Parameters for `CommandParameterMappings`

The base `DataMapper` class contains a ListDictionary that is expected to contain a list of any explicit parameters and their values. Helper functions exist to facilitate getting and setting the explicit parameters and their values. Any items in this list can be used during an update operation.

Suppose an enterprise application needed to manage information about orders and order details in addition to customers. Additionally, it may have requirements such that order and order detail information needs to be retrieved per customer. However, for this application's design, the customer ID is not a field in the *OrdersDS* typed DataSet that contains the order and order detail information. The database operations for this data access logic component can be configured similarly to the way the `CustomersMapper` was. One difference, however, is that since the stored procedures expect a customer ID and that field does not exist in the *OrdersDS* DataSet, it will need to be explicitly set at runtime. Figure A.16 shows the configuration for the `OrdersMapper` data access logic component and highlights the configuration node for CustomerID, where the `SourceColumn` is left blank to indicate that it should be explicitly set at runtime.

When an order needs to be added, the customer ID can be marked as an explicit parameter by using the helper methods that are part of the base `DataMapper` class. Listing A.6 shows how this can be accomplished.

Listing A.6: Setting Explicit Parameters Before Calling `PutObject`

```
[C#]
public int AddOrder(string customerID, DateTime orderDate,
                    DateTime requiredDate, DateTime shippedDate)
{
     OrdersDS orders = GetOrders();
     OrdersDS.OrdersRow orderRow =
               orders.Orders.AddOrdersRow
               (orderDate, requiredDate, shippedDate);

     ListDictionary explicitParameters = new ListDictionary();
     explicitParameters.Add(SR.CustomerIDParameter,customerID);
     set_ExplicitParameters
               (orders.Orders.TableName, explicitParameters);
```

```
        return PutObject(orders);
    }

    [Visual Basic]
    public int AddOrder(String customerID, _
                        DateTime orderDate, DateTime requiredDate, _
                        DateTime shippedDate)
    {
        OrdersDS orders = GetOrders();
        OrdersDS.OrdersRow orderRow = _
            orders.Orders.AddOrdersRow _
            (orderDate, requiredDate, shippedDate);

        ListDictionary explicitParameters = new ListDictionary();
        explicitParameters.Add(SR.CustomerIDParameter,customerID);
        set_ExplicitParameters(orders.Orders.TableName, _
            explicitParameters);
        return PutObject(orders);
    }
    End Function
```

Transactions

A data access logic component can be configured so that the database operations that it performs all occur in the scope of a transaction. For example, the transaction IsolationLevel for the `OrdersMapper` data access logic component can be configured so that as changes are made to order and order detail records, either all changes will be committed to the data source or none will. Setting the transaction IsolationLevel for a data access logic component can be done by modifying the setting for the `TransactionType` property for the `DataSetMapping`. Figure A.17 shows how the IsolationLevel is set to Serializable for the `OrdersMapper` data access logic component.

Sometimes, transactions may need to be set at a more granular level. It may be desirable, for example, to have some database operations occur in the scope of a transaction and others that do not. To allow for this, the base `DataMapper` class contains a protected property named `TransactionType`. Setting the `TransactionType` property to a transaction IsolationLevel before a call is made to `PutObject` will cause the database operations to be performed in the scope of a transaction. Listing A.7 shows how to add order and order detail information in the scope of a serializable transaction.

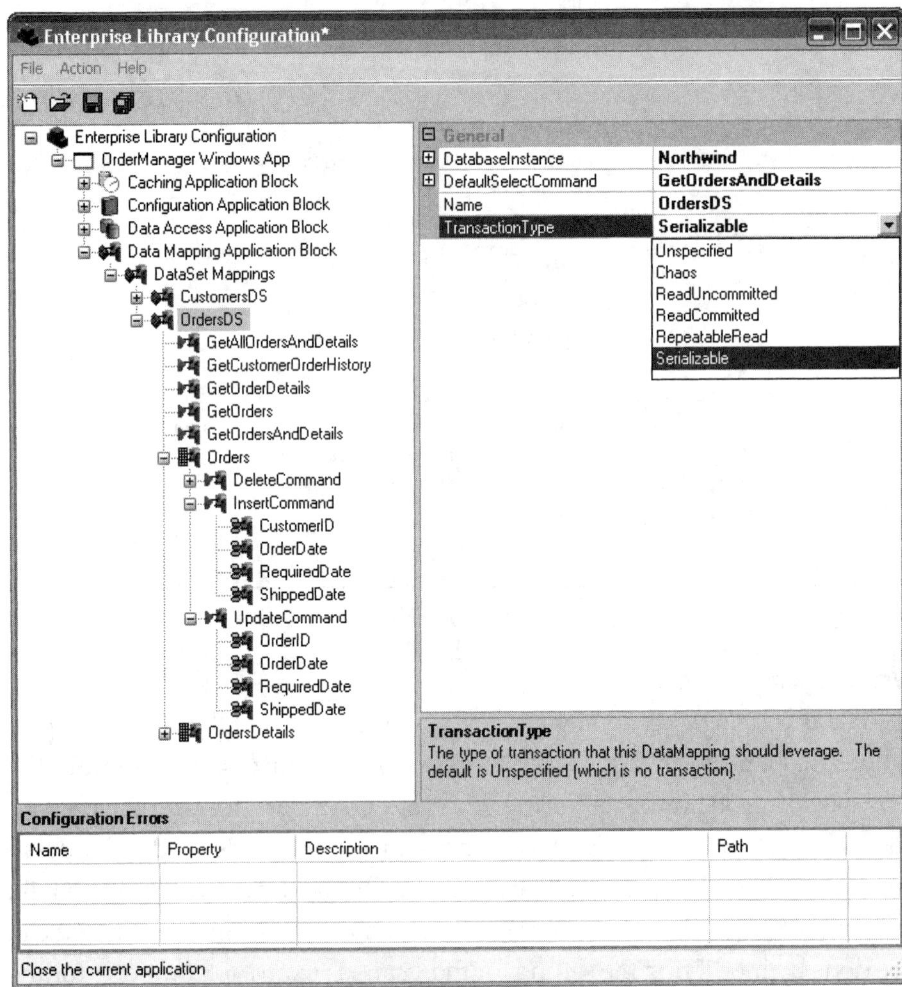

FIGURE A.17: Setting the Transaction IsolationLevel for a Data Access Logic Component

LISTING A.7: Programmatically Setting the Transaction Level

```
[C#]
public int AddOrderWithDetail(DateTime orderDate, DateTime requiredDate,
                              DateTime shippedDate, string productName,
                              short quantity, int discount)
{
    OrdersDS orders = GetOrders();
    OrdersDS.OrdersRow orderRow =
        orders.Orders.AddOrdersRow
        (orderDate, requiredDate, shippedDate);
```

```
    OrdersDS.OrdersDetailsRow orderDetailRow =
         orders.OrdersDetails.AddOrdersDetailsRow
          (productName, 0, quantity, discount, 0, orderRow);

    TransactionType = IsolationLevel.Serializable;

    ListDictionary explicitParameters = new ListDictionary();
    explicitParameters.Add(SR.CustomerIDParameter,customerID);
    base.set_ExplicitParameters
          (orders.Orders.TableName, explicitParameters);

    return PutObject(orders);
}

[Visual Basic]
public int AddOrderWithDetail(DateTime orderDate, _
                              DateTime requiredDate, _
                              DateTime shippedDate, _
                              string productName, _
                              short quantity, int discount)
{
    OrdersDS orders = GetOrders();
    OrdersDS.OrdersRow orderRow = _
              orders.Orders.AddOrdersRow _
              (orderDate, requiredDate, shippedDate);

    OrdersDS.OrdersDetailsRow orderDetailRow =
          orders.OrdersDetails.AddOrdersDetailsRow _
          (productName, 0, quantity, discount, 0, orderRow);

    TransactionType = IsolationLevel.Serializable;

    ListDictionary explicitParameters = new ListDictionary();
    explicitParameters.Add(SR.CustomerIDParameter,customerID);
    base.set_ExplicitParameters _
          (orders.Orders.TableName, explicitParameters);

    return PutObject(orders);
}
End
```

Summary

This appendix serves as a review of the design concepts of the Data Mapping Application Block and the steps needed to configure and develop an application to use it. The primary design goal for the Data Mapping Application Block was to make it easier for architects and developers to incorporate best practices for leveraging data access logic components in their applications. One of the most tedious and time-intense tasks related to developing a data access logic component is the mapping of parameters in a relational database to the fields or properties of a business entity. The Data Mapping Application Block's design allows the information about these mappings to reside in configuration data instead of requiring that a developer write code. Additional configuration-driven properties exist for settings, transactions, the command timeout value, and caching information.

This appendix showed how to configure the various features in the Data Mapping Application Block and demonstrated how the code that is needed to perform data mappings and execute database operations can be minimized by taking advantage of this configuration data. Specifically, it focused on how the name and parameters for a stored procedure can be completely driven by configuration, thereby decoupling an application from those stored procedures. It showed how to map data values that are not known until runtime into a stored procedure's parameters.

The appendix demonstrated how to configure and develop a data access logic component so that data can be cached and database operations can occur in the scope of a transaction. By making many of these decisions solvable through configuration, an application can not only be developed more expediently, but it can also be more isolated from changes that may occur in an enterprise's environment. For example, if a stored procedure's parameters change or a completely different stored procedures needs to be executed for a particular database operation, the likelihood that any code in the application will need to change is reduced by using the Data Mapping Application Block.

B

Creating a .NET Managed Data Provider

CHAPTER 3 DESCRIBED how to use database providers and demonstrated how to create a new one. A prerequisite for creating a database provider is the existence of a .NET managed data provider that provides an implementation for the interfaces that need to be returned for the virtual methods defined in the abstract `Database` base class. For example, the `SqlDatabase` class derives from the `Database` class and must return a class that implements the `IDataReader` for the virtual `ExecuteReader` method. It accomplishes this by using the `SqlCommand` and `SqlDataReader` classes that are provided by the .NET managed data provider for Microsoft SQL Server.

Listings 3-4 and 3-5 (in Chapter 3) provided examples for some of the code that needs to be written to create a new database provider that retrieves and stores data in an XML file. Part of the reason I picked this as an example was to demonstrate that you aren't without any options if a .NET managed data provider does not yet exist for the data source you need to use. It is possible to create a .NET managed data provider so that a database provider can be created to use it.

To create a .NET managed data provider that will support the needs of the Data Access Application Block, you need to develop seven classes that implement specific interfaces. These interfaces are `IDataParameter`, `IDataParameterCollection`, `IDataReader`, `IDbCommand`, `IDbConnec-`

tion /ICloneable, IDbDataAdapter, and IDbTransaction. This appendix shows how to create a .NET managed data provider for XML files by creating a class that implements each of these interfaces.

The IDataParameter Interface

Create, Retrieve, Update, and Delete (CRUD) commands are usually parameter driven. For example, retrieving data from a database often involves passing identity information to indicate which records in the particular data source need to be selected. The IDataParameter interface defines the methods that a .NET managed data provider must implement to pass parameters to its specific data source. The XmlFileParameter class implements the IDataParameter interface for the .NET managed data provider for XML files. The excerpt in Listing B.1 shows the code for this class that implements the IDataParameter interface for the .NET managed data provider for XML files.

LISTING B.1: XmlFileParameter **Class Implements** IDataParameter

```
[C#]
public class XmlFileParameter : IDataParameter
{
     DbType paramDbType = DbType.Object;
     ParameterDirection parameterDirection = ParameterDirection.Input;
     bool isNullable  = false;
     string paramName;
     string sourceColumn;
     DataRowVersion dataRowVersion = DataRowVersion.Current;
     object paramValue;

     ...

     public XmlFileParameter
            (string parameterName, DbType dbType, string sourceColumn)
     {
          this.ParameterName = parameterName;
          this.DbType = dbType;
          this.SourceColumn = sourceColumn;
     }
```

```
    public String ParameterName
    {
        get { return paramName; }
        set { paramName = value; }
    }

    public ParameterDirection Direction
    {
        get { return parameterDirection; }
        set { parameterDirection = value; }
    }

    public Boolean IsNullable
    {
        get { return isNullable; }
    }

    public String SourceColumn
    {
        get { return sourceColumn; }
        set { sourceColumn = value; }
    }

    public DataRowVersion SourceVersion
    {
        get { return dataRowVersion; }
        set { dataRowVersion = value; }
    }

    public object Value
    {
        get
        {
            return this.paramValue;
        }
        set
        {
            this.paramValue    = value;
            paramDbType = _inferType(value);
        }
    }
    ...
}

[Visual Basic]
Public Class XmlFileParameter : Implements IDataParameter
    Private paramDbType As DbType = DbType.Object
    Private parameterDirection As ParameterDirection = _
        ParameterDirection.Input
```

```
Private _isNullable As Boolean = False
Private paramName As String
Private _sourceColumn As String
Private dataRowVersion As DataRowVersion = DataRowVersion.Current
Private paramValue As Object

...

Public Sub New(ByVal _parameterName As String, _
               ByVal _value As Object, sourceColumn As String)
     Me.ParameterName = _parameterName
     Me.DbType = dbType
     Me.SourceColumn = _sourceColumn
End Sub

Public Property ParameterName() As String _
               Implements IDataParameter.ParameterName
     Get
          Return paramName
     End Get
     Set
          paramName = Value
     End Set
End Property

Public Property Direction() As ParameterDirection _
               Implements IDataParameter.Direction
     Get
          Return parameterDirection
     End Get
     Set
          parameterDirection = Value
     End Set
End Property

Public ReadOnly Property IsNullable() As Boolean _
               Implements IDataParameter.IsNullable
     Get
          Return _isNullable
     End Get
End Property

Public Property SourceColumn() As String _
               Implements IDataParameter.SourceColumn
     Get
          Return _sourceColumn
     End Get
     Set
          _sourceColumn = Value
```

```
            End Set
        End Property

        Public Property SourceVersion() As DataRowVersion _
                      Implements IDataParameter.SourceVersion
            Get
                Return dataRowVersion
            End Get
            Set
                dataRowVersion = Value
            End Set
        End Property

        Public Property Value() As Object Implements IDataParameter.Value
            Get
                Return Me.paramValue
            End Get
            Set
                Me.paramValue = Value
                paramDbType = _inferType(Value)
            End Set
        End Property

        ...
    End Class
```

The IDataParameterCollection Interface

Each of the Command objects (SelectCommand, InsertCommand, UpdateCommand, and DeleteCommand) exposed by a data adapter exposes a Parameters property to allow parameter values to be passed in at runtime. This saves the trouble of having to manually construct a string with runtime values and also provides type checking of the command parameters. The Parameters property returns a collection of the parameter objects that correspond to the particular data source (e.g., the XmlFileParameter created in Listing B.1). Therefore, for the .NET managed data provider for XML files, the XmlFileParameterCollection must exist to serve as the collection of XmlFileParameters. Listing B.2 shows how the XmlFileParameterCollection implements the IDataParameterCollection interface needed for the .NET managed data provider for XML files.

LISTING B.2: `XmlFileParameterCollection` **Implements** `IDataParameterCollection`

```
[C#]
public class XmlFileParameterCollection :
              ArrayList, IDataParameterCollection
{
     public object this[string index]
     {
          get { return this[IndexOf(index)]; }
          set {     this[IndexOf(index)] = value; }
     }

     public XmlFileParameterCollection() {}

     public bool Contains(string parameterName)
     {
          return(-1 != IndexOf(parameterName));
     }

     public int IndexOf(string parameterName)
     {
          int index = 0;
          foreach(XmlFileParameter item in this)
          {
               if (0 == _cultureAwareCompare
                     (item.ParameterName, parameterName))
               {
                    return index;
               }
               index++;
          }
          return -1;
     }

     public void RemoveAt(string parameterName)
     {
          RemoveAt(IndexOf(parameterName));
     }

     public override int Add(object value)
     {
          return Add((XmlFileParameter)value);
     }

     public int Add(XmlFileParameter value)
     {
          if (((XmlFileParameter)value).ParameterName != null)
          {
               return base.Add(value);
```

```
            }
            else
                throw new ArgumentException(SR.UnnamedParameter);
        }

        public int Add(string parameterName, DbType type)
        {
            return Add(new XmlFileParameter(parameterName, type));
        }

        public int Add(string parameterName, object value)
        {
            return Add(new XmlFileParameter(parameterName, value));
        }

        public int Add(string parameterName, DbType dbType,
                       string sourceColumn)
        {
            return Add(new XmlFileParameter
                         (parameterName, dbType, sourceColumn));
        }

        private int _cultureAwareCompare(string strA, string strB)
        {
            return CultureInfo.CurrentCulture.CompareInfo.Compare
                (strA, strB, CompareOptions.IgnoreKanaType |
                CompareOptions.IgnoreWidth |
    CompareOptions.IgnoreCase);
        }
    }

    [Visual Basic]
    Public Class XmlFileParameterCollection : Inherits ArrayList : _
                Implements IDataParameterCollection

        Public Default Property Item(ByVal index As String) As Object
            Get
                Return Me(IndexOf(index))
            End Get
            Set
                Me(IndexOf(index)) = Value
            End Set
        End Property

        Public Sub New()
        End Sub

        Public Function Contains(ByVal paramName As String) As Boolean _
                Implements IDataParameterCollection.Contains
            Return(-1 <> IndexOf(paramName))
```

```
End Function

Public Function IndexOf(ByVal paramName As String) As Integer _
        Implements IDataParameterCollection.IndexOf
    Dim index As Integer = 0
    For Each item As XmlFileParameter In Me
        If 0 = _cultureAwareCompare _
             (item.ParameterName, paramName) Then
            Return index
        End If
        index += 1
    Next item
    Return -1
End Function

Public Sub RemoveAt(ByVal paramName As String) _
        Implements IDataParameterCollection.RemoveAt
    RemoveAt(IndexOf(parameterName))
End Sub

Public Overrides Function Add(ByVal value As Object) As Integer
    Return Add(CType(value, XmlFileParameter))
End Function

Public Function Add(ByVal value As XmlFileParameter) As Integer
    If Not (CType(value, XmlFileParameter)).ParameterName _
             Is Nothing Then
        Return MyBase.Add(value)
    Else
        Throw New ArgumentException(SR.UnnamedParameter)
    End If
End Function

Public Function Add(ByVal paramName As String, _
             ByVal type As DbType) As Integer
    Return Add(New XmlFileParameter(paramName, type))
End Function

Public Function Add(ByVal paramName As String,
             ByVal value As Object) As Integer
    Return Add(New XmlFileParameter(paramName, value))
End Function

Public Function Add(ByVal paramName As String, _
             ByVal dbType As DbType, _
             ByVal sourceColumn As String) As Integer
    Return Add(New XmlFileParameter _
             (paramName, dbType, sourceColumn))
End Function
```

```
    Private Function _cultureAwareCompare _
            (ByVal strA As String, ByVal strB As String) As Integer

        Return CultureInfo.CurrentCulture.CompareInfo.Compare _
                  (strA, strB, CompareOptions.IgnoreKanaType Or _
                  CompareOptions.IgnoreWidth Or _
                  CompareOptions.IgnoreCase)
    End Function
End Class
```

The `IDataReader` Interface

Providing a solid DataReader is core to providing a reliable .NET managed data provider. DataReaders provide forward-only access over the ResultSets obtained by executing database commands. They also provide access to values for the fields in each DataRow through strongly typed accessor methods. Examples of strongly typed accessors are `GetInt32`, `GetString`, and so on. Additionally, DataAdapters use DataReaders to fill the DataTables in a DataSet. The Data Access Application Block returns a class that implements the `IDataReader` interface when the `ExecuteReader` method is called on a database provider.

The `XmlFileDataReader` is the implementation of the `IDataReader` interface for the .NET managed data provider for XML files. However, before showing you some of the code for this DataReader, I must provide a disclaimer: I have not made this DataReader as efficient as it should be. It uses a private DataSet member variable to read and write data from and to XML files, and uses the DataSet internally to return the values for column fields. While it is not optimized for performance, this DataReader will serve the purpose for providing a valid implementation for the `IDataReader` interface so a database provider can be created and used.

The DataReader could be enhanced to perform better. To do so, it would need to use the same inference process that .NET uses to determine the relational structure of the data when loading from XML. The inference process first determines, from the XML document, which elements will be inferred as tables. From the remaining XML, the inference process determines the columns for those tables. For nested tables, the inference process generates nested `DataRelation` and `ForeignKeyConstraint` objects. The following assumptions must be made during this process.

- Elements that have attributes are inferred as tables.
- Elements that have child elements are inferred as tables.
- Elements that repeat are inferred as a single table.
- If the document (root) element has no attributes, and no child elements that would be inferred as columns, it is inferred as a DataSet. Otherwise, the document element is inferred as a table.
- Attributes are inferred as columns.
- Elements that have no attributes or child elements and do not repeat are inferred as columns.
- For elements that are inferred as tables that are nested in other elements also inferred as tables, a nested DataRelation is created between the two tables. A new, primary key column named *TableName_Id* is added to both tables and used by the DataRelation. A `ForeignKeyConstraint` is created between the two tables using the TableName_Id column.
- For elements that are inferred as tables and that contain text but have no child elements, a new column named *TableName_Text* is created for the text of each of the elements. If an element is inferred as a table and has text as well as child elements, the text is ignored.

Listing B.3 provides an excerpt of the `XmlFileDataReader`.

LISTING B.3: `XmlFileDataReader` **Implements** `IDataReader`

```
[C#]
public class XmlFileDataReader : IDataReader
{
    ...

    public bool NextResult()
    {
        return (tableNum < dataSet.Tables.Count);
    }

    public void Close()
    {
```

```
        closed = true;
        if (xmlFileConnection != null) xmlFileConnection.Close();

    }

    internal void GetXmlFile(string strCommand)
    {
        fileName = strCommand;

        try
        {
            dataSet.ReadXml(strCommand);
            rowNum = -1;
            closed = false;
        }
        catch (Exception ex)
        {
            throw new
            ApplicationException
            (SR.ExceptionLoadXMLFile(command, ex.Message));
        }
    }

    internal XmlReader XmlReader
    {
        get
        {
            try
            {
                XmlReader retVal = new XmlTextReader
                     (new System.IO.StringReader
                     (dataSet.GetXml()));
                return retVal;
            }
            catch (Exception ex)
            {
                throw new
                ApplicationException(
                SR.ExceptionCreateReader(ex.Message));
            }
        }
    }

    public bool Read()
    {
        bool bRetVal = false;
        if (closed) return bRetVal;
        if (rowNum < (dataSet.Tables[tableNum].Rows.Count -1))
        {
            bRetVal = true;
```

```
                rowNum++;
            }
            else
            {
                tableNum++;
                rowNum = -1;
            }
            return bRetVal;
        }

        public int GetInt32(int i)
        {
            return (Int32)GetValue(i);
        }

        public byte GetByte(int i)
        {
            return (Byte)GetValue(i);
        }

        ...
    }

    [Visual Basic]
        Public Class XmlFileDataReader : Implements IDataReader
        ...

        Public Function NextResult() As Boolean _
                Implements IDataReader.NextResult
            Return (tableNum < dataSet.Tables.Count)
        End Function

        Public Sub Close() Implements IDataReader.Close
            closed = True
            If Not xmlFileConnection Is Nothing Then
                xmlFileConnection.Close()
            End If
        End Sub

        Friend Sub GetXmlFile(ByVal strCommand As String)

            fileName = strCommand
            Try
                dataSet.ReadXml(strCommand)
                rowNum = -1
                closed = False
            Catch ex As Exception
                Throw New ApplicationException _
                    (SR.ExceptionLoadXMLFile(command, ex.Message))
            End Try
```

```
    End Sub

    Friend ReadOnly Property XmlReader() As XmlReader
        Get
            Try
                Dim retVal As XmlReader = New XmlTextReader _
                    (New _
                        System.IO.StringReader(dataSet.GetXml()))
                Return retVal
            Catch ex As Exception
                Throw New _
                    ApplicationException _
                    (SR.ExceptionCreateReader(ex.Message))
            End Try
        End Get
    End Property

    Public Function Read() As Boolean Implements IDataReader.Read
        Dim bRetVal As Boolean = False
        If closed Then
            Return bRetVal
        End If
        If rowNum < (dataSet.Tables(tableNum).Rows.Count -1) Then
            bRetVal = True
            rowNum += 1
        Else
            tableNum += 1
            rowNum = -1
        End If
        Return bRetVal
    End Function

    Public Function GetInt32(ByVal i As Integer) As Integer
        Return CInt(GetValue(i))
    End Function

    Public Function GetByte(ByVal i As Integer) As Byte
        Return CType(GetValue(i), Byte)
    End Function
    ...
End Class
```

The IDbCommand Interface

The Command class is another core component for any .NET managed data provider. The Command object implements the IDbCommand interface and is responsible for formulating a database statement or command and passing it on to the underlying data source. This is the main class that is leveraged by a concrete `DBCommandWrapper` class. The `Command` object is responsible for returning results as a DataReader, a scalar value, or as parameters.

Classes that implement the `IDbCommand` interface must often define additional functions to add provider-specific functionality. For example, like the `SqlCommand`, the `XmlFileCommand` class defines the `ExecuteXml-Reader` method in addition to providing an implementation for all the other methods defined by the `IDbCommand` interface. Listing B.4 illustrates how the `XmlFileCommand` implements the `IDbCommand` interface.

LISTING B.4: `XmlFileCommand` **Implements** `IDbCommand`

```
[C#]
public class XmlFileCommand : IDbCommand
{
     ...
     public CommandType CommandType
     {
          get
          {
               return commandType;
          }
          set
          {
               // Only need to support text per SDK.
               commandType = value;
          }
     }

     public IDataReader ExecuteReader(CommandBehavior behavior)
     {
          // Must have a valid and open connection.
          if (connection == null ||
                    connection.State != ConnectionState.Open)
               throw new
                    InvalidOperationException
                    (SR.ExceptionConnectionOpen);
          return ExecuteReader();
     }

     public IDataReader ExecuteReader()
     {
          // Must have a valid and open connection.
          if (connection == null ||
              connection.State != ConnectionState.Open)
```

```
                throw new
                    InvalidOperationException
                    (SR.ExceptionConnectionOpen);
            XmlFileDataReader reader =
                new XmlFileDataReader(connection.Database);
            return reader;
        }

        public XmlReader ExecuteXmlReader()
        {
            // Must have a valid and open connection.
            if (connection == null ||
                    connection.State != ConnectionState.Open)
                throw new
                    InvalidOperationException(
                    SR.ExceptionConnectionOpen);

            XmlFileDataReader reader =
                new XmlFileDataReader(connection.Database);
            return reader.XmlReader;
        }

        //Updates file and returns number of records.
        public int ExecuteNonQuery()
        {
            // Must have a valid and open connection.
            if (connection == null ||
                connection.State != ConnectionState.Open)
                throw new
                    InvalidOperationException(
                    SR.ExceptionConnectionOpen);

            int recs;
            XmlFileDataReader reader =
                 (XmlFileDataReader)ExecuteReader();
            recs = reader.RecordsAffected;
            reader.Close();
            return recs;
        }

        ...
    }

    [Visual Basic]
    Public Class XmlFileCommand : Implements IDbCommand
        ...

        Public Property CommandType() As CommandType _
                Implements IDbCommand.CommandType
            Get
```

```
            Return commandType
        End Get
        Set
            ' Only need to support text per SDK.
            commandType = Value
        End Set
    End Property

    Public Function ExecuteReader _
           (ByVal behavior As CommandBehavior) _
            As IDataReader Implements IDbCommand.ExecuteReader

        ' Must have a valid and open connection.
        If connection Is Nothing OrElse _
                connection.State <> ConnectionState.Open Then
            Throw New _
                InvalidOperationException _
                (SR.ExceptionConnectionOpen)
        End If

        Return ExecuteReader()
    End Function

    Public Function ExecuteReader() As IDataReader _
                Implements IDbCommand.ExecuteReader
        ' Must have a valid and open connection.
        If connection Is Nothing OrElse  _
                connection.State <> ConnectionState.Open Then
            Throw New _
                InvalidOperationException _
                (SR.ExceptionConnectionOpen)
        End If

        Dim reader As XmlFileDataReader = _
            New XmlFileDataReader(connection.Database)
        Return reader
    End Function

    Public Function ExecuteXmlReader() As XmlReader
        ' Must have a valid and open connection.
        If connection Is Nothing OrElse _
                connection.State <> ConnectionState.Open Then
            Throw New _
                InvalidOperationException _
                (SR.ExceptionConnectionOpen)
        End If

        Dim reader As XmlFileDataReader = _
                New XmlFileDataReader(connection.Database)
        Return reader.XmlReader
```

```
        End Function

        'Updates file and returns number of records.
        Public Function ExecuteNonQuery() As Integer _
                Implements IDbCommand.ExecuteNonQuery
            ' Must have a valid and open connection.
            If connection Is Nothing OrElse _
                    connection.State <> ConnectionState.Open Then
                Throw New _
                    InvalidOperationException _
                    (SR.ExceptionConnectionOpen)
            End If

            Dim recs As Integer
            Dim reader As XmlFileDataReader = _
                    CType(ExecuteReader(), XmlFileDataReader)
            recs = reader.RecordsAffected
            reader.Close()
            Return recs
        End Function

        ...
    End Class
```

The `IDbConnection` and `ICloneable` Interfaces

Providing the ability to set connection and session information for a particular data source is vital to creating a comprehensive data provider. By implementing the `IDbConnection` interface, a .NET managed data provider can represent a unique session with a data source. Like the `IDbCommand` interface, some classes that implement the `IDbConnection` interface may define additional members that add provider-specific functionality. For example, the `SqlConnection` class defines the `PacketSize` property in addition to all the other inherited methods.

When designing the class that implements the `IDbConnection` interface, it is important to keep in mind that the Data Access Application Block needs for this class to also implement the `ICloneable` interface for dynamic discovery of parameters to work.

In the base `DbCommandWrapper`'s `DoDiscoverParameters` method, the `ICloneable`'s `Clone` method is used to make another copy of the `IDbConnection` to use for querying for the metadata in the data source. Although there's no reason to discover parameters for reading or writing to XML files, I have still implemented the `ICloneable` interface to be consistent for what you might need to do if you are creating your own .NET managed data provider. Listing B.5 illustrates how the `XmlFileConnection` class implements both the `IDbConnection` and `ICloneable` interfaces.

LISTING B.5: `XmlFileConnection` **Implements** `IDbConnection` **and** `ICloneable`

```
[C#]
public class XmlFileConnection : IDbConnection, ICloneable
{
     private string origConnString;
     private string fileName;
     private StringCollection parameters;
     private ConnectionState state = ConnectionState.Closed;
     private int connectionTimeout = 0;

     public XmlFileConnection()
     {
     }

     public XmlFileConnection(string strConnectionString)
     {
          ConnectionString = strConnectionString;
     }

     public IDbTransaction BeginTransaction(IsolationLevel iso)
     {
          return new XmlFileTransaction(this,iso);
     }

     public IDbTransaction BeginTransaction()
     {
          return new XmlFileTransaction(this);
     }

     public void ChangeDatabase(string newdb)
     {
          if (! newdb.Equals(fileName)) fileName = newdb;
          return;
     }

     public void Close()
     {
          state = ConnectionState.Closed;
          return;
     }
```

```
public IDbCommand CreateCommand()
{
     IDbCommand idbCommand = (IDbCommand)(new XmlFileCommand());
     idbCommand.Connection = this;
     return idbCommand;
}

public void Open()
{
     state = ConnectionState.Open;
}

public string ConnectionString
{
     get { return origConnString; }
     set
     {
          origConnString = value;
          fileName = String.Empty;
          if (parameters == null)
               parameters = new StringCollection();
          parameters.Clear();
          string[] arrConnString =
               System.Text.RegularExpressions.Regex.Split
               (value,";,");
          foreach (string strParam in arrConnString)
          {
               if (fileName.Equals(String.Empty))
                    fileName = strParam;
               else
                    parameters.Add(strParam);
          }
     }
}

public int ConnectionTimeout
{
     get { return connectionTimeout; }
}

public string Database
{
     get { return fileName;      }
}

public ConnectionState State
{
     get { return state;      }
}
```

```
        public void Dispose() {}

        public object Clone()
        {
            return new XmlFileConnection(ConnectionString);
        }
    }

    [Visual Basic]
    Public Class XmlFileConnection : Implements IDbConnection, ICloneable
        Private origConnString As String
        Private fileName As String
        Private parameters As StringCollection
        Private state_Renamed As ConnectionState = ConnectionState.Closed
        Private connectionTimeout_Renamed As Integer = 0

        Public Sub New()
        End Sub

        Public Sub New(ByVal strConnectionString As String)
            ConnectionString = strConnectionString
        End Sub

        Public Function BeginTransaction(ByVal iso As IsolationLevel) _
            As IDbTransaction Implements IDbConnection.BeginTransaction
                Return New XmlFileTransaction(Me,iso)
        End Function

        Public Function BeginTransaction() As IDbTransaction _
                Implements IDbConnection.BeginTransaction
            Return New XmlFileTransaction(Me)
        End Function

        Public Sub ChangeDatabase(ByVal newdb As String) _
                Implements IDbConnection.ChangeDatabase
            If (Not newdb.Equals(fileName)) Then
                fileName = newdb
            End If
            Return
        End Sub

        Public Sub Close() Implements IDbConnection.Close
            state_Renamed = ConnectionState.Closed
            Return
        End Sub

        Public Function CreateCommand() As IDbCommand _
                Implements IDbConnection.CreateCommand
            Dim idbCommand As IDbCommand = _
                CType(New XmlFileCommand(), IDbCommand)
```

```
        idbCommand.Connection = Me
        Return idbCommand
    End Function

    Public Sub Open() Implements IDbConnection.Open
        state_Renamed = ConnectionState.Open
    End Sub

    Public Property ConnectionString() As String _
            Implements IDbConnection.ConnectionString
        Get
            Return origConnString
        End Get
        Set
            origConnString = Value
            fileName = String.Empty
            If parameters Is Nothing Then
                parameters = New StringCollection()
            End If
            parameters.Clear()
            Dim arrConnString As String() = _
                System.Text.RegularExpressions.Regex.Split _
                (Value,";,")
            For Each strParam As String In arrConnString
                If fileName.Equals(String.Empty) Then
                    fileName = strParam
                Else
                    parameters.Add(strParam)
                End If
            Next strParam
        End Set
    End Property

    Public ReadOnly Property ConnectionTimeout() As Integer _
             Implements IDbConnection.ConnectionTimeout
        Get
            Return connectionTimeout_Renamed
        End Get
    End Property

    Public ReadOnly Property Database() As String _
            Implements IDbConnection.Database
        Get
            Return fileName
        End Get
    End Property

    Public ReadOnly Property State() As ConnectionState _
            Implements IDbConnection.State
        Get
```

```
            Return state_Renamed
        End Get
    End Property

    Public Sub Dispose()
    End Sub

    Public Function Clone() As Object Implements ICloneable.Clone
        Return New XmlFileConnection(ConnectionString)
    End Function
End Class
```

The `IDbDataAdapter` Interface

DataAdapters represent a set of commands and a database connection that is used to fill DataSets and reconcile changes made to the DataSets with the data source. They represent the bridge between a data source and a DataSet. The `IDbDataAdapter` interface and, optionally, the utility class `DbDataAdapter` make it easier for an inheriting class to create a DataAdapter. Like the `IDbCommand` and `IDbConnection` interfaces, classes that inherit `IDbDataAdapter` may define additional members to add provider-specific functionality. The `XmlFileDataAdapter` represents a set of data commands and a database connection that are used to fill the DataSets and update an XML File, but it doesn't include any additional provider-specific functionality. Listing B.6 provides an extract of the code for the `XmlFileDataAdapter`.

LISTING B.6: `XmlFileDataAdapter` **Implements** `IDbDataAdapter`

```
[C#]
public class XmlFileDataAdapter : DbDataAdapter, IDbDataAdapter
{
    XmlFileCommand selectCommand;
    XmlFileCommand insertCommand;
    XmlFileCommand updateCommand;
    XmlFileCommand deleteCommand;
    private bool disposed;

    private static readonly object EventRowUpdated =
        new object();
    private static readonly object EventRowUpdating =
        new object();
```

```
public XmlFileDataAdapter() { disposed = false; }

public XmlFileDataAdapter(XmlFileCommand cmd)  : this()
{
    selectCommand = cmd;
}

public XmlFileDataAdapter
     (String strCommand, XmlFileConnection conn) : this()
{
    selectCommand = new XmlFileCommand(strCommand, conn);
}

public IDbCommand UpdateCommand
{
    get { return updateCommand; }
    set
    {
        if (value.GetType() == typeof(XmlFileCommand))
            updateCommand = (XmlFileCommand)value;
        else
            throw new ApplicationException
             (SR.ExceptionMustBeXmlFileCmmands);
    }
}

public IDbCommand SelectCommand
{
    get { return selectCommand; }
    set
    {
        if (value.GetType() == typeof(XmlFileCommand))
            selectCommand = (XmlFileCommand)value;
        else
            throw new ApplicationException
                 (SR.ExceptionMustBeXmlFileCmmands);
    }
}

public IDbCommand DeleteCommand
{
    get { return deleteCommand; }
    set
    {
        if (value.GetType() == typeof(XmlFileCommand))
            deleteCommand = (XmlFileCommand)value;
        else
            throw new ApplicationException
                 (SR.ExceptionMustBeXmlFileCmmands);
    }
```

```
    }

    public IDbCommand InsertCommand
    {
        get { return insertCommand; }
        set
        {
            if (value.GetType() == typeof(XmlFileCommand))
                insertCommand = (XmlFileCommand)value;
            else
                throw new ApplicationException
                    (SR.ExceptionMustBeXmlFileCmmands);
        }
    }

    public new int Update(DataSet dataSet)
    {
        dataSet.WriteXml(this.selectCommand.CommandText);
        return 0;
    }

    public new int Update(DataSet dataSet, string srcTable)
    {
        if (dataSet.Tables[srcTable] ==
                dataSet.Tables[dataSet.Tables.Count])

        dataSet.WriteXml(this.selectCommand.CommandText);
            return 0;
    }

    override protected RowUpdatedEventArgs CreateRowUpdatedEvent
         (DataRow dataRow, IDbCommand command,
            StatementType statementType,
            DataTableMapping tableMapping)
    {
        return new XmlFileRowUpdatedEventArgs
            (dataRow, command, statementType, tableMapping);
    }

    override protected RowUpdatingEventArgs
        CreateRowUpdatingEvent(DataRow dataRow,
        IDbCommand command, StatementType statementType,
        DataTableMapping tableMapping)
    {
        return new XmlFileRowUpdatingEventArgs
            (dataRow, command, statementType, tableMapping);
    }
...
}
```

```
[Visual Basic]
Public Class XmlFileDataAdapter : Inherits DbDataAdapter _
            : Implements IDbDataAdapter
    Private _selectCommand As XmlFileCommand
    Private _insertCommand As XmlFileCommand
    Private _updateCommand As XmlFileCommand
    Private _deleteCommand As XmlFileCommand
    Private disposed As Boolean

    Private Shared ReadOnly EventRowUpdated As Object = _
        New Object()
    Private Shared ReadOnly EventRowUpdating As Object = _
        New Object()

    Public Sub New()
        disposed = False
    End Sub

    Public Sub New(ByVal cmd As XmlFileCommand)
        Me.New()
        _selectCommand = cmd
    End Sub

    Public Sub New(ByVal strCommand As String, _
            ByVal conn As XmlFileConnection)
        Me.New()
        _selectCommand = _
            New XmlFileCommand(strCommand, conn)
    End Sub

    Public Property UpdateCommand() As IDbCommand _
            Implements IDbDataAdapter.UpdateCommand
        Get
            Return _updateCommand
        End Get
        Set
           If Value.GetType() Is GetType(XmlFileCommand) Then
                _updateCommand = _
                CType(Value, XmlFileCommand)
            Else
                Throw New _
                    ApplicationException _
                    (SR.ExceptionMustBeXmlFileCmmands)
            End If
        End Set
    End Property

    Public Property SelectCommand() As IDbCommand _
            Implements IDbDataAdapter.SelectCommand
        Get
```

```
            Return _selectCommand
        End Get
        Set
           If Value.GetType() Is GetType(XmlFileCommand) Then
             _selectCommand = CType(Value, XmlFileCommand)
           Else
             Throw New ApplicationException _
                   (SR.ExceptionMustBeXmlFileCmmands)
           End If
        End Set
    End Property

    Public Property DeleteCommand() As IDbCommand _
            Implements IDbDataAdapter.DeleteCommand
        Get
            Return _deleteCommand
        End Get
        Set
           If Value.GetType() Is GetType(XmlFileCommand) Then
             _deleteCommand = CType(Value, XmlFileCommand)
           Else
               Throw New ApplicationException _
                   (SR.ExceptionMustBeXmlFileCmmands)
           End If
        End Set
    End Property

    Public Property InsertCommand() As IDbCommand _
            Implements IDbDataAdapter.InsertCommand
        Get
            Return _insertCommand
        End Get
        Set
           If Value.GetType() Is GetType(XmlFileCommand) Then
             _insertCommand = CType(Value, XmlFileCommand)
           Else
             Throw New ApplicationException _
                   (SR.ExceptionMustBeXmlFileCmmands)
           End If
        End Set
    End Property

    Public Shadows Function Update(ByVal dataSet As DataSet) _
                As Integer
        dataSet.WriteXml(Me._selectCommand.CommandText)
        Return 0
    End Function
```

```
    Public Shadows Function Update(ByVal dataSet As DataSet, _
            ByVal srcTable As String) As Integer
        If dataSet.Tables(srcTable) = _
            dataSet.Tables(dataSet.Tables.Count) Then
                dataSet.WriteXml _
            (Me._selectCommand.CommandText)
        End If
        Return 0
    End Function

    Overrides Protected Function CreateRowUpdatedEvent _
          (ByVal dataRow As DataRow, ByVal command As IDbCommand, _
           ByVal statementType As StatementType, ByVal tableMapping _
           As DataTableMapping) As RowUpdatedEventArgs
              Return New XmlFileRowUpdatedEventArgs _
                    (dataRow, command, statementType, tableMapping)
    End Function

    Overrides Protected Function CreateRowUpdatingEvent _
         (ByVal dataRow As DataRow, ByVal command As IDbCommand, _
         ByVal statementType As StatementType, ByVal tableMapping _
         As DataTableMapping) As RowUpdatingEventArgs
              Return New XmlFileRowUpdatingEventArgs _
               (dataRow, command, statementType, tableMapping)
    End Function
    ...

End Class
```

The IDbTransaction Interface

Many of the methods exposed by a database provider are overloaded to allow for an implementation of the IDbTransaction interface. This enables the Data Access Application Block to perform multiple database operations within a single manual transaction. That is, it can ensure that either all database operations are successfully committed or none of the operations are. To provide support for this feature, any .NET managed data provider for use with the Data Access Application Block should implement the IDbTransaction interface. For the .NET managed data provider for XML files, the XmlFileTransaction class implements the IDbTransaction interface. Listing B.7 shows the code for this class.

LISTING B.7: `XmlFileTransaction` **Class Implements** `IDbTransaction`

```
[C#]
public class XmlFileTransaction : IDbTransaction
{
     private XmlFileConnection oConnection;
     private IsolationLevel eIsoLevel;

     public XmlFileTransaction(XmlFileConnection _Connection)
     {
          if (_Connection == null)
               throw new ArgumentNullException(SR.Connection,
                                         SR.ConnectionNullError);
          oConnection = _Connection;
     }

     public XmlFileTransaction(XmlFileConnection oConnection,
                    IsolationLevel _iso) : this(oConnection)
     {
          if (_iso.Equals(null))
               throw new ArgumentNullException(SR.IsolationLevel,
                                         SR.IsolationLevelNullError);
          eIsoLevel = _iso;
     }


     //TODO: modify this so that it clears the data in cache.
     public void Rollback()
     {
     }

     //TODO: Modify this so that it writes out to the file.
     public void Commit()
     {
     }

     public IDbConnection Connection
     {
          get
          {
               return oConnection;
          }
     }

     public IsolationLevel IsolationLevel
     {
          get
          {
               return !(eIsoLevel.Equals(null))? eIsoLevel :
                    new IsolationLevel();
```

```
            }
        }

        public void Dispose()
        {
        }
}

[Visual Basic]
Public Class XmlFileTransaction : Implements IDbTransaction
      Private oConnection As XmlFileConnection
      Private eIsoLevel As IsolationLevel

      Public Sub New(ByVal _Connection As XmlFileConnection)
           If _Connection Is Nothing Then
                Throw New ArgumentNullException(SR.Connection, _
                                    SR.ConnectionNullError)
           End If
           oConnection = _Connection
      End Sub

      Public Sub New(ByVal oConnection As XmlFileConnection, _
                     ByVal _iso As IsolationLevel)
           Me.New(oConnection)
           If _iso.Equals(Nothing) Then
                Throw New ArgumentNullException(SR.IsolationLevel,_
                          SR.IsolationLevelNullError)
           End If
           eIsoLevel = _iso
      End Sub


      'TODO: modify this so that it clears the data in cache.
      Public Sub Rollback() Implements IDbTransaction.Rollback
      End Sub

      'TODO: Modify this so that it writes out to the file.
      Public Sub Commit() Implements IDbTransaction.Commit
      End Sub

      Public ReadOnly Property Connection() As IDbConnection _
                         Implements IDbTransaction.Connection
           Get
                Return oConnection
           End Get
      End Property

      Public ReadOnly Property IsolationLevel() As IsolationLevel _
                         Implements IDbTransaction.IsolationLevel
           Get
```

```
                Return IIf(Not(eIsoLevel.Equals(Nothing)), eIsoLevel, _
                         New IsolationLevel())
            End Get
        End Property

        Public Sub Dispose()
        End Sub
    End Class
```

C

Enterprise Library for the .NET Framework 2.0

THIS BOOK EXPLAINS the design of Enterprise Library for the .NET Framework 1.1 and how to extend, develop, and configure Enterprise Library's application blocks. As this book went into production, Enterprise Library for the .NET Framework 2.0 was released. The primary objective of the Enterprise Library for the .NET Framework 2.0 release is to unify the assets delivered with Enterprise Library with those delivered by the .NET 2.0 Framework. While most of the interfaces exposed by Enterprise Library remain unchanged, there are some important differences with how the blocks achieve the features they provide. This appendix highlights those differences.[1]

The Core

By far the biggest change between Enterprise Library for the .NET Framework 1.1 and Enterprise Library for the .NET Framework 2.0 is in the way configuration is handled. The Configuration Application Block has been deprecated because Enterprise Library now leverages the .NET Framework

1. A lot of information about the changes between Enterprise Library for the .NET Framework 1.1 and Enterprise Library for the .NET Framework 2.0 can be found at http://msdn.microsoft.com/library/default.asp?url=/library/en-us/dnpag2/html/entlibjan2006_aboutjan2006release.asp.

2.0 new configuration mechanisms. Additionally, the architecture around instrumentation for all of the application blocks has been refined, and new capabilities that promote the use of dependency injection in Enterprise Library now exist. These assets exist in an enhanced, common assembly known as the *Core*. This section highlights the primary changes in Enterprise Library that account for the Core.

`System.Configuration` and the Configuration Runtime

The features provided by the `System.Configuration` namespace in the .NET Framework 2.0 provide much of the same functionality that the Enterprise Library Configuration Application Block for the .NET Framework 1.1 provides. For example, it provides support for writing and reading configuration information as strongly typed object graphs to and from configuration files. The intent for Enterprise Library has always been to complement the .NET Framework, not to provide solutions that diverge from those offered by the .NET Framework. Therefore, many of the benefits offered by exposing the Configuration Application Block as a separate block are no longer needed when using the .NET Framework 2.0. Thus, the Configuration Application Block was deprecated and combined with the utilities that are found in the `Common` namespace.

Instead of a full-blown application block, configuration helper classes have been added to the `Common` assembly to facilitate the use of working with the `System.Configuration` namespace. These helper classes provide support for functionality needed by Enterprise Library that does not exist in the `System.Configuration` namespace. One such need is the ability to provide configuration support that allows for polymorphism for the types of objects that can be created. For example, an application can be configured to use the Logging Application Block (note that the word *Instrumentation* has been dropped from the name of this block) to log information to both a database and the Windows Event Log. Both providers for these logging stores derive either directly or indirectly from the abstract base `TraceListener` class. The configuration helper classes that exist in the Core of Enterprise Library allow the collection of Listeners to be configured as one group.

Another important need provided by the helper classes is the ability to read and write configuration data to data stores other than XML files. The .NET Framework 2.0 supports reading and writing configuration information to XML files, but without a lot of work, it is difficult to store configuration data in a different type of data store, like a database. In the latest release of Enterprise Library, the `ConfigurationContext` class has been refactored into the `ConfigurationSource` class in an effort to abstract away the need for developers to understand the intricacies needed to read or write configuration to a particular type of data store while also leveraging the .NET Framework configuration support (like declarative configuration serialization).

Wrappers exist over `System.Configuration` to write to the application domain configuration files (app.config or web.config) as well as external XML configuration files. Also, a `SqlConfigurationSource` is provided as a Quick Start that reads, writes, and monitors changes that occur with respect to configuration information stored in a Microsoft SQL Server database. Moreover, the factories that exist for every application block in Enterprise Library for the .NET Framework 2.0 accept a `ConfigurationSource`. Much like the `ConfigurationContext` in Enterprise Library for the .NET Framework 1.1, this can be used to programmatically set where configuration is read and written for a particular factory.

For example, in Listing C.1 a database provider is created from a `DatabaseProviderFactory` that is passed the name of a configuration file. Additionally, a much desired enhancement that was made in Enterprise Library for the .NET Framework 2.0 is the ability to create providers without the need to store any initialization information in a configuration source. That is, the provider can just be "newwed up."

LISTING C.1: Creating a Database Provider by Programmatically Setting the Configuration File

```
[C#]
FileConfigurationSource fileSource =
          new FileConfigurationSource("foo.config");
DatabaseProviderFactory factory =
          new DatabaseProviderFactory(fileSource);
```

```
Database db = factory.Create("PortalDatabase");

[Visual Basic]
Dim fileSource As FileConfigurationSource = _
         New FileConfigurationSource("foo.config")
Dim factory As DatabaseProviderFactory = _
         New DatabaseProviderFactory(fileSource)
Dim db As Database = factory.Create("PortalDatabase")
```

Change notifications still occur when changes occur in configuration data; however, by default only the Logging Application Block currently registers to receive change notification events. Handlers are exposed if you want to receive change notification for the other application blocks or in your own code.

Instrumentation

In Enterprise Library for the .NET Framework 1.1, instrumentation is turned on for every application block by default. Many of the common problems faced when deploying an application that uses this version of Enterprise Library is due to this fact. If the performance counters, Windows Management Instrumentation (WMI), and event logs are not installed properly and by a user with the necessary credentials (typically an administrator for the machine), then errors will occur when an application block tries to send instrumentation information. To resolve this issue, the counters and schemas need to either be installed properly (by running the InstallServices batch file or the InstallInstrumentation command file), or a version of Enterprise Library needs to be compiled that has instrumentation turned off.

In Enterprise Library for the .NET Framework 2.0, instrumentation is turned off by default for all application blocks, so you don't need to install counters and schemas if you don't intend to use them. In such a scenario, the application blocks can be deployed by simply copying them to the test or production server. This, however, leaves the application blocks without the ability to send instrumentation information, and instrumenting an application is considered a best practice. But rather than requiring the recompilation of the application block assemblies with different compiler directives, as is the case for the previous versions of Enterprise Library, this version made instrumentation configurable. For example, if it makes sense for an application to enable event logging and increment performance counters but there is no need to enable WMI, you can do this with the Enterprise Library Configuration Tool. Figure C.1 shows how to configure instrumentation for Enterprise Library for the .NET Framework 2.0.

However, what is even more interesting is how the instrumentation subsystem has been improved throughout Enterprise Library. It is based on a publish/subscribe design where the publisher of an instrumentation event is decoupled from Listeners for those instrumentation events. In the new version, an application block may contain `InstrumentationProviders` that are defined on an event (for example, removing an item from the cache, making a database call, etc.) in the block and specify the name of the event being fired. An `InstrumentationListener` in the block can be configured to handle the instrumentation event. In the Listener, an `InstrumentationConsumer` method can be defined that contains the logic for what to do when the event is handled, like incrementing to a performance counter or writing to the Windows Event Log.

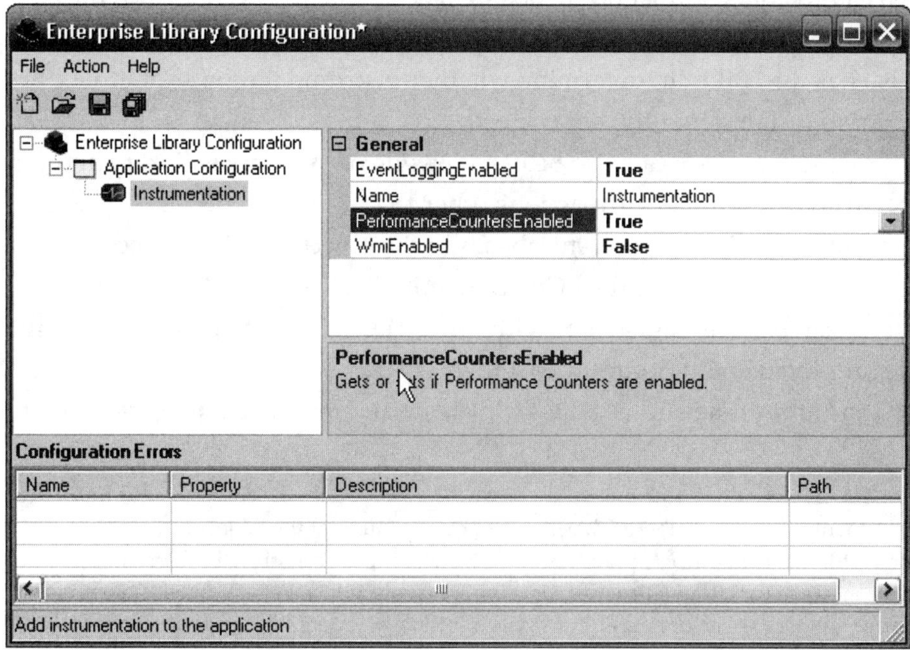

FIGURE C.1: Setting Configuration for Instrumentation

ObjectBuilder[2]

A lot of the feedback on Enterprise Library for the .NET Framework 1.1 was that extending the blocks was difficult because so much needed to be known about the configuration runtime. In an effort to remedy this, the latest release of Enterprise Library includes a new subsystem named `ObjectBuilder` that is a reusable, configurable dependency injection and object creation pipeline. In fact, it is so reusable that it was not actually created by the Enterprise Library team. `ObjectBuilder` was created by the team that developed the Composite UI Application Block (also known as CAB) to provide dependency injection capabilities. Because Enterprise Library's configuration needs were fairly similar to the Composite UI Application Block's needs, Enterprise Library adopted `ObjectBuilder` and it is now a shared asset between both teams. The idea behind `ObjectBuilder` is to provide capabilities for an easy and flexible way to create new providers or application blocks and that do not require an intimate knowledge of how the configuration runtime works.

The `ObjectBuilder` subsystem performs all the repetitive and necessary tasks for creating and disposing object instances. It provides the ability to read configuration data and *inject* that data to create new providers. It also has the ability to determine whether instrumentation should be used prior to instantiating the new object.

`ObjectBuilder` can also be used outside of Enterprise Library and can be customized to perform actions other than these. `ObjectBuilder` consists of a pipeline of different phases in the object creation process. These phases include PreCreation, Creation, Initialization, and PostInitialization. `Strategies` are registered with `ObjectBuilder` that determine the actions that should occur for each phase. Each `Strategy` can collect information at runtime and use it to help create and initialize an object. As men-

2. A lot of information about ObjectBuilder can be found at the ObjectBuilder workspace on Gotdotnet.com (http://practices.gotdotnet.com/projects/objectbuilder), in Brian Button's blog (www.agileprogrammer.com/oneagilecoder), Peter Provost's blog (http://peterprovost.org), and Brad Wilson's blog (www.agileprogrammer.com/dotnetguy).

tioned earlier, for Enterprise Library that involves collecting configuration data, creating an object with that configuration data, and connecting it to instrumentation if it applies.

As I have shown throughout this book, every application block exposes instance factories that are used to create an instance of a specific provider for that block. That does not change for Enterprise Library for the .NET Framework 2.0. What has changed, however, is that these instance factories don't really do much anymore. In the latest release, they just define the type of provider that needs to get created and call through to `ObjectBuilder` to create it.

The Configuration Design-Time API

The Configuration design-time API has also been improved in Enterprise Library for the .NET Framework 2.0. As highlighted in Chapter 2 and shown throughout this book, creating a design-time experience for an application block or provider involves creating the configuration node, a `ConfigurationDesignManager`, and setting an assembly attribute for the `ConfigurationDesignManager`. All these actions are still needed; however, the design for `ConfigurationDesignManager` has been improved to make registering nodes and commands much more logical.

In Enterprise Library for the .NET Framework 1.1, a lot of code was needed both in the configuration nodes and in the `ConfigurationDesignManager` to register the nodes and commands. In the latest release, `CommandRegistrars` and `NodeMapRegistrars` can be created to accomplish this and are simply called from the `Register` method in the `ConfigurationDesignManager`. A lot of the responsibility and logic needed in the configuration nodes can be removed in the latest release and the nodes no longer even need to contain an `OnSited` method.

Data Access

The Data Access Application Block has been simplified to provide better integration with ADO.NET 2.0. The tighter integration with ADO.NET 2.0 results in several benefits.

- The block uses the ADO.NET `<connectionStrings>` configuration section to house the configuration data for a connection string. This allows connection strings to be shared between the application block and other .NET classes that use this section. However, configuration information that is not supported by the `<connectionStrings>` section, like the name of the default database provider and information for all the database providers that are available to an application, still reside in the `<dataConfiguration>` section.
- `DbCommandWrappers` are no longer needed to wrap around the `DbCommand` exposed by a .NET managed data provider. With the latest release of the Data Access Application Block, the block uses the ADO.NET `DbCommand` instead of a `DBCommandWrapper`.
- The Data Access Application Block can be used with any ADO.NET 2.0 managed provider by using the `GenericDatabase` class. There is no need to use an Enterprise Library database provider that has been designed specifically for a particular database type. The database providers are still beneficial, though, as they provide increased functionality, like parameter discovery and transparency between different database implementations.

This version of the Data Access Application Block also makes it easier to use connection strings that are dynamically created instead of read from configuration. This was one of the most common requests in Enterprise Library for the .NET Framework 1.1, and while it is possible to accomplish this, it is not very straightforward. With the latest release, you can create a connection string programmatically and use it directly to create an instance of a database provider.

Logging

As mentioned earlier, the word *Instrumentation* has been dropped from the name of the latest Logging Application Block. This version of the block has been redesigned to take advantage of classes in the `System.Diagnostics` namespace in the .NET Framework 2.0, and a lot of time was spent by the Enterprise Library team to simplify the block and ensure that it performs faster than the previous version. The following are the primary changes for this block.

- Refactoring the LogSinks. The `System.Diagnostics` namespace includes classes called `TraceListeners` that serve the same purpose that LogSinks serve in the previous versions of the block. Therefore, in this version of the block, LogSinks have been replaced by concrete `TraceListeners`.
- Including the ability for a `LogEntry` to be associated with multiple Categories. Since Categories are used to filter and route a `LogEntry`, the ability to specify multiple Categories improves the flexibility of the block.
- Exposing `LogFilters` as an extension point to the block. In the latest release, a provider for a `LogFilter` can be developed and used to extend the filtering capabilities of the block.
- Eliminating the distribution strategies concept. This concept appeared overly complex to many users of the Logging and Instrumentation Application Block in the Enterprise Library for .NET Framework 1.1 version. The functionality for asynchronous logging that was provided by distribution strategies can still be achieved by "chaining" instances of the block together with `TraceListeners` like the `MsmqTraceListener`.

Security

In the latest version of the Security Application Block, the authentication, role management, and profile management features have all been deprecated because the .NET 2.0 Framework now provides the same functionality in the `System.Web.Security.Membership` class and `System.Web.Profile` namespace. Functionality for authorization and security caching remains unchanged.

Index

B

E

H

I

Microsoft .NET Development Series

0321154894

0321194454

0321113594

0321180593

0321334884

0321411757

0321160770

0321246756

032124673X

032126892X

0201760401

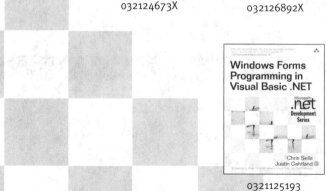

0321125193

0321169514

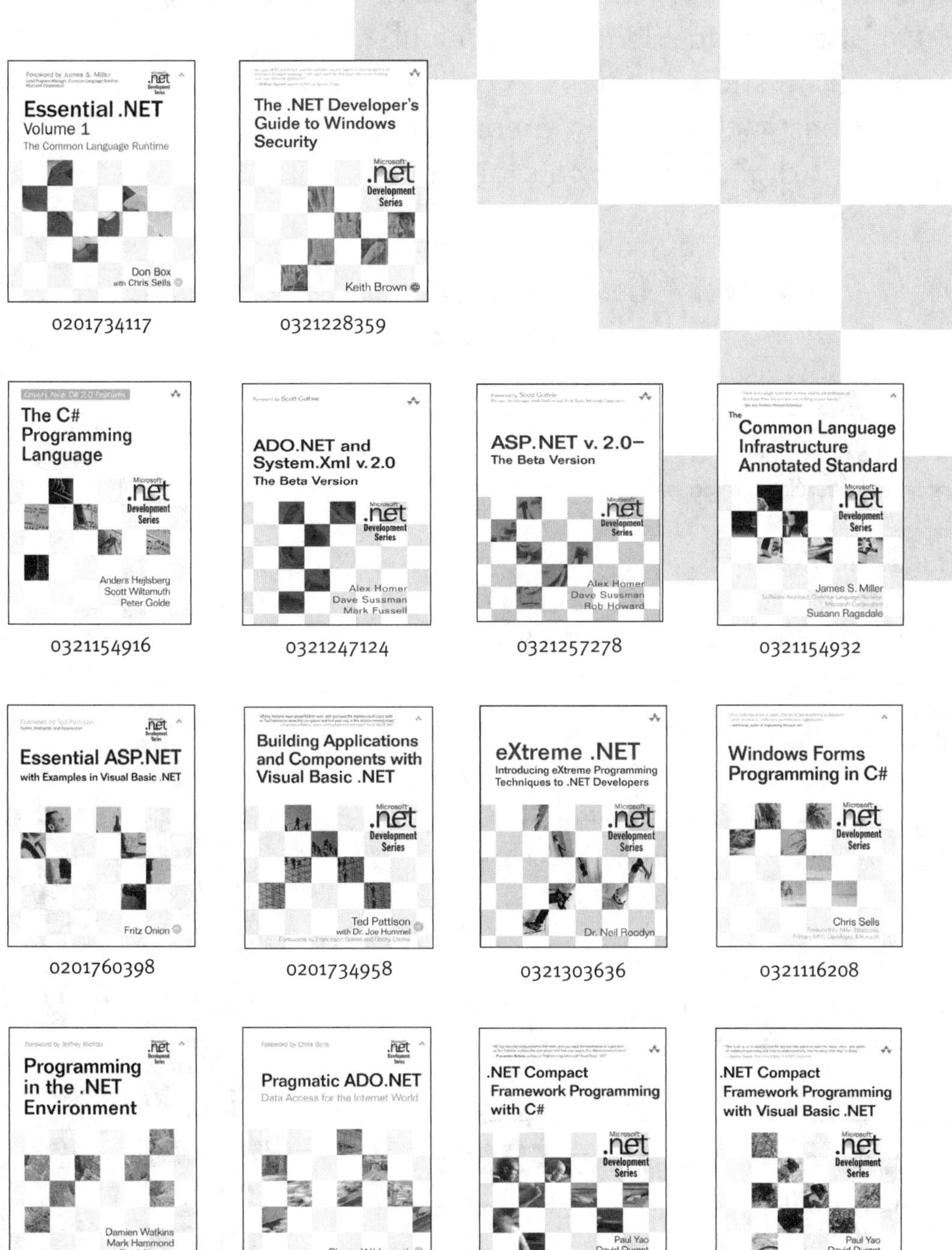

For more information go to www.awprofessional.com/msdotnetseries/